Children's
Literature
Review

Guide to Gale Literary Criticism Series

When you need to review criticism of literary works, these are the Gale series to use:

If the author's death date is: **You should turn to:**

After Dec. 31, 1959   ***CONTEMPORARY LITERARY CRITICISM***
(or author is still living)
for example: Jorge Luis Borges, Anthony Burgess,
William Faulkner, Mary Gordon,
Ernest Hemingway, Iris Murdoch

1900 through 1959   ***TWENTIETH-CENTURY LITERARY CRITICISM***

for example: Willa Cather, F. Scott Fitzgerald,
Henry James, Mark Twain, Virginia Woolf

1800 through 1899   ***NINETEENTH-CENTURY LITERATURE CRITICISM***

for example: Fedor Dostoevski, Nathaniel Hawthorne,
George Sand, William Wordsworth

1400 through 1799   ***LITERATURE CRITICISM FROM 1400 TO 1800***
(excluding Shakespeare)

for example: Anne Bradstreet, Daniel Defoe,
Alexander Pope, François Rabelais,
Jonathan Swift, Phillis Wheatley

SHAKESPEAREAN CRITICISM

Shakespeare's plays and poetry

Antiquity through 1399   ***CLASSICAL AND MEDIEVAL LITERATURE CRITICISM***

for example: Dante, Homer, Plato, Sophocles, Vergil,
the Beowulf Poet

Gale also publishes related criticism series:

CHILDREN'S LITERATURE REVIEW

This series covers authors of all eras who have written for
the preschool through high school audience.

SHORT STORY CRITICISM

This series covers the major short fiction writers of all nationalities
and periods of literary history.

ISSN 0362-4145

volume 20

Children's Literature Review

Excerpts from Reviews,
Criticism, and Commentary
on Books for Children
and Young People

Gerard J. Senick
Editor

Sharon R. Gunton
Associate Editor

 **Gale Research Inc.** · *DETROIT* · *NEW YORK* · *LONDON*

STAFF

Gerard J. Senick, *Editor*

Sharon R. Gunton, *Associate Editor*

Jeanne A. Gough, *Permissions & Production Manager*
Linda M. Pugliese, *Production Supervisor*
Jennifer E. Gale, David G. Oblender, Suzanne Powers, Maureen A. Puhl, Linda M. Ross, *Editorial Associates*
Donna Craft, *Editorial Assistant*

Victoria B. Cariappa, *Research Supervisor*
Karen D. Kaus, Eric Priehs, Maureen Richards, Mary D. Wise, *Editorial Associates*
H. Nelson Fields, Judy L. Gale, Jill M. Ohorodnik, *Editorial Assistants*

Sandra C. Davis, *Permissions Supervisor (Text)*
H. Diane Cooper, Kathy Grell, Josephine M. Keene, Kimberly F. Smilay, *Permissions Associates*
Maria Franklin, Lisa M. Lantz, Camille P. Robinson, Shalice Shah, Denise M. Singleton, *Permissions Assistants*

Patricia A. Seefelt, *Permissions Supervisor (Pictures)*
Margaret A. Chamberlain, *Permissions Associate*
Pamela A. Hayes, Lillian Quickley, *Permissions Assistants*

Mary Beth Trimper, *Production Manager*
Evi Seoud, *Assistant Production Manager*

Arthur Chartow, *Art Director*
C. J. Jonik, *Keyliner*

Laura Bryant, *Production Supervisor*
Louise Gagné, *Internal Production Associate*
Michelle M. Stepherson, *Data Entry Associate*
Wayne A. Jalava, *Internal Production Assistant*

Library of Congress Catalog Card Number 76-643301
ISBN 0-8103-2780-5
ISSN 0362-4145

Printed in the United States of America

Contents

Preface

As children's literature has evolved into both a respected branch of creative writing and a successful industry, literary criticism has documented and influenced each stage of its growth. Critics have recorded the literary development of individual authors as well as the trends and controversies that resulted from changes in values and attitudes, especially as they concerned children. While defining a philosophy of children's literature, critics developed a scholarship that balances an appreciation of children and an awareness of their needs with standards for literary quality much like those required by critics of adult literature. *Children's Literature Review (CLR)* is designed to provide a permanent, accessible record of this ongoing scholarship. Those responsible for bringing children and books together can now make informed choices when selecting reading materials for the young.

Scope of the Series

Each volume of *CLR* contains excerpts from published criticism on the works of authors and illustrators who create books for children from preschool through high school. The author list for each volume is international in scope and represents the variety of genres covered by children's literature—picture books, fiction, nonfiction, poetry, folklore, and drama. The works of approximately twenty authors of all eras are represented in each volume. Although earlier volumes of *CLR* emphasized critical material published after 1960, successive volumes have expanded their coverage to encompass criticism written before 1960. Since many of the authors included in *CLR* are living and continue to write, it is necessary to update their entries periodically. Thus, future volumes will supplement the entries of selected authors covered in earlier volumes as well as include criticism on the works of authors new to the series.

Organization of the Book

An author section consists of the following elements: author heading, author portrait, author introduction, excerpts of criticism (each followed by a bibliographical citation), and illustrations, when available.

- The **author heading** consists of the author's full name followed by birth and death dates. The portion of the name outside the parentheses denotes the form under which the author is most frequently published. If the majority of the author's works for children were written under a pseudonym, the pseudonym will be listed in the author heading and the real name given on the first line of the author introduction. Also located at the beginning of the introduction are any other pseudonyms used by the author in writing for children and any name variations, including transliterated forms for authors whose languages use nonroman alphabets. Uncertainty as to a birth or death date is indicated by question marks.

- An **author portrait** is included when available.

- The **author introduction** contains information designed to introduce an author to *CLR* users by presenting an overview of the author's themes and styles, occasional biographical facts that relate to the author's literary career or critical responses to the author's works, and information about major awards and prizes the author has received. Where applicable, introductions conclude with references to additional entries in biographical and critical reference series published by Gale Research Inc. These sources include past volumes of *CLR* as well as *Authors & Artists for Young Adults, Contemporary Authors, Contemporary Literary Criticism, Dictionary of Literary Biography, Nineteenth-Century Literature Criticism, Short Story Criticism, Something about the Author, Something about the Author Autobiography Series, Twentieth-Century Literary Criticism,* and *Yesterday's Authors of Books for Children.*

- **Criticism** is located in three sections: **author's commentary** and **general commentary** (when available) and within individual **title entries,** which are preceded by **title entry headings.** Criticism is arranged chronologically within each section. Titles by authors being profiled are highlighted in boldface type within the text for easier access by readers.

The **author's commentary** presents background material written by the author or by an interviewer. This commentary may cover a specific work or several works. Author's commentary on more than one work appears after the author introduction, while commentary on an individual book follows the title entry heading.

The **general commentary** consists of critical excerpts that consider more than one work by the author or illustrator being profiled. General commentary is preceded by the critic's name in boldface type or, in the case of unsigned criticism, by the title of the journal. Occasionally, *CLR* features entries that emphasize general criticism on the overall career of an author or illustrator. When appropriate, a selection of reviews is included to supplement the general commentary.

Title entry headings precede the criticism on a title and cite publication information on the work being reviewed. Title headings list the title of the work as it appeared in its first English-language edition. The first English-language publication date of each work is listed in parentheses following the title. Differing U.S. and British titles follow the publication date within the parentheses.

Title entries consist of critical excerpts on the author's individual works, arranged chronologically by publication date. The entries generally contain two to six reviews per title, depending on the stature of the book and the amount of criticism it has generated. The editors select titles that reflect the entire scope of the author's literary contribution, covering each genre and subject. An effort is made to reprint criticism that represents the full range of each title's reception—from the year of its initial publication to current assessments. Thus, the reader is provided with a record of the author's critical history. Publication information (such as publisher names and book prices) and parenthetical numerical references (such as footnotes or page and line references to specific editions of works) have been deleted at the editor's discretion to provide smoother reading of the text.

Entries on authors who are also illustrators will occasionally feature commentary on selected works illustrated but not written by the author being profiled. These works are strongly associated with the illustrator and have received critical acclaim for their art. By including critical comment on works of this type, the editors wish to provide a more complete representation of the author's total career. Criticism on these works has been chosen to stress artistic, rather than literary, contributions. Title entry headings for works illustrated by the author being profiled are arranged chronologically within the entry by date of publication and include notes identifying the author of the illustrated work. In order to provide easier access for users, all titles illustrated by the subject of the entry will be boldfaced.

CLR also includes entries on prominent illustrators who have contributed to the field of children's literature. These entries are designed to represent the development of the illustrator as an artist rather than as a literary stylist. The illustrator's section is organized like that of an author, with two exceptions: the introduction presents an overview of the illustrator's styles and techniques rather than outlining his or her literary background, and the commentary written by the illustrator on his or her works is called illustrator's commentary rather than author's commentary. Title entry headings are followed by explanatory notes identifying the author of the illustrated work. All titles of books containing illustrations by the artist being profiled as well as individual illustrations from these books are highlighted in boldface type.

- Selected excerpts are preceded by **explanatory notes,** which provide information on the critic or work of criticism to enhance the reader's understanding of the excerpt.

- A complete **bibliographical citation** designed to facilitate the location of the original book or article follows each piece of criticism.

- Numerous **illustrations** are featured in *CLR*. For entries on illustrators, an effort has been made to include illustrations that reflect the characteristics discussed in the criticism. Entries on major authors who do not illustrate their own works may also include photographs and other illustrative material pertinent to the authors' careers.

Other Features

- An **acknowledgments,** which immediately follows the preface, lists the sources from which material has been reprinted in the volume. It does not, however, list every book or periodical consulted for the volume.

- The **cumulative index to authors** lists authors who have appeared in *CLR* and includes cross-references to *Authors & Artists for Young Adults, Contemporary Authors, Contemporary Literary Criticism, Dictionary of Literary Biography, Nineteenth-Century Literature Criticism, Short Story Criticism, Something about the Author, Something about the Author Autobiography Series, Twentieth-Century Literary Criticism,* and *Yesterday's Authors of Books for Children.*

- The **cumulative nationality index** lists authors alphabetically under their respective nationalities. Author names are followed by the volume number(s) in which they appear. Authors who have changed citizenship or whose current citizenship is not reflected in biographical sources appear under both their original nationality and that of their current residence.

- The **cumulative title index** lists titles covered in *CLR* followed by the volume and page number where criticism begins.

Suggestions Are Welcome

In response to various suggestions, several features have been added to *CLR* since the series began, including author entries on retellers of traditional literature as well as those who have been the first to record oral tales and other folklore; entries on prominent illustrators featuring commentary on their styles and techniques; entries on authors whose works are considered controversial or have been challenged; occasional entries devoted to criticism on a single work by a major author; explanatory notes that provide information on the critic or work of criticism to enhance the usefulness of the excerpt; more extensive illustrative material, such as holographs of manuscript pages and photographs of people and places pertinent to the authors' careers; a cumulative nationality index for easy access to authors by nationality; and occasional guest essays written specifically for *CLR* by prominent critics on subjects of their choice.

Readers who wish to suggest authors to appear in future volumes, or who have other suggestions, are cordially invited to write the editor or to call our toll-free number: 1-800-347-GALE.

Acknowledgments

The editors wish to thank the copyright holders of the excerpted criticism included in this volume, the permissions managers of many book and magazine publishing companies for assisting us in securing reprint rights, and Anthony Bogucki for assistance with copyright research. We are also grateful to the staffs of the Detroit Public Library, the Library of Congress, the University of Detroit Library, Wayne State University Purdy/Kresge Library Complex, and University of Michigan Libraries for making their resources available to us. Following is a list of the copyright holders who have granted us permission to reprint material in this volume of *CLR*. Every effort has been made to trace copyright, but if omissions have been made, please let us know.

COPYRIGHTED EXCERPTS IN *CLR*, VOLUME 20, WERE REPRINTED FROM THE FOLLOWING PERIODICALS:

The ALAN Review, v. 11, Spring, 1984; v. 13, Fall, 1985. Both reprinted by permission of the publisher.—*Appraisal: Children's Science Books,* v. 5, Fall, 1972; v. 8, Winter, 1975; v. 9, Spring, 1976; v. 10, Spring, 1977; v. 11, Winter, 1978; v. 12, Winter, 1979. Copyright © 1972, 1975, 1976, 1977, 1978, 1979 by the Children's Science Book Review Committee. All reprinted by permission of the publisher.—*Appraisal: Science Books for Young People,* v. 14, Spring, 1981; v. 16, Winter, 1983; v. 17, Spring-Summer, 1984; v. 21, Summer, 1988. Copyright © 1981, 1983, 1984, 1988 by the Children's Science Book Review Committee. All reprinted by permission of the publisher.—*The Atlantic Monthly,* v. 209, March, 1962 for "The Saint and the Lion" by Edward Weeks. Copyright 1961 by The Atlantic Monthly Company, Boston, MA. Reprinted by permission of the Literary Estate of Edward Weeks.—*Best Sellers,* v. 46, January, 1987. Copyright © 1987 Helen Dwight Reid Educational Foundation. Reprinted by permission of the publisher.—*The Book Report: The Journal for Junior and Senior High School Librarians,* v. 4, March- April, 1986. © copyright 1986 by Linworth Publishing Co. Reprinted by permission of the publisher.—*Book Week—The Sunday Herald Tribune,* December 22, 1963; March 7, 1965. © 1963, 1965, *The Washington Post.* Both reprinted by permission of the publisher.—*Book Window,* v. 6, Winter, 1978. © 1978 S.C.B.A. and contributors. Reprinted by permission of the publisher.—*Book World—Chicago Tribune,* May 7, 1972 for "Grand Girls A" by Jane Langton. © 1972 Postrib Corp. Reprinted by courtesy of the author and *The Washington Post.*—*Book World—The Washington Post,* November 3, 1968. © 1968, Postrib Corp. Reprinted by courtesy of the *Chicago Tribune* and *The Washington Post.*/ April 10, 1983; May 8, 1983; June 8, 1986; June 12, 1988. © 1983, 1986, 1988, *The Washington Post.* All reprinted by permission of the publisher.—*Books for Your Children,* v. 11, Autumn, 1976; v. 17, Spring, 1982; v. 18, Autumn-Winter, 1983. © *Books for Your Children* 1976, 1982, 1983. All reprinted by permission of the publisher.—*The Booklist,* v. 70, May 1, 1974; v. 72, March 15, 1976. Copyright © 1974, 1976 by the American Library Association. Both reprinted by permission of the publisher.—*Booklist,* v.74, May 1, 1978; v. 74, May 15, 1978; v. 76, March 15, 1980; v. 76, June 15, 1980; v. 77, October 1, 1980; v. 77, December 1, 1980; v. 78, January 15, 1982; v. 78, March 15, 1982; v. 79, September 1, 1982; v. 79, May 15, 1983; v. 79, June 1, 1983; v. 80, November 15, 1983; v. 80, February 1, 1984; v. 82, November 1, 1985; v. 82, February 15, 1986; v. 82, June 1, 1986; v. 83, November 1, 1986; v. 83, March 1, 1987; v. 84, December 15, 1987; v. 84, February 15, 1988; v. 84, March 1, 1988; v. 84, May 15, 1988. Copyright © 1978, 1980, 1982, 1983, 1984, 1985, 1986, 1987, 1988 by the American Library Association. All reprinted by permission of the publisher.—*Books,* New York, v. 38, December 10, 1961; April 29, 1962. © 1961, 1962 I.H.T. Corporation. Both reprinted by permission of the publisher.—*British Book News,* Spring, 1982. © *British Book News,* 1982. Courtesy of *British Book News.*—*British Book News Children's Books,* March, 1986. © The British Council, 1986. Reprinted by permission of the publisher.—*British Columbia Library Quarterly,* v. 32, April, 1969. Reprinted by permission of the publisher.—*Bulletin of the Center for Children's Books,* v. XV, September, 1961; v. XV, October, 1961; v. 24, October, 1970; v. 26, September, 1972; v. 27, July-August, 1974; v. 28, April, 1975; v. 29, April, 1976; v. 30, October, 1976; v. 30, March, 1977; v. 30, July-August, 1977; v. 31, November, 1977; v. 31, February, 1978; v. 32, March, 1979; v. 34, March, 1981; v. 35, September, 1981; v. 35, January, 1982; v. 35, February, 1982; v. 35, June, 1982; v. 36, September, 1982; v. 36, February, 1983; v. 36, March, 1983; v. 37, December, 1983; v. 37, March, 1984; v. 38, April, 1985; v. 38, June, 1985; v. 39, October, 1985; v. 39, December, 1985; v. 39, February, 1986; v. 39, May, 1986; v. 40, May, 1987; v. 41, November, 1987; v. 41, February, 1988; v. 41, June, 1988; v. 42, October, 1988. Copyright © 1961, 1970, 1972, 1974, 1975, 1976, 1977, 1978, 1979, 1981, 1982, 1983, 1984, 1985, 1986, 1987, 1988 by The University of Chicago. All reprinted by permission of The University of Chicago Press.—*Canadian Children's Literature,* n. 1, 1975 for "Verve, Humour, and an Eye for Detail" by Patricia Morley. Copyright © 1975 by the author and Canadian Children's Press. Reprinted by permission of the author./ n. 5-6, 1976. Copyright © 1976 Canadian Children's Press. Reprinted by permission of the publisher.—*Canadian Library Journal,* v. 30, September-October, 1973 for "A Message from the Patron" by Farley Mowat. © 1973 The Canadian Library Association. Reprinted by permission

Children's
Literature
Review

(Albert) Chinua(lumagu) Achebe

1930-

Nigerian author of fiction and short stories and reteller.

Considered perhaps the most important figure in contemporary African literature as well as its best known novelist, Achebe is recognized for writing powerful and moving works which focus on the social and psychological conflicts created by England's colonization of Africa. Exploring the disparity between tribal and Western customs as well as the resulting changes which have occured in Ibo society, Achebe uses Ibo folklore and proverbs to underscore his exploration of the fundamental ethical questions facing his people. His four works for children—*Chike and the River* (1966), *How the Leopard Got His Claws* (1973), *The Drum* (1977), and *The Flute* (1977)—incorporate the same types of folktales, legends, jokes, and idioms which he uses in his books for adults. These stories, several of which are considered classics of African children's literature, are intended by Achebe to both instruct and entertain. All of them have strongly moral themes: in *Chike and the River,* an eleven-year-old boy receives his moral education when he leaves his village, crosses the Niger, and exposes a gang of thieves; with *How the Leopard Got His Claws,* Achebe creates an animal fable which shows the dangers of societal division and opportunism; in *The Drum,* Achebe examines the nature of power with a trickster tale about a tortoise and a magic drum; and in *The Flute,* a retelling of an African folktale to which Achebe adds original details, a young boy is rewarded for his honesty by the spirit world as he searches for his lost bamboo instrument. In his juvenile books, Achebe expresses such values of traditional Ibo society as courage, initiative, unselfishness, and tenacity to contemporary African children with the hope that they will continue to uphold these qualities in the future. Praised for his distinctive use of established literary forms to relate the realities of Ibo history and life, Achebe is lauded for contributing to the establishment of a relevant children's literature for his country. Achebe has received many awards for his adult works.

(See also *Something about the Author,* Vols. 38, 40; *Contemporary Literary Criticism,* Vols. 1, 3, 5, 7, 11, 26, 51; *Contemporary Authors New Revision Series,* Vols. 6, 26; *Contemporary Authors,* Vols. 1-4, rev. ed.; and *Black Writers.*)

AUTHOR'S COMMENTARY

[*The following excerpt is from an interview by Jonathan Cott, who also provides introductory commentary about Achebe's works.*]

"Literature," states I. B. Singer, "is completely connected with one's origin, with one's roots." And in his first children's book, *Chike and the River,* the Nigerian writer Chinua Achebe describes the adventures of his young, village-born hero—an eleven-year-old named Chike who, one day, reflects: "So this is me . . . . Chike Anene, alias Chiks the Boy, of Umuofia, Mbaino District, Onitsha Province, Eastern Nigeria, Nigeria, West Africa, Africa, World, Universe." And it is this reflec-

tion that reveals the roots and the trajectory of all of Achebe's writing for both children and adults. (p. 161)

As Achebe explains in the following conversation, both *The Drum* and *How the Leopard Got His Claws,* aside from being striking and enjoyable tales for both children and adults, are connected to the realities of Igbo life and history. And they were written both to delight and to instruct. It is this dialectical tension between delighting and instructing that is at the heart of Achebe's writings (as it is of much of children's literature). . . .

Today, as Nigeria . . . becomes increasingly developed economically and technologically . . . , we are continually reminded in Achebe's writings that as we inevitably move forward, we must at the same time remember where we began; and that if the adults forget, then the children and the stories they like best will remind them. (p. 169)

[Jonathan Cott:] As a person who grew up with the values of a village and who now lives in a country that is rapidly being modernized, you seem to be in the position of someone who has found himself standing at the crossroads.

[Chinua Achebe:] Those who live at the crossroads are very lucky, and it seems to me that there will never be this kind of opportunity again. My generation belongs to a group

1

whose fathers . . . my father, for instance, although a converted Christian, was really a member of the traditional society—he was already full grown in the traditions of Igbo life when he decided to become a Christian; so he knew all about our culture. My children, however, belong to the world culture to which American children belong. They went to school in America for several years, and liked the same kind of music that children in America and England enjoy. But I'm in between these two. And we can talk about "transitions"—it's a cliché, of course, since every day's a transition—but I think that I'm much more a part of a transitional generation than any other. And this is very exciting. Of course it carries its penalties, since you're in a no man's land, you're like the bat in the folk tale—neither bird nor mammal—and one can get lost, not being one or the other. This is what we are, we can't do anything about it. But it does help if you have the kind of temperament I have, which tries to recover something from our past. So you have one foot in the past—my father's tradition—and also one in the present—where you try to interpret the past for the present.

[Cott:] The folklorist Richard M. Dorson states: "Two main conditions for the study of folklore are just being realized in Africa: the appearance of an intellectual class with a culture partly different from that of the mass of all people, and the emergence of national states. In the tribal culture all the members share the values, participate in the rituals, and belong fully to the culture, even if some hold privileged positions as chiefs and diviners. In the national culture a schism divides the society. The intellectuals in the professions, on the university faculties, and in the government seem sometimes to have more in common with intellectuals in other countries than with their tribal countrymen." Now, the sociologist Philip Slater has written about the difference he sees between the "community" and the "network." By the former he means the people whom we live with, and by the latter he is referring, like Dorson, to the people we communicate with professionally throughout our own particular country or even throughout the world—just as you have a readership and attend conferences in many different countries.

[Achebe:] Let me touch on the difference between the network and the community, for this is what I meant by the challenge and the risk of being at the crossroads. I think there's a certain strength in being able to have one foot in the network and another foot in the community. But if one forgets the foot that's in the community—and this is quite possible—one can get carried away into the network system. And this is a real problem for us—for the African intellectual, the African writer. I've sometimes complained about African writers who blindly follow Western fashions with regard to what an author should be writing, saying, or even looking like . . . what ideas he should be expressing, what attitudes he should be having toward his community, and so on—all of them taken from the West—while we forget about the other part of our nature which has its roots in the community. So I think we have the responsibility to be both in the community and in the network. This is a challenge—it's very exciting and also very perilous.

[Cott:] You yourself are at the crossroads on many levels—spiritual, political, intellectual—and you have chosen to write for both adults and children. It's as if you've decided to balance and integrate all of these levels and activities.

[Achebe:] Yes, I do that consciously. I think this is the most important and fascinating thing about our life—the cross-

road. This is where the spirits meet the humans, the water meets the land, the child meets the adult—these are the zones of power, and I think this is really where stories are created. Noon—the middle of the day—is a very potent hour in our folklore. It is the time when morning merges into afternoon, the moment when spirits are abroad. When the adults go to the farm and leave the children at home, then the spirits can come into the village.

I've talked about the "crossroad hour" in one of my poems—this hour when the spirits appear—and it is this transitional period that manifests, I think, the great creative potential. It's an area of tension and conflict. So I deliberately go out of my way to cultivate what I call the crossroad mythology, because I think it's full of power and possibility.

[Cott:] In *Things Fall Apart,* Okonkwo tells his son Nwoye "masculine" stories of violence and bloodshed, but the boy prefers the tales his mother tells him about Tortoise the trickster, about the bird who challenged the whole world to a wrestling contest and was finally thrown by a cat, and about the quarrel between Earth and Sky—stories for "foolish women and children," as Okonkwo thinks of them. But in *No Longer at Ease,* Nwoye—now the father of the protagonist Obi—forbids the telling of folk tales to his son because he himself has become a Christian, and doesn't want to disseminate what he now thinks of as "heathen" stories. All of this reminds me of the constant attacks against fairy stories in Europe by Enlightenment spokesmen and by any number of rigid moralists and educators during the past two centuries.

[Achebe:] I think that stories are the very center, the very heart of our civilization and culture. And to me it's interesting that the man who thinks he's strong wants to forbid stories, whether it's Okonkwo forbidding the stories of gentleness, or whether, later on, it's a Christian who, so self-satisfied in the rightness and superiority of his faith, wishes to forbid the hidden pagan stories. It is there in those despised areas that the strength of the civilization resides—not in the masculine strength of Okonkwo, nor in the self-righteous strength of the Christian faith. The stone the builders reject becomes a cornerstone of the house. So I think a writer instinctively gravitates toward that "weakness," if you like; he will leave the "masculine" military strength and go for love, for gentleness. For unless we cultivate gentleness, we will be destroyed. And this is why you have poets and storytellers.

[Cott:] The psychologist James Hillman has talked of the importance of "restorying the adult."

[Achebe:] This is what I've been trying to say when I talk about weakness and strength. You see, "re-storying the adult" is a very interesting phrase. What, in fact, is the adult as distinct from the child? The adult is someone who has seen it all, nothing is new to him. Such a man is to be pitied. The child, on the other hand, is new in the world, and everything is possible to him. His imagination hasn't been dulled by use and experience. Therefore, when you restory the adult, what you do is you give him back some of the child's energy and optimism, that ability to be open and to expect anything. The adult has become dull and routine, mechanical, he can't be lifted. It's as if he's weighted down by his experience and his possessions, all the junk he's assembled and accumulated. And the child can still fly, you see. Therefore the story belongs to the child, because the story's about flying.

[Cott:] In your autobiographical essay **"Named for Victoria,"** you've mentioned that, like Nwoye, you were told stories by your mother and older sister. So you were lucky enough to be "storied" at an early age.

[Achebe:] I was very fortunate, but I would say that this was traditional. Any child growing up at that time, unless he was particularly unlucky, would be told stories as part of his education. It doesn't happen anymore. The stories are now read in books, and very rarely is there a situation in which the mother will sit down night after night with her family and tell stories, with the young children falling asleep to them. The pace of life has altered. Again, this is what I meant by saying that our generation is unique. And I was lucky to have been part of the very tail end of that older tradition. Perhaps we may not be able to revive it, but at least we can make sure that the kind of stories our children read carry something of the aura of the tales our mothers and sisters told us.

[Cott:] In traditional oral societies, the storyteller would employ intonation, gestures, eye contact, pantomine, acrobatics, and occasionally costumes, masks, and props in his or her dramatic presentation.

[Achebe:] Yes, that's right and the loss is enormous. And all I'm saying is that, rather than lose everything, we should value the written story, which is certainly better than no story at all. It's impossible in the modern world to have the traditional storytelling. But I think that perhaps in the home we should not give up so quickly. I find, for instance, that when I write a new children's story the best thing I can do is to tell it to my children, and I get remarkable feedback that way. . . . But the storyteller today has to find a new medium rather than regret the passing of the past. Television is there, we can't do anything about it, so some of us should use this medium, we should do stories for television.

[Cott:] You once wrote that "our ancestors created their myths and legends and told their stories for a human purpose (including, no doubt, the excitation of wonder and pure delight)." And you've often stated that stories impart important messages to us and that they are repositories of human experience and wisdom. Your children's stories are, of course, excellent examples of this notion.

[Achebe:] I realize that this is an area where there is some kind of uneasiness between us and the Western reader concerning just how much of a "message" is suitable for a story. I'm not talking about "preaching," which isn't the same thing as telling a story. But to say that a good story is weakened because it conveys a moral point of view is absurd, because in my view all the great stories do convey such a point. A tale may be fascinating, amusing—creating laughter and delight and so forth—but at its base is a sustaining morality, and I think this is very important.

In the Igbo culture, the relationship between art and morality is very close, and there's no embarrassment at all in linking the two, as there would be in Western culture. The earth goddess Ala—the most powerful deity in the Igbo pantheon—is also the goddess of the arts and of morality. (pp. 171-76)

[Cott:] You've given a beautiful description of the *mbari*—a ceremony performed at the bequest of Ala—and I imagine someone like Tolstoy would have loved this ceremony. I mention him also because his children's fables reflect his deep-seated notion of the connection between morality and aesthetics.

[Achebe:] Tolstoy, coming out of the great Russian tradition, is an excellent example of an artist who proves that purpose does not destroy art.

[Cott:] Your children's tale **"The Flute"** might also have come out of this tradition, too.

That's right. This story is, as you know, really a traditional folk tale, and what I've done is to retell it . . . while adding a few details—such as the one where the boy himself makes his own flute. I'm very much concerned about our consumer culture in which few people make anything themselves anymore. Our ancestors made things, and so I put this detail in the story, and I think that one is entitled and expected to do that. Of course the purist collector of folk tales would say this is terrible. But my concern is that stories are not only retrieved and kept alive but also added to, just as they always were, and I think this is really what a living, traditional storyteller would do. I loved the stories my mother and elder sister told me, but there were always little changes here and there. And this was part of the entertainment—you heard a tale a hundred times, but each day there was one additional little twist, which was expected.

[Cott:] This also suggests the personal style of the storyteller.

[Achebe:] Yes, there's that combination of stability and change. You mustn't alter the story so much that you don't recognize it. The child won't accept tinkering with the folk tale to the extent that it becomes something else. But little twists now and then . . . yes.

[Cott:] In *The Drum,* the tortoise, when retelling to the other animals the story of how he descended into the spiritland to find his magic drum, improvises little dramatic changes in order to make his tale sound more heroic and convincing—which is, of course, what people do quite often in everyday conversation.

[Achebe:] To serve their own ends [laughing].

[Cott:] It's strange but obvious that it is children—the seemingly least significant members of society—who are given stories about the most important matters: selfishness, pride, greed, the meaning of life and death.

[Achebe:] That's right, and this is wonderful for children. I think the adult sometimes loses sight of the nature of stories. But these great fundamental issues have never changed and never will. I mean, children always ask the same questions: Who made the world? How come some people are suffering? Who made death? And to think that we have somehow moved on to more "adult" subject matters is simply self-deception. What we do, of course, is quite often get trapped in trivia masked in highfalutin language. But the basic questions are still the same, and this is what children's stories particularly deal with.

I think that mankind's greatest blessing is language. And this is why the storyteller is a high priest, and why he is so concerned about language and about using it with respect. Language is under great stress in the modern world—it's under siege. All kinds of people—advertisers, politicians, priests, technocrats—want to get a hold of it and use it for their own ends; these are the strong people today; the storyteller represents the weakness we were talking about. But of course every poet is aware of this problem. . . . And this is where children come into it, too, because you can't fool around with children—you have to be honest with language in children's stories; mere cleverness won't do. (pp. 176-78)

[Cott:] You write in English, but which language—English or Igbo—do you use with your children?

[Achebe:] Both English and Igbo—even when we were in America. The youngest girl was just over a year old when we left Nigeria and went to America. And when she went to nursery school—she was just two—she refused to speak English, even though she was already bilingual like everybody else in the family—she had a few words of each language. She refused to talk to her teachers, and we realized that she was putting up a fight for her language. And it lasted a couple of months. Incidentally, one of the conditions she exacted from me for going to school was that I had to tell her a story in Igbo as I drove her there. And another coming back every day, too [laughing]. I didn't quite know what to make of it, but I think that it reveals the importance both of language and of stories. And if a child is deprived of these things I think he or she will be unhappy. The imagination becomes stiff. A lot of cruelty, in fact, comes from a lack of imagination—I think it's all very much connected. And I really feel that stories are not just meant to make people smile, I think our life depends on them.

[Cott:] I wanted to ask you about the background to your powerful fable *How the Leopard Got His Claws.*

[Achebe:] That story was made at a very difficult time politically—at the beginning of the Biafran struggle. A good friend of mine, a very fine poet named Christopher Okigbo, who was killed fighting for Biafra, had set up a publishing house. We had fled from different parts of Nigeria because our lives were in danger—he fled from Ibadan, I fled from Lagos, and we returned to Enugu. (He had been West African representative for Cambridge University Press, so he knew about publishing . . . and, in fact, he asked me to do my first children's book, *Chike and the River,* for Cambridge.) So when we both arrived back in Enugu, he suggested that we set up a press. I said, Well, you set it up, you know about it, and I'll join. He said, You'll be chairman and I'll be the managing director [laughing], so the Citadel Press was formed: The name came from the idea of the fortress—you flee from a foreign land, in danger, and return home to your citadel. Little did we know that Enugu wasn't safe—anyway, that's another story.

We were going to concentrate on children's books, and so we told our friends we were planning on publishing and asked for manuscripts from all the writers around. And a man named John Iroaganachi sent in a story called "How the Dog Became Domesticated"—it was a charming, traditional-type story, but it was rather weak. So I decided to edit it, and as I edited it, it grew . . . it grew until it just turned into something else, it wasn't about the dog at all anymore but rather about the leopard. And it was now a parable about Nigeria—the common house that had been torn apart.

I was possessed by that story, which works on very many levels. Biafra was represented by the leopard . . . but let's not talk about whom the dog represents; I think a good story remains valid even beyond the events described. It is however, interesting to mention that when the city where we were working fell to the federal troops, we had that book in press. In fact, the last time I saw Christopher Okigbo was when he came to discuss it with me. That day a bomb fell on my house. And the end of it was that Enugu was sacked, and we fled and abandoned the book.

Now, at the end of the war, we went back to the site of the publishing house, and it had been razed to the ground—it seemed to me that whoever did it didn't like publishing or at least this particular publishing house and perhaps this particular book. Fortunately, there was one proof copy that somehow survived—I think a friend of ours, a relation of Christopher Okigbo's who had a copy of the galleys, fished it out and brought it to me. And so I made a few more changes, not major ones, and it was published. Later on, one chap who was working as an intelligence officer with the federal troops said to me, "You know, of all the things that came out of Biafra, that book was the most important." . . . Children read the book and love it. Not only in Nigeria, but also in East Africa, where they did a special edition of it. In Nigeria it sold out very quickly—it was out of print for a long time—but a Nigerian publisher has just reissued it, and it's used as a supplementary reader in schools.

I don't believe children get all the levels—they're not supposed to—but I think they get the main point about the ingratitude and opportunism of the animals, and about the danger of not working together when they have a common problem. Of course, the villain is the dog . . . which is a problem, I understand, for readers in the West—it's very difficult for them to see a dog in the role of a villain, but I did that deliberately. John's original story had the dog as the nice guy, a wonderful fellow who became a slave. But I don't like slaves, so this is why I turned the plot around 180 degrees. (pp. 179-81)

[Cott:] I wanted to ask you, too, about your children's story *The Drum,* which begins: "In the beginning when the world was young . . ." Here you conjure up a kind of fairy-tale setting in which animals and trees talk to each other. . . . By the way, the number seven seems to come up in your children's books all the time. In *The Drum,* for example, there are seven steps to the underworld, seven times that the drum thanks the tree, and so on.

[Achebe:] Seven is a magical number. And this is almost a formula—crossing the seven rivers and the seven savannas in order to go beyond the world of the human to the world of the spirits. The Igbo week is four days, and seven weeks is one month. Seven weeks is a crucial measure of time. When a child is born, it's not really regarded as fully here until it has lived seven weeks. Then it is human and is given a name.

[Cott:] The tortoise, who's the protagonist of the story, follows the fruit he's let fall into the underworld abode of the spirits. And when he returns to his family and friends, he begins to make a grand speech.

[Achebe:] Yes, it's like an Igbo meeting. He's trying to become a king, which is anathema to the Igbo.

[Cott:] So here again we discover a parable. And when the tortoise has to repeat his journey to the underworld—since the magic drum has been destroyed and he wants to get another one from the spirits—

[Achebe:] He fakes it. So here is a way in which the story of *The Drum* and "The Flute," have the same theme. A true adventure isn't a faked adventure, and there's no mercy shown to the faker. You do something the first time, you do it honestly, that's okay. But then you go back and you plan something which doesn't arise out of necessity—that's fakery. And children understand this because they know about faking. Adults think that they can fool children [laughing], but they don't really succeed.

[Cott:] In **"The Flute,"** the "faked" situation is set up by the greedy first wife, who wants to get something for her son and herself.

[Achebe:] Yes. Stories often become far more evil when human characters move in—there's a greater possibility for evil. Somehow there's a limit to how evil the tortoise can be—you know that. He's a rogue, but he's a nice kind of rogue. And in the end he's punished, and that's it. (pp. 181-82)

[Cott:] Children seem to have a special affinity with Tortoise.

[Achebe:] Yes, they love him. He's a nice, unreliable kind of rascal, and the village is all the happier for that kind of character—as long as there aren't too many like him in any one community [laughing]. You know the kind of character he is, and when he appears everybody immediately knows that Tortoise is up to his tricks, and they protect themselves. Remember the story in which Tortoise wants to go with the birds to heaven and have a feast? They give him wings, and though he says he's converted, he actually intends to cheat them. As the Chinese say: If you fool me once, shame on you; fool me twice, shame on me. That's a very wise statement. Unfortunately the birds let themselves be fooled three, four, or five times. And so do we.

But getting back to why children, especially, like the trickster: Perhaps it's because this figure is very lively, like a child; he's always doing something unexpected. There's a difference between the kind of roguery Tortoise is guilty of and evil. I don't think children like an evil character, they prefer a lively and vivacious one. Even if he's not very honest, they know that anyway, so he can't fool them. And there's room for this kind of person in all stories. Even in adult fiction. Think of a villain like Chief Nanga in **A Man of the People,** who has an attractive character—yes, a trickster, he's really a Tortoise figure. And you're attracted to him in spite of yourself, in spite of what you know. There's always drama around him, something is always happening where he is. As with Tortoise, he isn't going to simply walk down the street and disappear, he's going to start something.

Finally, I think that children like Tortoise because he's a very small fellow—he's weak in relation to the giants of the animal world. The tortoise is the slowest of all slow creatures, and yet he wins the races.

[Cott:] I wanted to ask you about your first children's book, **Chike and the River.** The name Chike has *chi* in it, and so does your first name, Chinua. About *chi,* you've written: "There are two clearly distinct meanings of the word *chi* in Igbo. The first is often translated as god, guardian angel, personal spirit, soul, spirit double, etc. The second meaning is day, or daylight, but is most commonly used for those transitional periods between day and night or night and day. . . . In a general way we may visualize a person's *chi* as his other identity in spiritland—his *spirit* being complementing his terrestrial *human* being; for nothing can stand alone, there must always be another thing standing beside it."

[Achebe:] When we talk about *chi,* we're talking about the individual spirit, and so you find the word in all kinds of combinations. Chinwe, which is my wife's name, means "*Chi* owns me"; mine is Chinua, which is a shortened form of an expression that means "May a *chi* fight for me." My son is named Chidi, which means "*Chi* is there." So it's almost in everybody's name in one form or the other. Our youngest girl asked me why she didn't have *chi* in her name [laughing], she

thought it was some kind of discrimination, so she took the name Chioma, which means "Good *chi.*"

[Cott:] What does Chike mean?

[Achebe:] Chike is a shortened form of Chinweike, which means "*Chi* has the strength or the power." And that's what that frail-looking character has—he has the power.

[Cott:] Chike comes from Umofia, the village that is the main setting for **Things Fall Apart** and **No Longer at Ease.** And this village seems to me to be as rich an imaginary geographical setting as Faulkner's Yoknapatawpha County.

[Achebe:] I had the idea of its being more like Thomas Hardy's Wessex—someplace in the mind, occurring again and again . . . and thus in that way creating a geographical solidity for that zone of the mind. There's actually no place called Umofia, but its customs and its people are clearly those of Ogidi in Eastern Nigeria, which is where I'm from. (pp. 185-87)

[Cott:] **Chike and the River** is an adventure story that seems to have been written especially for ten- or eleven-year-old kids.

[Achebe:] Yes, it's a "children's novel," if you like. . . . It was my first children's book. I enjoy writing for children, it's very important for me. It's a challenge I like to take on now and again because it requires a different kind of mind from me when I'm doing it—I have to get into the mind of a child totally, and I find that very rewarding. I think everybody should do that, not necessarily through writing a story, but we should return to childhood again and again. And when you write for children it's not just a matter of putting yourself in the shoes of a child—I think you have to be a child for the duration. It's not easy to begin with, and I didn't know if I could do it, it never occurred to me until Christopher Okigbo said I must do a children's story. (p. 188)

[Cott:] Igbo history seems now to be unalterably connected to Nigerian history, and history has brought Nigeria to a critical point—as a country it, too, seems to be at the crossroads. What role do you think stories—and particularly stories for children—can have in these rapidly changing times? And might it not be possible for those of us in the West to learn something from your experience?

[Achebe:] Whether or not the West learns anything from the African experience is a matter for the West to decide. I can only say that a major prerequisite to learning is humility; and that on present showing this virtue is extremely difficult for the West, thanks to its immense material success.

But to the main part of your question. Igbo and Nigerian fortunes seem to be indissolubly linked again—for good or ill. Our responsibility as Nigerians of this generation is to strive to realize the potential good and avoid the ill. Clearly, children are central in all this, for it is their legacy and patrimony that we are talking about. If Nigeria is to become a united and humane society in the future, her children must now be brought up on a common vocabulary for the heroic and the cowardly, the just and the unjust. Which means preserving and refurbishing the landscape of the imagination and the domain of stories, and not—as our leaders seem to think—a verbal bombardment of patriotic exhortation and daily recitations of the National Pledge and Anthem. (p. 192)

Jonathan Cott, "Chinua Achebe: At the Cross-

roads," *in his* Pipers at the Gates of Dawn: The Wisdom of Children's Literature, *Random House, 1983, pp. 161-92.*

GENERAL COMMENTARY

JAMES MILLER

Achebe's belief that the modern African writer should teach, that he has a particular responsibility to shape the social and moral values of his society, has been a persistent theme of his various public statements. (pp. 7-8)

Given Achebe's outlook, it is not surprising that his vision of the rehabilitation of Nigerian society should extend to the entire population, not just to adults, and that he—as well as many other contemporary Nigerian writers—has devoted considerable attention to writing literature for Nigerian children.

The emergence of a significant body of literature written by African writers for African children is a recent development in Nigeria, closely connected to the upsurge in creative writing in English that has distinguished Nigerian literature in general during the past two decades. The increasing attention Nigerian writers have given to developing children's literature also reveals their recognition of the need for suitable reading materials for Nigerian schoolchildren, a relatively new and distinctive stratum of modern Nigerian society. (pp. 8-9)

During the colonial era, Nigerian schoolchildren were fed on a literary diet culled from the bookshelves of England. A product of the colonial educational system, Achebe once recalled the literary fare he had inherited as a child:

> I remember *A Midsummer Night's Dream* in an advanced stage of falling apart. . . . I remember also my mother's *Ije Onye Kraist,* which must have been an Ibo adaptation of *Pilgrim's Progress.* . . . I became very fond of those aspects of ecclesiastical history as could be garnered from *The West African Churchman's Pamphlet*—a little terror of a booklet prescribing interminable Bible readings morning and night.

And, in another context, Achebe reflects on the paucity of literature available for Nigerian students:

> I went years later to teach in one of the so-called private schools in my district and discovered that the school "library" consisted of a dusty cupboard containing one copy of the Holy Bible, five pamphlets entitled *The Adventures of Tarzan,* and one copy of a popular novel called *The Sorrows of Satan.*

Achebe clearly has a serious argument with the literary legacy English writers bequeathed to his society, and we can expect his literature for children to reflect many of the broad moral and political concerns which characterize his novels.

Given Achebe's preoccupation with the literary reconstruction of precolonial Ibo society, particularly in his novels ***Things Fall Apart*** and ***Arrow of God,*** it is somewhat surprising that ***Chike and the River,*** his first venture into children's literature, should have a contemporary setting. ***Things Fall Apart*** and ***Arrow of God*** reflect Achebe's preoccupation with the late nineteenth- and early twentieth-century history of the Ibo people, their religious, cultural, and political traditions,

and the tragic consequences of their encounter with the British. At the same time that these novels examine the historical forces which relentlessly and inevitably undermined precolonial Ibo society, they also reveal the tenacity, adaptability, and receptivity to change which seem to be characteristic of the Ibo society in general. The past, however ambiguous, however painful, must be accepted; it cannot be changed, Achebe implies in his fiction. (pp. 9-10)

If we consider all of Achebe's novels as a sequence of connected works exploring the changes which have occurred in Ibo society—from the initial contact between the Ibo and the British depicted in ***Things Fall Apart*** to the satiric portrait of contemporary Nigerian society in ***A Man of the People***—***Chike and the River*** can be seen as a short chapter in Achebe's epic. Whereas his novels depict a world in which traditional values are slowly disintegrating, a society drifting towards an uncertain present, ***Chike and the River*** offers Achebe's young readers an almost idyllic portrayal of independent Nigeria.

Historically, the Ibo people have participated in a highly individualistic, "open" society, emphasizing personal mobility and achievement. Traditional Ibo society provides a range of alternatives among which individuals must choose, based upon their own skill and knowledge. The British imposed new forms of cultural, political, and economic order upon Ibo society, but they did not necessarily alter the ethical framework of the society itself. While the context changed, the moral qualities of Ibo society remained the same; at least, this is what Achebe suggests in ***Chike and the River.*** Although he deliberately sidesteps many of the issues that he addresses in his novels, Achebe makes it clear to his young readers that the values of traditional Ibo society—hard work, perseverance, individual initiative—should continue to guide their lives in the modern setting.

Like the heroes of Achebe's novels, Chike comes from the village of Umuofia, but the story suggests that the traditional character of the village has already been transformed. Chike yearns to experience life in Onitsha, the site of the largest market in West Africa (before the Nigerian civil war) and the unofficial capital of Iboland. . . . (p. 11)

Inasmuch as attaining an education is one of the explicit values held before the reader throughout ***Chike and the River,*** the story almost inevitably moves from the countryside to the city. Unlike the sustained and nostalgic portraits of Umuofia we encounter in Achebe's novels, the village setting is quickly displaced by the urban landscape.

In contrast to the characters who exist within the tightly woven fabric of family and clan relationships depicted in Achebe's novels, Chike is often left on his own. Although he lives with his uncle (and, therefore, continues to exist in an extended family framework), Chike must rely primarily upon his own wit and upon the advice of a street-wise school companion whose nickname is S.M.O.G.

Having been warned by his mother to beware of the city and above all to stay away from the River Niger, Chike is, of course, compelled by his own curiosity to explore the streets of Onitsha and to devise a means of crossing the River Niger. In a series of loosely connected episodes, ***Chike and the River*** recounts the way in which Chike finally manages to cross the river and the adventures he encounters on both sides.

Chike's various efforts to secure the one shilling necessary to cross the river take place within a clearly defined moral framework in which Achebe upholds specific social and cultural values while condemning others. As in traditional African narratives, individual episodes in the story often convey an explicit moral statement. In one episode, for example, Achebe narrates the tale of Ezekiel, a spoiled child raised by an indulgent mother. Ezekiel quickly develops into a "lawless little imp," stealing small amounts of money from his mother and, finally, moving on to a more ambitious scheme: offering nonexistent leopard-skins to several pen pals in England in exchange for money and other presents. When the headmaster of the school discovers Ezekiel's scheme, he exposes him to ridicule and shame before the entire school:

> Think of the bad name which you have given this school. . . . Think of the bad name you have given Nigeria, your motherland. . . . Think how the school in England will always remember Nigeria as a country of liars and thieves. . . . Some of you will go to study in England when you grow up. What do you think will happen to you there? I will tell you. As soon as you open your mouth and say you come from Nigeria everybody will hold fast to his purse.

Since the headmaster never is treated satirically in *Chike and the River*—as this figure often is in contemporary African literature—his stern, moralistic warning must be taken seriously. His insistence upon the values of scrupulous honesty, dignity, and self-respect are precisely the same values Achebe himself upholds throughout the story.

Although the school setting provides a framework within which Chike—and presumably Achebe's young reader—receives his moral education, he must also learn the proper code of conduct through his experiences in society. Chike finds sixpence on the street, only to lose it when S.M.O.G. persuades him to take it to a "money-doubler" to increase its value. After considering various inappropriate means of securing money, including begging and borrowing, Chike discovers work, and it is only after he works on behalf of his goal that he earns enough money for his passage across the river.

Chike's subsequent adventures on the other side of the river, his role in bringing a gang of thieves to justice, and his public recognition as a hero bring the moral framework of Achebe's story into sharp relief. Chike emerges as a hero primarily because he has upheld the values of his society. His award, appropriately, is a scholarship that will take him through secondary school.

In *Chike and the River,* Achebe turns his attention away from the evocation of the past and addresses himself to the present. His portrayal of post-independence Nigerian life is buoyant, optimistic, and remarkably free of the tensions and conflicts that beset Ibo society in his novels. Chike is neither burdened by the conflict between "traditional" and "modern" values, as are many of Achebe's adult characters, nor degraded by the colonial legacy. Rather, he seems to represent the best qualities of a new society poised on the edge of its own destiny.

Ironically, the optimism of Achebe's outlook in this story quickly crumbles in his last novel, *A Man of the People.* Although published in the same year as *Chike and the River, A Man of the People* marks a fundamental change in Achebe's political consciousness. Many of the prominent themes of his earlier novels have disappeared. Europe no longer di-

rectly influences the lives of his characters, even though Achebe suggests that neocolonialism continues to shape the politics and culture of the society he depicts. The breakdown of traditional values is virtually complete, and the entire society seems overrun with greed and corruption. In this novel Achebe examines the conflict between a young university graduate and a corrupt politician, neither one of whom can be regarded as a repository of meaningful moral values, and concludes with an uncanny description of a military coup, accurately foreshadowing the military coup that occurred in Nigeria in January 1966—the month of the novel's publication. An angry, bitter novel, *A Man of the People* scatters its moral judgments freely and indiscriminately. Achebe's tirade extends to virtually everyone in his society—the intellectuals, the politicians, the military, the common people—and it is this sense of outrage that shapes the theme and tone of his second story for children, *How the Leopard Got Its Claws.* (pp. 12-14)

Deceptive in its simplicity, *How the Leopard Got Its Claws* appropriates the form of a traditional African animal story. The story is apparently one of the "how" stories so popular in oral tradition, but the underlying theme is one of betrayal, the dominant tone one of anger and outrage. Like *Things Fall Apart* and *Arrow of God, How the Leopard Got Its Claws* portrays with nostalgia a world that has now vanished. In the beginning all the animals live together in harmony, guided by the kindness and wisdom of the leopard. None of the animals has sharp teeth or claws except the dog—obviously a misfit in this idyllic setting. When a torrential downpour forces the dog to seek shelter in the common hall built by all the other animals, he viciously attacks them and drives everyone out. Faced with the choice of remaining in the rain or accepting the new regime established by the dog, the animals depose the leopard as their leader, driving him away with stones and taunts.

The rest of the story is concerned with the leopard's revenge. (pp. 15-16)

In an epilogue to the story, the beaten and exhausted dog staggers to the hunter's house for sanctuary, offering his assistance to the hunter in exchange for shelter. Thus, at the end of the story, the idyllic paradise is destroyed. . . . (p. 16)

The grim and pessimistic conclusion of the story raises a provocative question. Who was responsible for the destruction of the animal kingdom? The dog, whose antisocial values and behavior undermined the cohesion of the community? Or the animals themselves, whose collective lack of integrity and principles led them to support the dog's overthrow of the leopard? In the context of the story, the leopard's pride, his anger, and his revenge seem justified, yet Achebe suggests that perhaps the leopard's sense of outrage must be balanced against the greater danger that the hunter represents. Although he moralizes and condemns in the conclusion of the story, clearly pointing out the perilous consequences of disunity, Achebe offers no easy solutions.

In *How the Leopard Got Its Claws,* Achebe carefully manipulates the structure and symbolic meanings of traditional animal tales to achieve a powerful social and political statement. In oral narratives, animal characters are often imbued with symbolic significance. The tortoise, for example, is associated with wit and wisdom, while the dog, at least in Ibo narratives, is brutish and deceitful. Working with the traditional West African bestiary, Achebe has conferred new meanings upon established forms. In view of his sharp criticism of post-independence African societies, particularly during the Nigerian civil war, it is clear that *How the Leopard Got Its Claws* is a political parable about modern Nigeria. The spectacle of disunity within the animal kingdom is too suggestive of the disintegration of the Nigerian federation to be merely coincidental. And *How the Leopard Got Its Claws* reveals the same bitter anger, the same anguish and despair that we encounter in *A Man of the People.*

In his literature for children, as in his novels, Achebe has covered a considerable historical and ideological distance. Although he has been consistent in his moral concerns, in his preoccupation with the fundamental ethical questions facing his society, he has undergone a radical transformation of attitude. His earlier posture of dispassionate objectivity and moral certainty has given way to anger without a clear social or political focus. The buoyant optimism of *Chike and the River* has been replaced by the moral and political uncertainties of *How the Leopard Got Its Claws.* Two chapters in his spiritual and political autobiography, Achebe's stories for children present two radically opposed portrayals of Nigerian society. More importantly, however, these stories reflect the depth of Achebe's commitment to the belief that the novelist must also teach, holding up to his society—including its children—a mirror in which its best possibilities and deepest flaws are clearly reflected. (pp. 16-17)

> James Miller, "The Novelist as Teacher: Chinua Achebe's Literature for Children," in Children's Literature: Annual of the Modern Language Association Seminar on Children's Literature and The Children's Literature Association, *Vol. 9, 1981, pp. 7-18.*

HOW THE LEOPARD GOT HIS CLAWS (1972)

Perhaps it was a pity to advertise this book here as "the greatest news in children's literature in Nigeria". Advance in publishing it may be, but as the story is presented in English it has to be reviewed on level terms with our own editions of traditional tales. As such, the production seems rather drab . . . , while Anglicisation flattens out what must once have been interesting and appropriate sentence rhythms. The legend of the leopard begging claws of iron and bronze from the blacksmith in order to introduce violence into a peaceful kingdom follows the trend of today well enough but only the interpolated poem by Chinua Achebe gives an effective impression of the book's country of origin.

> Margery Fisher, in a review of "How the Leopard Got His Claws," in Growing Point, *Vol. 12, No. 1, May, 1973, p. 2173.*

When Leopard was king, the animals lived as friends and, except for the dog, none had sharp teeth. Together they build a shelter, but the dog drives them out. Afraid to oppose him, they declare him king. The leopard gets teeth of iron and claws of bronze from the blacksmith and a new voice from thunder. Thus armed leopard defeats dog, and the latter entreats man to be his protector. Unfortunately, the animal characters are unconvincingly portrayed—they clap their hands, shed tears, throw stones: the leopard " . . . eats up anyone he can lay his hands on." All of this is out of keeping with animal behavior and weakens the effectiveness of the tale. The black-and-white pen sketches [by Per Christiansen] are adequate but can't save this unsuccessful story.

> Mary B. Mason, in a review of "How the Leopard Got His Claws," in School Library Journal, *Vol. 20, No. 1, September, 1973, p. 54.*

THE FLUTE (1978)

> [*The following excerpt is from an essay on Achebe's short story "The Flute," a retelling of a Nigerian folktale that appeared in a different version in his adult novel* Arrow of God. *"The Flute" was written for Francelia Butler's* Sharing Literature with Children: A Thematic Anthology *in 1977 and was published in book form in 1978. The quotations from Achebe are from an interview by Marianne Whelchel conducted on 30 April 1976.*]

"The Flute" is Achebe's retelling of a folktale that occurs in many variations throughout Nigeria, other parts of Africa, and the rest of the world. (p. 248)

Because Achebe believes in the relevance to contemporary experience of the wisdom carried in the folktales, he is particularly interested in recording them before they are lost. Tales such as "The Flute" are part of Nigeria's rich oral tradition, a tradition now threatened by Nigeria's move toward universal literacy. As a culture becomes literate, the oral tradition is lost unless definite steps are taken to preserve it. Achebe believes those steps must be taken by serious artists and writers. He is not satisfied with word-for-word transcription of the tales as told by village storytellers, for each storyteller has his own version and unless one finds an outstanding storyteller, it is probably better for a writer like himself to re-create the original tale, which he may have heard in childhood from his mother or older sister or brother. According to Achebe, the recording of the oral tradition is "not a mechanical thing":

> The story has to be retold, has to be re-created for this age, and this is the work of people who make stories, not people who just stumble on things in the course of their other work, whether they're anthropologists, or district officers, or missionaries, or what have you.

Achebe envisions two steps in the recording of folktales: the first is recording the tale in the original Nigerian language and the second, translating it into English. Much of the original folktale experience is lost when one first encounters the tale in a book. For instance, if "The Flute" were told in an Igbo village gathering or within a family, visual and sound effects would play an important part. The two boys' flute songs would be sung by the storyteller and on certain lines the audience would join in. (p. 249)

Interestingly, Achebe uses this same folktale . . . in one of his adult novels, *Arrow of God*. . . . [That] the same tale can be told to both children and adults illustrates what Achebe believes to be an important quality of good children's literature. Speaking of his use of this particular story for both adults and children, Achebe talks of the various levels of interpretation a story may have:

> . . . a story is a story, but its interpretation is something else. You don't tell interpretation, you tell a story, and if it's a good story it will have these various levels of interpretation, and an adult will get a lot more out of it—not a lot more, but something different from it than a child. A child will see a story, will see dramatic situations and so on but would not be in a position to relate this to the

scheme of the universe. This is something that an adult can do and this is what tells you that those who made children's stories were not second-rate storymakers. That's what we tend to do today, to leave it to second-rate storymakers. It's only good storytellers who can create stories that have these various levels, you know, like *Alice in Wonderland.* A child can read it and it's just a nice, pleasant story, and an adult will read it and see the whole politics of society displayed there, and this is what makes a good story. So you can tell a story to children and tell the same story to adults for different reasons.

(pp. 249-50)

The child who reads or hears **"The Flute"** as presented in this anthology will find in the story both entertainment and instruction. On one level the story is a fine adventure tale, for the boy who owns the bamboo flute takes great risks to recover it and he succeeds better than he had dreamed. It is also a story of personal values pitted against social and cultural ones. In going to search for the flute at night, the boy defies a cultural taboo that requires him to respect the spirits' right to the fields after dark and he disobeys his parents. On the face of it, then, his defiance should evoke disapproval and punishment. We know, however, that the quest for the flute is not merely an act of defiance for its own sake—the boy is very afraid of the spirits but undertakes the trip anyway. The tale makes a point of the boy's fear; when he sees the spirits, fear freezes him, and when he sings to the spirits he reveals that he knows death may be the penalty for disrespecting them. Because he undertakes the search despite his great fear, we understand how much the simple bamboo flute means to him. In his song he explains to the spirits his devotion to the flute in terms that suggest it is almost human:

> How could you
> Contain yourself and sleep till dawn
> When your flute in damp and dew
> Lay forsaken and forlorn.

Thus, we know the trip is not made for selfish reasons. In going after the flute the boy asserts personal values that take priority over his parents' and the spirits' right to respect. And he is approved of for doing so. His devotion to his own simple flute when he has the opportunity to replace it with a seemingly more valuable gold or white one, his obvious fear of the spirits, and his scrupulous respect of them in everything except his coming to the fields by night make it clear that his motives are pure and that his action is not a question of mere defiance but of values held with conviction and courage. Impressed by the boy's courage and devotion, the spirits reward him grandly. Thus, one moral of the story is that the individual is sometimes right to place his own values above society's and that he is even to be admired for doing so.

In discussing his children's adventure story *Chike and the River,* Achebe points out that the teaching and entertainment aspects of stories are not necessarily separable. In that story the young boy Chike moves from a small bush village to a city where his curiosity and adventurous spirit lead him to capture some robbers. Achebe believes that many of his countrymen in Nigeria are generally in need of a more adventurous spirit, as there is less a premium on adventure there than in many Western cultures. Thus, the element of adventure in that story is itself a teaching aspect. The same might be said for **"The Flute,"** which approves an adventure taken on behalf of personal values.

There is, however, a delicate balance in **"The Flute"** between individual and social or cultural values. As a common function of folktales is to legitimize and to teach a society's values, we would not expect a tale from a culture that places high value on the family and respect for ancestors and spirits to treat lightly a child's defiance of these values. And this tale does not. Except for breaking the taboo against entering the fields at night when the spirits inhabit them, the boy respects the spirits. He even apologizes to them: " 'I did not mean to offend you but only to take back my flute.' " Further, his reward depends upon scrupulous obedience to their instructions about his return home and his opening of the pot. His reward also depends upon a display of respect for his parents.

The second boy's experience obviously underlines the moral points already made. Encouraged by his mother, he disregards for purely selfish reasons the taboo of visiting the fields at night, and he does not hesitate to insult and disobey the spirits and to show his greed in claiming the flute "of shining precious metal" and in choosing the larger pot. Further encouraging him in his greed and defiance of the spirits' instructions upon his arrival home, his mother seals her hut and opens the pot without inviting her husband. The boy and his mother are, of course, rewarded for their greed and defiance by death. The tale, then, manages to uphold the important cultural values of respect for family and for spirits, while at the same time it presents an instance in which personal values may rightly take precedence over social ones. And the second boy's story makes it clear that the values which may acceptably and temporarily replace social ones may not be rooted in the desire for mere selfish gain. The tale censures greed, envy, and self-seeking defiance of social taboos and affirms adventure, courage, and unselfishness. (pp. 250-51)

Marianne Whelchel, "Achebe's 'The Flute'," in Sharing Literature with Children: A Thematic Anthology, edited *by Francelia Butler, David McKay Company, Inc., 1977, pp. 248-51.*

Richard (George) Adams

1930-

English author of fiction and poetry.

The following entry presents criticism of *Watership Down*.

Applauded as one of the best contemporary writers of fantasy, Adams is well known as the creator of *Watership Down* (1972), the story of a valiant band of rabbits in search of a home where they can live in peace. Considered a work of exceptional originality and scope as well as the first book to make anthropomorphic rabbits into truly heroic figures, *Watership Down* is recognized as a modern classic which blurs the distinctions between juvenile and adult literature. It is also acknowledged as one of literature's most notable financial successes: marketed as both a book for children and an adult novel, *Watership Down* became an immediate best seller and is now considered an international publishing phenomenon. A lengthy, challenging work which explores the nature of leadership and the struggle for survival, *Watership Down* offers readers from the upper elementary grades through adulthood entry into the world of rabbits, a civilization complete with its own history, language, mythology, and government. Drawing from folklore and the animal fable as well as on the epic and the picaresque novel, Adams describes how Hazel, an inventive and determined rabbit, takes a small band of refugee bucks on a hazardous quest through the English countryside to find a new home after his brother, the visionary Fiver, senses the destruction of their warren by a developer. After of series of adventures which include a nearly fatal encounter with a group of lotus-eaters and a dangerous search for does, the rabbits try to settle in Watership Down, an actual location in Berkshire. After Watership Down is invaded by General Woundwort, a tyrannical and psychotic rabbit who leads a neighboring warren, the outnumbered troops emerge victorious and are ready to begin building a lasting democratic society. Adams breaks his narrative to introduce tales about El-ahrairah, the rabbits' folk hero, which outline the origins, characteristics, and religious beliefs influencing the behavior of Hazel and his band. Adams also provides a variety of literary, scientific, and historical references in *Watership Down:* for example, he introduces each of his chapters with quotes from dozens of masterpieces of Western literature and provides information on natural history both from personal observation and from R. M. Lockley's *The Private Life of the Rabbit,* a work considered a definitive source on lapine life.

A former civil servant in the Department of the Environment who has written two additional children's books and several works for adults, Adams wrote *Watership Down* to introduce his two daughters to literature by presenting them with the rules and principles of the adult novel. Underscoring the work is Adams's criticism of humanity as contrasted against rabbit society as well as his charge that nature is being destroyed by human technology. By using his rabbits to examine social organizations and responsibility, Adams outlines the elements necessary for creating a successful society, such as honor, courage, respect, cooperation, inherited culture, and religious faith. *Watership Down* has received a variety of interpretations since its publication: some critics see it as sex-

ist for portraying a male-dominated community which regards does merely as breeding stock, while other reviewers consider it a didactic, overly indulgent work which is too sophisticated and taxing for children. However, most observers admire *Watership Down* as a deeply moving story which successfully blends realism and imagination to create a credible rabbit world which parallels our own. Critic Alec Ellis has written that "*Watership Down* is a phenomenon the like of which only appears once or twice in a lifetime, and one could not reasonably ask for more of a treasure so scarce." Adams was awarded the Carnegie Medal and the Guardian Award in 1973 for *Watership Down.*

(See also *Contemporary Literary Criticism,* Vols. 4, 5, 18; *Something about the Author,* Vol. 7; *Contemporary Authors New Revision Series,* Vol. 3; and *Contemporary Authors,* Vols. 49-52.)

AUTHOR'S COMMENTARY

For years of my childhood I found solace and delight in the poems of Walter de la Mare. These are informed throughout, in the most disturbing manner, by a deep sense of mankind's ultimate ignorance and insecurity. ('The Children of Stare' is a really frightening poem in my opinion.) De la Mare scarcely mentions Christianity—if indeed he can be said to mention it at all. Cold, ghosts, grief, pain and loss stand all about the little cocoon of bright warmth, which is everywhere pierced by a wild, numinous beauty, catalyst of fear and weeping. Why ever should this be comforting? First, I think, simply because the words, sounds and rhythms are so beautiful. John Mouldy in his cellar is beautiful in the same way as Agamemnon's dreadful death-cry from within the palace. Secondly, the poems possess and confer dignity—they make you feel, though perhaps unconsciously, that the human race is nobler and grander than you knew. . . . Thirdly, they tell the truth. I used to weep at the grief of the Mad Prince, of poor Robin and his wife, of Dame Hickory and Mrs Gill. But I also felt that this poet treated me as a potential adult and showed respect for me by telling me the truth—and all in words of storm, rainbow and wave. His sorrow was better than Mabel Lucie Attwell's reassurance. From de la Mare I derived early the idea that one must at all costs tell the truth to children, not so much about mere physical pain and fear but about the really unanswerable things—what Thomas Hardy called 'the essential grimness of the human situation' . . . I would like to think that Silverweed, the story of the Black Rabbit and the Epilogue are in some degree in debt to the atmosphere of de la Mare's lyrics. Ultimately, of course, El-ahrairah *is* the Black Rabbit, but not in any way that we—or rabbits—can expect to comprehend in this world. But it is, perhaps, significant that Bigwig asks for the story of the Black Rabbit, to encourage him before he goes into Efrafa. He prefers the truth, as did I when a child.

My childhood—the twenties and early thirties—was the heyday of J. M. Barrie and of Christopher Robin, when children were seen by many people primarily as delicate, sensitive, small creatures, who ought properly to live in a world from which not only suffering, but to some extent reality, were excluded until they were older. This idea is not altogether false, of course, but at that time it was overdone. . . . (pp. 164-65)

I personally felt resentful of this general atmosphere, which thwarted one's natural aggression while at the same time unfitting one for the rougher side of life, so that one felt—and hated knowing that one was justified in feeling—at a disadvantage. . . . It was also a time when quite a lot of people tended to tell lies to children with a view to protecting them from apprehension, fear and grief. The trouble was that the lies tended to fall down. They told you the dentist wasn't going to hurt; but of course he did. They said the cat hadn't been run over. Later, the gardener told you it had. This kind of deprivation—deprivation of the natural human lot of physical fear, pain and hardship—should, I think, be considered as something separate from deprivation of the numinous and disturbing. The latter I never really suffered. The former I certainly did—and it has not really got much to do with the latter.

In this difficulty I derived a lot of help and comfort from the books of Ernest Thompson Seton. He didn't dodge danger, fear, bloodshed and death. Just the contrary—on the straightforward, physical level he laid it on with a trowel. He simply gave it to you perfectly straight. Raggylug and the snake, Molly Cottontail going through the ice, Hekla and the Silver Fox drifting down to death on the ice floes, the nest-building sparrow who accidentally hanged himself in a length of horsehair, the murder (for that is what it amounted to) of Krag, the Kootenay Ram—I have never forgotten these and similar incidents in Seton's work. They were honest and true,

as the horrors in Conan Doyle's *Brigadier Gérard* or R. M. Ballantyne's *Coral Island* were not. (Those seem, in several cases, the nasty, crypto-masturbatory offshoots of repressed minds—and that, too, I sensed instinctively at an early age.) If the physical truth is cruel and terrible, be a man and say so (but don't be a pervert and say so), and you may help your reader more than you know. This idea underlies the crushed hedgehog on the road in **Watership Down,** Bigwig in the snare and the gassing of the Sandleford warren recounted by Holly. (Should Bigwig have died after fighting Woundwort? Perhaps he should. I return to this below.)

The first 'great' book which I encountered with no holds barred was *The Pilgrim's Progress,* and I had the good luck to encounter it all by myself, without any intermediary, at a relatively early age—seven. The gardener was a devout 'chapel' man and he simply lent it to me as he might have lent it to anyone; in a little, square, dark-green, cloth-bound edition with tiny, but perfectly clear, marginal steel engravings; which you could treat fairly roughly because it was rather worn already and anyway the gardener wouldn't be particular about a book as, say, your godfather would. I felt a tremendous respect for the book (and perhaps for myself for reading it?) I read it stolidly, with all the disputes and doctrinal conversations, which I was quite incapable of understanding. Nevertheless, those conversations did something for me. Unconsciously, I realized that parenthesis has a valuable part to play in a relatively long book (at that age it seemed to me a relatively long book) by giving the reader a rest and by making divisions between 'peaks'—dramatic, objective adventures which would otherwise crowd each other. (Later, of course, I came across the same technique in *Pickwick Papers.*) I had little idea what Christian and Co. were disputing about, but I knew it must be something valuable, or the book wouldn't still be there after two hundred and sixty years, or whatever it was. I remembered this when deciding to include, in a book which was going to be long anyway, the parenthetical tales of El-ahrairah and the two narratives of Holly. Simply that the immediacy of the main action is taken away for a time, gives the reader a respite—which is what I got from Mr Bunyan's incomprehensible doctrinal conversations. (pp. 166-67)

At that date you could not escape the Pooh books—you were rolled in them by the grownups, who loved them. So did I, and I am ready to defend them now. . . . [One] thing the Pooh stories have, pressed down and running over. They have marvellous characters; clear, consistent, interacting upon each other, each talking like himself—as good as Jane Austen's, in their own way. The relationship of Pooh and Piglet is splendid. Tigger is unforgettable. So is Eeyore—as far as I know, the first portrait in English literature of a type of neurotic we all know only too well; though perhaps he owes a little to Mrs Gummidge, 'the lone, lorn crittur' in *David Copperfield.* From the Pooh books I learned the vital importance, as protagonists, of a group of clearly-portrayed, contrasting but reciprocal characters—though I wouldn't claim that Hazel, Fiver and Co, come anywhere near Pooh and his friends. It would take Tommy Handley, Colonel Chinstrap and Mrs Mopp to do that, though I'd also be prepared to admit Doctor Dolittle and his household.

But 'Journey', I can hear someone saying. Surely you derived from the Pilgrim's Progress the concept of Journey, didn't you? Perhaps I did—but here it is another book which I think of. No one told me about it. I had never heard of it. I found it by myself, in my prep. school library, at the age of eleven. It was a first edition (by Duckworth) and had at that time been extant only seventeen years—Walter de la Mare's *The Three Mulla-Mulgars* (now known for the worse as *The Three Royal Monkeys*). For me, this great work was a milestone of profound importance. It opened my eyes. A tear springs to my eye as I think of what I owe to it. At the time, it seemed that this alone was a story and that all others were mere attempts at stories. I need not speak of the Mulgars' journey. From it I understood, darkly, that we are all wandering in the snow, to an unknown destination beyond darkness and hypnotic water. Never pretend otherwise. I understood, too, for the first time, that the greatest achievement of a great novel is to create, by feeling, selection and emphasis, a particular world, having its own colours, its own sun and moon, climate, atmosphere and values (how inadequate are words), more real than those of the actual world, to which the devoted reader can return again and again for delight and comfort. (pp. 167-68)

To try to copy *The Three Mulla-Mulgars* would be like trying to copy *King Lear.* But involuntarily, certain specific incidents and features of **Watership Down** undoubtedly reflect, *mutatis mutandis,* that unparalleled work—rather as the William books may be said to reflect *Huckleberry Finn.* Most obviously, of course, there is the weakling hero with the second sight who guides and saves his friends, sometimes despite their disbelief or contempt. Fiver is Ummanodda, no danger. And Fiver's meeting, in a trance, with the man putting up the board in memory of Hazel, recalls Nod's dream of the Oomgar's spelling-book, which led him to save the Moona-Mulgar who had fallen over the ledge during the fight with the eagles. The Black Rabbit of Inlé owes something to the Immanâla; though she is wicked and hateful, while the Black Rabbit is not. He is, rather, a counterpart of the Hindu Kali—the terrible but necessary death-aspect of God's face.

One thing of a different nature I owe to *The Three Mulla-Mulgars.* My family, all of them, scoffed and jeered—a shade harshly, I fancy—at my passion for it. No doubt I was a bore, but the pain taught me, once and for all, never to mock any child's feeling for any book—you never know what it may mean to him. And it drove the Mulgars underground, to germinate in silence and darkness—the best conditions for such a process, I dare say.

Early, too, I came upon the ghost stories of M. R. James and of Algernon Blackwood, for my elder sister introduced me to them when I was about ten. Oh boy, was I frightened by those ghost stories? . . . In these stories I watched their writers building up tension by the use of little, vaguely-disturbing touches and incidents, and the worrying, harassing and baiting of the reader; the step-by-step technique; the use of some apparently innocuous phrase ('There *is* no kitchen cat') to turn the screw a little tighter and to lure the reader into frightening himself far more effectively than straight talk could ever frighten him. Then suddenly, the trap goes off. The awful figure of crumpled sheets sits up in the empty bed, and the devil-creature from Canon Alberic's scrapbook is crouching beside the reader's own chair. Undoubtedly, the mounting sense of unease and the feeling that something is wrong in Cowslip's warren owes something to M. R. James, even though the episode is not a supernatural one. Perhaps it is not entirely successful—one or two people have told me that they knew the answer before the trap went off (and Bigwig in it). Still, for the matter of that, one knows there's going

to be a ghost—but precisely *how* will it appear and when, and what will it do? (All James's ghosts are malignant.) But the other passage of tension-building—Bigwig in Efrafa—is, I fancy, reasonably effective. A bit of appropriate weather can help a lot in bringing off the atmosphere of such an episode, but I can't trace the Efrafan thunderstorm to any book of my childhood. I think that that may owe most to the heat in Moscow in *Crime and Punishment,* and to Walter de la Mare's short story *Crewe.*

Moonfleet is a wonderful book (and has quotations as chapter-headings—not very apt ones, for the most part, I fear—but a nice idea to borrow. . . . Nothing in it is more moving than the character of Elzevir Block, the strong, grim man who never complains of his wrongs and in the end gives his life to save the hero's. Actually, Elzevir hazards his life for the hero twice before the end on Moonfleet beach—once on the Zig-Zag and once at Carisbrooke well. I am sure that he contains the germ of Bigwig, who survives the snare, fights the cats at Nuthanger Farm and goes alone into Efrafa before he finally meets Woundwort in single combat. To live up to Elzevir, Bigwig should have died in that fight. It would have been right artistically, but I could not bring myself to do it, or face up to depicting the grief of the other rabbits. Nor did I really want to attempt that most difficult of feats, a muted, half-happy ending. Besides, my daughters did not want Bigwig to die—and would anyone else have preferred it, really? After all, the book is escapist fantasy. (pp. 168-70)

The El-ahrairah stories derive from folk-tales, of which any good nursery, of course, is full. We had Andrew Lang, naturally, but I also had a splendid book called *Stories of the Birds from Myth and Fable.* (Author's name forgotten.) I wish I had it now. (Could anyone help?) Only one of the El-ahrairah stories, however, was actually lifted from a real folk-tale—the one about Hufsa and the trial of El-ahrairah. In the Russian story, an old peasant finds a hoard of gold in the forest, but his wife is such an inveterate gossip that he dares not bring it home, or the whole village will get to know and the lord of the manor or the bailiff will have it off him. So when he and she go together to pick up the gold, he arranges in advance that their journey shall be full of fantastic incidents. E.g. he puts a pike up a tree. Later, she tells all the incidents to the village, with the result that no one believes a word about either the journey or the gold. All the other four El-ahrairah stories (one of which, of course, is not funny) are simply 'in the manner of'. Perhaps they have their prototypes, but if so I can't place them consciously. I think the Uncle Remus stories have some relevance, too, but no adventure of El-ahrairah is lifted from Brer Rabbit. What I do feel I owe to Joel Chandler Harris, however, is the meticulous care which he takes to render dialect in carefully-considered and accurate phonetics. Uncle Remus you can hear to perfection. Thus encouraged, I took a deal of pains over the speech of the farmhands and of Lucy and her father, and if they're not accurate Hampshire, then it can't be done, I reckon.

But Kipling unimitated, inimitable Kipling, how shall I describe thee? Beyond argument, no one has ever written books more full of enjoyment for children. *The Just-So Stories,* the Jungle Books, *Puck of Pook's Hill* and *Rewards and Fairies* have no equal; and while we are about it, I would like to include the Barrack-Room Ballads. I remember well a dormitory-full of twelve- and thirteen-year-olds laying aside their own books on a Saturday night to listen to one of us who felt impelled to read the ballads aloud, with passionate intensity.

Eleven years later he was killed in Normandy, and I can never read 'Ford o' Kabul river in the dark' without remembering him. Re-assessing these books as an adult, and in the light of Kipling's work as a whole, it seems to me that he was, in a sense, at his happiest and best in writing them, for to a child audience his fault of sententious didacticism is not irritating as it is to adults, and in these tales his fault of a certain insensitivity and banality—even vulgarity— . . . seems to fall away from him. The stories are often, in fact, extremely sensitive, and possess a sure imaginative empathy. It is very hard to find any fault at all with the best of them—*The King's Ankus, Red Dog,* the Sir Richard Dalyngridge stories and *The Knife and the Naked Chalk.* Can I claim to have been influenced by them, in the sense that my work shares any of their qualities? No, in that sense I cannot. But nevertheless, in two very important respects Kipling has his finger firmly in the **Watership Down** pie, and without him those lines would never have been written—or certainly not in the way they are. First, Kipling's illusion-formula for an anthropomorphic fantasy is an excellent one—so I deliberately copied it. The point is interesting, at any rate to any carpenter of tales. How exactly do you go about an anthropomorphic fantasy? Beyond one end of the scale altogether—a sort of ultra-violet—stands Henry Williamson. *Tarka the Otter* is superb natural history, but for that very reason it is neither a novel nor an anthropomorphic fantasy; nor is it meant to be either. It is simply an account of the life and death of a real otter. Next comes Ernest Thompson Seton. He wrote about real animals living their lives, but he shaped the stories a shade beyond straight *tranche de vie,* and was not concerned positively to stress, as Williamson does, that an animal *is* not a human being. At the extreme other end of the scale is Kenneth Grahame, whose animals are simply humans disguised in animals' bodies. All anthropomorphic fantasies have to pick a point along that line. The genre is an illusion-game. What's your particular formula? Kipling ensured retention of his animal protagonists' dignity (and also, I think, of their essential animal nature, albeit anthropomorphized), while leaving himself a very wide scope for his narrative powers. His rule is (and you need a rule to be bound by, to keep your invention within a disciplined and consistent frame) to attribute to his animal characters human thoughts, human powers of converse, even human values (e.g. loyalty) but never to make them do anything of which real animals would actually be physically incapable. I can't help feeling, with all due respect, that I may even have played a little fairer than Kipling in one way. His animals have some rather up-stage motives at times, based on the 'Law of the Jungle', etc., Hazel & Co., however, are never concerned with anything except food, survival and mating. Otherwise, like Baloo and Kaa, they certainly do things animals *wouldn't* do, but never anything they *couldn't* do.

The other Kipling influence can be simply stated. Don't be afraid to let your writing be difficult, or to make big demands on your readers. Say what you have to say and don't be deterred by wondering whether they're going to be able to follow you. I have been pleasantly staggered to receive letters of obviously sincere appreciation from eight-year-olds; I wouldn't have thought anyone under ten could tackle **Watership Down.** It only goes to show. Apparently straight writing carries some kind of readability of its own. But after all, eight-year-olds read the Authorized Version quite happily. When I began on Kipling, I was eleven. It seemed very difficult stuff then, but the difficulty was part of the fascination. No doubt he knew that.

I believe writing is rather like chess in the respect that although there are certain useful rules to bear in mind, a lot of these should really be torn up at discretion. As far as learning how to do it goes, there is no substitute for continually studying the games of the great players. As fast as you try to articulate rules for writing for children (or for anybody else), someone will triumphantly break them. What else did Lewis Carroll and Kenneth Grahame do? (Anyway, what are the rules about writing for adults—perhaps we ought to have a few of those too?) I would say, beware principles and rules about writing for children—the value of an established moral order and all that. One can easily get so blinkered by the rules that one can no longer judge a book by the light of the heart. That light, of course, is what is used by the children themselves— of whom the Lord, in one of His most enigmatic and dazzling utterances, said: 'In heaven their angels do always behold the face of my Father.' And we all want to do that, don't we? (pp. 171-73)

Richard Adams, *"Some Ingredients of 'Watership Down',"* in The Thorny Paradise: Writers on Writing for Children, *edited by Edward Blishen, Kestrel Books, 1975, pp. 163-73.*

THE TIMES LITERARY SUPPLEMENT

Watership Down has all the originality and depth so often lacking in children's novels. These are no cosy nursery bunnies, but very real rabbits. With great thoroughness Mr Adams leads us into a new lapine dimension. From blood and the thump of fear to the pleasure of good feeding, the discovery of new surroundings (a road or river) or the texture of the day, we are immersed in the rabbits' world. The immersion is helped by a lapine vocabulary and even mythology. . . . But, and it is this combination that makes the book remarkable, one might at the same time be reading some gripping escape story, the rabbit characters are so totally credible. . . .

The Berkshire Downs provide the novel's setting (there is even a reference map) and Mr Adams's love of the countryside is very apparent. His knowledge of wild flowers and trees is as thorough as his knowledge of rabbit lore. Once in a while the descriptive prose becomes a little windy, but for years children have swallowed all those purple passages in *The Wind in the Willows,* so they will swallow these too. Some might even enjoy Mr Adams's use of words. Grass, for example, "coruscated along the miles of escarpment"; rabbits hear "the continual susurration of trees" while elms are "multifoliate and powerful". One of the free rabbits pleads with the General that animals have "dignity and animality". These two qualities are embodied in **Watership Down.**

"The Burrowers," in The Times Literary Supplement, *No. 3692, December 8, 1972, p. 1489.*

THE ECONOMIST

A great children's book is always a great rarity; but this one deserves all the accolades it is currently receiving. It is right outside the mainstream of children's publishing. That is not to say that children's publishing is not, as a whole, remarkably good: for calibre, colour and price it compares increasingly favourably with adult literature. . . .

This book is a saga of the migration of a small group of

youngish bucks from a warren threatened by planning permission through dangerous and unknown countryside to Watership Down, and of the capture of does from a hostile warren to perpetuate their own new one. The trick is, at least partly, that Mr Adams has so exact a knowledge of the territory he describes, a real piece of downland and common on the Hampshire-Berkshire border, and so profound a knowledge of animal behaviour, that fantasy is contained within the real and not superimposed upon it; he colours and reinforces nature rather than obscuring or concealing ignorance of it. And he is, above all, a remarkable story teller. He can pile up suspense, convey urgency, relief or fear, melt his characters into the landscape or make them stand out from it with equal facility. This book was, it seems—in the tradition of all classics—rejected by three publishers. If there is no place for **Watership Down** in children's bookshops, then children's literature is dead.

"Pick of the Warren," in The Economist, *Vol. 245, No. 6748, December 23, 1972, p. 47.*

LEON GARFIELD

I don't know whether Mr Adams had one or a dozen purposes in mind in creating this large-scale narrative; certainly it has many parallels—political, social, philosophic—with our own society. But these parallels are only parallels; they are not the heart of the book. **Watership Down** is a grand, epic adventure, taking place in the Berkshire of here and now. It is not fantasy; it is not science fiction or historical drama. It is set in an aggressively present-day world, even to the housing-estates.

How has it been done? Quite simply Mr Adams has set his novel in the only world where such an epic adventure is still possible. He has set it in the fields and undergrowth—and in the rabbit-warrens. His protagonists are rabbits—wild rabbits.

Using the same raw materials as Beatrix Potter and Alison Uttley, Mr Adams has created an entirely absorbing and original novel. The sheer impudence of the notion takes one's breath away; but the integrity with which it is carried out provokes a deep sigh of satisfaction. The natural world is observed and rendered with wonderful precision; and the character of the wandering band of rabbits, with their language and their legends, becomes part of one's own experience as one progresses through the book.

This seems to me to be a measure of the book's excellence. When Hazel, Fiver or Bigwig silflay or pass hraka, one knows precisely what is meant and one feels that the language has been not so much invented as divined. The 'hedgerow patios' I found particularly sharp; for this book has its moments of really forceful comedy. An injured gull is as acute as any denizen of Soho.

Some writers have already commented on Mr Adams's choice of quotations for chapter headings. These range from Aeschylus to Napoleon Bonaparte to Dostoievsky and reflect the breadth and sagacity of the author's reading. Apart from their general aptness, I take them as being indicative of the scale and seriousness of the enterprise. At first glance it would seem bizarre that so substantial a book (there are more than four hundred well-filled pages) should be offered on the juvenile list; but on reflection, its appearance in such a place shows very plainly that the so-called 'juvenile list' is the last

refuge of the narrative novelist. Here at least, he can still achieve honour and dignity by 'telling a story.'

Leon Garfield, "Burrow in Berkshire," in The Spectator, *Vol. 230, No. 7545, February 3, 1973, p. 141.*

C. S. HANNABUSS

Fantasy as a genre appeals rather to a temperament than an age group, and the corollary of this is that the *manner* rather than the *matter* is likely to determine readership level. **Watership Down,** where the plot is not always able to keep the sheer business of writing afloat, presents a test case of the conflict between manner and matter, a conflict that does not exist in the work to which it is being persistently compared, The Lord of the Rings trilogy.

The traditional bunny rabbit, from Brer Rabbit in *Uncle Remus* to Peter Rabbit of Beatrix Potter, was humanised and could talk. Adams's first task is to establish his rabbits as credible heroes, and for this they have to talk. It is a great shame, therefore, that what they say is made up of so many tired middle-class conversationalisms 'What a frightful noise!', 'Confounded fool!'), anti-Gowers officialese ('He relapsed into hedgerow vernacular . . .'), and outdated pompous slang. Two things result from this: one, their heroism is reduced; two, they humanise across to types which are essentially boring.

Elaborate efforts are made to de-anthropomorphise them by the inclusion of excerpts on rabbitology from R. M. Lockley's *The Private Life of the Rabbit:* perhaps in imitation of the folk-wisdom embodied in traditional story-telling, these help to establish the rabbits as rabbits despite their textbook dogmatism. Further, at one remove, they underpin episodes in the story—for instance, Fiver's premonition about the destruction of the warren has a biological source. The more fictionally this material is used, the better it becomes: the rabbits have to go against their natures in order to survive at all, fighting their instinct to panic, adapting to new country, acquiring new skills. Again, the world is seen from the rabbit point of view, so that it is a world of plants and burrows and avoidance of enemies (men and their machines, dogs and stoats and weasels, and the white sickness), seen vividly from within.

The best material comes when Hazel and his friends attack the police-state warren of Efrafa in search of does. Under the relentless scrutiny of General Woundwort and his secret service of Owsla, the rabbits live a 1984 existence and feed and sleep in shifts. All have lost the will to live until Bigwig infiltrates himself in as a spy. The terrifying escape in a thunderstorm, down river on a makeshift raft, and even more terrifying reprisals it brings, are described with much of the excitement of *The Hobbit.* The last defence of Watership Down, Bigwig's last stand, the gruesome death of the fanatical Woundwort are moments when manner becomes matter, when we read apace.

But most of the time this fusion is absent. A continuous sense of artificial delay leads one to wonder whether the plot as it is conceived can really support over 400 pages. . . . [Even] by adult standards, the style gets in the way. Just as Adams has difficulty in telling a story for children, he has difficulty in communicating his love of nature to adults—and this is the attitude of Richard Jeffries with the mysticism replaced by a sense of ecology. Only in the mythic tale of the Black Rabbit of Inlé does a magic start to grow.

The book's strength lies in its adventures when disentangled from the complications of presentation, and this will place it on the children's shelves, besides Tolkien and Asimov's *Foundation.* It is also ideal cult-fantasy for adults, a schizoid area where matter/manner problems become hermaphroditic. Once upon a time, a book like this was bound to appear. (pp. 43-4)

C. S. Hannabuss, in a review of "Watership Down," in Children's Book Review, *Vol. III, No. 2, April, 1973, pp. 43-4.*

AIDAN CHAMBERS

Watership Down is presently a name to conjure with. An extraordinary feat of sustained narrative, the novel appeared in England towards the end of 1972. . . . [Everyone] who bothers at all about children's books (and some who don't) have now formed extreme opinions—this being one of those books about which it is not easy, if at all possible, to be neutral. I've no doubt that, as with Alice, the hobbits, and Batman, there'll be cultishness to cope with before long. (p. 253)

[Lapine] fantasy is not my literary cup of tea—be it for children or not, and I question whether *Watership Down* was ever really intended for children until the question of publication arose. Rabbits, to my mind, are best left to their own rodent activities. And had I not had to review the tome, I would certainly have given it the go-by. (p. 254)

Disconsolate, a reviewer in professional straits, I set to work. But work it remained for only a page or two. Thereafter, I was an addict. I could have stayed on Watership Down . . . as long as Mr. Adams wished to keep me there. Four hundred and thirteen pages seemed, when they were finished, a less than generous amount. Absorbing, sensational, staggeringly unexpected, flawed to the point of critical disaster, brilliant, exciting, evocative (the sense of place and atmosphere, climate and season is beautifully achieved), English to the last full-stop, tough, gentle, blood-shot, violent, satisfying, humorous. The list of epithets, superlatives, qualifiers, paradoxes, and blazoned blooming nouns could cover the rest of the space allotted me.

In sum, *Watership Down,* though not a comfortable nor even a lovely book, is deeply moving and vividly memorable in the way that all "good" books, all works of true art, are: They implant themselves—some by main force, others by subtle injection—into the living tissues of your being, to remain there, illuminating your view of life ever after. Most obviously and least importantly, rabbits will never be the same again for me, a warren never again be simply a collection of messy holes in the ground. But to say that is to say little. There are some who speak of allegory and hint at many hidden and profound meanings burrowed beneath the surface of the narrative. They may well be right. But I suspect there are as many different tunnels of meaning as one cares to dig. So, to return for now to the pleasantly simple and obvious: I shall never again watch a bobbed and white-lined tail stub its way across a field in pursuit of a hedge without believing it belongs to a lapine guerrilla from the warren Mr. Adams biographs in such rich and intimate detail.

The story is what one might expect had *Wind in the Willows* been written after two World Wars, various marks of nuclear bomb, the Korean and Vietnam obscenities, and half-a-dozen other hells created by the inexhaustibly evil powers of Man. In fact, the tale begins with a deliberate act of demolition,

when human beings destroy an ancient warren in order to clear a building site, inadvertently leaving alive a handful of ill-assorted rabbits to wander the countryside as refugees. Despite all the calamities that befall luckless Toad, no one ever dreamt Toad Hall would be bulldozed. And putting the pick into the medieval rooms inhabited by Badger would have been unthinkable. But that was 1908. And 1908 is gone, *Wind in the Willows* with it. *Watership Down,* if none the wiser than that wise and lovely book, is a great deal better informed. (pp. 254-55)

Aidan Chambers, "Letter from England: Great Leaping Lapins!" in The Horn Book Magazine, *Vol. XLIX, No. 3, June, 1973, pp. 253-55.*

GRAHAM HAMMOND

That *Watership Down* should have been acclaimed as an original first book by a writer of unusual talents is not difficult to see and to some extent justify: the rabbit is not an unfamiliar figure in children's fiction but he has never before been the hero of an epic tale of leadership and the struggle for survival; and the author's stamina, narrative skill, inventiveness, linguistic ingenuity, keen observation of nature and wide knowledge of literature in at least three languages form an impressive repertoire of skills. One might have thought that the book's great length and its self-conscious literariness would have diminished its appeal as a children's book, but its pace, liveliness and clarity of plot make it extremely readable and many children as well as adults will get much pleasure from it. What more could one ask of a children's book?

Richard Adams's book is interesting, apart from its merit and its enthusiastic reception, because it raises in a particularly striking way the familiar question, how are we to judge children's books? At one level, immediately accessible to children, we have the story about the rabbits and their adventures. At another level, intelligible to some children at some stage, is the significance of the anthropomorphic rabbits and the comment the author is making through them about human nature and the human predicament. The trouble with epics and literary allusions is that although they probably have little or no conscious effect upon the child reader, they flatter the adult reader, evoking in him echoes of his literary education and inducing expectations of profundity. Unless the author has taken us all for an elegant ride and never intended his moral, social, political and even metaphysical meanings to be taken seriously, we have in *Watership Down* a view of man which in many respects seems outmoded and scarcely adequate. A writer, whether for children or adults, may not always be aware of the values and assumptions which his work embodies, but it is part of the adult reader's responsibility to examine and evaluate them. With a children's book such considerations are complicated by the question, what shall we tell the children? We know, for example, that a child needs the assurance of a secure and dependable moral order in the universe, but if this means that a writer for children must either live in the past or suspend his modern consciousness, then this has crucial implications for the nature and status of writing for children. (pp. 48-9)

By devising the overarching narrative concerning the flight of Hazel and his followers and their quest to found a new warren, Richard Adams has hit upon a structure of remarkable flexibility and potential which not only generates and binds together the prolific succession of episodes and incidents in the main story, but also supports a number of subsidiary narratives. The author organizes his complex material with a sure touch and he is adept for the most part at making the apparent digressions functional in the book as a whole and plausible at the point of their introduction.

For example, the first of the legendary tales of El-ahrairah, the rabbits' folk hero, is told by Dandelion at Hazel's request to raise the morale of the dispirited band of fleeing rabbits and distract them from their gloomy preoccupations at a critical point in their flight. Together these tales constitute the mythology of the rabbits, explaining their racial origins, characteristics and religious beliefs which at various crises in the main story influence the rabbits' behaviour. But this endless capacity for telling stories, the apparent determination to miss not a single opportunity for elaboration, is the cause of a number of weaknesses in the book, leading not only to its excessive length but more seriously to the unsatisfactory dénouement, where the dramatic impetus is dissipated in a series of flashbacks culminating in the intrusive Lucy, whose appearance is as unnecessary and ill-judged as the choice of chapter heading *Dea ex machina* threatens. In this fondness for elaboration and in other ways the author shows a tendency to indulge himself at the expense of his book.

The author has taken pains to establish his characters' lapine credentials. Explicit references to his source of information appear in the text as well as in the Acknowledgments. . . . But fidelity to the ways of rabbits would be an intolerable restriction in a work of fiction, and in the best tradition of anthropomorphic animal stories, Richard Adams allows his rabbits, within certain physical limits, to think, feel and act as human beings. One never loses sight of their rabbitness and this mixture of realism and imagination enables the author to present an authentic and informative picture of life in the warren and at the same time, by giving his rabbits human attributes, to represent and comment upon the affairs of men. The authentic element is so pervasive and the distinction between fact and fiction so blurred that a child might be forgiven for believing that rabbits could and would, for example, free another rabbit from a snare or escape from an enemy by floating down a river on a punt released by gnawing through a rope. (pp. 49-50)

The story opens with Fiver's premonition of imminent disaster to Sandleford Warren. Though physically weak, Fiver has a strong influence on Hazel because of his visionary powers, which not only in their physical symptoms closely resemble Cassandra's, but the significance of which the author explicitly links with the *Agamemnon* by heading his opening chapter with four lines of Aeschylus in Greek. . . . (p. 50)

In order to urge the Chief Rabbit to abandon the warren, Hazel, accompanied by Fiver, persuades the guard, Bigwig, to arrange an audience, which he does with misgivings because the Chief Rabbit is held in some awe:

> The Chief Rabbit's name and style was *Threarah,* meaning 'Lord Rowan Tree'. For some reason he was always referred to as 'The Threarah'—perhaps because there happened to be only one threar, or rowan, near the warren, from which he took his name. He had won his position not only by strength in his prime, but also by level-headedness and a certain self-contained detachment, quite unlike the impulsive behaviour of most rabbits. It was well-known that he never let himself become excited by rumour or danger. He had coolly—some even said coldly—stood firm during the terrible onslaught of

the myxomatosis, ruthlessly driving out every rabbit who seemed to be sickening. He had resisted all ideas of mass emigration and enforced complete isolation on the warren, thereby almost certainly saving it from extinction. It was he, too, who had once dealt with a particularly troublesome stoat by leading it down among the pheasant coops and so (at the risk of his own life) on to a keeper's gun. He was now, as Bigwig said, getting old, but his wits were still clear enough. When Hazel and Fiver were brought in, he greeted them politely . . .

> 'Ah, Walnut. It is Walnut, isn't it?'

> 'Hazel', said Hazel.

> 'Hazel, of course. How very nice of you to come and see me. I knew your mother well. And your friend—'

> 'My brother.'

> 'Your brother,' said the Threarah, with the faintest suggestion of 'Don't correct me any more, will you?' in his voice. 'Do make yourselves comfortable. Have some lettuce?'

The Threarah listens politely, but never seriously considers the warning, because to give so unpalatable an order as to evacuate the warren would be to run the risk of losing his authority.

Sensing this, Fiver is smitten with another bout of tremors. The Threarah is compassionate:

> 'What a shame! What a shame! Poor fellow, perhaps he ought to go home and rest. Yes, you'd better take him along now. Well, it's really been extremely good of you to come and see me, Walnut, I appreciate it very much indeed. And I shall think over all you've said most carefully, you can be quite sure of that. Bigwig, just a moment, will you?'

> As Hazel and Fiver made their way dejectedly down the run outside the Threarah's burrow, they could just hear, from inside, the Chief Rabbit's voice assuming a rather sharper note, interspersed with an occasional 'Yes, sir,' 'No, sir.' Bigwig, as he had predicted, was getting his head bitten off.

In this passage the conditions of rabbit life and the conventions of 'civilized' society are worked together. But whether or not we enjoy this picture of life at the top with its rational basis for decision-making, we may pause to consider the question of the audience whom the writer wishes to address in and through his fiction. We may ask whether the author does not make demands of a kind and on a scale likely to overtax the child reader's understanding, experience and reading skills to the point where the book becomes something of an obstacle race, checking the reader's onward rush, and working against the author's otherwise swift narrative pace. One wonders, for instance, what children will make of the irony in the passage quoted, and there are linguistic and other features of the book which raise similar questions.

Four lines from *The Lotus-Eaters* are the signpost for another kind of political blindness which Hazel and his followers meet in Cowslip Warren. Having fled before the holocaust of Sandleford and having barely survived a number of hazards without loss, they are particularly susceptible to the allurements of a languid, well-fed life with the bland, immaculate Cowslip. The fact that this warren has a social and political system based on self-deception, reinforced by a taboo which prevents the rabbits from questioning their acquiescence in their inevitable death by snare, renders it a menace as sinister in its way as the totalitarian police state of Efrafa; for whereas General Woundwort is an obvious if fearsome adversary, Cowslip Warren is an insidious threat to the rabbits' will, eroding their resolve from within. (pp. 50-2)

The author's debt to Homer and Tennyson is acknowledged by the quotation from *The Lotus-Eaters,* for a good deal of the Cowslip Warren episode is one of the more expansive examples of a recurrent device, that of blending overt borrowings from literature with the author's own invention. It is a way of giving young readers their first taste of great literature which they will hopefully enjoy in the original later on. Some children will find the quotations at the head of each chapter a distraction and simply skip them. Most adults will enjoy the quotations for their own sake—the one from Malory, for example: ' . . . he plunged over the head in deep mires, for he knew not the way, but took the gainest way in that woodness . . .'—and will be intrigued to discover their aptness and what use Mr Adams makes of them in the story. There are over sixty of these quotations, two of them in French and one in Italian (without translation), and overall they contrive to give the book an old-fashioned flavour. *Watership Down* is a literary experience in a new sense.

The author's love of literature frequently runs over into his extensive knowledge and observation of wild life and his delight in explaining natural phenomena. He indulges himself in passages of considerable artistry but sometimes questionable literary taste. . . . (p. 53)

The author's love of nature and his intimate knowledge of the Berkshire Downs enable him to give his novel an unusually strong and vivid sense of place and to convey a powerful impression of the terrain in its varied forms and at various seasons. (p. 54)

But . . . there are signs of the excesses which mar many of the setpiece natural descriptions as for example when the sunrise is treated to the following device:

> Then the whole down and all below it, earth and air, gave way to the sunrise. As a bull, with a slight but irresistible movement, tosses its head from the grasp of a man who is leaning over the stall and idly holding its horn, so the sun entered the world in smooth, gigantic power. Nothing interrupted or obscured its coming.

The straining after effect, the self-conscious attempt at fine writing borders on the absurd and defeats the author's laudable desire to share with the young reader his delight in nature. [There is a] tendency towards a forced breathlessness and artifice. . . . (p. 55)

Another of the author's mannerisms is that of stepping out of the impersonal omniscient narrative stance to address the reader direct. (p. 56)

Frequently these asides are overtly didactic as, for example, at the height of the dramatic scene in which Hazel tries to negotiate with General Woundwort to save the warren, the writer gratuitously interposes:

> At that moment . . . there was offered to General Woundwort the opportunity to show whether he was really the leader of vision and genius which he believed himself to be, or whether he was no more

than a tyrant with the courage and cunning of a pirate.

(pp. 56-7)

[Persistent] didacticism is another aspect of the author's apparent desire to cram all the knowledge and wisdom he can into the book. One's doubts about this are not as to whether the ideas Mr Adams wishes to impart are interesting, valuable or even apposite, but rather they are about the author's choice of an overtly instructional mode which was once the fashion in 'improving' books, instead of allowing the insights to reveal themselves through situations and experiences which work upon the reader's imagination. In *Watership Down* much information is fed in at the factual textbook level; it is not synthesized into significant experience which enables the reader to develop an understanding through an intuitive response. The author's didacticism is at odds both with literary art and with effective education.

In places the space given to explaining an idea is disproportionate to the importance of that idea at the particular point in the narrative. It is as though the author cannot resist the temptation to inflate the situation with an elaborate flourish. . . . (p. 57)

There are many instances, especially when Hazel is establishing himself as leader both in relation to his followers and to other creatures encountered, that show [the author's] sensitivity to status. A particularly interesting example is the importance that is attached to Hazel's having a storyteller—Dandelion—of preeminent skill among his ragged band of followers. The function of the artist in society is, as in the old tradition, to divert, to remind rabbits of their cultural and religious inheritance, and to show other warrens how superior and civilized you are! In fairness one should add that the storytelling competition in the great burrow at Cowslip Warren—an event which has its own literary antecedents—is skilfully used to point up the cultural differences between Hazel's rabbits and their hosts who have abandoned their traditional beliefs epitomized in the figure of El-ahrairah and the legends which surround him.

In a sense El-ahrairah is the central figure in the theme of leadership and perhaps even of the book as a whole. (p. 58)

[At one level the legendary tales] contain some very amusing and entertaining episodes which children will greatly enjoy, such as the stratagems over King Darzin's lettuces and at the trial of El-ahrairah. At another level there is considerable skill in the way in which the oracles of El-ahrairah, the rabbits' equivalent of the Sibylline Books, are made to influence the action and supply an increasingly powerful religious not to say mystical element. Some of the events dictated by the religious demands that the author makes on his book seem less than well-judged. One instance of this is the mutilation of El-ahrairah (echoed in the mulilation and humiliation of Blackavar in Elfrafa, and corresponding both to Hazel's nearly fatal wounding at Nuthanger Farm and to Bigwig's ultimate bloody battle with General Woundwort) when he goes to offer his life to the Black Rabbit of Inlé in return for the safety of his people. The parallel between the legend and 'reality' is pointedly drawn when Bigwig, understandably thoughtful on the eve of his leading the extremely hazardous infiltration into General Woundwort's stronghold, claims the right to choose the evening's diversionary tale to be told by Dandelion. His deliberate choice is 'The Story of El-ahrairah and the Black Rabbit of Inlé', and Hazel's doubts about its suitability for raising their spirits seem justified. . . . (p. 59)

The link between legend and 'reality' is later reinforced when General Woundwort is referred to as 'first cousin to the Black Rabbit of Inlé himself,' and this is merely one of many complicated and at times confusing connections that are made between the various personal, political, religious and mystical elements in the course of the book. This complexity is handled with impressive skill and the book is on the whole a remarkable feat of organization and integration of many strands. But ultimately one is left with two questions: whether the rabbits' system of values and beliefs corresponds with the author's own and as such is being commended to the child reader; and whether these values and beliefs constitute profound insights or conventional wisdom. Leaving aside the political values explored in the book, the rabbits' theological and moral beliefs would seem to consist of fatalism ('For what is, is what must be'), a belief in El-ahrairah's power to protect and guide ('I believe El-ahrairah will save us from this Woundwort' and 'El-ahrairah has shown me what to do'), and a morality based on enlightened self-interest (see Hazel's policy of befriending strangers in case they should turn out to be useful in some future contingency). If this is a true interpretation, then it is to be wondered that so elaborate an allegorical apparatus should have been erected in order to deliver so orthodox a message. One may ask where the author stands in all this and in what relation to his child reader. (p. 60)

The book is almost inexhaustibly discussible. Whatever view one takes of it, the book cannot be ignored. Originality has been claimed for it, and certainly, taken as a whole, it is unique among children's books. And yet it has been shown to be a book in many ways so old-fashioned in style and outlook and so derivative in some of its elements as to test one's credulity that it could have been written and published in the 1970s. The most strikingly original aspect of the whole enterprise is that it has exploded many of the myths and limiting assumptions in the children's book publishing world as regards acceptable length, scope and subject-matter for children's books, and for this Mr Adams and Rex Collings should be congratulated.

However ambivalent one's views may be about the book, it is certainly better that we should have the book as written than that it should never have been published at all. (p. 62)

> *Graham Hammond, "Trouble with Rabbits," in* Children's literature in education, *No. 12, Fall, 1973, pp. 48-63.*

PETER S. PRESCOTT

I'll make a deal with you: if you won't say anything dumb like "I'm not interested in a story about rabbits," I won't say anything dumb like "this is a great novel." Because indiscriminate hostility toward modern animal fiction is generally sound critical practice, we must marvel that so fresh a twig can sprout from such a battered branch of literature. **Watership Down** is an adventure story of an epic scope that takes place within a few months and a few square miles of English soil. It is a story of exile and survival, of heroism and political responsibility, of the making of a leader and of a community. And it is more: through a remarkably sustained thrust of the imagination, Richard Adams has constructed a complete civilization, with its own governments, language and mythology. . . .

Adams handles his suspenseful narrative more dexterously than most authors who claim to write adventure novels, but his true achievement lies in the consistent, comprehensible and altogether enchanting civilization that he has created. His fantasy is firmly rooted in the world we know (which is why it may be enjoyed by readers allergic to J. R. R. Tolkien's hobbits, elves and walking trees). Beginning with what would appear to be all the information there is on how rabbits really behave, Adams provides us with a highly textured, ankle-high perspective on the English countryside. He convinces us that if rabbits were capable of conceptualizing their existence this is how they would think of themselves and the rest of the world—and he does it without anthropomorphism or sentimentality. The light sprinkling of rabbit language is linguistically interesting, as are the rabbits' ideas of freedom, the good life, even death: "We've all got to stop running one day, you know. They say Frith [the sun god] knows all the rabbits, every one."

But what is most extraordinary is the rabbit mythology, the legends of the first rabbit, a hero and prankster—legends that take the place of rabbit history (which couldn't very well exist) and are passed down in storytelling sessions. Adams has endowed these creatures with a spectacular creation legend and a deeply moving story of a rabbit redeemer who braves the palace of death to offer his own life for those of his people.

I cannot imagine that any sensible reader could come away from this novel unaffected and unchanged. A rabbit story it may be, but it is also about us, who live in communities and cope with the world. But then animal fables, like caricatures, get very quickly to essentials, unimpeded by surface distractions. I urge **Watership Down** upon you.

> *Peter S. Prescott, "Rabbit, Read," in* Newsweek, *Vol. LXXXIII, No. 11, March 18, 1974, p. 114.*

RICHARD GILMAN

I doubt that Richard Adams's **Watership Down** is really aimed at young children, despite his having said that it arose from impromptu stories he used to tell his small daughters. I can't imagine many readers under 13 or 14, an age when the lines between juvenile and adult fiction begin to blur, having the patience and grasp of extended allegorical strategies to persevere to the end of a 426-page epic about a community of rabbits. And while older teen-agers may well enjoy it, I suspect that this tour de force, the *Iliad* and *Odyssey* of *Oryctolagus cuniculus,* is going to find its true audience mainly among the people who have made a cult of Tolkien, among ecology-minded romantics and all those in need of a positive statement, not too subtle but not too blatant either, about the future of courage, native simplicity, the life-force, and so on.

I don't mean to be condescending. **Watership Down** is in some ways a delightful book, at times an affecting one. But faced with the extraordinary praise given the book in England, one has to draw back some distance. Lacking the high wit and imaginative force of *Alice in Wonderland* or the triumphant (if occasionally purple) lyricism of *The Wind in the Willows,* the book seems to me a good deal less than the "classic"—with the implication in the word of settled universal appeal—that British commentators have so reflexively proclaimed it.

Watership Down is a narrative of quest, in this case that of a group of male rabbits for a safe home. (p. 3)

The group is led throughout by a rabbit called Hazel, a figure of natural authority, whose chief assistants include Fiver, the clairvoyant, Bigwig, a tough, courageous fellow, and Blackberry, known for his cleverness. At times this division of qualities comes to resemble that of a Hollywood war movie, the kind with the brave guy, the prankster, the brooder, etc. But for the most part the characterizations work surprisingly well, and this is because Adams is able to get past the usual sentimentalities about bunnies and afford his creatures a rough plausibility as representatives of embattled life.

As in all such fiction, the plausibility issues from the detail and consistency with which the animal life is rendered, and above all from the resemblances we can discern to aspects of our own lives. (We can identify, for example, with the phenomenon of worker bees serving a queen, but not with the physiological process of making honey.) To this end Adams offers a remarkable wealth of information on rabbit existence . . . and wisely concentrates on matters of sustenance, living arrangement, behavior toward other animals, and the like.

But as anthropomorphic fantasy replaces observation (the book is set in an actual area of Berkshire, England, and Adams is particularly fine on landscapes and flora, weathers and seasons) he sees fit to give his rabbits a folklore and folk-heroes, a mythology complete with creation-myth and, finally, a language. It is a sparse tongue, consisting of a few dozen words like "frith" (sun) "hrududu" (motor vehicle) and "tharn" (hypnotized with fear), and because I could detect no principle to explain why only certain words are in Lapine, as it's called—"silf," for instance, is "outside" but "inside" is in English; a badger is a "lendri" but a mouse is a mouse—I suspect that the Lapine is there as a kind of whimsical bonus or, more dangerous for the enterprise, as an attempt to give the fantasy an extra dimension of "realism."

If I remember correctly, the great writers of animal fiction let their characters unselfconsciously speak the authors' own languages, and this is proper because the imaginative act is complete once the literary decision has been made to allow animals to speak in words; their own verbal language, is to tempt the pathetic fallacy beyond its acceptable limits. This may seem a small point, especially since the Lapine is a very minor element of the rhetoric, but I think it symptomatic of what is wrong with *Watership Down,* or rather what keeps it from being wholly right.

There is a subtle indecisiveness or doubt on Adams's part as to just how convincing his fiction is. This is manifested partly by his tendency to do too much (the Lapine, the rabbit-myths) and also by the frequent occasions when he steps outside the narrative to serve for a moment as a naturalist, dropping his anthropomorphic inventing to inform us that: "Rabbits, of course, have no precise idea of time or punctuality"; "the phenomenon of laughter is unknown to animals"; ". . . ideas of protection, fidelity, romantic love and so on . . . are, of course, unknown to rabbits."

Remarks such as these have the effect of somewhat undermining our commitment to the fiction. To be reminded of what we of course knew before we began reading the book, to be reminded really of the unhuman nature of rabbits, is to find it more difficult to accept a speech like this when it comes: "That Vilthuril's a beautiful doe. I'd like a chance to get to know her better." The point is that if you are going to anthropomorphize you had better do it all the way, relying

on the pure inventedness of your tale, the same outrageous conceit which is at the back of the March Hare, Mowgli and Pooh, however differing their literary realities.

Now I know there are going to be readers for whom such questions of literary strategy and imaginative rightness couldn't matter less. For some, particularly the younger ones, the narrative will be enough and, as I've said, that works perfectly well, as adventure and melodrama. For the other kind of readers I mentioned before, the ones I think will give *Watership Down* its cachet, the narrative will have more complex uses, being in the service of the book's "meanings," the lessons it teaches, its allegorical élan; such readers are just as unlikely to be troubled by inconsistencies or excesses.

For what is chiefly wanted from a book like this is *utilitarian* fantasy, qualities of reassurance and inspiration, a consoling legend. The morale it seems likely to instill, whatever its intentions, is that peculiar sort which consists in a strength gained through having been first made to feel ashamed, in this case ashamed of our oblique, acquisitive, "insincere" lives in the face of candid and undevious nature. It isn't that Adams has sentimentalized his rabbits—the book is no *Jonathan Livingston Seagull*—but that the shadowy presence of man is almost always characterized by hint and threat of evil, a theme on occasion made wholly explicit.

"Men will never rest until they've spoiled the earth and destroyed the animals," one of the rabbits says. And one of the quotations ranging from Aeschylus to Auden that preface each chapter and mainly serve to present human analogues to the events is this from Dostoevsky: "Love the animals. God has given them the rudiments of thought and joy untroubled. Don't trouble it, don't harass them, don't deprive them of their happiness, don't work against God's intent."

Why, yes, who would quarrel with that except hunters? The point, though, is whether love of animals is best served by a depreciation of the human. In the classics I have cited that is almost never present. It would seem that in Adams's ardor for wild creatures he has tried too hard to make a case for them instead of allowing them fully to be their own recommendation. I'm grateful for much of what he's done, but I'm not going to look at rabbits differently from now on. . . . (pp. 3-4)

Richard Gilman, "The Rabbits' Iliad and Odyssey," in The New York Times Book Review, *March 24, 1974, pp. 3-4.*

JANET ADAM SMITH

[*Watership Down,*] was published in Britain last year as a straightforward children's book. . . . But the American publishers present it simply as "A Novel," and by so doing may well encourage readers to go looking for the wrong things. For who would write a novel for adults about rabbits—unless the tale were a fable or a myth? I foresee an outbreak of symbol hunting in the burrows; mythic explications will drop like *hraka* on the grass. I think the publishers sniff a campus cult on the wind, and this underlies their proclaimed expectation that the book will be "one of the major literary and commercial successes of 1974."

Certainly, it appears at a time when we are becoming increasingly skeptical of our species' ability to live its life decently; there is an inclination to look, if only in fancy, for alternative models in other species, other worlds. I don't think that *Watership Down* has much to tell us of how to set about transforming ourselves and our institutions, or how to find a short cut to the promised land. In as much as Mr. Adams has a message for his readers, I'd say it is to make them more sensitive to the complex balance of nature, more aware of the needs and ways of other species (and the effect of human actions on them), more mindful that we are creatures too, and must live in harmony with the others who share our world.

The tale ends with Hazel, who has risked himself to save the warren, being captured by a little girl from the near-by farm. Advised by the kindly Dr. Adams (whose name can be no coincidence) Lucy lets the rabbit free on the down—far enough away to do no harm to the farmer. Man and rabbit *can* coexist; there is hope of a peaceable kingdom. . . .

Several times—in reading, for instance, of the old warren's destruction so that men might have homes—I thought of Thomas Hardy's "The Field of Waterloo":

> Yea, the coneys are scared by the thud of hoofs,
> And their white scuts flash at their vanishing heels,
> And swallows abandon the hamlet-roofs.
> The mole's tunnelled chambers are crushed by wheels,
> The lark's eggs scattered, their owners fled;
> And the hedgehog's household the sapper unseals. . . .

It is this sensibility that informs **Watership Down.** But if Hazel and Bigwig are to succeed Gandalf and Frodo as heroes of a cult, then a good book will have been demeaned and misunderstood. (p. 9)

Janet Adam Smith, "Exodus," in The New York Review of Books, *Vol. XXI, No. 6, April 18, 1974, pp. 8-9.*

JANE RESH THOMAS

In creating the new world of **Watership Down,** Richard Adams stands squarely in the old one. His novel draws upon not only epic and picaresque literary traditions but also an anti-feminist social tradition which, removed from the usual human context and imposed upon rabbits, is eerie in its clarity. . . .

Adams has created a splendid story, admirable for its originality as much as for its craft. Since the stereotype to which the female characters conform dictates their colorlessness and limits their social range, they are so peripheral they are scarcely noticeable. Its anti-feminist bias, therefore, damages the novel in only a minor way.

A literary work may survive such flaws as peripheral prejudice or cruelty or racism. It is important that the soldier in Andersen's "The Tinderbox" gratuitously murders the old woman and does so with impunity; it is important that the elephants in the Babar books sometimes seem more human than the "savages." But despite what may be viewed as ethical lapses, these stories still merit qualified praise. Just so, it is important that in **Watership Down,** Richard Adams has grafted exalted human spirits to the rabbit bodies of his male characters and has made the females mere rabbits. The males are superhuman and the females subhuman, creatures who occupy only a utilitarian place in the novel's world. That fact is important, notwithstanding the artistic merit of the work as a whole. (p. 405)

The refugees owe their survival and the establishment of a new warren to the variety of their talents. They exhibit admirable human traits—bravery to support their daring; the common-sense kind of wisdom; originality; reverence for his-

tory tempered by flexibility; compassion. The group includes a bard, a politician, a seer, a soldier, and even an intellectual. As they travel together, they improvise a new community which not only accommodates but values their great differences. Thus, it seems an enormously civilized and humane society, an association of equals whose personal gifts are recognized. But the members of this civilized society are all males.

To my mind, a just community is a cooperative venture which enriches individual lives instead of restricting them for the supposed good of the group. Even when membership is exclusive, one can admire fictitious community where one finds it—in a rathole with Mole and Ratty in *The Wind in the Willows* or on a journey through Mirkwood in *The Hobbit*—if one ignores any deprived class. So Kenneth Grahame and J. R. R. Tolkien wisely avoid the intrusion of females into the fraternity, just as cultivated gentlemen lock the massive doors of their oak-and-leather clubs. The illusion of civilization, of equalitarian warmth and respect, could hardly be maintained in the presence of a declassed group.

Richard Adams himself avoids that problem throughout the first half of **Watership Down,** which describes the itinerants' perilous journey. Like Grahame and Tolkien, he simply omits females from consciousness. However, when the rabbit troupe settle down, they begin to long for female companionship, a longing based on afterthought.

For one thing, they'd like to have some females around to do the work: In established warrens, nubile females do all of the serious digging. Adams has so skillfully bridged the distance between rabbits and people that, whoever digs the burrows in rabbit reality, one easily draws conclusions from Adams' rabbit fiction about the appropriate roles of men and women. The girl who rescues chief Hazel from a barnyard cat's jaws receives her orders from men with a lapine docility that reinforces this rabbit/human connection.

Additional considerations also bring females to the refugees' minds. As Hazel observes, "We have no does—not one—and no does means no kittens and in a few years no warren." . . . Although the males are rarely called *bucks* but are individually designated by name and collectively referred to as *rabbits,* the females are usually called *does,* a distinction analogous to the classifications *people* and *women* with reference to human males and females. For all its subtlety, that is a psychologically charged distinction, as Simone de Beauvoir suggested when she wrote that there are two classes of people, human beings and women. When women try to be human beings, she said, they are accused of acting like men.

Furthermore, the narrator makes it clear that only two alternatives exist in relations between sexes, the human way of romantic idolatry or the rabbit way of animal husbandry. In either case, the female is deprived of anything like the participation granted male members of the brotherhood by virtue of their maleness. Consorting with females seems to be an onerous necessity.

Eventually the refugees act on their longing and raid Efrafa, a neighboring rabbit police state. Of the ten does who willingly escape the totalitarian rule of General Woundwort, only two are even superficially characterized. One is a scatter-brained youngster who reveals the escape plan by chattering uncontrollably to Efrafan officers. All of the others, except Hyzenthlay, are powerless to act on their own initiative—paralyzed by fear at every critical turn.

Only Hyzenthlay possesses courage or dignity. She is a seer, gifted like the male Fiver, with prophetic vision. And like Dandelion, the refugees' bard, she is an artist, a poet whose lament resembles primitive poetry. But her artistic energies, like her determination to escape, are biologically directed, for what she laments is lost opportunities for reproduction. Although the males' sex makes demands upon them, as do their needs for food and shelter, sex does not dictate every form and detail of their lives. But Hyzenthlay is first and only a female, with her poetry seeming merely an aspect of her femaleness. Indeed, since her talents are neither admired nor even noticed, the rabbits of Hazel's warren consult her only as mate, not as prophet or bard. With motherhood, her poetry apparently ends.

A male victim of Efrafan violence says without correction when a fox kills one of the females, "What's a doe more or less?" He accepts the leader's decisions automatically, even forgetting his own opinions if they differ from those of the chief. Asked if her thought processes are like those of the Efrafan male, Hyzenthlay cryptically replies, "I'm a doe." After her brief heroism in the run for freedom, Hyzenthlay turns, in accordance with her sexual definition, to the roles of mate and mother. Her presence on stage is so brief, though, it hardly matters.

Watership Down survives the flawed characterization and the discrepancy between the richness of the male rabbits' lives and the spiritual penury of the females'. Although it seems odd that Adams counters an ugly totalitarian society with a system where females are merely interchangeable ciphers, one easily ignores that discrepancy too, because the females are unessential baggage, present only to motivate the male characters, not necessary to the story for their own individual sakes.

All of this is important, like the murder of Andersen's expendable old woman and like the beastiality of Babar's black neighbors. Within the framework of an otherwise delightful story, Richard Adams has embodied an anti-feminism which deprives his female characters of the spiritual fruit of community. (pp. 406-08)

> *Jane Resh Thomas, "Old Worlds and New: Anti-Feminism in 'Watership Down'," in* The Horn Book Magazine, *Vol. L, No. 4, August, 1974, pp. 405-08.*

DENNIS FLANAGAN

Watership Down is even more interesting for what it represents than what it says. It is a significant expression of the current state of relations between the literary culture and the scientific one.

"The two cultures" is now well-established as a figure of speech. As a concept, however, it has had its vicissitudes. When C. P. Snow gave his Rede Lecture titled *The Two Cultures and the Scientific Revolution* in 1959, the literary culture was, so to speak, laying for the scientific culture. It also seems as if it had been laying for Snow. He was riding high as a popular novelist, on the strength of his coping with "real" worlds of modern life: science, the government, academia and so on. He was nonetheless out of literary style in a time when most serious novels were more introspective. He was not much praised by literary critics, and there even seemed to be a certain amount of resentment that this somewhat old-fashioned approach was going over so well with serious readers—even

though it was fortified by inside knowledge and considerable storytelling skill.

In this critical environment Snow's metaphor of the two cultures was assaulted with remarkable violence. (p. 152)

Actually, of course, Snow was simply calling attention to the deepening fissure between the two cultures and fretting over it. What was really happening, in my view, was that many people in literary circles had become resentful of the rising influence of science, particularly in the universities, and Snow's fame as a novelist of the other culture gave them an uncommonly handy target. Such critics might have been doubtful of their ability to meet science head-on, since they knew so little about it, but Snow, after all, wrote novels, and that was something they did know about. Something had to be done to stop the intellectual juggernaut of science from overwhelming all the finer things of life: literature, painting, music, the dance and so on.

It is a pity that the idea of the two cultures should have been the locus of such a volcanic eruption of intellectual passions. It all came out as a scrimmage between the tribal institutions of literature and science, whereas the original intent had been to take a step in the direction of reconciling the two. Snow's original formulation is correct, and hardly anyone really doubts it: there are people who have considerable knowledge of the arts and very little knowledge of the sciences, and there are people for whom the reverse is true. This bifurcation is one of the main weaknesses in modern man's ability to improve his personal and social lot. The proper recognition of that fact, and efforts to do something about it, must surely rank high on the agenda of the perfectibility of man.

What does all this have to do with *Watership Down*? A good deal more than one might think. *Watership Down* is a book about rabbits. It is soundly based on modern knowledge of the rabbit. Who gathered this knowledge? Biologists. What is a biologist and what does he do? He is a scientist and he does science. . . . In other words, *Watership Down* is a scientific novel, a work that embraces the two cultures.

What happens in the creation of such a book, it seems to me, is that a thoughtful and imaginative nonscientist masters a certain body of scientific knowledge and begins to think on it. What would it be like, he might say to himself, to be a rabbit? How might I convey in human terms what it is like to be a rabbit? What could being a rabbit tell us about what it is like to be human? We are all the beneficiaries of such efforts to inform our factual knowledge with its potentialities. One can even argue that the main social function of art is to encompass factual knowledge and then to imaginatively dilate on it, to consider not only what is but also what might be.

Watership Down, of course, is about what it is like to be a rabbit. It is a gripping tale, full of adventure, deadly combat, blood, sadness and triumph (not much sex, in spite of what most of us are led to expect of rabbits). It is refreshing that the rabbits in the book are not cute little humans. . . . They are a far cry from Peter Rabbit, a homunculus who would not pay the proper heed to his mother. The difference is probably no accident; it may be that each generation has to have its own rabbit legend.

One may be grateful for *Watership Down*, but if Adams's main purpose is to tell us what it is like to be a rabbit (in the light of modern knowledge about what a rabbit's life is like), the book has some major flaws. For one thing, the rabbit characters in *Watership Down* talk, which automatically introduces a feature of human life that rabbits do not share. Adams even goes so far as to introduce a rabbit vocabulary called Lapine. . . . The choice here was clear: either use the more descriptive third person or the more dramatic first person.

There can be no doubt that human speech is the most highly developed form of communication in the biological world (at least on this planet). Speech, however, is only one of a great many different forms of communication. It is well known, for example, that many other mammals communicate intensively by means of odors. In *Watership Down* Adams refers to the fact that rabbits rub their chin on objects around their home burrows. He does not say, although he probably knows, that they do this because they have glands in their chin that secrete odorous substances. When a rabbit rubs its chin on a log near its burrow, it is leaving a message something like: "This is Joe's place. Keep out!" (pp. 152-54)

Rabbits frequently urinate on each other for communication purposes. If a rabbit smelling of strange urine enters a warren other than its own, the other rabbits will attack it violently. The rabbit also has a well-developed set of glands around its anus that secrete odorous substances; these substances give each rabbit's fecal pellets a unique smell. When rabbits pass *hraka*, as Adams would say, they often park the pellets in a place where they will be encountered and sniffed at by other rabbits. . . .

Adams may know these things too, but the point is that the social life of the rabbit may be even stranger, richer and more intriguing than his book makes out. If such notions as rabbits communicating with each other by the smell of urine and fecal pellets are offensive to us, that is not the fault of the rabbits. If we seek to understand another animal and its role in the same natural system to which we belong, we must allow it the dignity of its own way of life. (p. 154)

We live in a golden age of children's literature. The great classics endure, but the sheer weight of first-class children's books being published today dwarfs anything that has gone before. The best children's books are written by members of the literary culture, and under present circumstances that is inevitable and even right. The imagination of a child is not going to be stretched by books that merely recite facts. The present state of affairs does, however, reinforce the duality of culture. Here is where the case of *Watership Down* is particularly instructive. Even though Adams has not escaped the bonds of anthropomorphism, his epic of the rabbit does more to encompass the facts than anything that has gone before it. (p. 156)

Dennis Flanagan, "To Each Generation Its Own Rabbits," in Wilson Library Bulletin, *Vol. 49, No. 2, October, 1974, pp. 152-56.*

M. JEAN JORDAN

[*The following excerpt is from a letter to the editor of* The Horn Book Magazine *in reaction to Jane Resh Thomas's essay "Old Worlds and New: Anti-Feminism in 'Watership Down'," which appeared in the August 1974 issue.*]

Jane Resh Thomas has made some valid points re: anti-feminism in *Watership Down.* However, I feel that in her examination of this book some of the points she makes are not valid. Too often quotations and excerpts are manipulated or taken out of context in order to prove a particular point of view, and I feel that it would be a great literary loss if librarians were to cancel or avoid ordering this book on the grounds of anti-feminism—and I am sure there are some that would do so after reading Thomas' article. . . .

Certainly, in the first half of the book "[l]ike Grahame and Tolkien, he [Adams] simply omits females from consciousness." Anti-feminism is not a sound argument in my opinion, however, when no females are present in the story. We must look for anti-feminism in the attitudes and characteristics of the individuals, and it is here that I disagree with Thomas, particularly when she resorts to reversing some sequences of events.

At the bottom of page 406 Thomas states that the rabbit troupe would like to have some females around to do the work, but this statement is simply not true. The refugees' main concern is survival, and their survival depends on food, shelter, and sex, in that order. They realize, when they first arrive on Watership Down and need shelter, that they will have to dig the burrows themselves and they are not averse to changing some of their established habits if necessary. In fact, they could be described as "liberated" in the same sense that "liberated" human males do not balk at housecleaning or cooperating with a working wife in running a home. Hazel, the leader, states: "It never entered my head to try to make a lot of bucks dig regular holes but . . . we ought to do our best. I'm ready to try, anyway". And not once, while the bucks are digging, do they say or imply that they'd like to have some females around to do the work. While it is certainly true that most digging is done by does preparing for litters, this is a biological fact of most animal life and is commonly referred to as the nesting instinct; and this instinct is also being studied among humans. (Recent research shows that women, during the first few months of pregnancy, have strong housecleaning instincts.) . . .

I also disagree with Thomas' statement that the males are superhuman and the females subhuman. This is a generalization that simply does not hold true. I find that the rabbits in the book, both male and female, are products of their social environment, just as humans are, whether we like it or not. For example, how superhuman is the buck, Strawberry, when he asks to join the band? "All his urbane self-possession had vanished. He was staring and trembling and his great size seemed only to add to his air of stricken misery. He cringed before them". And how subhuman are Hyzenthlay and the other does of the Right Fore Mark in approaching the Council of Efrafa, a task requiring much courage and determination? Adams' description of Hyzenthlay does not support Thomas' argument that the females are simply subhuman, utilitarian creatures: "Bigwig realized that he had stumbled, quite unexpectedly, upon what he needed most of all: a strong, sensible friend, who would think on her own account and help to bear his burden". This description of Hyzenthlay also refutes Thomas's statement that "[c]onsorting with females seems to be an onerous necessity." While it is true that the other Efrafan does are paralyzed by fear at every turn, they have at least shown the courage to attempt an escape, and it is *not* because they are does that they are paralyzed, as Thomas implies, but because of the conditioning of their previous existence in Efrafa.

Another example of the rabbits as products of their environment is shown at Nuthanger Farm. The four hutch rabbits, two males and two females, are also products of conditioning, and their personalities and actions have nothing whatsoever to do with being male or female. In fact, it is Clover, a strong, active doe, who is the most excited about escape and life on the downs, and who shows the most initiative during the actual escape; while it is Laurel, one of the bucks, who becomes paralyzed by fear and does not succeed in escaping.

I also do not agree that the narrator makes clear only two alternatives existing in relations between sexes or that "one easily draws conclusions from Adams' rabbit fiction about the appropriate roles of men and women." In fact, I find that the example Thomas uses to illustrate this statement is completely erroneous. The girl Lucy, who rescues chief Hazel from the cat, acts completely independently in rescuing him and is definitely ready to defend her actions, if necessary, in her desire to show the rabbit to Doctor. She does not receive one single order from men, unless you call her father's suggestion to get dressed an order. Lucy's behavior, it seems to me, is entirely child-like and is neither characteristically male or female, but simply human. She shows curiosity, compassion, and intelligence; and her actions are impulsive and independent. . . .

I think the real danger in such an article is that, in trying to prove a particular point of view, so much of the essential story is lost or overlooked. The far-reaching message of cooperation and interplay among all animal life is far more important than the degree of anti-feminism present. Thomas states on page 406 that: "The refugees owe their survival and the establishment of a new warren to the variety of their talents. . . . But the members of this civilized society are all males." Initially, yes, but this civilized society cannot function without females any more than a civilized society of females could function or prosper without males. Although the does' primary purpose is reproduction, that fact does not necessarily rule out the possibility of their becoming contributing members of the prospering warren and eventually of the new warren, half Watership and half Efrafan. . . .

Let's not discourage our children from reading **Watership Down** on the grounds of anti-feminism. The benefits will far outweigh the disadvantages. (pp. 3-4, 93)

> *M. Jean Jordan, in a letter to the editor in* The Horn Book Magazine, *Vol. LI, No. 1, February, 1975, pp. 3-4, 93.*

JANE RESH THOMAS

[*The following excerpt is from a letter to the editor of* The Horn Book Magazine *in reaction to a letter by M. Jean Jordan which appeared in the February 1975 issue and is excerpted above.*]

In her recent letter (February 1975) opposing my essay about anti-feminism in **Watership Down,** M. Jean Jordan's evidence is less substantial than it seems, for she not only ignores some of the main points of my argument but distorts the facts of the novel as well.

Whereas Jordan claims, for example, that "not once, while the bucks are digging, do they say or imply that they'd like to have some females around to do the work," at the first necessity for such labor, Bigwig in fact complains, "[T]here's no need to do any serious digging, is there? . . . That sort of thing's all right for does, but not for us". Even if females do perform such duties in literal rabbithood, as Jordan wants to argue, Adams elsewhere ignores other biological facts.

Selma Lanes has cited R. M. Lockley's treatise on rabbits to make such a point: "Does are at the very center of any rabbit community, a decided matriarchy," Lanes writes. "Not only

do does provide the key to a warren's organization, but it is always young, dissatisfied females who initiate the founding of new colonies. Lockley also emphasizes the ferocity of mother rabbits in defense of their young." (*New York Times Book Review,* June 30, 1974, p. 39.) These sexual facts of literal rabbit life, Adams reverses. In addition, Jordan makes too much of minor characters and scenes which do not in sum begin to offset the picture of female ineptitude and passivity Adams paints.

More important than such faulty details are the weak foundations of Jordan's argument, the conclusions arising from spurious social scientific assumptions about the nature of rabbit/human personality and its conditioning by environment. She forgets that Hazel's is not a literal rabbit warren, but a created world. Whatever social conventions form these characters are instituted by the artist who created the universe of **Watership Down.** The society that limits Hyzenthlay's and Clover's participation did not grow accidentally. Adams is the novel's god, and every environmental detail affecting his characters is his own creation.

Jordan wishes to focus on the "far-reaching message of cooperation and interplay among all animal life" which she taxes me with overlooking. Comradeship is obviously a central theme of **Watership Down,** as I in fact made clear; but that theme coexists with the contrary, more subtle anti-feminist theme. Even slaves may love their masters, and masters may feel friendly toward their slaves, but if together they create a productive society founded on the slaves' sacrifice of their human gifts, personal fellowship does not alter the autocratic basis of their relations. Jordan's speculation about "the possibility of [the females'] . . . becoming contributing members of the prospering warren" at some post-novel date is irrelevant.

Finally, I am dismayed by Jordan's assumptions about the nature and function of literary criticism. She entirely ignores my praise of the work, but my private view that **Watership Down** is a treasure has nothing to do with the issue anyway. Although book reviewers are obliged to provide a balanced summary of a whole work, literary critics may and often do examine a limited subject. It is furthermore not the critic but the novelist who has the last word; one may read a novel in the light of a critic's ideas, but the novel is its own authority. . . .

Jordan's misgivings about the "dangers" of my article notwithstanding, it is not a literary critic's function to sell books, no matter how priceless they may be, but to cast a beam of light on a sliver of the truth. I trust that librarians share my aversion to censorship and that my article will not serve as an excuse to exclude **Watership Down** or any other masterpiece from the public bookcase.

> *Jane Resh Thomas, in a letter to the editor in* The Horn Book Magazine, *Vol. LI, No. 2, April, 1975, p. 99.*

MARGERY FISHER

Fourteen years allow long enough, I feel, to decide whether **Watership Down** is merely a long story about rabbits or a mock epic of an original and lasting kind. It has been read as anti-war propaganda, with the dauntless rabbit band as refugees and the psychotic General Woundwort as an arch fascist; it has been castigated as sexist, with the few does given totally submissive parts to play; it has been read most often as a tongue-in-cheek Odyssey, with all the paraphernalia of literary quotation and allusion and the interpolated myths of the rabbit god El-Ahrairah to dignify the authentic behaviour of rabbits nibbling, excreting, thumping for danger, digging scrapes for shelter. It is, in any case, a rattling good adventure story. . . . The journey to the upland which Fiver has unerringly in his sights is told with wit as well as with robust humour, with a scrupulous attention to distance, terrain and weather and with a jaunty, unabashed development of personality in the rabbits and their neighbours and enemies which never negates the biological accuracy of events. Above all—and this seems more evident to me at this later reading—it is a fine picture of Hampshire downland, worthy to be put beside Jefferies for its pointilliste detail, its sure perspective and its sensuous immediacy. (pp. 38-9)

> *Margery Fisher, "Animals as Characters," in her* Margery Fisher Recommends Classics for Children & Young People, *Thimble Press, 1986, pp. 32-9.*

DIANA WAGGONER

Richard Adams's two books, **Watership Down** and **Shardik**, have both been best-sellers and have suffered accordingly from perverse and shoddy criticism. *The New Yorker*, for example, castigated **Shardik** for its "odd names like Santil-ke-Erketlis, Gel-Ethlin, Mollo, and Rantzay." Worse than this, however, is the persistent, and wholly unwarranted, assumption of popular critics that the books are "novels" in a strict realistic sense. Nothing could be less true. **Watership Down** is a reworking of the *Aeneid* from the perspective of rabbits, while **Shardik** combines elements from the history of Mohammed and from the medieval romance of *Sir Gawain and the Green Knight*. The books can be justly criticized on other grounds, notably the leader-worship of the first book and the anti-climactic resolution of the second. But Adams's potential is enormous and, probably, almost untapped as yet. His future work may use the potential hinted at in these books, or he may degenerate into mere best-selling adventure fantasy. Too much fame has broken better authors. But if he can live up to his potential, he will be a major figure. (p. 46)

> *Diana Waggoner, "Some Trends in Fantasy," in her* The Hills of Faraway: A Guide to Fantasy, *Atheneum, 1978, pp. 36-64.*

PETER HUNT

[As a world bestseller **Watership Down**] has suffered inevitably from the schizophrenic critical response accorded to *The Lord of the Rings:* extravagant praise followed by round condemnation. In retrospect, it is easy to apply Adams's observation on Kipling—that he had "a certain insensitivity and banality—even vulgarity—to his own book; but it is equally easy to overlook his impressive technical achievement. Set the twin tasks of making rabbit behaviour into an interesting narrative, and of telling the story in such a way as to integrate this with necessary factual information, he was more successful than he is sometimes given credit for. The blemishes, as we shall see, often derive from unsureness about the validity of the narrative contract between author and reader.

The reactions to the book—as adult novel and as children's book—have been significant. Perhaps the shrewdest review appeared in *Newsweek* (18 March 1974): "I'll make a deal with you. If you won't say anything dumb like 'I'm not interested in a story about rabbits', I won't say anything dumb like 'This is a great novel' ". Quite so; **Watership Down** is good

of its kind: that is, an adventure narrative, efficiently told and sufficiently unusual to make it distinctive. It does not, generally, pretend to be more than this; although when it does, the pretensions show. Yet when we turn to Alec Ellis's comments on the book in connection with its Carnegie Medal award for 1972, we might get a different impression. "**Watership Down** is a phenomenon the like of which only appears once or twice in a lifetime, and one could not reasonably ask more of a treasure so scarce."

The implications here should give us pause. Is there a value scale running unbroken from adults' classics down to children's rubbish, with the acceptably second-rate adult books and the very best possible children's books sharing the same rung? Possibly not, but while that assumption is detectable, it is difficult to get a clear view of the books themselves.

Watership Down was, of course, a first novel and might be forgiven some of its defects on that score. (pp. 226-27)

Richard Adams's style is, by and large, unexceptional—possibly as a result of the base material he is working on. . . . (p. 228)

In an interview Leon Garfield observed that **Watership Down** was, like many significant children's books, "a freak book by somebody who is not naturally a writer". Certainly this shows on the surface of the text on occasion. Fred Inglis has written that it is "by turns, clumsy, portentous, longwinded, and magnificent"; he did not add that the vast majority of the book is also efficient (if not exactly elegant), unassuming, economical, and undistinguished. It is true that Adams is capable of surface felicities: "Then it was gone, and Bigwig's fur was blowing in the whack of wind that followed it down the hedges." "He sat still and his words seemed to come crawling up the sunlight, over the grass." And equally, of awkwardnesses: " '. . . . but I thought that first of all I ought to tell you how it is that we four—Silver, Buckthorn, Strawberry and I—have come back without any does.' "

But it should be noted that he very rarely lapses into children's book register so that, when he does, it is strikingly out of key (and, as happens with Garfield, sometimes vulgar, as if that is a natural concomitant). "He could smell the man. The man could not smell him. All the man could smell was the nasty smoke he was making." " 'Well, what is the charm?' said Chervil. 'You say: O fly away great bird so white, And don't come back until tonight.' "

Rather more interesting is the degree of consistency he shows in the implied narrative contract. We have noted his technical problems, and on occasion he can integrate pure information with scarcely a hiccough. . . . However, elsewhere, the authorial voice takes over and begins to preach:

> The short June darkness slipped by in a few hours. The light returned early to the high down but the rabbits did not stir. Well after dawn they were still sleeping, undisturbed in a silence deeper than they had ever known. Nowadays, among fields and woods, the noise level by day is high—too high for some kinds of animal to tolerate. Few places are far from human noise—cars, buses, motor-cycles, tractors, lorries. The sound of a housing estate in the morning is audible a long way off. People who record bird-song generally do it very early—before six o'clock—if they can. Soon after that, the invasion of distant noise in most woodland becomes too constant and too loud. During the last fifty years

the silence of much of the country has been destroyed. But here, on Watership Down, there floated up only faint traces of the daylight noise below.

It is noticeable that this hectoring is from the author, not the narrator; the story is put aside, the contract is broken. Along with this goes a lapse into language designed for a specific audience: "some kinds of animal", "people who", "cars, buses . . ." and into cliché and platitude: "during the last fifty years . . ." But cheek by jowl with this we find, perhaps, an implied resonance to a deeper level which is not actually there: "undisturbed in a silence deeper than they had ever known". Possibly both intent and effect here are literal—but the slight deviation of "deeper" seems to suggest that Watership Down is more than just a safe place for a warren. Is this signalling an implied general truth behind the story? Perhaps the falseness can be recognized in the cliché.

Elsewhere Adams could quite justly be accused in Ruskin's terms of being a second-order writer; a man who "feels strongly, thinks weakly, and sees untruly". The rabbits rest after a hard day's travel, and the author steps forward:

> To come to an end of anxiety and fear! To feel the cloud that hung over us lift and disperse—the cloud that dulled the heart and made happiness no more than a memory! This at least is one joy that must have been known by almost every living creature.
>
> . . . Here is a soldier who was waiting, with heavy heart, to suffer and die in battle. But suddenly the luck has changed. There is news! The war is over and everyone bursts out singing! He will go home after all!

And so on for half a page. Now this is not only cliched, but untrue, and the half-borrowing from Sassoon only points it up. The depth of the story (the contact with which gives an impression of value) simply will not support such artificial significances. This is not because the story is about rabbits, or because their heroisms are small. It is that nothing in the book goes beneath theme level; and that level itself is pre-digested. As some critics have pointed out, plot and character are not greatly different from a hundred B-picture war stories; which is only to say that the surface variations (rabbits, names) are ingenious transforms of a structural element that has ceased to have any real significance. Whatever the origins, this structure has become fossilized, and now stands for nothing but itself. It is, at best, only superficially disturbing—or true. (pp. 230-33)

Given the modest aims that Adams has insisted upon, this might scarcely seem to be a criticism; but the attempt, however unconscious, to imply that we are—or should be—reading something that has profounder levels, is not entirely honest to the narrative contract. As we have seen, the surface structure tends to betray such attempts, while elsewhere such flights end in bathos. When the rabbits first reach the River Test, Marco Polo at Cathay is invoked; or, when Bigwig is chewing the hinge of a rabbit hutch: " 'By Frith, that'll do', said Blackberry, for all the world like the Duke of Wellington at Salamanca."

It is also curious that Adams, who can evoke the weather so accurately and appropriately as a natural hazard and an element of naturalism, should attempt to use it as a pseudo-mystic element in the defeat of Woundwort. One might argue that the employment of such a discredited device is rather ap-

propriate to the level of incident he is working with. Yet the concatenation of extravagantly inaccurate mixed metaphors and clichés in which it is couched, suggests that he is deliberately trying to pull the book onto a different plane.

> Along the western horizon the lower clouds formed a single, purple mass, against which distant trees stood out minute and sharp. The upper edges rose into the light, a far land of wild mountains. Copper-coloured, weightless and motionless, they suggested a glassy fragility like that of frost. Surely, when the thunder struck them again they would vibrate, tremble and shatter, till warm shards, sharp as icicles, fell flashing down from the ruins. Racing through the ochre light, Bigwig was impelled by a frenzy of tension and energy. He did not feel the wound in his shoulder. The storm was his own. The storm would defeat Efrafa.

Where, one wonders, does "surely" come from? The shift into the present suggests, conventionally, some cohesion with the protagonist's consciousness. That it is clearly inappropriate to Bigwig's perceptions casts doubt on the last two statements. This piece of authorial self-indulgence seems to be not only underselling the pace of the story and infringing the narrative contract, but also attempting to impose significance by sleight of hand.

Despite authorial disclaimers, it seems to me that the chapter epigraphs share something of this intent. Apart from one excellent joke ("the General's unjust interference, so far from being injurious to their felicity, was perhaps rather conducive to it . . .") their effect tends to be to emphasize the comparative shallowness of Adams's own writing. This is especially the case with the interpolated tales of El-ahrairah, which are for the most part inept and vulgar pastiches and are not well served by being introduced with quotations from Yeats and the Psalms. In these attempts to provide a solid, and resonating, underpinning to the rabbits, the juxtaposition of the heroic and the childish (rather than child-like) seems to indicate an ambivalence about the status of the tale. (pp. 233-34)

> *Peter Hunt, "The Good, the Bad and the Indifferent: Quality and Value in Three Contemporary Children's Books," in* The Signal Approach to Children's Books: A Collection, *edited by Nancy Chambers, Scarecrow Press, 1980, pp. 225-46.*

FRED INGLIS

To bring off a bestselling achievement like **Watership Down** seems to me to meet a sufficiently tall order. Richard Adams's book satisfies both cult and culture much more impressively than *The Lord of the Rings*. . . . (p. 201)

Watership Down is so strong because it brims over the flow-charted stratification of cultural life. It is far more than the bestselling novel which in one month alone (October 1974) sold 145,000 copies in the thirteen languages into which it is translated, and went past the million mark before it had been in the Puffin list for three years. Adams's strength is that he draws upon the materials of popular culture but in such a way as to break critically with the conventions of the liberal novel for children. He draws together in a new synthesis old heroics and new psychology. That is, he seeks to render certain drastically changed features of the intellectual landscape, the contours of the mind, in such a way as to make children experience these changes for themselves.

One cannot doubt that Richard Adams intends to strike this

pedagogic note. Indeed, he strikes it often clumsily—he can be clumsy in many ways, both when trying too hard and when not trying enough:

> When Marco Polo came at last to Cathay, seven hundred years ago, did he not feel—and did his heart not falter as he realised—that this great and splendid capital of an empire had had its being all the years of his life and far longer, and that he had been ignorant of it? That it was in need of nothing from him, from Venice, from Europe? That it was full of wonders beyond his understanding? That his arrival was a matter of no importance whatever? We know that he felt these things, and so has many a traveller in foreign parts who did not know what he was going to find. There is nothing that cuts you down to size like coming to some strange and marvellous place where no one even stops to notice that you stare about you.

That is a lapse into avuncularity which occurs a number of times in the novel. Indeed it is not unendearing; it has the ring of someone who has come to teaching during middle-age, benign but often awkward. He has a teacherly point. Adams aims to create enough disorientation in children's minds to enable them to see the world in a new way. This new way becomes clearer when Adams begins the tricky business of making his rabbits both alien and familiar, non-human and sympathetic, to his readers:

> Rabbits, of course, have no idea of precise time or of punctuality. In this respect they are much the same as primitive people, who often take several days over assembling for some purpose and then several more to get started. Before such people can act together, a kind of telepathic feeling has to flow through them and ripen to the point when all know that they are ready to begin.

There is more than a touch here, as elsewhere in Richard Adams, of a Victorian explorer's bluff patronage which sorts perfectly well with the glimpses we get of the red-bereted officer elsewhere, with his Sergeant-major Bigwig, his Captain Holly, his 'Thus it fell to one of the rank-and-file to make a lucky find'. But the same pages give us a different cue as well; they make the connection, certainly, with the anthropologists, but not merely the anthropologists hired by the nineteenth-century Empire to report on the peculiarities of colonial peoples. Adams's novel has moved with the times which have dispersed that Empire, and it seeks to give a moral account of the change, an account which will explain some of the varieties of human experience, its openness and closures. To do this, it enters alien minds and experiences the world with the concepts and values of those minds.

Adams works to bring together two post-Romantic modes of thought in a common, though necessarily blurred focus. For he is a novelist and as such, he is committed to the understanding and inhabitation of other frames of mind. Because novels are the product of one tributary from the Enlightenment, he is engaged upon the traditional Romantic enterprise of examining subjectivities. But there is a different anthropology astir as well, and insofar as Adams seeks systematically to render an alien perception of the world, he is very much engaged in the new science, which, as Isaiah Berlin says, seeks for

> yet another type of awareness, unlike a priori knowledge in that it is empirical, unlike deduction in that it yields new knowledge of facts, and unlike

perception of the external world, in that it informs us not merely of what exists or occurs, and in what spatial or temporal order, but also why what is, or occurs, is as it is, i.e. in some sense *per causas*. This species is self-knowledge: knowledge of activities of which we, the knowing subjects, are ourselves the authors, endowed with motives, purposes, and a continuous social life, which we understand, as it were, from the inside . . .

What Berlin goes on to show is not so much 'self-knowledge' as the phrase is conventionally understood, as knowledge of others, and it is this technique of empathic interpretation which he commends to us as the life- and truth-giving tendency of a new hermeneutic, or system of understanding and explanation. (pp. 201-03)

[Adams's] unusual capacity for presenting the familiar as terrifyingly unprecedented is what—to return to the question of values—I would most want children to experience in the book. For the ten-year-old reading Captain Holly's description knows what a bulldozer is; he is in the traditional relationship of child to pet or doll or Peter Rabbit; for once, in a world otherwise full of giant grown-ups, abrupt and arbitrary eventualities, fixed authorities, wide open and hostile spaces, the child knows better than the hero. He can experience the rabbits' bewilderment while understanding what is going on. . . . More impressively yet, Adams takes us through the incomprehension of the rabbits into the moment at which they think themselves beyond what was hitherto thinkable. The first such moment arrives when the escaping rabbits come across a little stream called the Enborne, and their group intellectual, a rabbit called Blackberry, works out how to use a loose plank as a boat. Similarly, when, with the foresight which we share with the heroes, we know that the punt is ready for their escape with the captured doe rabbits, and we see Hazel and company drawn away into the current of the river Test under the nose of the pursuing tyrant General Woundwort, we experience at once the familiar satisfaction of relief at the last-minute safety of our side and at the same time the pleasure of understanding the incomprehension of the enemy as in his eyes solid ground moves magically away out of his reach.

It is this knot between *how* we see and the intellectual and verbal mechanisms we have for telling us *what* we see which Adams so vividly unties and ties again; to put it more technically, the central structure of the book builds and rebuilds the intricate, intercellular relations of perception and cognition, of image and idea. It gives us—and 'us' includes children—a strong, clear picture of how culture develops, and it does this broadly and simply in a dozen different ways. At one moment Adams notes in an aside that rabbits cannot count beyond four; after that numbers blur into 'lots'. The seagull Kehaar classifies 'all insects as beetles'—only their edibility is significant. At another moment, Fiver the seer struggles with the idea of shaking sounds and meaning out of 'the black sticks [which] flickered on the white surface' of a noticeboard as 'they raised their sharp, wedge-shaped little heads and chattered together like a nestful of young weasels'; a little before, we experience with the rabbits the stupefying glare of a car's headlights, the 'awful brightness [of which] seemed to cut into the brain'. In all these and many other instances we are made to know the strangeness and omnipotence of an alien human technology, or else we are made to recognize the singularity and, as one might say, *interestedness*, of our systems of concepts and the percepts which are a consequence of the concepts. Adams unfixes and refixes, in the way only a novelist can, the fluidity of experience, the facts of an intelligent eye and a brain which has to shape the world for the eye to see. This movement from dissolution to coagulation of ideas is sustained with the slow growth in the hero-rabbits' community of a dynamic culture. Hazel and company leave a static society, adroit and intelligent enough in its own way— its leader gives all the eerily familiar political reasons for not seeing crisis as crisis—and gradually construct a frame of thought capable of extension and adjustment, and of resistance and rejection too. Even from the doomed warren, which acts as the farmer's leader, they learn to carry and store food. They learn, against all their nature and their instincts, to travel long distances, to fight when they have to and not to run away from cats and dogs and foxes. They learn architectonics or how to build piered and vaulted underground halls. They learn friendship and dependence when their instinct is to scatter in a rout. These are the strengths of the book, that it insists upon the protracted difficulty of making a home out of exile, a society out of a gang of scared, forlorn, hungry bits and pieces, order and ceremony out of a sandy hill-top, a ride of sweet turf, and the cover of the tall pine trees. Culture is made out of the hard years, out of the permanence of fear, the threat of desert places:

> Rabbits above ground, unless they are in proved, familiar surroundings close to their holes, live in continual fear. If it grows intense enough they can become glazed and paralysed by it—*tharn,* to use their own word. Hazel and his companions had been on the jump for nearly two days.

This is the broad moral of his task, and when it issues in generalization, then for all Dr Adams's slight pomposity of manner, it rings true enough. In the long paragraph which opens chapter 22, he reconnects the **analogy between rabbits and communitarian** (i.e. non-individualist) **primitive peoples.** . . . And he goes on to modulate into bolder and, we may feel, justifiably strong moral assertion:

> Would that the dead were not dead! But there is grass that must be eaten, pellets that must be chewed, hraka that must be passed, holes that must be dug, sleep that must be slept. Odysseus brings not one man to shore with him. Yet he sleeps sound beside Calypso and when he wakes thinks only of Penelope.

The Homeric reference is typical of the man who so loads even the rifts between chapters with epigraphs from Congreve, Xenophon, Sidney Keyes, folksong, Clausewitz, Robinson Jeffers. Adams is a manly man, and none the worse for it. But to say so brings me to the point at which his special limitations must be named. For the strong, rich, savoury presence in this novel which comes from its cultural ancestry in Western literature seems to run, however strongly, into some very stereotypical forms.

In the first place, Adams is up against the structural difficulty of any anthropomorphic storyteller. He gives rabbits consciousness, which they do not have, but keeps them as rabbits. It won't do simply to say, with [*Guardian* reviewer] Richard Boston, that Germaine Greer would hate the book because the female rabbits are simply there to bear children and to dig burrows while all the real friendships and human qualities are shown by the men. Adams's creation of an alien set of values and ideas out of which to see the world resists our making the novel into an animal fable; it is not the

Nonne's Preeste's Tale, nor is it *Animal Farm.* . . . The trouble with this sprawling, immoderate, unreflective book is that Adams has such an uneven touch in making [his rabbit] language. He is by turns clumsy, portentous, long-winded, and magnificent. What makes the book into an unprecedented bestseller is this adventitious mixture.

There is, as they say, something for everyone. For the intellectual child or adult there is the rabbit lore, the creatively non-positivist animal behaviourism, and there are the makings of other cultures. Crossing into this territory, there is the ecology and the heady stuff of the conservation polemic, lapsing at times into an involuntary parody of *The Observer's Book of Wild Flowers.* Woven into this thick technicolour, with all its living detail and the samples pasted in from the author's commonplace book, is the war thriller. Richard Boston has very amusingly ripped out this structure, and mocked the 'onion-seller French and organ-grinder Italian' of Kehaar and 'maquis mouse'. Certainly the main group of rabbits are portioned out with a haversack of iron moral rations which would look best in a commando sortie: 'Leadership for you, Hazel'; 'Brainbox for you, Blackberry'; 'Bulldog Drummond kit for you, Bigwig'; 'Nervous loyalty for raw recruits, Pipkin'; 'Mad poet's outfit to Fiver'—'Now, who's for a futile gesture?' But the success of any book for children in part depends on a simple moral structure and a rattling good yarn; its strength and its weakness and, because of both, its sales, depend on having hit the right moment with this cultural recipe. It is a depressing consequence of such success that as Adams becomes a more accomplished writer, if **Shardik** is anything to go by, the limitations of his mind and his imagination, once his ambitions draw him away from that simple, honest morality, leave him with nothing but the fashionable camp of Aztec cruelty, of a slow, ceremonious, picturesque, and brocaded dose of the horrors. (pp. 205-09)

Watership Down is vital . . . to children's novels in general . . . because it truthfully and livingly imagines a frame of mind, both human and lapine, which makes new values rational and intelligent. It is not a way of doing social science (a dreadful thought—'Here, have a dose of Marx with your *Tale of Ginger and Pickles*'). It *is* a way of learning to understand other cultures and the modes of living things as they make up culture and society. If these claims are fair, its status as cult novel can only be a matter for rejoicing. Its novelty and its strong traditionalism make it one of the best examples we shall find of a brave effort to maintain continuity across deep historical chasms. (pp. 209-10)

> *Fred Inglis, "Cult and Culture: A Political-Psychological Excursus," in his* The Promise of Happiness: Value and Meaning in Children's Fiction, *Cambridge University Press, 1981, pp. 182-210.*

SHEILA A. EGOFF

In **Watership Down** and **The Plague Dogs**, Adams is an Old Testament prophet thundering out his disapproval of humans and their injustice, cruelty, dishonesty, manipulation, and blind hatreds, contrasted in a Manichaean manner with the goodness of the animal world. Although **The Plague Dogs** can be seen as the penultimate beast tale with its Swiftian, misanthropic vision toward the human race, **Watership Down** can be said to straddle the gulf between Aesop and de la Mare. It is both moral and mythic. Basically it is a survival story given epic proportions by means of the utilization of lapine history, language, and mythology. (p. 111)

Adams's greatest triumph is the creation of a complete rabbit society, all the more astounding since rabbits have not been considered in any way the intelligentsia of the animal world. Therefore his success in suspending the reader's disbelief is really a greater achievement than that of Tolkien's creation of Middle Earth. But despite the book's wholeness and its poetic vision, it is Adams's view of humanity that severs its link with animal fantasy, particularly of the past. (p. 112)

[With] *Watership Down* Adams, single-handedly, has given the talking animal story back to an adult audience from which it has been divorced since Aesop. (p. 119)

> Sheila A. Egoff, "The New Fantasy," in her Thursday's Child: Trends and Patterns in Contemporary Children's Literature, *American Library Association, 1981, pp. 80-129.*

ANN SWINFEN

[*Watership Down*] is a book notable for many different qualities. . . . [While] the political theme is only one among many, the whole form of the novel is the quest for a new home, the drive towards a more perfect community, so that the political and social issues . . . are highly relevant to the whole. (pp. 192-93)

In the warrens of the Berkshire countryside, surrounded by the everyday human pursuits of a contemporary farming community, Adams depicts four main types of human political systems: a totalitarian state, a community of lotus-eaters, a once healthy social group sinking into stagnation and complacency, and an attempt to set up a utopia.

Watership Down is not a straightforward political allegory like *Animal Farm,* but like Orwell's animal society it shows the influence of particular aspects of twentieth-century history on the author. Adams himself served in World War II, and a parallelism with the political atmosphere of the 1930s and 1940s lies behind all the Efrafan sections of the book. One cannot draw up a precise table of equations, as one can between *Animal Farm* and revolutionary/post-revolutionary Russia, but General Woundwort has all the attributes of the ruthless head of a totalitarian state, whether he be Franco, Mussolini, Hitler, Stalin or Amin. In particular, the police states of Nazi Germany and Stalinist Russia provide the background for Efrafa. Woundwort has none of the sophisticated technology, but he has the mentality of the twentieth-century dictator, and the most illuminating characteristic of this is the determination to prevent his subjects from escaping from the state. In the past, rulers' energies were almost entirely directed towards preventing a political coup at home or an attack from outside. Exile was a common punishment for political dissidents. It is a modern tendency to fear and prevent the departure of 'citizens'. This is also one of the most notable features of Efrafa.

Like other totalitarian states also, Efrafa has a highly efficient army, the Owsla, kept in regular fighting order, and a secret police, the Owslafa, chosen for their strength and brutal nature. Obedience must be unquestioning and is enforced by punishment, torture, mutilation and even death. The expression of views possibly unacceptable to the state is suppressed by fear of retribution. The inhabitants of the warren are divided into 'Marks', and a bite in ear or flank scars them for life with the appropriate mark. The different Marks live in separate burrows with no intercommunicating passages, in order to prevent the spread of disease or rebellion. They are allowed outside for exercise and feeding only at certain set times, to prevent rabbits of different Marks from meeting. The Owsla officers have considerable powers within their Marks, although they too are always subject to Woundwort and his Council. The attitude of the Owsla towards the other rabbits is summed up in Chervil's remark to Bigwig about the does: 'If you want a doe you have one—any doe in the Mark, that is. We're not officers for nothing, are we? The does are under orders and none of the bucks can stop you!' In Efrafa individual rights and individual liberty count for nothing.

When Woundwort originally established Efrafa, his intention was to create a warren which was safe from the attacks of predators, men or disease, but his insatiable longing for power has developed into the determination to conquer and enslave all surrounding warrens, and to reduce his subjects to mere cyphers in his power game. Woundwort thus sets out . . . to establish a utopia, and finishes by creating a dystopia. The dignity of the individual has become meaningless in this totalitarian state. Only the strength of the warren and the size of the geographical area which he controls through the Wide Patrols of his Owsla matter to Woundwort. As a result of these policies, the ordinary inhabitants of Efrafa are either cowed or rebellious. The unhappiness of the does has resulted in fewer and fewer litters being born, and here Adams uses one of his excellent touches of realism. It has been observed that in overcrowded warrens pregnant does reabsorb their unborn kittens instead of giving birth to young who will starve. Adams uses this biological fact in two ways: first, as an illustration of the rabbits' religious belief in the divine dispensation of the Lord Frith, and secondly, to make a moral point about the deterioration of life under a political regime like that in Efrafa.

Efrafa is not entirely ruled by terror, although this is the main instrument of discipline. General Woundwort is more than a mere bully. He is clever, courageous and shrewd, with a genius for organization. Young bucks compete to gain entry into the Owsla, not only for the privileges, but in a spirit of emulation of the general. Once there, they are eager to volunteer for the Wide Patrols, on which many lose their lives, and their admiration for Woundwort is warm-hearted and sincere. (The Owslafa, or Council Police, are a different matter. They are ruthless and inhumane almost without exception.) The attitude of the Owsla illuminates Woundwort's good qualities, and even after the final battle with the dog some of the Efrafans refuse to accept that Woundwort has been killed (his body is never found). However, the General's attitude towards the courageous exploits of the members of his Owsla is not altogether attractive:

> the casualties . . . suited Woundwort's purpose, for numbers needed keeping down and there were always fresh vacancies in the Owsla, which the younger bucks did their best to be good enough to fill. To feel that rabbits were competing to risk their lives at his orders gratified Woundwort, although he believed—and so did his Council and his Owsla—that he was giving the warren peace and security at a price which was modest enough.

At the opposite extreme from Efrafa is Strawberry's warren, which the band of wandering rabbits finds after a nightmare journey across heather and bog. As Efrafa is Adams's depiction of a totalitarian state, so this warren is his presentation, in rabbit terms, of a community of self-deluding lotus-eaters. (Significantly, this is the only warren in the book which has no name. Sandleford, Efrafa, Watership Down, even the briefly mentioned Nutley Copse, all have an identity, in which the inhabitants can take a pride.) To all outward appearances this warren seems to the weary travellers, with the exception of Fiver, to be a veritable utopia. All the rabbits are large, sleek and healthy. There is plenty of room for newcomers, for the warren is by no means overcrowded. It seems that the wandering rabbits have reached their goal.

The lives of the rabbits in this community are totally unnatural: they neither have to avoid *elil* (enemies) nor to defend themselves against them—the warren is open and conspicuous, and they rush out of the runs heedless of danger. (In Efrafa there is a headcount at the mouth of each run, supervised by the Owsla officers.) They do not even need to seek for food: *flayrah* (royal food) is provided for them, and they have developed the curious habit of storing and eating food underground, so that they need not go outside in inclement weather. (Efrafan rabbits tend to be somewhat undernourished. Feeding sessions are policed, and may be cancelled because of rain or a security scare for as long as twenty-four hours.) Unlike all the other rabbit communities in the book, they have lost their traditional rabbit culture, having forgotten the folk-tales and ceased to believe in the traditional religion of Frith and Inlé. Instead they have developed a curious, inward-looking culture of their own: they perform a ceremonial greeting dance, the does make a kind of singing noise to their young, and they devise pictures by pressing pebbles into an earth bank—but all of this is very superficial, only the outward forms and gestures of culture. It has no inner meaning for these rabbits, who are obsessed with the illusory surface of their lives, and will not confront reality. All their tales are introspective, shutting out any speculation about the world outside, while their decadent poetry expresses in veiled language what they dare not speak of openly—a longing for escape, even to some dream-shrouded, peaceful death kingdom. The fear and horror which permeate this warren are the fear of violent death, the horror of sudden strangulation by the wire snare. Fiver senses at once that this warren is a place of deceptive luxury and hidden terror, roofed with bones.

The wandering band of rabbits, led by Hazel and incited by Fiver, comes originally from the Sandleford warren, a third type of society which Adams implicitly criticizes. Midway, in terms of social organization, between the extremes of Efrafa and Strawberry's warren, this is an old-established community (a parallel to modern Britain?) whose Chief Rabbit is the Threarah, and where many of the migrating band were 'outskirters', young rabbits with no social status within the warren. The Threarah possesses courage, resourcefulness, tact and strength of character, and his behaviour during the myxomatosis crisis has saved the warren. However, he is settled now, growing older, secure in the complacent estimate of his own wisdom and foresight, and he ignores Fiver's warning of impending disaster.

This warren is comfortable, secure against wild *elil,* happy and well organized. Nothing, of course, can protect it against the vicious destructiveness of man. Moreover, it is becoming overcrowded, and the young bucks feel that they have little future there. They decide to go in quest of a new home partly in response to Fiver's prophecy, and partly in order to make a better life for themselves. This tendency to colonize in order to absorb overpopulation is a natural phenomenon amongst rabbits, as it is amongst primitive peoples. After the departure of the small band, almost the entire population of the warren is deliberately exterminated by poison gas. In a com-

munity where there is no room for mental growth or the appreciation of fresh ideas, Adams suggests, social stagnation sets in, political development atrophies, and the community becomes a natural victim to outside forces. This happens at Sandleford. Complacency culminates in disaster.

All of these communities are rejected by Hazel and his companions, and so, by implication, by Adams: Sandleford is deteriorating from what was once a desirable society; Efrafa and the 'warren of bones' are both dystopias. The two dystopias are powerfully admonitory. The community of lotus-eaters appears to be a utopia, but the utopian superstructure is built on a foundation of horror and sudden death. On the other hand Efrafa, which is patently a dystopia, has evolved—and become distorted—from the utopian projections of its founder, whose obsession with ultimate ends has led to a corruption in the means, in this case in the lives of the members of the community. This is a reflection of much human experience, in which utopian ideals too narrowly conceived can, perversely, destroy human happiness. Warned by these examples, Hazel has only simple, but wide-reaching, objectives for Watership Down: that all the rabbits should be free and happy, and that the weaker members of the community should not be tyrannized by the stronger. The community established on Watership Down has no rules, only commonly accepted patterns of behaviour, and Hazel is accepted and respected as leader not because of superior physical strength (which is the attribute of Bigwig) or the gift of prophecy (Fiver) or ingeniousness (Blackberry), but for the breadth of his humane vision, and his compassionate understanding of his fellows.

Adams uses dystopias to illustrate what is necessary in a utopia. Inherited culture and religious faith give a strength and cohesion to the community. Both have virtually been stamped out in Efrafa (only the rebellious doe Hyzenthlay recites a poem, an elegy for the vanished freedom of the spirit), and have died a natural death in Strawberry's warren, where the fear of facing even the reality of their situation stunts any spiritual or imaginative growth in the rabbits. Hazel's group, by contrast, have a rich store of inherited tales, and a robust and unshakeable belief in the Lord Frith and the hero Elahrairah. In addition, the overprotected life of the lotus-eaters has stultified all political energy and vigour. Their passive acceptance of their fate is as degrading as the submissive obedience of the majority of the Efrafans. They combine physical well-being with mental torpor, demoralization and depression. This has led to such disintegration of personality under the strain of their unspoken knowledge of the snares which wait to end their lives, that it can only find expression through the decadent poetry of Silverweed, which is filled with the death-wish. On the other hand, the tyranny of Efrafa has resulted in a total loss of personal freedom and the victimization of dissidents. In both of these communities, the inhabitants are protected from the outside world, from disease and from predatory animals, but become instead the victims of the politically powerful within the community: in Efrafa of Woundwort and the Council, in the other warren of 'the man', the farmer who is effectively the ruler of the community, protecting it, providing its food, and killing its inhabitants.

By contrast with these two dystopias, and with the warren of their childhood, the rabbits on Watership Down establish a small and modest utopia. It is a loose democracy with a popularly acclaimed leader or prince, which looks back to the traditional culture and faith which the inhabitants, like human colonists, have brought with them to their new home, and forward to the good life which is to be lived in their new and freer community. It is a society without bigotry, in which there is adequate accommodation for individual talents and eccentricities, and each member can be valued for his own qualities. Above all there is complete freedom of action, of thought and of speech, within the limitations imposed by consideration for other members of the community.

This respect for the individual within the political system is the most notable feature of Adams's portrayal of Watership Down. Hazel is the prince, Hazel-rah, but only by the consent of the community. The relationship between the individual and the political system is fundamentally different in the two dystopias. Strawberry's warren has no political head, because of the danger that the leader might be the next victim of the snares, but it also has no sense of direction or purpose. The lives of the individual members are not restricted by political controls, but they are essentially futile; all have equal rights, and all run an equal risk of death. At the other extreme, Woundwort is a ruthless dictator, a psychopath with a lust for bloodshed and tyranny. The rules of the warren have a logical basis in the safety of the community as a whole, but they have been pushed beyond the limits of reason. Individuals are cruelly suppressed. Dissidents, even if their only desire is to leave the community, are tortured and killed. The inhabitants of Efrafa are healthy enough, although not as sleek and well-fed as the lotus-eaters, but the sense of oppression and mental deprivation leads to discontent, psychological troubles, the death of unborn young, and a spirit of rebellion. Bigwig senses when he first meets them that the discontented does have become so desperate under oppression, so much in need of escape from the imprisoning atmosphere of Efrafa, that he is almost too late to rouse them to action. They are sinking into suicidal despair. Yet so strong is the will for freedom that even Blackavar, cruelly mutilated and condemned to death, brain-washed, bullied and half-starved, summons up the last of his strength to join in the escape, and reaches the utopia of Watership Down.

Watership Down is never described by Adams or any of the characters as utopian, but it functions, like most imagined utopias or visions of the Golden Age, by negatives. In presenting the two dystopias, Adams has prepared the reader for the utopian quality of Watership Down. It is utopian by what it is *not*. There are no snares in the grass, no sudden death, no tyranny, no sense of hopelessness, no secret police, no informers, no military law, no repression of individual freedom. The positive qualities . . . are modest: a sense of personal and communal self-respect, faith and culture, security, and personal liberty. Modest riches to those who have always possessed them, but infinitely precious to those who have not. (pp. 219-25)

In depicting the cruelty and oppression of Efrafa, Adams directs our anger against other totalitarian states. (pp. 225-26)

[In *The Mouse and His Child,* Russell] Hoban sets the squalor of the dump against the countryside in which the fight for survival is equally ruthless; Adams, however, paints a varied and minutely detailed picture of the beauty of the countryside as a corrective to an urban-centred view of life. What do these writers offer as a goal? Certainly nothing so clear-cut as a simple utopia: The Last Visible Dog and the Watership Down warren are only tentative attempts at a utopia. The first is seen as fragile, probably transient, but the mouse and

his child and their friends have found personal fulfilment. At the end of **Watership Down** Hazel dies, and leaves the warren in the company of the legendary rabbit hero El-ahrairah. Yet the sense here is not one of ending but of promise for the future. . . . (p. 227)

Ann Swinfen, "Idealisms: Social and Political," in her In Defense of Fantasy: A Study of the Genre in English and American Literature since 1945, *Routledge & Kegan Paul, 1984, pp. 190-229.*

KATHLEEN J. ROTHEN AND BEVERLY LANGSTON

Engaging characters and fast-paced action make [**Watership Down**] readable; rich imagery and provocative implications make it rich with possibilities for study. . . . Besides generating enthusiasm, the work presents concepts which re-emerge through the year.

Our sophomore honors curriculum, like many others, focuses on classical works from the Greek to the Renaissance. Replete with heroes, **Watership Down** offers a starting point to link Odysseus to Beowulf, King Arthur to Julius Caesar. First, the novel has epic elements which parallel those of other works, especially *The Odyssey.* Also, it lends itself to activities for analysis we use throughout the year: close reading and group analysis of character, setting, structure, mood, theme, and conventions of genre, such as epic, allegory, and myth. (p. 56)

Since our honors curriculum parallels the sophomores' study of world history, we structure our study of works chronologically. **Watership Down** dovetails beautifully into the study of *The Odyssey* because similarities are innumerable. In chapter five Adams says, "Odysseus himself might have borrowed a trick or two from the rabbit hero," El-ahrairah, the rabbits' mythical hero. Other characters combine qualities students will later recognize in Odysseus: Hazel shows his courage and fairness, Bigwig, his superhuman strength; Blackberry, his ingenuity and craftiness; Dandelion and Bluebell, his powers of poetry and story telling.

Individual character parallels include:

> the doe Hyzenthlay (shine-dew-fur in lapine), who combines shining Kalypso's beauty with Penelope's courage and circumspection;
>
> Strawberry, a young Telemachos, who leaves his home to find not only a father figure but his own true nature as well.
>
> General Woundwort, portraying an extreme of Odysseus' negative qualities as he leads his followers to total destruction.
>
> Fiver, Hazel's mentor, with a gift of vision that provides Athene-like aid to Hazel.

Another similarity is the journey motif. Like Odysseus, the rabbits wander through a vast setting (about twenty square miles of English countryside) as all-encompassing as Odysseus' whole world (the Mediterranean Sea). Both heroes encounter either hospitable or hostile foreign communities on journeys fraught with dangers. In Cowslip's Warren, for example, Hazel finds rabbits living in Lotus-like luxury and resignation. Like Circe, the farmer who feeds them changes them into something unnatural. Fiver senses the danger when he hears the poet Silverweed sing his siren song. . . . This beautiful lyric enchants and repels Fiver, a poet himself. Like Athene on Circe's island, he warns Hazel and reminds the others that a rabbi. s instinct demands survival, not surrender.

The rabbits survive other obstacles that parallel those of Odysseus in relative dimension. Hrududil (construction machines) destroy Sandleford Warren with the cold-blooded cruelty of Skylla and Charybdis. The stream the rabbits cross seems as wide and dangerous as the sea between Kalypso's island and the land of the Phaiakians. Monstrous enemies—foxes, hedgehogs, badgers, and dogs—as frightening (and stupid) as the Laistrygones and Polyphemos are defeated more often with craft and quickness than with physical strength. But with rabbit enemies, Hazel and his band show amazing but believable physical strength as they battle to save their warren with the same energy and tenacity as Odysseus purging his hall of the suitors.

Another similarity is in the role of fate or chance. As for Odysseus, the agents of fate for the rabbits take many forms. Pursued by hostile Efrafans, the rabbits are rescued by Frith's "fiery thundering angel" who speeds down an iron road. In "Dea ex Machina," little Lucy Crane plays an unlikely Nausikaa to Hazel's Odysseus when she rescues him from her cat and helps him return home. Kehaar, the rabbits' seagull ally, swoops like the furies upon Efrafans who endanger the heroes. (Viewing these events from both the rabbits' and their own perspectives, students begin to recognize the origins, nature, and functions of myth.)

Besides analogies in character and plot, other similarities exist. Though linear in plot compared with *The Odyssey*'s cinematic structure, **Watership Down** introduces the young reader to rhetorical complexity. Stories are interspersed throughout the narrative about the rabbits' mythical hero, El-ahrairah. . . . These stories, like the many digressions in *The Odyssey,* provide both mythical insights and examples of simple variation of a narrative pattern. (pp. 56-7)

Noting all these parallels (more of which arise on each reading), we structured our study of **Watership Down** to focus on elements the work shares with other works covered. First, we structured the unit as a group study so that students may share details from close reading and help each other with critical thinking. After a day discussing general reactions to the novel, we identify the basic conventions of epic: vast setting, heroic characters, episodic structure, national or racial significance, deeds of great valor or superhuman courage, a hero's descent to the underworld, and elevated style with epic similes. To their amazement, students find examples of each of these which they share with the class. . . . Besides providing practice in close reading, this activity prepares students for similar analyses of more complex works, especially *The Odyssey* and *Beowulf.*

After group presentations of epic elements, we move to a study of allegory. First we discuss allegory in forms they know—fable and Biblical parable. As we turn to **Watership Down,** discerning students see that the entire book has an allegorical nature. The rabbits' search for a home parallels Odysseus' pursuit—a quest for origins and identity which permeates much of Western literature. The rabbits' quest clarifies for them the essence and potentials of their rabbithood.

This over-all allegory, however, is not an easy concept for most sophomores to grasp. They seem more capable of finding allegorical interpretations of the various rabbit communities:

Sandleford Warren, where unquestioning adherence to tradition and resistance to change leads to total destruction;

Cowslip's Warren, in which love of luxury robs rabbits of freedom, natural instincts, and joy;

Nuthanger Farm, whose rabbits live in cages in plain view of cat and dog enemies so that they have lost the will to escape;

Efrafa, whose fearless leader demands complete isolation and obedience in exchange for complete safety;

Watership Down, not a utopia but a new beginning where each rabbit has a part to play in assuring a natural and fulfilling life for all.

In examining one of these societies, each group must:

describe its attributes

find advantages and disadvantages of the system

tell how it differs from the other societies

tell how the system affects the rabbits who live there

find parallels to the system in past history or in the modern world.

These questions offer practice in critical thinking, including comparison, contrast, association, interpretation, and evaluation. These steps need only minor adjustment for use with *The Odyssey.* Having worked with allegory in the novel, students more readily accept the possibility of symbolic implications of Odysseus' encounters with the Sirens, Polyphemos, the Lotus-Eaters, and Circe.

The final question our groups address is that of myth and myth-making. Since the word *myth* is misused—even reviled—by some, we review the concept of myth as opposed to *lie,* myth as opposed to fiction. . . . Reviewing the students' past readings of myths, the class comes to a consensus on definitions and functions of myth. **Watership Down's** El-ahrairah stories offer a non-sectarian view of the essence and purposes of myth. Adams uses all of the following functions of myth:

as an explanation of creation;

as an explanation of a natural phenomenon;

as a chronicle of a racial hero's adventures;

as a concrete embodiment of a people's perceptions of a deep truth;

as an attempt to explain the meaning of life and death.

Each group rereads one of the El-ahrairah stories and its surrounding chapters. Then they

summarize the story for the class,

decide what function of myth the story illustrates and explain how it shows that function,

explain what the story reveals about the nature of its people, i.e., the rabbits. (How do they view their world and their place in it?)

show why the story is positioned in its particular

place in the narrative. (Why is it here, not some-where else? For plot advancement? Foreshadow-ing? To parallel a situation in the narrative?), and

tell how the story is similar to or different from other myths read.

Adams includes a creation story (chapter six), various hero's exploits (chapters fifteen and twenty-two), a profound meta-phor of sacrifice, death, and rebirth (chapter thirty-one), and an irreverent barb at the nature of dogs (chapter forty-one), in which El-ahrairah, disguised as the Fairy Wogdog, makes a fool of the huge, slobbering, dim-witted Polyphemos of the novel, Rowsby Woof. (Students have nearly come to blows vying for the choice of "Rowsby Woof"—or "The Black Rabbit of Inle," a curious second in popularity.)

After group reports, the class discusses the implications of the end of the book in which stories of El-ahrairah are told to the young rabbits in episodes the reader recognizes to be Hazel's own exploits. The focus on myth and its functions in society promotes understanding in later studies of *The Odys-sey, Beowulf,* Arthurian legends, and *Julius Caesar.*

For teachers unfamiliar with the book who feel reluctant to venture into 400 pages of unexplored territory, we offer en-couragement. Adams draws us so quickly and so completely into the lapine world that we're sorry that the book ever ends. To those overwhelmed by the activities, we invite you to pick and choose. To those who wish for more writing suggestions, we submit that a first reading will suggest endless possibili-ties. To those who doubt the book's validity, we remind them of *Gullilver's Travels* and *Alice in Wonderland,* which were both dismissed at some time as children's fare. To any who question student interest and involvement, we offer countless testimonials from a variety of students. (pp. 58-9)

Kathleen J. Rothen and Beverly Langston, "Hazel, Fiver, Odysseus, and You: An Odyssey into Critical Thinking," in English Journal, *Vol. 76, No. 3, March, 1987, pp. 56-9.*

PETER DICKINSON

When a book suddenly rages through the minds of the chil-dren of a nation, as if it were a highly infectious disease, you'll often find out that despite its apparent novelty it's in some ways much more traditional than many apparently more or-dinary books. **Watership Down** is a case in point. It's an im-mensely artful book, written with conscious brilliance and elaboration, with the various episodes in the plot carefully echoing those of Virgil's *Aeneid.* That's not the sort of tradi-tionalism I'm talking about, although the values which drove Richard Adams to write it in that way are, indeed, highly tra-ditional and literary ones. But what you might call the moral tenor of the book is also traditional, the Victorian boy's ad-venture story—*The Coral Island* rather than *Treasure Is-land*—inculcating, throughout, the virtues of the imperial of-ficer class and teaching smaller lessons in natural history by the wayside. (pp. 97-8)

Peter Dickinson, "The Burden of the Past," in Inno-cence & Experience: Essays & Conversations on Children's Literature, *edited by Barbara Harrison and Gregory Maguire, Lothrop, Lee & Shepard Books, 1987, pp. 91-101.*

L(eonard) Leslie Brooke

1862-1940

(Also wrote as Leslie Brooke) English author and illustrator of picture books and reteller.

The following entry emphasizes general criticism of Brooke's career. It also includes a selection of reviews to supplement the general criticism.

One of the most beloved creators of picture books, Brooke is credited with providing warm and appealing works for children which accurately reflect what they most enjoy. He is best known for the "Johnny Crow" series—*Johnny Crow's Garden* (1903), *Johnny Crow's Party* (1907), and *Johnny Crow's New Garden* (1935)—which describe in verse how an amiable crow entertains his animal friends, and for his collections of Mother Goose rhymes and folk and fairy tales, of which *The Golden Goose Book* (1905) and *Ring o' Roses* (1922) are among the most familiar. Depicting the serene English countryside in line and wash drawings which reflect his refined but spirited optimism, Brooke is often likened to his eminent predecessors Randolph Caldecott, Kate Greenaway, and Walter Crane. Brooke's work, however, is acknowledged as unique and distinctive: his genial personality emerges in his affectionate view of animals as well as in the winsome humor and dramatic yet playful quality of his drawings. He is lauded for his outstanding ability to portray animals with a wide range of human expressions engaging in diverse activities while remaining fully animalistic in nature. Drawing upon the tendencies of barnyard and jungle animals, Brooke consistently presents his readers with kindly but discerning portrayals of very human personalities.

Although he had already illustrated numerous books by other authors, including nonsense rhymes by Edward Lear and several works by Mary Louisa Molesworth, it was not until *Johnny Crow's Garden,* the first book that he both wrote and illustrated for children, that Brooke is acknowledged to have fully realized his inimitable style. In this story, which is often considered a landmark of children's literature, Brooke transforms a simple verse game his father had played with him, in which the child names an animal and the adult provides a rhyming couplet, into a robust, mirthful view of Johnny Crow's visitors and a sympathetic regard for Johnny Crow, the ever-patient and considerate host. With an effective use of demanding vocabulary and portmanteau rhyme coupled with cheerful ink drawings and watercolor paintings, Brooke presents young readers with an amiable view of life through the microcosm of the garden. The same confident glee can be found in his renditions of traditional nursery rhymes and tales; the three bears, the three little pigs, and other favorites are shown with intimacy and fondness while remaining subject to Brooke's sweet-tempered but incisive wit. Brooke's charming stories and illustrations, with their abundant treasures of drama and comic detail, have made many of his works recognized as timeless and enduring classics of juvenile literature. Brooke was awarded the Lewis Carroll Shelf Award in 1960 for *Johnny Crow's Garden.*

(See also *Something about the Author,* Vol. 17.)

R. E. D. SKETCHLEY

Mr. Leslie Brooke succeeded Mr. Crane in 1891 as the illustrator of Mrs. Molesworth's stories, and the careful unselfconscious fashion of his drawing, his understanding of child-life and home-life as known to children such as those of whom and for whom Mrs. Molesworth writes, make these pen-drawings true illustrations of the text. His drawings are the result of individual observation and of a sense of what is fit and pleasant, though neither in his filling of a page, nor in the conception of beauty, is there anything definitely inventive to be marked. On the whole, his children and young people are rather representative of a class that maintains a standard of good looks among other desirable things, than of a type of beauty; and if they are not artistic types, neither are they strongly individualized. In his 'everyday' illustrations Mr. Leslie Brooke does not idealize, but that his talent has a range of fancy is proved in illustrations to **'A School in Fairyland'**, and to some imaginings by Roma White. Graceful, regardful of an unspoilt ideal in the fairies, elves and flower-spirits, there are also frequent hints in these drawings of the humour that finds more complete expression in **'The Nursery Rhyme Book'** of 1897, and in the happy extravagance of **'The Jumblies'** and **'The Pelican Chorus'**. (p. 99)

R. E. D. Sketchley, "Some Children's-Books Illus-

trators," *in her* English Book-Illustration of Today: Appreciations of the Work of Living English Illustrators with Lists of Their Books, *Kegan Paul, Trench, Trubner and Co., Ltd., 1903, pp. 94-120.*

THE BOOKMAN, LONDON

Since that memorable Christmas when Mr. Leslie Brooke came to brighten the home with his inimitable volume, **Johnny Crow's Garden,** we have scanned Messrs. Warne's autumn list annually for something in the nature of a sequel to that masterpiece. Now it has come, and we find to our delight that Mr. Brooke has achieved that which is generally considered impossible—he has produced a sequel which is equal to the original volume. Here we see again "the Lion, with his green-and-yellow tie on," and as he listens to "the Bear, as he sings a sentimental air," he certainly rivals his earlier portrait. There are many amusing and beautiful books this year, but in its own line this one will be hard to beat.

> A review of "Johnny Crow's Party," in The Bookman, *London, Vol. 33, Christmas, 1907, p. 70.*

Old tales become as new ones when Mr. Leslie Brooke sits down to illustrate them. A year without a book from his hands is a disappointing one, for, whatever others may do with their fairies and gnomes, their robbers and princesses, it is to Mr. Leslie Brooke we turn for the acme of expression on the faces of his animals. We are always faithful to the creator of Johnny Crow and his friends, and we give a cordial welcome to the procession of birds and beasts who mingle with the humans in [the] old, old fairy-tales [Brooke illustrates in **The House in the Wood**]. Besides **"The House in the Wood,"** with its pretty hidden moral that it is well to be kind to animals, we have in this volume "The Goblin and the Grocer," "Snow-white and Rose-red," "The Bremen Town Musicians," "Red Jacket; or, the Nose Tree," and many others. And the special end-papers, which show a delicate wreath of honeysuckle suspended as a fairy swing, are deserving of special notice too.

> A review of "The House in the Wood," in The Bookman, *London, Vol. 37, Christmas, 1909, p. 76.*

The old rhyme of **The Tailor and the Crow** affords Mr. Leslie Brooke an opportunity for exceptional distinction. The artist has seldom advanced a stronger claim upon public consideration than in this work. The illustrations—of which there are something like thirty-six, six of them being also reproduced in colour—are full, not only of fine drawing, but of genuine humour. . . .

> "The Tailor and the Crow," in The Bookman, *London, Vol. XLI, No. 243, Christmas, 1911, p. 24.*

It has lately been the fashion to write books of nonsense verse, presumably for children. As a rule, these books are simply portrayals of the child mind. The child cares nothing for them; the humour passes him by, and they are read largely by his elders. Mr. L. Leslie Brooke clearly believes that there are no rhymes like the old rhymes; at any rate, in his **Nursery Rhyme Picture Book,** he has attempted no modern verse, and his illustrations are wonderful. The pig in **"To market, to market,"** is an animal to have known, and the poor man whom the robbers came to rob when he had nought, and who subsequently ran fifteen miles in fourteen days and never looked behind him, will delight any nursery. His treatment

of colour is excellent, especially in the two full page illustrations of **"Humpty Dumpty."** It is certainly one of the best books of its kind, and cannot fail to be a source of endless pleasure to thousands of children.

> A review of "The Nursery Rhyme Picture Book," in The Bookman, *London, Vol. XLV, No. 267, Christmas, 1913, p. 196.*

WILLIAM ROSE BENÉT

Leslie Brooke, now seventy-three, a famous English illustrator, brought **Johnny Crow's Garden** into being over thirty years ago, followed it in 1907 (the year I graduated from college) by **Johnny Crow's Party,** and now, recently, on his birthday **Johnny Crow's New Garden** claims his audience. Even as a college graduate I remember I took to the drawings of Leslie Brooke; and though the slight thread of rhyme is distinctly for "tots," it is still so amusing, and the light-footed animals so delicious, that no adult need be ashamed of a taste for Johnny Crow. Brooke belongs with Caldecott and Walter Crane, Lewis Carroll and Lear.

> William Rose Benét, in a review of "Johnny Crow's New Garden," in The Saturday Review of Literature, *Vol. XIII, No. 3, November 16, 1935, p. 27.*

"Good King Arthur." From The Nursery Rhyme Book, *edited by Andrew Lang.*

MAY LAMBERTON BECKER

They told me last year in London, "There will be a new Johnny Crow—that's news for you!" . . . Now we have [*Johnny Crow's New Garden*], the gay and dancing little book, and I had the surprise of my life when I found it was published on Mr. Brooke's seventy-third birthday.

He did not look within many a year of that when I visited him last summer in Hampstead—a tall, slender English country gentleman, light on his feet as becomes a first-rate walker. I asked him how he made his creatures so light on theirs; how, for instance, he could draw a pig doing something a pig could not possibly do—dancing—and make him do it precisely as he would if he could. Mr. Brooke understood at once this somewhat involved question. He said he took a sketching block down to the farmyard fence and leaned and looked and made sketch notes all over the paper, until at last he would come home convinced that nobody could draw a pig. He would then draw one. Same with other creatures. In this way, I suppose, he gets the right distribution of weight when a four-footed creature stands on two legs, as most of his are in the habit of doing, or when a cow sits down and leans her back against a tree. Five-year-olds will not know this is one of the things that make his comic animals so convincing; they will know only that their own dear animals are getting a chance to be all they would wish them.

The story bumps along in verse at the foot of the pictures, not more than a couplet to a page, recurring to the refrain "In Johnny Crow's new garden." This classic bird has enlarged his grounds and asked in the same old friends to celebrate. Thus the Lion had the same old tie on and even the Llamas wore pajamas and the Donkey sang in the wrong key and the Pheasant said "It's most unpleasant," in Johnny Crow's new garden. . . .

Make no mistake, the publication of this picture-book is an event. It is in the great tradition. Little children won't know that, of course. All they will know is that it is Right.

> May Lamberton Becker, in a review of "Johnny Crow's New Garden," in New York Herald Tribune Books, October 20, 1935, p. 10.

ANNE T. EATON

As we register our gratitude that, in 1935, Johnny Crow has seen fit to enlarge his little Garden [in *Johnny Crow's New Garden*], we find ourselves wishing that for every Christmas season we might have a new Leslie Brooke picture book. . . .

A few complications result for Johnny Crow, the assiduous host, and his other guests, but the patients make a rapid recovery, tea and muffins are handed by the puffins, in their best style, and everything ends happily with dancing and singing.

> Each Visitor's attitude
> Was his very best way of ex-
> pressing his gratitude,

and this the reader, as he gazes on the general hilarity of the final picture, will be the last to deny. (p. 21)

No one enters more perfectly into the enchanted garden of childhood than Leslie Brooke, whose books have delighted thousands of children and will delight thousands more. *Johnny Crow's New Garden* has all the charm and humor and freshness of invention of *Johnny Crow's Garden,* published thirty years ago. No child should be allowed to grow up without making the acquaintance of all of the Johnny Crow books. (pp. 21, 25)

> Anne T. Eaton, in a review of "Johnny Crow's New Garden," in The New York Times Book Review, November 17, 1935, pp. 21, 25.

MARCIA DALPHIN

Mr. Brooke was an English water-colorist and portrait painter, but he is probably best known in America as an illustrator of children's books. By those who loved his work he will always be remembered as the creator of Johnny Crow, the perfect host, and of the hero of *A Roundabout Turn,* that adventurous toad that lived on Albury Heath and wanted to see the world. True, it was Robert Charles who made the verses for the latter book, but it was Leslie Brooke who made them live for us.

His imaginative and humorous interpretations of such old nursery favorites as **"The Three Bears," "Tom Thumb"** and **"The Three Pigs"** have delighted people of all ages since first they appeared in 1906, and his collaboration with Andrew Lang in a Mother Goose for which Lang did the selection and comment and he the illustrations resulted in an edition of that classic that is indispensable. He also reinterpreted freshly and most amusingly many of Lear's nonsense rhymes, as well as some of the Grimm fairy tales.

Many of us feel that no child can be properly brought up without *Johnny Crow's Garden* and its sequels, *Johnny Crow's Party* and *Johnny Crow's New Garden.* And if proof were needed of the inexhaustibility and freshness of Leslie Brooke's fancy it could be found in the fact that in 1935, when the third book of the series was published, thirty-two years had elapsed since the drawings for *Johnny Crow's Garden* were made, and yet this book had all the charm and humor, the gay, engaging quality of the early work.

To make well-nigh perfect illustrations for stories and verses which have been the favorites of generations is not so simple as it seems: there is too much room for lapses in taste and judgment. Leslie Brooke was incapable of such lapses. Every page of his reflects his lovely personality. Let any discriminating person take up one of his books. On laying it down he will say,

> Here was an artist who had the great gift of natural gayety. He had an unusual feeling for animals and their essential characters: he had fun with them in his mind. He was a great lover of gardens and of the English countryside. He loved children, and he could draw the kind of pictures they understand and enjoy. They will always remember him.

> Marcia Dalphin, "Leslie Brooke," in The Horn Book Magazine, Vol. XVI, No. 4, July-August, 1940, p. 268.

ANNE THAXTER EATON

Every house where there is a child should start a Leslie Brooke shelf to be added to until by the time the child is seven he has at his disposal all of Mr. Brooke's books—to be returned to again and again, to be looked at by himself or with an adult. In the latter instance the occasion will probably turn into a delightful game, child and grown-up vying with each other to see who can find the most amusing details and clever touches supplied by the artist's humorous imagination.

Children from three to six delight in the gaiety and humor of *Johnny Crow's Garden* and its companion volumes, *Johnny Crow's Party* and *Johnny Crow's New Garden,* in the neatly capped rhymes, and in the suspense of having to turn a page in order to come to the end of a sentence. **"The Three Bears," "The Three Little Pigs,"** and **"Tom Thumb"** and **"The Golden Goose"** make up *The Golden Goose Book.* These old stories, simply and irresistibly illustrated, make a good beginning for the fairy tales to be enjoyed by a child before he can read to himself. (pp. 54-5)

Anne Thaxter Eaton, "Through Magic Doorways," in her Reading with Children, The Viking Press, 1940, pp. 41-64.

REGINALD BIRCH

The illustration of stories and books for children is of such vital importance to the cultural upbringing of youth, that it is disturbing and disheartening, to note in books of today, a radical change in the point of view which threatens to destroy the high aim which distinguished the work during that golden period, when the books of the inimitable Randolph Caldecott and the gifted Walter Crane literally showered down upon crowds of happy and privileged youngsters—engendering in them a love for gentle fun and a cultivation of a taste for all that is good and desirable in illustrative art.

Caldecott's books embodied everything children's books should contain—the drawings in color, superbly reproduced, the black and whites, or sepias printed with ample margin—were masterpieces of the printer's skillful art.

The fire of enthusiasm started by these artists, fed by the contributions of John Tenniel, Kate Greenaway, Leslie Brooke, Hugh Thomson and others, spread rapidly across the Atlantic and soon was blazing furiously.

Due to the able stoking of A. B. Frost, "Hop," Howard Pyle, Alfred Brennan, Robert Blum and their followers, the conflagration grew into a veritable pillar of fire that was to illuminate the imagination of American children for many years to come.

The light so gloriously kindled and generously handed down to us by the stars of that great galaxy has been dimmed, as one by one they left us, to undertake bigger tasks and to work on a mightier scale, in closer touch with the Master Artist and Creator of all things good and beautiful.

Fortunately they left with us an almost inexhaustible supply of materials for enlightenment, so that one has only to open a book to discover pages brilliantly illuminated by their inspiring genius.

And I found this to be a boon on hearing that one of the last of this puissant company had received his promotion and been called to a better front—and I sought to renew my acquaintance with the output of that amiable and admirable artist, Leonard Leslie Brooke, who so carefully and consistently carried forward in his work all the fine old traditional excellencies—every line evincing the same meticulous care given to the smallest detail, whether in the more important, or minor drawings.

His conception and treatment of many old and hackneyed themes is noteworthy in the giving of novelty and new life to these old favorites.

His technique, though somewhat lacking in that spontaneity and easy flow which disguises any sign of effort, has, as a substitute, a certain ingratiating honesty of endeavor that creates a warm interest and curiosity to see more of the drawings,

and one is amply rewarded by an ever-increasing desire to learn more about this clever being whose good fortune it was to be born at a time when the world in general was convinced that Security, Peace and Plenty had arrived for a permanent stay and so life in the future promised to become a sort of perpetual picnic, and there were good grounds for this belief.

Music, Literature and Art were flourishing and it was an age of liberal thought and spacious living—above all, it was the era that produced the most glorious nonsense that has ever been known.

Edward Lear, Richard Barham, Bon Gaultier, Douglas Jerrold, Artemus Ward, Halliburton, Leland, Lever, Lover, Dickens, Thackeray and their contemporaries amusing themselves and incidentally a delighted public by constantly producing all kinds of irresponsible literary absurdities.

In the Ingoldsby Legends, the Book of Nonsense, Hans Breitman, "The Fight with the Snapping Turtle," together with pictures by Leech, Cruikshank, Hablot Brown (Phiz) and Darley, the youthful Leslie must have found much food for cogitation.

That he was a thoughtful child, is evinced by his wisdom in choosing a father possessing a traditional story which he conveyed orally to his little son and which was destined to become the keystone of that masterpiece—*Johnny Crow's Garden* and its sequel, *Johnny Crow's Party.*

Not content with this, however, after a lapse of thirty-two years, a new version, or rather a second sequel, *Johnny Crow's New Garden,* was published—proving conclusively the inexhaustibility and youthful fancy of this genial man's delightful personality.

These books are all about Johnny Crow, the perfect Host to an ever-varying crowd of extraordinary guests and should have a niche in every healthy, fun-loving child's library.

In *A Roundabout Turn,* a happy conceit, Mr. Toad's remarkable adventures are uproariously funnily depicted, and in many of his books, small pen-and-inks, by virtue of a largeness of conception, become of extreme importance.

His use of color complementary to the line work, is always pleasing and appropriate—one drawing in *Oranges and Lemons* depicting a cluster of Fairies disporting themselves on the roof of a church, with adjacent spires, being atmospherically very convincing.

A word too for *The Jumblies* of Lear . . . where he manages to invent a new approach, of which I am sure the author would have heartily approved.

The Grimm Fairy Tales, and Mother Goose—in fact all his work, is full of charm and gaiety that never grow old and we are indebted to him for giving us so freely and lavishly of his delightful whimsies.

He was also a generous and impartial critic and not only could use a pen as a tool wherewith to display his fancy, but wield it as a weapon in defense of his opinions.

In answer to a letter, commenting adversely on his attitude in regard to the presentation of animal personalities, Leslie Brooke answered trenchantly and wittily,

Of course Mr. Nameless is fundamentally right. Animals should be themselves and treated so by us and not as imitation human comedians, and I should be doing far better to be interpreting the toadal toad by observation only. But then it's not my job. I'm a human, not an animal artist. Also there have been legends of animals acting as humans in all the early civilizations so it seems an ingrained form of original sin. Finally, let us concede that C. L. Dodgson, a strictly trained mathematician, would have done more worthily to confine himself to statistics as to the recurrence of albinos among wild rabbits and to the effect of their trying-on profession upon the mentality of hatters, with a view to alleviation of its deplorable result to the state. Let us concede all this and more and then say what sort of a world it is that we are going out into this afternoon with the memory of a virtuously scientific Dodgson before us as our only legacy from him.

Brooke's very name carried happy presage, for his fancy flows like a strong current, from time to time forming limpid pools on whose surfaces are mirrored reflections of delightful hidden pictures which arouse children's curiosity and tempt them irresistibly to wade in and explore their magic depths.

An admirable article on Arthur Rackham by one who, in my opinion, is today's best and most versatile illustrator for children, emboldens me to make a plea for a continuation of the sturdy, honest sanity expressed in Leslie Brooke's work and the cessation of offering hokum, whether literary or pictorial, to the youngsters of the present age. (pp. 168-72)

> Reginald Birch, " 'Johnny Crow's' Creator," in The Horn Book Magazine, Vol. XVII, No. 3, May-June, 1941, pp. 168-72.

GLADYS ENGLISH

My own nephew was the first child I knew to wear **Johnny Crow's Garden** and **Johnny Crow's Party** literally to shreds by his constant poring over them, but I have known many since. David is thirty now, but when **Johnny Crow's New Garden** appeared in 1935 it brought the same delighted response from him as the earlier volumes did when he was three. I can see him now, head thrown back, laughing out loud, just as the children do when they find in the new garden their old friends, "the lion with the green and yellow tie on," and the bear who before "had nothing to wear," clad in the very latest "slumber wear."

No wonder Johnny Crow in the thirty-odd years between the publication of the two garden books found it necessary to "enlarge his little garden." Thousands of children have poured through that enchanting gate with the sign *Welcome* above it, set in a garland of flowers. And every child who has gone into that garden has lingered there, leaving behind him all mundane thoughts to savour to the full the good company awaiting him. In all three of the Johnny Crow books there is the joy of familiarity—"John," as the Swan calls him, always the solicitous and kindly host, then the friendly Bear, the benevolent Lion and the solemn Goat, ever ready to pounce upon a guest who shows the slightest indication of a temperature.

The timid weasels with the measles are popped into the self-same bed with the identical flowered valance around it where the beaver languished with a fever thirty years before. True, there's an official looking chart above the weasles' bed, and a competent thermos on the floor, while neat medicine glasses have replaced the ominous bottle of earlier days, but Johnny

Crow hovers near them just as sympathetically as ever and Dr. Goat takes their illness just as seriously.

It is delicious nonsense, but there's far more than this in the three slender volumes. There is a philosophy and a way of life. Leslie Brooke dedicates *Johnny Crow's Garden,* first published in England in 1903, to the memory of his father, who first told him about Johnny Crow, and to his two boys. The Party book appeared four years later and the flowers in the little garden have grown apace.

Johnny Crow's New Garden is for [Brooke's grandson] Peter, and though it did not appear until 1935 it has recaptured exactly the same quality that enchants the mind and heart in the two earlier books. The gaiety and genuineness in these three books have a universal appeal. Not English children alone, but children all over the world respond to these qualities, and to the warm feeling of friendliness and kindliness. (pp. 173-75)

> Gladys English, "Expressing Our Gratitude," in The Horn Book Magazine, Vol. XVII, No. 3, May-June, 1941, pp. 173-75.

LEONORE ST. JOHN MENDELSON

A few days ago I had an air mail letter from New York telling me that the May number of *The Horn Book* was to be a tribute to Leslie Brooke. Would I write something about the Leslie Brooke picture books as I remembered them long ago in

And they all sat down
to their dinner in a row

From Johnny Crow's Garden, *written and illustrated by L. Leslie Brooke.*

the Central Children's Room of the New York Public Library, or even better, perhaps I could tell something of how I used them in Japan during the fifteen years I had lived there. (p. 176)

Of course I remember Leslie Brooke, he of Johnny Crow fame, and yes, I had sent a good supply of his picture books to the International School in Yokohama fourteen years ago. . . .Once, in a nursery in Yokohama, I made a scene from **Johnny Crow's Party** out of animals from a Noah's Ark and a miniature garden set. The little girl I was amusing was down with chicken-pox and she had a marvelous time doing the talking inspired by Leslie Brooke's verses, while I dressed up the animals for the party. It's a pity we did not have **Johnny Crow's New Garden** then, as it would have been great fun to put the Bear into Slumber Wear and the Llamas into beautiful striped pajamas!

Following the procession of gay animals that is marching up out of the depths of my memory come very fair Princesses, kindly Kings in fine raiment, merry farmers' boys; in the background are village scenes, with houses, meadows and boys and girls busily engaged in carrying out a story. The whole scene is flooded with sun and lovely delicate colors. There was always a friendly atmosphere in these scenes as I recall them; here written and illustrated for children was an appraisal of life that was intensely human and good. It is easy to see that children looking at Leslie Brooke's picture books knew just what his humor meant; they knew that Father Bear wiping his spectacles just that way was funny; they knew that the fuss made by animals with colds and sore throats was a reflection of their own troubles in similar circumstances, and they felt that the artist was letting them in on a secret. We all love being in on a secret and it is not often that an artist can beckon children to come and see the secrets he has discovered about the things of this world and have them agree with chuckles that what he sees is good fun and true. They understand his secret relish of the comic traits and the dear idiocies of men and animals. It is this intangible something that lifts Leslie Brooke, the artist, out of the ranks and makes him a star. (pp. 176-77)

> *Leonore St. John Mendelson, "Out of the Orient," in* The Horn Book Magazine, *Vol. XVII, No. 3, May-June, 1941, pp. 176-77.*

LOUISE P. LATIMER

As everyone knows, when an experienced reviewer takes up a children's book for consideration, two questions are kept in mind. One question is, Will it appeal to children? The other, Has it quality? A lack of either appeal or quality makes a book of little or no worth. In these two essentials Leslie Brooke reigns supreme. Nowhere else in picture books for little children can be found such perfect union.

Thinking of his predecessors, Randolph Caldecott, Walter Crane, Kate Greenaway, those three distinguished creators of the picture book, Walter Crane, decorative, stylized, detailed, attracts few children of picture-book age; Randolph Caldecott, of blessed memory, needs to be introduced; Kate Greenaway, prim, patterned, appeals only to certain children. But Leslie Brooke is taken to heart instantly by all children and by all grown-up children. He has art, storytelling quality, detail that appeals to a child, warm color, characterization, humor. (p. 178)

While Walter Crane is strong in detail, it is not detail that

From The Golden Goose Book, *written and illustrated by L. Leslie Brooke.*

strikes home to a child. While Kate Greenaway makes a picture, she rarely tells a story. Though Randolph Caldecott, who may have inspired Leslie Brooke somewhat, has all the attributes of a master picture-book maker, he introduces American children to a scene, not quite familiar, to which they must be led, perhaps to a somewhat adult scene.

But Leslie Brooke has universal appeal. See his beautiful Goose standing at the top of the stair poised on the lovely rose-colored carpet, righteously angry at the old man who would not say his prayers. He is a Goose that would be a friend of the family to any child. (pp. 179-80)

Leslie Brooke's work is childlike and homelike. What a beautiful mind, what a tender heart and what a rare talent have met in this man to give to the world the perfect picture books for little children. (p. 180)

> *Louise P. Latimer, "The Little Child's Artist," in* The Horn Book Magazine, *Vol. XVII, No. 3, May-June, 1941, pp. 178-80.*

ANNE THAXTER EATON

The maker of a truly childlike picture book must give himself up to a game of make-believe in the thoroughgoing fashion of a child. No illustrator has ever thrown himself more whole-heartedly into the playing of the game than Leslie Brooke.

For the little child not yet able to use the magic of print to enlarge his horizon, Mr. Brooke's pictures provide a new and vastly entertaining world; a world in which the creatures behave with a delightful and completely reasonable absurdity. On the flower-bordered paths and green lawns of Johnny Crow's Garden there is the fun of unexpectedness and at the same time a feeling of complete assurance and safety.

Children like to be surprised; they like also to see cause and effect neatly tied together. The smallest of the Three Bears playing in the Bear family's charmingly cultivated garden, aims his pea-shooter at a bird among the flowers. The child turns the page and one glance at the smug expression of the bird, the exasperation of the Little Small Wee Bear, and the motherly amusement of the Middle-Sized Bear, is all that is needed to show what has happened between one picture and the next.

In *A Roundabout Turn* the adventurous Toad returns to the identical home he left in order to investigate the rumored report of the world's roundness, but the increased length of Mrs. Toad's knitting indicates that he has been absent for some hours. Growth and change make Mr. Brooke's picture-book world convincing. Can one ever forget the cat, who, when "the mouse built himself a little house, in Johnny Crow's Garden," sat down upon the mat and, becoming visibly thinner while the daisies go to seed and the grass grows tall, watches patiently in vain, all unaware that the energetic householder comes and goes by the back door of his cottage. Leslie Brooke's pictures are eventful but at the same time permeated with that blessed consistency that means all the world to the little child. The animals who

> . . . before they went their several ways
> . . . all joined together
> In a hearty vote of praise
> Of Johnny Crow and his garden,

are actually the animals whose doings at the party the child has been following. Leslie Brooke always plays fair; never through forgetfulness or carelessness does he substitute a new character for the old friend the child is expecting. The lion, be it noted, in *Johnny Crow's New Garden* (written thirty years after the first Johnny Crow book) "had the very same tie on."

And so along with the glorious fun to be had in Leslie Brooke's pages, there is always a happy sense of security. The child knows that his universe will obey its laws, that old friends will not change and that at the end of the story the artist will still remember the details and the characteristics he had in mind at the beginning. (pp. 193-94)

> *Anne Thaxter Eaton, in a letter in* The Horn Book Magazine, *Vol. XVII, No. 3, May-June, 1941, pp. 192-94.*

LILLIAN H. SMITH

We are often told that little children require this or that kind of illustration in their picture books and I have seemed to detect an underlying suggestion that this is the kind of pictures children *ought* to want whether they do or not. Such an approach to any human being is the least "literary" and certainly the least understanding that can be imagined. It implies also an omniscience that one commonly associates only with deity. There are too many people who have listened to the streamlined bookseller who piles up his "big little books," his "animated cartoons" and his "talking books" in front of the classics of childhood, and then declares that the modern child demands his literature slick, smart and snappy. But it is the

children after all who have the last word, and it is they who, in the end, dispose of the fads of each generation of advertisers of the ephemeral and mediocre. (p. 197)

Little children's first reaction to pictures is always a literary one. They expect a picture to tell a story and to take the place of the words they cannot read. This ability for putting into pictures all that words imply is perfectly exemplified by Leslie Brooke and is immediately, if unconsciously, recognized by very little children, but because this artist addresses himself to people so new in the world that they can give no reason for the faith that is in them, they merely turn to his pictures as they would to the sun, less happy with any others. A three-year-old was shown a profusely illustrated Mother Goose at the house of a friend and when the book was opened before her, she pointed to a picture. "Who's 'at?" "That's Wee Willie Winkie." "No!" "But it *is*." "No!" repeated the three-year-old, "Wee Willie Winkie's in my *Ring o' Roses* at home."

When I ask myself what is this *living* quality in these classics of the nursery, timeless and ageless in their power to charm, my thoughts fly to Caldecott and Leslie Brooke. With both these men their lasting value is in the understanding that informs their pictorial interpretation of life in a topsy turvy world when animals and inanimate objects assume the foibles of the human race. It is this understanding that gives strength to the artist's ideas expressed so perfectly picture by picture in "The frog he would a-wooing go" or in *Johnny Crow's Garden.* When Caldecott died, some one said, "The children will laugh less now," but children's laughter has always kept his books alive as it will those of Leslie Brooke.

Children are always attracted by the warmth and colour of Leslie Brooke's pictures but they are even more captivated by their droll humour. His line drawings in black and white are pored over as much as the coloured ones because of their action and their laughter-making situations, pictured in simple familiar detail. To the adult connoisseur his slightest line can beautify the page.

All Leslie Brooke's animals (and no one else draws pigs and bears so well) are carefully and humorously observed as well as decoratively rendered, and he never forgets for a moment the children's fondness for them. He had formed the habit of making his pictures under the eyes of his own children, and in a letter written after they were grown he explains how he had come to need the criticism and collaboration of a small child. "Now-a-days," he wrote, "I am not in constant touch with any small people, and it is almost ridiculous how much, when drawing for them, one misses the corroboration, as it were, of the rightness of one's half-formed idea, and still more the look of boredom which warned me when I was going off the line." That he heeded the warning and did not go "off the line" is seen in his ability to picture all sorts and degrees of emotion—jaunty self-confidence, bewilderment, anticipation or dejection. More than once children have been heard to say of "the beaver" who "was afraid he had a fever," "Oh, look how sick he feels!"

Year after year when dropping chestnuts and whirling maple leaves bring back the picture-book hour to the children's libraries, it is usually "Johnny Crow" who first appears, for as you turn the pages and show the pictures the jolly chant "in Johnny Crow's garden" that rises so spontaneously to the lips of the boys and girls brings back into the room the fun and laughter so necessary for a happy winter's work. Indeed a library without "Johnny Crow" would seem sad and lonely like Hamelin Town after the worthy burghers lost their children for the sake of a thousand guilders.

In these days, so dark and fretted with care, we can ill spare for our children the jovial and kindly humour of Leslie Brooke. We can ill spare his light-hearted enjoyment of the animals and his sunny landscapes where the trees are always in blossom and daffodils, delphiniums and foxgloves scatter their fragrance around. It is true that without Leslie Brooke we would still have **The Three Bears,** but we would no longer see Father Bear smiling so benignly through his spectacles and no longer know that the Little Wee Small Bear had so impeccably chosen "Tom Bruin's Schooldays" for his bedside book. "It is the first time the Three Bears have looked like a family" was one child's comment as she gazed at the pictures. And what other pictures than Leslie Brooke's of **The Three Little Pigs** could convey the affable self-confident air of the little pigs as they set out into the world, and the final victory over the wolf of the third Little Pig who not only ate him but used his skin as a cosy hearthrug so that he could warm his hooves on the back of his ancient enemy? (pp. 198-201)

There are probably no books that useful grown-ups are called upon to read aloud as often as those of Leslie Brooke. Little Pamela who peeks over the edge of the desk to say "Here's **Johnny Crow**—six times I have taken him home. Eighty times my daddy has read him" gives some hint of the endurance of parents in the cause of literature. Leslie Brooke, doubtless, had the resuscitation of tired daddies in mind when he placed on the cottage wall of the Three Bears the subtle motto: "Thyme is honey. Save it," and when he placed the morning paper, "The Bear Truth," on the breakfast table where Goldilocks tasted the Bear's porridge, and when he buried Mr. Toad of Albury Heath deep in the pages of his favourite tabloid, "The Weekly Croak." And surely it is for the enlightenment of the old rather than the edification of the young that the Tailor's Wife finally locates the brandy bottle in the lower workings of the great hall clock!

Leslie Brooke's humour stands with that of Tenniel and Lear and Mr. Punch. His country gardens of blossoming trees and perennial borders, low stone walls and trimmed hedges, link him with Kate Greenaway and Caldecott. His kindly yeoman folk, the jovial innkeeper, the parson, the sexton and the good-natured village simpleton are akin to Hardy's rustics making merry on the Heath. (pp. 201-03)

> *Lillian H. Smith, "A Canadian Tribute to Leslie Brooke," in* The Horn Book Magazine, *Vol. XVII, No. 3, May-June, 1941, pp. 197-203.*

JAMES DAUGHERTY

We shall be missing you here in America, Leslie Brooke. . . . (p. 204)

But there is nothing missing of you when we turn again with timeless delight to those surprising and persuading creatures that live so enduringly between the covers of **Johnny Crow's Garden, The Three Bears** and **The Three Little Pigs.**

Take, for instance, the carbuncled hero of **A Roundabout Turn** as you have drawn him to the life. How completely and winningly you have rendered him, his background, environment and companions,—yes, and even those mysterious impulses that drove him to his amazing exploit and its realization, but not without perils, doubts and difficulties. The same

whimsy and pervading humanity enlivens the cavortings of all the gay companions of Johnny Crow.

Out of the shy and subtle essence of the English spirit you have drawn such stuff as Alice and *The Wind in the Willows* are made of.

Under the bright valour and quiet courage of your people in their ordeal by fire is a vast and enduring humanity that is the steadfast and peculiar characteristic of the English genius and its faith.

It is because your lyric talent was based on and evoked by this great thing, expressed so modestly and so sincerely, that we salute your passing and treasure the fine things that remain of you.

It is this persistent humor and unfailing courage which are so magnificent in England's darkest and finest hour.

I am not one to know how important in the world of art is the work of Leslie Brooke. I am no critic, other than when I love a man I love his work and that makes a very bad critic. But since I feel that your work is pervaded with the spirit which moves the children of a common tongue to warmth of feeling, to laughter, to generous friendship and to staunch comradeship, I look upon it with admiration and gratitude for all that you have given to children and childhood on both sides of the Atlantic. (pp. 204-05)

> *James Daugherty, "A Letter to Leslie Brooke," in* The Horn Book Magazine, *Vol. XVII, No. 3, May-June, 1941, pp. 204-05.*

MAY HILL ARBUTHNOT

One edition of *Mother Goose* that no child should miss is **Ring o' Roses,** illustrated by Leslie Brooke. Here is an imaginative and broadly humorous interpretation of the traditional verses. The lovely English countryside is done in soft, pastel colors, with yellows and tender greens giving a springtime brightness to the pages. The characters are in English period costumes and are utterly satisfying interpretations. Simple Simon *is* Simple Simon, daft and delightful. Goosey, Goosey Gander and the outrageous old man "who wouldn't say his prayers" will be forever your vision of that remarkable pair. But above all you will remember Leslie Brooke's pigs and after chuckling over them you will never again see pigs as just plain pigs. Instead you'll see pigs with a smirk or a leer, pigs looking coy or shocked, pigs on the rampage, or pigs of complacence. This is, after all, the test of great illustrations: they do more than illustrate—they interpret the text so vividly that they become the visual embodiment of the words. There are only some twenty rhymes in **Ring o' Roses,** but every child should have it to pore over and absorb until the pictures are his forever. Whether it is a *Mother Goose* rhyme or a folk tale, Leslie Brooke's illustrations illumine and add unforgettable humor to the text. (pp. 44-5)

> *May Hill Arbuthnot, "Mother Goose," in her* Children and Books, *Scott, Foresman and Company, 1947, pp. 32-49.*

M. S. CROUCH

Leslie Brooke's self-portrait shows a genial old buffer, baldheaded, bespectacled, wrinkled from a lifetime of kindly laughter. With one of his incomparable pigs on the blackboard, he holds forth like the nicest of professors on the relative merits of going to market and staying at home.

From The Golden Goose Book, *written and illustrated by L. Leslie Brooke.*

This cheerful caricature contains the essence of Leslie Brooke and his sincere, humane and humorous art. Of the distinguished band who made picture books under the Warne imprint, Caldecott, Greenaway, Crane, Brooke and Beatrix Potter, only the last was his equal in humanity, and he surpassed her in draughtsmanship. (p. 86)

[Brooke's fame rests] on the picture books which Warne's published between 1897 and 1935. The first of these was Andrew Lang's *Nursery Rhyme Book,* on the whole a typical product of the Nineties, strongly reminiscent of the style of Crane, and showing the effect, I fancy, of Brooke's earlier work in illustrating Mrs. Molesworth. It is the least characteristic of the books still in print, although there are a hundred hints—a pig here, an old man there—of what was to come. It is interesting to compare the treatment of these rhymes with that in *Ring o' Roses,* which came at the very height of his power twenty-five years later. In the *Jumblies,* a book of Edward Lear's rhymes . . . , some of the qualities which were later to be so familiar appeared, notably in "The Owl and the Pussy-Cat." *Johnny Crow's Garden,* in 1903, showed him at his best (it was on the whole his most perfect book), and thereafter he was always completely himself, supremely competent, entirely individual. *Johnny Crow's New Garden,* his last book, is so precisely in the spirit of the earlier book that it seems incredible that thirty years lay between them. (pp. 86-7)

The impressions which Brooke left among those who worked with him are of painstaking technical ability and infinite personal kindliness. To both these qualities his books bear convincing witness. No books of his period are better made.

Every detail, from endpapers and preliminaries to each page of text, is designed to contribute to the general effect. In every process of production he took a keen and leading part, as the crowded files of his publishers testify.

The sweetness of his nature glows in every page. Johnny Crow is the type of this quality. Courteous, kindly, and unobtrusive, he is the perfect host. When all the other animals have fled from the whale's very long tale, Johnny Crow stays politely to the end and then escorts his guest to the seashore and sees him off. . . . Johnny never occupies the centre of the stage, but he is always on hand with a helpful word or deed. One feels for him the quite personal affection reserved for the very best and closest of friends.

Kindliness is indeed the first characteristic of every drawing. Brooke sweetens his subject, without once falling into the pit of sentimentality. In *This Little Pig*—one of his finest conceptions—he cannot resist giving a good square meal to the pig who had none. The lion and the unicorn, who fight so fiercely for the crown, sit amicably side by side afterwards in the most enchanting of rustic settings, and share their bread and cake. This sweetness is far from the softening up of folk tale so characteristic of one school today; he is not protecting the young from a hard world, but rather colouring everything with the warm glow of his own personality.

The most original and characteristic of Leslie Brooke's contributions to the child's picture book is the completeness of the world he depicts. Each character in the stories lives his own life independently of the action of the story. This interior action adds enormously to the charm and interest of the books, while it distracts not at all from the force of his main theme. He is at his happiest with stories which he has written or remembered himself, like the timeless nursery rhymes and stories which he has pondered and dreamed for a lifetime, or where, in the Edward Lear rhymes, he finds himself intimately in sympathy with the author. In these best books there is an inner consistency rare in children's books. As a very young critic said to me: "He never forgets anything." In the sad story of the man who "had nought, and robbers came to rob him," there is a nice example of cause and effect. The man, it will be remembered, "crept up the chimney pot," and in getting down "on t'other side" he left his hat blocking the chimney. The consequent discomfort of wife and cat is admirably caught in a lovely 'double-spread,' in which loving treatment of lichened roofs and distant ships does not distract from the force of dramatic action. The barest hint in the words of the old nonsense rhyme have called up a most vigorous picture.

Nowhere is the independent action of his characters more clearly seen than in the incomparable Johnny Crow books. I like particularly the two penguins who patrol with solemn and superior step through the three stories, unspeaking, self-absorbed, only once even joining in the tributes to their generous host. Brooke developed a technique for introducing his characters somewhat similar to that of the cinema. He shows, as the camera does, out of the corner of the eye, the person who is shortly to occupy the centre of the stage. Children can play a good game of 'spotting the winner' on almost every page. So each character is introduced and departs to enjoy in his own characteristic way the charms of this enchanting garden. The detail in these books is rich, and rewards that prolonged and searching study which children delight to give, but it never spoils the exquisite balance of the pictures. (pp. 87-90)

Brooke delights in the details of domestic interiors, whether the simple rustic comforts of the crooked man's pleasantly asymmetrical parlour, or the greater luxury in which the three bears live. Every detail of this delightful home is lovingly drawn, folk-weave rugs, chair covers, pictures on the wall, even the Ursa Major symbol on Father Bear's bed. The jokes are naive but always good.

Although Leslie Brooke created some charming human characters, and was particularly happy with the deeply-lined faces and expressive hands of old people, he is best remembered and loved for his animals. These are nearly always seen engaged in essentially human activities, but whether shopping, eating at table, singing or dancing, they are never distorted or inaccurately drawn. . . . Brooke's skill in casting is unfailing. His animals play just the parts for which nature designed them. All his pigs are, in the final reckoning, friendly, sweet-smiling and intelligent. His ganders are stupid and malevolent; his goose—"well, the goose *was* a goose." The goat, whose medical skill was so often called upon, portentous, absorbed, has the perfect bedside manner. . . . All these creatures, in fact, simple line-and-wash characters though they are, exercise a strange and irresistible fascination; they *exist*, as few more elaborately worked-out characters in fiction do.

There is only a small handful of children's authors and artists whom children of all ages and classes recognise as their friend. Leslie Brooke belongs to this company. His sweetness of temper, kindly humour and clear sight, allied to technical skill of the highest, have resulted in a series of the most delightful books, in which fun and beauty walk hand in hand.

In the last resort it is of Leslie Brooke himself that one thinks. The stamp of his personality, lovable, honest and sincere, is on everything he did. (pp. 92-3)

> *M. S. Crouch, "Homage to Leslie Brooke," in* The Junior Bookshelf, *Vol. 16, No. 2, July, 1952, pp. 86-93.*

LILLIAN H. SMITH

The picture books of Leslie Brooke are of special note. The tradition begun with Randolph Caldecott has been carried a step further in **Ring o' Roses, Johnny Crow's Garden** and **The Golden Goose Book.** Leslie Brooke has the same capacity as Caldecott for seeing with the eyes of a child. He has a similar gift of unfailing fancy and lively humor. And, like Caldecott, his pictures are full of activity in dramatic happenings.

What could be more expressive than his pictures for **"The Three Little Pigs"**? On the first page we see them leaving home to seek their fortunes, airy, self-confident and eager to appear worldly-wise. On the final page we find the single survivor, grown to be a cautious and wise little pig, as he sits snug and complacent in the little house made of bricks. Family portraits adorn the walls, and before the hearth is spread a rug made from the skin of the wicked wolf. (p. 121)

Leslie Brooke draws creatures familiar to children and shows them in such unexpected circumstances, drawn with such particularity of detail, that they acquire an exciting freshness and romance to children. He never forgets children's affection for animals, and his appreciation of their comic traits is always warm and friendly. Leslie Brooke's, perhaps more than most picture books, belong to all childhood, not just to one generation alone. Like the nursery rhymes and fairy tales he illustrates, his picture books are ageless and timeless. (pp. 121-22)

> *Lillian H. Smith, "Picture Books," in her* The Unreluctant Years: A Critical Approach to Children's Literature, *American Library Association, 1953, pp. 114-29.*

ANNE CARROLL MOORE

[*The following excerpt originally appeared in the March 1925 issue of* The Horn Book Magazine.]

"Who is Leslie Brooke?" we asked, as we delightedly turned the pages of Andrew Lang's **Nursery Rhyme Book** at Christmas time, 1897. "Who dares make new pictures for Edward Lear?" we said in 1900, with a scornful look at **"The Jumblies"** and **"The Pelican Chorus"** in gay new picture book covers. "Why, it's Leslie Brooke again," we exclaimed. "Now, can that be the real name of an artist—be it man or woman—or is it a name out of a nursery rhyme? 'The most beneficent and innocent of all books,' this artist, with his own sense of nonsense, calls the Nonsense Books of Edward Lear, and wants the children of a new generation to know and love them. That's why the books were given a new form, and I do believe more children are going to like them. This artist ought to make a picture book of his own. He is no mere illustrator. He's a picture book artist."

And that is precisely what Leslie Brooke did do. He made a picture book of his very own and called it **Johnny Crow's Garden.** This jolly, timeless book, with its priceless gifts of true humor and original interpretation, went straight to the hearts of children of all ages, and for twenty years and more has held first place in the affection of American children.

With the coming of *Johnny Crow's Garden* we began to feel personally acquainted with Leslie Brooke, for the words of its dedication are revealing words:—

> To the memory of my Father, who first told me of 'Johnny Crow's Garden,' and to my Boys, for whom I have set on record these facts concerning it.

And as the Christmas holidays brought one after another of his inimitable picture books—*The Three Bears, The Three Little Pigs, The Golden Goose, Tom Thumb, The Man in the Moon, Oranges and Lemons,* and all the rest—we said: "These are picture books out of England itself. There have been none to compare with them in their simplicity of drawing and clearness of color since the golden days of Randolph Caldecott, Kate Greenaway, and Walter Crane. Why doesn't some one tell us who Leslie Brooke is?" (pp. 60-1)

It was close upon Midsummer Eve in 1921 that, by invitation of [a] dear friend of Leslie Brooke, I visited his studio on behalf of thousands of American children who love his picture books. Unfinished drawings for *Ring o' Roses,* published in 1922, were there, but I was taken back and back, as I had hoped to be, by earlier work and delightful talk, to the days when Leslie Brooke began to paint portraits.

As a young artist, he had painted Barrie, then a young writer, and from memory he had painted his friend, Arnold Glover. Over and over again he had painted the beautiful face of his wife, with the golden hair, and I saw at once that she lives for children in *The Golden Goose Book.* One of the two sons for whom *Johnny Crow's Garden* was made did not come back from the War, and Leslie Brooke had published no new picture book since 1916.

"I'd like to do another *Johnny Crow* if you think the children would still get fun out of it," he said wistfully.

"There's no shadow of doubt about it," was my reply. "They love *Johnny Crow* and it's the best book on gardening I've ever seen."

For many years, Leslie Brooke's studio was in his garden at Hampstead, and there an immense amount of work was done with the modesty and degree of technical skill which have given him his unique place among living artists of children's books of the first rank. (pp. 61-2)

"His extraordinary powers of observation and delicate sympathy with every phase of life have linked his own creative faculties as an artist to a rare understanding of 'the inner side of things.' Even his thumb-nail sketches bring a smile of happy amusement to any one who understands 'children,' whatever the age may be.

"He is a lover of the countryside and a first rate walker. As a companion on the open road, or by the running stream, his charm is a part of the surroundings, and leaves the same memory of 'far-off days,' never to be forgotten. A keen sense of humor is his by inheritance, and speech is hardly needed to illustrate his intuitive appreciation of wit or wholesome fun."

Such is Leslie Brooke, lover of Caldecott and Edward Lear, himself no less beloved by the fortunate children of his own time. (p. 62)

Anne Carroll Moore, "Leslie Brooke: Pied Piper of English Picture Books," in A Horn Book Sampler

They all joined together
In a Hearty Vote of Praise

From Johnny Crow's Party: Another Picture Book, *written and illustrated by L. Leslie Brooke.*

on Children's Books and Reading: Selected from Twenty-five Years of the Horn Book Magazine, 1924-1948, *edited by Norma R. Fryatt, The Horn Book, 1959, pp. 60-2.*

MARCUS CROUCH

Beatrix Potter's nearest contemporary in time, and the only artist to challenge her in humour and shrewdness, was L. Leslie Brooke. Brooke, for all the strong individuality of his style, is the heir of Caldecott. He has the master's robust imagination and delight in physical movement. He is kinder, possibly softer; at least Caldecott's equal in technical virtuosity.

Brooke did competent, uncharacteristic illustrations to some of Mrs. Molesworth's books (notably *The Carved Lions*), before finding his own style in two collections of poems by Edward Lear. *Nonsense Songs* and *The Pelican's Chorus* showed a ripe appreciation of nonsense allied to practical good sense. This is the quality shown most strongly in *Johnny Crow's Garden.* Brooke had learnt from his father a ridiculous rhyme about Johnny Crow who made a little garden, in which each animal visitor had a couplet describing his improbable activities. Remembered and augmented, this made perfect material for his exuberant and exact art. He could draw animals supremely well, and he had a rich sense of humour. The result was that the lion, the bear and all Johnny Crow's other friends were depicted with a zoological accuracy which accentuated the incongruity of their actions. This book was so greatly loved that the artist had to produce *Johnny Crow's Party* in 1907, and nearly thirty years later he added *Johnny Crow's New Garden* in the same vein and with all the old sparkle.

Leslie Brooke's drawing is full of movement and dramatic detail. The text is a starting point for all kinds of action and detail which may be latent but are never stated in the words. The lasting success of these books comes partly from their beauty and humour, partly from this richness of texture. Children love to 'read' the pictures, to follow the activities of minor characters in the Johnny Crow books and to study the topographical detail of the three bears' house in *The Golden Goose Book,* a picture-book version of four English fairytales ["Three Little Pigs," "Tom Thumb," "Three Bears," and "The Golden Goose"] which shows him at his most mature. Brooke published very little . . . , but everything he did shows the hand of a master, firm, precise, with fine technique directed by a keen, kindly eye. (pp. 26-7)

> *Marcus Crouch, "The Edwardian Age," in his* Treasure Seekers and Borrowers: Children's Books in Britain 1900-1960, *The Library Association, 1962, pp. 12-31.*

ELIZABETH NESBITT

The name of L. Leslie Brooke is well known and discerning and deserved tribute has been paid him. There should be no need to stress that he belongs to that fine English tradition to which children's literature owes an immeasurable debt; the tradition of men great in heart and mind and spirit, of Caldecott and Lear and Carroll, of Kipling and Grahame and Milne and Tolkien and others, who have infused children's books with gentleness and tenderness and gaiety, with fundamental goodness and sanity, and with optimism and beauty for all of which the adult, as well as the child, is grateful.

More than most illustrators, Brooke has revealed in his work the charm of his own personality. To be familiar with his pictures is to have an intensely intimate feeling of personal acquaintance with the man who made them, with his geniality and warmheartedness, his quick interest and sympathy, his peculiar power of imagination, his delightfully uninhibited and spontaneous enjoyment of the inner spirit of the stories and rhymes he illustrated. It is possibly this feeling of personal friendship with him which, in part, has made his name so revered on this side of the Atlantic. But the debt which America feels is owed to him is also due to our respect for his knowledge of children, a knowledge founded on genuine interest and sympathy and appreciation of a child's preferences. He knew that whereas an adult, at first sight, gains a general impression of a picture as a whole, and is frequently oblivious to small details, the child begins with the small details and from them achieves a cumulative appreciation of the totality of the picture. The details must be stimulating to the imagination and must have storytelling quality within themselves. They must also be harmonious with the picture as a whole and consistent in their continuity. Leslie Brooke had many great gifts, but his genius for detail is at one and the same time the underlying factor of much of his gaiety and humor and imaginative insight, and the secret of his great appeal. The *Johnny Crow* books are loved as living things, intimately associated with the child, are loved by him, and it is easy to see why, once one has seen what a little child sees in these books. At the end of *Johnny Crow's Garden* each ani-

mal has become a definite personality and a friend with Johnny Crow, the ubiquitous and generous host, the friendliest of all. In *Johnny Crow's Party* and *Johnny Crow's New Garden,* no change has been allowed to mar the reality of that hospitable garden. All things remain securely and serenely the same; the lion has his "green and yellow tie on"; the bear still possesses his striped pants and tailcoat. Johnny Crow still plies rake and hoe and improves his garden, coping patiently and politely with the troubles and idiosyncrasies of his guests. Every picture tells with graphic and faithful detail the incident described in the accompanying mnemonic and nonsensical verse.

The Golden Goose Book is a thing without price in its insight into the appeal such stories as *The Three Bears* or *The Three Little Pigs* have for little children. In one of Leslie Brooke's letters, quoted by Reginald Birch in his article in the Leslie Brooke memorial number of *The Horn Book* (May-June 1941), there is an implication that the illustrator had been taken to task for his personification of animals by some ardent realist. Such prosaic and literal-minded people miss the whole point of the classic appeal of the nursery folk tale. That appeal lies in the combination of the familiar and unfamiliar which only the folk tale and its faithful imitations possess. Bears, as such, are familiar animals, and home life a familiar experience; but bears living in a house, sleeping in beds, sitting in chairs, and eating porridge, constitute a novel and utterly fascinating deviation from the thoroughly realistic and therefore unexciting, commonplace. How well Leslie Brooke knew this, and how thoroughly he entered into the spirit of the little child's response to such stories is eminently revealed in the illustration for *The Three Bears* and *The Three Little Pigs.* The bears live in a typical English cottage, but it is unmistakably clear that this is a bear's cottage. The bed on which Goldilocks takes her nap has tiny figures of bears upright on the footboard. Bears are stenciled about the edge of the coverlet, and bears' heads form the design on the rug. The bedside book is *Tom Bruin's School Days,* and the newspaper lying carelessly on the table is *The Bear Truth.* Statues of bears and small models of beehives form the mantel decorations. The ancestral portrait hanging on the wall is that of Major Ursa, D. SO., and the motto of the framed family tree is "Bear and Forbear." Such delightful whimsy is more than superficial fancy. It is the result of an uninhibited imagination at play within the literature being illustrated. This same quality of imagination enabled Brooke to create additional little side stories which invariably harmonize with the main story, rather than detract from it. In fact, such side issues as the pictorial story of the little bear aiming his sling shot at a robin, and missing it, or that of the family walk, with the little bear turning somersaults down the hill, add immeasurably to the spirit of the story. Incidentally, the emotion of parental complacent pride in offspring has never been more faithfully portrayed than in the faces of the parent bears, as they walk arm in arm, beaming at the antics of their child.

It has been said of Caldecott that he was master of the fine art of leaving out, and that he could express a whole story in a few lines or a single figure. The same thing could well be said of Brooke. Among his most delightful and expressive work are the tail pieces to the stories in *The Golden Goose Book.* The black-and-white sketch of the small bear, parading triumphantly around the garden with Goldilocks' big hat, wrong side to, tied under his chin—the utter satiety implied by the back view of the little pig, finishing his dinner of wolf, are not only perfect finales, they are masterpieces of simplicity.

Underlying Brooke's humor and merriment, his story-full detail and the play of his imagination, the fineness of his technical skill and the quiet beauty of his workmanship, is a sustaining quality comparable to that of Beatrix Potter—a quality of old-world peace, of pleasure in the simple and gracious things of life. This is, indeed, a quality which in some kind or degree pervades the best picture books of all times. It constitutes their greatest single gift to children who find in picture books a world which is their own world of wonder and delight—and to adults, who, it may be suspected, find in picture books an anodyne for the confusion and contradiction of the modern world. By its very nature and intention, the picture book is freed, as is fantasy, from any necessity to reflect the present, and like fantasy, the picture book speaks an international language. (pp. 373-75)

> *Elizabeth Nesbitt, "The March of Picture Books," in* A Critical History of Children's Literature *by Cornelia Meigs and others, edited by Cornelia Meigs, revised edition, Macmillan Publishing Company, 1969, pp. 369-76.*

HENRY BROOKE

[In the early 1900s], Leslie Brooke was turning his thoughts to the production of a children's picture book all of his own: a book in which the words would be his, as well as the illustrations. His wife and son, of course, knew of the Johnny Crow game which he and his brother had played with their father on Sunday evenings thirty years ago and more; and it was she who suggested that he might try plaiting together the old Johnny Crow rhymes into a story and call it *Johnny Crow's Garden.* (p. 38)

It would be a test of his originality. . . . In the old Johnny Crow game there had been no continuity. Each animal stood alone, in what a later reviewer described aptly as that state of life to which rhyme had called him.

The Lion who had a green and yellow tie on, and the Bear who had nothing to wear, came straight from the old game and were certain claimants for inclusion in the new book. So were others, but it swiftly became apparent that to weave them into a story, or to weave a story out of them, was going to demand the invention of a number of new rhymes too. Some of these were easy enough to compose, but not all. One day Leslie Brooke walked over from Harwell to the village of Blewbury about three miles away, to tea with a friend who lived there, possibly Kenneth Grahame, author of *The Wind in the Willows* and *Dream Days.* On the road back he set himself to find an appropriate rhyme for hippopotamus, to follow after the couplet 'The Stork Gave a Philosophic Talk'. He tussled with it all the way home, and as he reached Harwell the answer came; 'And the Hippopotami said, "ask no further what am I".'

To this the Elephant added 'something quite irrelevant'. Occasionally Leslie Brooke was asked how he came to risk using so difficult a word as 'irrelevant' in a book designed for children. There was no hesitation about his reply. Children are not a bit troubled when they come in a picture book to a word they do not understand, provided that the picture accompanying it is something which they do understand. In this instance they can see that the remark described as irrelevant has obviously annoyed the Stork as much as it has secretly pleased the Elephant. This sufficiently indicates to children the sort of remark it was, and that is all that children want to know. In confirmation, he would sometimes add that he had read *Johnny Crow* aloud to numberless children, beginning with his own boys, and not one of them had ever asked him what 'irrelevant' meant. (pp. 38-42)

Leslie Brooke now had two children on whom to try out the humour of each of his drawings at the sketch stage. Sometimes, though rarely, it happened that they did not see anything particularly funny in it. In that case there was nothing for it but to scrap and start again. 'Little Henry' had no influence on *Johnny Crow's Garden,* as he was only six months old when it was published, but he had grown to be a powerful and trusted consultant when *Johnny Crow's Party* appeared four years later.

These two books mark the development of Leslie Brooke's skill in bringing into the background of his pictures small points which a child can look for and find, but which many a grown-up might miss. Doubtless this in part explains how the Johnny Crow illustrations have held the imagination and won the love of British and American children in generation after generation.

When the Lion, proud of his tie and with tail erect, is one of the first guests to arrive at the garden door, everyone will see Johnny Crow peeping round the door as he opens it. But not everyone will notice that the latch and the keyhole are not in their normal position but quite close to the ground: at crow-height, that is, not lion-height. Always perfect in courtesy to each of his guests, Johnny Crow in the very next picture has

AND THEN THEY THOUGHT THEY HAD HIM

From Ring O' Roses: A Nursery Rhyme Picture Book, *written and illustrated by L. Leslie Brooke.*

managed to slip an unobtrusive tie round his own neck, so that the Lion may be assured that he has come correctly dressed for the occasion. The Ape, mischievously mimicking the Lion, overdoes it in neckwear.

Members of his family and friends used sometimes to tease the artist with allegations that they could see a strong facial resemblance between some of the Johnny Crow animals and some human relations of his. He staunchly denied that any such resemblance was ever intended—though the evidence to the contrary in one or two cases seems very strong. But part of his genius lay in his ability to draw an animal so that it brought to mind irresistibly a human type. (p. 43)

For the following Christmas Leslie Brooke embarked on fresh seas. He took two of the old nursery stories, **The Three Little Pigs** and **Tom Thumb,** and illustrated them with bold drawings in colour and black and white. (p. 47)

In these books the purpose of the pictures is to illustrate the letterpress, and there is less opportunity for imaginative humour and bye-plots in the background, but the perceptiveness of the artist is as acute as ever. There was no animal whose facial expressions he could make more of than pigs, as the pictures of the old sow testify when she is sending her three little pigs out into the world to seek their fortunes. Two of them are so pleased with themselves that they walk off without even giving their mother a good-bye glance. It is only the third, the one that outwits the wolf, who turns to wave farewell to her. This is the one also who has a loyal taste in family portraits. Over the wash-stand in his bedroom hangs a portrait entitled FRIEDRICH BACON, and over his fireplace and his wolf-skin hearthrug are pictures of his two less prudent brothers.

Tom Thumb is a simpler tale, in which the artist has to come to grips with the problem of delineating with sufficient clarity and detail, in a world of otherwise normal size, a small boy who was born no larger than his father's thumb. As Tom is leaning over the edge of the batter pudding which his mother is making, the batter dripping from the spoon she has been using makes a face. On the next page, as Tom falls into the pudding bowl, the batter makes a different and a graver face. The small child who spies Tom hiding in a flower-pot from the King's anger, and subsequently rescues Tom from a royal watering-can, is reputed to have been modelled on Leslie Brooke's younger son, his first appearance in any of the picture books.

A twelvemonth later, this series was completed by the appearance of two further stories, **The Golden Goose** and **The Three Bears.** (pp. 47-8)

The Three Bears is a thoroughly human story. Goldenlocks enters the house of the Great Bear, the Middle Bear and the Little Bear while they are out for a walk, eats up the Little Bear's porridge because she is hungry, sits through the Little Bear's chair because she is too heavy for it, and lies down on the Little Bear's bed and goes to sleep.

She might have guessed that the house was lived in by bears, if she had looked around. On the wall of the room where breakfast is laid out there is a family tree with the family motto, 'Bear and Forbear', and a portrait of a bear in military uniform entitled 'Major Ursa'. The morning paper, not yet unfolded, is *The Bear Truth;* upstairs, above a wash-stand is the precept 'Thyme is Honey—Save it'. At the foot of the Great Bear's bed one can see the constellation called by his name, and the book which the Little Bear has been reading in bed is *Tom Bruin's School Days.*

None of Leslie Brooke's books for children exemplifies better than **The Three Bears** his special power to draw animals which are formidable without being frightening, and whose feelings any child or grown-up can instantly share. (p. 50)

Johnny Crow's New Garden . . . was completed and published in 1935. . . . No one looking at the three [Johnny Crow] books together could have deduced from the nature or quality of the pictures that whereas the 'Garden' and the 'Party' were done at the age of forty and forty-four respectively, the 'New Garden' was the work of a man of seventy-two. The magic was still there. The secret was that in his mind and his art Leslie Brooke remained as close to the child's outlook as ever he had been.

Part of the skill was to design the pictures so that the child, if he looked carefully enough, would find in them the answers to the many questions he might ask. The Deer came over very queer because he had rashly been nibbling the laburnum; there is no mention of that in the letterpress, but the background in a previous drawing has disclosed it. The Bear with the help of the Chimpanzees changed into his day-time clothes so that the loan of his slumberwear could help in the process of getting the Deer better by degrees; this is inferred but not stated. (pp. 115-16)

One of the rare ambiguities in the Leslie Brooke books was the identity of John, who was at risk of catching the weasel's measles. Some have supposed it to refer to Johnny Crow himself, but this was not so. John was the fluffy cygnet whom the two swans in the frontispiece were ready to defend against all comers, including germs. In the picture of all the animals expressing their gratitude, Johnny Crow can be seen having a word with them. Naturally every animal can be found there, if one looks.

The Lion had been the first to arrive in 1903, and was the last to leave in 1935. To show that it was all over, he had taken off his green and yellow tie and draped it between two upright evergreens, and was saying good-bye with an almost human expression to Johnny Crow, who was modestly confident of having been a successful host once more. (p. 116)

The expressions on the faces of animals which [Leslie Brooke] was constantly drawing, such as bears and pigs, came straight out of his own head. Also, for most of his working life, he was within reach of the London Zoo, where he could study and sketch wild animals in their cages, if he had any doubts about the set of their heads or the ripple of their muscles. There was also the Natural History Museum in South Kensington, where he could find almost anything from skeletons of dinosaurs and pterodactyls to stuffed hedgehogs rolled up into prickly balls.

In addition he kept and used all his life as his constant stand-by a large book entitled *All about Animals,* consisting of some 240 superb photographs published about 1895 by George Newnes in collaboration with the Zoological Society. He did not copy from these or other photographs, but used them as a check or a reminder when he had to draw an animal which was not familiar to him. What he would never do was to fudge or blur a drawing so as to conceal any uncertainty existing in his own mind. Because he had had no previous occasion to draw a llama or a tapir, for example, he paid a special visit to the Natural History Museum to study their shapes and the pattern of their muscles. (pp. 122-23)

[Leslie Brooke] never lost his enthusiasm for art, and never, so to speak, laid down his pencil or paint-brush. In the last year of his life he was actually planning a new children's book. This was to be a collaborative venture between him and [his wife] Sybil. Years ago she had written a short story for children about Mr Nobody, who lived up to his name and had no body, and longed to be like other people and have a body. There was a goose in the tale, and also a pig, two creatures which he relished drawing. He had completed six of the black-and-white drawings for *Mr Nobody* and was still working on the book, when he fell ill. His hand kept up its gaiety to the end.

One of the features of his career as a children's artist was that his workmanship and his humour never flagged. It was by the friendliness and the kindliness which shone through all his drawings that he first captured the minds of children and then held them for over fifty years; and there was no falling away, as age crept on him. He paid children the compliment of putting into their hands pictures which of themselves tell almost the whole story; pictures which gave children the answers to their natural questions, if they will look carefully enough to frame their questions, and then turn over the pages to find the answers. The doings of the animals may be absurdities, but they are essentially reasonable and understandable absurdities; and they were never frightening or horrific. The expressions on the faces of pigs or bears are the fruit of life-long sympathetic observation; one has never caught quite that emotion on the face of a real pig, but it would come as no surprise if one did. (p. 127)

Like most young art students Leslie Brooke set out on his chosen profession with the ambition and the hope to become a great artist, to earn the initials R.A., to rise to the top, and to make a name for himself in the history of art. Man proposes, God disposes. In the form which it took originally, that ambition was unfulfilled. But in the end would Leslie Brooke have wished it otherwise? In a tribute to him in the *Horn Book* of May, 1941, the librarian of a New York City Branch Library with a sense of humour wrote: 'How wonderful to have created those books! I've been studying *Hamlet*. But I don't know; it has its points, to be sure, but oh, to have given such rapture to children. Yes, I think I'd rather be Brooke than Shakespeare!'

Many years later, a member of the Brooke family received in a letter from a friend perhaps the most penetrating tribute ever paid to Johnny Crow, and implicitly to his author. 'We were very much fascinated about Johnny Crow, who is one of our favourite characters, one of the best of all books on Pastoral Care, comparable to the learned treatise on the subject by Pope Gregory the Great.' The writer was Professor of Ecclesiastical History in the University of Cambridge, so he ought to know. (pp. 129-30)

> *Henry Brooke, in his* Leslie Brooke and Johnny Crow, *Frederick Warne, 1982, 144 p.*

GRACE HOGARTH

Johnny Crow's Garden, the first of L. Leslie Brooke's picture books, was written and illustrated in 1903; the second, *Johnny Crow's Party,* in 1907. The miracle is that in 1983 these books still delight children fortunate enough to see them. After so many years it is now possible to take not just a sec-ond look, but a third, and indeed a fourth, as each generation of children discover that garden in which Johnny Crow, who "Would dig and sow," entertained his many animal friends. (p. 77)

What gives these simple, ridiculous rhymes and the simple, ridiculous illustrations their immortality? Of course, animals do not date as humans do, and no humans disturb Johnny Crow in his garden. What is more, these animals wear very few clothes and vividly express themselves through their smiles or tears or accurately active bodies. There is, however, a more profound reason why the books have survived. I think, looking back, that Leslie Brooke was *with* his own children and, through them, with many others in England and America when he set down the verses with which his father had delighted his childhood. As an artist, he was able to add the pictures almost to order. One senses that the small boys and girls were there beside him as he worked, whether in his mind and heart or in the flesh. They made suggestions; they laughed at the odd words, the silly jokes, and the animal antics. They applauded, and they criticized. This ability to *be* the child one used to be is rare among people who write and draw pictures for the very young.

When I first met L. Leslie Brooke in 1935, he was living in Hampstead, England, and I wrote of this meeting: "When he smiled, he seemed to be enjoying a secret joke that he would be only too willing to share with anyone who could enjoy his kind of humor." And, of course, it is children who most appreciate that humor. But many adults can laugh, too, and it is fortunate for the preservation of these books that those who must do the buying, the reading aloud, and the sharing can enjoy the experience. As with the children who stood round the artist, the adults who are asked to turn the pages over and over again find that Johnny Crow and his friends are *fun.* Everybody can laugh together. (pp. 78-9)

Both of the first two Johnny Crow books are still available today—remarkable at a time when many new picture books seem to have a brief life. Almost eighty years after the publication of the first book, there is still a place at Johnny Crow's table for my grandchildren, and I can take yet another delighted look at their genial host. (p. 80)

> *Grace Hogarth, "A Second Look: Johnny Crow," in* The Horn Book Magazine, *Vol. LIX, No. 1, February, 1983, pp. 77-80.*

MARGERY FISHER

The very first picture in the first of these three inimitable picture-stories [*Johnny Crow's Garden, Johnny Crow's Party,* and *Johnny Crow's New Garden*] hardly prepares one for consistency, since we see Johnny Crow placing seeds in a trench dug, seemingly, with a spade rather bigger than himself. Turn over, though, and he is watering a healthy row of pansies with a can exactly the right size to be held in a claw and for the rest of *Johnny Crow's Garden* sizes are carefully related (for instance, in the tomes which the stork has consulted for his 'Philosophic Talk' and the delectable little villa built for himself by the Mouse). Scale is important, in fact, because of the conglomeration of animals, even including a whale, all of them humanised, tactfully in posture but dramatically as regards facial expressions; though some of them are clothed and they often handle domestic objects more suitable to human life, they are proper animals, certainly not turned into people in the manner of the Bruin Boys, for instance. Besides, the role of each animal is chosen to suit its nature; the sheep snoozes in the middle of *Johnny Crow's Party,* the chimpanzees are buffoons and mimics and Johnny Crow's alert curiosity is always apparent as he wanders through his garden, an observant and perhaps a mildly sardonic host.

These impressions arise as much from text as from pictures, for there has seldom been a tighter and more total balance and consonance between the two in any nursery book. It must be admitted, though, that the plots, if they may be so called, are dictated to a great extent by the exigency of rhymes, which get wilder and more experimental with each book. If the pictures, with their happy humour of shape and situation, are a delight few can resist, the words are so chantable and so provocative that they confirm the books as classics just as firmly. Browning himself was no more cavalier with words than Leslie Brooke, with simple-sounding but unexpected rhymes like elephant/irrelevant, camel/enamel or llamas/pyjamas and with the more extreme portmanteau rhymes when the 'Porcupine said: 'Wake me if for talk you pine' and the Pelican, essaying to caper, assured the tiger 'When I'm feeling well I can'. The story seems to depend on the rhymes, indeed (the sheep has to go to sleep, the armadillo has to use him for a pillow, the fox has to put the guests of the first gathering in the stocks) but in fact there is no need to determine any responsibility in the matter. The books as a whole have a superbly spontaneous, ingenuous, cheerful air about them. They are for children but made by an adult completely uncondescending who was happy to enjoy his own jokes and the employment of his notable talents in line and colour. The three books, now reprinted in a small format which is entirely acceptable, must be placed in that small section of nursery-literature about which we can feel entirely at ease, whatever changes in taste and attitude may separate us from their first publication. . . . Small masterpieces, they were built to last and will surely continue to do so.

Margery Fisher, in a review of "Johnny Crow's Garden," "Johnny Crow's Party," and "Johnny Crow's New Garden," in Growing Point, *Vol. 25, No. 6, March, 1987, p. 4753.*

Paula Danziger

1944-

American author of fiction.

Danziger is one of the most popular writers of young adult literature among the audience to whom she directs her books. Her appeal can perhaps be attributed to the fact that she combines realism with humor and addresses some of the more difficult aspects of growing up with candor and empathy. As they move between school, family, and friends, Danziger's funny, somewhat self-effacing middle-class heroines face a variety of problems. Her novels present dilemmas to which teenagers can relate, ranging from simple feelings of inadequacy to the trauma of divorce. A former junior high school instructor, Danziger has based much of her work on her own life and on the experiences of her students. For instance, her first book *The Cat Ate My Gymsuit* (1974) stemmed from the stormy relationship Danziger had with her father; like protagonist Marcy, she was a perpetual failure in gym and had a younger brother who stuffed his teddy bear with orange pits. Despite some accusations that Danziger's fiction is trite and offers simplistic solutions to complex problems, a wide readership of young adults has affirmed their appreciation of her sensitive portrayals of their concerns and feelings.

(See also *Contemporary Literary Criticism,* Vol. 21; *Something about the Author,* Vols. 30, 36; and *Contemporary Authors,* Vols. 112, 115.)

AUTHOR'S COMMENTARY

When I was student teaching in 1966½, the faculty evaluator said that if the length of my skirt were any indication, I would have to make a choice between being a go-go dancer and being an English teacher.

The choice was to teach (and not just because I have trick knees). My first full time job was as a permanent substitute, an occupation that could have been a punishment in Dante's *Inferno.* That lasted half-a-year, and then I was a high school Title I teacher for a year. (I was fired.) Teaching junior high school English for two years came next. After that there were two graduate assistantships, one in an urban junior high, the other with a college reading program. Then, for several years I worked as a college counselor and then went back to junior high English teaching. During that year my slip fell down in class and two students crazy-glued desks to the floor. The realization came that it was incredibly hard to be a good creative writer and a good creative teacher. Each was a full-time commitment.

My choice was to write full time. I was never good at taking attendance, doing lesson plans, or getting papers back on time. I sold two book ideas to Dell, took the advance money, and hoped for decent royalties from the first three books. It was a risk—no major medical, no guaranteed pay check, and no imposed structure.

I survived. However, I still miss the kids, the day-to-day developing relationships, as well as the excitement when learning takes place.

How does my teaching past affect my writing? Let me count the ways—

1. The experiences have been useful in my storytelling.

2. Character development has been influenced by the "characters" who were in my classes.

3. School situations create a common sense of place for my readers. We've all been there in one way or another.

4. Whenever I have a writer's block and get scared, I say. "Well, Paula . . . You can always go back to teaching." That's usually enough to get me started writing again.

I do miss teaching. Every once in a while, I ask my friends to raise their hands and say things like, "Can I go to the bathroom—pl - - - ease?", "Is it an *A?*", and "Is 'the lion's fingernails' an example of a noun claws?"

It's appropriate that *English Journal* has asked that this "assignment" be completed in 450 words or less. I want to raise my hand and say things like, "Do articles count?" That's what many of my students would have done. That's what I would have done as a student.

Sure, having been a teacher affects my writing. Everything in my life offers a connection to my writing and some have more of an impact than others. Teaching was and continues to be one of the most important influences on what I do. I write to the kids that I once taught and to the ones who, I hope, still learn from what I write. (p. 26)

> *Paula Danziger and others, "Facets: Successful Authors Talk About Connections between Teaching and Writing," in* English Journal, *Vol. 73, No. 7, November, 1984, p. 24-7.*

GENERAL COMMENTARY

ALLEEN PACE NILSEN AND KENNETH L. DONELSON

Few critics would place Paula Danziger's novels in the pantheon of YA fiction, yet Danziger is among the most popular writers for young adults. Her novels are, admittedly, loaded with puns and jokes and one-liners and visual humor, but they are far more than mere collections of laughs. *The Cat Ate My Gymsuit, There's a Bat in Bunk Five, The Pistachio Prescription, Can You Sue Your Parents for Malpractice?* and *The Divorce Express* remain favorites with junior high school students because they do not talk down to their readers, because they present real issues and real problems facing their readers, and because they do not pretend that there are easy answers to any problems. Danziger's inability to develop characters, particularly adults, and her willingness to toss glib comments around as if they were profound may annoy adults, but her humor is exactly what her readers want. (p. 339)

> *Alleen Pace Nilsen and Kenneth L. Donelson, "Poetry, Drama, and Humor: Of Lines and Laughs," in their* Literature for Today's Young Adults, *second edition, Scott, Foresman and Company, 1985, pp. 335-69.*

THE CAT ATE MY GYMSUIT (1974)

The Cat Ate My Gymsuit is such an unusual title that it is sure to arouse curiosity. If readers expect humor, they will get it, but it is well blended with worthwhile values and character development. (p. 333)

For all its marvelous humor, this book is still realistic. Marcy's sense of humor is a counterbalance to her father's negative influence and helps keep her going.

The Cat Ate My Gymsuit is a thoroughly enjoyable, tightly written, funny/sad tale of an unglamorous but plucky girl who is imaginative, believable, and worthy of emulation. (p. 335)

> *A review of "The Cat Ate My Gymsuit," in* Journal of Reading, *Vol. 19, No. 4, January, 1976, pp. 333-35.*

Many of the children's novels grownups admire are unpopular with children; meanwhile, many children enjoy novels grownups consider to be trash. Rather than conclude that grownups understand nothing about excellence in children's literature, we must assume that children simply have bad taste. I think that many of them do, and I suspect that they do at least partly because of the expectations we create in them, at very early ages, about reading—not just about what they should read, but about how and why they should read. We create such expectations unconsciously, simply by pro-

viding stories for children and talking about stories with children in ways that imply our own unconsidered assumptions, both about children and about their reading. (p. 177)

Every novel contains assumptions about its intended audience. Harlequin Romances, for instance, assume their readers will be deeply interested in the way well-turned-out young ladies do their hair and fall in love in exotic locales. The novels children like frequently imply, not just that their readers have certain characteristics and interests, but also that those readers understand the books they read in a certain way. The popularity of these novels suggests that many children share these assumptions about themselves.

The most important of them is that children are either incapable of understanding subtlety or terminally impatient with it. But popular novels like Paula Danziger's *The Cat Ate My Gymsuit* lack subtlety for a specific reason: they have no distinctive detail, apparently on the assumption that their readers dislike such detail. They make little attempt to create the sense that the events they describe take place in a particular place at a particular time to particular people; in fact, quite the opposite happens. In *The Cat Ate My Gymsuit,* readers find out many things about Marcy Lewis, her family, her appearance, and her attitudes. But interestingly enough, not one of these details is unusual or surprising; none of them separates Marcy from the vast sea of theoretically typical teenage girls we all assume exist somewhere outside our immediate acquaintance in towns we have never visited. It seems that readers who like these books prefer clichés to carefully described experience.

We develop our clichés of the typical by considering only those qualities we believe masses of people share with each other; in doing so, we eliminate all the things that do make people different from each other. Many teenagers have acne; but some have acne and play the flute, and some have acne and cerebral palsy. The odd thing about Marcy Lewis is that she has none of these distinguishing qualities; at least we don't hear of any. Even descriptions of her appearance are carefully controlled, so that while we know nothing of the particular shape of her nose or the particular colour of her eyes, we do know that she is "an adolescent blimp with wire-frame glasses, mousy brown hair, and acne." She is, in other words, a fantasy version of a popular cliché, a person so typical that she lacks reality.

In fact, Marcy is so typical that she is impossible, a paradoxical summation of everybody's clichés about teenagers. She is both fat and flatchested, an unusual combination of two sorts of typical teenage problems. And she typically hates everything about her life; but she is untypical enough to realize exactly how typical she is: "sometimes I feel guilty being so miserable, but middle-class kids have problems too."

The generalization is suggestive; Marcy assumes that it is typical of her to feel different, that it is, in fact, normal. She also assumes that most grownups don't like untypical behaviour, particularly in teenagers. And in fact, the novel shows us that they don't. Marcy's father tells her, "Just be good and play by the rules and you'll be a much happier person." Her principal drives the point home: "Marcy, the younger generation just doesn't understand they've got to play by the rules." And her mother reinforces it: "It's just that it's safer being like everybody else." It seems that all grownups speak with a single, typical voice.

Marcy's response to all this is, once again, typical: "some

people can be different and still be happy." Perhaps they can; but neither Marcy nor her creator (nor, apparently, those who enjoy reading about her) have much patience with people different from themselves. Parents and principals who live by less "different" values are shown to be idiots, and Marcy despises her other teachers for not acting just like the amazing Ms. Finney, apostle of individuality: "we kept asking the teachers to be more like her, but they made faces and told us to keep quiet." Marcy wants everyone to be "different" in exactly the same way, and *The Cat Ate My Gymsuit* promotes differentness by assuming that people ought to be exactly like each other. It replaces both reality and individuality with typicality, and describes a world in which absolutely everybody is "normal" enough to do exactly what normal people normally do. (pp. 177-79)

[The] typicality of *The Cat Ate My Gymsuit* appears to be quite deliberate, a way of encouraging a particular relationship between Marcy Lewis and those who read about her. . . .

In other words, one can only enjoy *The Cat Ate My Gymsuit* by "identifying" with it, or "relating" to it. While those who usually use these words use them vaguely, they imply a close relationship between a reader and a character. "I could really identify with Marcy's fat problem," a fat teenager might say; or, "My principal is strict too; I can relate to that." In other words, one "relates" or "identifies" when one perceives oneself in the characters or situations one reads about. And that can happen to a sizeable body of readers only when characters are described vaguely enough to lack distinctness. The less realistically a character is described, the more typical that character can be; and the more typical a character is, the more readers can see similarities between that character and themselves. (p. 180)

Paula Danziger seems to assume, with some justice, that children read and will like books about people much like themselves set in worlds much like their own. *The Cat Ate My Gymsuit* proceeds on the assumption that children read looking for information about themselves—for something to identify with. (p. 181)

The important question is, why do so many children demand identification with the characters they read about? A distressing answer to that question is that we work hard at teaching them to do it.

Learning how to read is not just learning what sounds the symbols represent. In continually offering children the same kind of story, we necessarily suggest that all stories ought to be that way. In offering young children story after story which demands identification, we teach them that one understands stories precisely by identifying. When Fuzzy Fred or Fuzzy Harold or Fuzzy Matilda learns, through bitter and comical experience, that good little animals should trust their mothers and stay safely at home, the children who read about them have no choice but to put themselves in the position of Fuzzy Fred or Fuzzy Harold or Fuzzy Matilda. Given my personal experience of children, I doubt that such stories actually teach good behaviour; but they do seem to persuade children that all stories actually are or ought to be about themselves, and that reading is primarily a matter of self-recognition.

Not surprisingly, the stories for young children grownups admire usually put some distance between their characters and their readers. Even a simple book like Margaret Wise

Brown's *Goodnight Moon* demands that its readers stand back from the "great green room" it depicts in order to find the specific objects in the room the text mentions; few readers of any age care much about the young rabbit whose presence in the room is dwarfed by the vibrancy of the objects surrounding him. Similarly, no-one could enjoy the delightful joke of Pat Hutchins' *Rosie's Walk* if he identified with Rosie. Rosie does not see the fox who keeps almost catching her; but people who read the book do, and in so doing, find themselves at some distance from Rosie, wiser than she and enjoying their superior wisdom. They also find themselves at some distance from the fox, who is too stupid to be identified with. In fact, the pictures in any good illustrated book capture the atmosphere of the world they create so specifically that enjoyment of them inevitably depends on our consciousness of the peculiarities of the atmosphere.

Ironically, young children are capable of responding to such stories without identifying with their main characters; my own four-year-old son tells me that stories take place in "another world," a world clearly unlike his own that he enjoys hearing news of. Unfortunately, many children lose their capability for such enjoyment. I think that happens mainly because grownups insist on identification even when stories do not demand it, because they point out how Rosie the hen or the rabbit in *Goodnight Moon* are really like the children hearing about them, and how they ought to be wary of evil strangers or how they ought to go to sleep quickly—just like Rosie or the rabbit. For children who learn to respond to stories in this way, stories which make identification difficult finally become boring and irrelevant.

Why, then, do we insist on teaching children something so obviously limiting? Simply, I guess, because we think it useful for us to do so. If we can teach children to see themselves in the characters they read about, then we can make things happen to those characters that will teach children important truths about themselves. Our conviction that the main purpose of fiction is education causes us to turn fiction into propaganda; as Marcy Lewis insists toward the end of *The Cat Ate My Gymsuit*, "I think I'm learning a lot." Not surprisingly, Paula Danziger's publishers tell us that she is "currently studying bibliotherapy"; *The Cat Ate My Gymsuit* is the archetypical bibliotherapeutic novel.

The assumption of such novels is that identification leads to manipulation. If you see yourself as Fuzzy Harold, then you will learn never to run away from home, just as Fuzzy Harold does. If you see yourself as Marcy Lewis, then you will develop a good image of yourself, just as Marcy eventually does. If you were like her in the first place, and it happens to her, then it can happen to you, too.

That is the theory; but it is, of course, a deception that bibliotherapists perpetrate upon themselves. For novels like *The Cat Ate My Gymsuit* are not therapeutic at all, except insofar as they are designed to make their readers feel good. But they cannot possibly make their readers learn to accept reality, since they contain no reality. On the other hand, they do act as wish-fulfillments; they present the world as some grownups imagine young people would like it to be.

Even to begin with, *The Cat Ate My Gymsuit* confirms the usual teenage prejudices about the world that grownups assume to be typical. Marcy is fat and ugly, but she is much smarter and much more sensitive than any of her parents or her teachers. She does not just imagine that her father has no time for her; he actually says, "I've worked hard all day for this family. . . . I don't have to talk to all of you too, do I?" She does not just imagine that her principal is stupid and reactionary; he is. She does not just imagine that her teachers are insensitive and lazy, and give only multiple-guess tests "because they're easier to correct"; they are, except, of course, for the marvellous Ms. Finney, the novel's superheroine. In other words, the book describes, not things as they are, but things as grownups imagine teenagers think they are. That is what readers are meant to identify with.

One might expect an adjustment to a saner and less self-indulgent reading of the world. And not surprisingly, after the identification comes the manipulation. Things happen to Marcy that change her. But ironically, none of them moves her any closer to a convincing reading of reality. Each of them simply fulfills a self-satisfying fantasy.

Marcy discovers that, even though she is fat, she is still desirable; and as soon as she stops feeling sorry for herself, she finds the love of a terrific guy. She becomes a leader after years of being a follower; in fact, a high school student tells her, "Wish we had more excitement at that stupid high school. Maybe it'll get more interesting next year, when you get there." Her mother becomes a better person by adopting her daughter's values and rejecting all her own old ones: "so now, at my age, I'm learning, and you're my teacher." Above all, Marcy meets exactly the kind of grownup teenagers are supposed to wish all grownups were—one who cares for her deeply as a person, admires her intelligence and her sensitivity, and never does anything to suggest that Marcy, at age thirteen, is anything other than absolutely right and absolutely wise about everything there is to know in the whole world.

That grownup is the marvellous Ms. Finney. She is young, dedicated, and perfect. She makes learning fun (mostly by never teaching anything except how to be yourself). She never yells at anybody, ever. She is capable of making every single thirteen-year-old in her class adore her, and become a sensitive genius, and always do his homework; every single one. She is, of course, not appreciated by the more ordinary grownups she works with, who try to get rid of her and her guitar and her sensitivity group. But her divinity is spectacularly confirmed when the School Board is forced to reinstate her, despite their obtuse dislike of her. Finally, she moves on to even greater heights, and resigns her job so she can "get a doctorate in something called bibliotherapy," obviously a perfect calling for a perfect human being. And at the end, Marcy dedicates herself to the faith, saying, "That sounds good. Maybe someday I'll do something like that."

This is hardly therapeutic in the clinical sense; while the book claims to show Marcy adjusting wisely to reality, it actually shows her moving off into a weird wish-fulfilling fantasy of a decidedly unrealistic sort—a world where one always gets what one wants, where one is always right about the inadequacies of others, and where one's consciousness of a problem automatically leads to its solution. It is not surprising that young people like such novels, just as it is not surprising that they like Superman or Nancy Drew, which depict reality in the same way; what is amazing is that grownups take the therapeutic value of these books seriously. (pp. 181-84)

In training children to identify, to read only about themselves, we sentence them to the solitude of their own consciousness. Less significantly but just as sadly, we deprive them of the pleasures of genuinely admirable fiction—the ability of carefully chosen words to evoke experiences we have never experienced and to show us lives we have never lived. The more we teach children to read about themselves, the smaller will be the audience for writing about people different from ourselves—and good writing, whether for children or for grownups, is never about anything else. (p. 184)

> *Perry Nodelman, "How Typical Children Read Typical Books," in* Children's literature in education, *Vol. 12, No. 4, Winter, 1981, pp. 177-85.*

This is one of those books for teenagers in which the author solicits the reader's sympathy by portraying an adult world of almost unrelieved gloom, a misunderstood group of teenagers and one adult martyr to bridge the gap. . . .

Although obviously well meant, it is all unbelievably trite. The adult characters are predictable stereotypes—even Ms Finney fails to convince, being too weakly drawn to sustain the Messianic role assigned to her. The style is jerky and stilted, the dialogue artificial, the American idiom lacking all the charm and colour characteristic of our favourite transatlantic authors. The most successful aspect of this novel is the portrait of Marcy, her tentative discovery of friendship, and her increasing confidence in herself. But there's not enough here to make a book.

> *Jane Inglis, in a review of "The Cat Ate My Gymsuit," in* The School Librarian, *Vol. 35, No. 1, February, 1987, p. 58.*

THE PISTACHIO PRESCRIPTION (1978)

Thirteen-year-old Cassie starts her first-person story with the assertion that "Pistachio nuts, the red ones, cure any problem," and she ends with "Twinkies, I bet, are the answer"—a fair enough indication of the level of growth that has transpired in between. And though Cassie does indeed have problems that neither pistachios nor twinkies can solve—chiefly, divorcing parents whose insensitivity brings on her frequent asthma attacks—her tone throughout is so glib and inauthentic that it's hard to believe in a real suffering child under all the predictably triggered hysterics. ("Sometimes I think my parents are wonderful, and sometimes I hate them" is a typical Danziger illustration of adolescent psychology.) Cassie does better outside the home, acquiring a kissing boyfriend, running for freshman class president and beating out the candidate from the elite in-group, and winning the right to wear sunglasses in class after she has disastrously plucked out her eyebrows. Not improbable, but shallow—a synthetic slice of "typical teenage" life.

> *A review of "The Pistachio Prescription," in* Kirkus Reviews, *Vol. XLVI, No. 7, April 1, 1978, p. 379.*

This is a novel no thoughtful 9- to 13-year-old should let parents see. They may not survive the instant ego deflation of viewing themselves through adolescent eyes. Of her mother, the gangly, asthmatic heroine Cassie says: "She's like one of those dolls: you pull the string, and the doll says the same phrases all the time. They should market a doll just like my mother. I'd buy one, cut the strings . . . and stick pins in it." On the other hand, Cassie's peers will surely identify with the ugly duckling heroine's inferiority complex, her hypochondria, her first love and her unexpected nomination for president of "the freshperson class" (my favorite phrase in the entire book). The work is really an extended monologue with lots of snappy one-liners, some good, some not (just like those red pistachio nuts Cassie compulsively consumes). And though her parents clearly seem headed for the divorce court by book's end, the heroine is beginning to make her own peace with them, and with the world as it is.

> *Selma G. Lanes, in a review of "The Pistachio Pre-scription," in* The New York Times Book Review, *March 18, 1979, p. 26.*

The notion of family attitudes, especially sibling opinion toward self-image is clearly depicted in Paula Danziger's *The Pistachio Prescription.* Cassie, the protagonist, has spent her life receiving insults from a sister she sees as being blonde, beautiful, and popular while Cassie perceives herself as dingy, unpopular, and uninteresting. She claims the whole family is attractive—except herself. She observes that "the only one I resemble is Mutant, my brother's pet gerbil". Apparently this picture of herself does not come from a close look in the bathroom mirror because her best friend Vickie tells her that she does have worth. Cassie records that:

> Vickie's always saying that I internalize all the things my family say I am, that I let them define me rather than making up my own definition for who I am. She says I am prettier and brighter and more talented than they can admit too. But I think Vickie just says all that so I don't feel bad.

The brainwashing is deep. Cassie has come to believe that when Stephie, her older sister, calls her dumb and ugly, which she frequently does, she really is. Even her mother, in more subtle ways, keeps telling Cassie how unattractive she is. . . . During a confrontation at the dinner table, Stephie calls Cassie a giraffe whereupon Mama jumps into the fray angrily reprimanding Stephie by saying, "You know how sickly she is". After Stephie leaves, Mama tries to comfort Cassie, but what comes out only deepens the wound. She says, "Cassie, don't worry. You'll probably stop growing some day. Anyway, you've got some wonderful qualities". The message is clear again. Mama thinks Cassie looks like a giraffe too and is hard-pressed to expand on her daughter's "wonderful qualities." Is it any wonder Cassie sees herself as unattractive and unworthy? (p. 15)

> *Jan B. Allen, " 'How Do I Know Who I Am?' " in* The ALAN Review, *Vol. 11, No. 3, Spring, 1984, pp. 14-17, 44.*

CAN YOU SUE YOUR PARENTS FOR MALPRACTICE? (1979)

"It's absolutely disgusting being fourteen." Bobby Taylor has jilted you for Sandy Linwood because she goes farther than you do, and Miss Crawford, the health-class teacher, tells you to put a telephone book on a boy's lap before you sit down. This book takes place in the airless chamber of early adolescence.

The heavy problems of Lauren and Linda and Bonnie are: 1) Does it hurt to get your ears pierced? 2) Should ninth-grade girls go out with eighth-grade boys? 3) Should fifth-grade girls wear training bras?

The atmosphere is close and sweaty and mildly titillating, with cute boys on the telephone, copulating Ken and Barbie dolls, hair appearing or not appearing under the arm, and

parents who are always fighting and deserve to be sued for malpractice.

Can You Sue Your Parents for Malpractice? by Paula Danziger, author of *The Cat Ate My Gymsuit,* is clever and funny. The chapters rush by in a catapulting present tense. Adolescent and preadolescent girls, and even chubby children who might otherwise be reading "Winnie-the-Pooh," will giggle and pass it from hand to hand.

The author is a junior-highschool teacher, and she might say that the book is an honest picture and that she does, after all, wave some kind of flag for decency and general morals. But the flag is about the size of the Barbie doll's bikini. Case in point: As Zack and Lauren go upstairs to his room "to study," Zack's "nice" mother warns them kittenishly not to "study too hard." Oh, civilization! Oh, chastity! Oh, a hundred years of chaperones on Sunday afternoon park benches! Oh, the creak of the bedsprings as Lauren and Zack lie down! Six minutes later they sit up. What have they been doing? The world of early adolescence is certainly hot and perspiring and scruffy. Open the window, somebody.

> *Jane Langton, in a review of "Can You Sue Your Parents for Malpractice?" in* The New York Times Book Review, *June 17, 1979, p. 25.*

Can You Sue Your Parents for Malpractice? is a fast-moving novel, with a title to entice most teenage readers. Actually, the title has little to do with the story itself, but reflects beautifully the feelings of many young people who desire to be "divorced" from their parents.

The character development in this book results in the ultimate paradox in communication between parents and their children. Lauren is now the mature young woman willing to accept people and their divergent beliefs; her father is the preadolescent, who demands his way and refuses to accept any way of life different from his.

Danziger's skillful balance between humor and pathos makes this novel yet another to add to her growing list of successful efforts in literature that's particularly appropriate for junior high students.

> *Michele Simpson, in a review of "Can You Sue Your Parents for Malpractice?" in* Journal of Reading, *Vol. 23, No. 5, February, 1980, p. 473.*

Lauren's troubles, in *Can You Sue Your Parents for Malpractice?*, stem partly from home, where Mom and Dad prefer fighting to discussion, partly from complex personal affairs. . . . It is all very familiar, rather touching. I find that the action is not helped by being narrated in the historic present; it is a difficult literary device to pull off well and Paula Danziger is less than master of the technique. But in its smart, wise-cracking way, the story bustles along, introducing us to some clearly drawn characters in a believable environment. Thoroughly readable—but I would not guarantee to remember any of it after the passage of a couple of months.

> *M. Crouch, in a review of "Can You Sue Your Parents for Malpractice?" in* The Junior Bookshelf, *Vol. 51, No. 2, April, 1987, p. 97.*

THERE'S A BAT IN BUNK FIVE (1980)

There's a Bat in Bunk Five, continues the saga of Marcy Lewis from the earlier *The Cat Ate My Gymsuit,* in which

Marcy at 13 was fat and insecure; it takes her through the summer when she turns 15, loses weight and begins to develop some confidence. Loveless in *Gymsuit,* she forms early in *Bunk Five* a loving relationship with Ted, a fellow counselor-in-training at the creative-arts camp run by "Ms. Finney," whom readers will remember as the innovative, charismatic teacher from the previous novel. Nearly all the action in this new book takes place at camp, and while there Marcy takes a great many more steps toward maturity. (p. 36)

In spite of its trendy title, *Bunk Five* is not a funny story any more than its predecessor was—notwithstanding the frequent one-liner zingers in both—and Marcy's family life continues to be miserable, her father a monster, the communication gap a chasm. Marcy begins, of course, to learn tolerance and understanding at camp, to become, presumably, more "adult." But in the world Miss Danziger presents, adults, with a couple of exceptions, are two-dimensional, egocentric and small-minded. If this is really the case, why try to be one? But Miss Danziger is playing pretty much flat out for the audience. You of the new generation, she seems to be saying, will be fine folk someday, unlike the poor saps from whom you sprang. That stance has increased her popularity, but it's pretty simplistic and questionable considering the complexity of the problem.

Some parents and librarians have come down hard on Judy Blume for the occasional vulgarities in her stories. Mrs. Blume's vulgarities, however, exist in real life and are presented in her books with honesty and full acceptance. Miss Danziger, on the other hand, by romanticizing the distortions that complicate the healing of family rifts, may be perpetuating some of the very miseries for which she shows much sympathy. (pp. 36-7)

> *Natalie Babbitt, in a review of "There's a Bat in Bunk Five," in* The New York Times Book Review, *November 23, 1980, pp. 36-7.*

The author has skillfully balanced her insight into the daily trauma of the young adult years with liberal doses of humor. The book is neither didactic nor reeking of bibliotherapeutic intentions; yet junior-high readers should feel reassured by it. The easy-to-read style will attract numerous reluctant readers, and the book is sure to be extremely popular from the moment the appealing cover is seen.

> *Harriet McClain, in a review of "There's a Bat in Bunk Five," in* School Library Journal, *Vol. 27, No. 5, January, 1981, p. 68.*

From Barbara's exemplary surrogate-parenting to Marcy's continuing lack of communication with her father and her new fear of her feelings when kissing Ted, this gives us pop-psychology profiles instead of imagined characters and shallow with-it attitudes instead of sincere probing. Danziger's fans probably won't mind, but neither will they be stretched an inch.

> *A review of "There's a Bat in Bunk Five," in* Kirkus Reviews, *Vol. XLIX, No. 1, January 1, 1981, p. 12.*

THE DIVORCE EXPRESS (1982)

Phoebe Brooks spends a good deal of time on the "Divorce Express" shuttling to her old home in New York City to spend weekends with her mother, a successful decorator, and back again to rural Woodstock, New York, to spend the weekdays with her father, a would-be painter. As might be expected, conflicts abound in such diverse households. Her busy mother loves her, but she has a prospective husband whom Phoebe loathes; her father is caring but adamant in his refusal to keep her pet raccoon. Old friendships with boys and girls in New York shrivel up when Phoebe must attend high school in Woodstock, but new ones develop—despite her fears. Many of these situations may seem familiar to children of divorce—the need to keep two different rooms tidy and to have two sets of clothes as well as the threat of new stepparents. The author has a sympathetic eye for the ups and downs of her characters and a quick ear for adolescent conversation. If her treatment of divorce is timely rather than profound, it is to her credit that she resists the temptation to depict abusive and destructive adults in order to attract her teenage audience.

> *Ethel R. Twichell, in a review of "The Divorce Express," in* The Horn Book Magazine, *Vol. LVIII, No. 5, October, 1982, p. 516.*

"If you take the letters in the word DIVORCES and rearrange them, they spell DISCOVER," the heroine says at the end of this story. Well, maybe. But there's a lot of grief along the way for the children of divorcing or divorced parents, and this book aims both to detail the grief and to show that kids can survive it successfully. . . .

Some of the characterizations in this book border on the simplistic (Phoebe's awful grandmother and stepfather-to-be, Rosie's wonderful mother). Similarly, Woodstock's beauty and purity are set against New York City's presumed superficiality and crassness. And the breezy, fast-paced, often humorous first-person narrative, which makes the book an undeniable "good read," occasionally muffles the impact of the emotional traumas described.

Nevertheless, the specific problems—and seeming resiliency—of the children of divorced parents, as well as the general concerns of young teenagers, are ably evoked. And it's a pleasure to have a heroine who, without undue angst, is popular and gets the boy she wants too.

> *Diane Gersoni Edelman, in a review of "The Divorce Express," in* The New York Times Book Review, *February 13, 1983, p. 30.*

Adults enter junior fiction almost on sufferance when the generations are in conflict. The points of view of Phoebe's joky father and Rosie's independent mother inevitably come to us through the very articulate and wryly cynical comments of the girls as they travel to and from New York for their statutory exchange visits, in *The Divorce Express.* As Phoebe the narrator remarks, 'The transportation industry would be practically bankrupt if it weren't for divorce' and Rosie's comment on popular 'teenage novels about divorce marks the theme of the book:

> They're mostly for the kids who are just starting it. There should be one about a kid who's lived with it for a long time. Then you'd see that we all survive.

This particular couple survives partly because both girls are extrovert enough to be able to discuss their situation coolly (or, at least, to seem to do so as far as the author pursues their thoughts) and partly because with a predictable symmetry they end up as step-sisters. Perhaps it is with readers rather younger than these fourteen-year-olds in mind that the author keeps her tale on a light, even studiedly humorous, throwaway note; there are no depths of loneliness here, no moments of alarming edginess between parent and child, and only an occasional touch of bitterness (though once or twice Phoebe's mother threatens to push the book into deeper waters). Mercifully avoiding the inspissated gloom and wearisome heart-searching of so many novels on this highly topical subject, *The Divorce Express* makes its point in an agreeably relaxed and shrewd manner. (pp. 4673-74)

> *Margery Fisher, in a review of "The Divorce Express," in* Growing Point, *Vol. 25, No. 3, September, 1986, pp. 4673-74.*

IT'S AN AARDVARK-EAT-TURTLE WORLD (1985)

In *The Divorce Express* . . . Phoebe was the narrator, and her perceptive story of two broken families ended with an alliance between her father and the mother of her best friend Rosie. In this sequel it's Rosie who tells the story, equally perceptive and just as lively. There's friction between Phoebe and Mindy (Rosie's mother) and it's a difficult adjustment for everyone. Rosie's disappointed, because she had hoped her new sister would continue to be her best friend. There are some problems because Mindy and Jim (Phoebe's father) are not married. There are further problems when Phoebe resents, while they're on a trip together, the fact that Rosie spends time with other people. Eventually, after an estrangement, Phoebe decides that she'll accept counseling and stay with Mindy and Jim and Rosie rather than her mother and stepfather. Rosie is open throughout about the fact that her father's black and her mother's white, indeed, she's proud of her double heritage; only once in the story is there an unpleasant incident, when a bigoted stranger yells at her to stay with her "own kind." Fortunately, the boy she's with responds for both of them "We are the same kind—human." This has moments of sweetness to balance some tartness, an honest approach to problems, a lively and natural writing style, and strong, consistent characterization. (pp. 182-83)

> *Zena Sutherland, in a review of "The Divorce Express," in* Bulletin of the Center for Children's Books, *Vol. 38, No. 10, June, 1985, pp. 182-83.*

[In this book there] is something for everyone: Comedy—especially the title incident (in which Aardvark, the dog, eats turtle, Nerdlet's latest "pet-of-the-month"); Romance—Rosie's first kisses; Race—Rosie's father is Black and Rosie is " . . . stuck with the whole black/white issue"; problems of maturation—Phoebe has a very difficult time adjusting to the changes in her life; and, a happy ending—Mindy sells her book, Phoebe comes home, Jason comes to visit and all seems well.

Highly energetic beginning to Danziger's latest; second half doesn't quite live up to the promise of the first. YAs probably won't mind; junior highs will buzz to it.

> *Carole A. Barham, in a review of "It's an Aardvark-Eat-Turtle World," in* Voice of Youth Advocates, *Vol. 8, No. 2, June, 1985, p. 129.*

This is the first YA novel I've come across that approaches the subject of interracial children and some of the problems they encounter. The author handles the subject well, and even though the issue is only a minor part of the story, I welcome and recommend this book. . . .

[Rosie and Jason face] an ugly confrontation with a racist who yells at Jason: "Stick to your own kind." Rosie is hurt; it is the first time she has had to deal with something like this (which is highly unlikely). Rosie goes on to say her mother had tried to prepare her for this kind of incident by telling her some of the unpleasantness she dealt with when she was married to Rosie's father. Rosie concludes by noting her parents are freer in a sense since they have re-formed their own groups and in essence she is stuck with the problem. She and Jason deal with the incident briefly and move along—perhaps more quickly than is realistic.

Jason, his father and Canadians in general are portrayed as less racist than people in the U.S.—the insulter "must have been a tourist," Jason concludes—and that *may* be true. Still, setting the incident outside the U.S. seems something like a cop out.

This book, a sequel to the one in which Rosie and Phoebe meet, could well serve as a launching pad for another in which an older Rosie could tell us even more about growing up as an interracial child.

> *Emily Leinster, in a review of "It's an Aardvark-Eat-Turtle World," in* Interracial Books for Children Bulletin, *Vol. 16, No. 8, 1985, p. 18.*

THIS PLACE HAS NO ATMOSPHERE (1986)

This new novel by the popular Danziger features a heroine who lives in the year 2057 but whose problems will seem familiar to today's teens.

Aurora Williams, 15 and a sophomore, is in the right crowd with the right best friend, and even has a date for the big dance with the right boy. When her parents announce that they are joining a colony on the moon, she is devastated and considers every option, from pregnancy to being nice to her sister to escape. Dragged sulkily to her new home, having wrung from her parents the promise of a return to earth after a year, she begins a reluctant adjustment and, of course, finds that the kinds on the moon are not as bad as she thought they'd be, that there are values beyond the ones she's held so dear, and that she'd like to stay after all. An understanding friendship with a boy helps.

A Danziger book is rarely distinguished by plot, characterization or literary style. She does hone in, unerringly, on the concerns of her audience, using a style that rat-tats out wisecracks—not great, but funny and on the mark. Her audiences will not be disappointed.

> *A review of "This Place Has No Atmosphere," in* Kirkus Reviews, *Vol. LIV, No. 17, September 1, 1986, p. 1368.*

This is a good family story with characters that have believable faults. Danziger has a keen ear for teenage jokes and chatter; puns, some witty and some corny, punctuate the realistic dialogue. Aurora's story suggests to middle school readers that the teens of 2057 will suffer the same bittersweet emotions as those of today, and that caring friends, a loving family, and a sense of humor are important anywhere. (p. 100)

> *Phyllis Graves, in a review of "This Place Has No Atmosphere," in* School Library Journal, *Vol. 33, No. 3, November, 1986, pp. 99-100.*

Danziger, a popular writer of lively, rather mindless teenage fiction, can always be counted on for a smoothly placed narrative. She appears initially skillful in concocting this tale of teen life in the twenty-first century. Her characters "hang out" in Monolith Mall and window shop for mood clothing that changes color according to the emotions of the wearer. High school attendance is taken by thumbprint squares, discipline is maintained by humorless robots, and the curriculum includes courses in ESP. Ultimately, however, Danziger's story does not maintain its momentum, but moves to a predictable conclusion of adolescent reconciliation with environment and parents. Danziger resorts to formula construction and even the occasional gag (for example, the film *Rocky 415* is shown on a space shuttle). . . .

Few sf addicts of any age are likely to be impressed by this book, though Danziger's usual teen audience will not be disappointed.

> *Allene Stuart Phy, "Malls on the Moon," in* Fantasy Review, *Vol. 10, No. 5, June, 1987, p. 42.*

REMEMBER ME TO HAROLD SQUARE (1987)

This lightweight, romantic teen novel floats atop a tour of New York City.

Like oil and water, the two don't mix well. Westsider Kendra Kaye (14) and her cheeky little brother Oscar ("So what does S.W.A.K. mean? She Was A Kangaroo?") are saddled for part of the summer with Frank (15), a Wisconsin farm boy from a troubled family. Rather than have the young folk sit around, their parents present them with a sort of scavenger hunt, a list of things to do, places to visit, cuisines to sample and questions about NYC to answer; they'll have to scramble, but if they get through the list their reward is a trip to England. Despite some obstacles, Frank and Kendra hit it off, and by the end of the summer their friendship has become something more intense. This much Danziger handles in her usual cheery, sympathetic way, with plenty of rapidfire puns delivered by a cast of sane characters willing to recognize problems and talk things out. The travelog doesn't come off so well. The list is confined to Manhattan places below about 125th Street (they go to a Mets game, but that's an afterthought), so readers get only a tourist's-eye view of the city, and except for an excited visit to the set of *All My Children*

and a sobering one to the Jewish Museum, the characters' reactions range from "Awesome!" to "It is so sad." Most of the meals, performances, museums, and sights are hardly noticed, much less described.

The author does communicate an upbeat, positive impression of life in the Big Apple, but it's a vague impression, from a single angle.

> *A review of "Remember Me to Harold Square," in* Kirkus Reviews, *Vol. LV, No. 17, September 1, 1987, p. 1318.*

Danziger's irrepressible chatter is further hyped up here by the running gags and puns characteristic of all three kids, occasionally clever but mostly the corny product of Kendra the narrator's admittedly "smart-aleck mind." Readers will whiz through it all, however, enjoying the predictable romance and the exploration-game aspect (including lists of questions and answers), with glamorous glimpses into New York on a seemingly unlimited budget (the reward for completing the scavenger hunt is a trip to England). The one serious experience of a Holocaust exhibit seems forced into a glib context, and in fact only a few of the excursions are developed; the focus is on dialogue and dynamics among the young characters, which will make this all the more popular.

> *Betsy Hearne, in a review of "Remember Me to Harold Square," in* Bulletin of the Center for Children's Books, *Vol. 41, No. 3, November, 1987, p. 46.*

Danziger has scored a hit again with her realistic characters, believable dialogue, and smooth style. As in ***This Place Has No Atmosphere,*** she makes good use of puns and seems to have fun in developing her characters. It's refreshing to read a book whose characters develop a special friendship without the subject of sex intervening. Readers will also learn many facts about New York City (through the scavenger hunt); Danziger incorporates these into the story without making it too heavy. An entertaining story. (pp. 114-15)

> *Bonnie L. Raasch, in a review of "Remember Me to Harold Square," in* School Library Journal, *Vol. 34, No. 3, November, 1987, pp. 114-15.*

Henrik Drescher

1955-

Danish author and illustrator of picture books, fiction, and nonfiction.

The creator of works often praised for their freshness, originality, and inventiveness, Drescher is acknowledged as one of children's literature's most promising recent contributors. His stories, often absurd and surrealistic tales in both textual and wordless form which place their human and animal protagonists in exciting situations, are noted both for their sophistication and for stretching the limits of the picture book. Drescher's illustrations are considered as fantastical and jubilant as his plots. Influenced by the European graphic artists whose books he read during his childhood, Drescher has designed distinctive illustrations which are characterized by their wit and animated quality. The pictures, which include splotches of paint, scratches of pen-and-ink, and engaging borders which often integrate elements from the text, show an imaginative playfulness in keeping with Drescher's declaration that children's books should be pleasurable. Although his art initially appears childlike in its execution, upon closer study it is apparent that Drescher has taken great care to craft drawings which reviewers acclaim for their unobtrusive complexity and skill. His best known works are his first book, *The Strange Appearance of Howard Cranebill, Jr.* (1982), which relates the tale of a human couple who raise an infant left on their doorstep only to find that he is in fact a stork, and *Simon's Book* (1983), a story within a story about how two pens and a bottle of ink assist a boy who is being pursued by a monster. Drescher is also the creator of two informational books that introduce young children to African and Australian animals and are credited with challenging their audience beyond the usual level of concept books directed to them.

AUTHOR'S COMMENTARY

[The following excerpt is from an interview by Jim Roginski.]

Selma Lanes, in her *New York Times* review of *The Strange Appearance of Howard Cranebill, Jr.,* gave Henrik Drescher the title, "graphic magician." This 29-year-old artist will be known by this description for a long time.

European-born Drescher, primarily a self-taught graphic artist, is one of those artists who presents—or re-presents—the world in a new way. His ideas, offbeat as they may seem, work: He can create sophisticated pictures and stories for young children in a manner so fresh and original that children and adults return to his books, discovering something new each time.

His books are not tame. They provide excursions in ideas. Children find them accessible because their views of the world are not severally defined as are many adults. His highly graphic artwork is so unique and his voice so inventive that once you've seen a Henrik Drescher book, you will never forget it. Henrik has published four children's books in three

years. Few artists receive such distinction for artwork or recognition of talent in such a short time. . . .

[Roginski:] You have an extraordinary style, one that is at once fresh and original. Is this the result of many years of study and hard work?

[Drescher:] No, it's not from training or study. Style doesn't come from training. Style is secondary to the art. What you are seeing is not style, but, I think, my experience in art.

[Roginski:] What type of illustration did you do when you were younger?

[Drescher:] Political illustration. I started doing political drawings for myself, not for publication. A friend of the family inspired me. His name is Klaus Albrechtsen, a great political satirist in Denmark. . . .

[Roginski:] How did you come to move from political illustrations, which you still do, to children's book illustration?

[Drescher:] Julie Quan, a friend who works in children's books as a designer, encouraged me to do children's books, or to try one anyway. I always put it off. Eventually I got to the point when I thought I had something in me. That was *Howard Cranebill.*

I spent about a month doing it and left the work on Julie's desk at her office. It was in a dummy format, black-and-white, and very rough.

Barbara Lalicki (Henrik's editor at Lothrop, Lee & Shepherd Books) was visiting Julie. She saw the dummy and told Julie she was interested in my work. A week and a half after seeing Barbara, I had a contract. It was a real big accomplishment for me!

[Roginski:] One of the distinguishing elements of *Howard Cranebill* is the borders in the book. They incorporate sentences from the story, and put the images and text together. Is there a story behind them?

[Drescher:] I had been looking at a lot of Persian paintings, Indian miniatures, and icons. Borders are so important in them. And in a book, borders are natural things to do.

It was my first book so I was afraid of playing with it too much. I decided that if I was going to do borders they should relate to the pictures inside of them with words and pears and storks and other elements from the story.

[Roginski:] And the book that followed was *Simon's Book,* the book that brought you more closely into the public eye?

[Drescher:] Yes. After I had done *Howard Cranebill* I assumed I was going to do another book. I went away to New Orleans for the purpose of finding a new book. That was *Simon's Book.*

[Roginski:] Do you start with an image first with a story following, have the story first with an image following, or work on the story and image simultaneously?

[Drescher:] The art. I'll work on an image until I find one I like. Then I'll find a story I like for the image. Simon's Book came out of one drawing. I wanted to do a book about a story happening inside a book. I love the idea of a story in a story, a circle story.

For *Simon's Book* I drew one germinating image, the hole in the page. I kept going back to the hole in the page. Then the monster was drawn, and then the boy. I realized that was the book I was looking for. . . .

[Roginski:] One distinguishing element in all your books are your—for lack of a better word—"squiggles." They're everywhere! They make your books almost look like artists' notebooks.

[Drescher:] Actually all that stuff comes from my notebooks.

I travel often. Notebooks are my way of keeping in touch with bookmaking. I draw in little theme books. This is where a lot of my ideas come from. All the squiggles, the lines, the textures—all graphic and sensual.

(Henrik showed me one of his notebooks that he happened to have with him. It is a wondrous object, filled with squiggles and doodles, images that have caught his eye; pages of colors and notes, ticket stubs, a piece of bamboo curtain and the like. It is immediately apparent how heavily he leans on his notebooks as one source of continuing inspiration for his published books.) (p. 11)

[Roginski:] What new ideas are you working on now?

[Drescher:] I'm trying to figure out a new structure for my stories. Maybe not so much the circular motif. I'm at the point where I'd like to change.

[Roginski:] Selma Lanes has referred to you as a "graphic magician" in *The New York Times Book Review.* Your work strikes me as being very European because of the way you use line, color, space and the page. Perhaps you are a "magician," but are you influenced at all by European artists?

[Drescher:] As you know I grew up in northern Europe. Drawing is a cultural phenomenon there; it's all around you. My line quality, my spontaneity, my sensibility is northern European. I draw very heavily from their traditions and bookmaking.

Drawing is looked at more carefully in Europe. There are wonderful traditions from Rembrandt, Durer, Escher, and others.

Northern Europe is to graphics as Italy is to painting. I'm impressed particularly by the Polish and Czechoslovakian artists. I pick up color and concept from them. And also graphically the way a page is used, the way a page engages you.

The Polish are so wild! They play around. They have more fun, I think, with the printed page than anyone else. That is the right idea. . . .

To me, illustration is a *big* thing! It's publication and mass dissemination of ideas. It's a great medium for art.

Children like pictures. They can look at a picture book, modern art, contemporary art, anything, and get engaged with the pictures.

As far as I'm concerned, my purpose with children's books is to open the book up, engage the mind. That's if I have a "Big Purpose" at all. My personal purpose is to make children's books *fun!* (pp. 11, 26)

> *Henrik Drescher and Jim Roginski, in an interview in* Parents' Choice, *Vol. 8, No. 3, Autumn, 1985, pp. 11, 26.*

THE STRANGE APPEARANCE OF HOWARD CRANEBILL, JR. (1982)

The freshness and charm of Henrik Drescher's first picture book owe much to the Danish-born illustrator's virtuoso handling of colored pencils, eraser, pen and ink—objects he lovingly pictures on the title page of the work. Like Saul Steinberg, Mr. Drescher is a graphic magician who can turn an ink blot or smudge to high pictorial advantage. Whether he is simulating an elephant's leathery hide with airy, black-line scribbles or improvising rainbow-hued page borders comprised of sprouting greenery and awesomely inventive comic calligraphy, Mr. Drescher makes every squiggle enhance the visual richness of the story he tells.

The tale itself has its own matter-of-factly zany appeal. A baby in a basket arrives, stork-delivered, at the door of a childless couple, the Cranebills. Their delight is only briefly tempered by concern over the infant's elongated, stiletto-tipped nose. But, wisely, they decide to ignore the anomaly and, as all good parents should, lavish loving and attentive care on their offspring.

How infant Howard ultimately achieves the destiny to which his most prominent facial feature leads him makes for a logi-

It perched silently above them, waiting for the right moment to leap.

From Simon's Book, *written and illustrated by Henrik Drescher.*

cally perfect, if mildly disconcerting, denouement to this latter-day Ugly Duckling—actually Storkling—saga.

> Selma G. Lanes, in a review of "The Strange Appearance of Howard Cranebill, Jr.," in The New York Times Book Review, *October 10, 1982, p. 25.*

This is a slight, zany book, deceptively simple in its unembellished, deadpan text, and illustrated with originality, humor and skill by the author, whose drawings have occasionally appeared in the *New York Times Book Review*. On first glance, the drawings seem to be the colored-pencil scribblings of a four-year-old. However, they are in fact crafted, intricate, sophisticated and done with technical excellence. They are closest, perhaps, to the well-known and lovely drawings of Harold Jones. The placement of the illustrations on the pages, and the magical borders especially, are intriguing. The unusual typeface is unappealingly crowded and unattractive. Perhaps the most interesting question raised by this book—a question pertinent to so many picture books that stretch the limits of conventionality—is: what, precisely, is the relationship between the artificially childlike and the taste, preference and comprehension of children. (p. 82)

> Peter Neumeyer, in a review of "The Strange Appearance of Howard Cranebill, Jr.," in School Library Journal, *Vol. 29, No. 3, November, 1982, pp. 81-2.*

SIMON'S BOOK   (1983)

Action drawings, with a kinetic energy and a more sophisticated, tricksy play on the *Harold and the Purple Crayon* motif, illustrate what happens between Simon and a big furry beast when the little boy who draws them both gets tired and goes to bed. "First it was a faint shuffle, then a louder rustle," as the boy's pens slither "like caterpillars" from their coffee can to introduce themselves. ("Simon shook their tails.") Soon the beast leaps, the fastest pen draws a hole in the page for Simon's escape, the beast follows them through, and the chase is on. (At this point the ink bottle stumbles and spills and, on the next page, we see only the pursuing beast's eye and bared teeth gleaming through the black splatter.) In a bit of a let-down, it turns out that the beast just wanted to kiss Simon, and everyone goes home together, to bed. And the boy who drew them wakes up in the morning to find the filled-in book, the same one that "you have been reading." Clever and offbeat like last year's **Strange Appearance of Howard Cranebill, Junior,** and alive and crackling with its scratches, splashes, charged-up beast, and Simon's stand-up Struwwelpeter hair.

> A review of "Simon's Book," in Kirkus Reviews, *Juvenile Issue, Vol. LI, Nos. 13-17, September 1, 1983, p. J-147.*

Simon's Book is a modernist fable of art rising out of its own materials and includes a tale within a tale. But this seems a trifle abstract for 3-to-6-year-olds, for whom the aliveness of a book's contents is an obvious truth requiring no special proof or elaboration.

It is an illustrator that Mr. Drescher knows his audience well. . . .

Furiously scratchy line work, prankish caricature and a tendency to splatter paint are among the engaging elements of his zestful graphics, which range lightly among the wild immediacies and heady chaos of a small child's world.

> Leonard S. Marcus, in a review of "Simon's Book," in The New York Times Book Review, *November 20, 1983, p. 39.*

Using the story-within-a-story format, the author-artist embarks on an exhilarating exploration, in a childlike yet sophisticated manner, of the elusive border separating dream and reality. The opening sequence sets tone and mood with remarkable economy. . . . In succeeding pages, while the small artist slumbers, the ink bottle, pens, and drawing become animated participants in a surrealistic pursuit as they try to help Simon escape from the threatening creature who, at the climactic moment, turns out to be a friendly monster. The denouement is equally imaginative—satisfying yet enigmatic, the stuff of which dreams are made. Dramatic pauses in the text are complemented by the cinematic vibrancy of the pictures, changes in perspective, and skillful modification in page design. Definition of characters and movement is established through a marvelously sinuous and delicate line which tempers visual excitement with humor to achieve the light touch necessary for bringing events full circle to a logical, reassuring conclusion. Original, fresh, and engaging, the book is deliciously thrilling but never terrifying.

> Mary M. Burns, in a review of "Simon's Book," in The Horn Book Magazine, *Vol. LIX, No. 6, Decem-*

ber, 1983, p. 699.

LOOKING FOR SANTA CLAUS (1984)

Praised for **Simon's Book** and **The Strange Appearance of Howard Cranebill,** Drescher presents an even more preposterously diverting Christmas Eve lark. Little Maggie's mean aunts hate Christmas so the child flies off on the back of her cow Blossom, in search of Santa Claus. Surrealistic, full-color paintings illustrate the journey into far-out space. In Russia, Switzerland, Egypt and other countries, Maggie and Blossom collect Santa look-alikes and take them back home, where everyone revels in a grand celebration. There is no explanation for the aunts suddenly becoming warm, hospitable hostesses, laying on a feast for all including Blossom. But then there is no sense to any part of the book, just plenty of good reasons to laugh out loud.

> *A review of "Looking for Santa Claus," in* Publishers Weekly, *Vol. 226, No. 8, August 24, 1984, p. 79.*

By the light of a crescent moon, Drescher provides a bizarrely-illustrated colorful story of the spirit of Christmas. His outrageous humor and sophisticated story may limit the appeal of this atypical Christmas story, but he certainly can't be faulted for lack of imagination or originality in these wacky illustrations that are filled with verve.

> *Elizabeth M. Simmons, in a review of "Looking for Santa Claus," in* School Library Journal, *Vol. 31, No. 2, October, 1984, p. 173.*

Looking for Santa Claus . . . is an off-the-wall fable whose great charm is in its fantastic drawings. It has a happy ending and Christmas spirit and all that good stuff, but this is to most childrens books what "Doonesbury" is to most comic strips. . . . The eccentric humor is in the illustrations: the expressions on the flying cow are wonderful and probably belong in The New Yorker.

> *Molly Ivins, in a review of "Looking for Santa Claus," in* The New York Times Book Review, *November 11, 1984, p. 58.*

LOOK-ALIKES (1985)

Going far beyond the fantastic inventions in **The Strange Appearance of Howard Cranebill, Jr.** and his other acclaimed books, Drescher presents a staggering feat of storytelling. Mr. and Mrs. Pearson, their son Rudy and Buster the monkey are at home on their "small green planet in space." Spacy is the word for events when Buster babbles some rhymes and takes Rudy to a treehouse, where they watch as their toy look-alikes experience a series of fast, tense crises. A snake with an elephant's head, a shark with airplane wings, a two-headed human are just a few of the monsters involved in the excitement before Rudy and Buster return home in time for a staid dinner. Drescher's artistry is astounding. Combining realistic landscapes with cartoons in contrasting dark and garish hues, he creates the feeling that this craziness is possible.

> *A review of "Look-Alikes," in* Publishers Weekly, *Vol. 238, No. 3, July 19, 1985, p. 53.*

When Drescher transfers his quirky imagination into graphic form, zany things happen. . . . The story ends and begins on

a "Small green planet in the middle of space," providing dimension to the tale. Also, librarians using picture books as art examples will find Drescher an excellent introduction to the fantastical work of Hieronymus Bosch.

> *Barbara Elleman, in a review of "Look-Alikes," in* Booklist, *Vol. 82, No. 5, November 1, 1985, p. 404.*

Drescher's scrawly full-color illustrations, with many frenetic scribbles within and without the borders, are filled with activity. The changing perspectives and busyness of the pictures, the Escher-esque stairway, the splashes and doodles and stick figures create a sensation of chaos and confusion. The text is spare, descriptive and unremarkable; one sentence or phrase per large page. The book seems to be trying for a combination of humor, scariness and novelty, but the effect is merely bizarre. If the point is that we are all small creatures being watched and manipulated by larger ones like us, as we tumble through life battered by absurdity, it will be lost on the picture book audience.

> *Susan H. Patron, in a review of "Look-Alikes," in* School Library Journal, *Vol. 32, No. 4, December, 1985, p. 71.*

WHOSE FURRY NOSE? AUSTRALIAN ANIMALS YOU'D LIKE TO MEET; WHOSE SCALY TAIL? AFRICAN ANIMALS YOU'D LIKE TO MEET (1987)

Who better to go tramping around Australia and Africa with than Henrik Drescher—whose every book seems to be a fascinating artistic safari. With his newest couple of creations the author-illustrator introduces young children to a small menagerie of animals in pleasingly unorthodox, full-color illustrations. Drescher pulls readers right into the books by initially showing only part of a specific creature. One double-page spread, for example, features a pair of hairy legs springing through the multicolored border and off the paper while the text asks "Whose leaping legs?" A flip of the page reveals that the appendages belong to a wallaby. In ensuing pages readers of **Whose Furry Nose?** meet numbats, yellow belly gliders, koalas, and three other animals from Down Under. **Whose Scaly Tail?** features seven African creatures, including porcupines, elephants, pangolins, and aardvarks. In both books a slightly scruffy, bristly-haired little boy appears in each illustration to peer or point at the animals and, in some cases, to hold or touch them. More contained than the artwork in **Simon's Book** but full of bright colors, scratchy lines, and wobbly, interesting borders, the illustrations depict the animals vividly and with a sense of fun. For readers wanting more than just a pictorial introduction, two pages at the end of each book offer a brief descriptive paragraph about the physical characteristics of each animal. (pp. 626-27)

> *Karen Jameson, in a review of "Whose Furry Nose? Australian Animals You'd Like to Meet" and "Whose Scaly Tail? African Animals You'd Like to Meet," in* The Horn Book Magazine, *Vol. LXIII, No. 5, September-October, 1987, pp. 626-27.*

This companion set provides an introduction to a variety of African and Australian animals, from such familiar creatures as the elephant, giraffe and koala to less widely known species like the pangolin and numbat. The books employ a simple question-and-answer format to good effect; a partial view of each animal is accompanied by a query ("Whose tubby snout?"), and turning the page reveals both the pictorial and

From Looking for Santa Claus, *written and illustrated by Henrik Drescher.*

verbal solutions (in this example, "an aardvark's"). A small boy plays the role of discoverer: he and the animals are friendly and expressive, which elevates the lessons beyond mere rote. A concluding spread provides information about each animal and, in many cases, its young. With Drescher's zany, offbeat illustrations, these books offer an engaging introduction to the specialized animals of the African and Australian continents. (pp. 62-3)

> *A review of "Whose Furry Nose? Australian Animals You'd Like to Meet" and "Whose Scaly Tail? African Animals You'd Like to Meet," in* Publishers Weekly, *Vol. 232, No. 24, December 11, 1987, pp. 62-3.*

Two alluring and sophisticated picture books that introduce young children to intriguing animals. . . . The ebullient full-color illustrations are entertaining and informative. Framed illustrations are used to their full advantage as, for emphasis, the redtail monkeys hang out of the border and the giraffe's neck stretches beyond. So too will young readers be stretched beyond the usual "name-the-animal" concept book. (pp. 181-82)

> *Catherine Wood, in a review of "Whose Furry Nose? Australian Animals You'd Like to Meet" and "Whose Scaly Tail? African Animals You'd Like to*

Meet," in School Library Journal, *Vol. 34, No. 7, March, 1988, pp. 181-82.*

[**Whose Furry Nose?** is] a fascinating little picture book, presenting a few Australian animals in a novel manner.

Not a bad picture book introduction to some unusual animals.

Whose Scaly Tail? is another book which presents the reader with a question and a view of only part of the interesting animal, giving the reader something to think about before turning the page to see this time African animal revealed.

The flap copy claims that "This is a book that will stir the imagination and curiosity of all would-be adventurers and animal lovers," and indeed it is a book which does just that. Young children enjoy the tension of having to wait to see the entire animal, even after they have gone through the book numerous times.

This may very well be the kind of picture book experience which encourages the young child to think and speculate; if so, it is certainly a science book worthy of note. Who knows what the picture book precursors of scientific speculation may look like? Perhaps now we know. (p. 18)

> *Clarence C. Truesdell, in a review of "Whose Furry*

Nose? Australian Animals You'd Like to Meet" and *"Whose Scaly Tail? African Animals You'd Like to Meet,"* in Appraisal: Science Books for Young People, *Vol. 21, No. 3, Summer, 1988, pp. 17-18.*

THE YELLOW UMBRELLA (1987)

In this wordless picture book, a bright yellow umbrella warms the black line drawings and pale lemon scenes. . . . Although the artistic styles are utterly different, Drescher's themes recall John Goodail's *Jacko* (HBJ, 1972) in which a monkey ingeniously returns to his jungle family, and *The Surprise Picnic* (Macmillan, 1977) in which an umbrella is used as emergency transport for mother and young. Still, the book's engaging narrative pace and droll depictions of both the natural and manmade worlds in Drescher's quirky drawings give it an appeal of its own.

> *Patricia Dooley, in a review of "The Yellow Umbrella," in* School Library Journal, *Vol. 34, No. 3, November, 1987, p. 89.*

Remember when, while helplessly toddling about, you wanted to read the book someone gave you at your party, but you couldn't: you were disadvantaged. You had no words yet. And the book was filled with words and it was all brouhaha to you, and to get some sense you had to go get an adult, and tug and whine, and maybe the adult would care to explain, from her or his all-impressive height and might, what on earth might be in your book. But most likely not.

The Danish-born artist Henrik Drescher, who lives in New York, is a savior in the world of books for very small children: he uses no words. **The Yellow Umbrella,** with pictures only, is dedicated to his newborn son, who will, in due course, reach out and be perfectly able, all by his small self, to figure out what's what, making up his own story as he follows his father's pictures of monkeys at play with a magical free-floating umbrella. They beautifully dart from page to page, luring him (and us) along, gently and with humor. The child will be cheered too, for there's a great message in this descriptive journey: hope in despair, freedom in flight, positive pursuit of harmonious happiness at the end.

The Yellow Umbrella is recommended for rainy mornings, sojourns in dentists' waiting rooms, traffic jams spent in a cramped carseat and other opportunities for blissful unwinding. It is guaranteed to benefit the search for freedom. Watch the monkeys flee from evil, swoop through storms, overfly disaster, overcome, overjoy.

> *Janwillem van de Wetering, "Float and Slither," in* The New York Times Book Review, *November 8, 1987, p. 42.*

Black, white, and yellow, the scratchy and lively pictures in this small book have more substance than does the story they tell. This doesn't quite achieve what a wordless book should, since the pictures tell a story that requires more knowledge (visual signs for wind currents and a conventional depiction of bends in a river) than most young children have.

> *Zena Sutherland, in a review of "The Yellow Umbrella," in* Bulletin of the Center for Children's Books, *Vol. 41, No. 6, February, 1988, p. 115.*

Paul Fleischman
1952-

American poet and author of fiction.

Fleischman is noted as a writer for readers from grade school through high school whose prose and verse ranges stylistically from a lighthearted sentimentality to a haunting eeriness reminiscent of the masters of dark tales. In his fiction, Fleischman's fluid, polished texts relate stories of complex psychological and moral import in which characters display deep emotional needs and make surprising discoveries about themselves and each other. Fleischman's stories, several of which are set in the past, present young readers with an otherworldly and mysterious picture of life. When writing his poetry, Fleischman has most often chosen to express his distinctive observations of the natural world. In *Joyful Noise: Poems for Two Voices* (1988), for example, he not only recounts the habitats and physical characteristics of various insects, but humanizes his subjects by providing them with feelings and personalities; while relating each poem from the point of view of a different insect, Fleischman modifies the tone of his verse, which he designed to be read aloud, to disclose the distinctive character of his subject. Noting that Fleischman's lyrical duet would lend itself dramatically to oral interpretation, critics commend *Joyful Noise* for its sensitivity and imaginativeness, qualities which have been noted consistently in all of Fleischman's work. *The Half-a-Moon Inn* was selected as a Golden Kite Award honor book in 1980; the same distinction was given to *Path of the Pale Horse* in 1983. *Graven Images* was named a Newbery honor book in 1983 and Fleischman received the Newbery award for *Joyful Noise* in 1989.

(See also *Something about the Author,* Vols. 32, 39 and *Contemporary Authors,* Vol. 113.)

THE BIRTHDAY TREE (1979)

When Jack is born his parents plant an apple tree, and as Jack grows they notice that the tree shivers when he has a fever, droops when he is sad, and so on. The parents are lonely and frightened when Jack goes off to sea and as they had lost three sons to the sea and moved to escape it before Jack was born, but they watch the tree for signs of his progress and condition. The news they read in the tree involves a shipwreck, hunger and thirst, and what appears as winter comes to be death—but in spring the tree perks up and tells of a land journey, and sure enough Jack turns up back home. Fleischman tells the story with a pleasant oral ring . . . ; but instead of using the birthday-tree conceit as a springboard, Fleischman gives in to its obvious sentimental disposition.

> *A review of "The Birthday Tree," in* Kirkus Reviews, *Vol. XLVII, No. 10, May 15, 1979, p. 573.*

A soft, homespun texture pervades the text: "Jack's mother ran her fingers through the leaves as through her son's hair." The style is fine for independent reading but the imagery would find its due in the hands of a good storyteller. Marcia Sewall's blunt-faced characters and sparse illustrations evoke

the rustic spirit of the words. The pencil sketches and subdued beige backgrounds are simple reinforcements for a well-told tale.

> *Judith Gibbons, in a review of "The Birthday Tree,"in* School Library Journal, *Vol. 26, No. 1, September, 1979, p. 110.*

THE HALF-A-MOON INN (1980)

The day before Aaron's 12th birthday, his mother asks him to stay home alone while she goes out to market. She wants to bring him back a birthday surprise. This separation would be nothing momentous to an ordinary boy of Aaron's age, but Aaron is not ordinary—he is mute. (p. 45)

Aaron agrees to wait patiently and never to leave sight of the house; his mother, for her part, promises to be home by noon the next day. But that night, snow falls and quickly becomes a raging blizzard. When Aaron awakes the next morning, it is still snowing. He sits next to the stove, waiting, his eyes and ears tensed to the wind. . . .

Another dawn, and he wakes to find the snow still coming down, the house empty. Fearing for his mother's safety, he puts aside her warning, leaves the house and wanders off in search of her. Blinded by the blizzard, he soon becomes lost. For three days Aaron stumbles through the woods, until he finds a ragman whose cart is stuck in the snow. Unable to explain himself, Aaron writes out some words; the ragman is impressed, especially because he cannot read. . . . A sequence of misunderstandings and misadventures lands Aaron at the Half-a-Moon Inn.

At the Half-a-Moon Inn, Aaron is seized by the proprietor, Miss Grackle. She needs a boy to keep the fires going. The guests are brigands, kings and wealthy men traveling as beggars, and Miss Grackle is a thief. . . .

Miss Grackle, ever-watchful, seizes Aaron's notes, steals his shoes and coat, and beats his feet, so that he can barely stand, much less walk out. Miss Grackle even reads Aaron's dreams, as she reads the dreams of all her guests—in order to unmask and rob them. . . .

The Half-a-Moon Inn is a haunting tale; its descriptions of nature alone are striking and memorable. And, yes, it has a happy ending, but its main strength is not in its power to reassure or its realism but, rather, in its dreamlike intensity and compelling inner momentum. The book is startling in its evocations of the muteness that surrounds each of us, the straining, gesturing, supplicating qualities of speechless things. Waiting for his mother, Aaron stares at the wall and sees it "almost imperceptibly bulge and sink, like skin over a heart." Lost in the woods, he looks up to see the wild bending of the branches in the wind, "as if desperately struggling to be understood." . . .

The only distraction in the book is an occasional overindulgence in simile. But such lapses are few and easily forgiven. (p. 67)

> *A. G. Mojtabai, in a review of "The Half-A-Moon Inn," in* The New York Times Book Review, *April 27, 1980, pp. 45, 67.*

A story of grisly threats, daring, and foul play, spelled out in an atmosphere and style somewhat reminiscent of Leon Garfield. Vivid, imagistic writing describes the problems of mute twelve-year-old Aaron. . . . When his mother fails to return, Aaron sets forth to find her, and he does—but not until he has confronted a wild assemblage of adversaries. A succinct and fast-moving piece of fiction.

> *Virginia Haviland, in a review of "The Half-A-Moon Inn," in* The Horn Book Magazine, *Vol. LVI, No. 3, June, 1980, p. 294.*

In folkloric style, Fleischman creates a suspenseful tale with archetypal characters and a haunting atmosphere. . . . The brisk pace and steady accumulation of events build tension, while Fleischman's fine writing begs to be read aloud and signals a storyteller to watch.

> *Barbara Elleman, in a review of "The Half-A-Moon Inn," in* Booklist, *Vol. 76, No. 20, June 15, 1980, p. 1531.*

GRAVEN IMAGES: 3 STORIES (1982)

From the author of *The Half-a-Moon Inn;* three polished tales set in the past and told with dexterous application of old genre techniques. The first makes a cracking little whodunit of a reclusive old woman, her deaf hired girl who can lip-read secrets, and the mysterious death of a whole ship's crew. The second makes a light courtship comedy of a lovesick shoemaker's apprentice who reads personal guidance into the direction faced by the saint on a broken weather vane, and constructs love messages in the language of flowers that only he is aware of. In the third story, a poor, snobbish sculptor is given a commission by an unsavory ghost, who destroys the sculptor's illusions about his high-and-mighty idols. Fleischman establishes a storyteller's hold on his audience; they can put themselves in his hands with the assurance that they won't be disappointed—and that all the surprises will be well within the established conventions.

> *A review of "Graven Images," in* Kirkus Reviews, *Vol. L, No. 16, August 15, 1982, p. 937.*

The three stories in *Graven Images* concern characters who are deeply affected, maybe even possessed, by sculpted figures. In the lightest of these tales, **"Saint Crispin's Follower,"** a young shoemaker's apprentice lets his search for a servant girl's love be guided by the saint's figure on a broken weathervane. A series of comic misunderstandings leads him to his goal.

The other two tales are grimmer, and more powerful. . . .

The focus of **"The Binnacle Boy"** is on the unraveling of the mystery, rather than its underlying horror. Therefore it emerges as a safe and fascinating tale that, treated differently, might have been highly disturbing to young readers.

Paul Fleischman's last story, **"The Man of Influence,"** also views horror from a distance, but with the added emotional resonance that comes from focusing on one character's moral dilemma. . . .

Graven Images occasionally fails to explain its events—it's not really clear, for example, why the townspeople of **"The Binnacle Boy"** choose to tell their secrets to a statue—and sometimes Mr. Fleischman's narrative veers toward sentimentality—would a starving sculptor throw a fat purse into the sea, no matter how reprehensible he found a ghostly patron? Still, *Graven Images* is a strong book. It poses psychological and moral issues in a way that will engage older children; and it will certainly satisfy their hearty appetites for the mysterious and bloodcurdling. Mr. Fleischman's darker tales will prickle the back of the neck, without leaving nightmares behind.

> *Ann Cameron, in a review of "Graven Images," in* The New York Times Book Review, *November 28, 1982, p. 24.*

Three fanciful tales harking back to the spirit of Poe and of Hawthorne are linked by the central theme of a sculptured figure and by a pervading atmosphere of mystery and suspense. . . . Unusual in our day, the young author's timeless, elegant, figurative prose is fashioned with fluency and skill.

> *Ethel L. Heins, in a review of "Graven Images: Three Stories," in* The Horn Book Magazine, *Vol. LVIII, No. 6, December, 1982, p. 656.*

Three short stories are linked because each focuses on a chiseled figure. . . . The macabre tone is deftly maintained in the tales, which themselves have the combination of strength, mass, structure, and delicacy in portraying details that are the characteristics of graven images. (pp. 125-26)

> *Zena Sutherland, in a review of "Graven Images,"*

in Bulletin of the Center for Children's Books, *Vol. 36, No. 7, March, 1983, pp. 125-26.*

THE ANIMAL HEDGE (1983)

Fleischman builds an entrancing story on themes he has used to effect in all his tales: the power of love and the resiliency of the human spirit. A farmer and his sons grieve when their crops fail and they must sell the animals that the father, in particular, is devoted to. They settle in a small cottage, surrounded by a flourishing hedge. In time the farmer eases his sorrow by clipping the hedge into the shapes of his dear hens, cows and pigs. But the author has more profound incidents to relate, growing out of the father's understanding of his sons' needs, feelings that he also expresses by cutting different forms in the hedge.

A review of "The Animal Hedge," in Publishers Weekly, *Vol. 223, No. 8, February 25, 1983, p. 88.*

"There once lived a farmer whose heart glowed like a hot wood stove with the love of animals." So begins a gentle, original story narrated in the style of a traditional tale, which chronicles the misfortunes, resignation to fate, and ultimate triumph of a kindhearted farmer with three sons who sang while they toiled. . . . Although the farmer remained at home, the three sons left to pursue their respective callings; but when they returned, they realized that the hedge did not choose their occupations but only reflected "what lay deep in their hearts and heavy on their minds." The theme is subtle, yet the tale's brevity, flowing style, and [Lydia Dabcovich's] copious animated illustrations—slightly cartooned—suggest its use in picture-book story hours.

Mary M. Burns, in a review of "The Animal Hedge," in The Horn Book Magazine, *Vol. LIX, No. 3, June, 1983, p. 289.*

PATH OF THE PALE HORSE (1983)

The 1793 adventure of Lep, short for Asclepius, a devoted doctor's apprentice who goes to bed with his *Materia Medica.* Traveling overnight to Philadelphia when that city is in the grip of a yellow fever epidemic, Lep and Dr. Poole plan to purchase medicines and return home. But the two become separated and end up lodged in different homes: Dr. Poole with Mrs. Uffington, a disagreeable woman who misuses her servants, and Lep with Mr. Tweakfield, a kindly man who is being cheated by his servants. Lep's sister Clara is also in Philadelphia, working for a man who sells "electric" rings to ward off the fever; and Lep, charged by his mother to bring her home, must convince her that her employer is a charlatan and an imposter. But Lep, who scorns fraudulent and super-

Fleischman at his desk.

stitious medicines, has the utmost faith in medical science, and is filled with idealistic excitement when Dr. Poole decides to stay and fight the fever. An early success encourages Lep's faith in his own powers as well, but when Mr. Tweakfield expires of the fever despite Lep's fervent ministrations, he learns something of Dr. Poole's humility. Lep's Philadelphia encounters are neatly interconnected variations on the theme of fraud, faith, and science; Mr. Tweakfield's treacherous servants and Clara's escape from her oily employer keep the plot perking; and Fleischman's period tone and narrative artifice assure the comforts of a tale well told. (pp. 375-76)

> *A review of "Path of the Pale Horse," in* Kirkus Reviews, *Vol. LI, No. 7, April 1, 1983, pp. 375-76.*

Path of the Pale Horse deals with an unusual but exceptionally interesting historical event: the yellow fever epidemic that decimated Philadelphia in 1793-94. The author treats a fascinating historical issue: the relationship of science, superstition and religion as ways of comprehending and dealing with a crisis, in a time when modern scientific ideas still had to contend with magic and folklore. His hero is well chosen to present these issues to us. He is young Asclepius ("Lep") Nye, apprenticed to a country physician, a naive devotee of a "scientific" medicine that is itself still innocent of modern method; and as a child, he is still susceptible to the appeal of superstitious fear and religious interpretations of the catastrophe.

But Fleischman's book is weakened by both novelistic and historiographical flaws. Philadelphia in the plague-year calls for a Dickensian recording, or at least a rendering that gives us the sense of the urban scene—which must have appalled and overwhelmed a country lad like Lep. Instead the setting seems flat and empty.

Fleischman relies too much on allusiveness to place his characters historically. He tells us at the start that a certain wealthy man is revered on a level otherwise reserved "for President Washington, selected saints, and Almighty God" might be going it a bit strong; and the vague reference to "selected saints" seems wrong for 18th-century Protestants.

This inauthenticity of language carries over into the characterization of Lep. An 18th-century boy ought to have stronger reactions to religious ideas. Lep's inner dialogue about the things he sees and feels is psychologically and historically flat. The author's language does not rise to emotional crises; and he *alludes* to feelings and issues instead of recreating them from the inside out. (pp. 15, 18)

> *Richard Slotkin, "Tales of Two Cities," in* Book World—The Washington Post, *May 8, 1983, p. 15, 18.*

The author, in rich resonant language and fluid writing style, presents an insightful glimpse into the state of medical knowledge at that time as well as into the beliefs and superstitions for curing [yellow fever].

Excellent for sharing in the history class, this book also presents possibilities for role playing, dramatic interpretation, and researching the known facts about yellow fever.

> *Ronald A. Jobe, in a review of "Path of the Pale Horse," in* Language Arts, *Vol. 60, No. 6, September, 1983, p. 771.*

PHOEBE DANGER, DETECTIVE, IN THE CASE OF THE TWO-MINUTE COUGH (1983)

Ten-year-old Phoebe Elizabeth Dangerfield (alias Phoebe Danger) and her friend Dash have just started their own detective agency. When a relative's rare antique bottle is stolen from the Willingtons' house, Mrs. Willington calls for help. The kids take the few clues they have and eventually use them to prove that it was Mr. Willington himself who stole the bottle for his own collection. Although the revelation that Mr. Willington is the thief comes as no surprise, the manner in which he tried to pull off the crime while arranging an airtight alibi is quite clever and makes for a fun mystery.

> *Drew Stevenson, in a review of "Phoebe Danger, Detective, in the Case of the Two-Minute Cough," in* School Library Journal, *Vol. 29, No. 9, May, 1983, p. 92.*

There's a bit of an arch tone to this light mystery. . . . Suspense is extended by Phoebe's seemingly impossible same-day-service guarantee for solving the case. But her actions are quick and to the point, and the tale is credible in the convention of kid detectives. An alternative for Encyclopedia Brown and McGurk mystery readers.

> *Denise M. Wilms, in a review of "Phoebe Danger, Detective, in the Case of the Two-Minute Cough," in* Booklist, *Vol. 79, No. 19, June 1, 1983, p. 1275.*

Certainly not a spellbinding, uproarious mystery story, but just the thing for readers right out of the first and second grade, eager for their first book with real chapters and a little excitement.

> *A review of "Phoebe Danger, Detective, in the Case of the Two-Minute Cough," in* Children's Book Review Service, *Vol. 11, No. 13, July, 1983, p. 133.*

FINZEL THE FARSIGHTED (1983)

Fleischman's favorite folk-motif, the tell-tale object, is used with panache in this tale of Finzel the fortune-teller—who, in true Fools of Chelm tradition (the jacket says it, but it's so), can see a person's past or future in a lemon or a walnut . . . but can't see well enough to tell whose lemon is whose. Specifically, he mixes up the lemon and the walnut, and the lettuce, of young simpleton Pavel and elderly ailing Mashka, and has Pavel convinced he's near death. When Pavel's wily brother Osip catches on to Finzel's blindness, he hatches a scheme to steal Finzel's money—by having Finzel read a poppy plucked from his own window box . . . and telling him where he (Osip) keeps his (Finzel's) money. In true Chelm tradition, too, Finzel outwits Osip by mistake—also making nothing more of him, as a thief, "than a mouse." . . . A droll and shapely little book—on a par, in its way, with **Graven Images.**

> *A review of "Finzel the Farsighted," in* Kirkus Reviews, *Vol. LI, No. 17, September 1, 1983, pp. J147-J148.*

By the time this involved plot has reached its denouement, the humor of the initial premise has worn a little thin. However, the continuous action will appeal to younger readers and the lively style and humor make this a tale which merits reading aloud. [Illustrator Marcia] Sewall's full-page drawings with their solid figures, sure design and hint of Eastern

Europe in the details of architecture and costume echo the warmth and wit of the text.

> *Joanna Rudge Long, in a review of "Finzel the Farsighted," in* School Library Journal, *Vol. 30, No. 4, December, 1983, p. 65.*

Paul Fleischman's briskly paced original folk tale of crime and punishment in Plov, a Slavic village of uncertain location, is a pleasure to read aloud. The prose is fresh and dramatic, with words carefully chosen for comic effect, and readers will love the fact that the plot of *Finzel the Farsighted* turns on a seemingly unimportant act—a mouse's theft of cheese.

> *Sally Holmes Holtze, in a review of "Finzel the Farsighted," in* The New York Times Book Review, *March 4, 1984, p. 31.*

COMING-AND-GOING MEN: FOUR TALES   (1985)

Silhouette cutter Cyrus Snype, skilled at reading character in his subjects' shadowed profiles, travels the country in search of the devil, whom he blames for destroying his once-illustrious career. In New Canaan, Vermont, Snype is hired by a parsimonious tanner to find an honest woman for the tanner to wed; but the innocent girl he selects is certain that Snype is the devil himself. (Doesn't he collect people's souls with their shadows, and keep them in his scrapbook?) The cross purposes of this trio leads to further entertaining complications in **"The Shade Cutter,"** the first of Fleischman's four proficiently turned tales about traveling men who pass through New Canaan in the year 1800.

The second story, about a candle-maker's apprentice sent out to shoot crows, is enjoyably creepy. Toward the end, the apprentice learns from a ballad seller's song the terrible reason for his master's obsessive war with crows.

One can easily imagine Fleischman himself as a coming-and-going man, fabricating his way through his storybook Early America and enthralling the populace with his illusionist's wordcraft. (J32-J33)

> *A review of "Coming-and-Going Men: Four Tales," in* Kirkus Reviews, *Juvenile Issue, Vol. LIII, Nos. 5-10, May 15, 1985, pp. J32-J33.*

The car, the radio and the television set have gradually opened up the valleys of Vermont. You can buy quiche in the restaurants now and bean sprouts in the supermarkets, but not so long ago it was common to meet people who had never been more than 20 miles from home. They were curious about the great world where the flat-landers lived, but the world had come to them.

Paul Fleischman has written a short book about Vermont at the beginning of its long isolation—four tales of itinerant "coming-and-going men" who made their livings (when they made anything at all) by cutting silhouettes, peddling notions (pins and needles, tinware and a host of other portable goods that locals could not make for themselves), selling poems and ballads of a sensational or sentimental nature, and showing panoramas painted on a long scroll of canvas. The stories unfold in a town called New Canaan in the year 1800, just after the death of George Washington.

Isolation can breed some pretty strange ideas about the world, but it is the traveling men in these tales who are really odd. . . .

I read these stories with interest. They are intricately plotted, briskly paced and filled with forgotten sights and smells. But I found myself wondering just what sort of children they were intended to amuse or instruct. The world they describe is crabbed and narrow—far from the picturesque images of Currier and Ives, but not so far from Hieronymus Bosch. The man chasing the Devil is a poisonous figure. His weird behavior convinces an innkeeper's daughter that *he's* the Devil. It seemed plausible to me.

What would an 11-year-old make of this twisted tale—or any of the others, all clever in their way but centered on episodes of perverse ill will or outright horror? I confess I am puzzled. But maybe, isolated in Vermont, I just don't understand the reading habits of children, the requirements of libraries or the business of publishing.

> *Thomas Powers, in a review of "Coming-and-Going Men," in* The New York Times Book Review, *September 8, 1985, p. 35.*

Sardonic and gentle wit, a full measure of irony, surprising twists and turns and polished, figurative prose characterize four fastmoving short stories. . . . Here is good reading from start to finish, four tidily-crafted tales that will appeal to those who appreciate skillful revelation of character, subtly realized themes and deftly turned phrases.

> *Althea K. Helbig, in a review of "Coming-and-Going Men: Four Tales," in* The ALAN Review, *Vol. 13, No. 1, Fall, 1985, p. 25.*

I AM PHOENIX: POEMS FOR TWO VOICES   (1985)

Devotés of the almost lost art of choral reading should be among the first to appreciate this collection of poems designed for reading aloud by two voices. Printed in script form, the selections, all of which are about birds, have a cadenced pace and dignified flow; their combination of imaginative imagery and realistic detail is echoed by the combination of stylized fantasy and representational drawings in [illustrator Ken Nutt's] black and white pictures, all soft line and strong nuance. An exciting book.

> *A review of "I Am Phoenix: Poems for Two Voices," in* Bulletin of the Center for Children's Books, *Vol. 39, No. 2, October, 1985, p. 26.*

The collection fails to offer any new insights and degenerates to the merely silly, especially if the attempt is made to read it aloud. The viewpoints expressed and the imagery used (**"Doves of Dodona"** or **"The Common Egret"**) will mean nothing to most children. Wonderful, accessible poems about birds already exist. Why bother to clutter up the skies with **"Warblers"** ("Warblers warbling / Warblers warbling") when Edward Thomas' "Sedgewarblers" exists? The poem **"Owls"** ("Sun's down, / Sky's dark,") cannot evoke the mood of Randall Jarrell's poem "The Bird of Night." In this year of Audubon's anniversary, honor the beauty of birds with poetry worthy of them—poems found in collections like Cole's *The Birds and the Beasts Were There* (Collins, 1963: o.p.) or MacKay's *A Flock of Words* (HBJ, 1970: o.p.).

> *Kathleen D. Whalin, in a review of "I Am Phoenix:*

Poems for Two Voices," in School Library Journal, *Vol. 32, No. 3, November, 1985, p. 84.*

This bird won't fly. Try as hard as it might, it just doesn't have the energy to pull itself out of its ashen drawings and sing. These words nest, scattered sparsely on the page, repeating themselves in patterns that don't emerge. The similes die from creative starvation: a Phoenix "as large as an eagle," a sun "hot as fire." The drawings alone hold sustained interest. Delicately detailed, there is more story, color and variation in each of the 15 black-and-white illustrations than in all the 15 poems.

> *Richard K. Moore, in a review of "I Am Phoenix: Poems for Two Voices," in* The Book Report, *Vol. 4, No. 5, March-April, 1986, p. 33.*

REAR-VIEW MIRRORS (1986)

As the title suggests, **Rear-View Mirrors** is a remembrance of things not long past. More prose elegy than novel, this thematically rich and well-written book recounts 17-year-old Olivia Tate's memories of her first encounter, the previous summer, with the father she has never known, her parents having been divorced when she was 8 months old. The first-person narrative cuts back and forth between two journeys: the one, in the present, is a bicycle ride which, as a rite of passage, completes the other, which was a journey to both knowledge of her father *and* herself begun the summer before. Each mile traveled, each day remembered, uncovers a new layer of personal self-discovery much as each stroke of an archaeologist's shovel uncovers a new layer of the past. And, so, it is not insignificant that Olivia decides, at the first summer's end, that archaeology will be her life's work. The skill with which Fleischman creates the characters of Olivia and her writer father Hannibal and with which he evokes the rural New Hampshire setting are occasions for joy and celebration and can only be matched by the extraordinary felicity of his prose style. (pp. 102-03)

> *Michael Cart, in a review of "Rear-View Mirrors," in* School Library Journal, *Vol. 32, No. 9, May, 1986, pp. 102-03.*

In a new departure from his earlier rather Gothic and twisted tales of Colonial times, the author has written a tight, realistic story of a girl's relationship with her father. . . . Hannibal Tate, the author of several mystery novels, is a man who likes his solitude, his organ, his pipe, and the state of New Hampshire. He is by no means inclined to curry favor with this unknown daughter by speaking with kindness of her mother or the marriage. His ideas and ideals are diametrically opposed to those of Olivia's upbringing. . . . Olivia, however, starts to get used to him, finds she likes New Hampshire, discovers some agreeable relatives and friends, and plans to visit again the following year. When he is killed by lightning, she comes and commemorates his life by repeating a one-day bicycle ride that he took every year. The story is told, somewhat confusingly, during the ride with flashbacks to their visit of the previous summer. A great deal is packed into a small space; Olivia is a stout character, well able to stand up for herself, and Hannibal, despite the fact that he's a curmudgeon, is rather interesting. But the strength of the story is in the realistic perception of the sort of relationship and understanding that can be achieved between two such diverse people and under such circumstances. (pp. 329-30)

> *Ann A. Flowers, in a review of "Rear-View Mirrors," in* The Horn Book Magazine, *Vol. LXII, No. 3, May-June, 1986, pp. 329-30.*

Fleischman has written a marvelous rite of passage story for young girls. Olivia's apprehension and determination are shown as she matures through the flashbacks. Her father's legacy of a butterfly collection, a love of the Boston Red Sox and an imaginary winter baseball league, and Virgil Stark mysteries offers her a new view of herself and the world.

> *Beverly B. Youree, in a review of "Rear-View Mirrors," in* Voice of Youth Advocates, *Vol. 9, No. 2, June, 1986, p. 78.*

JOYFUL NOISE: POEMS FOR TWO VOICES (1987)

A splendid collection of poems in many moods about the lives and dreams of insects. Vivid language, strong images, and the masterful use of two voices in musical duet make this an excellent choice for reading aloud.

A charming pair of book lice ("We're book lice / fine mates / despite different tastes") set up home in Roget's *Thesaurus* to be "close to his Horace" and the mysteries she enjoys. Fleischman captures the character of empty-headed water striders, single-minded water boatmen, and the serene queen bee with her complaining worker.

More somber pieces include **"Requiem,"** an elegy for the insects that have died in the first killing frost; and **"The Digger Wasp,"** who laments "I will never / see my children." . . . A joyful noise that should find a wide audience.

> *A review of "Joyful Noise: Poems for Two Voices," in* Kirkus Reviews, *Vol. LV, No. 24, December 15, 1987, p. 1732.*

In this collection of 14 "Poems for Two Voices" about insects, Fleischman surpasses its companion volume, *I Am Phoenix.* He has combined the elements of sound and meaning to create clear, lively images of a variety of insects. Elements of repetition, onomatopoeia, and alliteration are effectively used to create a character for each of these creatures, with fireflies "Flickering, flitting, flashing" and mayflies "lying, dying," which make these poems a joy for reading aloud. In addition, elements of personality, both fictional and real, are presented with charming effect. The lovelorn moth who yearns for the lightbulb and the book lice who overcome their differing "tastes" represent the lighter side, while the digger wasp's reflection on the home it digs for children it will never see and **"Requiem,"** written for the victims of "Fall's first killing frost," represent real behaviors. . . . This book can join *Bugs* (Viking, 1976) by Mary Ann Hoberman and *Never Say Ugh! to a Bug* (Greenwillow, 1979) by Norma Farber as proof that insects are indeed the stuff of poetry.

> *Barbara Chatton, in a review of "Joyful Noise: Poems for Two Voices," in* School Library Journal, *Vol. 34, No. 6, February, 1988, p. 79.*

Similar in style and format to the author's *I Am Phoenix,* a book of poetry concerning birds, this collection of poems for two voices explores the lives of insects. Designed to be read aloud, the phrases of the poems are spaced vertically on the page in two columns, one for each reader. The voices sometimes alternate, sometimes speak in chorus, and sometimes echo each other. Fleischman steps imaginatively inside each

Fleischman, with his sister and father, author Sid Fleischman, at the Newbery/Caldecott/Wilder Awards banquet in 1989.

insect and in fine, free verse gives that creature's own point of view on its unique qualities, life cycle, and habits. . . . While the book may need introduction to children, it could be used successfully for offbeat choral readings in the classroom or auditorium.

> *Carolyn Phelan, in a review of "Joyful Noise: Poems for Two Voices," in* Booklist, *Vol. 84, No. 12, February 15, 1988, p. 1000.*

Every so often a book is published which demands accolades. This marvelous, lyrical evocation of the insect world belongs in that category. Scored for two voices, "one taking the left-hand part, the other taking the right-hand part," it is a companion volume to *I Am Phoenix,* but, unlike many such complementary works, stands on its own merits, equaling—perhaps even surpassing—its predecessor. The subjects, ranging from grasshoppers to butterflies, represent familiar insect classifications. Each is personified according to its particular habitat and notable habits so that the poems flow from the nature of the subjects: symbolism and emotion are thus logical derivatives rather than artificial impositions. Consequently, there is variety in tone, mood, and theme, making the collection one which can be used selectively with younger children but with broad appeal for intermediate and older audiences, including adults. **"Water Boatmen,"** for example, with the insistent refrain "Stroke" punctuating short, straightfor-

ward, descriptive lines could be used for voice choirs in the early grades; in contrast, **"Mayflies,"** with its references to "birthday / and dying day, / this particle of time / this single sip of living," needs a more sophisticated audience. Similar demands are made by the humor of **"Book Lice,"** chronicling the romance between two insects with differing literary tastes, and **"Honeybees,"** contrasting the worker's with the queen's perspective. In these latter two poems Fleischman has achieved an effect similar to that used in opera in which voices blend in a duet, yet each part has a different message to convey. The imagery throughout the volume is as remarkable as the technique: memorable but never intrusive, again because the words seem exactly right for the particular voice. . . . Each selection is a gem, polished perfection. If Paul Fleischman never wrote another book, his reputation would remain secure with this one. (pp. 366-67)

> *Mary M. Burns, in a review of "Joyful Noise: Poems for Two Voices," in* The Horn Book Magazine, *Vol. LXIV, No. 3, May-June, 1988, pp. 366-67.*

This delightful two-voiced poetry enlightens the readers and/or listeners about the habits and lives of insects while enjoying the sounds, blends and poetic devices of the poetry. My two favorite poems are **"The Book Lice"** and **"The Digger Wasp,"** but all 14 of the insects covered have an endearing quality. Young and old could enjoy the book because of the poetry . . . , and the knowledge to be gained from it. As an added feature, this book could be used in a drama, reading, or speech class to help students learn choral reading and express intonation.

Every library should have a copy of this book; it fits in the same category as Shel Silverstein's books of poems, *Where the Sidewalk Ends* and *The Light in the Attic.*

> *Donna Houser, in a review of "Joyful Noise: Poems for Two Voices," in* Voice of Youth Advocates, *Vol. 11, No. 3, August, 1988, p. 145.*

RONDO IN C (1988)

From a gifted novelist and poet for children, 13 neatly phrased lines of verse, each a succinct expression of the memory that Beethoven's piano piece evokes for one of the listeners at a recital in a large, comfortable living room: "The first squint of sunlight on the water in Maine/Lightning bolts! Thunder! Rain pounding the plains! Watching Ray's train leave the station last fall/Life back in Vienna—the concerts, the balls . . ." . . . An unusual tribute to the power of music, and to the depth and diversity to be found in any group of people.

> *A review of "Rondo in C," in* Kirkus Reviews, *Vol. LVI, No. 18, September 15, 1988, p. 1402.*

Though the text and concept may be difficult for children to understand, there are riches in this book well worth the mastery. . . . Fleischman's rhymed couplets present poetically condensed moments from each listener's life. "Bravo . . . for that 'Rondo in C'!" (pp. 67-8)

> *A review of "Rondo in C," in* Publishers Weekly, *Vol. 234, No. 14, September 30, 1988, pp. 67-8.*

Each portrait, lovingly and warmly rendered, combined with the memory it touches off, is a character study. The poetic text sings with the music, and [illustrator Janet Wentworth's] pastel drawings change with each personality: stormy, nurturing, romantic, or wild and free. The book is a loving tribute to the versatility of music and its power to evoke different responses from each listener. Recordings should be in great demand as parents and teachers share this lovely book and music with their children.

> *H. B. Z., in a review of "Rondo in C," in* The Horn Book Magazine, *Vol. LXIV, No. 5, September-October, 1988, p. 614.*

Russell (Bruce) Freedman

1929-

American author of nonfiction and journalist.

Freedman is applauded for creating a variety of informational books, characteristically biographies and works on animals and animal behavior, which are considered informative, well-written, and entertaining. Several of these books, which are addressed to young readers from preschool through high school, are acknowledged as outstanding examples of their genre. Praised for his ability to represent accurate technical information without becoming overly technical, Freedman provides his audience with a wide range of subjects, many of which are regarded as unusual topics for children's literature. The majority of his works focus on animals; collectively, these books describe the abilities and behavior of both wild and domestic animals from the birth process through their early lives and into adulthood and parenthood. Many of these books center on the attributes which the animals use to survive, including their instincts, defense techniques, and even the games they play as youngsters which prepare them for later life. In addition, he has written related works which discuss brain research on animals and humans, animal homes, and world animal records, and has created studies of specific animals such as snakes, fish, birds, and dinosaurs. Freedman is also celebrated for writing outstanding biographies of both individuals and groups which are noted for their thoroughness and objectivity. He is especially well regarded in this area as the creator of *Lincoln: A Photobiography* (1987), a work which is often lauded as the best children's book on its subject. Approaching his works by viewing them in visual terms, Freedman includes a large selection of rare historical and natural history photographs and prints in his books, a characteristic which is credited with making them even more illuminating and engaging. *Children of the Wild West* (1983) won the Western Heritage Award from the National Cowboy Hall of Fame in 1984 and was designated as a *Boston Globe-Horn Book* honor book in the same year. *Lincoln: A Photobiography* won the Newbery Medal in 1988.

(See also *Something about the Author,* Vol. 16; *Contemporary Authors,* Vol. 17-20, rev. ed.; and *Contemporary Authors New Revision Series,* Vols. 7, 23.)

AUTHOR'S COMMENTARY

We take it for granted that good fiction will be a pleasure to read. Nonfiction is supposed to be utilitarian. It's expected to do its duty—to inform, instruct, and enlighten. The idea that a hard-working, nose-to-the-grindstone nonfiction book also should be a pleasure to read is provocative enough to inspire a panel discussion. (p. 27)

If I'm excited enough about a subject to spend months researching and writing about it, I want my reader to be excited, too. I want to convey something about that subject as clearly and accurately and honestly as I can. But just as important, I want to hold the reader's attention from first page to last. I want to motivate the reader, to stimulate the reader's curiosity and enthusiasm, so that I'm not just blowing in the wind. I want the reader to actually read what I've written—and to read it with pleasure. (pp. 27-8)

My own books have changed quite a bit in the past ten or fifteen years. When I first started writing about science and natural history during the 1960s, I had what might be called a definitiveness complex. For example, James E. Morriss and I coauthored a series of books called *How Animals Learn, Animal Instincts,* and *The Brains of Animals and Man.* They were solid, substantial books, comprehensive and up-to-date, and they were well received. By the time they came out, however, I had become dissatisfied with writing that kind of definitive, comprehensive volume. I wondered, does anyone really sit down and read a book like this from beginning to end? Or do they just dip into it and use it to write reports?

That thought was a depressing one, so I began to experiment with different formats and approaches. After a period of trial and error, I discovered that for me the most satisfying way to approach natural history was to narrow my scope—to focus sharply, for instance, on particular kinds of animals or on particular kinds of animal behavior and to illuminate my subjects by using striking and revealing photographs. I began to think in visual terms as soon as I had the idea for a book. Sometimes a particular photograph I had chanced upon suggested the idea in the first place.

One day I was browsing through a book on bats, and I came upon a close-up photograph of a mother bat flying past the camera. Clutching her furry chest was a scrawny, helpless baby. Its eyes were closed, and it was hanging on with its teeth and claws as its mother flew about, hunting for insects. She was a bat, to be sure, but the photo presented a timeless and powerful image of a mother and her infant. The photograph was an enormously affecting one and fascinating because the infant's very life depended on its ability to hang on to its mother.

Hanging on, I thought. That's a terrific title for a book. So I made up a list of baby animals that hitch rides with their parents and began searching for photographs. The hardest photo to find, believe it or not, was the mandatory one of a plain, ordinary house cat carrying a kitten. I had collected rare and unusual photographs of baby-toting pangolins, anteaters, scorpions, beavers, and marmosets—but a house cat? My editor, Margery Cuyler, came up with a solution. She knew a photographer whose pet cat had just given birth to some kittens. We got in touch with him, and he agreed to stand by with his camera ready, waiting to catch his cat in the act of carrying a kitten.

The cat wouldn't cooperate. What she did behind the photographer's back is anyone's guess, but she refused to pick up a kitten while he was watching. After her kittens had grown too big to be picked up by their mom, we finally found the cat-and-kitten picture we needed at a commercial photo agency.

My next book was suggested by a scene I had witnessed as a child—a scene that also involved a house cat. I can remember sitting cross-legged on the kitchen floor beside my mother, my father, and my sister as our pet cat, Sally, gave birth to her first litter. It was late at night. My parents, finding Sally in labor, had awakened my sister and me so we could watch the kittens being born. (pp. 28-30)

That night my attitude toward Sally changed. She was a wonderful pet, mischievous and cuddly, and I had always loved her. But now I had to respect her. She had delivered four kittens with dignity and skill, and though it was her first experience as a mother, she knew exactly how to clean them, feed them, and protect them. Sally, I realized, was a lot more complicated than I had suspected. I could never look at her in quite the same way again. And it was Sally who inspired my book *Getting Born.* Since then, I've done many other books about animals and animal behavior that combine photographs and text. The photos, of course, are more than just a come-on. They're an essential part of the story I want to tell, the information I want to convey. Ideally, the photographs should reveal something that words alone can't express. And the text, in turn, should say something that isn't evident in the photographs. In my recent book *Rattlesnakes,* for instance, there is a wonderful photograph of a rattlesnake yawning, taken especially for the book by Jessie Cohen, the photographer at the National Zoo in Washington, D.C. Few people have ever seen a rattlesnake yawn. If you want to find out why the snake is yawning, you have to read the text. But no words could possibly capture the priceless expression on the face of that yawning rattler—only photographs can do that.

Recently I've become interested in doing a different kind of photographic book. A few years ago I went to see an exhibit of old photographs at the New York Historical Society. The exhibit, "New York Street Kids," commemorated the 125th anniversary of the Children's Aid Society. Many of the photographs in the show dated back to the nineteenth century and showed children, primarily poor children, playing, working, and just hanging out on the teeming New York City streets of that era. What impressed me most of all was the way that those old photographs seemed to defy the passage of time. They were certainly of their own time, for they depicted, in their vivid details, a particular era from the past. And yet those same photographs were also timeless. They captured scenes from life that are as familiar and recognizable today as they were then, scenes that have been frozen and preserved for future generations to see.

There was a photograph of a newsboy and a newsgirl standing on a New York City street corner. The picture had been taken a century ago, or more. The boy and girl had grown up and grown old. As I stood there in the New York Historical Society looking at them, I knew they were dead and gone. But in the photograph they were still children, grinning at me from out of the past. Their clothing, the horses and wagons passing by on the street, the architecture of the buildings around them all showed that these children were time-bound—locked in their own era. But the expressions on their faces were timeless and made me wonder at what is timeless in all of us.

I also had a personal interest in those photographs. My grandparents had arrived in New York City as immigrants at the turn of the century, and my father had spent his earliest years playing on the New York City streets that the photographs depicted. I actually began looking for the child that was my father among the photographs. I didn't find him, of course, but the photographs made me feel closer to him, to his past, and to my own past. I asked my editor, Ann Troy, to visit the exhibit with me, and the outcome was my book *Immigrant Kids.* It was followed by *Children of the Wild West* and by a companion book, *Cowboys of the Wild West.* Other books using historical photographs are in the works for the future, and meanwhile, I've continued to write natural history books.

Whenever I'm starting a new book, I often think of a story that my father liked to tell about himself. He was still a small child when his family moved from New York City to a rockbound farm near Windsor, Connecticut. One afternoon, as my father would tell it, he ran across a field to meet *his* father, who would soon be coming down the road with his horse and wagon. As my father waited and dawdled, he noticed a big stone on the other side of the field. He ran over, picked up the stone, which was almost too big for him to hold, and started carrying it back toward the road, stopping here and there to put the stone down and catch his breath, then picking it up again and carrying it a bit farther. When he reached the side of the road, he carefully put the stone down for good.

When his father came rolling down that dirt road and climbed out of his wagon, my father said, "Do you see that big stone? I picked it up and carried it all the way across the field."

"Why did you do that?" his father asked.

And my father replied, "God put the stone down over there, and *I* moved it over here!"

My father loved to tell that story because to him it signified that he had the power to effect change—and that everyone big and small has that power. Today when I begin a book, I'm hoping to move a stone or two myself. I'm hoping to change the landscape of the reader's mind, if just a little—to leave the reader with a thought, a perception, an insight, perhaps, that she or he did not have before. If I write about rattlesnakes, I want the reader to come away from the book with a greater appreciation of these remarkable living creatures and their place in nature. If I write about immigrant children or frontier children, I want to leave the reader with a deeper understanding of our nation's history and a feeling of kinship with youngsters from another time. But most of all, I want to write a book that will be read willingly, read from beginning to end with a sense of discovery and, yes, with a feeling of genuine pleasure. (pp. 30-2)

> *Russell Freedman, "Pursuing the Pleasure Principle," in* The Horn Book Magazine, *Vol. LXII, No. 1, January-February, 1986, pp. 27-32.*

GENERAL COMMENTARY

FRANK J. DEMPSEY

The term *Renaissance Man* has been overworked in recent decades, but how else would you describe someone who has written books about famous teenagers, poisonous snakes, the Boy Scouts, farm animals, Jules Verne, killer fish, Indian chiefs, immigrant children, and Abraham Lincoln? Since some of these things weren't around during the Renaissance, perhaps *Twenty-first Century Man* would better describe Russell Freedman.

Over the past thirty years Russell has written at least one book a year and has built up a solid reputation among teachers, librarians, and the reading public for his craftsmanship, reliability, and intellectual integrity. (p. 452)

Russell's first hardcover book, *Famous Teenagers Who Made History,* [is] a remarkably durable title that remained in print for nearly twenty years. "I never expected or planned to become a writer of nonfiction for young people," Russell remarked recently, "but I certainly have no regrets." The book was followed by *2000 Years of Space Travel, Jules Verne,* and *Scouting with Baden-Powell, Thomas Alva Edison*—and then came the animals.

The first of the animal books, which were to total twenty-three before he turned elsewhere, appeared in 1969, *How Animals Learn.* It was also about this time that Russell decided to make what would be a major shift in the format of his books: using striking, informative photographs, rather than drawings to illustrate his texts. This approach, which he still follows, proved popular and successful, and he began to develop a well-deserved reputation among book buyers for a consistently informative and entertaining style. This format also led to countless hours of research in photo archives the country over to locate just the right picture. . . . The last animal book, *Sharks,* surfaced in 1985, when Russell decided to return to the human comedy for future productions. "But I may write some more animal books," he recently cautioned.

Right away a built-in restriction asserted itself regarding the use of photographs. Wishing to continue the heavy and successful emphasis on photography in his books, he was necessarily limited to people and events occurring after the 1840s, the decade photography was invented. This problem turned out to be not-at-all insurmountable.

Further motivation was provided, if not needed, by Street Kids: 1864-1977, an outstanding photography exhibit at the New York Historical Society featuring wonderful photos of New York City's children in the nineteenth century. "I was deeply moved and impressed by this show," Russell remarked later, "and by the poignant expressions on the faces of these children, most of whom had never had their picture taken before." This experience led directly to *Immigrant Kids.* Reviews, as usual, were very good, but sales were modest.

But sales were not a problem with the next book. *Children of the Wild West,* which resulted in Russell being awarded the prestigious Western Heritage Award from the National Cowboy Hall of Fame for the outstanding juvenile book that year on a Western theme. The award ceremony, as it always is, was held in Oklahoma City, and he reported to me in rather awed tones, "I sat on the dais next to Kirk Douglas and Burl Ives!"

Since he had treated cowboys, there obviously should be equal time for Indians, and, sure enough, *Indian Chiefs* came out the following year. Because he wanted to give fair and equal attention to all six of the native American leaders he was describing, Russell said that this book was the hardest one he had attempted to date.

Then came *Lincoln: A Photobiography.* I grudgingly admit that I was one of the mistaken Jeremiahs who predicted, "Another book on Lincoln? It is not needed and won't sell"—so much for calamitous prophets. Even before the Newbery announcement, his colleagues were saying "what a wonderful book," "his best yet," and other such encomiums. From the handsome cover and binding all the way to the back cover photos of Lincoln with McClellan at Antietam, the book is a class act. (pp. 454-56)

I think Lincoln would . . . have been pleased to have such a gifted and caring biographer. (p. 456)

> *Frank J. Dempsey, "Russell Freedman," in* The Horn Book Magazine, *Vol. LXIV, No. 4, July-August, 1988, pp. 452-56.*

TEENAGERS WHO MADE HISTORY (1961)

A collection of brief biographies about eight people who had distinguished themselves in their professional lives before they had reached the age of twenty. The eight are Arturo Toscanini, Wernher von Braun, Samuel Colt, Louis Braille, Babe Didrikson Zaharias, Galileo Galilei, the Marquis de Lafayette, and Edna St. Vincent Millay. The binding motif, as shown in the title, is somewhat tenuous, and most of the material is available elsewhere; however, the writing has pace and a nice sense of drama. A divided list of suggestions for further reading is appended.

> *Zena Sutherland, in a review of "Teenagers Who Made History," in* Bulletin of the Center for Children's Books, *Vol. XV, No. 1, September, 1961, p. 7.*

TWO THOUSAND YEARS OF SPACE TRAVEL (1963)

Russell Freedman has written three concurrent surveys, of varying quality, in *2000 Years of Space Travel.* One is a history of astronomy, which is excellent, smoothly written and absorbing; another is a history of aviation and space flight—truncated, but to the point and accurate. The third is a history of science fiction blended in with the other two.

Mr. Freedman begins with Lucian's journey to the moon by sailing ship, written in 160 A.D., continues with fiction by Johannes Kepler, Edgar Allan Poe, H. G. Wells, Jules Verne and many others. Of course, only the bare bones of each tale are presented, and each suffers mightily. They also seem often to interrupt the general flow of the book.

What is particularly interesting is Mr. Freedman's demonstration of the relationship between fact and fiction. Each author gathered all available evidence and theory up to his time for a solid footing, and then let imagination carry his tale forward, and up.

> *Henry W. Hubbard, in a review of "2000 Years of Space Travel," in* The New York Times Book Review, *February 9, 1964, p. 24.*

This interesting book is a mixture of scientific history and science fiction. . . .

For the young reader who wants to know the main facts of the history of astronomy, this book is ideal: if, at the same time, he is interested in reading some of the extracts from the fiction of the subject, he will find himself equally well served.

> *B. J. Hopper, in a review of "2000 Years of Space Travel," in* The School Librarian and School Library Review, *Vol. 14, No. 1, March, 1966, p. 114.*

Teenagers, and others, who recall faint memories of Icarus, da Vinci and Jules Verne will be delighted with this account of ideas of space travel put forward in fiction and research during what may loosely be called the Christian era. . . . Mr. Freedman has the gift of explaining technicalities without being dishearteningly technical and he also has a sense of humour which prompts him to choose the most effective extracts from the fantasies of Lucian, Kepler, Bishop Godwin and Bishop Wilkins and later exponents of space fiction in the widest sense of the words. Interspersed with such are adequate summaries of the more scientific work of Ptolemy, Copernicus, Galileo, and the Herschels, not to mention the Great Lunar Hoax. The story so told is a fascinating one well worth the reading for pleasure or instruction.

> *A review of "2000 Years of Space Travel," in* The Junior Bookshelf, *Vol. 30, No. 2, April, 1966, p. 130.*

JULES VERNE: PORTRAIT OF A PROPHET (1965)

This is an excellent biography of the Frenchman who masterminded the 19th century classics of science fiction and whose imaginative projections of submarine life and aerial conquest have become matters of fact in the mid-20th century. In the days before electricity, Verne had what can be called an atomic imagination. Mr. Freedman uses very little invented dialogue to keep the story of Verne's life moving. He is successful at showing the restless writer at work, learning his craft. The biography is also a revealing source of French family life and behavior. Verne insisted on his independence but remained ever the dutiful son in a life pattern foreign to Anglo-Saxon attitudes. Each of his books is discussed and briefly analyzed. "In Verne's methods as a writer, we can find the clue to his success as a prophet. By looking carefully at

the present, he was able to look into the future . . . with his rich imagination, he made the facts and figures he used spring dramatically alive." Good point, good book. There is a bibliography of Verne's works, and an index.

> *A review of "Jules Verne: Portrait of a Prophet," in* Kirkus Reviews, *Vol. XXXIII, No. 8, September 15, 1965, p. 988.*

Accurate biography, though somewhat plodding. Mr. Freedman has used the Allotte de la Fuye, the Kenneth Allott, and the G. H. Waltz biographies as his main sources, since Verne jealously guarded his privacy and burned many personal papers. . . . Freedman spends a great deal of time comparing the author's novels with Verne's background and the times. This technique should have added interest, but unfortunately it was overdone. Nevertheless, this biography is much better than the Catherine Peare book and is less eulogistic than the Franz Born biography. There is not much material on Verne for boys and girls, and this is a competent work.

> *Janet Hellerich, in a review of "Jules Verne: Portrait of a Prophet," in* School Library Journal, *Vol. 12, No. 5, January, 1966, p. 138.*

Jules Verne: Portrait of a Prophet is a superbly analytical and absorbing life of this man of many talents, who did incredible research in the preparation of his books. The author gives an impressive introductory summary of the many scientific fields in which Verne was almost prophetic of future developments. There is also a complete list of Verne's writings, ranging from his plays to his "extraordinary journeys," and his output was truly prolific. (p. 275)

> *May Hill Arbuthnot, "Biographies for Older Children," in her* Children's Reading in the Home, *Scott, Foresman and Company, 1969, pp. 271-75.*

SCOUTING WITH BADEN-POWELL (1967)

The operative word is *with*—you'll fetch tea for the "uppers" at Charterhouse, travel from London to Wales by collapsible boat (and a few portages), go pigsticking in India, reconnoitering in Afghanistan and Zululand, draw maps in the guise of butterflies' wings as a Malta-based spy, stalk the Ashanti on the Gold Coast and the Matabele in Rhodesia, and finally withstand the siege of Mafeking that made Baden-Powell the hero of Britain. You'll go with him not only because the adventures are continually intriguing or exciting but also because the fresh, lively telling, based on and incorporating excerpts from Baden-Powell's accounts gives them a convincing immediacy. This was the first of his two lives; the second, long since begun in little ways, was his initiation of the scouting movement, beginning with twenty-one English boys camping for a week on an island . . . and a guidebook drawing on these and other experiences. How the movement grew and Baden-Powell was honored is told with pride that stays this side of idolatry. Boys—who needn't be Scouts—will enjoy it thoroughly.

> *A review of "Scouting with Baden-Powell," in* Kirkus Service, *Vol. XXXV, No. 20, October 15, 1967, p. 1287.*

[**Scouting with Baden-Powell** is a] well-written story. . . . The growth and development of the [Boy Scout] movement is traced along with the activities of its founder in a generously illustrated work that most boys will have difficulty putting down. The author worked extensively from Baden-Powell's own writings, and librarians should be aware that Brian Gardner's recent adult history, *Mafeking: A Victorian Legend* presents strong evidence that Baden-Powell's accounts of the siege at Mafeking were highly distorted and embellished to glorify his own role in the proceedings. But Mr. Freedman's long account of the siege follows the traditional story that lauds Baden-Powell. (pp. 83-4)

> *Ralph J. Folcarelli, in a review of "Scouting with Baden-Powell," in* School Library Journal, *Vol. 14, No. 5, January, 1968, pp. 83-4.*

HOW ANIMALS LEARN (with James E. Morriss, 1969)

Kids will learn *How Animals Learn* from this cogent presentation—everything from Pavlov to problem-solving, well illustrated with photographs and diagrams (even some elementary line graphs) and salted with projects for home testing. Instinctual behavior is distinguished from different areas of learning—habituation, association, imitation, practice (but not motor skills *per se*). Intelligence is defined as "the ability to change behavior as a result of experience"; the authors point out, however, that intelligence is ultimately tested in the animal's ability to learn "things important to his way of life" rather than in lab test situations and that rats are especially suited to experiments because "they normally live in dark, narrow passageways that resemble lab mazes." Lorenz and imprinting, Pavlov and conditioning, Thorndike, Skinner and puzzle boxes are carefully examined and other significant research (Kohler, Krushinsky), is also reported. The chapter "Animal Tricks and Training" describes much of the entertainment-oriented Brelands' work and includes tips for shaping behavior. No reference to Piaget's work with human animals but there is a chapter on "A Time to Learn" which implicates developmental stages. As discerning as Kay's *How Smart Are Animals,* emphasizing learning types rather than the representative animals, and avoiding some psych class labels (generalization, discrimination), which may make this more accessible to more (and younger) readers.

> *A review of "How Animals Learn," in* Kirkus Service, *Vol. XXXVII, No. 8, April 1, 1968, p. 461.*

Investigations of animal behavior, traditionally called "comparative psychology," also are comprehended under the newer term "ethology" which is the subject of this excellent young people's book. Some classical experiments and demonstrations by well-known experimental scientists such as Konrad Lorenz and Ivan Pavlov are mentioned. But many of the ongoing studies and investigations of the present day are unknown to the average general reader, and here he will be introduced to many of them. Accompanied by photographs, basic terms and concepts such as *instinct, habituation, association,* and *imitation* are explained and defined. In discussing *animal intelligence* and its measurement the authors explain why human standards of evaluation are not significant (e.g., if a dog were to attempt to teach a man to follow a scent through a heavily wooded area, the dog could and probably would conclude that man is a stupid clod). The concept of *imprinting* is developed by excellent case histories, as is the theme "can animals think." The great dividend in this excellent acquisition for inquiring young minds is the treatment of problem solving, and the description of open-ended investigations in which the student may engage. These potential

"science projects" are not exhibits that can be cooked up over the weekend before a deadline date into some sort of a visual exhibit, with the help of an indulgent parent. They are genuine learning and investigative activities that will require several weeks or even months if they are developed and reported adequately. The biliography, both books and magazine articles, is a rich resource for the investigator-reader or others who may want more information. Indexed. In addition to its usefulness as a school or public library acquisition, some science or social studies classroom teachers may find it worthwhile to acquire multiple copies as an accessory text. (pp. 6-7)

> *A review of "How Animals Learn," in* Science Books: A Quarterly Review, *Vol. 5, No. 1, May, 1969, pp. 6-7.*

A fascinating book on the way animals learn . . . .

A particularly stimulating chapter raises the questions: "Our investigations of animal learning have led us to ask some critical questions about ourselves. . . . When is the best time to learn certain skills and certain kinds of behavior? And what happens if we miss a time to learn?" Fine photographs harmonize well with the text, and a book list and simple experiments to be done with animals are included for especially interested readers. An entertaining exposition, particularly useful in school libraries.

> *Alma De Loney, in a review of "How Animals Learn," in* Library Journal, *Vol. 94, No. 12, June 15, 1969, p. 2500.*

ANIMAL INSTINCTS (with James E. Morriss, 1970)

In their previous book, *How Animals Learn* the authors presented an admirable introduction to comparative psychology. . . . Although neither book is intended to be read and studied first, potential readers, and teachers especially, should use them to complement one another. *Animal Instincts* deals with those functions, actions or activities an animal "knows how to do" or does instinctively, sometimes even automatically, in response to an appropriate "signal" or stimulus. The various chapters explore the nature of instinct, offer suggestions for studying instinct, explain migration and suggest how the reader can conduct and participate in migration studies, describe the delimiting and protecting "home boundaries" with a suggestion for an experiment involving fishes, describe several variations in animal courtship with descriptions of investigations that determine the factors in the instinct displayed by different species, and tell about the raising of a "family" by various species. The last chapter, "Blueprint for survival," mentions some of the fundamentals of genetics, natural selection, and behavior. The discussions are documented by citations from the literature. . . . The bibliography is excellent and indicates the scholarly research of the authors and their desire to share those resources with the reader who wants more information on various subjects. The various experiments and observations suggested for the reader are open-ended and the instructions and suggestions offered are minimal. After carrying out the suggested observations and experiments, the enterprising reader should be able to distill suggestions for other similar studies from the text as supplemented by exploration of appropriate references. Perhaps one of the chief merits of this book is that it deals with many familiar animals the young reader recognizes by sight, and offers him explanations of some of their actions and reactions that he may have observed but has not hitherto understood, and points out still other features that may have escaped his attention. To be a good student of nature, one must observe, tabulate, compare, and interpret, and the authors' books, *How Animals Learn* and *Animal Instincts,* are among the best for beginning naturalists. (pp. 2-3)

> *A review of "Animal Instincts," in* Science Books: A Quarterly Review, *Vol. 6, No. 1, May, 1970, pp. 2-3.*

Natural and experimental examples expand a word to the dimensions of a concept: instinct is first defined—"behavior that is inborn and does not have to be learned"; then its properties are refined—the term is *descriptive* but not fully *explanatory*. Internal stimuli (hormones) function chemically to prepare for a given action, and external stimuli trigger the action by exploiting, in the case of courtship for instance, the animal's best-developed sense (sight, sound, smell). His relative position on the evolutionary scale is what dictates the extent to which his innate or inherited 'outline' is filled in by 'learned' details. Word and picture portraits of particular species balance theory with a variety of intricate instinct-controlled behaviors: in courting, reproduction, and family-raising; in migration—the urge (glandular), navigation (sun- or star-oriented), and claiming of territory ("Is Man Territorial?"). However, "Instinct is too inflexible to cope with every situation that may arise. . . . Many species have become extinct because they were unable to adjust to changes in their environment"—here, discussion of genes, DNA, and mutation (re natural selection). Would-be observers are offered projects-in-context for inducing and conditioning instinctive reactions; further-readers will find a list of books (including juveniles) and accessible magazine articles for additional, de-limited investigation. The authors know *How Animals Learn*—human animals—and they foster a sense of discovery.

> *A review of "Animal Instincts," in* Kirkus Reviews, *Vol. XXXVIII, No. 9, May 1, 1970, p. 518.*

Using the same format and clear, simple writing style as in *How Animals Learn,* Freedman and Morriss have again collaborated to produce an outstanding book on animal instinct, suitable for both general and science-prone readers. Animal behavior is not just simply described as in many children's books, but it is analyzed and interpreted with reference to the best research data available to ethologists. . . . Facts, theories and hypotheses are clearly separated. Reader involvement is encouraged through suggestions for practical, simple experiments—a feature that makes the book particularly useful to educators. This very well done title should be a premium choice in the area of animal instinct.

> *Albert C. Haman, in a review of "Animal Instincts," in* Library Journal, *Vol. 96, No. 12, June 15, 1971, p. 2130.*

ANIMAL ARCHITECTS (1971)

Though the subject lacks the inherent conceptual interest of the author's *Animal Instincts* or *How Animals Learn,* this treatment of animal homes, from air-conditioned termite cities to the huge underground Texas metropolis housing 400 million prairie dogs, is up to his high standards of clarity, relevant detail, and respect for subject and reader. A short but stimulating first chapter telling "Why Animals Build," and

how they respond instinctively to sunlight or seasonal secretions, adds dimension to the examples that follow—and the examples are often intriguing. And as homes are built for living, the reader learns incidentally about the animals' mating, child-rearing and food-getting habits. A congenial and informative tour.

> *A review of "Animal Architects," in* Kirkus Reviews, *Vol. XXXIX, No. 10, May 15, 1971, p. 556.*

Freedman offers a wealth of scattered bits of information, but the material as a whole is not well organized. The first chapter, "Why Animals Build," is good, but in the rest of the book an attempt is made to cover too much territory in too little space. The second chapter, ostensibly on homes of insects and spiders, deals primarily with social Hymenoptera; spiders and two or three other insects are relegated to the section on solitary wasps. Caddis flies (repeatedly referred to simply as "caddises") are discussed in the following chapter on underwater architects, together with a water spider and several fishes and frogs. The last two chapters are concerned with birds and mammals. For no obvious reason some animals are allotted a great amount of space—ten pages for termites and seven for beavers, for example—whereas a number of other animals are dismissed with a single sentence. The longer sections are well written and interesting, but the brief references, with no description of the animal mentioned, are often confusing. It is regrettable that much of the material included here can be found in other books for young people, yet no mention is made of the equally interesting homes constructed by such creatures as fan worms, coral polyps, moss animals, or millipedes. (pp. 138-39)

> *A review of "Animal Architects," in* Science Books: A Quarterly Review, *Vol. 7, No. 2, September, 1971, pp. 138-39.*

Interesting examples of fish, bird and mammal architecture are given. The author's descriptions are both accurate and lively—for example, when describing the habits of beavers he writes, "Swooshing out of their underwater tunnels like torpedoes. . . . " The book overall is a worthy acquisition even for those libraries that already have George Mason's *Animal Homes;* it's more comprehensive and can appeal to slightly older readers.

> *Janet Kuenstner, in a review of "Animal Architects," in* School Library Journal, *Vol. 18, No. 2, October, 1971, p. 110.*

THE BRAINS OF ANIMALS AND MAN (with James E. Morriss, 1972)

This is not an introduction to the structure and function of the brain but a review of interesting brain research on the order of Margaret O. Hyde's commendable *Your Brain* (1964). Unfortunately for Freedman and Morriss, Hyde has already covered many of the same topics and even the same experiments: Penfield's mapping of the cerebral cortex, Olds' discovery of the pleasure center, Hyden's research on the biochemistry of learning and memory, McConnell's findings on memory transfer in planaria, Delgado's development of ESB (electrical stimulation of the brain). Freedman and Morriss, however, offer a trimmer presentation, and supplement their lucid reports with intriguing speculation: Imagine getting your optic and aural "wires crossed" so that you could see sound and hear reflected light. Or an international crisis developing because diplomats assigned to negotiate a disagreement were mismatched alpha types and simply couldn't get along. Or injections on demand of courage or musical talent, algebra or French. Or the political implications of behavior control by electrode. *The Brains of Animals and Man* is likely to inspire further investigation, and the bibliography of popular books (including juvenile) and *Scientific American* articles will provide some direction.

> *A review of "The Brains of Animals and Man," in* Kirkus Reviews, *Vol. XL, No. 10, May 15, 1972, p. 583.*

The Brains of Animals and Man is a very well-written and thought-provoking book. It fills an important place in required reading for advanced biology students. The authors trace the development of the brain from lower animals to man. The explanation of how the brain regulates our thoughts, emotions and actions is very well handled. The final chapter, "Behavior by Remote Control," may be too deep for some of the more immature students, and the individual teacher will have to decide if his students are able to handle the concepts.

> *Ryan B. Walden, in a review of "The Brains of Animals and Man," in* Appraisal: Children's Science Books, *Vol. 5, No. 3, Fall, 1972, p. 19.*

I am not much of a biologist or physicist, but I have tried to form a mental picture of just what is going on in my gray matter when I visualize the atomic structure of beryl, or try to memorize "All Through the Night" in Welsh, or when I am trying to form the aforesaid mental picture itself. I suppose most other people have done the same.

Maybe since it both supported and extended my mental picture, I greatly enjoyed *The Brains of Animals and Man*. . . . I am not qualified to pick any holes in the factual statements of this book; they all seem reasonable to me and seem well-backed by experimental evidence. Other statements are frankly announced to be hypothesis or speculation. I don't think I'll give this book to the school library (as I usually do with review copies); I may occasionally lend it to selected students, but I want to keep it where I can get my hands on it at a moment's notice. It is a fine piece of work.

> *Harry C. Stubbs, in a review of "The Brains of Animals and Man," in* The Horn Book Magazine, *Vol. XLVIII, No. 5, October, 1972, p. 490.*

THE FIRST DAYS OF LIFE (1974)

Following an introductory overview of eggs and fertilization, the first days of a cod, green turtle, herring gull, robin, wolf, elephant, dolphin, and chimpanzee are described. The text is clear and interesting and is illustrated with attractive charcoal drawings [by Joseph Cellini]. This fills the gap between Selsam's *When an Animal Grows* and Schwartz's *When Animals Are Babies* for primary graders and Selsam's *Animals As Parents* which is for grades five to nine.

> *Cecile M. Reid, in a review of "The First Days of Life," in* School Library Journal, *Vol. 21, No. 7, March, 1975, p. 87.*

The title of this book is somewhat misleading; only a brief (three-page) discussion of the generalized aspects of reproduction and the very beginning of life is included. It is not clear whether this section is a preface, an introduction or a chapter. No drawings of pictures are included to illustrate the rather abstract topics being discussed. Terms, such as ovaries, sperm, fertilized, yolk, embryo and womb, are used without clarification other than the somewhat imprecise descriptions and definitions in the written material. This is unfortunate because in subsequent sections of the book the terms are used without additional clarification. The main body of the book is divided into eight sections which focus on the development and care of eight different animals. The "story-type" accounts of each are generally interesting and accurate. The accompanying illustrations are occasionally confusing and seem to do little to augment the text. In all cases, a natural history description of early life and care of young is provided. For some reason, perhaps it is the writing style, the depth of the discussion seems very shallow. An anthropomorphic tone surfaces in the material, and the reading level seems uneven. Although the content is limited, the book may be of interest to some young readers as a source book for report preparation.

> *David H. Ost, in a review of "The First Days of Life," in* Science Books & Films, *Vol. XI, No. 1, May, 1975, p. 35.*

A reader may generalize from this book that nature has provided different methods to insure the survival of a certain number of offspring of each species. The stories about each animal young are well told and enjoyable. The writing style is clear and captivating, but it is curious that half the animals included are mammals, and unfortunate that nothing new is really added to the literature on any one of these species by this book.

> *Diane Holzheimer, in a review of "The First Days of Life," in* Appraisal: Children's Science Books, *Vol. 8, No. 1, Winter, 1975, p. 16.*

GROWING UP WILD: HOW YOUNG ANIMALS SURVIVE (1975)

What happens after *The First Days of Life*—to a tadpole becoming a frog, a rattlesnake during his first summer, an eagle getting ready to go off on her own, and two beaver kits between their first temporary displacement for their mother's next litter and their permanent expulsion from the family lodge a year later. Freedman also gives a cub's eye view (based on George Schaller's reports) of a lion pride's kill and feast and describes an uneventful encounter, also from Schaller but observed here by a four-year-old female (an "awkward age"), between a band of gorillas and two men with camera and binoculars. There is no attempt at parallelism among the six different sketches, which could make for a slackness overall, but Freedman does give you the feeling (with his frog escaping from a boy's grasp by emptying her bladder and screaming like a human baby, or his rattlesnake swallowing and digesting a lizard) that you are sharing firsthand observations, not just enduring another regurgitation.

> *A review of "Growing Up Wild: How Young Animals Survive," in* Kirkus Reviews, *Vol. XLIII, No. 22, November 15, 1975, p. 1290.*

Growing Up Wild: How Young Animals Survive considers the maturation of differing wildlife in six tightly constructed essays. Unifying the topics is the theme of survival, in particular the unique characteristics and instincts young animals are born with and acquire which will enable them to exist in particular environments. These environments are subtly unfolded within the descriptions of the early lives of a leopard frog, timber snake, bald eagle, beaver kit, lion cub, and gorilla. The prose is action packed and compelling, which should draw intermediate readers despite the small number of drawings [by Leslie Morrill], appearing only at the beginning of each essay. Although there is no index, there are suggestions for further reading. The work is a very good example of descriptive natural science writing.

> *Debbie Robinson, in a review of "Growing Up Wild: How Young Animals Survive," in* Appraisal: Children's Science Books, *Vol. 9, No. 2, Spring, 1976, p. 20.*

Most impressive is the author's ability to present a wealth of data in an interesting way; even minute details of a young animal's life are covered, including predator-prey relationships, population dynamics, thermoregulation, parental care and more. The last three chapters on mammals are the best and concepts are well presented. The author's data are factual. . . . My only criticisms are that there is no unifying theme tying the chapters together and that the descriptions are sometimes anthropomorphic. However, this book has more facts about animals than most others, for this educational level, and I recommend it for any future young zoologist.

> *Richard L. Lattis, in a review of "Growing Up Wild: How Young Animals Survive," in* Science Books & Films, *Vol. XII, No. 1, May, 1976, p. 40.*

ANIMAL FATHERS (1976)

The seahorse who hatches the female's eggs in his pouch is a commonly cited example of a nurturing father; it's less widely broadcast that both the Siamese fighting fish and the stickleback famous for his male aggression also preside over their hatchlings. The sea catfish "uses his mouth as a nursery," and similar patterns occur in certain frogs and toads, while the bird parents cited here divide things more equitably and even the gray wolf and gibbon who leave the bulk of infant care to their mates are faithful helpers. Here too of course is that picture of paternal devotion—the penguin who starves and shivers on top of his young while their mother fattens up for her shift. Freedman's fourteen simply written double-page profiles, each one illustrated in soft black and white [by Joseph Cellini], are enlightening in themselves—and, together, they'll help to balance all those on animal mothers.

> *A review of "Animal Fathers," in* Kirkus Reviews, *Vol. XLIV, No. 8, April 15, 1976, p. 475.*

Fascinating facts about 15 animal fathers and their parental habits and behavior are enhanced by Joseph Cellini's soft pencil drawings. Included are the father seahorse who carries the eggs in his pouch and actually gives birth; the sea catfish who uses his mouth as a nursery; and the gray wolf who devoutly guards his young. Selsam's *Animals As Parents* is more scientific, but this is interesting for its paternalistic approach to the family life of a variety of animals.

> *Pam Pearson, in a review of "Animal Fathers," in* School Library Journal, *Vol. 23, No. 1, September, 1976, p. 115.*

Freedman takes the unusual approach of examining the role of the male parent in rearing the young. All of the animal species discussed are vertebrates, and they range from the sea horse to the white-handed gibbon. One of the major strengths of the book is that Freedman avoids the anthropomorphic style so common in children's books on animal behavior. Another interesting feature is that the scientific name of each species is given in the table of contents, thus introducing the reader to biological nomenclature. (However, no explanation of the purpose of the taxonomic designations is offered.) . . . The text is well written, factual and some of the terminology introduced will serve as an excellent vocabulary builder. The book could serve well as the basis for a general discussion of animal behavior.

> *Erik Paul Scully, in a review of "Animal Fathers," in* Science Books & Films, *Vol. XII, No. 3, December, 1976, p. 160.*

ANIMAL GAMES (1976)

"These young gorillas are playing follow the leader . . . Wrestling is a popular animal game. Bear cubs stand on their hind legs when they wrestle . . . Tag is a favorite game of hoofed animals." Agreeable as the subject is, Freedman's flat, unemotional descriptions of animal play and its relationship to later survival, fail to develop any momentum or kick. So while St. Tamara's graceful line drawings set the mood of benign good humor, the double-page scenes of frolicking chimps, dolphins, and beaver kits invite only passive admiration.

> *A review of "Animal Games," in* Kirkus Reviews, *Vol. XLIV, No. 19, October 1, 1976, p. 1098.*

Freedman discusses the young of sixteen animals, pointing out that the way they play prepares them for the skills they will need in order to survive. Much of the text, however, is simply descriptive; the double-page spread on elephants, for example, describes the mud-rolling, climbing, and spraying that a herd of elephants does when at a river, and there is no comment about how this prepares the young for a task. There is, of course, some repetition: wolf pups and bobcat kittens pounce and tumble in similar fashion. The book is factual but only minimally informative.

> *Zena Sutherland, in a review of "Animal Games," in* Bulletin of the Center for Children's Books, *Vol. 30, No. 7, March, 1977, p. 106.*

[Freedman's] behavioral descriptions are good although sometimes a bit too anthropomorphic. For example, it is said that gorillas play king-of-the-mountain, fawns play tag and seals play tug-of-war. Such terms suggest that animal play is much more organized and rule bound than is actually the case. Nevertheless, the book is entertaining and excellently illustrated. It should appeal to elementary school children.

> *James W. Kalat, in a review of "Animal Games," in* Science Books & Films, *Vol. XIII, No. 1, May, 1977, p. 43.*

HANGING ON: HOW ANIMALS CARRY THEIR YOUNG (1977)

A collection of animal profiles, for junior behaviorists who'd like to see a beaver carrying its kitten like a stack of wood, or a sea otter roping itself to a pup with seaweed. Subjects, ranging from the familiar kitten-toting cat to the piggybacking pangolin, are illustrated by assorted sequential and close-up black and white photos. Though specific differences in parental dependence are mentioned, the general procedural approach adds little to the many animal baby books available.

> *A review of "Hanging On: How Animals Carry Their Young," in* Kirkus Reviews, *Vol. XLV, No. 5, March 1, 1977, p. 226.*

Freedman's theme is the animal behavior of carrying young, found mostly among the mammals. Twenty-two different examples are carefully presented. A mother beaver takes her kit in her arms and holds it in place with her chin. Opossums ride on their mothers' backs. Nonmammal carriers are represented by swans, grebes, wolf spiders and scorpions. Effective inclusions are the excellent black-and-white photographs taken from different sources. Freedman admits that the available pictures were a factor in his choice of animals. Every animal discussed is clearly shown carrying its young. Some photographs detail development of the young, pouches in the mother and carrying techniques. Young readers will enjoy the pictures of the koala and of the brush-tailed opossums riding on their mothers' backs. An excellent aid for readers is the inclusion of phonetic pronunciations of some of the more difficult names. More children's science books should do this. **Hanging On** is unique and very well done.

> *Paul R. Boehlke, in a review of "Hanging On: How Animals Carry Their Young," in* Science Books & Films, *Vol. XIII, No. 3, December, 1977, p. 166.*

This is a winning book of photographs and brief text, fine for reading and showing to the preschooler, a mixture of empathy in caring and the diversity of life.

The young author, with several similar books to his credit, is plainly a man of parts. He dedicates his book to the T'ang poet Tu Fu, and he begins it all with a noted 20-character poem, quite untranslated because it is only of personal relevance. (pp. 34, 36)

> *Philip Morrison and Phylis Morrison, in a review of "Hanging On: How Animals Carry Their Young," in* Scientific American, *Vol. 237, No. 6, December, 1977, pp. 34, 36.*

HOW BIRDS FLY (1977)

This excellent account of how birds fly is clearly written, using a minimum of technical terms, with artistically rewarding drawings illustrating the main points of the text [by Lorence F. Bjorklund]. The flight-adapted structure of a bird's body is carefully described, and the dynamics of flight, uplift, forward motion, gliding, soaring, take-off, steering, landing and hovering comprise the major portion of the text. There are some weak spots, such as the explanation of how the bird's tail helps in flight turns, but these faults are minor. There is a final section on the speed of flight and the relationship between a bird's wing and tail shape and its average speed. The glossary and index are useful. The average adult reader will find this book as interesting as children will.

> *Betty Cochran, in a review of "How Birds Fly," in* Science Books & Films, *Vol. XIV, No. 2, September, 1978, p. 113.*

Freedman accepting the Newbery Medal in 1988 for Lincoln: A Photobiography.

Brief, thoughtful, convincing, **How Birds Fly** makes clear what we know and do not know about bird flight, without any mathematics but with careful analysis in words of the needs and task of flight. It has simple diagrams, no less than whole-bird pencil drawings, of real utility and beauty. Feathers, muscles, weight, the wing slots and the propellerlike sweeping motions are made real for young readers. Gliding, soaring and hovering flight are distinguished from the strong wing-beat form in an introduction that does not demand too much and yet satisfies. The simple Bernoulli demonstration—blowing over the curving droop of a page held before the lips—is the earnest of a book that genuinely increases understanding.

> *Philip Morrison and Phylis Morrison, in a review of "How Birds Fly," in* Scientific American, *Vol. 239, No. 6, December, 1978, p. 37.*

GETTING BORN (1978)

Getting Born is not a sex education book; it shows exactly what the title suggests—the birth process of animals. Progressing logically from the genesis of fish to amphibians, to reptiles and birds, and finally to mammals, well-done diagrams [by Corbett Jones] and photographs clarify the information in the text. Packed with interesting and surprising details, e.g., the egg tooth of birds and reptiles, the metamorphosis of tadpoles, and a father seahorse giving birth, this title would be enjoyed by even very young children hearing it read aloud.

Drew Harrington, in a review of "Getting Born," in School Library Journal, *Vol. 25, No. 3, November, 1978, p. 61.*

Confronted straight off with the photoenlargement of brown trout eggs about to hatch, children won't have to be prodded to turn the page to the less spectacular-looking but well laid out drawings of *sperm, egg,* and *embryo*—and on to more photos of the emerging trout. Freedman then points out that some fish, like the molly, grow inside the mother's body, and he turns then to the seahorse, with an accompanying photo of the male in process of giving birth. The same combination of straightforward generalization (reptiles' and birds' eggs hatch on land), notable exception (garter snakes don't lay eggs—the one seen here has just given birth to 57 babies), eased-in vocabulary (*uterus, amnion*), and impressive, well-timed photos distinguishes Freedman's progression through different orders and species right up to the cat, dolphin, and horse. Freedman's survey of **How Animals Carry Their Young** was too diffuse and incidental to carry much weight; in this case the combination of wide range (trout to horse) and narrow focus (the process of birth) makes for a particularly effective lesson—and the photos add considerably to the impact.

A review of "Getting Born," in Kirkus Reviews, *Vol. XLVII, No. 1, January 1, 1979, p. 9.*

An outstanding collection of unusual black-and-white photographs combined with a simple, but highly interesting text convey the diversity of life in this latest book on parturition for primary grade children. Unlike other recent authors who have confined themselves to a single species, Freedman covers eleven, ranging from fish, through frogs, turtles and snakes to chickens and finally mammals. The author does not oversimplify. Examples of both egg-hatched and liveborn fish are included, and excellent diagrams show the difference in structure between fish and reptile eggs. . . . The book does have some weaknesses. It ends abruptly after a series of photographs already published in Jane Miller's *Birth of a Foal,* without any summary, and without any mention of the birth which interests many young children the most—their own. Several mistakes in accent in the pronunciation guides must also be noted. Nevertheless, this is a book highly recommended for purchase.

Rea Alkema, in a review of "Getting Born," in Appraisal: Children's Science Books, *Vol. 12, No. 2, Spring, 1979, p. 18.*

HOW ANIMALS DEFEND THEIR YOUNG (1978)

Unusually skillful at choosing and arranging an interesting variety of examples to support central concepts, Freedman draws widely on other sources (Jane Goodall, Ross E. Hutchins, Millicent Selsam, etc.) but manages to complement rather than duplicate them. He explores categories of behavior animals employ in protecting their young: sheltering, use of signals, escaping, camouflage, attack, and herd activity. Attractive black-and-white photographs and a bibliography of readily accessible titles along with the readable text comprise a creditable account which children will read both for pleasure and information.

Margaret Bush, in a review of "How Animals Defend Their Young," in School Library Journal, *Vol. 25, No. 7, March, 1979, p. 138.*

Too many popular books on animal behavior, especially for young readers, are riddled with inaccuracies, myths and anthropomorphism. Freedman's book, dealing with various aspects of protection of young animals by their parents, is a happy exception. Surveying a broad range of defensive behaviors displayed by diverse taxonomic groups, Freedman relies on scientific literature rather than fabulous anecdotes that are either fabrications or misinterpretations of some behavior that may not even be typical of the animal species. The book is clearly written, accurate and packed with fascinating information. Although perhaps most suitable for sixth or seventh graders, I suspect that any high school student could find much of interest here and might be stimulated to watch the behavior of animals more carefully.

B. Dennis Sustare, in a review of "How Animals Defend Their Young," in Science Books & Films, *Vol. XV, No. 4, March, 1980, p. 228.*

TOOTH AND CLAW: A LOOK AT ANIMAL WEAPONS (1980)

Unlike Schlein's *Snake Fight, Rabbit Fight, and More,* this makes no generalizations about animal fighting and no attempt to introduce concepts or provide a theoretical framework. Instead, Freedman proceeds from one type of weapon to another—essentially, sprays, quills, teeth, claws, horns, and poisons—and for each, takes a close look at two or more animals who exhibit some variety of the weapon in question. Spectacular photos from various sources truly illustrate the points at hand; and Freedman's direct, well-focused descriptions inform without trumped-up dramatics.

A review of "Tooth and Claw: A Look at Animal Weapons," in Kirkus Reviews, *Vol. XLVIII, No. 12, June 15, 1980, p. 781.*

In the same well-organized, informative style and inviting format of the author's **Getting Born** and **Hanging On: How Animals Carry Their Young,** Freedman examines some common and unusual animal weapons and shows how they are used for hunting and self-defense. . . . The black-and-white photographs on every page are clear and exciting and will help make this an especially appealing book for five to eight year olds.

Diane Holzheimer, in a review of "Tooth and Claw: A Look at Animal Weapons," in School Library Journal, *Vol. 27, No. 2, October, 1980, p. 134.*

Freedman has collected enlightening material on the weapons of various animals. Excellent black-and-white photographs, correlated with crisp text, detail the adaptations of more than 30 animals. . . . Carefully selected from many different sources, the sharp photographs comprise more than half the book. Pains have been taken to picture each adaptation. When the text states that zebras can kick and bite, the photograph shows both actions. Children should enjoy this book and it would be a valuable addition to any school library. An excellent aid for readers is the inclusion of phonetic pronunciations of some of the more difficult terms. Freedman's following of a theme through the animal kingdom has again produced a unique and interesting book.

Paul R. Boehlke, in a review of "Tooth and Claw: A Look at Animal Weapons," in Science Books & Films, *Vol. 16, No. 2, November-December, 1980, p. 93.*

IMMIGRANT KIDS (1980)

A nicely integrated, refreshingly un-woeful introduction to the experience of being a young urban immigrant around the turn of the century. As the text describes the arduous crossing, the terrifying health inspections, the cramped apartments, strange schools, etc., photos by Riis and Hine (and others) make the scenes real and recollections of immigrant childhoods give them a personal dimension. If there was hardship, Freedman makes clear, there was also compensation—for women, in the water magically available from a hall or apartment tap; for kids, in the freedom and vigor of street-life. And though we see kids working at adult-sized tasks, we also see the "newsies" (one of them a girl!)—"independent business people" whom not all kids will pity. Freedman also cites, matter-of-factly, the split between quickly-Americanized children and their Old-Worldly parents; indeed, he falters only on the last page when he states, blandly and ahistorically, that today's immigrants face similar experiences. Otherwise it's concise, graphic, and designed in every respect to catch and hold the reader's interest.

A review of "Immigrant Kids," in Kirkus Reviews, *Vol. XLVIII, No. 16, August 15, 1980, p. 1082.*

Period photographs from the late 1800s and early 1900s tell a poignant story of the struggle of immigrant families to find a better life for themselves in America. The smoothly worded text is attractively arranged, complementing the understated eloquence of the photographs. Freedman, himself a child of Russian immigrants, brings insights into the joys and problems of families of many cultures who crossed the Atlantic, arriving in New York City, established homes, worked, went to school and played. (pp. 145-46)

Sherry De Borde, in a review of "Immigrant Kids," in School Library Journal, *Vol. 27, No. 2, October, 1980, pp. 145-46.*

Freedman's essay, plus some 48 well-chosen photographs of the times, will illuminate a most important subject—the lives and life-styles of the children who immigrated to America during the period of the largest European influx—1880-1920. The author takes pains to re-create the day, with quotations and detailed descriptions that highlight the vast differences, and sometimes the similarities, between childhood then and now. The systematic order of his material—passage, home life, school, work, and play—makes good sense while it reveals aspects of the subject not often found in children's books. And, although he occasionally skirts around the very grimmest of facts, his addition of real-life good times more than makes up for any apparent lack of thoroughness.

Judith Goldberger, in a review of "Immigrant Kids," in Booklist, *Vol. 77, No. 3, October 1, 1980, p. 208.*

THEY LIVED WITH THE DINOSAURS (1980)

Though he doesn't say how "the animals' bones turn to stone," Freedman explains at the outset how "scientists learn about prehistoric animals by digging up fossils." He does less well with the idea that some prehistoric animals who "lived on" have "changed greatly as time passed." (This can be a stumper for kids unless it's explained how the species, not the individuals, changed.) But this is about those "living fossils" that have not changed—beginning with starfish, horseshoe crabs, cockroaches, and others which, a chart makes clear, long predated the dinosaurs. Again, there are problems with levels of understanding: coelacanths, we learn, give birth to live young—interesting, but only when you know that other fish don't. However, Freedman's descriptions of the animals are generally on target, their unique and interesting features are brought out without frivolous dramatics, and the detail is well integrated into the overall "living fossil" concept. And, as usual with Freedman's books, the text is considerably sharpened by an excellent selection of photos, showing both the fossils of prehistoric specimens and their contemporary counterparts.

A review of "They Lived with the Dinosaurs," in Kirkus Reviews, *Vol. XLVIII, No. 23, December 1, 1980, p. 1519.*

This fresh approach to ancient animal forms is a welcome change from the usual concentration on static bones. . . . Pictures of mostly familiar mammals, birds, reptiles, fish and insects combined with succinct descriptions of their structures and habits now and in ancient times establish a tangible link to an almost imaginary prehistoric world. The ancient world and the reasons for these species' long-lived success are described in a manner sure to draw readers on. Minor defects in format, such as the partial obscuring of the time chart and one misplaced photograph, do not seriously detract from the book's careful design. Name pronunciations and a good index are included. Herbert S. Zim's *Dinosaurs* compares dinosaur anatomy to that of various living creatures, but no other book deals exclusively with insects and animal life that shared the dinosaurs' world and still exist today. A valuable book for the dinosaur shelf. (pp. 64-5)

Ann G. Brouse, in a review of "They Lived with the Dinosaurs," in School Library Journal, *Vol. 27, No. 6, February, 1981, pp. 64-5.*

At first glance, this book appears to offer a novel and refreshing thematic approach; focusing attention upon those less familiar forms of animal life that shared the [Mesozoic] world of the dinosaurs. Unfortunately, however, that promise falls short of fulfillment. The dinosaurs, even in their "supporting role" as objects of comparison and contrast, manage to "upstage" many of the creatures who are billed as the "stars" of this paleontological drama.

A more serious flaw is to be found in the book's organization, which is basically historical, yet bewilderingly non-chronological. The text seems to shift unpredictably from the present to the Paleozoic and back again, with random stops en route. For those who can follow the itinerary, the trip may be worthwhile; but I suspect that too many young readers will get lost along the way.

Ronald J. Kley, in a review of "They Lived with the Dinosaurs," in Appraisal: Science Books for Young People, *Vol. 14, No. 2, Spring, 1981, p. 16.*

WHEN WINTER COMES (1981)

How do animals stay alive through the winter? After posing the question, Freedman shows us a range of answers: saving food, as squirrels do with nuts; hibernating, as woodchucks and other animals do; hunting other animals or digging for seeds and roots; and migrating, as some birds do. As Freedman pans past the various animals, he also notes the features that help them stay warm or hide from enemies in winter, and he points to interesting examples beyond the standard squirrel-nut level. For example, he shows a beaver amassing a pile of tree branches, then nibbling at the bark "as though it were eating corn on the cob" throughout the winter. With pleasant soft-pencil drawings of the different animals in snowy settings [by Pamela Johnson], an agreeable early nature book.

> *A review of "When Winter Comes," in* Kirkus Reviews, *Vol. XLIX, No. 12, June 15, 1981, p. 738.*

The black-and-white sketches of [the] animals are very realistic and add significantly to the text. The information is accurate, but rather "blah". Embellishing the bare bones text with more detail would make it more valuable and interesting to readers in grades 1-3. For example, the author explains that monarch butterflies are insects that migrate. Why not include that they fly all the way to the Yucatan Peninsula in lower Mexico? Facts such as this would not take much space, yet would add more meat to this "easy-to-read" book. (p. 20)

> *Martha T. Kane, in a review of "When Winter Comes," in* Appraisal: Science Books for Young People, *Vol. 14, No. 3, Fall, 1981, pp. 19-20.*

The preparations animals make for survival through the winter, including hibernation and migration, is the subject of Mr. Freedman's book, and the outstanding illustrations make this subject come alive! Pamela Johnson's soft black-and-white drawings lovingly evoke the snowy landscape with its busy (or sleeping) inhabitants, and when combined with the accurate but unrelentingly "reader" text (the book is called a Smart Cat 2A) succeed in making the book most attractive. The wintering of squirrels, rabbits, beavers, woodchucks, bears, frogs, winter birds, foxes, mice, deer and some insects are pictured and discussed—just briefly enough for a seven-year-old. A very desirable purchase for any nature-oriented child, class or group. (pp. 19-20)

> *Heddie Kent, in a review of "When Winter Comes," in* Appraisal: Science Books for Young People, *Vol. 14, No. 3, Fall, 1981, pp. 19-20.*

FARM BABIES (1981)

Specific information, accompanied by sharp black-and-white photographs, is given about nine different newborn animals and two kinds of birds often found on farms. . . . The text stresses the abilities and behavior of each new animal. The narrow purpose of this book is well achieved.

> *Barbara Hawkins, in a review of "Farm Babies," in* School Library Journal, *Vol. 28, No. 5, January, 1982, p. 63.*

Farm Babies describes eleven farm animals during their first days of life, and it should be of general interest to early elementary readers. The reading level of the text, however, seems more suited to grades three and four, but the book could be used as a "read to" book at the lower levels. Information is quite accurate, complete, and carefully avoids anthropomorphism. Although clearly written, the vocabulary, length, and complexity of some sentences may prove difficult for some readers. Children's general interest in this topic should help compensate for this. Some of the black-and-white

photographs lack the clarity and contrast that one reasonably expects in such a book, but others are good to excellent.

> *Donald C. Edinger, in a review of "Farm Babies," in* Science Books & Films, *Vol. 17, No. 3, January-February, 1982, p. 162.*

First comes a new-born calf, and then, more briefly, ten other "babies"—about which we learn some things that are different, and some things that are the same. But Freedman, practiced in presenting this subject matter to the young, makes no overt attempt to instruct—and that, along with the simple fluency of the text and the simple clarity of the pictures, reinforces the book's natural appeal. (The text almost never refers to the animals as "babies"—save to say "baby goats" as an alternative to "kids," or "baby pigs" as an alternative to "piglets.") Instead, the brief remarks accompanying each picture take as reference points the picture itself ("These piglets are about a week old. They are beginning to leave their pen and explore the barnyard"); a child's instinctual response or natural queries ("If you touch a small piglet, it feels like velvet. . . . When it is about ten days old, it begins to grow soft bristles"); or the animal's distinguishing traits ("Baby pigs make lively pets. . . . In fact, pigs are probably the smartest animals on the farm"). Virtually all the information, in sum, is of immediate interest and some consequence—for a listening five-year-old or a second- or third-grader. A routine undertaking, discerningly executed.

> *A review of "Farm Babies," in* Kirkus Reviews, *Vol. L, No. 3, February 1, 1982, p. 137.*

ANIMAL SUPERSTARS (1981)

A cut above the usual comparison and record books, this compilation is presented in an informative, though choppy, narrative form. Among the subjects covered are the fastest, the biggest eaters, the champion survivors and the "super moms." Comparative charts and lively black-and-white photographs add to the appeal this will have for browsers and reluctant readers.

> *Ilene Cooper, in a review of "Animal Superstars," in* Booklist, *Vol. 78, No. 14, March 15, 1982, p. 957.*

If you have been looking for a Guinness-type book of world animal records, look no more. It's here. The slowest, the fastest, the biggest, the strongest, the most prolific—from shrimp to slug, dog to dolphin. Arranged in various categories, sprinkled with black-and-white photos, this takes a little more reading than do the Guiness books but can be fun for the curious. I am happy to report that it's indexed.

> *Patricia Manning, in a review of "Animal Superstars," in* School Library Journal, *Vol. 29, No. 3, November, 1982, p. 83.*

CAN BEARS PREDICT EARTHQUAKES? UNSOLVED MYSTERIES OF ANIMAL BEHAVIOR (1982)

The real question seems to be not *whether* animals can sense approaching earthquakes, but *how*. Still, that's only the first of several mysteries considered here. Why do elephants cluster around dead comrades—and do they sometimes bury their dead? Why do groups of whales fatally strand themselves on beaches? How smart are dolphins? Curiositypiquers all, with enough examples for lively reading, and enough facts and theories to launch further investigation.

> *A review of "Can Bears Predict Earthquakes? Unsolved Mysteries of Animal Behavior," in* Kirkus Reviews, *Vol. L, No. 22, November 15, 1982, p. 1237.*

Freedman offers an exploration of interesting and unusual animal behaviors, utilizing scientific research that has disclosed questions as well as answers. . . . Subjects are presented in a clear and logical manner, and are illustrated with photographs. A useful book for motivating the study of scientific research and animal behavior.

> *Catherine Wood, in a review of "Can Bears Predict Earthquakes? Unsolved Mysteries of Animal Behavior," in* School Library Journal, *Vol. 29, No. 6, February, 1983, p. 76.*

Raising more questions than it answers, this book explores some of the mysteries of animal behavior that humans have wondered about for years. The author cites new studies and ties the information together in a readable way. There are eight chapters dealing with a different phenomenon in each, a few b/w photographs, a useful index, and a bibliography of recent books and articles to spur on the curious student to do more reading. Science teachers will be happy to know about this book, but librarians and literature teachers should be able to tie it into career talks and lead-ins to other reading. One of the techniques the author uses is to show the reader that many of these riddles are still unsolved . . . maybe the young reader will be contributing to this knowledge in the future. Fun and informative book!

> *Ruth Cline, in a review of "Can Bears Predict Earthquakes? Unsolved Mysteries of Animal Behavior," in* Voice of Youth Advocates, *Vol. 6, No. 1, April, 1983, p. 49.*

KILLER SNAKES (1982)

"If such a snake"—a 37-foot anaconda—"climbed up the side of a three-story house, its head would reach the roof before its tail left the ground." "A baby cobra is ready for action as soon as it hatches." "Two drops of black mamba poison can kill a grown man within ten minutes." "When [the death adder] bites, it hangs on and chews to get more poison into the wound." "A gaboon viper can bite through a person's foot." No doubt about it, Freedman's crisp characterizations are as sharply on the mark as a rattler's one-second attack. The equally apt photos include a slithery tangle of Australian taipans ("the most ferocious snake in the world"), a close-enough look at a gaboon viper's fangs, and, altogether, a snappy variety of views and angles.

> *A review of "Killer Snakes," in* Kirkus Reviews, *Vol. L, No. 23, December 1, 1982, p. 1294.*

I have to confess to a slight prejudice against books which paint the snake as killer at the same time they're trying to embrace the notion that these animals have venom for practical food-getting and protection reasons and not to "get" people. Nevertheless, this book does a good job of straddling, if straddle you must. It's nicely laid out, has wonderfully clear photographs and will made kids shiver joyfully as they read about how little venom it takes to die at the hand, or rather the fangs, of a mamba or a cobra. I think it would have been interesting to at least make mention of the rear-fanged snakes, which have a whole different venom delivery system, but which have killer capacity, though not as much.

> *Barbara Brenner, in a review of "Killer Snakes," in* Appraisal: Science Books for Young People, *Vol. 16, No. 3, Fall, 1983, p. 26.*

The justified fears that are likely to be raised by the dangers of venomous snakes are neither balanced by appreciative insights into the beauty of their intricate solutions to nature's challenges for survival nor into their role in nature's balance. In addition, the danger of snakebite is not placed in the perspective of other dangers we face in life. Although the black-and-white photographs of snakes and snake skulls are generally of high quality and include some good closeups, nearly all are taken from zoos, and the coral snake pictured looks diseased.

> *Wade C. Sherbrooke, in a review of "Killer Snakes," in* Science Books & Films, *Vol. 19, No. 2, November-December, 1983, p. 97.*

KILLER FISH (1982)

Killer Fish is an interesting book with an unfortunate title—*Dangerous Sea Creatures* would be better. The text describes animals that bite, sting, shock, or grab. Diverse creatures such as sharks, sting rays, stone fish, electric eels, octopuses, and jellyfish are presented. Coverage is brief. Although the text contains nothing new, it is well written. Freedman takes care to place appropriate, well-captioned photographs opposite the text about each type of animal. The book is thin and perhaps not much for the price, but young readers will find it interesting. **Killer Fish** is the type of book that is likely to be very popular in a public library.

> *David Feigenbaum, in a review of "Killer Fish," in* Science Books & Films, *Vol. 18, No. 3, January-February, 1983, p. 146.*

This will be a super resource for seven and eight year-olds who are just learning to write reports. After mastering the index, they will find the information pertinent to each creature all in one place and, except for sharks, never of more than one or two pages in length. Although brief, each section is precisely written and contains many facts for the beginning researcher. The black and white photographs are clearly labelled and close to the text which they illustrate.

While the subject matter is enticing, the author doesn't exaggerate the danger posed by most sea creatures, and explains at the start what causes some few of them to attack people. Then he groups them into four categories: the biters, the stingers, the shockers and the grabbers. While the last—octopuses, squids and jellyfishes—aren't fish at all, who would deny Mr. Freedman a title with the allure of **Killer Fish**? I would quibble, however, and point out that the jellyfish doesn't grab people anyhow. It stings 'em.

> *Lavinia C. Demos, in a review of "Killer Fish," in* Appraisal: Science Books for Young People, *Vol. 16, No. 1, Winter, 1983, p. 24.*

Well, it starts off on a weak note with, "The greatest fear of any swimmer or diver is to be grabbed by the jaws of a man-eating shark." It just isn't true. I'm a swimmer, and I have no fear of sharks at all. In the first place even if one did mysteriously get through the Mississippi and then the Missouri Rivers to come close to where I swim, I believe I would notice the darned thing before I got into the pool. Freedman's second sentence has the same sort of broad-based inconsistency, "Luckily, this does not happen often." Luck has nothing to do with my not being nabbed by a shark; it may be cowardice on my part, or even perhaps lack of opportunity, but I just don't happen to be where the sharks are.

"Greatest fear," "any swimmer," and "luckily" are words English teachers consistently mark with red pencil on freshman themes, and I believe this is the major flaw in the book— poor writing. I'm not sure that anyone needs yet another book on dangerous sea creatures, particularly one that deals with several animals superficially, but if they do, this one does have good black and white photographs and an index. It may be a good book for a browsing table, but I would look further for any serious look at these creatures.

> *Norma Bagnall, in a review of "Killer Fish," in* Appraisal: Science Books for Young People, *Vol. 16, No. 1, Winter, 1983, p. 25.*

DINOSAURS AND THEIR YOUNG (1983)

As the only title on this level to concentrate on dinosaur young, this is a good summary of the little that is known about the subject. Although several well-known fossil finds of dinosaur eggs are discussed, half of the book is devoted to a 1978 find of duck-billed dinosaur eggs and nests in Montana. Careful study of the various-sized skeletons at the site indicate that duck-billed dinosaurs cared for their young for many months after their hatching, unlike most modern reptiles. The almost obligatory chase scene involving a Tyrannosaurus Rex near the end of the book lends an air of drama to the hadrosaurs' otherwise peaceful life style. The text inaccurately states that modern reptiles lay hard-shelled eggs, as did the dinosaurs. It is true that some reptiles lay hard-shelled eggs; but others lay tough and leathery eggs. The eggs and young of several dinosaurs are compared in weight and size to their adult counterparts and a pronunciation guide for each name is included within the text. . . . Children will also enjoy Lambert's more general *Dinosaurs* as a follow-up depiction of the life styles of adult dinosaurs.

> *Ann G. Brouse, in a review of "Dinosaurs and Their Young," in* School Library Journal, *Vol. 30, No. 6, February, 1984, p. 58.*

This excellent book on dinosaurs is intended for young children. It is short, simple, direct, and easy to read, and the illustrations are superb. Most children already know that dinosaurs are huge beasts that lived long before humans appeared. Beginning at this point, Freedman tells the story of some recent, remarkable findings of baby dinosaur fossils. Implications drawn from the study are simply and accurately explained. Children, young people, and even adults will enjoy this book.

> *Marie M. Jenkins, in a review of "Dinosaurs and Their Young," in* Science Books & Films, *Vol. 20, No. 1, September-October, 1984, p. 33.*

RATTLESNAKES (1984)

In addition to a discussion of rattlesnake behavior and life cycle, Freedman includes information on different kinds of rattlers as well as safety advice when walking through areas inhabited by these poisonous snakes. A wide selection of black-and-white photographs include some fascinating pictures of males performing their "combat dance" during mating season and of a rattler striking. There is also an appropriately grisly sequence showing how rattlesnakes kill and eat their prey. The writing is clear and never stilted, and the photographs are well-coordinated with the text. The brief index is preceded by descriptions of six common rattlesnakes. There are several good books about snakes available, especially poisonous ones. Seymor Simon's *Poisonous Snakes* and George S. Fichter's *Poisonous Snakes* provide information about rattlesnakes for the same age group. However, the Freedman book would still be an attractive, informative addition to a popular subject area. (pp. 73-4)

> *Cynthia M. Sturgis, in a review of "Rattlesnakes," in* School Library Journal, *Vol. 31, No. 5, January, 1985, pp. 73-4.*

Such a fascinating topic needs to be presented in an equally stimulating manner to children. Despite being well structured and clearly concise in style, the book does not achieve the fascination that such a topic merits.

Striking black-and-white photographs attract attention: eye to eye with a rattler! Although lacking the intensity of the cover, the photos are sharply focused and clearly defined. Close-up shots detail the forked tongue, dry rattle, needlelike fangs, and the high-speed strike sequence.

Alas—no color! The power of the book is greatly diminished; the reader misses the beauty of the natural coloration and confusion is created by conflicting shadow and ground configuration. With such remarkable photographs it seems somewhat disappointing that a traditional format has been adopted for this book.

Despite these drawbacks, the book may very well extend the appreciation of children for snakes. (pp. 424-25)

> *Ronald A. Jobe, in a review of "Rattlesnakes," in* Language Arts, *Vol. 62, No. 4, April, 1985, pp. 424-25.*

CHILDREN OF THE WILD WEST (1984)

A successor of sorts to ***Immigrant Kids***—but a less focused, more diffuse entity. The title, indeed, is something of a misnomer: though the period photographs that are the book's prime attraction frequently show frontier children, much of the volume has simply to do with the westward travel and settlement of which children were a part. On the other hand, the chapter on the lives of Indian children is really ethnography, except for mention of Indian boarding schools. Subsequent chapters—on frontier schools, on chores and paid employment (Nat Love and other black cowhands, Lotta Crabtree and other performers), on assorted diversions—are somewhat less fulfilling than reading Laura Ingalls Wilder. (They're also somewhat less frank: "Discipline . . . was not usually a serious problem for female teachers," we're told. "In those days they were respected because they were women.") As an account of frontier conditions, however, the text is as unromantic as the photos (e.g., "Accidents and disease killed far more emigrants than the Indians did"); and the endpaper photo alone—a multiethnic, multiracial crush of children in Central City, Colorado—will make the book memorable for some.

A review of "Children of the Wild West," in Kirkus Reviews, *Vol. LI, No. 21, November 1, 1983, p. J-195.*

Mr. Freedman's book follows the fortunes of . . . resilient children of the West from the first wagon trains of the 1840's to the turn of the century, when the Indian wars were over and store-bought toys, the circus and other civilizing influences arrived to mitigate the harshness of their young lives.

As the contemporary photographs in this attractive book indicate, the children of the Old West had the infinite adaptability of children everywhere. They sit in front of their sod houses with the empty prairie all around them, clearly at ease in their everyday world of fantastic dangers and hardships.

Mr. Freedman has given space not only to the settlers but to the people they usurped. His chapter on Indian children would be more interesting if it were not quite so relentlessly elegiac. We are told, for instance, that the Indians were appalled by white hunters' wholesale slaughter of the buffalo because this "sacred animal . . . was to be killed only as needed, to be worshiped before every hunt, to be praised and thanked for its many gifts." This is true, but it's also true that to get hold of the three or four buffalo carcasses they could carry away, Indians drove whole herds over cliffs. The stark record of the white conquest of the continent is eloquent enough not to need sentimental embellishment.

For the most part, though, this engaging book tells the story of Western children through a clearly written text and 61 well-chosen photographs. And since the story of children is inevitably the story of the civilization in which they live, the book also serves as a good introduction for young readers to the patterns of life in a Wild West that had nothing at all to do with gambling halls and shootouts.

Richard Snow, "Prairie Smarts," in The New York Times Book Review, *November 13, 1983, p. 52.*

With the same outstanding quality that characterized his ***Immigrant Kids,*** Freedman has written a memorable book that is notable both for its subject and for its use of exquisite documentary photographs. ***Children of the Wild West*** presents a significant overview of what children of pioneer families experienced as they traveled west in a wagon train. This is a west that is not glamorous, a fact made clear by the photographs throughout the book. Yet, Freedman explores all aspects of daily life in a way that is refreshing in its honesty. Stories about school days, Indian raids, the American Indian, holidays and life on the wagon train are included. The format is inviting, the text memorable and the captioned photographs, which are of especially good quality, stunning in their matter-of-fact nature. The combination is a fascinating look at our past that vividly makes that past meaningful. Though suitable for third through sixth graders, younger children would enjoy the photographs and teachers might glean materials for units on the west, pioneer life and Indians. There are many fine books available on the west and frontier life, among them Laycock's *How the Settlers Lived.* Freedman's book is a splendid contribution to this subject area.

Elena C. Carvajal, in a review of "Children of the Wild West," in School Library Journal, *Vol. 30, No.*

5, January, 1984, p. 75.

COWBOYS OF THE WILD WEST (1985)

Large type; clear, historic black-and-white photographs and no-nonsense but readable writing give this volume style, punch and character. Basic information is sufficient to satisfy casual readers as well as school researchers, and the good bibliography could lead one to more extensive, adult literature, such as William W. Savage, Jr.'s *Cowboy Life: Reconstructing an American Myth.* The genuine vividness of some of the illustrations may escape readers unfamiliar with the terrain and working conditions of the cowboy; however, such pictures can be read at several levels, and primary impact is satisfying. Certainly a book to linger over and to turn to again and again. (pp. 99-100)

George Gleason, in a review of "Cowboys of the Wild West," in School Library Journal, *Vol. 32, No. 4, December, 1985, pp. 99-100.*

Russell Freedman has prepared an interesting look at a perennially popular topic. . . . The text is arranged by subject—"Cowboy Clothes and Equipment" and "Up the Trail," for instance—rather than chronologically. The photographs are a combination of historic and modern ones, but in each case they are used sparingly and appropriately to clarify and add depth to the text. This book is not as specific as *Cowboys and Cattle Country* (American Heritage) or *Once in the Saddle* by Laurence Seidman and is written for a younger reader than are those books. It is most similar in style and readability to *The Cowboy Trade* by Glen Rounds. Freedman says, "Like all legends, this one [the American Cowboy] was a complex mixture of fact and fancy." The author does a fine job of presenting us with information without belittling the real place the cowboy has in both history and fiction. Bibliography and index. (pp. 220-21)

Elizabeth S. Watson, in a review of "Cowboys of the Wild West," in The Horn Book Magazine, *Vol. LXII, No. 2, March-April, 1986, pp. 220-21.*

Ordinarily, *WAL* does not review children's books. We are making an exception for ***Cowboys of the Wild West*** because Russell Freedman has attempted what few authors of children's literature attempt: to counteract rather than perpetuate a stereotype. He does not do so, however, with the intent of stomping on a cherished myth, gleefully exposing childhood heroes as frauds. Instead, he simply explains the development of the American cattle industry, from the "barefoot Indian cow herders called *vaqueros*" to "the last herd . . . driven north to Kansas in 1896." Throughout the narrative, Freedman compares the "real" cowboy to his Hollywood counterpart. He says, for instance, "Today, in movies and TV shows about the Old West, cowboys are usually white. In real life, they were often black or Mexican." The photographs which supplement the text back up his words, revealing cowboys of various shapes, sizes, ages, and races. Children who read this book will learn that not all cowboys were handsome, clean-shaven white men with six-shooters permanently attached to their hips. Freedman includes quotes from the memoirs of cowboys who actually rode the range, like Teddy Blue Abbot, Charles Siringo, and Andy Adams, to further prove his point. Abbott, for instance, is quoted as saying he "never . . . saw a cowboy with two guns." Another Texas cowboy reveals he "always took plenty of novels . . . and usually a cat" when he went out to work on the winter range.

Freedman dispels a lot of the glamour surrounding the image of the American cowboy, but he does so gently, in the manner of one who was himself brought up believing the cowboy was a "fellow who says 'yup' and 'nope,' who never complains, who shoots straight, and whose horse comes when he whistles." By portraying a more accurate and complete picture of cowboy life, Freedman is telling children that cowboys were heroes enough as they were—without the embellishments others later deemed it necessary to add to their image. (pp. 172-73)

> *Charlotte M. Wright, in a review of "Cowboys of the Wild West," in* Western American Literature, *Vol. XXII, No. 2, Summer, 1987, pp. 172-73.*

SHARKS (1985)

This brief but nicely organized book discusses the physical characteristics of several kinds of sharks, their behavior and uses to man. The numerous black-and-white photographs are well coordinated with the text. The writing is lucid and succinct; most unfamiliar terms are explained. Freedman uses some interesting analogies to better illustrate facts about sharks. For example, the whale shark may reach 60 feet in length—almost the length of a bowling alley. There is enough astounding, grisly information here to satisfy the voracious curiosity of youngsters fascinated by these creatures. Although nothing new is offered, **Sharks** will make a useful, entertaining addition to an already large array of shark books.

> *Cynthia M. Sturgis, in a review of "Sharks," in* School Library Journal, *Vol. 32, No. 5, January, 1986, p. 56.*

[The author] has completed an entire absorbing volume on "one of nature's most perfect designs." Information—some of it quite startling about the physical characteristics, locomotion, reproduction, and, of course, feeding habits of sharks—is clearly set forth. In its straightforward presentation of facts, however, the writing also conveys a subtle but perceptible sense of drama—just enough to slide readers to the edge of their chairs: for example, once a shark picks up the scent, "it swims toward the source like a guided missile"; and "they hug the shore, prowling for food in shallow water where they may meet swimmers." The author quickly points out, however, that only less than a dozen members of the shark family actually pose a threat to people. Although other books, such as Rhoda Blumberg's **Sharks,** for a slightly older audience, also give the fish substantial coverage, Freedman's work is distinctive for its readability and for its visual appeal. A generous number of clearly focused photographs show not only many species but also some excellent close-ups of the shark's jaw and saw-edged teeth and a few scenes of the fish attacking and gulping down their dinner. (pp. 69-70)

> *Karen Jameyson, in a review of "Sharks," in* The Horn Book Magazine, *Vol. LXII, No. 1, January-February, 1986, pp. 69-70.*

A perennially favorite subject gets solid, selective treatment here as Freedman covers general characteristics of the shark family, plus specifics of its 350 members that read like Ripley's believe-it-or-not. There's certainly no need to sensationalize such interesting material, and the text never does. From the basic mechanism of a shark's moving teeth to a listing of stomach contents documented from several catches, this gives a careful picture of one of the best adapted creatures in the aquatic environment. The style is smooth ("This shark is doing what a shark does best"), the coverage well considered, and the black-and-white photographs clearly composed for added information.

> *A review of "Sharks," in* Bulletin of the Center for Children's Books, *Vol. 39, No. 6, February, 1986, p. 106.*

INDIAN CHIEFS (1987)

In this remarkable book, six Plains and Northwest chiefs from tribes swept by the tide of white expansion are profiled. The humanity, courage, compassion and steel resolve of these dignified, resourceful leaders make a strong impact. With a true biographer's dispassion, Freedman simply tells what happened, what was said, and what effects actions had. He does not condemn the cavalry, for example, for the massacre at Wounded Knee Creek, but merely gives the facts. In these stories, though, the facts are enough to elicit strong compassion for the Indians. . . .

Each of these powerful biographies can stand alone (in fact, some material is repeated in the parallel stories of Red Cloud and Sitting Bull), but the cumulative effect is staggering. Remarkable photographs from many collections on the American West, including the Smithsonian's glowing portrait photographs of the chiefs, illustrate the times and events. Bibliography, index, and photo credits are included.

> *A review of "Indian Chiefs," in* Kirkus Reviews, *Vol. LV, No. 8, April 15, 1987, p. 636.*

These six biographical essays on Red Cloud, Satanta, Quanah Parker, Washakie, Joseph, and Sitting Bull form a gripping historical portrayal of Native American resistance to whites' taking their western lands. The story is a tragic one, and this is a moving account. Yet it also shows glimpses of the humor with which the Indians sometimes lightened their own load. The Nez Perce, for instance, while fleeing from the army in 1877, "paced themselves to stay two days ahead of Howard. They began to call him 'General Day-After-Tomorrow.' " Freedman has selected leaders who showed superlative courage and wisdom in the face of a doom that most of them foresaw as inevitable. Without becoming repetitive, he gives a sense of the trail of broken treaties, encroachments, and reprisals that ended an ancient way of life. The perspective in the first and last chapters, framed by Sitting Bull's inauguration as Sioux chief in the 1860s and his murder two weeks before the Wounded Knee Massacre in 1890, gives readers a general context from which the individual stories will emerge to make an unforgettable impression. The writing, selection of historical photographs, bookmaking, and subject combine to make this an exceptional piece of nonfiction. A bibliography, index, and list of photographic sources conclude the book.

> *Betsy Hearne, in a review of "Indian Chiefs," in* Bulletin of the Center for Children's Books, *Vol. 40, No. 9, May, 1987, p. 167.*

Written in the fluent and engaging style that we've come to expect from Russell Freedman, the book chronicles the lives of six renowned Indian chiefs, each of whom served as a leader during a critical period in his tribe's history. . . . The text relates information about the lives of each chief and aspects of Indian/white relationships that illuminate his actions. Interesting vignettes and quotations are well integrated into the narrative as are dramatic accounts of battles. While the tone of the text is nonjudgmental, an underlying sympathy for the Indians' situation is apparent. The illustrations and photographs and an especially clear map [by Leonard Everett Fisher] augment the text well and add to the overall appeal of the book. The volume will be welcomed equally by readers interested in development in the West and those eager to learn more about great leaders of the Indian people. Bibliography and index. (pp. 482-83)

> *Elizabeth S. Watson, in a review of "Indian Chiefs,"*
> *in* The Horn Book Magazine, *Vol. LXIII, No. 4,*
> *July-August, 1987, pp. 482-83.*

LINCOLN: A PHOTOBIOGRAPHY (1987)

AUTHOR'S COMMENTARY

[The following excerpt is from Freedman's Newbery Medal acceptance speech in 1988.]

My father was a great storyteller. The problem was, we never knew for sure whether the stories he told were fiction or nonfiction. He was also a dedicated bookman. In fact, my parents met in a bookshop. She was a sales clerk, and he was a sales representative for Macmillan. They held their first conversation over a stack of bestsellers, and before they knew it, they were married. I had the good fortune to grow up in a house filled with books and book talk.

As a young man, I worked as a journalist and later a television publicity writer before discovering my true vocation. One day I happened to read a newspaper article about a sixteen-year-old boy who was blind; he had invented a Braille typewriter. That seemed remarkable, but as I read on, I learned something even more amazing: the Braille system itself, as used today all over the world, was invented by another sixteen-year-old boy who was blind, Louis Braille. That newspaper article inspired my first book, a collection of biographies called *Teenagers Who Made History.*

I hadn't expected to become a writer of nonfiction books for children, but there I was. I had wandered into the field by chance, and I felt right at home. I couldn't wait to get started on my next book. As Sid Fleischman said in his acceptance speech last year, "It was as if I had found myself—and I didn't even know I had been lost."

That was during the early sixties. Since then, children's nonfiction has changed significantly in form and content. Consider biography. Until recently, children's biographies tended to be heavily fictionalized, dressed up with imaginary scenes and manufactured dialogue—as in " 'Drink your tea, Eleanor,' " said Franklin." There's an old tradition for this. In the United States, fictionalized biography has been a publishing staple ever since the Reverend Mason Locke Weems made up the cherry tree anecdote and inserted it into his *Life of George Washington.* The fifth edition of Weems's biography appeared in 1806; there we find the earliest known version of little George's immortal confession: "Father, I cannot tell a lie." (pp. 446-47)

I grew up during the cherry-tree era of children's biography.

Recently I looked again at a Lincoln biography I read as a boy; it contains my favorite example of invented dialogue. Abe is eleven years old in this scene, and his father is bawling him out: " 'Books!' said his father. 'Always books! What is all this studying going to do for you? What do you think you are going to be?' 'Why,' said Abe, 'I'm going to be President.' "

I read that book as an elementary school student in San Francisco. Apparently the lessons of Lincoln's virtues were lost on me, for I was always being summoned to the principal's office. From the school corridor I would enter a small waiting room, and from there a door with a frosted glass pane led into Mrs. Koeppe's inner sanctum.

I would sit on the wooden bench in that waiting room—waiting for the ghostly form of Mrs. Koeppe to appear behind the frosted glass as she rose to open the door and say, "Come in, Russell." On the waiting room wall hung a pendulum clock, tick-tick-ticking off the seconds as I waited. And looking down at me from an adjacent wall was the bearded visage of Abraham Lincoln. George Washington may have been the father of our country, but Lincoln was the one who always knew when I was in trouble.

His picture reminded me that in America a boy could travel from a log cabin to the White House. Or rather, a good boy could. And from what I had read, young Abe was definitely a good boy. He was never late to school, and he always kept his clothes clean. As a young man working in a general store, he was so honest that he walked, or maybe ran, miles through drifting snow to return two cents change to a forgetful customer. Honest Abe—always fair in games and work, always kind to man and beast. That's the Lincoln I grew up with, a first cousin to Goody Two-shoes. (p. 448)

If there was a man behind the Lincoln myth, I knew little about him. It wasn't until years later that a passing remark in a piece by Mary McCarthy ignited my interest in Lincoln. Mary McCarthy, hardly a sentimentalist, said that she was fascinated by Lincoln's intellect and melancholy. Melancholy? That was my first inkling that a complex and paradoxical man—a believable human being—was concealed behind the layers of historical make-up. After that, Lincoln intrigued me, and when Clarion Books suggested that I write a presidential biography, Lincoln was my first and immediate choice.

One of the great joys of writing nonfiction for youngsters is the opportunity to explore almost any subject that excites your interest. I picked Lincoln as a subject because I felt I could offer a fresh perspective for today's generation of young readers, but mostly I picked him because I wanted to satisfy my own itch to know.

Approaching a biography of Lincoln is daunting. There have been more books written about him that any other American—thousands of titles covering every imaginable aspect of his life and career. Luckily, a friend told me about the Abraham Lincoln Bookshop in Chicago, so I made a beeline to that shop. I introduced myself to Daniel Weinberg, the proprietor, and told him what I was planning to do. Dan Weinberg saved me. He helped me chart my course through the Lincoln literature and decide which books to focus on. If it weren't for him, I'd probably still be researching Lincoln. My book wouldn't be finished today.

Along with my reading, I had a chance to enjoy the pleasures of eyewitness research. I visited Lincoln's log-cabin birthplace in Kentucky, his boyhood home in Indiana, and the reconstructed village of New Salem, Illinois, where he lived as a young man. I went to Springfield, with its wealth of Lincoln historical sites, and to Washington, D.C., for a firsthand look at Ford's Theatre and the rooming house across the street where the assassinated president died.

There's something magic about being able to lay your eyes on the real thing—something you can't get from your reading alone. As I sat at my desk in New York City and described Lincoln's arrival in New Salem at the age of twenty-two, I could picture the scene in my mind's eye, because I had walked down those same dusty lanes, where cattle still graze behind split-rail fences and geese flap about underfoot. When I wrote about Lincoln's morning walk from his house to his law office in downtown Springfield, I knew the route because I had walked it myself.

I'll never forget my visit to the Illinois State Historical Library in Springfield. One afternoon while I was working there, Tom Schwartz, the curator of the Lincoln Collection, came over and asked, "How would you like to see the vault?" I followed him through narrow aisles past crammed library shelves to an impressive bank vault. He twirled the big combination lock, swung open the heavy door, and invited me to step inside. It was cool and still in there, with temperature and humidity precisely regulated. Tom began to show me original documents written in Lincoln's own hand—a letter to his wife, a draft of a speech, scraps of paper with doodles and notes scrawled during long-ago trials in country courthouses. Each document had been treated with a special preservative that removed all traces of acid from the paper. Tom Schwartz pointed to one of Lincoln's courtroom notes and told me, "This will last a thousand years."

I didn't actually learn anything new in that vault or see anything that wasn't available in facsimile. And yet looking at those original documents, I could feel Lincoln's presence as never before, almost as though he had reached out to shake hands.

The more I learned about him, the more I came to appreciate his subtleties and complexities. The man himself turned out to be vastly more interesting than the myth. Of course, I was never able to understand him completely. I doubt if it's possible to understand anyone fully, and Lincoln was harder to figure out than most people, "the most secretive—reticent—shutmouthed man that ever lived," according to his law partner, William Herndon, who knew him as well as anyone. That's something I wanted to get across to my readers—a sense of the mysteries of personality, the fascinating inconsistencies of character.

I was never tempted to write an idealized, hero-worshiping account. A knowledge of Lincoln's weaknesses throws his strengths, and his greatness, into sharper relief. And it certainly wasn't necessary to embellish the events of his life with imaginary scenes and dialogue. Lincoln didn't need a speech writer in his own time, and he doesn't need one now. (pp. 448-50)

I've been asked, "How long did it take to write your Lincoln biography?" Well, **Lincoln** was my thirty-fourth book, so let's say it took thirty-three books to write it. And it took the help and support of a great many people. . . .

The poet John Keats once said: "A life of any worth is a con-

tinual allegory." Maybe that's why I started with a book of biographical sketches and, after some byways, was drawn back to biography, to Lincoln. Perhaps, after all, it is that sense of worth, that allegorical illumination, that both fiction and nonfiction are after. And I take your support to be the recognition of that secret yearning in us all. (p. 451)

Russell Freedman, "Newbery Medal Acceptance," in The Horn Book Magazine, *Vol. LXIV, No. 4, July-August, 1988, pp. 444-51.*

Few, if any, of the many books written for children about Lincoln can compare with Freedman's contribution. More than 80 photographs and prints illustrate the crisp and informative text. The pictures have been well-placed to coordinate with the text; captions have been written with care as well. While many of the photographs are well-known, many less familiar pictures are also included. Freedman begins by contrasting the Lincoln of legend to the Lincoln of fact. His childhood, self-education, early business ventures, and entry into politics comprise the first half of the book, with the rest of the text covering his presidency and assassination. Freedman's extensive research is apparent in the liberal use he makes of quotations from original sources (letters, contemporary newspaper articles, etc.). Freedman makes clear the controversy and vilification that Lincoln engendered and endured during his presidency. A listing of historic sites open to the public and a sampler of wise and witty excerpts from Lincoln's writings complete the book. Well-organized and well-written, this is an outstanding example of what (juvenile) biography can be. Like Lincoln himself, it stands head and shoulders above its competition. (pp. 93-4)

Elaine Fort Weischedel, in a review of "Lincoln: A Photobiography," in School Library Journal, *Vol. 34, No. 4, December, 1987, pp. 93-4.*

Relying on the recent scholarly biographies that have argued that many famous Abraham Lincoln stories are myths, Freedman carefully introduces a more realistic portrait than is usually found in juvenile biographies. The well-loved tales of Abe (a nickname he hated) courting Anne Rutledge, splitting rails in New Salem, or walking miles to obtain books are put into perspective with a few sentences. Lincoln comes alive as a conscientious lawyer who put clients at ease with stories but was a hopeless slob with files and papers. Freedman also offers a concise but excellent picture of Lincoln's struggle with the ethics and the politics of slavery, as well as his frustrating search for the right general to lead the Union troops.

The 90 black-and-white photographs are highlighted by fine book design and by Freedman's comments about the nature of photography in the mid-1800's. While the photographs contribute much, it is Freedman's talent for putting the right details in uncomplicated prose that provides a very sharp focus for this Lincoln portrait. Appendixes include Lincoln quotes from 1832-1865, a description of Lincoln sites, notes on materials consulted, and an index. This is a necessary purchase for all collections—and an opportunity for librarians to scrutinize earlier biographies on Lincoln that have long occupied their shelves.

A review of "Lincoln: A Photobiography," in Kirkus Reviews, *Vol. LV, No. 23, December 1, 1987, p. 1674.*

In a calm, unemotional style Freedman seeks to dispense

with the romanticized folk-hero imagery and misconceptions; for example, he notes that the long "freeze" exposure photography process of the time, which resulted in stiff and formal poses, never did justice to the real Lincoln. The author points out that while Lincoln was witty and talkative in company he rarely betrayed his inner feelings and was never fully understood by even his closest friends. Freedman traces Lincoln's early years and study of law and comments on his fierce ambition to rise above his log-cabin origins. The harsh emotional pain, melancholy, and depression endured by Lincoln and his wife Mary throughout their lives are also made clear. The antidote Lincoln so frequently used—his wit and rollicking humor—is seen in sharp contrast, making the accomplishments of this complex man all the more awe-inspiring. Following the account of the presidential/war years and assassination, Freedman includes a sampler of quotations from Lincoln's writings and speeches and a listing of historic sites. This eminently well-researched photo biography is outstanding; the man, his times, and his contemporaries are compellingly portrayed. (p. 706)

> *Phillis Wilson, in a review of "Lincoln: A Photobiography," in* Booklist, *Vol. 84, No. 8, December 15, 1987, pp. 705-06.*

In **Lincoln: A Photobiography,** Russell Freedman has succeeded in writing a well-balanced book—no small achievement, considering that some modern historians are still coming up with new visions and revisions about the 16th President's political and personal motives. Indeed, several revisionist academics have advanced the incredible theory that Lincoln really wanted the Civil War, with its 600,000 casualties, in order to eclipse the Founding Fathers and insure his own place in the pantheon of great Presidents. . . .

[Mr. Freedman] has done his research, visiting the Lincoln sites in Illinois and elsewhere as well as some of the Civil War battlefields. Apparently he has also immersed himself in the literature by and about the President. The author has faced the problem of any children's book writer who deals with a complex subject—do you talk up or down?—by choosing to trust in the intelligence of the youthful reader.

For example, on the central question of Lincoln's attitude toward slavery, he begins long before the Emancipation Proclamation. As a 28-year-old Illinois state legislator, Lincoln recorded his belief that slavery was "founded on both injustice and bad policy." As a Congressman 10 years later, he voted to stop the spread of slavery and introduced a bill to outlaw slavery in Washington. Again, 10 years later, Lincoln kindled those ideas and made them glow brightly during his seven debates with Senator Stephen A. Douglas.

Lincoln's arguments were made on moral as well as legal grounds, and they are spelled out and recalled by the author. . . .

Here and there, Mr. Freedman omits some needed perspective for his modern young readers of all races. In 1858, Lincoln spoke incendiary words during the debates; today, after civil rights legislation that took another century to pass, and judicial decisions upholding desegregation, the words seem relatively mild. But the author has to be praised for avoiding a number of pitfalls: he has not made too much of the Ann Rutledge legend that she was Lincoln's one true love; he has not turned Mary Lincoln into a monster, although conceding that the marriage had its difficulties; he has given Lincoln credit for being an intelligent lawyer instead of a country bumpkin; and he has not built up the assassination into some kind of national plot.

There is useful material at the end of this well-designed photobiography, including a sampler of Lincoln's language, a list of places to visit, such as the reconstructed village of New Salem, Ill., and a small (though inadequate) list of books about Lincoln for further reading.

> *Herbert Mitgang, in a review of "Lincoln," in* The New York Times Book Review, *January 24, 1988, p. 37.*

In some respects the title of this finely rendered account is misleading; the handsome photographs illuminate the text, but the book is far more than a photographic account. Used generously but judiciously, the pictures have been selected from the archival collections of several libraries, museums, and historical societies. There are numerous photographs and drawings of Lincoln, political friends and foes, family members, and notable documents and the expected scenes of presidential events, the Civil War, the assassination, and funeral processions. The compact and cohesive narrative is a chronological examination of the times and the life, personal characteristics, and career of Lincoln, with a major portion of the book devoted to the shifting political complexities engendered by slavery in the 1840s and 1850s and the dismal events of the resulting war in the divided nation. Freedman's intent is to move beyond the simple folk hero to the human dimensions of the Lincoln so much admired today and so strongly criticized in his own time. The author represents Abraham Lincoln as somewhat enigmatic and as a man of contrasts; he is humble but ambitious and even wealthy, humorous but melancholy, unpolished in manner but highly intelligent. Above all, he is seen as a man of great integrity, gradually acquiring a willingness to speak out against slavery, deeply pained by the human loss and suffering of the war, chagrined at the delays and reluctance of his generals, and ever steadfast in his commitment to a united country.

> *Margaret A. Bush, in a review of "Lincoln: A Photobiography," in* The Horn Book Magazine, *Vol. LXIV, No. 2, March-April, 1988, p. 222.*

Alan Garner

1934-

English author of fiction and picture books, playwright, reteller, and editor.

Recognized as a brilliant and original writer of modern myths who has created several works for children and young adults which have achieved classic status, Garner takes elements from legend, history, and folklore and transforms them into a world view which reflects his respect for the past and his belief in its importance to modern life. His powerful works demonstrate the enduring vitality of the themes of ancient myths. Using contemporary situations to give emphasis to these themes, which he feels endlessly repeat through time, Garner is praised for displaying an intensity and immediacy which captures the interest of middle school and high school readers. Although he has retold several volumes of British folk and fairy tales which recreate their oral tradition and has written picture books drawing on these same traditions as well as a nativity play and four unconventional stories for younger children about the continuity of life, Garner is perhaps best known as the author of innovative fantasies which contain intricacies beyond the basic confrontation between good and evil on which they are based. While his earliest books were tales of adventure in which average young protagonists were confronted by imposing powers of malevolence, many of Garner's later books are emotion-laden modern dramas in which young people struggle against formidable forces of the past along with their own tempestous sexuality and self-doubts. In his award-winning novel *The Owl Service* (1967), for example, Garner portrays three impressionable young adults as they involuntarily act out the mythical tragic love triangle of a Welsh tale from *The Mabinogion;* through the reverberations of the past, lives in the present are changed immeasurably.

Although he is lauded for his creation of atmosphere and place as well as for his polished style, Garner is considered one of England's most controversial children's writers. Due to the profundity of his themes, his excision of beneficial explanatory material, and his exploration of languages and dialects, critics question whether many of his works are truly appropriate for, and meaningful to, school-age readers. His experimental novel *Red Shift* (1973), for example, which is set in three centuries and written almost entirely in dialogue, is considered one of the most difficult books ever written for young people. Garner's works address such themes as jealousy, revenge, betrayal, and dislocation. In his "Stone Book Quartet," however, he seems to have reached some resolution with this latter issue. In these works—*The Stone Book* (1976), *Granny Reardun* (1977), *Tom Fobble's Day* (1977), and *The Aimer Gate* (1978)—Garner follows a family of Cheshire working-class people through several generations and eulogizes the artistry and emotional gratification of traditional craftsmanship. Many reviewers have lauded his success in expounding the unadulterated, impassioned mastery of craft unfamiliar to readers immersed in twentieth-century adulation of technology and mass production. Praised as a writer of both integrity and fervent iconoclasm, Garner is acknowledged for providing children's literature with works that are

challenging and stimulating for readers at many levels of experience. In 1965 *Elidor* was commended for the Carnegie Medal, an award Garner received in 1967 for *The Owl Service.* The latter work was also given the Guardian Award in 1968. *The Weirdstone of Brisingamen* received the Lewis Carroll Shelf Award in 1970. In 1978 Garner was selected as a highly commended author by the Hans Christian Andersen Awards committee of the Board on Books for Young People (IBBY).

(See also *Contemporary Literary Criticism,* Vol. 17; *Something about the Author,* Vol. 18; *Contemporary Authors New Revision Series,* Vol. 15; and *Contemporary Authors,* Vol. 73-76.)

GENERAL COMMENTARY

With his latest novel, **The Owl Service,** Alan Garner has moved away from the world of children's books and has emerged as a writer unconfined by reference to age-groups; a writer whose imaginative vein is rich enough to reward his readers on several different levels, whether they are old or young. This is a novel of love and of jealousy, that destructive and not often explored ingredient of human nature. The word "love" is never mentioned in the book. The primitive power of jealousy is given a dimension of poetry through the grafting of the story upon the Celtic myth of Blodeuwedd, the flower goddess. . . .

In the remote Welsh valley that is the setting for the novel, the legend of Blodeuwedd is commemorated by the pierced Stone of Gronw. The tale in its essentials has been reenacted some years before in the lives of Huw, Nancy and her dead lover. When an English family take over the house where Huw and Nancy are employed as servants, it is a younger generation who must live through the ancient drama: Alison, her stepbrother Roger, and Nancy's son, Gwyn. . . .

This is not a story which "uses" supernatural aids to induce effects of brooding uneasiness and fear. The forces that linger in the valley could be said to "use" the protagonists of the story, and, as in Mr. Garner's other books, it is the girl through whom the ancient powers work; it is she who must endure the uncomprehended terror, must relive and exorcize the pain. . . .

The book is a complex of attractions and hostilities between persons, classes, myth and modern day reality. In the end, it is to Roger that Alison turns, and by a subtle reference to, almost a summoning of, Blodeuwedd's original conception as a flower goddess, the destructive owl-power is exorcized. Sceptical, joking, normal Roger restores Alison to herself, "and the room was full of petals from skylight to rafters". And Gwyn? He is not simply an impersonation of Gronw, the lover who must die. The drama can never be exactly repeated and in Gwyn it enters a new phase. Like his Celtic forebear, the Blessed Bran, Gwyn could claim with truth: "He who is chief let him be a bridge. I will myself be the bridge." Alison may be the medium for the old powers, but it is Gwyn, the "educated peasant" as Roger rather cruelly calls him, who is the bridge to a synthesis of the old and the new.

What gives this book an added tension is the sense of inevitability—centuries ago it would have been called fate—that broods over the valley and its people. Mr. Garner may write in terms of Blodeuwedd's power and its supernatural manifestations in the scratch of owls' claws, the scent of meadowsweet hanging in the air near the stone where Gronw died, and other palpable evidences of the secret powers that Huw and Nancy recognize, but what is clearly implicit in the story is that these are forces that we must admit and accept *in ourselves*. The legend and Alan Garner's use of it cannot be regarded as beautiful myth-making except by those who do not recognize that poetry is truth and often terrible.

To read this author's books straight through in their order of writing gives the reader a sense of the distances he has travelled. The first novel, *The Weirdstone of Brisingamen,* is somewhat overloaded with legend, congested names and cryptic allusions. Susan and Colin, the children who endure the hardships and rewards of their encounter with the world of Fundindelve, are themselves rather negative. They are people to whom things happen. They listen to the "folk-talk" of Cadellin the wizard, and the reader learns something of Celtic legend he may never have known, but he is not seriously involved except in the excitement of the adventures themselves. These are prolonged and sometimes contrived. The book seems an experiment in fear, and much of the mythical machinery must be regarded as trappings to produce an agreeable chilling of the blood.

In the sequel, *The Moon of Gomrath* it was clear that Mr. Garner had taken a step in a new direction. It is one of the rewarding things for a reviewer who is reading through a

writer's output chronologically, to find that each book contains the seeds of the next. Though Susan and Colin are at first the same rather drab, colourless children, the writing is wonderfully colourful and concentrated. The magic takes charge of the book and works *through* the characters rather than *at* them. Mr. Garner is moving towards the synthesis realized in *The Owl Service.* As though driven by the Wild Hunt, so splendidly described in its pages, the second half of *The Moon of Gomrath* moves into a new and urgent rhythm. Susan, hitherto unmemorable, becomes an interesting figure, one who looks forward to Helen and Alison in the two later books. Again, the old magic works most powerfully and disconcertingly through the distaff side. It is the girls who must bear the pains of involvement in powers beyond their comprehension, but it is also Susan and Helen who take the longest and most daring journeys into the interior, and upon whom is bestowed the gift of finding the wisdom of the heart, as opposed to that of the intellect, a wisdom that has always in mythology belonged to goddesses.

It seems hardly a coincidence that the street that leads to the land of Elidor should be called Thursday Street. Alan Garner is acutely aware that the old myths embody some permanent truths about human nature and about the workings of the imagination, but those who would find them must travel far. The age-old theme of the journey, often underground, plays a large part in his books. In this third novel, *Elidor,* four children explore the Manchester backstreets, and after finding themselves in a derelict area are swiftly drawn into another world. Roland throws a ball through the window of a partly demolished church and Helen—Burd Helen?—runs round the church widdershins, to disappear with her brothers into the land of Elidor. The words "Burd Helen" are deliberately queried, for it would reduce the authority of Mr. Garner's writing to derive it too closely from the legend of Childe Roland. In this novel, myth erupts far more violently into the present world. The unicorn thunders down the Manchester streets, a proud and terrible creature, pursued by ghostly knights.

In *Elidor* an attempt is made to explain some of the magic in scientific terms. The four treasures, the stone, sword, spear and cauldron, hidden by the children, give off static electricity. Far more disturbing and convincing, however, is the manifestation of powers that could be more readily translated into psychological rather than electrical terms. Mr. Garner is not postulating a world of abstract evil warring against good, nor has he in any book suggested that by reaching back for what we have so largely forgotten we shall find a lost paradise. He is too intelligent and unsentimental for this. "Do not let darkness into your minds", cries Malebron, the wizard-minstrel of Elidor. There emerges clearly the twin theme that while the primitive dark powers cannot be vanquished but only contained, there are also rich worlds upon which the mind can draw, beneficent forces which can be evoked, and which are in danger of being destroyed by modern ways of thinking and living: "Findhorn and the Song are forgotten".

Alan Garner is an uncompromising writer who demands much of his readers. Sometimes his elusiveness is a stumbling-block. A lack of any knowledge of the myths on which he draws—and they are often little-known ones—makes certain episodes and allusions hard to follow. Perhaps this induced him to put at the end of *The Moon of Gomrath* a somewhat grudging note on the sources of his material. On the other hand, Mr. Garner has some justification for refusing to enlighten us about what we really ought to know.

Now that one can look back over the four novels that Alan Garner has written in seven years, it is possible to see a pattern. *Elidor* is perhaps the most experimental, and like many experiments is not wholly successful, in spite of its undoubted originality and powerful style. *The Weirdstone of Brisingamen* occupies the least important part in the pattern, but its sequel, *The Moon of Gomrath,* carries undertones both splendid and sinister that sound even more surely and resonantly in *The Owl Service,* and make this latest novel an augury for a brilliant future.

"Alan Garner: Thursday's Child Has Far to Go," in The Times Literary Supplement, *No. 3431, November 30, 1967, p. 1134.*

MARCUS CROUCH

Laughter is quiescent in Alan Garner's first book, *The Weirdstone of Brisingamen* [a] story devoted to the struggle with the forces of evil, here commanded by the Great Spirit of Darkness, Nastrond. This was a remarkable first book by a young writer but hardly a successful one. The narrative is confusing and confused, always whipping itself into a further frenzy of activity. The terms of reference are Norse rather than Celtic, and the Norse gods were always a complicated lot. There are some fine moments, mostly marred by a turgid style. Where the book excels is in the use of an actual landscape whose topography plays an essential part in the action and in relating the nightmares of the story to commonplace figures of the everyday world. . . . (p. 126)

This skill in harnessing the modern scene and its inhabitants was more marked in Garner's *Elidor* where the magic starts to work in Piccadilly, Manchester. It is not chance that when Roland spins the wheel which operates the index to a street plan it comes to rest at Thursday Street. For Thursday Street has disappeared into a heap of rubble in a slum-clearance scheme. And why is an old street Musician playing his fiddle among these inhospitable ruins? From this confusing scene, strange yet typical of a modern city, the Watson children are shot into 'a magic land and full of song' where Malebron of Elidor holds back the night. The children—it seems improbable—have been sent to 'bring back light to Elidor'. It is never quite clear why. As in the 'Narnia' stories, the weakness lies in casting such commonplace children as the agents of destiny.

The scenes in Elidor are unconvincing. The book picks up when the children return to their own world with their Treasures. In Elidor these were a spear, a golden stone, a sword and a chalice; back in Manchester they turn into a bit of iron railing, a stone from a demolished church, a wooden sword and a cracked cup, but they retain their magic potency. Much of the interest lies in Garner's use of technology, not to explain away but to make the magic credible. The Treasures, buried in the Watsons' back garden, ruin reception on television, start the family car, and make Mrs Watson's washing machine churn all night with the plug out. These are effective devices, but neither they nor the clear presentation of the Manchester and Cheshire scene and its inhabitants make the central theme sufficiently important to justify the book.

Garner reached maturity in *The Owl Service.* Here the real and the magical worlds are very close and there is no awkward transition between them. The characters, too, are ac-

ceptable, and their social problems in the everyday world are relevant to the main theme. (pp. 126-27)

The conflict in the nature of Blodeuwedd between flowers and owls, beauty and cruelty, is echoed in the storm which sweeps the valley at the climax of an extraordinary story.

Wisely, Garner does not make his theme explicit. The clues are scattered throughout the action but the reader is left to pick them up as he goes. What gives contemporary meaning to the ancient tale is that it is played out by modern people whose personal problems are curiously connected with the old drama. (pp. 127-28)

Garner draws a disturbing picture of a modern scene in which timeless forces are at work. (p. 128)

Marcus Crouch, "Magic Casements," in his The Nesbit Tradition: The Children's Novel in England 1945-1970, *Ernest Benn Limited, 1972, pp. 112-41.*

BRIAN ALDERSON

[Garner's earliest books, *The Weirdstone of Brisingamen* and *The Moon of Gomrath*] are direct, fast-moving, fairly conventional stories about baneful supernatural powers; but, with hindsight, one can see in them preoccupations which come to dominate his subsequent work. Indeed, one of the fascinating aspects of Alan Garner's development as a writer is the way in which each book seems to be a preparation for the one that is to follow.

The preoccupations now discernible in these early books may crudely be described as landscape and language. *The Weirdstone* is sub-titled "a tale of Alderley", and one of the distinguishing features of it and its companion volume was the immediacy with which they brought an actual location to life; then, despite the inexperience of the beginner craftsman, there was also in the writing of these books an urge towards exactness of expression, whether of description or of the conversation of Alderley farmers, wizards and shape-shifters.

As Alan Garner's work has progressed these characteristics can be seen more clearly as part of a profound concern for history.

It is not history in the schoolroom sense (although the Roman-British and Civil War scenes in *Red Shift* have more to contribute to such a thing than ever textbook did); and it is not "working-class" history in the tendentious modern interpretation of that term. It is history coming up through the bones of the land, or flowing through the rhythms of a sentence—casting the people of a locality, for good or ill, in the mould of their own landscape.

The Owl Service and *Red Shift,* despite moments of outstanding perception, were flawed in their construction—but, perhaps because of his work on two remarkable anthologies . . . : *The Book of Goblins* and *The Guizer,* Alan Garner has come to a richer sense of the part played by folk-lore in the texture of narratives. Since the publication of *The Guizer* in 1975 his art has reached new heights in the two short tales: *The Stone Book* and *Tom Fobble's Day.*

Like the best work of William Mayne these two books seem to lie beyond any making. They were just there, in some stratum of the Cheshire countryside, and Alan Garner, by a fortunate magic, has brought them to the light of day. They combine direct accessible accounts of child experience (Mary climbing ladders up St Philip's steeple in *The Stone Book*) with closely realized detail of one place at one time—so that when, at the end of **Tom Fobble's Day** he writes of young William sledging alone down a hill: "The line did hold. Through hand and eye, block, forge and loom to the hill and all that he owned . . . " Alan Garner encapsulates both the fact of a tale and the warrant for its telling. To the citizens of Chorley, and, indeed, of the British Isles, it will have a potency all its own.

Brian Alderson, "A Wizard in His Own Landscape,"
in The Times, <i>London, August 24, 1977, p. 16.</i>

BOB DIXON

The creation of other worlds . . . leads, naturally, to a preoccupation with landscape and terrain. . . . [This] is a natural development but in the case of Garner it's something more than this. All his work shows a strong, mystical sense of place. (p. 146)

Often, as in Garner and Le Guin, there's a strong sense of a vague, disembodied but menacing force which is just hovering around waiting to be loosed, a process which might be as accidental as springing a trap. This is very noticeable in Garner. In Le Guin, it's more a case of meddling with danger. Once loosed, the evil can take a variety of fantastic forms or can possess people. There are many cases of possession in these books. Sometimes the evil is seen to be innate, as in Adams and Lewis and then, of course, it's original sin. All the writers draw upon words denoting blackness or darkness to portray this evil and use 'white' and all kinds of words associated with whiteness or light to show the opposite. (pp. 146-47)

Another very striking feature of this group and one which links it strongly to the religious tradition in the past is class antagonism and manipulation. This is in its most obvious and usual form in Garner's **The Owl Service:** it's strange that very few people seem to have noticed that this book is riddled with anti-working-class feeling. (p. 147)

Garner resembles Tolkien in several ways, even in details sometimes as when his 'svarts', evil underground creatures, mostly black, recall the evil dark men called 'swertings' in *Lord of the Rings.* Both writers have specialist interests in language and they probably took the word from the Common Teutonic word for 'black' now only remembered in modern English, in the word 'swarthy'. It's a small point, but an insight into attitudes. What comes out very strongly, especially in Garner's first three books, **The Weirdstone of Brisingamen, The Moon of Gomrath** and **Elidor** is the overpowering sense of black evil. Towards the beginning of the second novel, we read that men have 'loosed the evil a second time', in a typical Garner expression. But what's it all for? What do the forces of evil want? What's the matter with them?—There aren't any answers to these questions. . . . The forces are just 'evil' and we have to take it at that. Even the power-crazed scientist of the comics, bent on world domination, is rather more understandable. Another question needs to be asked with this particular group of writers in mind. It's often said that children prefer a 'black and white' world, a world where heroes and villains, goodies and baddies are sharply distinguished one from another. I think it needs to be asked how much this is promoted by adults.

In Garner's later work, **The Owl Service** and **Red Shift,** two elements that were there but not very noticeable in the books already mentioned, come to the fore. In general, taking Garner's work as a whole, his characters grow in importance with each successive book although they never free themselves from the domination of place. However, as they grow in importance, social conflict grows, so that, because of Garner's class stance, in **The Owl Service** he foists upon the reader an ending which just doesn't seem to grow out of the rest of the book, at all. He gives us the unlikeable, selfish prig, Roger, as hero, and passes over Gwyn, who has been more attuned to the legendary background of the book all along. Garner has tried to pass over this class prejudice by saying that it's Gwyn's illegitimacy which makes him 'incapable of coping with the epic quality of the situation'. Thankfully, it's very much to be doubted whether anyone else will share such a weird and destructive view. The class prejudice, in fact, could be foreseen in **Elidor** where it was emphasised by [illustrator Charles] Keeping's crude drawings of Paddy, the Irishman. The other element which has now come to the fore in Garner's latest book, **Red Shift,** is perhaps more to the point in this chapter though not separable from Garner's attitudes as a whole. A rather doom-laden and pretentious manner could be seen as far back as **The Moon of Gomrath.** In **Red Shift** it has developed into a general atmosphere of hopelessness and degeneration which recalls William Golding, a writer Garner admires, at his worst. (pp. 149-50)

Bob Dixon, "The Supernatural: Religion, Magic
and Mystification," in his Catching Them Young:
Political Ideas in Children's Fiction, Vol. 2, Pluto
Press, 1977, pp. 120-64.

MARGARET MEEK

Ten years ago, in June 1968, Alan Garner wrote in this journal an article called **"A Bit More Practice".** Speaking of his readers he said:

> the age of the individual does not necessarily relate to the maturity. Therefore, in order to connect, the book must be written for all levels of experience. This means that any given piece of text must work at simple plot level, so that the reader feels compelled to turn the page, if only to find out what happens next; and it must also work for me, and for every stage between. . . . I try to write onions.

This last phrase is now well known and is sometimes used to explain the "difficulty" of the books. Garner does not acknowledge (did he really not know?) his link with Barthes in this image, but the clue for the reader is in the idea of layers, the interplay of surfaces and meanings in the text. Because so much of our and our children's reading of prose is for the retrieval of information, the grasp of a linear meaning, we forget that the young also need experience in this kind of competence once they can deal confidently with "what happens next". Garner's bond with his younger readers is to show them what fiction can do.

In his earlier books he often moved the emblems, mythologies, symbols and modes of writing just slightly out of the reach of his readers, hence the complaints about incomprehensibility. The allegoric fragments in **Elidor** are carried by the traditional shape of the plot, which the young reader recognizes. But in order to engage in the play of the text in **The Owl Service** the reader needs other expectations if he is not to be tantalized to exasperation. The narrator has disappeared, the reader is shown, not told. So in the opening sequence of **Red Shift,** the familiar tropes are missing. For those who can tolerate the uncertainty long enough to see fear in the handful of dust that Jan puts down Tom's shirt, and to hear overtones of *King Lear* in the opening conversation, it is a vertiginous experience. But it is opaque, boring, for the reader who, when presented with a picture of cosmic uncertainty, expects "once upon a time".

In the **"Stone Book Quartet"** the complications of showing-not-telling have been resolved with an artistry that is nothing short of breath-taking, a simplicity that engages everyone who can hear the voices of the characters on the page. The youngest readers (of nine or ten, I guess) may need the help of reading aloud and knowledge of the historical setting. That done, the episodes in each book stand out clear against the sky and the landscape of Garner's north-east Cheshire; a place where history is now and England. . . .

As the first movement, establishing the tonality and the themes, **The Stone Book** is still the most prodigious tour de force in Garner's writing. It is also the least elegiac. Robert's story continues in **Granny Reardun.** He is now old, building a wall with the reluctant help of his grandson Joseph, for whom stone means also the threatening weight of Robert's skill. . . . As "a granny reardun", Joseph has to make his own way with his own skill. His half-brother, Charlie, has to do the same. Charlie, a baby in Joseph's book, reappears in **The Aimer Gate,** with Joseph's son, young Robert. We are now at the time of Kaiser Bill's war. Joseph's great skill at the forge has been brought down to making horseshoes for army horses. The Allman in this story is Faddock, a legless Boer War veteran, who breaks up stones for roadmending. Robert's secret place is under the pinnacle of the chapel steeple. On the last day of Charlie's leave from the front, Robert climbs to the highest point and finds his name, left there by his great-grandfather, under the capstone. His father explains how the clock works, by "escapement", and wonders about Robert's future. "I don't know what there is for you to get aback of, youth." Charlie, who spends his day reaping the field where once the house was, polishing his rifle, says, "Get aback of me", as with a sniper's accuracy he shoots the rabbits cornered in the last standing corn. This is the most searing moment in all four books.

No more is heard of Robert, but Joseph and his grandson, another William, appear in **Tom Fobble's Day.** The time is the Second World War. Bombers are overhead on a starry night as William and Stewart Allman sledge down the familiar hill. It is Joseph's last day at the forge. With wood remaining from Old William's loom, the iron from Charlie's pram and the handle of the forge bellows, he makes for William a sledge that runs fast and true—the last of its kind and an epitome of skilled craftsmanship. In the talk that accompanies the work, Joseph, in the oral tradition of genealogy, tells William of his forebears. . . .

But even at the simplest plot reading there are resonances, themes, recapitulations and developments, perspectives and meanings conveyed by the text itself. The author is exploring at different levels, differentially focused, the significance for each character in his own time and in relation to past and future. Each time is crucial: Mary's, as the railways shorten distances and time; Charlie's, as men slaughter each other in wheatfields; William's, as the sledges fly like bombers. The way into this multi-consciousness is by means of the speech of the characters, a direct vernacular, with its own vocabulary and information. . . . Garner links the continuity of the oral tradition with the modulations of a classical style of great clarity. This counterpoint produces the reverbation of meanings. Without ever intruding as the omniscient narrator, he

shows that he is adopting a significant attitude to large problems that are social, moral and artistic.

For example, what Raymond Williams calls "the long revolution" is apparent throughout. For Garner it is the depreciation of human strength and skill, decline in the craftsmanship that comes from working elemental materials into artifacts of use and beauty. Mary's father makes stones into jewels. Joseph holds time in minute adjustments of a pendulum. Knowledge grows as strength increases in the smith's grip, and is measured in learning to hoist anvils and ladders. In writing about what, one guesses, has roots in his personal history, Garner makes us all re-create our own past. This gives the reader a freedom which extends beyond the text.

As the stories grow into one story, so one's awareness of the emblems and symbols deepens. Mary astride the weathercock is matched by Robert "wearing the steeple all the way to the earth". These unforgettable scenes act as metaphors which condense meaning into an image that defies linear description and resists explanation. Garner's quite definite moral and political stance is offered, not as a series of propositions, but as a pattern of images. Mary's father teaches her geology—a kind of reading that reveals creation beyond the prayer book. The church, "the prints of chisels in the sky", is both "Lord Stanley" and "only a bit of stone round a lot of air". Music and hymnody, cornet and ophicleide, soothe anger and pain and rejoice the heart, linking a variety of voices and languages to the cry of the summer fields that goes with cap waving. Mary swings aloft, Joseph declares himself, and Charlie sights his rifle at the rabbits in the cornfield. Then it is heard no more.

As we read, this use of metaphor, a characteristic of all Garner's writing, becomes clearer. Where once it was a stumbling block (at the end of **The Owl Service,** for example), now it has a diamond-like quality that makes us read his text as an exciting exploration of writing. He binds the reader to him and he shows us the author working with language to make his book as his characters worked with stone and iron. Not a word is wasted. As the reader sees the structure, the thematic unity, so it becomes impossible to say any more what the work is "about", because the story is also "about" the author's relation to what he has made and the reader's response to it. In this way the reading of the child who looks for "what happens next" is linked to interpretative reading of the most experienced adult.

In the **"Stone Book Quartet"** we have moved away from a kind of nineteenth-century writing which is still found in books for twentieth-century children. This is a book of our day, for all its Victorian and Edwardian settings. Its conventions and codes derive not from the time of the events, but from our world of television dialogue and the experimental forms of adult fiction. Only thus can books for children be genuinely continuous with adult literature, where the story is not delivered to the reader but is re-created by him. Garner, who has always written out of a deep realization of mythic re-creative force, now invites his readers to see themselves "at the intersection of the timeless with time". The experience of this kind of reading makes readers of passion and power. To match this experience with a comparable literary competence is the challenge to all writers.

Margaret Meek, "A View from the Steeple," in The Times Literary Supplement, No. 3991, September 29, 1978, p. 1081.

FRANK EYRE

Alan Garner's first book was *The Weirdstone of Brisinga-men.* In this and its sequel, *The Moon of Gomrath,* he made use of much of the material of earlier attempts at creating contemporary sagas and it seemed likely at first that he was planning a sustained series. These stories of the knights bound in sleep until they can be wakened to fight the forces of evil have moments of strength, but are marred by uncertainty in their organisation, roughness in the writing and a general sense of unsureness of touch. Although they were warmly received when they were first published they are clearly prentice work and the author abandoned this vein when he moved on to stronger work. He is at his best with the natural surroundings of the stories, which are set at Alderley Edge in Cheshire, and at his worst with the children, who are not fully realised and do not come alive.

The same defect is apparent in *Elidor,* an otherwise far better book. Four children in one of the poorer districts of Manchester explore a ruined church and suddenly find themselves not transported to, but living a parallel life in the terrifying land of Elidor. The two worlds overlap and the disturbing, at times frightening, fusion of this other world and the everyday world makes this a highly original book. . . . (pp. 143-44)

Elidor has been a much praised book and I am going against the weight of critical opinion in saying that to me it seems a contrived one. In an article in *The Times Literary Supplement* about his work, the author said of this book:

> For instance, in the third book, *Elidor,* I had to read extensively textbooks on physics; Celtic symbolism; archaeology; study the writings of Jung; brush up my Plato; visit Avebury, Silbury and Coventry Cathedral; spend a lot of time with demolition gangs on slum clearance sites; and listen to the whole of Britten's *War Requiem* nearly every day. A major block in the writing was resolved by seeing Robert Stephens' performance as Atahualpa in *The Royal Hunt of the Sun* at Chichester.

Such an approach may be admirable (the author goes on to admit that this is 'an absurd list' but clearly intends it to be taken seriously) but is not likely to produce enduring writing for children. When writers for children talk in this way of their work the suspicion is aroused that it is being written as much for adult critics to admire as for children to enjoy. An infinitely greater amount of knowledge and research lies behind *The Lord of the Rings,* but that was not research undertaken in order to write an impressive children's book. The writer already possessed the knowledge, it had become a natural part of his own culture, and its contribution to the book was no more and no less than that made by any other man's natural equipment.

It seems likely from statements that Garner has made about his writing that he works best when he can use a framework of this kind on which to build his stories—Leon Garfield has quoted him as saying that he 'uses fantasy as a crutch'. Whether or not this is so, his next, and best-known book, *The Owl Service,* is based on a story in the *Mabinogion,* about Lleu Llaw Gyffes and his wife, who was made for him out of flowers, but who destroyed him and was then herself turned into an owl. Garner has explained that he was fascinated by this story, and turned it over in his mind for some time, but could make nothing of it until he saw somewhere a dinner service with an elaborate pattern of flowers which the owner had touched up until the model of an owl appeared. The dinner service is used as a symbol of the legend, and plays an important if at times confusing part in the story, which is essentially a modern one of tension between youth and age, class and class, Welsh and English, with powerful forces of hatred and revenge, illegitimacy and adultery brooding over the protagonists. (pp. 144-45)

On a first reading, especially to a reader unfamiliar with the *Mabinogion,* much of [the plot] seems inflated and insincere, but on a second reading, with the symbolism more familiar, the tension and power that the author has built into the relationships become impressive. The themes of jealousy, social distinction and past hatreds are painfully real. It is obviously a powerful and significant novel and though there is an atmosphere about it that is at times snobbish and unpleasant this is possibly intended.

The Owl Service, more than any other book for children, puts critics, librarians, teachers and everyone else professionally interested in the matter of children's reading, on their mettle. Is it, or is it not, a book suitable for children? And is it, or is it not, successful? Is it a good book? The last question is the easiest to answer simply. Yes, of course it is. It stands head and shoulders above the average book written for children and is obviously the work of a genuinely creative artist. Nevertheless it does not seem to me wholly successful. Too much is made, I feel, of the legend and the dinner service, and the author is so convincing at human relationships and the development of his characters that he could almost certainly have made as good a book, perhaps even a better one, without the elaborately contrived symbolism. I wonder, in fact, whether more than one in ten of the children who read the book even notice it. Children, as we all know, are capable of reading books at several different levels, and the application of the legend is so involved and the incidents in which it is worked out so complex that they must be difficult for any but the most intelligent and widely read child to follow. I suspect, therefore, that they don't even try, and that most children read this simply as a story about people, aware no doubt of a kind of horrid and unnatural fascination that they find emotionally and sensually disturbing, which attracts them to the book without being understood, but largely unaware of the fact that the author has an underlying purpose. (pp. 145-46)

It will be very interesting to see along what lines Alan Garner develops his work. He is also one of the few contemporary British writers for children. Having aroused so much controversy and attracted so much critical interest so early in his career he must inevitably feel the need to live up to it. He is unlikely, therefore, ever to turn to a simpler kind of writing. But it cannot be altogether healthy for a writer for children to be so conscious of the need to be intelligent, different, challenging—the need always to produce a new work that is more demanding than the last. It is this obvious perfectionalism that makes him so unusual even among his contemporaries. He takes his craft very seriously, gives far more time to each book than the majority of present-day writers and has probably given more thought to the theory and practice of writing for children than anyone else. (p. 146)

If thinking were all that is necessary to make a good book, Alan Garner would undoubtedly in time produce some of the best children's books ever written. But loving is at least as important, and in this quality he seems less well endowed. (p. 147)

Frank Eyre, "Fiction for Children," in his British Children's Books in the Twentieth Century, *revised edition, Longman Books, 1979, pp. 76-156.*

JOHN ROWE TOWNSEND

[Alan Garner's books, though few, have had an extraordinarily powerful impact; they have been felt and not forgotten. (p. 81)

Because Garner's novels have come out at fairly long intervals, they show their differences—and the author's development—more clearly than do the works of more prolific writers. Alan Garner has never stood still. The novels have grown less complicated but more complex, less crowded but more intricately ramified, and more demanding. (p. 82)

The deepening and strengthening of the human element in *The Owl Service* is . . . a key difference between that book and the three earlier novels. . . . To my mind *The Owl Service* shows a new maturity and authority; it is the work of a man who has mastered his craft and knows just what he is about. The theme is characteristic of Garner: the irruption of old legend into modern life. But this time the author is concerned with the emotional realities of a situation existing here and now. In earlier books, the people were little more than pawns; the power lay in external forces. In *The Owl Service,* the legend and its re-enactments are in their true place as phenomena arising out of the nature of humanity rather than working on it from outside. People—unthinking, vulnerable, little knowing what harm they can do to themselves and others—carry the potentiality for disaster within them. They also carry within them the potentiality for avoiding disaster. (p. 86)

I have said and still say that *The Owl Service* is—against formidable competition—the most remarkable novel to appear on a British children's list in the 1960s. (p. 88)

Red Shift is a complex structure. Artistically, is it a sound one? I am not sure. For all the ingenuity with which the three stories are woven together, I feel that the relationship of the earlier two to the contemporary one is not fully organic. This last, which is the outer and clearly the principal story, stands up perfectly well without the others. They add, but they do not inhere. They could be removed from the book and the outer story would still be there. And it would be seen to be rather a banal little story, no better than many other portrayals of young love and worse than some. The highly intelligent yet ineffectual and ultimately destructive Tom is probably Garner's most successful characterization so far, but his dreadful parents come close to being stereotypes, and even Jan does not emerge clearly as a person. Her account of her previous brief affair with a married man is almost novelettish. The dialogue has what Eleanor Cameron, writing of *The Owl Service,* described as a staccato beat giving the impression of choppiness. (This can, however, be brilliantly effective at times. On the day when Tom has learned of Jan's former lover, one can clearly hear his silent inward screaming beneath the ordinary words.)

In spite of what seem sizeable flaws, *Red Shift* comes across as a strong, disturbing and memorable novel. Possibly Garner has turned his main weakness into a strength. In past books, as I have already indicated, one has felt that his characters did not match the size of their stories. In *Red Shift,* Tom, his girl and his parents match the size of *their* story, because it is not a big one; it is not the size of the whole book.

The image left in my mind is a visual image: an image of small, vulnerable present-day people with great black shadows of the past looming over them. This may not have been the author's aim, but I think it is his achievement. (pp. 90-1)

[As with *Red Shift,* a question of readership] arises over the four linked stories which Garner published in 1976, 1977 and 1978. They are a quartet of brief books printed in large type, and look as if intended for children of the middle years, perhaps eight to ten or eleven. But they have no strong plot line, no easy appeal; and probably they require a more patient, thoughtful and mature reader than one might suppose at first sight. The four—in order of the events they describe, not in order of publication—are *The Stone Book, Granny Reardun, The Aimer Gate* and *Tom Fobble's Day.* (pp. 91-2)

[*The Stone Book* is] a beautifully told and balanced story; its two halves are Mary's climb into the sky and descent into the earth; it is full of echoes and resonances. Yet I confess I find it the least sympathetic of the four books, largely because it leaves me worrying over an obvious but surely important point. Father can read. Mary wants to read, too, and one feels quite passionately that she should be taught to do so, not fobbed off with an imitation book. Whatever wisdom may reside in stone and in the mason's craft, a stone book is no substitute for a real one; indeed, it is a contradiction in terms, almost a perversion of the nature of stone.

The other three books, though rich in implication, are simpler and, I think, better. (pp. 90-3)

Though I have, as indicated, a reservation about *The Stone Book,* I have no doubt that the quartet as a whole is a fine achievement. The sense of landscape, of people, of the passage of time but the continuity of families and crafts, is marvellously sure and solid; voices ring true and clear with the vigour and dignity of the common folk. In *Red Shift* it was still possible to feel a lack of depth and sympathy in Garner's portrayal of people, and to wonder whether this would turn out to be a crucial limitation of his talent. But no such lack is felt in the quartet; there is more humanity here than in any of his previous work. 'He is always likely to do something one would not have guessed at until it was there,' I wrote in 1971; and these last four books are a good instance. Alan Garner's potentiality is obviously still great, and there is still no telling what he will do next. Whatever it is, it will be eagerly awaited. (p. 94)

John Rowe Townsend, "Alan Garner," in his A Sounding of Storytellers: New and Revised Essays on Contemporary Writers for Children, *J. B. Lippincott, 1979, pp. 81-94.*

DAVID REES

It has always seemed to me that Alan Garner is capable of writing a work of major importance and that *The Owl Service* and *Red Shift* should have been such works, not the flawed masterpieces they are. The lines in T. S. Eliot's "The Hollow Men"—"Between the conception/And the creation/ . . . Falls the Shadow"—are very relevant to Garner's work.

This is not to say that reading his stories is not a fascinating and absorbing experience. From *The Weirdstone of Brisingamen* to *The Aimer Gate* the technical expertise and the exploration of powerful emotions in areas where myth and the world of everyday reality meet show a remarkable development, even if the reader is left unsatisfied in some way or other with every single one of his books. Garner himself said of **The Weirdstone of Brisingamen** that he thinks it "is one of the worst books published in the last twenty years." It depends, of course, on what criterion is used to define *worst*, but neither it nor its sequel **The Moon of Gomrath** are particularly interesting or profound. Both novels are like any hackneyed thriller or TV serial; they merely hold the reader's attention by placing the good characters in one dangerous situation after another and then rescuing them. There is nothing more. Evil is in no way internalized in the characters, who are either flat, uninteresting figures (Colin and Susan), talking notice-boards issuing instructions or explanations (the wizard and the various dwarfs), or caricatures (Gowther Mossock). Garner's note at the end of **The Moon of Gomrath** that Gowther Mossock is taken straight from life may well be true, but the Cheshire farmer does not come through as anything other than the standard English rustic of fifty or a hundred years ago. The writing in both books is quite adequate, despite some bejeweled and mannered passages, but it is not especially exciting. This extract from **The Moon of Gomrath** is characteristic:

> The notes rose and fell in a sadness that swept the children's minds with dreams of high landscapes of rock, and red mountains standing from them, and hollows filled with water and fading light, and rain drifting as veils over the peaks, and beyond, in the empty distances, a cold gleam on the sea. And into that distance the voice faded like an echo, and Atlendor came towards the children from the shadows of the house.

Why are these novels so unmemorable? The explanation may lie in part in Garner's own comment that he felt "if I could not write for people twice my age, I could perhaps . . . say something which would be of interest to people half my age." In other words, they are written specifically for children, indeed for the child whose major interest in a book is simply what happens next, which is not to say that such books should not exist or should not have an important function in many children's lives. The point is that too many pretentious claims have been made for Garner's first two novels. (pp. 56-7)

Now, [it] seems to me that books which offer only conveyed fear and nothing more to interest the reader—whether they have plots wrapped up in a lot of mythological paraphernalia and difficult Celtic names or are science fiction or cops-and-robbers stories—are readable once and once only. They're the equivalent of *Kojak* or *Star Trek,* however well written or well researched. (p. 58)

Elidor, however, shows Garner emerging as a rather more interesting writer than either **The Weirdstone of Brisingamen** or **The Moon of Gomrath** suggested. The plot has greater unity and purpose—we are not merely subjected to a series of disconnected danger sequences—and it is possible for the reader to feel that the story is not aimed just at a certain kind of child. It has something interesting to say, on a number of different levels, about imagination and reality, about the position and importance of myth in a modern context, about the power and significance of place. The derelict church and the cobbled working-class streets of Manchester, with their years of private and public history swept away by the bulldozer in the name of progress, are portrayed convincingly, particularly when paralleled with the blighting of the world of Elidor and contrasted with the security and safety of the Watsons' house, graceless though that house may be. Everyday life

may be dull, but it is stable and necessary if the children are to survive; yet if they are to grow up as complete human beings and not become the television-obsessed automata that their parents are, they also need to know Elidor as it once was and realize the importance of restoring it to its former glory, so that it may take its part in their own adult lives, a symbol of the powers of the imaginative and creative life. Only Roland is able to appreciate this fully; for Helen, Nicholas, and David, Elidor will in time probably fade to nothing more than a disturbing memory.

So myth, then, in **Elidor** is a way of expressing certain fundamental truths about human behavior. That is a right and proper function of myth; using it as a glorified cops-and-robbers tale is not. The book has other strengths; the Watson parents, observed with a tolerant amusement, are the first credible characters that Garner created. They are in fact more interesting than the children—who are still cardboard creations as in the previous two books—and the parents show that the author has a talent for social comedy which, unfortunately, he has not employed elsewhere:

> Mrs Watson took the evening paper, and made a point of reading it. Every minute or so she would turn the pages fretfully, as if they were responsible for the television breakdown.

These cardboard children are a problem, the major flaw in the novel. Their speech does not serve to differentiate character, nor does it always sound very realistic; the dialogue could be rearranged so that David could speak Helen's lines, or Helen Nicholas's, and the book would not suffer. . . . They simply aren't flesh-and-blood people. The closeness of the plot to C. S. Lewis's *The Lion, the Witch, and the Wardrobe* is uncomfortable. Alan Garner's dislike of Lewis's novels is well-known, yet in **Elidor,** as in the Narnia stories, four rather uninteresting children are taken to lands ruined by the powers of darkness, which need the children to help restore them to their former grandeur. Was Garner attempting to rewrite Lewis, using the same idea for what he thought were better ends? Or was the parallel less conscious? The answer is not clear.

Nor is the ending of **Elidor** particularly clear; it is the first example in Garner's work of an obscurity that bedevils much of the two subsequent books, as if the author were deliberately cloaking himself in a veil of secrecy because he did not seem to want the reader, for some reason, to peer too closely into the sources of what he had to say. Garner's own words about the conclusion of Elidor are not very helpful. "If the book had gone on another page Roland would have gone mad . . . When he watches the dying Findhorn (based heavily on Platonic philosophy), it's not the back of the cave he sees when he looks into the creature's eyes, but rather he is in the cave himself: and he sees that in order to achieve another shadow he has killed the reality." I cannot think that any reader, child or adult, would realize that the concepts expressed here form the ending of **Elidor:** madness, Plato, the cave, the shadow—they may be in the author's mind, but they are not there in the words. And in any case, what does Garner's statement mean? It sounds even more obscure than what it is intended to elucidate.

It is **The Owl Service** and **Red Shift,** however, on which Alan Garner's reputation stands, and they are undoubtedly the books for which he would like to be considered a serious and important writer. **The Owl Service** has received an acclaim permitted to few novels. It also appears to have been extremely widely read. *Red Shift* was treated less kindly, many people finding its obscurity very nearly impenetrable. This seems rather odd, as *The Owl Service* presents at least as many problems to the reader as the later book, and, in any case, subsequent rereadings solve most, though not all, of the difficulties of both novels. The final puzzle is not that they are so obscure, but why the author should wish to try and make them so, a puzzle to which there does not seem to be an easy answer.

Both books demand an excessively close attention to nuance, to what is being stated beneath the words, to what is left out; this requires an intensity of intellectual concentration that is, curiously, at variance with Garner's own statement that "because I am writing a novel I am primarily in the entertainment business, providing an emotional experience, not an intellectual one." In fact, there is not much in either book that is entertaining in the conventional sense of the word, but there is a great deal to be admired. The dovetailing of three stories in *Red Shift,* widely separated in time but linked in theme and in the use of the same locale, is masterly and satisfying; there is the opportunity, which the author fully employs, for each story not only to comment obliquely on the other two and thus underline what he wishes to say, but also to point to difference and similarity between then and now and to push the reader into thinking about people in a context of history even wider than the two thousand years that separate the first and last stories. In *The Owl Service,* especially, there is the power of place. . . . (pp. 58-61)

There is, too, a similar contrasting of the effect of that place and the myth that rules it on different generations of people. And in both books there is the excitement of a totally gripping suspense that works in every rereading, because it is not so much an external danger as one that exists inside characters who see themselves on the brink of disintegration when confronted by people and events that force their weaknesses to the surface.

The Owl Service, I repeat, is a flawed masterpiece, however, and it has suffered from a generally uncritical adulation that is blind to both its virtues and its defects. Regrettably, it is often studied in the schoolroom; if any book needs to be read whole, and privately, this one does: Read it aloud and ask questions about *The Mabinogion,* and its spell is destroyed. Many people feel that is is a profound and searching study of adolescence; Penelope Farmer has spoken of its influence on her writing, particularly on *Charlotte Sometimes* (an influence, I must confess, I fail to see). If it's really a marvelous portrait of adolescence, then all teenagers must be maimed and tortured: Gwyn, Roger, and Alison are emotional cripples—Gwyn, in fact, says this to Alison—corrupted by their selfish, crippled parents, and they will probably go on to inflict the same patterns on their own children. Not all, not even most, adolescents are like this. Penelope Farmer, in fact, has a much wider and more generous view of that period of life in *A Castle of Bone,* as does Ursula Le Guin in *A Wizard of Earthsea*. . . . (p. 62)

Aidan Chambers says he is "amused to observe how difficult the middle-class enclave find the ending [of *The Owl Service*] . . . They say it mars the story and is a weakness when, in fact, it is the book's great strength." The ending is, by any standards, confused and not a strength. The problem Aidan Chambers is referring to is that many readers feel the wrong boy gets the girl, and they may indeed honestly feel

that they have been cheated, as they have been asked by the author throughout the book to identify with Gwyn, to be inside his thoughts and feelings, hopes and fears and to regard Roger as insipid, humorless, and repugnant. "She could have had a Heathcliff, but instead she gets a Young Conservative," someone once remarked. The point is that Alison inevitably is not going to find a Heathcliff; she is too trapped and crushed; she can never be herself, as Gwyn so often urges her, dominated as she is by her revolting mother. The reader, by identifying with Gwyn, is lulled into forgetting that he is just as maimed even though he is more sympathetic; he is no Heathcliff and is never likely to be. The ending, then, is surely right intellectually, but it is fair to say that the author should not have asked us to be so much on Gwyn's side emotionally; it leads inevitably to confusion, to a sense of letdown.

Aidan Chambers's remarks point, rightly, to the interesting class tensions in the book, but here again there is weakness, not strength. Gwyn is any working-class boy with a chip on his shoulder that grows to an enormous size when confronted with the closed doors of the moneyed English middle class; he is not really specifically Welsh, despite the author's impeccable handling of the Welsh speech rhythms. And Roger and Clive seem to me as phony as Gwyn's Welshness. They are standard caricatures of the chinless, witless, public-school type, observed externally with all the inaccuracies and flatness that are characteristic of the outside observer, particularly the frustrated working-class observer. No one ever uses so many stereotyped clichés of speech as Clive does; he really isn't credible. Alison's mother Margaret might make up for this, but unfortunately she doesn't appear at all in person. (In fact she's left to surface as Tom's mother in *Red Shift* in all her totally credible nastiness, changed though she is into a working-class woman.) Margaret's absence is interesting; and Alan Garner's own views about this seem a weak justification for the device: "I was half way through the book before I realized she hadn't [appeared]. I thought, 'Now why hasn't she? I wonder if it works if she doesn't? . . . I wouldn't have kept it that way if I thought it hadn't.'" I don't think it does work; why her? one asks. It's so arbitrary. Why not leave out Nancy or Clive or even Gwyn? It is a hole, an unnecessary one; and the trouble is that without Margaret's presence Roger and Alison seem more unsympathetic than they should be. If we could have seen her effect, in person, on her daughter and stepson we would feel for them more, and the reader's sympathies would not have been tilted so dangerously towards Gwyn, resulting in the unsatisfying cheated feeling at the end.

Another problem, perhaps less important, is what happens to Nancy. Does she walk over the pass to Aberystwyth or literally vanish into thin air, dead? The latter seems more probable, but why? And why isn't it clear? Perhaps one of the reasons for the obscurities in both books derives from the author's method of working. For *The Owl Service* he says, "I put myself on a two-year crash course of Welsh economic history, Welsh political history, geology, geography. I went into Welsh poetry, I learned Welsh," and *Red Shift* involved "nearly seven years of unbroken work" and "a bibliography of something like two hundred books. I got that out of the way in the first two years. It's like reading for a degree—that intensity." Yet the actual writing process, he tells us, is fairly brief, in the case of *The Owl Service* very brief—twelve weeks. Is it possible that all that Welsh economic history (its relevance may seem somewhat marginal), those hundreds of books, got in the way rather than helped? Garner's statements about his method of working are curious in another way, too; they are more like the kind of statement that one of his more tortured characters might make (Tom in *Red Shift* is the most likely one) rather than deeply-felt verbalizations about the creative processes, which have more to do with a conscious and subconscious linking of the different parts of a person's experiences and needs than self-conscious research.

It would perhaps be only repetitive to launch at this point into a similar analysis of *Red Shift,* for the same puzzles and dissatisfactions arise to mar its very considerable virtues, especially, once again on the last page. Do the characters survive or not? What happens to the relationship between Tom and Jan? Is it over? Is there hope for any of them, or not? The reader would like to know. (Decoding the letter doesn't help much, either.) It is, however, worth saying again that a great number of the book's difficulties do resolve themselves on a second or a third reading, and it is also worth pointing out that the general comment made on its publication—that it is not a children's book—is unimportant, though it was perhaps not quite honest of the publishers to place it on a children's list. It is not a children's book any more or less than is *The Owl Service,* although some young people may derive enjoyment from it.

A more fitting conclusion would be to speak of Alan Garner's most recent work, the quartet of stories that begins with *The Stone Book.* The last of them, *The Aimer Gate,* seems to be falling into the old fault of unnecessary obscurity—what *is* the Aimer Gate? one asks—and the middle two, *Tom Fobble's Day* and *Granny Reardun,* are less good than *The Stone Book.* In this first story, very brief though it is, there are signs that bear out Justin Wintle's view that here is "a major talent . . . remarshalling its resources," whereas *The Owl Service* and *Red Shift* point to that talent "energetically destroying itself." Story line, relationships, tension, underlying significance all marry in total harmony—the conveyed fear in *The Stone Book,* for instance, is Garner's best yet, a scene on a church spire which fills the reader with an appalling sense of vertigo—and it is much to be hoped that this new-found inner harmony will be expressed in a full-length novel in which the shadow does not fall between the conception and the creation. Alan Garner has all too frequently reminded me of one of the castles in his own Elidor, magnificent but ruined, waiting like Roland for "the glories of stone, sword, spear, and cauldron" to hang "in their true shapes." In *The Stone Book* they have begun to hang in their true shapes, and when they do so in a more extended work, they will certainly make a masterpiece worth the reading. (pp. 63-6)

> *David Rees, "Hanging in Their True Shapes: Alan Garner," in his* The Marble in the Water: Essays on Contemporary Writers of Fiction for Children and Young Adults, *The Horn Book, Inc., 1980, pp. 56-67.*

HUMPHREY CARPENTER

"The Stone Book Quartet" is scarcely a work of literature for children. The language is simple (apart from dialect words) but profound, and it requires several readings even by adults before anything like full comprehension is reached. The four stories virtually reject plot of the conventional sort, and even the characters are not clearly defined by the standards of children's fiction. In fact within Garner's whole *oeuvre* this makes sense, is even predictable: "The Stone Book Quartet" stands at the end of a long progression from conventional adventure-fantasy (*The Weirdstone of Brisingamen* and its se-

quel) via more sober, plausible, serious fantasy novels (*Elidor* and *The Owl Service*) to an enigmatic book dealing with present-day adolescents interpreting themselves through history (*Red Shift*). It is partly a process of refinement and improvement—Garner becomes a far better literary craftsman during it—but also a desire to write about what matters, to create fiction of integrity and maturity.

Alan Garner seems to stand at the culmination of the post-war movement in modern English children's writing. It is hard to imagine anyone bettering what he has done in **"The Stone Book Quartet,"** giving a finer expression to the theme of the child finding its place in the world by understanding history. (p. 221)

> *Humphrey Carpenter, "Epilogue: The Garden Revisited," in his* Secret Gardens: A Study of the Golden Age of Children's Literature, *Houghton Mifflin Company, 1985, pp. 210-23.*

MARGERY FISHER

["The Stone Book Quartet" contains] four meticulously linked books about strata (of people and stone), about continuity (of families and buildings) and about change (of occupations and outlooks). They count as landmarks for me because of the stratified prose, whose simplicity of precisely selected words, defined by context, could engage a reader of nine or so and whose imagery, repetitions and reverberances should satisfy the most exacting adult reader—a dual capacity easier to find in children's books of the last century than in ours. Each book centres on a child significantly stirred by a single event. In *The Stone Book* Mary finds that the stone from a mine can contain a story. Her son Joseph, in *Granny Reardun,* decides his future must be in iron rather than stone. In *The Aimer Gate* Joseph's son Robert is made aware, by marks he feels rather than sees, of his forebears. And his son William, in *Tom Fobble's Day* riding his toboggan in a night lit by searchlights of war, is at one with past and present. The stories compass five generations of one family of craftsmen (stone workers, smiths) in the part of England Alan Garner terms North Mercia, and the highly wrought yet supple language he uses is not Latinate but Saxon, resoundingly concrete and yet a proper form for thought, as each of the men who shapes the minds of the young passes to them, as it were, the continuous thread of pride in the work of hands. Hands, indeed, provide one of many links in the stories; dominant symbols (the metal used in the clock that records time and the stone that records the past) mark the theme of the quartet. The counterpointed narratives have the inevitability of master-writing.

> *Margery Fisher, in a review of "The Stone Book Quartet," in her* Margery Fisher Recommends Classics for Children & Young People, *Thimble Press, 1986 p. 65.*

ELAINE MOSS

"The Stone Book Quartet" seems likely to survive as a literary peak; one can imagine observers of the future remarking that Alan Garner's work was a symphony rousing the intellectual young reader of the seventies to an awareness of the dying crafts that once gave man his dignity, and the local dialects that used to distinguish him from his fellow countrymen. In the year 2001 the historical researcher may handle the first editions of the Garner quartet printed (well, photolithographed) on fine cream paper and illustrated with etchings by Michael Foreman, and marvel at the skill with which author, artist, publisher and printer could interweave their crafts and make the medium—a finely produced book—reflect the author's message. (p. 145)

> *Elaine Moss, "Signal Contributions: 1970-1980," in her* Part of the Pattern: A Personal Journey through the World of Children's Books, 1960-1985, *Greenwillow Books, 1986, pp. 45-160.*

MICHAEL DIRDA

Every so often a "children's book" so exceptional appears that it seems a shame that only kids, librarians and a few lucky parents will read it. Russell Hoban's *The Mouse and His Child,* for instance. Or Daniel Pinkwater's *Alan Mendelsohn, The Boy from Mars.* To this select company belongs Alan Garner's *Stone Book Quartet. . . .*

For Garner the past isn't past or prologue: it is present, here and now. Because every word gradually becomes charged with meaning, his chronicles of "inner time" achieve a dour kind of poetry, with a power hard to convey by quotation or summary. To readers of the right sympathy they suggest all the momentary wonders and inevitable sorrows of life, especially as each book builds to a moment of ecstasy or epiphany—Mary deep in the earth, Joseph seeing the work of the smith in everything around him, Robert alone amid the giant workings of the clock tower, and William sledding down the hill and down the years of his family's history.

A history that, one learns, is in fact the author's own. As Neil Phillip says . . . : The story of a man who makes marks on paper as his forefathers made them on stone and metal.

Alan Garner was throughout most of the 1960s and '70s the most talked-about children's author in Britain. His first books were a pair of related fantasies, an amalgamation of quest romance, Arthurian myth, and Celtic folklore, set around his hometown of Alderley Edge in Cheshire . . . .

Much of the tremendous excitement of this [*The Weirdstone of Brisingamen*] grows out of the way Garner makes the familiar uncanny, transforming the Cheshire countryside into a haunted realm. A neighboring spinster, ordinary hikers and commonplace locales loom as agents of evil, places of mystic power and danger. One feels that, after their adventure, the children will be rightly paranoid for the rest of their lives. . . .

The Weirdstone suggested a Celtic Tolkien, what with its blind dolmen-like Mara, sniffing for victims, its black magician who moves as a cloud, its strange and unseasonal cold, the "fimbulwinter." By contrast *The Moon of Gomrath* shows the darker and more unsettling influence of Robert Graves' *The White Goddess,* countering a masculine High Magic of calculated spells and sorcery with a feminine Old Magic of blood, sexuality and instinct.

While the prose of these two novels is lush and occasionally overwrought, that of *Elidor* and *The Owl Service* is more strictly controlled, with greater emphasis on dialogue. Magic grows increasingly ambiguous; as in Greek tragedy or Celtic myth, these stories are fraught with foreboding. Their heroes are lonely, isolated, confused, angry. (p. 14)

A marvel of compression, *The Owl Service* displays classical unities, telling its chilling, claustrophobic story in a single place, in a short space of time, and largely with three characters. Its end is a shocker.

It took six years for Garner to finish his next book, *Red Shift,* sometimes described as the most difficult book ever published as children's literature. Here Garner constructs a contrapuntal narrative of three strands, all connected by a Cheshire hill called Mow Cop, a neolithic stone axe, and a shared impotence among the main characters. . . . Garner elaborates his theme—the relationship of violence and sexuality—almost entirely through dialogue, at first making clear that he is shifting from one time period to another, but eventually mingling matters so that it becomes difficult to know for sure whether Tom, Thomas or Macey (a diminutive of Thomas) is talking.

Red Shift is clearly the high point of Garner's focus on the experimental and elliptical. For instance, all the sexual activity—and there's quite a bit—takes place between the lines, and yet seems graphically, even brutally, described. Still, the book does seem to have exorcised the demons that embittered Garner's early fiction and allowed him to compose *The Stone Book Quartet,* a quiet text, all passion spent, forgiving, almost sacerdotal.

Alan Garner has not published any fiction for 10 years now, though he has edited several excellent collections of British folktales. He is still relatively young, only in his mid-fifties, and is, I hope, at work on a new novel. It will be interesting to see what it is like. (p. 15)

> *Michael Dirda, "England, His England," in* Book World—The Washington Post, *June 12, 1988, pp. 14-15.*

THE WEIRDSTONE OF BRISINGAMEN: A TALE OF ALDERLEY (1960; also published as *The Weirdstone: A Tale of Alderley*)

Susan and Colin are staying with farmer friends in Cheshire and meet the wizard of local folk-lore. He tells them the story of a lost precious stone—the weirdstone of Brisingamen—which is necessary to awake a band of sleeping knights to fight Nastrona the spirit of evil. Susan finds that she herself has this precious stone as a bracelet. This bracelet is seized by the evil powers and Susan and Colin, aided by the wizard's friends, set out to recapture the stone and bring it, after a long chase, back to the wizard. This is the author's first book and his great enthusiasm permeates his writing, making the book rich and sparkling with movement and people. The folk-lore of his native countryside forms a background for a jostling crowd of characters and drama. This is an all-round book where reality and fantasy are intertwined until they are indistinguishable. In his enthusiasm, however, the author conjures forth too many characters and too many names, and while some of the latter are mellifluous and haunting, others are ugly and confusing. The children's long chase and subsequent long drawn out flight tire and perplex the reader. Mr. Garner should, perhaps, have restrained himself a little and deleted some of the repetitive action and a few of the characters. (pp. 363-64)

> *A review of "The Weirdstone of Brisingamen," in* The Junior Bookshelf, *Vol. 24, No. 6, December, 1960, pp. 363-64.*

The writing has flavor and atmosphere, but the combination of the realities of the children's lives and their involvement with supernatural beings is not completely successful; in part the book is weakened, too, by the elaborate intricacies of the magic world: many invented terms, unfamiliar dialect, magic spells, mists and swamps, odd creatures, etc., and the further complication of having some of the adults in the real life of Colin and Susan participating in their magical adventures.

> *Zena Sutherland, in a review of "The Weirdstone: A Tale of Alderley," in* Bulletin of the Center for Children's Books, *Vol. XV, No. 2, October, 1961, p. 29.*

The tense and often horrifying episodes of the plot are centered around the attempt, finally successful, to restore the weirdstone to Cadellin. As in **Elidor,** but perhaps not with the same balance, reality and fantasy are played against each other. The feeling for terrain and dwelling, for Gowther's dialect and humor, are earthy and of this world. But the inrush of beings familiar from Germanic and Celtic mythology and folklore add the richness as well as the terror of a bygone world to the everyday surroundings of the children. . . . However, "beauty and terror" are presented as "opposite sides of the same coin," and the almost unbearably tense events closing the story end on a chord of triumph. (pp. 45-6)

> *Paul Heins, in a review of "The Weirdstone of Brisingamen: A Tale of Alderley," in* The Horn Book Magazine, *Vol. XLVI, No. 1, February, 1970, pp. 45-6.*

[*The following is a review of a revised edition of* The Weirdstone of Brisingamen.]

This slightly revised edition of a book first published in 1960 remains the spellbinding story of the struggle between the forces of good and evil. . . . Like Tolkien and Lloyd Alexander, Garner borrows heavily from legend, folklore and mythology (especially the Welsh) in telling his story. Yet Garner's voice is uniquely his own: his novels in general are less diffuse, more controlled, and, in a sense, darker and more sophisticated than those of Tolkien and Alexander. Garner's superb interweaving of our apprehended "real" world with that of marvelously alive, differentiated, and believable wizards and warlocks, witches and dwarfs, lends to his books a breathtaking immediacy not so readily discernible in those of Tolkien and Alexander, in which all of the action takes place in the mythological environment. **The Weirdstone of Brisingamen** can stand on its own merits without reference to the body of Garner's work (capped in 1968 by the superb **The Owl Service**), as a nearly perfect example of literature which is not simply fantasy nor the simple retelling of myth but the creation of a world in which good and evil are more than words, a world in which they become eternal personifications engaged in an eternal struggle. And, on a simpler level, the book offers, from start to finish, gripping, bewitching adventure.

> *Michael Cart, in a review of "The Weirdstone of Brisingamen," in* School Library Journal, *Vol. 16, No. 6, February, 1970, p. 86.*

THE MOON OF GOMRATH (1963)

For Alan Garner, the power of Celtic myth is inseparable from the power of magic; as he renews the one he frees the other in a remarkable interpretation that leaves the reader wondering. Colin and Susan are already living in two worlds (introduced in **The Weirdstone,** established concisely here) when the enterprises of men unlooses the formless, speechless Brollachan, blacker than the blackest night, to join the Mor-

rigan or witch-queen, and when the children's own carelessness releases the Einhariar, the Wild Hunters and their antlered leader Garanhir. Ranged against them are the spirits withdrawn since the Age of Reason: Cadellin the wizard, Uthecar the dwarf, and Atlendor the elf-lord (whose lios-alfar are retreating from the dirt and foul air of men). To wizards and their High Magic of thoughts and spells, the Old Magic is a hindrance, a power without shape or order; they have tried to destroy it before but it would only sleep. Now it threatens the children, especially Susan because she wears the bracelet of ancient silver, the Mark of Fohla. Susan is almost lost, and Colin is captured, before the Old Magic is dispersed but not destroyed in a harrowing confrontation. The words of the hunters trail behind: "Leave her. . . . It will be. But not yet." This exists on a more mythic plane than William Mayne's *Earthfasts;* both take simultaneity for granted, but here the interest is primarily in the inhabitants of "the world of magic that lies near and unknown to us as the back of a shadow." In a reluctant afterword, Mr. Garner identifies his sources; he has already transcended them in a story that requires but repays close attention.

> *A review of "The Moon of Gomrath," in* Kirkus Service, *Vol. XXXV, No. 17, September 1, 1967, p. 1055.*

In Alan Garner's story the moon of Gomrath rises over an unmistakably British countryside and over a hidden, ageless underworld of frighteningly evil powers and almost equally fearsome champions of the good. Colin, and Susan, who possesses the magical Mark of Fohla, are pursued by the daemonic witch Morrigan and the shapeless monster Brollachan but are saved by the wizard Cadellin Silverbrow and other fabulous creatures. The story jumps abruptly from one Tolkienish shiver to another, but there is a gripping power to these episodes of creeping horror, reminiscent of those in Charles Williams's adult novels of the occult.

> *Andrew B. Myers, in a review of "The Moon of Gomrath," in* The New York Times Book Review, *October 22, 1967, p. 62.*

This action-packed novel is almost as good as its predecessor, but it suffers somewhat from a rather heavy dose of expository material in the beginning chapters, and also from the introduction of too many characters throughout the course of the narrative. The reader begins to feel like a stranger at a cocktail party who is introduced to a dozen or so guests and is then expected to remember not only their names but also something about their backgrounds. This is especially true when the Einheriar of the Herlathing appear on the scene about midway through the book. (p. 89)

> *Marshall B. Tymn, Kenneth J. Zahorski, and Robert H. Boyer, "Core Collection: Novels and Short Story Collections," in their* Fantasy Literature: A Core Collection and Reference Guide, *R. R. Bowker Company, 1979, pp. 39-184.*

ELIDOR (1965)

Elidor is the third long novel by a writer much involved with the meeting of ancient world and new: this, if the least wildly poetic, is also the most skilful of the three. It is ambitiously imagined and worked out with a hard economical tension: the reader is kept—except for some dazzling visionary moments—well on the present-day human side of the arena. It is, you might say, a reanimation of the Roland/Burd-Ellen legend in a modern industrial setting. There are cracks where the fabric of time and place is weak—and a Manchester bomb-site with a ruined church, already on the eve of demolition, is such a one. It is there, on an autumn evening, that Roland's sister Helen and his two brothers vanish in their search for a lost ball; Roland, the youngest, climbs the dark church tower, and in a thrilling episode encounters Malebron, proud spirit of doomed Elidor ('the death of Elidor would not be without echo in your world'). The four go back to their suburban home with the Treasures (sword, stone, spear and cauldron) in which the virtue of this ancient kingdom lives. Troubled, they bury them in the garden, deep in the earth. But the old magic runs athwart the new. All the electric gadgetry begins to riot—razors, television sets. A great wounded unicorn thrashes through the hedge. The burden must be passed on. The climax, a peak after chapters of mounting terror, is brilliant. The threads of myth make a nice unravelling. (pp. 748-49)

> Naomi Lewis, "Other World," in New Statesman, Vol. LXX, No. 1809, November 12, 1965, pp. 748-49.

We have tried before to illuminate the special technique Alan Garner employs to marry magic and reality because it seemed necessary. Other reviewers have apparently found it necessary also, and although no firm point of agreement seems to have been reached it is clear that **The Weirdstone of Brisingamen** and **The Moon of Gomrath** have created for the author a reputation which will take a lot of keeping up. It will not be kept up by such hastily germinated hybrids as **Elidor** in which four Manchester children "break through" into a benighted kingdom in which, it seems, "light" can be restored only through their agency as the chosen. The individual incidents are exciting and stimulating but the balance of elements is less certain than before. One feels not only that the magic is too thinly and too meanly spread but that the humorous and domestic elements of real life are better reading on the whole than the magical. Perhaps Mr. Garner is reacting to reader and critic reaction of a kind not revealed to us; he would do better to go his own way. (pp. 360-61)

> A review of "Elidor," in The Junior Bookshelf, Vol. 29, No. 6, December, 1965, pp. 360-61.

Pedants through the ages have tried to banish all forms of fantasy on the grounds that it is immoral, untrue; or, as now, because its darker violent side is psychologically harmful—hence wolves may no longer devour grandmothers nor spiders frighten little girls.

Yet surely it is this edge of darkness that gives fantasy its depth, meaning and value. As for its lack of truth in the scientific sense, the best of it contains a poetic and imaginative truth quite as valid, precisely because it can leap the barriers of physical possibility.

All the books chosen for review here [**Elidor,** R. E. Jackson's *The Witch of Castlekerry,* Nicholas Stuart Gray's *Mainly in Moonlight,* Patricia Wrightson's *Down to Earth,* Elaine Horseman's *The Hubbles' Treasure Hunt,* and Barbara Wersba's *The Land of Forgotten Beasts*] have perhaps something of this quality, whatever their other faults. First comes certainly the darkest, most powerful and probably also the most successful of them, Alan Garner's third book, *Elidor.*

This, like his others, sets a conflict between a mythological good and evil against a contemporary background. . . .

[Of] course, one thinks of Tolkien. Yet here, unlike in **The Weirdstone of Brisingamen** or **The Moon of Gomrath,** the myths are the mere backbone of fantasy, enriching it, while the story is worked out economically in contemporary, even scientific terms. The result is Garner original as the earlier books for all their power are not, perhaps because the children there never seem quite vivid enough to balance the primeval fascinations of witches, warlocks and goblins.

Here are no witches; the terrors are more modern and subjective, some taking the shape of the children's half-conscious fears. Their struggle is partly to overcome these fears, and also, accepting their responsibilities, to face the implications of what is happening rather than to reject it as nightmarish hallucination, as all except the youngest, Roland, wish to do.

Tension mounts through quite ordinary things—domestic machines run mysteriously wild; plastic toys from crackers; the suburban front door visualized by Roland in Elidor which has become the route for the evil into his own world. Fantasy and reality exactly balanced interweave logically and subtly.

The writing, moreover, has a bared even bleak precision, quite new it seems, forcefully though Mr. Garner wrote before. Each detail, ordinary or sinister, establishes atmosphere, background or character exactly. One reservation comes to mind as it does with Tolkien; that by contrast with the vitality of the evil, the good—golden towers and all—seems hazy, conventional, even self-indulgent. The solid contemporary reality may help a little here, but the reservation remains for all that.

Nevertheless **Elidor** is a remarkable book; intelligent, rich and terrifying. Too terrifying? Perhaps for the impressionable but worth ten of most prettier things.

> "Heirs of Tolkien, Nesbit and Carroll," in The Times Literary Supplement, n. 3328, December 9, 1965, p. 1130.

HOLLY FROM THE BONGS: A NATIVITY PLAY (1966)

Alan Garner and his photographer friend Roger Hill have produced this most unusual Christmas book—the story of the preparation and acting of a Nativity play in the Cheshire village of Goostrey. There are two traditional carols set to music by William Mayne. The play was actually performed by the local children in the stable of an inn, but it could be adapted for general use. In the first part of the book, in black and white photography, we see the children themselves, the part they play in ordinary village life, and their preparations for the play. Then follows the text and music, and lastly, in a section of glorious colour photography, the actual acting of the play in the stable. Those who know Alan Garner's work must be prepared for something unusual and beautiful; there is something of Christopher Fry in the poetry of the play, and the version of an old mummers' performance introduced into it, gives humour and an opportunity for fun in the midst of the seriousness of the occasion.

> A review of "Holly from the Bongs," in The Junior Bookshelf, Vol. 31, No. 1, February, 1967, p. 39.

Holly from the Bongs is a peak in Alan Garner's work. He achieves in it—the only occasion in his apprentice work, by which I mean everything up to *The Owl Service*—a balance and harmony of heart, mind, content, and technique. *Holly from the Bongs* is a moving and brilliant nativity play.

The words *nativity play* provoke, in my country, groans even from quite innocent people—like five-year-olds, for example. Quite understandably. Nativity plays can be, and usually are, twee, sentimental, inept, embarrassingly trite, ego-tripping disasters. Garner tackled that minefield in 1965 when he wrote *Holly* for his local village school. But he brought to it a quite exceptional mix of ideas; threads of ancient home-region folklore to set against the Christian myth, for example; a miracle play-within-the-play given vaudeville treatment. Working with seven-to eleven-year-old actors, whom he also directed, and performing the finished play in the stable of the Crown Inn, Goostrey, with the audience sitting on bales of straw, all helped, no doubt. But it was Garner's talent that wrote lines like these:

> First Shepherd: Is this the place?
> Second Shepherd: I cannot see.
> My eyes are mithered
> By that light
> Outside. The bright
> Flame and wings and the sky
> All feathered fire;
> And now the fierce cold star
> Like a dagger.

Or these, when at the end, modern children—the children of Goostrey itself—brought gifts to the New Born. Not gifts of gold and incense but things of a more modest and English kind they themselves picked from places round their homes, whose names Garner wove into his tapestry:

> Modern Children:
> I can bring him holly with berries
>   from the Bongs,
> And leaf of linden light from Galey Wood;
> Bracken from Bomish, Broadway and Blackden:
> Apple and medlar from No Town Farm.
>
> I can bring alder, birch bark, a pine branch
> From Top Dane, Jodrell, Petticoat Wood:
> Sycamore, beechmast, hazel, a thorn twig
> From Twemlow, Fullers Gate, Shawcroft Hall.

And so on. There's Joseph, abashed by gold:

> That's more than
> I can earn
> In all my years.
> You shouldn't have.

                                                    (pp. 227-28)

Humor, lyricism, an encoding of the Christian message so subtle and yet so accessible, language based on the Cheshire vernacular but poetically handled. If nothing else had to date, this little piece of pure masterliness ought to have told us that Garner was primarily a dramatic poet, rather than a novelist, and that one day, with luck, he would write work of outstanding brilliance. It took him ten years to get from *Holly* to **"The Stone Book"** quartet, which begins the redemption of that promise. (p. 228)

> *Aidan Chambers, "Letter from England: The Play's the Thing . . . ," in* The Horn Book Magazine, *Vol. LV, No. 2, April, 1979, pp. 224-28.*

THE OLD MAN OF MOW (1966)

Tempted by a signpost, two English boys are off to Mow Cop (cop: *Brit. dial.* crest), a craggy, windswept village where they lark about and look for the Old Man of Mow as per the words painted on a rock. "He's up top," they're told over and over, but John and Charles gaining the top again and again can't see him. A farmer's wife chases them out of her field, the foreman at a brick factory explains how they're made—it's all very fluid which is also to say unhinged: "There wasn't anyone to ask. So they thought they would have a fight. So they did." Whereupon (no transition from tumbling in the grass) "They found themselves in the way of a bus" (a doubledecker), find themselves several old men who deny being the Old Man in question, and at last locate him, a stone face above the painted legend. What appeal this has is in the getting there and that . . . is likely to seem quixotic to American children when it's not lost on them altogether.

> *A review of "The Old Man of Mow," in* Kirkus Reviews, *Vol. XXXVIII, No. 18, September 15, 1970, p. 1028.*

A selection of photographs [by Roger Hill], some in color and some in black and white, is accompanied by a text that often seems contrived to fit the pictures. . . . Some of the pictures are very good, others quite ordinary both technically and esthetically; the writing is adequate, tending to be fragmented by the format but mitigated by flashes of humor.

> *Zena Sutherland, in a review of "The Old Man of Mow," in* Bulletin of the Center for Children's Books, *Vol. 24, No. 2, October, 1970, p. 25.*

THE OWL SERVICE (1967)

AUTHOR'S COMMENTARY

The Owl Service contains elements of fantasy, drawing on non-Classical mythological themes. This is because the elements of myth work deeply and are powerful tools. Myth is not entertainment, but rather the crystallization of experience, and far from being escapist literature, fantasy is an intensification of reality.

When I first read the Welsh myth of Lleu Llaw Gyffes, it struck me as being such a modern story of the damage people do to each other, not through evil in themselves, but through the unhappy combination of circumstance that throws otherwise harmless personalities together. Then I happened to see a dinner service that was decorated with an abstract floral pattern. The owner had toyed with the pattern, and had found that by tracing it, and by moving the components around so that they fitted into one another, the model of an owl could be made.

Welsh political and economic history; Welsh law; these were the main areas of research. Nothing may show in the book, but I feel compelled to know everything before I can move. This is a weakness, not a strength. I learnt Welsh in order not to use it. Through the language it is possible to reach the mind of a people. By learning the language I hoped to discover how a character would feel and think, and hence react, in situations.

On a more general level—the ideas have struck a spark, and the spark has been fed. There is nothing else to be done but to write. At this stage panic sets in, because the ground has been covered, and there just is no story. Coming to terms with this phase has been difficult. Then a sudden, unpredictable brilliantly original idea erupts, an idea woven from strands of that book, and that film, and that conversation, and that book, and those notes, and that book, and that book. . . . There follows a string of such unexpected flashes of worked-out ideas, which have to undergo another process of shaping and selection, but this part is relatively straight-forward, and it is possible to get on with the excitement of telling the story. The details are never planned, but grow from day to day, which helps to overcome the deadly manual labour as well as to give the whole an organic development.

This has been, of course, merely a statement of intent, since all books fall short of the vision. There is always the hope that, with a bit more practice, a real book will emerge. If it is good enough, it will probably be for children. (pp. 143-44)

> *Alan Garner, "The Owl Service," in* Chosen for Children: An Account of the Books Which Have Been Awarded the Library Association Carnegie Medal, 1936-1975, *edited by Marcus Crouch and Alec Ellis, third edition, The Library Association, 1977, pp. 143-44.*

The 1967 Carnegie Medal was given to this brilliant, haunting novel of many dimensions—myth, fantasy, mystery, horror, a sorrowful portrait of how men live yet brushed with a final touch of hope. Teen-age Alison owns the house, legacy from her dead father, in the Welsh valley where she, her mother, her new stepfather and his son Roger are spending the summer. Also there and native to the valley are Gwyn, his mother (the family housekeeper), and Huw, the caretaker they regard as at least half mad. Alison and Gwyn discover in the attic a strange dinner service; its pattern: owls composed of flowers. Alison becomes obsessed with tracing the plates' pattern, thus setting free the owls and the power of a legend—that of Blodeuwedd, the maiden made of flowers and the two men who loved and killed for her. The valley is haunted by this myth, set down in the *Mabinogion,* which for centuries has been re-enacted by three members of every generation. The tension among Alison, Roger and Gwyn grows relentlessly, based on present-day class tensions and the inexorable workings of the legend, compounded by the fatalistic attitude of the valley inhabitants, especially Huw. At the end, proud Gwyn cannot bend to save an Alison filled with the power of Blodeuwedd, but he allows Roger, who has found the strength to rise above his own hatred, to do so and the chain is broken, at least for this generation. Complex and powerful, *The Owl Service* is told in an oblique, elliptical style which exactly suits the story but which demands, and no doubt will find, willing readers . . . ones who will read, comprehend, and never forget it. (pp. 166-67)

> *Margaret A. Dorsey, in a review of "The Owl Service," in* School Library Journal, *Vol. 15, No. 2, October, 1968, pp. 166-67.*

From a tale in the Welsh *Mabinogion* Alan Garner has woven an eerie and suspenseful fantasy of three people who, possessed by forces only dimly understood, are driven to reenact an age-old legend of jealousy, betrayal and revenge. It is a story rich in excitement and foreboding, yet at the same time mercurial in its delineation of the young and astonishingly honest in its exploration of their attitudes toward each other and toward their parents. Because Alison, Roger and Gwyn

are not sentimentally conceived, they have the stature to convince us that the impending evil is dreadfully real.

Mr. Garner's story is remarkable not only for its sustained and evocative atmosphere, but for its implications. It is a drama of young people confronted with the challenge of moral choice; at the same time it reveals, like diminishing reflections in a mirror, the eternal recurrence of the dilemma with each generation.

> *Houston L. Maples, in a review of "The Owl Service," in* Book World—The Washington Post, *November 3, 1968, p. 12.*

Alan Garner's *The Owl Service . . .* reveals that he is not a man to rest on the laurels awarded him by those enthusiastic children who read with pleasure *The Weirdstone of Brisingamen, The Moon of Gomrath,* and *Elidor.* For *The Owl Service* (a set of dishes, not a train run) is entirely different from his other three, having in common with them only that it is fantasy and takes off from legend. But because certain of Garner's tendencies as a writer are noticeable in all of his books and because these tendencies play an important part in the final effect of *The Owl Service,* it is rewarding to go back to the beginning and consider his work as a whole.

Garner is one who, from the start, has found his inspiration in Scandinavian mythology, Celtic legend, and Hebridean and British folklore. Rich is his knowledge of old spells, of the *Mabinogion,* and such volumes as Murray's *The God of the Witches,* Robert Graves's *The White Goddess,* and Watkins's *The Old Straight Track,* which has to do with prehistoric man's use of long-distance tracks marked by cairns, stones, and beacons. Old Britain and its ancient powers and presences waiting to be released over the English countryside are what are felt most strongly in the first two books. Garner has a splendid sense of place. When he shows Colin in *The Weirdstone* searching for the old straight track, and its eventual revelation by moonlight, he is at his best, involved purely in scene and feeling and overtone.

Nevertheless, even given Garner's knowledge and his particular qualities as a writer, neither *The Weirdstone* nor *The Moon of Gomrath* can begin to compare with the first fantasies of Lucy Boston, for instance, or Mary Norton or Philippa Pearce when it comes to subtlety and depth. It may be that the average child devoted to fantasy will prefer Garner's books for their movement, their tension, and continuous threat of evil about to be fully unleashed. But I am speaking of artistry from the point of view of the critical adult who is considering the following elements: a combination of cleanness and strength of structure, no matter how complex; sense of reality (and fantasy must have this); the communication of the visual perceptiveness of the writer; the way in which his mature thought and imagination compels and shapes action with full respect for his audience; originality in the handling of materials (all materials have been worked and reworked a thousand times); characterization; and style which, in its involvement with the whole impact of the book, cannot be separated from content.

Concerning the folk of his novels, there is in *The Weirdstone* a great bustling of all sorts of mythic and legendary beings, and in its sequel, *The Moon of Gomrath,* the bustling becomes positively overcrowded. In both of these books, all action stems from a fierce battle between the forces of Black Magic and the Old Magic, which works through feeling and intuition and which was driven into hiding when the Age of

Reason arrived. The basis of action is a cops-and-robbers chase, the Bads after the Goods, and the Goods then turning and stealthily tracking the Bads. But no amount of curious creatures, svarts and trolls and goblins and elves, can offset the balance of memorable individuals whose qualities might play upon one another to create unique situations of more lasting value and interest than the excitement of constant action. In neither *The Weirdstone* nor *The Moon of Gomrath* do the children, Susan and Colin, evolve into individuals. Except for their superhuman courage, they are almost completely at the mercy of plot, possessing no other qualities with which to affect it. (p. 425)

Elidor is a better book than the first two, not only because it is more original in its various conceptions of the impingement of magic upon the everyday world, but because both scene and action are no longer cluttered with too many beings, too many wills at cross-purposes. Here, again, the Bads are tracking the Goods and the Goods are then turning and searching out the Bads to save Elidor from extinction. But Garner's disclosure of a realm of existence, invisible to us but interpenetrating ours, is typical of his sensitivity to place, his imaginative power of seeing, and his ability to reveal what he sees to his reader. He is no longer describing the English countryside, but his own country of the mind. And in his conjuring of a desolate landscape, menacing, drained of all color, intensely seen as in a nightmare or in some surrealist film in stark black and white, we again experience Garner's gift of poetic overtone released by certain kinds of circumstances. I was reminded of that sequence in Ingmar Bergman's film *Wild Strawberries* in which the elderly protagonist dreams of his own funeral carriage moving along a warped and deserted street where a giant watch hangs overhead pointing to some doomed moment. For it is exactly this premonitory sense of dream, in which events seem insanely warped yet exude, as one progresses through the dream, a kind of arcane logic, that is best in *Elidor*. It is there as Garner prepares for and carries off the instant when the four children, Helen, Nicholas, David, and Roland are, through apparently their own decisions, led to that fateful cross-roads of incidents which ejects them from our plane of existence into that other that has awaited their coming since the days of the starved fool. It is there when Roland discovers the empty fingers of Helen's recently lost mitten clutched in layers of smooth-growing turf and, underneath, the cuff frozen in ancient quartz. It is there when the children are shown an ages-old parchment on which the fool had foretold their coming and painted their small pictures in figures of medieval beauty. (Here, in these last two details, are the first hints of Garner's captivation by the idea of past, present, and future existing in a timeless moment which comes to fuller fruition in *The Owl Service*.) It is there, this arcane, dreamlike logic, in those later events in which the children are besieged by men of the other world who are attempting to reclaim the treasures of the four kingdoms that the children are preserving until Elidor shall be safe and light shines in Gorias again.

In many of these last chapters, Garner makes use of one of the principles of physics, yet in doing so in no way sends his fantasy over into science fiction. Here we are reminded of William Mayne's *Earthfasts*. Garner's fantasy was first published in Britain in 1965 and Mayne's in 1966, so that both must have been brooding their own special uses of scientific knowledge within the context of fantasy at about the same time. But there is an interesting difference between the two men's employment of science. Garner makes direct use of the

effects of static electricity upon the children and all electrically run objects within the force field surrounding whatever place the children have hidden the treasures. But Mayne mingles poetic and scientific insights and awarenesses throughout *Earthfasts* not only to make more precisely felt by the reader the experiences of his two boys in a situation of released magic in the twentieth century, but to pinpoint those qualities and points of view which differentiate David and Keith. It is a much richer and more subtle use than Garner's.

Character portrayal, a deficiency in Garner's writing which was apparent in his first two books, is again a problem. For in *Elidor* too there is a lack of characterization of the children, with the exception of Roland, the child most concerned with all that is unbelievably happening to the Watsons. It is through his eyes that we see the landscape of the other world, and through his thoughts that we experience most of the action and emotion of the book. It is he who in the human world remains faithful to the idea of Elidor in the face of the flip, slangy cynicism of his two brothers, set down in a more staccato style than the conversations of the two previous books. Yet what we have of him, simply because we are "seeing" through his senses, does not approach the complexity and felt humanity of either David or Keith in *Earthfasts*. And I cannot in recollection separate Garner's Nicholas from his brother David, nor remember anything about Helen except that she is a girl. (pp. 426-27)

In *The Owl Service* Garner again takes off from legend, specifically from the fourth book of the *Mabinogion,* and relates the effects of this legend upon a small group of people living in the valley of Ardudwy in Wales. Susan Sontag, in her essay "Against Interpretation," advises that in order to do any creative work the highest justice, the critic must never show what a work means, but rather "show how it is what it is," and "even that it is what it is." Nonetheless, Garner himself has placed in the front of *The Owl Service* a quotation from the *Radio Times* concerning possessive parents and selfishness, and there in the fewest possible words is the minor theme of the book, one that determines, actually, the progression of the major theme, which the reader can scarcely avoid seeing as an explication of how the evil that men do lives after them. (p. 428)

One sees within the structure of *The Owl Service* a series of three triangles. The first triangle was formed in legendary times by Blodeuwedd, her husband, and her lover. The second triangle was formed centuries later, before the action of the book, by Huw Halfbacon and Nancy, servants in the house which is the main scene of the book, and Bertram, Nancy's lover. The third triangle is formed in present time by the teen-agers Gwyn (Nancy's son), Alison, and Roger, who is Alison's stepbrother. The story begins with the act by which Blodeuwedd's accumulated agony is given power and direction when Gwyn and Alison recover the owl service from its hiding place, a service decorated with a design which could be either owls or flowers. When Alison chooses to see the design as owls and acts accordingly, she brings upon herself the concentrated hatred of Blodeuwedd and at length becomes her emotional and spiritual captive. Only through a fresh "seeing" of the design can both Blodeuwedd's and Alison's release be affected after continuing discoveries by Gwyn and Roger concerning the past. Nancy acts always as the impassioned obstacle to these revelations, and Huw Halfbacon as the fateful voice of timelessness.

Garner's method in this book (the first time he has used it to such an extent) is to allow almost all information regarding place, previous events, character, and plot to be revealed through explanations by the author. And it is a tribute to his craftsmanship that with a few deft strokes these relationships are all made clear, though in the interests of tension and suspense the legendary ones come through by degrees.

As in his three previous works, Garner is at his best in the evocation of place, but there is little actual description in *The Owl Service* and what is given is laid on in almost pointillist strokes, now here, now there, in single sentences or short paragraphs having to do with feeling and action. Presently one realizes almost by osmosis, that it is the same valley, Ardudwy, where the legendary lover, Gronw Pebyr, met his death at the hands of Lleu Llaw Gyffes. Wales as place is a necessity, given the Welsh origin of the legend, and the ancient Cantref of Ardudwy in particular. But Garner takes advantage of Wales as the small, insular bit of the British Isles, where the inhabitants are even more deeply aware than in the rest of Britain "of time as an eternal moment rather as something with a separate past and future," to make of *The Owl Service* a time tale. And not only because of Welsh nature and its awareness of the Globe of Time, but because the spirit of Blodeuwedd, a creation of magic, exists in timelessness. He also takes advantage of the fact of Ardudwy as a valley to conceive of it as a reservoir in which force, power, energy (Blodeuwedd's wild agony at being imprisoned) builds up until it must find release through whatever humans are in a particular emotional state with regard to one another. Under extreme duress, they must find it possible to give comfort instead of express hate and so bring to an end the evil that Gwydion had begun. Both Blodeuwedd's imprisonment and the desolation of the valley have continued over the centuries because hatred and murder have been the choice.

With respect to character portrayal, we are struck by Garner's aesthetic growth since his first and, indeed, since his third book, where only the child Roland came through as an individual. In *The Owl Service* Garner works not only with the relationships of the teenagers Gwyn, Roger, and Alison, but with the bitter resentments generated between parent and child and between servant and employer, between classes, backgrounds, and these resentments are continuously laced through the progression of the main theme.

Huw Halfbacon, caretaker of the house and man of all work, who would seem to have existed in the valley since time immemorial, is in his own mind both the magician Gwydion and the betrayed husband Lleu Llaw Gyffes; to the English Roger and his father Clive, he is nothing but an especially moronic type of Welsh clod, "a great hairy Welsh freak"; but to the inhabitants of the valley he is their master, their father, their lord. He it is who holds within himself the weight of the legend, who has taken on its burden, who must protect his people from it, and see that Gwyn does not escape the inheritance of that burden.

Nancy, the housekeeper, who was once, according to Huw, "the winds of April," is now lean and knotted with hard work and bitter with memory, with frustrated destiny; one sees and feels her strongly, as one does Huw and Gwyn, purely through their own words and actions. She hates the valley and what it represents of her own low beginnings, and thus still nurses her hatred of Huw, not only because of their previous relationship, but because he is the spirit of the valley: "I own the ground, the mountains," he says, " . . . the song of the cuckoo, the brambles, the berries, the dark cave is

mine." And yet all these years Nancy has been instilling in Gwyn such an intimate vision of the valley that, though he has never been there until now, he knows every inhabitant, every house, every path and turn and rise and vista and meadow.

As for Gwyn, he is torn between his love of Welsh earth, Welsh singularity, and his fierce determination to better himself away from Welshness in the face of English self-possession, English "superiority," the kind that so takes itself for granted that it is scarcely conscious of its own power to enrage those who suffer under it. And while Gwyn loathes, not his mother's Welshness, but her crudity and illiteracy, he at the same time detests these thick-skinned Birmingham snobs, who come here simply to be able to boast to their friends that they own a Welsh cottage.

Furthermore, this loathing of his mother's class, her commonness, and what it means for his own future, is all entangled with his fury at her blind, raw, selfish power over him, a fury so intense that his moment of revenge on "the old cow" is one of the jolting scenes of the book. Neither Roger nor Clive are any more capable of sensing Gwyn's terrible, self-devouring sensitivity than they are capable of seeing Huw for what he really is. Gwyn says of his own future that he ought to be in Parliament, but Roger calls him a Welsh oaf, and is amused that he wants to better himself. Clive says of his kind that they turn out to be nothing but "barrack-room lawyers. . . . They're the worst . . . brains aren't everything, by a long chalk. You must have background." Clive blandly takes for granted that he and Roger have background, mistaking the possession of a comfortable income for breeding. And Roger shares with his father the morality that, "You'll not go far if you don't learn to bend with the wind." Yet he can say of his father, "Anything for a quiet life; that is why he never gets one." Nancy sees right through Clive. She calls him Lord Muck, the man who looks on pebbledash, a kind of cheap stuccoed surface, as being "rather tasteful," and who is delighted with a hideous little "Kelticraft" object made, revealingly enough, in England. Neither Roger nor Clive are aware of the fact that the clichés that litter their utterances are symbols of their own too-easy, unreflecting attitudes toward life and human relationships.

Alison seems an echo of them. Though she can say to Gwyn in a moment of comradeship that it doesn't matter how he speaks, and that she likes his way because it is Gwyn and not "ten thousand other people," still, she, like Clive and Roger, bends with the wind (Mummy's desires) and, as part of her effort not to upset Mummy, deals Gwyn a mortal hurt in such a way as to reveal herself as either incredibly stupid or incredibly insensitive. We cannot be sure which because we don't know enough about Alison.

I have gone into these character portrayals at some length because Garner's ability to imbue with felt life (Henry James's phrase) his three Welsh protagonists, and his lesser ability to do so for his three English protagonists, is interesting and has a bearing on the final effect of the book. By "felt life" I mean the depths and complexities, the cross-currents of desire and repulsion communicated to the reader from fictional persons. Garner's three English characters are vapid and superficial, and are no doubt meant to be so. But were they meant to be merely *types* of English, or rather *a* type of English? Were they meant to be lacking in interesting qualities, in uniqueness? They are, and here we are faced not only with the communication of their superficiality, but also with this quality in the rendering of them. It is true certainly that something of their personalities can be caught, but there is really not a great deal more to be said of them than what is reported here, except possibly the fact of Clive's stinginess. Were they minor characters, this would be sufficient, but they are not. The book therefore suffers as it would not have done had Garner depicted the vapidness of those three English people as acutely as he has the qualities of his three complex Welsh protagonists. Assuredly the portrayal of an uninteresting or ordinary person can, in the hands of an artist, prove just as fascinating and revelatory of cross-currents as the portrayal of an extraordinary one. There are simply no human beings who do not possess their fascinations, even including those like Roger and Clive and Alison. Alison, to a disappointing degree, is reminiscent of Susan in Garner's first book: the puppet of plot.

One of the weaknesses of Garner's presentation of his English characters is the lack of past. We see backward along the vistas of Huw's and Nancy's and Gwyn's lives, but Alison and Roger and Clive seem scarcely to have existed before the action of the book begins. In Garner's portrayal of Gwyn we even discern with sadness his possible future in London where he will become like those Welsh artists Dylan Thomas speaks of, who "ape the narrow 'a.' They repudiate the Welsh language, whether they know it or not." They stifle "their natural ardour so that they may disparagingly drawl, and with knowledgeable satiety, of the paintings, the music, the guests, their host, corseting their voices so that no lilt or inflection of Welsh enthusiasm may exult or pop out." We know enough of Gwyn, however, to suspect that there will be a time beyond that when he will become himself again.

Dialogue, which can be the means of communicating individuality above all else, raises a question here: can the too faithful echoing of reality result in an injury to art? In *The Owl Service* the dialogues are even more staccato in rhythm than in *Elidor.* And the number of cliché phrases and expressions is truly astonishing. . . . Smart-aleck retorts made their appearance to some extent in *Elidor,* but here their use is carried to such an extreme that they strike us as almost an ingratiation with that ten-to-eighteen age group Mr. Garner says he is writing for: as if he were slanting his book, and this is a regrettable impression. It is no use protesting, "But this is the way people—especially teenagers—talk." Art is selective; the artist *must* select, for strict naturalism is a dead end. Oddly enough, Garner says that he learned Welsh in order not to use it, to avoid the "superficial in characterization— the 'Come you here, bach' school of writing." And he says of the possible insertion here and there of "a gratuitous, and untranslated, line of the language" that "This is reality laid on with a trowel, and it remains external and false." He clearly understands the danger of strict naturalism, and might well have looked farther into the gratuitous use of another kind of language, using the word 'gratuitous' in the legal sense to mean something given without receiving any return value. It is true that these clichés reveal one quality of Roger and Clive, and that Gwyn tries always to be less Welsh. But what Garner has succeeded in doing in his use of this TV type of dialogue (in the unsparing and unselective use of worn phrases in the utterances, quite often *as* the utterances, of those of his characters who would use them) is to lessen the number of opportunities he has to convey facets of individuality and to cheapen the texture and therefore the content of his work.

As well, Garner makes tedious his pages of dialogue by his persistence in using a rhythm which could just possibly be used among his particular characters but which, in art, in a created work, strikes insistently on the inner ear to the point of exhaustion. Two persons, devoted to fantasy, upon finishing *The Owl Service,* accused it of being "confusing," "choppy," of failing to hold together as a unified structure. And I believe that while the effect of confusion could have resulted from the fact that the book is so lean and spare that one must note each small detail, each pointillist stroke in order to understand the whole, it is the staccato beat of the dialogue which may give the effect of choppiness rather than the progression of the action. Furthermore, the tedium of the often unrelieved beat results in weariness on the part of the reader and an ensuing lack of attention and therefore of understanding.

Two questions occur to me in the last pages of *The Owl Service.* The first arises out of the fact that Garner's third triangle is composed of teenagers, young teenagers, though of their exact ages we cannot be certain. One reader thought they could be around thirteen. I felt they were fifteen or sixteen and might well have been older: three persons capable of mature sexual passion and love in order that the full drama inherent in the releasing of Blodeuwedd's agony in the valley of Ardudwy might have been more powerfully realized. Assuredly a novel of teenage struggle can be as full of drama and emergence in any direction as the creator is capable of making it. Possibly here it is the seethe and leap of old fires, still burning fiercely in timelessness, that renders the relationships of these particular young people pale by comparison. Alison appears to have no particular feeling for anyone: for Roger a vague friendliness, and in Gwyn a brief interest. Roger, as far as emotions are concerned, entertains only one: scorn for both Huw and Gwyn. Only Gwyn, of them all, seems capable of passion in the large sense, though his love of Alison (it may simply be an attraction because she is feminine and appealing and is aware of him as a human being as Clive and Roger are not), sinks once he discovers how passively and completely she is at the mercy of her mother. Gwyn suffers. Who else does, of the three? One questions Garner's purpose in determining the members of his triangle to be immature teenagers, two of them uninvolved, if he desired to bring to their fullest fruition the potentialities of his conception. One recalls Rosemary Sutcliff choosing, after a series of novels on early Britain written for youth, to put the story of Arthur and Guinevere and her lover into a novel for adults, because in no other way could she come at its deepest imaginative truth. My question is this: Has Garner wasted his material in thus debilitating it? If one agrees that he has, the question could then be asked if it is wise, having conceived one's idea, to tailor it to an audience of teenagers rather than to allow the material itself to dictate the way in which it shall be handled.

This weakness, this lack of passion and power and force from the depths (what one feels to be an emphasis on the working out of plot: "My concern for the reader is not to bore him"), brings me to a second question, that of the ending. Given Garner's implied necessity that only forgiveness can release Blodeuwedd from her imprisonment, one finds the concluding lines of *The Owl Service* conveying mere prettiness of conceit, a disappointing ease of solution. In fact Roger says, "Is that all it is? As easy as that?" And it turns out to be a matter not of inner struggle but of the repetition of words, the repetition of a single word. Nor is it Gwyn, the inheritor of Huw's burden, who forgives, who comforts. It is Roger, who has suffered nothing—and what does he forgive? A few angry words of Gwyn's. And when one considers the degrees of forgiveness man has wrung out of himself in the face of the most appalling indifference, hypocrisy, and brutality since history began, we find ourselves again faced with weakness, with not nearly enough brought to bear if Garner is concerned, as he declares himself to be, with layers of meaning.

By way of contrast, I keep thinking of another fantastical work, one that has at its heart, as does **The Owl Service,** the brazen act of a magician taking upon himself too great a power, daring too much, and bringing into life a being who should never have existed, an act out of which only suffering can come. I am referring to Ursula K. Le Guin's *A Wizard of Earthsea.* . . . It is a work that is never satisfied simply with the act of magic, but goes beyond to the truth behind it, to the battle of human beings, surrounded as they are by a doom wrought of misapprehension and indiscipline. The final effect of the book is built up through gradual realization and not any easily brought about magical change. It is a work that reveals the human condition as calling for the painfully slow effort to understand one's self and others and then to act upon that understanding, something inevitably as difficult as all that has gone before. As for **The Owl Service,** my second question is this: Isn't it possible that the ingeniousness of conceit which commences it, the fact of Alison seeing one thing rather than another in the design of the plates, may fatally have led to a mere ingeniousness of conceit in the last pages?

For myself, though I appreciate what is best in the craftsmanship of the book, neither the texture nor the final effect is such that I shall go back to it again as I have been compelled to go back to *Earthfasts* and *A Wizard of Earthsea* for that almost indefinable aesthetic reward which arises out of implications, out of the whole ambience of a work, which is always more than a sum of the meanings of the words. (pp. 428-33)

> *Eleanor Cameron, " 'The Owl Service': A Study," in* Wilson Library Bulletin, *Vol. 44, No. 4, December, 1969, pp. 425-33.*

Alan Garner has taken the Celtic legend of Blodeuwedd as the driving force for an intricately plaited narrative in which the ancient tragedy changes each time it is played out. In Alison, Roger and Gwyn it canalizes the unstable, indefinable stresses of adolescence as well as the intangible effects of class difference. The legend is no mere decorative parallel; the mystery of Blodeuwedd and the aura of ancient sorrow deepen the emotional problems that rise from a simple family holiday. The complex material of the book is contained almost wholly in dialogue, the best and most difficult tool any novelist has for revealing character. Spare, short sentences are exchanged between the three young people and their parents; Alison's mother, Margaret, who never speaks or appears, is revealed vividly in the comments or reported speech of the others. Dialogue in **The Owl Service** has to imply action, to sustain atmosphere, to reveal nuances of character, to build tension and to suggest the endless repetitiveness of human passion, and still sound unforced and natural. The power and the passion of the story justify the method Alan Garner has chosen. (pp. 17-18)

> *Margery Fisher, "Who's Who in Children's Books: Alison," in her* Who's Who in Children's Books: A Treasury of the Familiar Characters of Childhood, *Holt, Rinehart and Winston, 1975, pp. 17-18.*

THE HAMISH HAMILTON BOOK OF GOBLINS (1969: U.S. edition as *A Cavalcade of Goblins;* also published as *A Book of Goblins)*

Every child that lies in bed and sees the shadows looming on the wall is reacting to the potential strangeness of the universe. The smaller we feel in relation to the world around us, the more we are conscious of the otherness of things and if modern man has built himself a bastion of science to fend off this world, he is none the less vulnerable to the stars that lie beyond. In Garner's words: "We have lost our faith in the terror of the cornfield and the dark wood, but we still need terror." Folk tales are to some extent an attempt to externalize our fears and to establish a community of terror.

For this reason we should not be afraid of letting our children have such stories. It is often said that children enjoy frightening themselves, and so they should. They are young and highhearted and it is right that the unknown should excite them. It is only the old who flinch away.

[*The Hamish Hamilton Book of Goblins* has] . . . a certain directness, a refusal to compromise which makes [it] real in a way, that retellings of stories handed down from oral tradition are too often not. Alan Garner's interpretation of "goblins" is broad and idiosyncratic. He has chosen stories with a particular quality of imagination which appeals to him. Their provenance is wide and includes many Celtic, Japanese and Indian sources. The absence of tales from Greece and Rome may be due less to the fact that classical myth leaves him, as he says, "cold as marble" than to the strong literary associations of those stories we have. The common folk of Greece and Rome had their bugbears too, still to be found today in the remoter countryside as a living tradition.

A distinguishing characteristic of Alan Garner's book is the scrupulousness with which he has indicated the origins of his stories. His editing in all cases is confined to bringing out the most striking qualities of the original and ranges from discreet clarification of some dialect words to almost complete rewriting of a good idea in a poor setting. Here, as with Sir George Dasent, it is the quality of the English presentation which allows the stories to be almost themselves.

Alan Garner's own talents and imagination are placed at the service of his material rather than striving to dominate it, carrying it back to the oral traditions from which it sprang.

> *"The Long Tradition," in* The Times Literary Supplement, *No. 3513, June 26, 1969, p. 688.*

Central to Alan Garner's offering of spirits and specters is the chapter entitled **"The Secret Commonwealth"** in which he expands upon his belief in fairies "as real people at war with their neighbors" (to quote from the introduction to another chapter), specifically, in Britain, the early inhabitants displaced by the Celts. Which seems not at all obscurantist or oddball after reading the insidious legends adapted here from not only British but also American Indian, Japanese, Serbian and Norse sources to say nothing of the reports of apparitions (including a recent transcription). As Mr. Garner notes in his Notes, he has reworked them in varying degrees; inherently diverse in tone and theme, they retain their individuality of idiom and rhythm. **"Hoichi the Earless,"** from Lafcadio Hearn, tells of a blind balladeer who conjured up graveyard ghosts thinking he was entertaining the Emperor, and the agony of his exorcism; **"Yallery Brown,"** a Lincolnshire legend, demonstrates the danger of heeding the fairy folk ("For harm and mischief and Yallery Brown/ You've let out your-self from under the stone"); **"Moowis,"** one of several Algon-quin tales, involves a cruel maiden cruelly mocked. Not to mention the elusive episodic **"Trade that No One Knows,"** of Serbian origin. Or the poems, mostly of recent authorship. If this series can be considered the aristocracy of anthologies, Alan Garner's contribution both maintains the literary stan-dard and extends the base of interest—not only beyond the British Isles but back to beginnings. (pp. 680-81)

> *A review of "A Cavalcade of Goblins," in* Kirkus Re-views, *Vol. XXXVII, No. 13, July 1, 1969, pp. 680-81.*

An excellent international collection of lurid horror stories, poems and anecdotes that will fill readers with fear and won-der. Some stories appear in their original form while others have been freely adapted; all move very quickly and sustain the mood. Useful source notes and [illustrator Krystyna Tur-ska's] skillful black line drawings intensify the drama. The blood-curdling qualities of the stories, along with their strange settings, exotic names and unusual dialogues, will ap-peal to an older, more sophisticated audience than Manning-Sanders' *A Book of Ghosts & Goblins* (Dutton, 1969), which is a collection of fantasy stories that are lighter in spirit and simpler in plot. Garner's unique, more horrifying and more varied assortment includes: Norse and American Indian my-thology; Oriental, African, European and Russian legends; stories from ancient times to the present. Since there is no du-plication in the two books, Garner can be used to follow up Manning-Sanders as readers progress in ability and mature in taste.

> *Edith F. Anderson, in a review of "A Cavalcade of Goblins," in* School Library Journal, *Vol. 16, No. 4, December, 1969, p. 50.*

RED SHIFT (1973)

Red shift, says the *World Book Encyclopedia* with character-istic clarity, "is a shift in the *spectrum* (color pattern) of a gal-axy or another astronomical object toward the longer (red) wave lengths." Among other things, apparently, it shows that "every galaxy is moving away from every other galaxy, and therefore that the universe is expanding." Knowing this, you might be forgiven for supposing that a novel entitled *Red Shift* dealt with a science-fiction plot. When you found it didn't, you might also be forgiven for guessing that the choice of title was intentionally symbolic and reach the not very pro-found conclusion that the story ponders the way people—individual human galaxies—are forever moving away from each other so that real contact, understanding, and close rela-tionships become less possible every day. (p. 494)

The book's top tune—the main plot and the easiest to fol-low—tells of an intelligent, oversensitive teenager, Tom (his wit saves him from being an emotionally spotty bore), who lives in a trailer with his disagreeably possessive mother and weak-willed army pa (overworked stock characters in teen-age fiction, but given some vitality and individuality here). Tom is in love with a better-balanced, equally intelligent girl, Jan, whose own parents enter the story only as absentee land-lords, because they are busybody social workers always out helping other people. (pp. 494-95)

Orchestrated with the top tune are two subplots, one set in an immediately post-Roman time, the other in the seven-teenth-century civil war period. Both involve the places lived in and visited by the twentieth-century protagonists. I call them sub-plots, but I fancy Garner means them to be co-plots, the function of which is not simply to support the top tune but to add variations to the main theme. In other words, and changing the image, the book is a decorated prism which turns to show—incident by incident—first one face, then an-other. In the last section, the prism spins so fast that the three faces merge into one color, one time, one place, one set of peo-ple, one meaning.

I cannot dwell here on the fascinating details of the novel. The way, for example, Garner suggests his historical periods, and especially the way he uses the brutal gutter talk of Ameri-can commandos in Vietnam to suggest the post-Roman inci-dents. Or the grueling description of the massacre of a village in the civil war scenes. Nor have I space to say anything about the transitions between plots, made by using painful moments in the characters' experiences to break through the time barrier, as though pain were a kind of telepathic switch-ing gear. If I could expand on anything, I'd choose what for me is Garner's most admirable achievement in *Red Shift:* the terrible accuracy of his dialogue, not only as lingua verita, but in the way he uses it to reveal his characters, powering the words with meanings beyond the obvious. (pp. 495-96)

[But] I can do no more now than prepare you for the central dilemma of this complex and difficult work. Is it a technically brilliant literary crossword puzzle, or is it masterpiece? Is the red shift symbol all inclusive of the book or to be interpreted more cautiously?

There are plenty of clues to work on. Indeed, as I read, I was acutely aware of being tested. Can you or can't you find the hidden references? How many did you score? Hit the hun-dred, and join the author's elect (for he, schoolmasterly, can't lose because he set the traps and knows the answers). Consid-er, for example, some of the evidence laid rather too obvious-ly on the surface. Jan tells Tom, "You're always so tolerant with strangers. . . . You savage the people near you." "We're," says Tom pompously, "bits of other futures." And he "sees everything at once," makes witticisms about the M6 (a road route) and M35 (a galaxy near our own), telling Jan meanwhile, "We were born grown up." "We've both be-trayed," says one of the historical characters. "There'll be a price." Tom could almost be replying when he says, "It's a pretty mean galaxy."

Put this sort of thing together, and you feel convinced the book has as its larger theme the red shift of parting worlds, of the impossibility of reconciliatory contact. If, however, you apply the symbol only partially and reinterpret the clues, you come out with a very much less metaphysical solution supported by another speech of Tom's: "I see and can't un-derstand. I need to adjust my spectrum, pull myself away from the blue end. I could do with a red shift. Galaxies and Rectors have them. Why not me?" Follow that hint, and you must decide the book is really saying nothing more startling than this: Everyone needs a little distance from the deepest pains of living before the pain is understood and can be coped with, before experience can be given perspective, and be made bearable. And I suppose you could add that adolescence is a time when emotional pain is raw and intensely felt, is often exaggerated and too closely inspected.

Literary code-cracking aside, what I find critically worrying is not the novel's complexity but its failure to work on the plane on which it asks to be accepted. We are intended, I'm sure, to feel very deeply, to empathize with Tom and his predicament. *The Owl Service* worked memorably in this manner despite its technical faults and constructional weaknesses. It didn't matter whether you understood completely and intellectually the below-surface meanings. You felt them strongly. *Red Shift*—brilliantly organized though it is, inventive, so tautly written it nearly snaps, honed, scrubbed, made concentratedly dense—is yet too clever by half. It doesn't touch the nerves of feeling that it reaches out, somewhat coldly, to finger.

In *The Owl Service* mythical history repeated itself in the lives of two boys and a girl and was, for me, utterly convincing in the telling. In *Red Shift* a boy and a girl are once again swept along with historic inevitability, trapped in the red shift effect; and though the idea is attractive, though I admire the technical achievements, I am neither convinced nor much moved except by isolated scenes.

Maybe the fault is mine; perhaps I need to give the book more time. After all, Garner has spent six years making it. Why should I expect to plumb its depths in a couple of readings? But of one thing I'm sure. Garner has given up any pretense of writing for children and is now writing entirely to please himself and those mature, sophisticated, literate readers who care to study his work. I'm not moaning about this; it is a fact of the writer's life. But because Garner is one of our most talented and exciting authors, I hope he won't forget where his career began and will occasionally let down his literary hair and again tell a story to children. (pp. 496-97)

> *Aidan Chambers, "Letter from England: Literary Crossword Puzzle . . . or Masterpiece?" in The Horn Book Magazine, Vol. XLIX, No. 5, October, 1973, pp. 494-97.*

Red Shift expresses the significance of place and the insignificance of time. Instead of plunging underground in the ruins of a Manchester church or vanishing into Alderley Edge to be plagued by svarts and aided by benign wizards, Alan Garner now leaves the fantasy worlds of his earlier books behind, eschewing even the legendary paths of *The Owl Service,* and becomes instead an older, more tortured mental traveller. Here the hole is in no mere hillside: it is a hole through which to look back through history, a hole which telescopes one endlessly through space, a hole into the brain of a man trying to come to terms with the notion that time is simply a convenient way of ordering experience. 'We're bits of other futures,' says Tom to his girl friend Jan, whom he meets for snatched weekends at Crewe, 'and the instant you step off that train it's the beginning of parting. Time runs out on us. I'm not living. I'm on Crewe station. I wake each morning hoping the day's the dream and the night real.' From such conceits are metaphysical poems made; and, certainly, in its singular way, *Red Shift* (to savage Donne) 'makes of Crewe an everywhere' while regarding Time as the invulnerable enemy. The significance of place is established through setting the narrative in three different periods in the history of a few square miles of Cheshire countryside around the village of Barthomley, Mow Cop and Crewe: the insignificance of time is suggested by the way the author interleaves the narrative's contemporary strand about the relationship of Tom and Jan, with the story of Thomas and the other villagers from the seventeenth century and that of Macey and his splinter group of Roman soldiers from the Ninth Legion. The shifts from one strand to another are managed skilfully such that

while one is kept busy associating characters and relationships, noticing the common thread of violence, responding to the tangible link of the stone axe-head which is handed from one time level into the next, yet the three narrative lines remain sharply distinct. For example, Tom, Thomas, and Macey are all prone to brainstorms when they apprehend the instability of man's place in the scheme of things yet they articulate their experiences quite differently. Macey 'flips' and becomes the frenzied killer of the Ninth Legion, Thomas's hallucinations and fears parallel Macey's and in his fits he too glimpses various colours and hears 'Sounds. All sorts. Echoes backwards.' Whereas Tom expresses Garner's ambitious attempt to link macrocosm and microcosm in twentieth-century terms, lacking the aid of the Elizabethan consciousness:

> I see and can't understand. I need to adjust my spectrum, pull myself away from the blue end. I could do with a red shift. Galaxies and Rectors have them. Why not me?

The sense of cosmic terror and violence which the writing unleashes when Macey flips and Thomas has his fits, and the uneasiness generated by Tom's constant awareness of the expanding universe are enough to render the most complacent reader's view of reality a precarious one. Moreover, Alan Garner stamps on one's fingers at the end for, predictably perhaps, the three time levels coalesce in the last few pages. Time is collapsed. A sort of artistic red shift has been effected.

Unevenness of commitment on the part of the author is a natural pitfall in this tripartite structure and there are indications that Alan Garner is emotionally caught up in the story of Tom, Jan and Tom's parents in ways he cannot be in the other strands. Tom, a highly intelligent eighteen-year old waiting to go up to Oxford, embodies amongst other things, the writer's hang-ups about his Cheshire upbringing and his education at Manchester Grammar School. It is not confessional writing, more an exorcism; through Tom, Alan Garner appears to be reliving a significant period of his own youth. (pp. 5-8)

The row with Tom's parents, the excruciating scene over his birthday cake, the jigsaw sequence where he tries to communicate with his mother and father are brilliantly written, relying (as indeed the whole book does) upon the writer's superb ear for natural dialogue. Tom is an irritating character at first, too clever by half, using his quick repartee to score easy verbal victories over his parents. His intelligence appears to be used insensitively as a weapon, alienating the reader until the parental background is sketched in and one's sympathies readjust. This development is handled carefully: the jigsaw of tensions is only slowly pieced together and Alan Garner holds back the sad scene in which Tom discovers Jan's lover until two-thirds of the way through the book with fine structural and psychological judgment.

The triangular relationship which is revealed late in the contemporary strand of the narrative and used as a means of exploring Tom's and Jan's life more intimately, is also present in more violent form elsewhere. Thomas and Madge are both threatened and aided by Venables; Macey and the girl salvage some tenderness despite Magoo and the other soldiers. All act out the timeless dilemma of striving for honesty and permanence in love and of trying to come to terms with its reality in a universe of perpetual flux. The most interesting feature of the seventeenth-century strand is the way the reader is focused on Thomas's terror. Thomas is on watch on Barthomley church tower shortly before a force of Irish who support the King attack the village. He gazes at Mow Cop and the hallucinations of his fit capture him. He tries to explain his visions to John Flowler, the young curate, who merely taunts him about Venables, Madge's former suitor. Thomas reacts violently and Madge bursts in to break up the fight between the two men. The interesting thing is that this incident is rerun on the next two occasions that the seventeenth-century strand is taken up; slightly varied and giving us a different slant and a little more information each time. The technique is cinematic; its effect is to intensify our interest in Thomas's state of mind and to relate it to Macey's brainstorms and Tom's periods of mental anguish. This device, while being unique, is symptomatic of **Red Shift** where every incident, like a stone thrown into a pond, reverberates through the rest of the pages. Events in Alan Garner's narrative assume spatial relationships rather than linear ones. (pp. 8-9)

Red Shift is a lean, spare book. Throughout there is a threat of incipient violence which periodically flares out, like a burning star, in psychological or physical terms. It is not a violence that is conceived of in a socially explicable manner; it is the violence engendered in the release of that energy which permits life and upon which the very notion of a created universe rests. Ted Hughes's poetry often approaches the same theme and one feels it is no accident that Alan Garner's style of writing is as hard-edged and evocative in its vocabulary and speech rhythms as are the poems of *Wodwo* and *Crow*. Certainly in style and structure the book is uncompromising: the familiar literary surface of the conventional novel is stripped away and one is constantly picking up hints, catching at clues, making associations and allowing the chiselled quality of the writing to suggest new mental landscapes. Perhaps **Red Shift** asks to be read as a poem. Inevitably, there are losses. There is the feeling of reading an over-digested book. It is seven years since **The Owl Service** and there is a distinct impression that **Red Shift** represents a distillation of years of reading and ruminating until the intellectual pattern of the book emerged. The result is, undeniably, a daring, intense piece of writing which, for those who approach the novel as they might an archaeological 'dig', proves a richly rewarding experience. They are plenty of hidden riches to unearth. The reader who enjoys the expansiveness of fiction, however, will be craving greater fullness and wishing the writer had allowed himself more room for reflection. On occasions there is certainly the uneasy feeling of dealing with a skeleton rather than a body and that the author requires the cooperation of the detective imagination in his reader to puzzle out everything from the original cosmic mystery to the intricacies of Lewis Carroll's code which Tom and Jan use in their letters to each other. . . . It's that sort of book: clever, infuriating, brilliantly conceived and beautifully written. (pp. 11-12)

> *Michael Benton, "Detective Imagination," in Children's literature in education, No. 13, March, 1974, pp. 5-12.*

[In **Red Shift** the] time-shifts are not accomplished by technology or explained by logic. The device that breaks through time-distance is psychic pressure—human pain. In the end the pain becomes intolerable, and the three times become one. As if the "red shift" of the titles were reversed, as in the expansion-contraction model of the cosmos, and all the souls and stars that drift helplessly farther and farther apart were brought back in together, gripped, crushed in a final and terrible implosion.

A bitter, complex, brilliant book.

Above all, brilliant. Garner writes in fireworks. The dialogue is as mannered as Compton-Burnett's, but wittier, more alive, more powerful. Everything cut to the bone. No transitions, no explanations. The reader, as with poetry, must work: and is rewarded for it. Pace—the driving pace of the 1960s—the American Sunday motorist in his highpowered car—"Nice town we're coming to, wasn't it?"

The danger of such brilliance: preciosity. It is not wholly escaped. Bareness becomes quirkiness, density become opacity; the crossfire of allusion and symbol becomes a flashy pedantry.

The function of such brilliance: well, delight . . . And also, it saves the book. It saves the protagonist, Tom, from being merely pitiful, sick, lost. Thomas and Macey, his other manifestations, are psychotics, quite out of reach, and correspondingly less interesting. Tom fights his madness, which is the world's madness. He fights it with wit, with the mind's grace, with verbal and intellectual brilliance. A cold light, but better than the darkness. You realize that when in the end he loses his fight and goes, mumbling platitudes, into the darkness.

Verbal originality of another kind saves the Roman-British sequences from banality. The legionaries of the Ninth talk G.I. It is absolutely right, and its rightness gives flair and intensity to the rather conventionally primitive-brutal episodes.

The Civil War sequences are the dullest to my taste: overcomplicated, and seldom relieved by stylistic rockets and pinwheels.

Garner's earlier book **The Owl Service . . .** rests upon a solider but less ambitious structure: a tale from the *Mabinogion* re-enacted, rather than an original, and difficult, invention of the author's mind. Some of the power of **Owl Service** is borrowed—and why not? The Blodeuwedd myth is very subtle and very strong; only a dolt could spoil it in the retelling. Far from spoiling it, Garner worked into his recreation of it a restrained passion that is entirely his own. There is only one character in the book, Gwyn; the others are stereotypes; but Gwyn is quite enough . . . Real passion is a very rare thing in modern novels. We skip from sentimentality to perversity, missing the centre, the real thing. Gwyn's love and desire, his despair, ambition, obstinacy, courage, the awful absoluteness of adolescent emotion: in these are the makings of tragedy, and of the tragic hero. The book would be, indeed, fully comparable to *Wuthering Heights*, if only Gwyn's Alison were a Catherine Earnshaw. Alas, she isn't. She isn't much of anything; not enough to stand up to Gwyn, anyway.

Jan, in **Red Shift,** is a person of force and grace; she is quite able to stand up to Tom, and their love story begins to build up the same kind of yearning, desperate power. But Tom lets us down. Not through hubris, but through weakness, like a Hardy hero. Listen to the footsteps of Doom. Watch the galaxies recede. Why does Tom give the stone axe his soul, her soul, their hope, away? Because he's sick. His parents are sick, so he's sick. What should hit the reader as an unbearable betrayal comes merely as a clinical symptom. Jan's strength and sweetness seem less wasted than merely irrelevant.

Though one may know the Welsh legend and so know "what's going to happen" in **Owl Service,** the dramatic tension never relaxes. In **Red Shift,** though the possibilities are unlimited, the story does not drive forward to its conclusion.

The sense of necessity falters. The book's gait is fast but mechanical; its motive force seems not so much emotional as geometrical. This may, of course, be quite deliberate.

I have read that Garner spent six years writing the book. Oh that some sf writers would spend six years, or even one year, writing their books! The number of raw first drafts passed off as sf novels is appalling. Write it on Tuesday, publish it on Wednesday. And remainder it on Thursday . . . But there is a danger, a rare one to be sure, in the other direction. **Red Shift** is wonderfully wellmade, pared down, honed, polished, refined, every rift loaded carefully with ore, every line of dialogue razor-edged. There is not one word too many. But, when one begins to go thus towards the perfection of silence, is not even one word, at last, too many?

Certain disturbed children, set to painting, paint startlingly beautiful and original pictures. And the doctor, observing, must struggle with his values: Art or Therapy? For if he does not intervene, take the picture away and put a new sheet on the easel, the child will go on painting the same one. On and on, adding, deleting, working, reworking, perfecting . . . When he stops he is satisfied, but nobody else on the hither side of autism can see the painting any more. All the carefully drawn and redrawn lines and masses cancel one another out, fill the paper from edge to edge. He has painted a solid blank, and hidden his soul behind it.

The root of the word "meticulous" is *metus,* fear.

There is a quality in **Red Shift** of withdrawal: it is its own symbol. That is both just and beautiful. But withdrawal, in an act of communication, which (alas) is what a novel is, can go only so far. Perfectly finished, the object refers only to itself. The lack of reference to anything outside is meaninglessness. The search for perfection turns inward, only inward. Desire, morality, perception, finally even pain, the last thing to go, recede, withdraw, implode. The Grail vanishes. One is left with a flicker of brilliance, a breath of coldness, a sense of loss. (pp. 110-12)

> *Ursula K. Le Guin, "No, Virginia, There Is Not a Santa Claus," in* Foundation, No. 6, May, 1974, pp. 109-12.

THE BREADHORSE (1975)

Alan Garner has found a perfect complement for his concentrated, philosophical text in the casual-seeming water-colours of Albin Trowski. This is a brief, telling parable of Ned who "can't whistle and can't spit" and who is never allowed to have his turn of riding in what proves to be a rough playground knockabout game. In bed, though, Ned finds new courage in visions of splendid horses who show him that they too have borne their burdens, and proudly. So, next day, the timid boy boldly makes his way to the playground, ready to join in not as victim but as the equal of his persecutors. In the jostling crowds of children faces and clothes are neatly differentiated. Faces express the changing moods of malice, amusement, boisterous high spirits and amazement; dreams evoke chargers and legendary horses shown in fluid, exciting line and colour. Topical, energetic play and the mystery of thought and feeling have taken an inevitable form in this outstanding picture-book.

> *Margery Fisher, in a review of "The Breadhorse," in* Growing Point, *Vol. 14, No. 2, July, 1975, p. 2666.*

Ned is the butt of other children, always the taunted and terrorized "Breadhorse" in the traditional game. By dreaming himself into a Pegasus figure, the real Ned becomes stronger and better able to cope with playground bullying. When Maurice Sendak boldly chose a mere temper-tantrum as the theme for *Where the Wild Things Are* he was illuminating a transient and ordinary phase in child development: even so, only genius of his stature could transcend the problems inherent in exploring its theme in picture-book terms. Alan Garner, with the aid of a new artist, has chosen to tackle an abnormal psychological state which proves, not surprisingly, resistant to picture-book analysis.

> *Elaine Moss, "The Unclassified Appeal," in* The Times Literary Supplement, *No. 3826, July 11, 1975, p. 771.*

THE GUIZER: A BOOK OF FOOLS (1975)

The Guizer, in this book, is many things. He may be called Fool or Trickster; he may be animal or human or both. He is almost always ambiguous—as Alan Garner puts in his introduction, "he is at once creator and destroyer, bringer of help and harm". In the Winnebago Hare Cycle he tries, and fails, to win immortality for his race, but in the story of **"Leza the Besetting One"** from Northern Rhodesia and, less directly, in the tales of Finn and the Fianna, he identifies Death. The Epilogue in fact states one line of argument—or rather, of feeling—in the sequence of tales, quoting a Ba'Ila proverb that says "A man does not die except at the hour of his birth". But more direct perhaps than words is the unspoken message of the extraordinary face on the book-jacket, a Celtic stone head whose date is conjectured as "circa 1st century A.D.". What are those eyes, that mouth, communicating? Is it an expression of pain, of quiet menace, of acceptance? It is a face full of secrets, and so is the book.

Alan Garner has chosen stories that come distantly from many oral traditions—from Africa, Polynesia, Ireland, Alaska, Flanders, as well as from his own county of Cheshire. He has arranged them in three sections, to "impose a sense of order, however fleeting, if the Guizer is to be presented with a valid face". So, in the first section he is seen as Fool, often either in animal guise or in an inexplicable combination of human and animal, as in the Akan-Ashanti tales of Ananse. In the second, he is Man—sometimes a kind of berserk, as in the strange cycle, 'Sir Halewyn', made by a nineteenth century French scholar from fragments collected in Brabant and Flanders, and again a coarser but less brutal disrupter like Robin Goodfellow. In the third section the Guizer is redeemer, fire-bringer, mediator between Heaven and Earth, or Under and Over Worlds, like Hare in North American myth or the Polynesian Maui, whose breaking of tribal tapus is seen as a brave attempt to force life to do his will. I find the choice of stories for the last section clear enough but the first two sections overlap a good deal. Moreover, they show (as the final and most searching section does not) how subterranean the "argument" of the book really is. We all find in myth what we are and what we have to bring to an understanding of it, and it is hardly likely that any of us will read the pieces in the way Alan Garner has read and used them.

The solution, as with all his books, is to read the stories. Something will emerge, even if it is partial and confused, something of the way people have in the past, and all over the world, sought to explain themselves and their surroundings.

Themselves, most of all. An enigmatic phrase in a note on Robin Goodfellow suggests that in arranging the stories, variations of the irrational in humanity, Alan Garner blames the Puritan ethic in England at least for the conscious separation of soul and body, of choice and impulse, of duty and pleasure, a separation which psychologists of our century are now trying to redress, not by license but by self-awareness. Certainly the lack of formal or moral logic is as obvious in most of the tales—notably, those from Africa—as the existence of a *stylistic* logic. Many of the tales have now been retold or compressed or in one way or another shaped to be clearer in the reading; as Alan Garner has said in another context, when a version works, "the writer is a transmitter, not an archivist". He has, all the same, gone back to the earliest possible versions of the chosen stories, altering only where it seemed essential. Most notably, he has used Antony Alpers's texts for the Polynesian myths, texts which happily bypassed the bowdlerised, trivial versions of the '30's to the transcripts made by Governor Grey in the middle of the last century, from conversations with Maori tohungas. Altogether, in Alan Garner's chosen pieces we escape from the prettified "How the kookaburra got its laugh" type of story, for metamorphosis or simpler kinds of change both reflect something wider and more numinous. (pp. 2783-84)

> *Margery Fisher, in a review of "The Guizer: A Book of Fools," in* Growing Point, *Vol. 14, No. 7, January, 1976, pp. 2783-84.*

This is Alan Garner's most ambitious work. His introduction explains his concept of the Fool, whom he chooses to call by the anonymous mediaeval name of Guizer: he is that element from which our emotions are built which marks us most, "the advocate of uncertainty: he is at once creator and destroyer, bringer of help and harm. He draws a boundary for chaos so that we can make sense of the rest". And Alan Garner divides this movement of the soul from animal instinct to divinity and self-knowledge into three, the Guizer as Fool, as Man and as God. In each section the myths range all over the world, from primitive folk-lore to local European legends and traditions. The title-decorations are from mediaeval church graffiti. We are meant to experience the book for itself, but there are (fortunately) careful notes giving sources and background, and an important bibliography. We find that some of the stories most suited in style to their mood and setting have been retold by Alan Garner himself. Elsewhere, he has chosen, where possible, the earliest version of his material in English. Some episodes are mere snippets, others long stories in several chapters, like the Finn legends and, in particular, the horrific Flemish chivalry tale, **"Sir Halewyn"** (in Harold Taylor's compelling translation). There is something sinister about the whole elaborately conceived work, and one falls under its spell even while not fully understanding. The Guizers are many of them cruel, with crude tastes: one wonders about all sorts of things, for instance why the Spider Ananse is here, but not the comfortingly familiar Brer Rabbit, Mr. Punch or even Pierrot. It is certainly a book that should be read, and not only by imaginative children. (pp. 42-3)

> *M. Hobbs, "The Guizer: A Book of Fools," in* The Junior Bookshelf, *Vol. 40, No. 1, February, 1976, pp. 42-3.*

THE STONE BOOK (1976); *GRANNY REARDUN* (1977)

AUTHOR'S COMMENTARY

[The following excerpt is taken from an interview by Aidan Chambers conducted on March 20, 1978.]

I had no idea that **The Stone Book** was going to beget others. I did not know there was a quartet until I was nearly at the end of **The Stone Book.** Through talking to Linda Davis, my editor, and hearing other conversations, I was aware that there was a problem over the nature of the material available for young readers today and that there was concern among teachers that readers were being lost because a child with the technical ability to read was being provided with material which insulted his intelligence and therefore he would quite rightly go and watch something on the television. So—as part of a simple general conversation—I did discuss it some two or three years before I had the basic drive to write **The Stone Book.**

When I was starting to write **The Stone Book,** I remembered the earlier conversations with great clarity; I thought, I must now forget those conversations because I am a writer. I'm not a technical linguist who can feed into the language the right proportion of difficulty, interest, and so on. I do not have that skill, or the training, or the background. But I did want to give the child as much room to expand as the child could take, without making the child feel that if he hadn't expanded far enough he was losing something.

Now this I think is the definition of a children's book. If a child can read with a totality of experience and the adult can too, that is a good children's book. Therefore I would say that *Lord of the Flies* is not a children's book, because I doubt if a ten-year-old can read the whole of the text without sensing gaps in his comprehension. This is not to criticize the author, it is to criticize the use of the book by other people.

I was faced with the fact that at the time, ostensibly, my editor and I were engaged on an educational project; it was as simple as that. And, I thought, Well, how am I going to do it? Then I did something instinctively. I went back to my own childhood for the first time, and I remembered that when I learnt to read, the act of reading was more important than the content. It was a physical act: I could feel the shape of the words in my mouth as concrete objects. And so I started to tell the story of **The Stone Book** in a vocabulary that I could taste—I could actually feel the words in my mouth. That was the simple level of doing it. When I looked back at the text, I see what the twenty years of writing had enabled me to do.

It is why, of all the work I've done so far, the only work which I would permanently want to hold on to is this quartet of four books, because what I set out to achieve, I surpassed. In other words, I did it despite myself. Because integration set in, and when I look back at the text it is far better than I, the organism, the trained male, could have done. Something else took place, and I can only put it down to the fact that at last I stopped being defensive towards my background. I did not have a chip on my shoulder. I had something far worse, I had one on my soul.

I also was very well read in a lot of abstract languages, so the simple language of **The Stone Book** is a complete trick, at one level. I chose a lot of the words because I wanted them to taste as I remembered their taste from childhood. That was my only criterion. But when I look at it I see that, incidentally, sections of **The Stone Book** obey rules which are demand-ed of poetry, both in medieval Welsh and in early English. Now that is something that you have to know even to under-stand. But I think that you can get it emotionally. In Welsh poetry there were certain rules which involved sequences of consonants and vowels which had to be maintained. Some-thing similar was present in Old English. At the beginning of **The Stone Book** you can see how it works as a piece of po-etry and also how it works for the teacher. I may have, almost by default, supplied the teacher with a reader. There are two paragraphs I'd like to use as an example, but what I'm saying is true in all four books:

> The new steeple on the new church glowed in the sun: but something glinted. The spire, stone like a needle, was cluttered with the masons' platforms that were left. All the way under the Wood Hill Mary watched the golden spark that had not been there before.
>
> She reached the brick cottage on the brink of the Moss. Between there and the railway station were the houses that were being built. The railway had fetched a lot of people to Chorley. Before, Father said, there hadn't been enough work. But he had made gate posts, and the station walls, and the brid-ges and the Queen's Family Hotel; and he had even cut a road through rock with his chisel, and put his mark on it. Every mason had his mark, and Father put his at the back of a stone, or on its bed, where it wouldn't spoil the facing. But when he cut the road on the hill he put his mark on the face once, just once, to prove it.

In the first paragraph there are links of assonance (such as "glowed" and "golden", "steeple" and "needle") and of con-sonantal sequence. "The new steeple on the new church glowed in the sun: but something glinted", is a sentence formed by contagion. It is this aspect that has affinities, with Old English and Welsh poetry, and it comes without con-scious thought. If I tried to write like this knowingly the re-sult would be a mess.

Something else happens in the second paragraph. "Brick", "brink", "bridges" are eased together by a word that isn't there. "Brought" is hiding under "fetched", which itself has been preferred because of the growing "ch, ch" of the working mason's hand: "church", "watched", "cottage", "reached". And so "fetched" instead of "brought". Then all is resolved in the word that is making the noise: "chisel".

If you'll look at the two paragraphs you'll see other examples.

As I've said, I found myself engaged on an educational proj-ect that I was not equipped to fulfil. Therefore, I was thrown back on something instinctive, which didn't fulfil it: it sur-passed it. And enabled me to write. (pp. 312-15)

Alan Garner, in an interview with Aidan Chambers in The Signal Approach to Children's Books: A Collection, *edited by Nancy Chambers, Scarecrow Press, 1980, pp. 276-328.*

Probably the best books I've read all year are Alan Garner's masterful and inspiring **The Stone Book** and **Granny Reardun** written in a most rich, economical English, in-formed by Garner's own childhood Cheshire dialect. The po-etic resonance of these sequential books is that of the most penetrating fairy tales, of the truest tales of journeys of the

soul. But Garner writes about plain people and focuses on the crucial decisions, or acts, that lead to man- or womanhood.

The Stone Book is set in the mid-19th century when the rail-roads were spreading throughout England. Mary, who gath-ers stone in the fields for her father, a master stonemason, brings him his midday ration. He's finishing work on a new church steeple. Mary climbs the spire, even climbs fearlessly atop the weathercock for a spin at the top of the world. Later, at home, she tells him she wants to learn to read, but if he won't allow it, she still wants a book to carry to chapel like her friends. Instead, her father takes her for a late walk down an old shaft where the stone has been nearly quarried out. She has to go the last bit alone, armed only with a light and his instructions, to find . . . what? A painting of a huge bull, and the mark of a hand as big as her own, that she thinks is her father's. But the hand mark is ancient: Her father had been taken down there when he was her age, his father before him, and so on. "It puts a quietness on you, does the bull." Later, he carves her a prayerbook of stone.

That's the outline. Garner's eye is keen for mood and gesture, for light and sound, for the intimate, humble details that be-speak other untold stories, for the look of a thing and for its weight in the life of his characters. Garner carries the girl from the brightest eyrie on the steeple to the blackest pit, and roots her back in her daily life nourished by a gift whose meaning she has grown to understand.

By the time of **Granny Reardun,** the good building stone has petered out: A house in the village is being torn down for the stone it's made of. And the boy, Joseph, reared by his grand-parents, must decide his future. He decides not to follow his grandfather (the stonemason of **Stone Book**), but to cut him-self loose from that dominating presence whose work is ev-erywhere he looks and declare his independence. Joseph ap-prentices himself to the blacksmith, to the labor that fires his imagination.

What is comforting about Mary and her father and Garner's other characters, is the solidity and clarity of their relation-ships, their truthfulness, their contemplativeness that leads unswervingly to concrete acts in an ordinary world. And it's in this matrix of ordinariness, of familiarity, that they show their fires. The stonemason loves and esteems his craft, his way with stone, cutting and polishing. It nurtures him and honors him. So he gives his daughter a book, not just to please her vanity, but a book out of the body of the world. (p. 98)

Burt Supree, "Kid's Books: 'Don't Eat Me!',"in The Village Voice, *Vol. XXIII, No. 52, December 25, 1978, pp. 98-100.*

Many of Garner's books for older readers are superbly writ-ten but too intricate for many children; with **The Stone Book** he begins a cycle of related short novels for younger children and combines a profound depth and compassion with simpler writing and an intriguing story. The four stories are set in Cheshire, and both the setting and the dialogue, rich in local idiom, give color to the writing. . . . The first book is set in Victorian times, but it and the second have a timeless quality; they are elemental, honest, touching vignettes of a simple life lived by good people, and they are small gems.

Zena Sutherland, in a review of "The Stone Book" and "Granny Reardun," in Bulletin of the Center for Children's Books, *Vol. 32, No. 7, March, 1979, p. 115.*

Thematically [*The Stone Book*] is symbolic and multilayered, but the ultimate idea shines through with an elemental wisdom: the continuity of life, the perception of a collective past. Laced with Mercian words still used in rural Cheshire, the prose is clean, cadenced, and simple, its images sharpened by the elliptical style. Worlds away from the clever contemporaneity of much modern realism, the book makes one want immediately to seek out some children to share it with. . . .

The luminous style [of *Granny Reardun*] is so simple and direct that there is scarcely a complex sentence in the story, but the combination of Mercian expressions with the unpretentious, everyday English words gives the writing an unexpected texture. Although the story lacks the narrative compulsion of *The Stone Book,* it is impossible to judge its structural significance without a knowledge of the final two books of the quartet, which will be published in 1979. On the other hand, it can be independently savored for its atmosphere, mood, and verbal overtones. (p. 193)

> *Ethel L. Heins and Paul Heins, in a review of "The Stone Book" and "Granny Reardun," in* The Horn Book Magazine, *Vol. LV, No. 2, April, 1979, pp. 192-93.*

[*Granny Reardun*] is beautifully crafted and vividly conveys Joseph's exhilaration at finding his future as well as his grandfather's satisfaction in his own past. Though the writing, overall, is straightforward, even simple, one problem for American readers may be the rural English vocabulary. Though context clues abound, the heavy sprinkling of strange words may initially intimidate all but the most self-confident readers. Still, its sense of inevitable change and the passing of enduring values from one generation to another make the story a rewarding reading experience for those who will persevere.

> *Margaret A. Dorsey, in a review of "Granny Reardun," in* School Library Journal, *Vol. 25, No. 8, April, 1979, p. 55.*

Each of these fine stories portrays a child determining his or her place in the continuum of past, present and future. . . . These splendidly written short tales will need to be read aloud to many children, for the pace is contemplative and the settings very British. But the ideas will stay forever with the hearer. (pp. 42, 44)

> *Kathleen R. Roedder, in a review of "The Stone Book" and "Granny Reardun," in* Childhood Education, *Vol. 56, No. 1, October, 1979, pp. 42, 44.*

TOM FOBBLE'S DAY (1977); THE AIMER GATE (1978)

In *The Aimer Gate,* the chronological third volume in the quartet that began with *The Stone Book,* Joseph—who chose the smith's trade in *Granny Reardun*—is now reduced to making horseshoes for World War I and concerned that there might be nothing for his son Robert, still a boy, to "get aback of." At present Robert's job is to transport legless Faddock Allman, a Boer War veteran, to the field, and to fetch the stones Allman breaks for road flints. On this day Robert's Uncle Charlie, a soldier home on leave, is also in the fields, helping to scythe the corn hill and then, with his army rifle, shooting the rabbits so uncovered. In *Tom Fobble's Day,* where we learn that Charlie was killed in his war, we follow Joseph's grandson William through a day and an evening of

sledding with Stewart Allman under World War II bombers and spotlights and anti-aircraft fire. It is Joseph's last day at the forge and, it turns out, his last day of life. ("I really do not know," he sighs early on, considering what times have come to.) Through both these short, beautifully crafted stories, which have even less conventional plot structure than the first two, the keynotes of time, change, timelessness, and generations first struck in *The Stone Book* are developed by means of parallels, bonds, and variations among the books themselves. In *The Aimer Gate,* Faddock Allman's delight in "the best stone" (readers will remember that it is from the old Allman house) both recalls and contrasts with old Robert's in the previous volume; and Robert's climb to the church clock-tower, where he finds old Robert's sign and his own name on the perfectly finished capstone, echoes and extends Mary's heady steeple-top ride in the first book. In *Tom Fobble's Day* old Robert's pipe ends up with Joseph's "prentice piece" forge key and his wedding horse-shoes; and Joseph makes young William a sled of old William's loom (he was Mary's technologically bypassed uncle in the first book) and iron from the forge. On the sled, in the concluding sentence, "through hand and eye, block, forge and loom to the hill and all that he owned, he sledged sledged sledged for the black and glittering night and the sky flying on fire and the expectation of snow." More could be said, but needn't be here. Garner says it in his layered images, in regional speech that is somehow both direct and glancing, and in moments like the final passage, which contain the whole.

> *A review of "The Aimer Gate" and "Tom Fobble's Day," in* Kirkus Reviews, *Vol. XLVII, No. 13, July 1, 1979, p. 740.*

The final two books of a quartet which explores the themes of man's relationship to the earth, to his work, and to the rest of mankind. (p. 533)

The men in the books continue to seek answers to the same questions Mary asked as she "sat by the fire and read the stone book that had in it all the stories of the world and the flowers of the flood." Garner shows that the answers have to be discovered anew by each generation and that each one's answers are different yet somehow the same.

Mary is the only woman in the story; other significant characters are men who become stonemasons or blacksmiths. Each one is able through his work to make his own "pattern left on sand and air." The language of the books is a combination of modern English with the old Mercian dialect, giving the stories a unique flavor and dynamic quality but possibly making them forbidding to young readers. The cadenced text makes abundant use of dialogue. In both books the etchings [by Michael Foreman] are mere suggestions of images drawn from the text; their shadowy, impressionistic quality touches on the mythical elements throughout. (pp. 533-34)

> *Karen M. Klockner, in a review of "The Aimer Gate" and "Tom Fobble's Day," in* The Horn Book Magazine, *Vol. LV, No. 5, October, 1979, pp. 533-34.*

Alan Garner has written a sort of *Forsyte Saga* for children, a series of four novels spanning a century and five generations. *Tom Fobble's Day,* which is the last in the series, takes place in Chorley, a small town in Cheshire, England, and follows the lives of a working-class family. The language Garner uses is a combination of modern English and words from the past, still in use in rural Cheshire. He springs them on his young readers without apology or explanation: " 'I see,' said Grandad. 'And what are you doing clagged up so you can't hardly walk?' 'I keep stopping to scrawk it off,' said William." I have no idea what this means, but it doesn't matter, for the book's power is somehow enhanced by these occasional lapses into Mercian dialect. . . .

In its concern for character, in its contrapuntal treatment of themes, in its strongly rendered setting, and in its vivid language, **Tom Fobble's Day** succeeds as a children's book and as a work of literature.

> Ted Morgan, in a review of "Tom Fobble's Day," in Saturday Review, *Vol. 6, No. 23, November 24, 1979, p. 65.*

THE GIRL OF THE GOLDEN GATE; THE GOLDEN BROTHERS; THE PRINCESS AND THE GOLDEN MANE; THE THREE GOLDEN HEADS OF THE WELL (1979; omnibus edition as *Alan Garner's Fairytales of Gold*)

To transmit folk-tale, you must first listen to the rhythms and sounds of the spoken word which, from whatever culture they come, will most *naturally* carry the *essence* of a story, its force of magic and its inner mysteries. Listener and creator, Alan Garner has devised four 'Golden Tales' for Collins 'Colour Cubs' series; his miniatures will bring to the ear of the very young a rare quality of style. One of the stories, **The Three Golden Heads of the Well,** has from Tudor times at least gathered accretions of mystery. It is a tale whose piercing pity and terror cannot be spoilt even by psychiatric comment, a tale whose force comes through incantation rather than reason. Here, Northern notes localise the tale:

> She came to a moorland and to a pony, that was tethered with a rope to a tree . . . And the queen's daughter said, 'You nasty beast, do you think I'll flit you? I'm a queen's daughter!'
>
> So she wouldn't loose the pony, and the pony wouldn't give her a ride over the Moor of Hecklepins. She had to go in her bare feet, and the hecklepins cut and pricked her till she could hardly walk.

The blunt cruelties of folk-tale are spelled out strongly and directly in **The Golden Brothers,** a story that takes off from the familiar 'Fisherman and his wife' into myth-situation coloured by the concept of gold and its basic virtues. Terror and the power of love conflict in **The Girl of the Golden Gate** and **The Princess and the Golden Mane,** stories again teasing the ear with echoes of old motifs and situations in words scrupulously selected and arranged to tether imagination, lightly, to earth:

> So the princess killed the horse. She threw its ribs towards the sun, its head towards the moon, and its legs to the four horizons of the sky.
>
> And the legs were four gold poplar trees with emerald leaves, and from under the ribs came villages and fields and meadows, flowing over the desert of the end of the world, and the ribs were a golden castle. And out of the head came a river of silver water, and on the river was a boat, and in the boat was the stableboy.
>
> And so the princess found her husband, and the children their father, and the stableboy took the

iron from his heart. And they lived together in that green and golden land.

> Margery Fisher, in a review of "The Princess and the Golden Mane," "The Three Golden Heads of the Well," "The Golden Brothers," and "The Girl of the Golden Gate," in Growing Point, *Vol. 18, No. 6, March, 1980, p. 3648.*

A 200-page picture book? Yes. This is essentially four 50-page picture books reduced to 6"x 9"and bound together. There is no more (and usually much less) than half a page of concise text in generous type per double-page spread, a spread washed by Michael Foreman's simple, luminous (and often droll) full-color illustrations. The tales lead us a breathless pace. Although in a sense "original," they rely on well-known folk-tale plots and motifs (e.g., "The Fisherman and His Wife," "Diamonds and Toads," the life-token, the sacrificing animal, etc.), linked in a surprising and unflagging series, so that all the familiar elements suddenly seem new and unpredictable. Unlike some old (and many recent) folk tales, here storytelling is not subservient to dispensing morsels of morality or reveling in romanticism; no obtrusive hurdles of meaning slow down the action. Just when you think the tale will end, it takes an unexpected turn, so the ending catches you unawares. As in traditional tales, the arbitrary is made to seem ineluctable, by the forthright authority of the narrative voice. However limited your resources, invest in . . . *Gold.*

> Patricia Dooley, in a review of "Alan Garner's Fairytales of Gold," in School Library Journal, *Vol. 27, No. 7, March, 1981, p. 132.*

The old adage, "You can't tell a book by its cover" (or its illustrations) is an appropriate warning for this book. Although the text is highlighted by beautiful watercolors, this collection of four modern fairytales is always sexist and often violent, with plots tedious to follow.

Each story has a golden aspect to it—a gold fish, a golden head, bags of gold. In all stories, males are active characters in control of their lives. All male characters are positive and sensitive, with the exception of a jealous (but reasonable) king and a mean cobbler. In contrast, the females are nagging wives, witches, cruel mothers and passive daughters. The one exception is the king's daughter in **"The Three Golden Heads of the Well."** She is gentle and kind, though the queen's daughter in this story is mean and ugly.

There are numerous other examples of sexism. In **"The Golden Brothers,"** the husband is responsible for catching a golden fish which brings his family good fortune. The wife's role is to bother the husband until he catches the fish again.

Even when women are in great danger, they remain passive. In two stories, females are trapped and escape only through the aid of magic, and not by their own planned actions. In two instances, kings choose their daughters' husbands, and then "give" the daughters to their spouses.

It is interesting to note how child-bearing is depicted. In one tale, a wife bears two sons by eating two pieces of a golden fish. Another woman has two children instantly, because her husband tells her to do so as he leaves town!

Incidents of violence are also common. Child abuse, wife-beating and murder are all treated matter-of-factly, and thus condoned. In **"The Girl of the Golden Gate,"** a mother dislikes her daughter so she "made her do all the hard work in the house, and she beat her and sent her to bed hungry each night." The girl eventually solves her problem by floating across deep water on a golden ball and leaving her mother to drown! In two stories, animals are killed to assure human good fortune. And, in **"The Three Heads of the Golden Well,"** the queen's daughter is so unkind that she "was married to the old cobbler, and he leathered her with a strap every day. And that's all." That's plenty!

The stories tend to ramble and wander, as fates change unexpectedly. They are often simplistic, with "love at first sight" and happily-ever-after endings. (pp. 20-1)

> *Jan M. Goodman, in a review of "Fairytales of Gold," in* Interracial Books for Children's Bulletin, *Vol. 12, Nos. 7 & 8, 1981, pp. 20-1.*

THE LAD OF THE GAD (1980)

There is something just the least bit perverse in the way that Alan Garner keeps even his most devoted admirers guessing. Which way is he heading now? After pushing the conventional structure of the novel about as far as it would go in *Red Shift,* he turned to the profound simplicities of the 'Stone' quartet. Now he is doing strange things to the folk-tale—or perhaps the folk-tale has been doing strange things to him!

The Lad of the Gad is a reworking of five Celtic folk-tales. This area of oral story-telling has always been one of the most difficult, long-winded (especially in its Irish manifestations), wayward, pointlessly violent. Mr. Garner has listened to these remote voices and tried, in the words of his difficult introduction, "to give the stories something of the sequential structure of a controlled fiction while retaining an impression of the original dream". Has he succeeded? Frankly, I don't know. He has substituted for the prolix esoteric mysteries of the original some characteristic mysteries of his own. One can follow his narrative, all right, but it is difficult to understand why he has thought it necessary, or desirable, to tell these strange stories or to tell them in this way. Nor is it clear for which audience, if any, he is writing. Surely not for children, who, when they are ready to accept fairy-tales, are likely to be impatient, or baffled, when confronted by these inconsequential sequences of strange events. Presumably Mr. Garner has, as the best writers do, written for himself, and for those chosen people who can follow him down these bewildering byways. (pp. 122-23)

> *M. Crouch, in a review of "The Lad of the Gad," in* The Junior Bookshelf, *Vol. 45, No. 3, June, 1981, pp. 122-23.*

Alan Garner reworks five stories from the Goidelic layer of British folktale. They celebrate above all the sheer power of the word to make things happen; decorated with due forms of words and ritual repetition, falling into incantatory verse on occasion, all strangeness and violence is absolutely accepted and contained. In *The owl service* and *Red shift* Alan Garner used myth to interpret the world in which we now live; in **"The Stone Book Quartet"** he made serious and successful efforts to celebrate a continuity between past and present. This collection seems to me almost a gesture of despair. The stories are thick, heavy, profound, beautiful and true; this was a way people had of understanding the world once upon a time in a place where we no longer live and to which we cannot go back. It is an archaic mode beautifully worked but

alas not resurrected, not alive. One remembers the pleasure children get from simpler versions, Seūmas MacManus's *Billy Beg and his bull,* for instance; wonders how many will get as much from this far more uncompromising approach; and regrets that it may be very few.

> *Dorothy Nimmo, in a review of "The Lad of the Gad," in* The School Librarian, *Vol. 29, No. 2, June, 1981, p. 133.*

Believing that "by nature, fairy tale is oral rather than literary," the author states, "The art is not to record the oral tradition but to recreate the effect of it, so that, for the reader, the printed word sings." The book contains five Gaelic stories, four drawn from J. F. Campbell's *Popular Tales of the West Highlands* and one based on an Irish manuscript tale, "The Adventures of the Children of the King of Norway." Although he was able to follow the Campbell texts closely, the author has reworked the Irish story, which he considers "opaque, confused and dull." The Campbell retellings are swift, with a preponderance of monosyllabic words, and the loosely constructed sentences not only suggest natural, oral cadences but are rich with idiomatic and poetic expressions. The patterns of humor, heroism, and magic in these retellings are successfully transmitted, but the drawn-out Irish narrative continues to be opaque, confused, and ultimately dull.

> *Paul Heins, in a review of "The Lad of the Gad," in* The Horn Book Magazine, *Vol. LVIII, No. 2, April, 1982, p. 174.*

ALAN GARNER'S BOOK OF BRITISH FAIRY TALES (1984)

Alan Garner's language is for the first instrument, the voice. He believes fairy tales are for everybody. They've been polished too much, they should be rescued from literature, and to do this he reverts to the tale told round the fire, depending for its magic on form, the impact of heard language, like poetry. Only poetry can appeal to instinct, and only instinct can make the connections which give meaning to irrational events.

"Fairy tale" is a term that should be taken out into a field and buried. These twenty-one tales [are] true stories of the supernatural, of barbaric terror, bold endurance, primitive belief. The teller is audible in the language, especially in dialect words which should be puzzling but aren't. We come to "a dark and ugsome glen" or find ourselves caught in the open "at darklins one night". We hear that "the daughter, a ramping young maid, was growed white and waffling like a bag of bones" and "the waves came big and gurly". It's not all like this. These are scattered instances, but the effect is powerful, a language not quite ours yet connected to what we know, and connected in such a way that it tells us more than we know. It's like our relationship to the supernatural, strangeness at a distance, its importance acknowledged by instinct while the intellect is baffled.

The book begins with the story of Tom Tit Tot in a Gloucestershire version. Edward Clodd found variants of this tale in fourteen countries. So how British is it? It is as told in Britain, anyway, like the variants here of the Cinderella story and Bluebeard and Beauty and the Beast. These appear under different names but all express the continuing theme of resurrection, spring following from winter, life from death, hope from despair. In the last story, **"The Castle of Melvales"**, an old man's head is struck off and a young man emerges.

The visible cycle of growth and decay and rebirth is man's most pressing experience. In some of these stories the strange transformations which are his artistic expression of this mystery are more directly related to natural causes. **"The Green Mist"** is a title which refers to the first faint greening of the earth in the spring. In this delicate and beautiful tale a girl's life strengthens with the surge of nature, but at the end there is a corresponding decline. She withers and dies with the ebb of life in a flower, just as Barkis goes out with the tide in *Great Expectations.*

These stories are magical and immediate. They have all the ingredients we expect—the obligatory three sons, not forgetting three daughters, and seven tasks, thwarted giants, gruesome horrors, animals on the same footing as men, only wiser. Alan Garner seems to have gone to work like Kate Crackernuts, the heroine of one of these tales, who solves her problem by "plucking nuts from trees and filling her apron". In Celtic legend the nut symbolized wisdom—truth in a nutshell.

The book is finely produced for the eye as well as the ear. The stark and startling woodcuts by Derek Collard are, like the stories, more telling for being, with intent, only obliquely related to the recognizable world.

Idris Parry, "Natural Causes," in The Times Literary Supplement, *No. 4261, November 30, 1984, p. 1381.*

Alan Garner celebrates our native tradition in **Alan Garner's Book of British Fairy Tales.** The twenty-one tales are 'adapted', for the most part only lightly; the versions chosen (from Joseph Jacobs, for instance, or from J. F. Campbell's versions of West Highland tales) show a simple interweaving of magic and domestic detail which needs no editing. The case of the Cinderella-variant **'Mossycoat'** is different because it comes, by way of K. M. Briggs, from a gypsy in Lancashire who told it to a folk-tale collector in 1915. The dialect, besides being irksome to eye and ear, has an unfortunate resemblance to Uncle Remus idiom; for whatever reason, Alan Garner has made the change to plain, neutral speech, with little syntactic alteration. The story as taken down originally sounds like this:

> It goes wi'out saying as de tother kitchen-girls was fair beside theirsel's wid jealousy; and it didn't mend matters as de new girl was a dam sight beautifuller nor what any o'dem was. Here was dis wagrant i' rags put above dem when all she was fit for at best was to be scullery girl. If anybody was to be under-cook, it stands to sense it sud'ev ben yan o'dem, as really knowed about things, not dis girl i' rags and tatters, picked up off 'n de roads. But dey's put her in her place, dey would.

It must be a matter of opinion whether Alan Garner's translation has lost more in pungency than it has gained in consistency with the rest of the tales in this volume:

> The other kitchen girls were fair beside theirselves with jealousy; and it didn't mend matters that the new girl was a sight beautifuller than what any of them were. Here was this vagrant in rags put above them, when all she was fit for at best was to be scullery girl. If anybody was to be undercook, it stands to sense, it should be one of them as really knew

about things, not this girl in rags and tatters, picked up off the roads. But they'd put her in her place, they would.

Apart from the considerable changes in 'Mossycoat', most are minor alterations such as re-paragraphing, an occasional alternative to archaisms or the omission of repetitions, all of which go to make a smoother sound in the interests of story telling—for these are not chamber-pieces but robust, strongly localised narratives strung on the thread between speaker and listener. . . . 'The meaning is in the music', Alan Garner says in his introduction, in 'pitch and cadence, and the colour of the word'. In these selected tales he has successfully carried out his intention. (pp. 4398-99)

Margery Fisher, in a review of "Alan Garner's Book of British Fairy Tales," in Growing Point, *Vol. 23, No. 6, March, 1985, pp. 4398-99.*

Garner has been faithful to the oral tradition of early times. These stories are for the ear rather than the eye, the plot evolving through physical action and repetition (often in rhyme), with the language, full of unusual expressions and dialect, adding to the authentic style. Most (except for **"Tom Tit Tot," "Kate Crackernuts"** and **"Mally Whuppy"**) are not found in present-day collections. Many are about poor peasants' superstitions and folk ways in rural England and belief in witches and bogles. In his introduction, Garner explains why the traditional stories of the fantastic and supernatural were relegated to children's literature by the middle of the 19th Century. Sources are given for the tales in this collection. Excellent material for reading aloud, for telling and for just plain reading enjoyment.

Mary Wadsworth Sucher, in a review of "Alan Garner's Book of British Fairy Tales," in School Library Journal, *Vol. 32, No. 4, December, 1985, p. 88.*

A BAG OF MOONSHINE (1986)

Taking its title from a nonsense rhyme included, this is a wonderful collection of 20 tales and 2 rhymes from England and Wales. Most are unfamiliar, although almost all contain variants of recognizable elements of European folktales. They are zestfully told, and their magic is not dark. Compare Joseph Jacob's "Jack Hannerford" with Garner's spirited "up galloped the farmer, all of a dither-a-wack, like a new-baked custard." He gives these tales the pepper of folktelling without letting them become arty or obscure. Readers will enjoy the lilt of the phrasing and can intuit meaning of unfamiliar words. A peevish changeling hides all but his eyes, which "keeked out like a ferret's"; the magic stick to beat a thief "wriggled like a snig in a bottle"; and the "Wicked Sparrow" starts on his mad career with "a thorn in my foot . . . and it's giving me gyp!" Numerous sketches and eight color illustrations [by Patrick James Lynch] convey the same combination of the zany and the supernatural. No sources are included. These selections will be appreciated by independent readers; they will also make fine read-alouds for younger listeners.

Ruth M. McConnell, in a review of "A Bag of Moonshine," in School Library Journal, *Vol. 33, No. 3, November, 1986, p. 76.*

The success of this new collection of some two dozen tales, re-created from the folklore of England and Wales (and the Isle of Man), will surprise few of Alan Garner's followers.

The range of the collection is striking—prose and verse; long and short; riddles and puzzles as well as tests and guests; gold and greed as well as love and loss; the familiar treacheries of mermaids and witches alongside the more singular threat of the ugsome Foawr, a kind of remotivated Rumpelstiltskin.

The world view of these tales never surrenders to bland simplicities or comfortable pieties. There seem few prizes for the gormless overreacher, be he the witless Jack Whopstraw, or the wicked sparrow, or the boneheaded Billy Bowker, the hobthrust with delusions of boggarthood; and yet it is hard not to warm to the unpuncturable cheerfulness of the bungling Mr Vinegar, a sort of Boethius of the hedgerows, whose refrain "But never mind" is squirted like a pain-killing spray over successive disastrous acts of entrepreneurial folly. Signs of a more positive heroism are discernible in several quick-footed, clear-sighted young protagonists, yet not all is *rites de passage* optimism and whimsy. **"Hom Bridson"** is an uneasy tale of develish possession as well as of childish innocence; the **"Salmon Cariad"** offers an intriguing and, in its way, powerfully symbolic tale about a predatory and sensuous mermaid and her young male victim; while **"Belaney of the Lakes"** reveals folk poignantly ensnared in ill-luck's meshes with no happy ending in sight. The narrator stares the truth in the eye: "It was hard for Hewin. But that's how it was in old days." Elsewhere, however, good cheer is soon restored, whether through a surreal verse fantasy, in which distant echoes of "The Twelve Days of Christmas" can be heard, or through the ingenious slapstick and triadic symmetries of the tale of Harry Cap and his magic table, purse and stick.

The Russian poet Mayakovsky urged an aspiring young writer to "fill your storehouse constantly, fill the granaries of your skull with all kinds of words, necessary, expressive, rare, invented, renovated and manufactured". This collection of tales reveals on every page that Alan Garner's granaries are characteristically well stocked with rich and rare words and expressions—blunging, skenning, granched, keeked out, skrawked, nowt, gowk, blob-tongue, nazzy crow, thrutching piece, lob's chance, big bart of fern, as short as old sticks, wriggled like a snig in a bottle, quiet as a tater, blinked like a duck in thunder, you great gawp-sheet, by the cringe, cob this for a game—all of them subtly and affectionately deployed, easily understood from context, and likely to intrigue and delight young readers. These pungent expressions are embedded in prose marked by a brisk yet evasive colloquialism, brightly flecked with alliteration, internal rhyme, "wrongly" formed past tenses and determinedly archaic tag phrases, and with a telling fondness for patterned repetition

and for studied avoidance of terracings of subordinate clauses. The cumulative effect is invigorating, disarming and eerie. Rarely can the voice of "once upon a time, in such and such a place, not near nor far, not high nor low", have been more engagingly caught.

> *Andrew Wawn, "Slapstick and Symmetry," in* The Times Literary Supplement, *No. 4365, November 28, 1986, p. 1346.*

The storyteller's voice in the twenty two tales from England and Wales retold in ***A Bag of Moonshine*** is immediate and colloquial and in the main jocose or robustly knockabout. We are almost invited to visualise the speaker—'Once upon a time, when I was young and handsome, and that hasn't been so very long ago, as you can see'; or, more indirectly, 'Now this is an old tale the Cornishmen brought out of Cornwall with them when they came getting copper in the mine holes thereabouts, I recollect Old Perrin used to tell it'. There is enchantment here, for example in the gentle tale of **'The Salmon Cariad'** or **'Belemary of the Lake'**, but most of the tales describe how changelings, witches or giants were outwitted or how fools and tricksters got their deserts. Racy prose, relaxed in sound but carefully disposed, and punctuated by snatches of homely verse, presents tales of the folk and suggests background for the hard-working, shrewd peasantry. Here is a typical passage from **'Harry Cap and the Three Brothers'**:

> And the stick wriggled like a snig in a bottle and began at the innkeeper's daughter, and it thrashed her in through the window and round the room, and gave her the hiding of her life. And Jack wouldn't tell it to leave off till she said she'd fetch him a table and a purse that were magic, if he'd only stop the stick from giving her such a hiding.
>
> So Jack told the stick to stop, and the innkeeper's daughter went and got the table and the purse and handed them over; and Jack told her what he'd do if he ever saw her and her hanky-panky again.

The black and white illustrations match the robust flavour of the text with a crowd of weird beings and crusty country folk, at times with an edge of terror quite in keeping with the magical aspect of the tales. . . . (pp. 4726-27)

> *Margery Fisher, in a review of "A Bag of Moonshine," in* Growing Point, *Vol. 25, No. 5, January, 1987, pp. 4726-27.*

(Margaret) Rumer Godden

1907-

English author of fiction, poet, reteller, and editor.

Recognized as one of England's most distinguished creators of children's literature, Godden has entertained young readers from preschool through high school for more than forty years with books which demonstrate her understanding of their thoughts and emotions as well as the things they enjoy most. A diverse writer who has written fantasy, realistic fiction, picture books, and retellings of Scottish and Indian folktales, she presents her audience with works which contain such themes as friendship, forgiveness, and the indomitability of the human spirit. Godden is especially well known for her doll stories, most notably her first book for children, *The Dolls' House* (1947), which describes a family of Victorian dolls whose wishes for a proper home are granted. Miniature dramas full of the complexity and conflict of real life, these books depict doll characters who, although they depend upon humans for their movement and freedom, are positive influences on their young owners. Godden has also written several coming-of-age stories; originally written for adults, several of these works are popular with young people and a few have been reissued as young adult novels. Portraying life as seen through the eyes of their young protagonists, who are often suspended between two cultures, these works often include autobiographical elements, drawn especially from Godden's childhood in India. Depicting the growing awareness of the youngsters to love, sexuality, deception, and death, the novels are marked by a sophistication and pessimism not found in Godden's juvenile literature. Nevertheless, these works show a concern for and appreciation of the child's world, a characteristic shared by her books for children. Most observers commend Godden as a talented literary stylist whose works reflect her sensitive perception of both the traumas and joys of childhood. Godden was awarded the first Whitbread Award in the children's book category for *The Diddakoi* in 1972.

(See also *Something about the Author,* Vols. 3, 36; *Contemporary Authors New Revision Series,* Vol. 4; and *Contemporary Authors,* Vols. 5-8, rev. ed.)

AUTHOR'S COMMENTARY

If you find a child with its nose in a book—and you do find them—it is just as likely not to be a book of our vintage but an old one, something like *The Little House on the Prairie* or *The Jungle Book* or *Black Beauty;* with the very young of course it's still A. A. Milne and Beatrix Potter. . . . I cannot help wondering how many of ours will still be read in fifty years' time? This isn't to say only the old are good, of course not; we have some outstanding writers for children. Nor am I talking about books of information such as our splendid nature books. I'm talking about books that are meant to give a child pleasure, sheer enjoyment; and it seems to me, in the writing of these books nowadays, something is being lost, something that children have always wanted, obviously wanted. I believe that "something" is the story.

Before the nineteenth century children's books were not very interesting. Why? They didn't really have a story—they usually had a moral. Then, in the nineteenth century, especially the latter half, up to Edwardian and Georgian times there came what one can only call an immortal flowering, a galaxy of names that are still with us today. If you come to look at those writers you will find that almost all were unself-conscious; they simply wrote.

In the Bible we are told that God created man by taking dust and breathing life into it; I hope it's not presumptuous to claim that a storyteller can do something like that, or should do something like that. A story is life even when it's a fairy tale—fairy tales are still loved in spite of what people say, look at the sales of Andersen and Perrault—and it seems to me that, with the loss of the story, life too has gone out of our books. So often these days it is overlaid, principally because of two dangers.

The first is very obvious. It is that a story cannot be in any way dictated by anybody else and yet so often it is—the publisher interferes, telling the author what will or will not sell. Perhaps it is degraded by having to be put into basic words and its drama is strained out of it in case it gives offence. That practice is dying out now—the result of a long and vigorous campaign. But the other danger is more subtle. It has crept into children's books from the adult world of the novel, in which it is almost disreputable to tell a story unless for a thriller or spy-fiction; it must, rather, be hinted at, symbolized. This may be good impressionism—often it's very beautiful, often weird—but it doesn't suit children's books. (pp. 115-16)

Nowadays, far from bothering too little about children's books perhaps we bother too much. We, who care about them as literature—editors, publishers, illustrators, authors—are immensely preoccupied with standards, standards of texts, of taste, of art. I used to be occupied with this myself, and made passionate speeches about it believing that this primarily was what mattered. Of course it matters; we don't want shoddy work, but that is not the primary concern. A little while ago I was asked by the *New York Times* to write a review, for its fiftieth anniversary, of *The Secret Garden* and was appalled at how badly Frances Hodgson Burnett wrote! There was no gainsaying it, and yet the power of the story overrode everything else. As you know *The Secret Garden* is more alive today than it was in her own time; it sells not in thousands but in millions, ... Frances Hodgson Burnett was what children want, a true storyteller, and that is a proud title.

It takes courage to tell a story, to endure the discipline of writing it, and doing that for children is a far more difficult art than writing a novel: courage not to listen to what people tell you, to what your publishers say will sell. Even they do not always know. It is difficult not to think about money when one is writing. We keep one eye on the critics, the other on the grownups who after all buy the books—but we shouldn't think about them. As a matter of fact we shouldn't even think about the child. Only about the story; to let ourselves be entranced by it, not be ashamed to be rapt away.

We hear a lot about the toil and frustration of writing but not nearly enough about the joy. We should have the courage to let our story take its time in growing, let it choose its own words however surprising; not let ourselves wonder how good or bad it is but consent to be its instrument not its master; in fact, to be what children want—a storyteller.

Then if we are lucky it may breathe; and if we are luckier still perhaps, perhaps not turn back to dust. (pp. 116-17)

> Rumer Godden, "Opening the Children's Books of the Year Exhibition," in Signal, No. 21, September, 1976, pp. 115-17.

GENERAL COMMENTARY

ELEANOR CAMERON

The influence of place upon the work of Rumer Godden is a . . . complex affair. . . . For one thing, Rumer Godden's childhood was lived in two countries, first in India until she was five, then in England until she was six, then in India again for five years, and she has gone back and forth between the two many times in the years that followed childhood, possibly feeling—as her sister Jon confesses of herself—always homesick for one or the other. Eudora Welty writes, "Sometimes two places, two countries, are brought to bear on each other, as in E. M. Forster's work, and the heart of the novel is heard beating most plainly, most passionately, most personally, when two places are at a meeting point." One feels this strongly in Kipling, but unlike Kipling, Rumer Godden has put all of her children's books in England save *The River,* one of her finest, which bridges childhood and adolescence,

and *Home is the Sailor,* which takes place in Wales and which, for this reader at least, seems remote and pale and to lack force compared to the clear, compelling vitality of *The Dolls' House* and *Miss Happiness and Miss Flower.* The fact that, for the most part, she has given an English background to her children's books is fascinating when we reflect that, as she and Jon tell us in *Two Under the Indian Sun,* they were far happier in India than in England and not only because in India they were with their own family but because "children in India are greatly loved and indulged and we never felt that we were foreigners, not India's own; we felt at home, safely held in her large warm embrace, content as we never were to be content in our own country. . . . Even as children we knew it was a wonderful land. . . . Even in the small compass of our home, a child's world, some of that wonder filtered through to us."

Mystifying it is, then, that this love and warmth and wonder and contentment have never compelled Rumer Godden to fuse these emotions through stories of childhood in India for children (*The River* is not, strictly speaking, a children's book in the sense that her other children's books are, though any child would be enlarged by reading it). One would have thought these inevitably to be the most fertile and potent years in their influence upon her books for children, but on the contrary it is that year spent in London, grieving for what was gone: "A year is not long if one is grown up; to five and six and a half, then six and seven and a half, it is an eternity."

> Never, in all that tall dark house, was there a gleam of laughter or enterprise or fun, and slowly, slowly our lives began to loosen from their roots—far away now, Mam, Fa, Nancy, Rose, seemed like little figures in a frieze looked at long ago and were being slowly covered over in the quiet gloom of the succeeding London days. That is perhaps the secret agony of children separated from their family—the agony that slowly, inexorably, they must forget.

It is this that Rumer Godden has put into *Miss Happiness and Miss Flower* in which Nona must be a memory, a reliving, of the small Rumer in London.

> When Nona was alone she went and stood by the window and presently a tear splashed down on the windowsill, then another and another. A home and a family of your own . . . 'Coimbatore, old Ayah,' whispered Nona, and the tears came thick and fast.

Here, precisely, is where we recall those words of Eudora Welty's: "the heart of the novel is heard beating most plainly, most passionately, most personally, when two places are at a meeting point." And it took the child, Rumer, living in the tall dark house in London and longing for the light, spacious, laughter-filled house in India to provide that special "place" for the writer out of which, years later, she would bring to tender and moving life Nona and the two little Japanese dolls in *Miss Happiness and Miss Flower,* for whom Nona insisted upon building a real Japanese house of their own, and Totty and Birdie and Mr. Plantagenet in *The Dolls' House.* (pp. 190-92)

Houses in India (*The River, Breakfast with the Nikolides, Thus Far and No Further, Kingfishers Catch Fire*), houses in England (*Take Three Tenses, China Court*), houses for dolls, for mice, houses for humans—these are Miss Godden's passion, her symbolic "place," so that there is almost, within the space of each imagined enfolding of four walls, a cataloguing of colors, surfaces, names, times of day, flowers, possessions, fabrics—but never tediously so. Because of her mode of expression, because for her each house is a symbol of some profound necessity which has to do with cleanliness and order, because the house is the root-place of life, all is integral. As the action of the story is set in motion and the inhabitants of the house begin to take on individuality (as they do almost at once in any Rumer Godden novel, be it for adults or for children, be these inhabitants of wood or china or of flesh and blood), objects belonging to the house acquire meaning and dimension beyond their simple physical existence, and their meaning and dimension have of course to do with the family. *Take Three Tenses* begins:

> The house, it seems, is more important than the characters. "In me you exist," says the house. For almost a hundred years, for ninety-nine years, it has enhanced, embraced and sheltered the family, but there is no doubt that it can go on without them. "Well," the family have retorted, "we can go on without you." There should be no question of retorts, nor of acrimony. The house and the family are at their best and most gracious together.

As a prelude to *Take Three Tenses,* Miss Godden quotes from T. S. Eliot's "East Coker":

> Home is where one starts from. As we grow older
> The world becomes stranger, the pattern more
> complicated
> Of dead and living . . .
> . . . In my end is my beginning.

"In my end is my beginning." This idea as well, but only in two of the adult novels, is present: the idea of Time as a whole, which is expressed continually throughout the evocation of place, thus giving it a vibrancy it would not possess in one tense alone. In relation to both *Take Three Tenses* and *China Court,* the sentences Miss Godden places above "East Coker" that describe Bach's fugues and which were written by Lawrence Abbot, are full of meaning. Bach's music, says Mr. Abbott, consists of "two, three or four simultaneous melodies which are constantly on the move, each going its own independent way. For this reason the underlying harmony is often hard to decipher, being veiled by a maze of passing notes and suspensions. . . . Often chords are incomplete; only two tones are sounded, so that one's imagination has to fill in the missing third tone."

In both of these books, so different in actual story but parallel in effect in many ways, Rumer Godden fully reveals her magician's ability to weave all three tenses—surely not simultaneously, yet one almost has that illusion—throughout the action of the story, drawing the reader backward and forward without misstep or obscurity. There is a technical device involved, on first thought rather a simple one: for all that happens in the past and in the future, she uses the present tense; for all that happens in the present, the past tense. It might seem to some nothing more than an arbitrary whim, but the effect is stunning, which it would not have been worked the other way round. By use of it she carries on the mingling of thoughts, actions, conversations taking place within the house at many different times to a truly impressive degree, particularly in *China Court,* where the proliferation of family within any one generation sets the house ringing with longings, joys, regrets, frustrations, unfulfilled passions, as though all that is gone and all that is yet to come is continually echoing and re-echoing upon the present. Yet "the underlying harmony . . . veiled by a maze of passing notes and suspen-

sions" is heard always with unfailing clarity, the echoes only serving to make all feeling, all emotion, the more keen and poignant. Nevertheless, the secret of her ability to create this resonance lies, I think, not alone in the technical device but even more in those words of Eudora Welty's already quoted: "The moment the place in which the novel happens is accepted as true, through it will begin to glow, in a kind of recognizable glory, the feeling and thought that inhabited the novel in the author's head and animated the whole of his work."

" 'In me you exist,' says the house." And because The House, which one starts from, which enhances, embraces and shelters the family, is of such profound importance to Rumer Godden, once she has come into imaginative and aesthetic possession of whatever House she has created, she can call upon any of her characters to speak and act in any tense of The House's time, at random it might seem, with voices which should be heard in the last chapter speaking out in the second, and voices from the future speaking in the first. But not in the least random, each note being struck with the most subtle intent, and the emotion which charges the whole arising always out of her pervading sense of place.

The art of Lucy Boston is animated by a combination of two ideas: the idea of Time as a coexistent whole and the idea of displaced humanity, and this combination finds expression through the love of a unique and special place. So, it seems to me, is the art of Rumer Godden animated by the idea of The House in most of her books both for children and adults, and combined most successfully in two adult books with the idea of Time as a whole, and still with this idea, but in a different way, in *The River.* It is the only one of her books which arises clearly out of her childhood in India, recreating the first loved house and revealing what must have been the source of her preoccupation with the idea of Time as a coexistent whole—or with timelessness, put it as you will. It is there in so many words in *Two Under the Indian Sun:* "Our lives were conditioned by our big rivers; they gave a sense of proportion, of timelessness to our small township and our family." (Indeed, Laurens van der Post has written of Indian rivers, "I should perhaps have envisaged [the Indian] as a creature of the river, for the role that rivers play in the Indian imagination and life does not appear to exist among other peoples. This is all the more mysterious because Indian rivers, great as they can be, are (with the possible exception of the the Brahmaputra) not particularly picturesque, dramatic or unusual. Yet it is in India that the river, from far back in recorded history, has remained a transforming and transfiguring factor in the path of spiritual salvation.") In *The River,* Harriet (Rumer) says, quoting from one of her own childish writings, "The day ends. The end begins . . . "

In none of Rumer Godden's adult novels is Time used to create fantasy as it is in Lucy Boston's books for children. The words of voices in the past and the future, heard in the present, are never the voices of ghosts. All takes place within the world of reality. It is only in her children's books, where mice and dolls speak, that she enters the world of the fantastical, but her giftedness for enclosing layers of time within a single drop she never calls upon for those who, it seems to me, would greet it most eagerly, with the hungriest, the most agile and uninhibited imaginations. Why? What underlying, perhaps unconscious reasons, keep her from weaving a story for children, as she has for adults, out of the idea of timelessness within some loved house? It is a combination that, in her hands, would take on a special artistry, and one hopes that on some unexpected day she will give the children this pleasure. (pp. 192-96)

Eleanor Cameron, "A Country of the Mind," in her
The Green and Burning Tree: On the Writing and
Enjoyment of Children's Books, *Atlantic-Little,
Brown, 1969, pp. 163-202.*

FRANK EYRE

[An] established novelist who has written children's books [with] . . . serious intentions is Rumer Godden. Her range is wide but the descriptive simplicity of her tales is best illustrated by **The Dolls' House,** a farthing novel that brilliantly succeeds in depicting adult situations and conflicts in a story that on the surface is no more than a simple tale about dolls. Many of her stories are told in this miniature form. There are others about dolls, and one, **The Mousewife,** derived from a note in Dorothy Wordsworth's Journal about the friendship between a caged dove and a mouse, that becomes, in Rumer Godden's hands, a parable about oppression. (p. 68)

Frank Eyre, "The In-Between Books," in his British
Children's Books in the Twentieth Century, *revised
edition, E. P. Dutton & Co., Inc., 1973, pp. 59-75.*

ELAINE MOSS

Rumer Godden, born in Sussex and now living in Rye, spent the formative years of her childhood in a remote part of Bengal where she drew into herself, through the roots she struck, the many-sidedness and the contradictions of Hindu philosophy as well as the mysterious power to reconcile them. This gives her and her work a "peculiar richness" whilst leaving the observer perhaps not utterly, but certainly partially, baffled. For the woman seems, in so many ways, at variance with the work.

And why not?

That an author is necessarily reflected in her novels or stories for children was the first of my preconceptions that Rumer Godden waved gently but firmly aside.

> Writing and painting are not self-expression as people think they are. They are nothing to do with self. Self probably gets in the way, I should say. When I was writing **The Kitchen Madonna** I was not expressing myself, I was expressing the boy, Gregory.

But then we went on to talk at length about the central characters of her books for children, how Gregory in **The Kitchen Madonna,** Kizzy in **The Diddakoi,** Nona in **Miss Happiness and Miss Flower** are all lonely children caught between two cultures or two ways of life and forced by circumstances to make a bridge between, through the power of their imagination and their strength of will. It is not Miss Godden herself but her experience of two cultures, of being a hybrid, that is reflected in the strains and stresses and emotional growth of the children she creates, both in her stories for the young and in her adult novels. For many of her adult novels (notably **The River,** perhaps the most poignant and honest book about adolescence ever written) focus on children.

What is it that distinguishes writing for children from writing for adults? We are so often told that an author does not write for anyone, he writes for himself; that children's books and adult books are part of "literature" and should be evaluated on the same critical principles. Rumer Godden has a great deal to say on this subject; most of it, running counter to fash-

ionable pronouncements, embodies good sound sense—an assessment she will eschew because, as she said in another context (concerning Mohammedanism), "It's very sensible, and I have never had much time for sense!"

Both **The Kitchen Madonna** and **The Diddakoi,** published here for children, were published in America for adults as well as for children. "They became 'twilight books'," says Miss Godden, "and were reviewed as if inadequate adult literature. When you write for children you don't write in a childish vein, but you do write differently. It's a much stricter discipline. You have to have a story, and the only interest in a story is conflict. If you remove all the adult problems you can't make a story, and *it's the story that makes the young reader want to turn the page.*

"When you are writing an adult novel you can really do anything, anything you like; whereas writing for children you know perfectly well that the child is going to lose patience if, for instance, you have a lot of introspective thought or if you have a lot of description. You can't use the classic way of describing someone that you would use in an adult novel, slowly dropping in hints of character over a number of pages. Children want to know *at once* what somebody looks like."

When Rumer Godden speaks of "children" she really *means* children; the lack of innocence in so much entertainment that is ostensibly "for children" appals her, which is why she describes the musical version of **Holly and Ivy,** on which she is working with David Henneker at the moment, as "for little children and real adults," adding, "Nobody between the ages of ten and thirty should see it." It is probably true that few young people between those ages would respond to Rumer Godden's books for children either, which is why, in her thinking, there is this sharp divide between two distinct techniques: writing for "real adults" and writing for children.

She gave me a superb example, from **Holly and Ivy** since that was the book we had been discussing. Ivy, the six-year-old heroine with (note the direct description) "straight hair cut in a fringe, blue-grey eyes and a turned-up nose", had had a very pathetic past—no father, no mother, no grandparents. "In an adult novel you would have used flashbacks to Ivy's past—her father, her mother, her home—but for the very young reader flashback is too confusing and the description has to be pared right down." So, to convey Ivy's past, Rumer Godden invented a short scene in which Ivy suddenly realizes that, unlike all the other boys and girls at St. Agnes's, she is the one who has not been "asked for by a kind lady or gentleman" for the Christmas holiday.

> "I don't care," said Ivy.
>
> Sometimes in Ivy there was an empty feeling, and the emptiness ached; it ached so much that she had to say something quickly in case she cried, and, "I don't care at all," said Ivy.

In that one tiny paragraph—in the two words "at all", really—the whole feeling of Ivy's orphan past is instantly conveyed.

"Children apprehend where they don't comprehend," says Rumer Godden, who, like Beatrix Potter, uses the most exact words she can find, regardless of whether children will know their meaning: Mr. Plantagenet, in **The Dolls' House,** for instance, had been "hurt, *abused* and lost". (pp. 55-7)

Rumer Godden clearly has a great regard for childhood, a period of growth, struggles, ferment, unfettered imagination and creativity. Dolls' houses, a miniature garden, the careful acquisition of materials for making a collage madonna and the intense concentration needed to assemble them into an icon, are each the catalyst in a Godden story for the young. So exact are the details the author gives of how the Japanese dolls' house or the miniature garden or the collage madonna are made, that any boy or girl reading the books can set about constructing them at once. Many do—and they write to tell the author of the pleasure this has given them. (p. 58)

Diminutive objects are as alive for Rumer Godden as they are for children, with whom she shares an obsession for dolls of character.

Of character?

Dolls set the imagination coursing with the possibility of their interaction, and Miss Godden's stories make a passionate appeal to children, to *consider* dolls' feelings and give them life—otherwise they are helpless and mute.

> "There will be some little girl who is clever and kind," [says Miss Happiness, one of the exiled Japanese dolls in *Miss Happiness and Miss Flower*].
>
> "Will there be?" asked Miss Flower longingly.
>
> "Yes."
>
> "Why will there be?"
>
> "Because there always has been," said Miss Happiness.
>
> All the same Miss Flower gave a doll shiver, which means she felt as though she shivered though it couldn't be seen. Miss Flower was always frightened; perhaps the child who made the chip in her ear had been rough. "I wish we had not come," said Miss Flower.
>
> Miss Happiness sighed and said, "We were not asked."

The story continues with the words "Children are not asked either"; it is this feeling of being impotent—if adults are inconsiderate—that Rumer Godden transfers from the child to the dolls in their relationships with their "mothers and fathers", the children who own them. Her books make a plea for communication, consideration and understanding but they make it magically in a way that the seven-, eight- or nine-year-old can perfectly "apprehend".

Because so much of a child's life is spent in interior dialogue Rumer Godden has adopted a unique and arresting way of using speech as merely the breakthrough point in thought, the short, intense switch-on of current between people that sets thought travelling again in, perhaps, a slightly different direction. In *The Kitchen Madonna* Gregory, trying to make an icon but lacking the money to buy what he believes he needs, is despondent; it was a foolish idea anyway, he says.

> Then, "It wasn't," said Janet and Gregory lifted his head. He did not often let his younger sister contradict him.
>
> "It was if I can't make it," said Gregory.
>
> "You can make it."
>
> "How can I make it without money?"

"You can make it with think," said Janet.

It was not what she meant to say, yet oddly it said what she meant.

Gregory and Janet are the children of middle-class professional people. Kizzy, in *The Diddakoi*, is a gypsy child who finds herself "ridin' in Rolls Royces" when the Admiral takes pity on her; the Plantaganets' behaviour in *The Dolls' House* mirrors the comfortable world in which the children who own the dolls' house live. Is Rumer Godden an anachronism, or is she relevant to today's child? How does she fare in a world where teachers search for reflections in books of the life of the inner-city child, and where critics use the words "middle class" as though they were pejorative? Rumer Godden smiles. "I am always told I have a Kensington voice," she says, without a hint of embarrassment.

> If they mind, I am very sorry for them. I'm not going to try to be anything I am not. To me, if you are a writer or a painter you are lucky enough to be in a totally classless society. It doesn't matter who you are or what you do or how you talk, so long as you don't let it worry you. You are just a person doing your thing and whoever you encounter it's because of your work. You are free of all these pettinesses: I remember Katherine Mansfield saying 'Artists are the cleanest people in the world: mentally clean.'

This philosophy is borne out in Rumer Godden's work. Whether she is writing a long, complex novel for adults like *In This House of Brede*, which has no less than eighty threads of women's lives woven into its intriguing pattern, or a short simple tale like *The Diddakoi* for children, Rumer Godden is "clean" and sure and timeless in her appeal—for she is a prince among storytellers, combining rich imagination with minute attention to detail. (pp. 58-60)

Elaine Moss, "Rumer Godden: Prince of Storytellers," in Signal, *No. 17, May, 1975, pp. 55-60.*

BOB DIXON

[Girls'] active lives . . . are much more restricted than boys'. Therefore, they tend to live substitute lives, and, increasingly, dream lives through fiction. Doll stories illustrate the point well, I think. On the one hand, girls have now been sufficiently initiated into the mother/housewife stereotype to take it up for themselves (even if only for want of something better) and, on the other, they can live make-believe lives through the dolls.

The many doll stories by Rumer Godden illustrate these points very well. In *Miss Happiness and Miss Flower* a quick association is made between the two Japanese dolls of the title and Nona, the little girl with an Indian-tea background, whose mother died when she was a baby and who wasn't asked whether she wanted to come to England. Neither were the two dolls. They all feel lonely, timid and out-of-place. The book is concerned with the making of a Japanese dolls' house but it is Tom, eleven years old, who makes it, his fourteen-year-old sister Anne and Nona, who's eight, merely acting as his servants. In fact, he's a proper little male chauvinist piglet: 'He did not beg Anne, he ordered her. "I wish I were a boy," thought Nona.' A large part of the book consists of conversations between the two dolls. Dolls can converse with each other but can only direct silent wishes at humans. This is the convention Godden keeps to in her doll stories.

We've already seen boy and girl roles contrasted. *Impunity Jane,* again a doll's name, gives us further insights. Here, the doll is passed down through the generations in a family. From the start, she'd longed to have adventures in the world and envies the brothers of two of her girl owners as they can do this. Then, Gideon comes. He's the main 'real life' boy character in the story and he wants to do all sorts of exciting things, such as putting the dolls' house up a tree. His cousin, Ellen, won't let him. Impunity Jane, though, who's been excited by the life of adventure proposed by him, but turned down by the humdrum Ellen, transmits thoughts to him (as he's the right kind of person) and he steals her. They have delightful adventures together till Gideon is caught, with Impunity Jane on him, by a gang. They call him a 'sissy'. He has the inspiration of passing Impunity Jane off as a 'model', joins the gang and the doll has more adventures with them. Then, Impunity Jane *has* to wish Gideon to take her back, as she was stolen. However, Ellen gives the doll to Gideon and Impunity Jane rides on his bike, as his 'mascot', goes about in his pocket and has adventures as before. Here, the girl reader, identifying with the doll, can lead a fantasy life, although at one remove and even then only through the boy. His furtive interest in the doll should also be noted.

The use of dolls for the reinforcement of 'feminine' sex-roles is seen quite clearly in another story by the same writer, *The Dolls' House:*

> It is an anxious, sometimes a dangerous thing, to be a doll. Dolls cannot choose; they can only be chosen; they cannot 'do'; they can only be done by; children who do not understand this, often do wrong things and then the dolls are hurt and abused and lost; and when this happens dolls cannot speak, nor do anything except be hurt and abused and lost.

Here, dolls stand in for girls. They share an oppression. They are objects (pp. 4-6)

> *Bob Dixon, "Sexism: Birds in Gilded Cages," in his* Catching Them Young: Sex, Race and Class in Children's Fiction, Vol. 1, *Pluto Press, 1977, pp. 1-41.*

ALEXANDRA HUNT

I have never been sure what a book intended for young people should ideally be; at the age of ten, I myself read *Mary Poppins* and then *Gone With the Wind,* and from the latter I learned more about America's Civil War and war's real horrors than I did about crinolines and love affairs. Surely a good thing to learn.

If I try to imagine what a book for young people *should* ideally be, then I think Rumer Godden has fulfilled it and has beguiled me at the same time, since I found *The Peacock Spring* and *The Greengage Summer* delightful and utterly engrossing as adult books as well. . . .

I was told that the decision to reissue these two as Young People's Books was made because the plots center around teenagers. Yes, that is true, but the books have enough subtlety and substance to stand also as adult literature. (With respect to young readers, I feel girls might be more drawn to them than boys.)

Both books involve families of children living in a foreign country, as the young Godden herself did. *The Greengage Summer* takes place in France, and *The Peacock Spring* in

India. I learned a lot about India without feeling that the author was deliberately spelling out something for me to learn. She writes so gracefully of the customs, colors, sounds, languages and people of India that I absorbed without trying—a painless way to learn. And she did the same for a small town in France.

Even more important to learn about, I think, is the code of honor which the children in both books live by. Dissembling and lying (stealing becomes a by-product of these) are taboos in their ethic, and that's not a bad thing to learn either.

The plots of both books are intricately worked out with perfect momentum but with some ends left untied—which is as it should be and as it is in life. The characters are humanly complex, and therefore utterly believable. Even minor characters are beautifully portrayed—sometimes only a few vivid words suffice.

Few contemporary writers could equal Godden, I suspect, in conjuring up the feel of a place, as well as its appearance and smells, in so few effortless words. How difficult is it to describe a smell? Many different smells? To describe movement—a peacock's dance? Godden must be considered one of the masters of our time in this art; she succeeds over and over, and with such economy.

> *Alexandra Hunt, in a review of "The Greengage Summer," and "The Peacock Spring," in* Best Sellers, *Vol. 46, No. 10, January, 1987, p. 405.*

THE DOLLS' HOUSE (1947)

To her first book for children Miss Godden brings the same sensitive play of imagination and delicacy of characterization which mark her adult novels. The Plantagenet family of dolls will surely enchant little girls of 6 to 9 for a long time to come.

Tottie is the heroine and the mainstay of the household, a little old wooden doll who drew her courage and endurance from the tree of which she was made. Poor Mr. Plantagenet, who never quite recovered from the callous treatment suffered before he became Charlotte and Emily's doll; Birdie, not quite right in the head but with a gift for happiness; Apple, the naughty, engaging baby, all leaned on Tottie's strength. It was she who taught them how to wish hard for things, such as a proper house instead of a shoe-box. And then, after they were snugly ensconced in a Victorian mansion (with real lace curtains) their newfound happiness was spoiled by the advent of a haughty beauty, but again Tottie's hundred-year-old patience and wisdom prevailed.

There are genuine suspense and intensity of emotion in this miniature domestic drama because the dolls, each sharply individualized, are as alive as the little girls who gave them life by loving them. The real and the unreal are deftly mingled with a perfect logic and the whole is illumined by tenderness and humor.

> *Ellen Lewis Buell, in a review of "The Dolls' House," in* The New York Times Book Review, *September 12, 1948, p. 35.*

It is an event when the gifted Rumer Godden turns to a children's book. She is one of our most sensitive writers and, in *The River* and elsewhere, has written about children with understanding and tenderness. Now she writes for them with freshness, assurance, and artistry.

In *The Dolls' House* she brings to life four delightful London dolls, caught in the shortage of doll houses and forced to live in shoeboxes when the story opens. Her dramatic sense in their characterization, their dialogue among themselves, and the careful separation between them and reality are exquisitely maintained. Tottie, the heroine, is a very small Dutch doll, originally bought for a farthing. But she is made of wood and has lasted 100 years in the same family. She has character and firmness. Her eyes are painted bright blue and are very determined. To her companions Tottie talks of the wonderful doll house she first lived in. As she describes its minute perfection their enchanted exclamations will be echoed by the children.

Then that very doll house is discovered in Great-Great Aunt Laura's attic. How it is cleaned, while the dolls watch anxiously from the mantel, how the furniture is reupholstered and covered with petit-point, how the curtains in the end are of real lace will be followed as eagerly by small readers as by the dolls themselves. In the course of the story Tottie is put on display at an exhibition of dolls, is admired by the Queen, and meets an old enemy. Marchbane, a mid-nineteenth-century doll of white kid and china, bland faced and elegant, becomes the mistress of the dolls' house. After a dramatic climax, she is whisked off to a museum and Tottie is reinstated.

Dolls' House can be added to that narrow shelf where such fine books as *Hitty—Her First Hundred Years* wait to give pleasure to young readers. (pp. 24-5)

> *Joan Vatsek, in a review of "The Dolls' House," in* The Saturday Review of Literature, *Vol. XXXI, No. 46, November 13, 1948, pp. 24-5.*

If we look at Rumer Godden's story of *The Dolls' House,* . . . there is much to delight us as it is, on its face value: the miniature scale of domestic activity, the perfection of detail, the drama of the story. We can look further into it, as into a picture, and enjoy it also as a period piece, with its Victorian atmosphere and its well-grounded setting in London. But if we see no more than that, enjoyable as it is, we miss the quality that sets *The Dolls' House* apart from other doll and toy fantasies.

This book reaches out beyond its doll characters into the fundamental questions of human life: good and bad; right and wrong; the recognition of true as opposed to ephemeral values. These are questions that are universally important. They are themes found in all great literature. To find them treated in this microscopic way does not lessen their importance; perhaps it even clarifies them and brings them into perspective. It will be argued that this inner meaning eludes children and that their enjoyment of the book is solely in the story it tells. But perceptive children cannot help hearing some of these overtones and so becoming more sensitively aware of the world about them. (pp. 151-52)

> *Lillian H. Smith, "Fantasy," in her* The Unreluctant Years: A Critical Approach to Children's Literature, *American Library Association, 1953, pp. 149-62.*

THE MOUSEWIFE (1951)

Based on an anecdote in Dorothy Wordsworth's journal, this is the story of a mouse who sets free a captive dove. It is as simple as that, but those who know Miss Godden's adult novels and her memorable story for children, *The Dolls' House,*

will rightly expect something special. They will not be disappointed. There is a kindly mousewife, longing for something more than the humdrum routine of picking up crumbs and raising a family. There is the caged bird, starving himself to death, who tells her of the free world outside. It was because of her sympathy for him that the mousewife caught one wonderful glimpse of the stars, which made her forever different.

Not every child will understand this parable. Some will, undoubtedly, find it slight, but the imaginative ones will remember it and respond to the precision of its prose, the rightness of its detail. Hans Andersen would have liked it.

> *Ellen Lewis Buell, "Mousewife's Progress," in* The New York Times Book Review, *March 25, 1951, p. 22.*

Rumer Godden has taken a short and simple incident related in Dorothy Wordsworth's *Journal* and has changed it into a thing of beauty. The mousewife is not given character against an artificial background, she wears no clothes to make her appealing, she is just a little grey mouse living with her babies and her selfish husband and always struggling to find food for her family. It is in her spirit that she is different from other mice, for although she does not know what it is for which she longs, she "wants more." "I think about cheese," says her mouse husband, "Why don't you think about cheese?"

Into the mousewife's life comes a captive dove and in return for her friendship he tells her of the world outside. The mousewife can feel in her heart as the dove can feel, and so she helps him to freedom. (p. 184)

From a simple story Rumer Godden's imagination has created a parable, perceptive and moving and universal in its meaning. Most children will read it for its story interest, but for the right child it will be an unforgettable experience. Aided by [illustrator William] Pène du Bois' delicate drawing of the tiny mousewife and the stars, the spirit of the story will reach the child. Long after other stories are forgotten, *The Mousewife* will be remembered. (p. 185)

> *E. H. Colwell, "Of Mice and Men," in* The Junior Bookshelf, *Vol. 21, No. 4, October, 1957, p. 180-86.*

Stories which combine . . . three strains—small size, busy courage and daring and the multitudinous life that makes it so easy to imagine mouse towns or societies near us and yet just out of sight—are the most successful and memorable. Rumer Godden's *The Mousewife,* retold and developed from Dorothy Wordsworth's story of the friendship between the mouse and the pigeon, though short, has all three. The story is touching, beautifully told and has deep human implications. The Mousewife does nothing that mice do not, or could not do, stealing the food from the dove's cage and eventually—her presence tolerated—jumping on the catch so that the dove is free and flies away. The human parallel is not explicit, yet it is there. The mouse is free (mice in stories usually are, even in the *Miss Bianca* books—the bars of her cage are far enough apart for her to slip through) and the dove is trapped. Yet the Mousewife has a routine, cramped, circumscribed existence; there are no cats or traps, but there is no true freedom either. The Mousewife's husband is even worse, because his mind is cramped, too. 'I think about cheese,' he says. 'Why don't you think about cheese?' or 'The proper place for a mousewife is in her hole, or coming out for crumbs and frolic with me.'

The busy little Mousewife, so occupied with foraging and

care, ends by having some conception of what the outside world is like through the dove's escape. Freedom, flight, wind, stars, have a meaning that the mouse can guess at, even if she can never experience it. One cannot say that Dorothy Wordsworth, or Rumer Godden have 'used' mice to say things about humans; the mice were there first, and one can read into the story what one wishes. (p. 159)

> *Margaret Blount, "Lilliputian Life: The Mouse Story," in her* Animal Land: The Creatures of Children's Fiction, *William Morrow & Company, Inc., 1975, pp. 152-69.*

IMPUNITY JANE: THE STORY OF A POCKET DOLL (1954)

Impunity Jane, though a little china doll, was so sturdily made "you could drop her with impunity." The several generations of small girls to whom she belonged were quite insensitive to her wishes to go out in a pocket and see the world, and they kept her in a doll house, seated on a hard, bead cushion. Then one happy day Gideon rescued her and her life of adventure began.

Impunity Jane is a new and very engaging personality with an appeal for little boys as well as girls. Her story does not have the substance or the overtones of this author's *The Doll's House,* but it is quite perfect in its own way, a fresh, gay story written with such charm and skill that adults will enjoy sharing it with children.

Rumer Godden brings to her writing not only careful craftsmanship but that quality so essential to good children's books, yet so rare, the sharp memory of childhood and the things of childhood.

> *Ruth Hill Viguers, in a review of "Impunity Jane: The Story of a Pocket Doll," in* The Saturday Review, *New York, Vol. XXXVII, No. 34, August 21, 1954, p. 34.*

Six years ago Rumer Godden gave us *The Doll's House,* a novel in miniature which is well on the way to becoming a classic. *Impunity Jane* is also a doll's story—shorter in length, designedly narrower in scope, with fewer philosophical overtones, yet so far as humor, imagination and style are concerned it is all of a piece with the first book.

Jane, a product of late Victorian England, is the prototype of all tomboys. For fifty years Jane lived a safe, dull existence, but she longed, in every one of her four china inches, for adventure. It is Gideon, who has not yet outgrown a small boy's secret liking for dolls, who rescues Jane and introduces her to the gay, adventurous life she has always dreamed of. And because of her—and his own wits—Gideon is accepted into a much-admired gang of bigger boys. Yet there is the nagging question as to whether Jane should go back to the dolls' house from which she had been most unethically released. This problem will give any right-minded child some uneasy moments, just enough to sharpen the pleasure of the ending.

Reality and fancy are compounded here into a story at once gay and moving, wholly convincing to any child who believes that dolls have their own emotions and needs.

> *Ellen Lewis Buell, in a review of "Impunity Jane: The Story of a Pocket Doll," in* The New York Times Book Review, *August 29, 1954, p. 18.*

[This] short tale gives us the same qualities of understanding of children, the same original attitude toward dolls, as we have in Miss Godden's longer tale, *The Doll's House,* an outstanding children's book. The concentration of action, the brevity of text, are accomplished with the usual art of this skilled poet and novelist. We read it quickly, but we have covered years, and shared colorful little adventures all over London. Many a six or seven-year-old boy has felt a secret, shamed affinity for a doll; here it is released and justified in a very clever way. But, of course, little girls will love it too. And both will learn that odd, hard word "impunity," for the tiny doll did "escape without hurt," forever and ever.

> *Louise S. Bechtel, in a review of "Impunity Jane," in* New York Herald Tribune Book Review, *September 5, 1954, p. 7.*

THE FAIRY DOLL (1956)

Rumer Godden's perceptive, almost intuitive understanding of the inner world of childhood illumines this beautifully restrained account of a small girl's discovery of her own spirit. A great-grandmother in her wisdom helps, but it is a decoration from the top of the family Christmas tree—a fragile fairy doll—whose magic releases a pathetic eight-year-old from bumbling stupidity to shining self-confidence. The writing is delicate and full of grace.

> *Eulalie Steinmetz Ross, in a review of "The Fairy Doll," in* The Saturday Review, *New York, Vol. XXXIX, No. 46, November 17, 1956, p. 54.*

Miss Godden has the perfect touch for a story like this. Her prose is as delicate as a cobweb and as carefully designed as a snow-flake. One could no more change a word than one could improve a Chinese poem of Arthur Waley. This is a perfect little tale, told with style and infused with wisdom.

It would be easy for an artist to upset the balance of this story, tipping it into vulgarity or sentimentality. [Adrienne] Adams, however, has something of Miss Godden's poetry matched with realism, and her decorations blend so exquisitely with the words that it would be difficult to say which came first.

> *A review of "The Fairy Doll," in* The Junior Bookshelf, *Vol. 20, No. 6, December, 1956, p. 324.*

Like Hans Christian Andersen, Rumer Godden can give overtones of wonder and magic to everyday happenings. Here is a happier magic, however, to delight children under ten, although it too does not pretend that unhappiness can always be avoided. Elizabeth has a long struggle, but she cherishes the little figure and believes in her power to give aid and guidance. Not since Miss Hickory have we read of such a charmingly detailed home for a doll as Elizabeth arranges, a broom of twigs, a burr for a door scraper, honeycomb pigeonholes over the desk and a different flower hat each season. Adrienne Adams' illustrations in soft gray and pink have caught the elusive quality of the story, especially the mingling of the matter of fact and the almost miraculous.

> *Margaret Sherwood Libby, in a review of "The Fairy Doll," in* New York Herald Tribune Book Review, *December 9, 1956, p. 14.*

Godden, aged three, with her sister Jon, aged four.

MOUSE HOUSE (1957)

Miss Godden's beautiful prose makes a lovely thing of this simple tale about a little red house, "like a doll's house, but not for dolls, for mice." It was a present to Mary but it was not very interesting, for the mice who lived in it were made of felt and never moved even when she lifted the roof off, hoping to catch at least a tail or a whisker in motion. Young children will like to hear what happened when the house was discovered by a real mouse whose family was suffering from a housing shortage.

> *Jennie D. Lindquist, in a review of "Mouse House,"*
> *in* The Horn Book Magazine, *Vol. XXXIII, No. 6,*
> *December, 1957, p. 483.*

There is no more skilled dispenser of delights today than Miss Godden. Her books for children have that quiet perfection which passes almost unnoticed; style is so much a part of her being that it cannot be dissected or analysed.

Mouse House is a result of the same partnership which made *The Fairy Doll* such an enchanting book. . . . The story is simple enough for the smallest children and springs from accurate observation; it is in the fullest sense a true story. The difficulty of a story told from both the human and the mouse point of view is that of proportion. Miss Godden, and her illustrator [Adrienne Adams], maintain perfect perspective. The reader shares in the fortunes of the mouse family, while keeping the standpoint of Mary.

Mouse House is that rarest of books, a product of complete sincerity and impeccable taste. How one dreads most stories of talking mice! Here there is no slightest fear of inanity or sentimentality; the author's strength and inflexibility are evident behind the delicate strands of this most memorable and enchanting tale. (pp. 121-22)

> *A review of "Mouse House," in* The Junior Book-
> shelf, *Vol. 22, No. 3, July, 1958, pp. 121-22.*

THE GREENGAGE SUMMER (1958)

Late in its pages, *The Greengage Summer* explodes into adroitly contrived melodrama, upon the elements of which a reviewer must not trespass at all. This doesn't matter, for while that abrupt compilation of plot has its own interests, it is not here that the real merits or rewards of the book lie.

The pleasures that Rumer Godden brings as she goes to work in what is for her a new setting, are of a subtle and delicate order. They may hover, at times, at the brink of the precious, but they do not stumble and fall over it, for her essential artistry and control of her materials are safeguards.

The story tells of the summer adventures of a group of English children, in somewhat shadowed circumstances, at a second-rate hotel on the Marne, near the forest of Compiègne. The five Grey children are ranked from Joss, who is 16, through Cecil, 13; and Hester, 10; to the two "Littles"—Will, called Willmouse, and Vicky. Each of these is realized with sharp individuality and distinctive appeal. Cecil—a girl, there is but one boy—is the narrator, from the vantage point of some years after the events.

Their mother is taken seriously ill as they are en route to the hotel Les Oeillets, at Vieux-Moutiers. Upon arrival, she is rushed to the hospital for a long stay. The disconcerted children are stranded at the hotel where neither the proprietress, Mademoiselle Zizi, nor her henchwoman, Mme. Corbet, want them. It is the somewhat mysterious Englishman, Eliot, apparently romantically involved with Mlle. Zizi, who takes them under his wing and casually superintends their stay.

The summer is filled with the special responses and perceptions of childhood, which Miss Godden understands magically. . . . From the first, we feel the specific stresses of crucial maturing, of a physical order for Cecil and an emotional order for Joss. The involvements with adult lives become increasingly complex, acting as precipitants to drastic events, the secret of which belongs to Miss Godden. I think the book would have had greater depth if those events had culminated in some less flamboyant way—the effect now being to make a particular fictional invention of something basically universal.

It is an experience to share the impact upon these middle-class English children of the less inhibited ways of France, especially as they encounter them much in the company of servants and without the protective supervision that would ordinarily have shielded their lives. Realities, some of them ugly and potentially dangerous, advance upon the five Grey children. The basic soundness of their often bewildered responses lend the substance to a slight, but warming, sometimes joyously funny, and exquisitely wrought tale.

Edmund Fuller, "Unprotected Nest," in The New York Times Book Review, *March 23, 1958, p. 4.*

Miss Rumer Godden has always written well about children, and in *The Greengage Summer* she writes particularly well. . . . [It] is not the plot which makes *The Greengage Summer* memorable. It is beautifully worked out, for no one knows better than Miss Godden how to sow the seeds of suspense and how on occasion to make one's flesh creep. That moment when the pseudo-Eliot is discovered by the river! But the sensational plot is somehow out of key with the rest—the evocation of the burning August weather, the impact of the hotel and its staff—all the "foreignness"—on the minds and imaginations of the children, their awakening to a life in two worlds—a world of truth and a world of untruth. When the police come in, poetry is apt to go out. By some miracle Miss Godden extracts this delicate poetry and shimmering lyricism from facts which are always hard and often sordid—for who will quickly forget Mme. Corbet's meanness, Paul the writer's nastiness (they both had other, pleasanter qualities), and, between bouts of ostentatious bonhomie, the ruthless materialism of the whole setup at Les Oeillets? Nor is her portrayal of childhood at all sentimental; we seldom feel she is balancing youth against age, innocence against its opposite,

but the contrast is always there and always poignant. (pp. 17-18)

L. P. Hartley, "Children's Aura," in The Saturday Review, *New York, Vol. XLI, No. 14, April 5, 1958, pp. 17-18.*

Wit being the soul of this story, it is, appropriately, wit that gives it brightness and a consistent quality and at the same time limits its power; ease and cleverness predominate, while a sense of the genuine—and a genuine concern on the part of the reader—is forfeited.

But for one more child and different names, the cast of characters is that of Miss Godden's earlier novel, *The River,* even to certain identical speeches. This is curious but unobjectionable since the children are still very appealing and so are their speeches. The viewpoint is again that of a pre-adolescent girl placed effectively in the midst of a large family—two little sisters, cherubic and placid, and a whimsical, self-contained little brother (these serve to emphasize her own vanishing serenity) and an older sister of maturing beauty who has passed disturbingly over a threshold before which the younger girl hesitates resentfully and longingly.

The Greengage Summer depicts, as did *The River,* a season of change, significant events, the discovery of good and evil unfathomably mingled, a season of gently inexorable growth. . . . (pp. 162-63)

In *The River* the same theme of discovery and growth emerges naturally, almost organically, out of its own setting, with a quiet, believable dignity that is truly moving. In *The Greengage Summer,* it is a matter of gimmicks; the devices being so extrinsic and so unlikely—even the necessity of removing the children to a foreign habitat in order to introduce them to "life"—that acceptable or not they necessarily reduce the scope and impact of the book.

It will appeal to some as sophisticated fare, because it gets around a fairly tender theme with a light touch. Yet with respect to the various raw elements involved—passion, murder, homosexuality . . .—the reader gets neither an adult's treatment nor the vivid observations of a Colette ingénue, and these elements emerge as if from a milk bath, not very alarming or real. That the narrator and protagonists are wide-eyed English children could, of course, have a particular advantage, but this point of view is not notably handled in *The Greengage Summer,* largely because, as happens more often than not, the whole device of the precious, unexpected naiveté of the child is pushed too relentlessly and ardently.

This is not to complain but only to try to place the book carefully in its own category and to offer some resistance to the wrong kind of praise. It *is* in a way delightful, but it is certainly nothing *more* than delightful. It is difficult to say of this kind of book that it is superficial because it is far too knowing, because it avoids superficiality so adequately (it is filled with appropriate profundities and the correct insights into motivations) and yet the total effect is, nevertheless, superficial. At its best it is very funny; at its worst it is never really moving unless one good-naturedly allows oneself conditioned reactions. *The Greengage Summer* would, in fact, make an excellent movie; the plot is symmetrical and picturesque from all angles, and it employs the kind of sensitivity that could be translated to the screen in its entirety without loss or injustice to the original in the process. (pp. 163-64)

Alice Saxon, "The Godden Cast," in The Common-weal, *Vol. LXVIII, No. 6, May 9, 1958, pp. 162-64.*

THE STORY OF HOLLY AND IVY (1958)

Holly was a doll, in a red dress, red shoes, with a green petti-coat and socks, and, like all the dolls in the toyshop, she wanted a little girl for Christmas. Ivy, 6 years old, (green coat, red gloves), was an orphan in search of a nonexistent grandmother, and she was wishing for a doll too. Mrs. Jones, a policeman's wife, had neither doll nor child, but she had a Christmas tree, trimmed and waiting for something or some-body—she didn't quite know what. These are the principals in the cast Rumer Godden has assembled in a story of purest Victorian sentiment (although its setting is of today).

An adult might well be surprised at a writer of Miss Godden's originality indulging in such a conventional theme. But this story is for little girls who are still of an age to believe that "dolls are not really alive until they are played with," and *they* never object to sentiment—or coincidence, either. For them it should be completely satisfactory because Miss God-den, with her sensitive touch and pellucid prose, evokes the essence of wistfulness and loneliness. Mrs. Jones wishing and waiting; Ivy, bravely denying reality in her stubborn search through strange streets; Holly, hoping uncertainly—all these are made for the brief space of this story real and touching. And even though you know the way it will end, you are on edge to find out just how it happens. And that is the measure of a real story-teller's skill.

Ellen Lewis Buell, in a review of "The Story of Holly and Ivy," in The New York Times Book Review, *September 28, 1958, p. 48.*

Christmas is a time for sentiment and for stories like *The Story of Holly and Ivy* that underline the power of fervent wishing. Rumer Godden can weave such a tale, using old and tried ingredients, in skillful and beautiful prose to enchant lit-tle girls and even to induce in skeptical grownups a willing suspension of disbelief. . . . [This] is a story of wishes that are fulfilled almost miraculously. However, so poignant and delightful is the telling . . . that whether you are child or grownup you will not want to miss a word.

Margaret Sherwood Libby, in a review of "The Story of Holly and Ivy," in New York Herald Tribune Book Review, *November 2, 1958, p. 5.*

In *The Story of Holly and Ivy,* by Rumer Godden, which is sure to be a favourite with girls of about five to seven, the wish theme is . . . delicately and naturally sustained. A little or-phan named Ivy longs to have a grandmother and sets out to look for one; Mrs. Jones, the childless wife of a police con-stable, longs for a daughter; and Holly, a Christmas doll, yearns for a little girl to play with her. All are united in an incredible (but to an uncritical child wholly satisfactory) se-quence of events. Miss Godden may not here by quite at her best, but there are places where she illuminates in a touching way basic truths about personal relationships. One weakness of the plot is that running away from an orphanage has such rewarding results—there is no suggestion that Ivy was in any way to blame for her behaviour. But perhaps this is a deplor-ably adult attitude to adopt. Holly, Ivy, and Mrs. Jones are all charming figures, and their coming together is certain to delight.

"Soft Soap or Commonsense?" in The Times Liter-ary Supplement, *No. 2960, November 21, 1958, p. xv.*

CANDY FLOSS (1960)

When Rumer Godden writes a doll story you may be sure that it will not be like anyone else's or even like her earlier ones. There is always about her dolls an air of difference, of being just a little more interesting than common ones. Admit-tedly, this story is slight, lacking the substance of her *Dolls' House,* or the subtle motivation of *Impunity Jane* and *The Fairy Doll.* Still and all, little girls will surely be captivated by a doll who is as pretty as Candy Floss . . . and who lives glamorously in a coconut shy (properly explained as a kind of English side show) and travels about with a fair.

Candy Floss' owner said she brought him luck and absolutely refused to sell her when Clementina, a spoiled, bratty child set her heart on the doll. So Clementina, unable to under-stand a simple no, made off with Candy Floss. And then, with that special art of hers, Miss Godden persuades us that a doll can have volition and emotion. Of course, a realist might claim that it was Clementina's guilty conscience alone which made her realize the enormity of her act. Almost any little girl, however, will be sure that Candy Floss had a great deal to do with the happy ending. Either way it's quite satisfacto-ry—even for Clementina.

Ellen Lewis Buell, "A Doll for Luck," in The New York Times Book Review, *March 20, 1960, p. 42.*

It would be hard to imagine a better name than "Candy Floss" (English English for American "Cotton Candy") for this doll heroine. "Her eyes were glass, blue as bluebells; her hair was fine and gold, like spun toffee." . . . All in all *Candy Floss* is the right name for the book too. Its threads of sweet-ness have been spun into soft whirls of nothingness that leaves nothing but pleasantness behind it.

P. M., in a review of "Candy Floss," in The Chris-tian Science Monitor, *April 28, 1960, p. 11.*

Rumer Godden's little stories have a fragile perfection which one finds nowhere else in children's books. They do not admit criticism, for it would be impossible to amend them in the smallest detail. Speaking in London this year Miss Godden said that she found writing for children valuable for the "dis-cipline" which it imposed. One can see this discipline at work in *Candy Floss,* but the children will not see the numerous drafts of each paragraph but enjoy instead the simple right-ness of every word.

Miss Godden is the finest master in our day of the "doll" story. . . .

Any young writer could with profit study *Candy Floss* in de-tail. Not that study will enable anyone else to match Miss Godden's luminous prose or the firm sweetness of her vision; but it is possible to observe how she uses details of descrip-tion, how she selects incidents, how she never cheats her reader. Candy Floss is a doll. She has character, but she is never, physically, anything but a doll. She defeats the objec-tionable Clementina purely by doll-like manoeuvres. Miss Godden earns her reader's respect by respecting the reader; she may purify and re-purify her style until it is simple enough for the smallest children: she never confuses simplification with falsification. *Candy Floss* is, in the most profound sense, a true story.

A review of "Candy Floss," in The Junior Book-shelf, *Vol. 24, No. 5, November, 1960, p. 292.*

MISS HAPPINESS AND MISS FLOWER (1961)

Sent away from her home in India to live with her three cousins in England, homesick little Nona found the ways of her relatives strange and difficult to understand. Certainly Belinda was no help, jealous of Nona's very presence in the household and intolerant of her mistakes. Then one day a package arrived for the two girls containing two Japanese dolls, Miss Happiness and Miss Flower. Like Nona they were strangers in a new environment, and so immediately she felt a sympathetic kinship towards them. How the silent wishes of the dolls inspire Tom to build them a Japanese house, and how they cause friendship to spring between the girls and to alleviate Nona's loneliness combine to make pleasant whimsical reading. Nobody writing today has quite the "feel" for dolls that Miss Godden reveals.

A review of "Miss Happiness and Miss Flower," in Virginia Kirkus' Service, *Vol. XXIX, No. 7, April 1, 1961, p. 328.*

It's something of a surprise to find Rumer Godden writing a story that is, in one sense, a do-it-yourself guide to building a miniature Japanese house—including directions at story's end. It's a persuasive guide but also something more than that with its theme (reminiscent of Miss Godden's *The Fairy Doll*) of finding oneself in doing something for somebody—even if that somebody is only a pair of Japanese dolls. . . .

Running in double counterpoint to the main story are the secret life of the dolls and the jealousy of Nona's obstreperous little cousin which other girls will find acutely realistic. Miss Godden weaves these strands together with her customary dexterity, manages to stay this side of sentimentality and provides genuine suspense on a scale as small and as charming as the doll's house.

Ellen Lewis Buell, "Something to Do," in The New York Times Book Review, *April 9, 1961, p. 34.*

[There] is cause for special joy in finding . . . books which have not been tailored to the standard needs of the reader, in which the authors are content to be themselves. Miss Godden fills her work with a rare and natural kindness, which must surely be her own. . . . In outline the story [of *Miss Happiness and Miss Flower*] is simple, but in fact it is never dull. The building of the doll's house, a true scale model of a traditional Japanese home, becomes an absorbing task, the sort of practical challenge which would quickly appeal to a child. There are footnotes and technical details for children who would like to make this doll's house for themselves. Such footnotes seem strange in a book for younger children (from eight to ten, at a guess); yet it is a mark of respect for the readers that the author treats them like this. The children in the story, too, are handled with respect: they are serious and natural, good on the whole but sometimes bad, and always genuine people who happen to be young. The story is in no way didactic, yet its ups and downs have a distant moral ring.

Miss Godden's book would appeal most strongly to the serious, gentle, practical child. (p. 721)

Jennifer Bourdillon, "Dolls' Distress," in New Statesman, *Vol. CXI, No. 1573, May 5, 1961, pp. 721-22.*

ST. JEROME AND THE LION (1961)

Do many children, or adults, I wonder, still read *Beasts and Saints,* that exquisite shaft of light on the Dark Ages? Miss Waddell's book has already given Ian Serraillier material for several poems. Now Rumer Godden has gone to the same source for a congenial theme. Let it be acknowledged at once that the best things in the poem come from the original, like Jerome's appeal to the monks, when the lion is under suspicion of ass-eating, not to "nag at him and make him wretched!" What Miss Godden has added is subtle rhythm, local colour of a pleasant kind, and an occasional neat phrase. Not in fact as good as we might have hoped for from this distinguished writer, *St. Jerome and the Lion* is a competent narrative.

A review of "St. Jerome and the Lion," in The Junior Bookshelf, *Vol. 25, No. 6, December, 1961, p. 339.*

[This book's] special charm lies in the combination of picturesque details of monastic life in ancient Bethlehem with keen, humorous, affectionate and reverent feeling for the characters, the situation and the period. Never has this lion, wrongly accused of killing an ass he was set to guard, been shown in a more beguiling way, nor his saintly friend as more strong and lovable.

Margaret Sherwood Libby, in a review of "St. Jerome and the Lion," in Books, *New York, December 10, 1961, p. 13.*

In her graceful narrative poem *St. Jerome and the Lion,* Rumer Godden retells the legend of the grave saint and his embarrassing convert in pleasantly conversational verse, supported by helpful footnotes, designed for young readers. The poem itself is for any age, provided one brings to it the credulity, at once simple, humorous, and practical, of the medieval imagination. Miss Godden has reproduced this kind of fancy, which saw nothing incongruous in combining a celebration of the power of the Christian faith with sly satire on the limited wit of Christian clerics, extremely well. . . .

Edward Weeks, "The Saint and the Lion," in The Atlantic Monthly, *Vol. 209, No. 3, March, 1962, p. 142.*

LITTLE PLUM (1963)

Little Plum by Rumer Godden contains one idea that could have been a winner: the development, through their respective ownership of Japanese dolls, of a relationship between the clumsy, friendly, extrovert Belinda and her difficult, lonely, rich little girl neighbour. Miss Godden's poetry and taste for the miniature always give pleasure, but the plot is curiously mishandled: it seems as if some obligation to introduce "happenings" had inhibited the author's usual delicacy of touch.

"Bread, Gruel or Stones?" in The Times Literary Supplement, *No. 3222, November 28, 1963, p. 988.*

Although this delightful story receives its name from a tiny

Japanese doll, Miss Plum, the little creature's role is a completely passive one. She does not even send doll-thoughts to influence the children's actions as Miss Happiness and Miss Flower did in Miss Godden's last book about the cousins Nona and Belinda. This does not mean that she is unimportant, however, for she is the cause of as savage and bitter a feud as any lively children would care to read about.

Booby traps, nasty notes, slashing of proffered presents to bits and eventual seizure of Miss Plum by Belinda (all for her good, of course) were but a few of the moves in this bitter game of which Nona only knew the mildest part and the grownups nothing. How Belinda managed to survive her perilous climbs using a poorly secured board as a bridge from the tree to Gem's balcony, and how that wonderful Japanese doll's house—every detail of which was described so interestingly in *Miss Happiness and Miss Flower*—became the scene of a Doll Festival and the end of bawling, make a splendid story.

Miss Godden uses with freshness and vitality many of the devices dear to the heart of Victorian writers. The disagreeableness of Gem's aunt and the ineffectualness of her father, as well as the hothouse atmosphere of this poor little rich girl's home, are a bit overdone, but Belinda and Gem are vivid, exciting and passionate children, superbly characterized, and it is chiefly their story. We are sure it will give pleasure to little girls for years to come.

> *Margaret Sherwood Libby, "Feuding with the Girl Next Door," in* Book Week—The Sunday Herald Tribune, *December 22, 1963, p. 13.*

HOME IS THE SAILOR (1964)

Anyone who has read Miss Godden's earlier books will not be surprised by the charm of this story. The author never treats her readers as children, she never attempts to "write down" to them, there is nothing "precious" about her style, consequently her books have a sense of reality which is sadly missing from so much of children's fiction to-day.

The story concerns a dolls' house and its occupants. These dolls, though outwardly filled with sawdust or made of china, have lives and problems of their own. They are real people, in fact the personification of real people, to the child who owns the house and to her family. They become real to the reader very quickly. The story is in many ways pure fantasy, but yet highly probable. There are coincidences, but these do not detract from it in any way. Perhaps the key to Miss Godden's success lies in the fact that her book can be read at many levels. The eight year-old will read it at face value, the twelve year-old as an improbable, but acceptable, adventure and the teenager as an amusing reflection on life. (pp. 294-95)

> *A review of "Home Is the Sailor," in* The Junior Bookshelf, *Vol. 28, No. 5, November, 1964, pp. 294-95.*

The doll house belonged to Sian Llewellyn, whose home overlooked the waterfront of the little Welsh town of Penhelig. At one time the doll-house family had included a father, Captain Raleigh, and his son Thomas, a sailor doll, engaged to marry Miss Charlotte the governess. But long ago Captain Raleigh had been lost in a sand dune and Thomas had been thoughtlessly given away and had sailed across the Channel. Now the only male in the household was seven-year-old

Curly, who, being a doll, would remain seven years old forever. Curly longed to go out into the world to find Thomas and bring him home. Then perhaps Miss Charlotte would not spend her days staring sadly out the doll-house window. There was a stranger in Penhelig one year, a lonely French boy, Bertrand, a member of the Sea School which, his uncle hoped, would drill some of the conceit out of him. The Sea School boys were marching past the Llewellyn house one day when a duster flicked Curly off the windowsill and into a puddle at Bertrand's feet. That was the beginning of adventures for Curly and of a happy new day for the doll house. The characters, human and doll, are alive, the atmosphere of the seacoast village vivid, and like Miss Godden's other doll stories, particularly *The Dolls' House,* the book has more than one level of interest and meaning. The drama of human life is somehow sharpened when seen through these stories of dolls, in much the way the world through the wrong end of a telescope may seem small and far away but especially clearly defined. A beautiful, enchanting book. (pp. 56-7)

> *Ruth Hill Viguers, in a review of "Home Is the Sailor," in* The Horn Book Magazine, *Vol. XLI, No. 1, February, 1965, pp. 56-7.*

A doll story by Rumer Godden is always eagerly awaited. Even more than her *Impunity Jane,* this story of a real sailor doll can be enjoyed by boys as well as girls, despite the rather too sweet pictures [by Jean Primrose]. Miss Godden's books appeal to children, but they are not contrived for children. Beautifully and skillfully written, completely without condescension, they are literature (in the restricted, complimentary sense of the word). . . .

The two sailor characters are vivid and convincing, the rest more conventional and shadowy, yet the dolls and Sian back in Penhelig, waiting and longing for the sailor's return, give the story much needed suspense, and the ending, although a little too dependent on luck, is eminently satisfying.

> *Margaret Sherwood Libby, "Plenty of Dolls in Port," in* Book Week—The Sunday Herald Tribune, *March 7, 1965, p. 23.*

THE KITCHEN MADONNA (1967)

Once again Rumer Godden has used the experiences of a child as the theme of her book. In this novella her protagonist is a shy withdrawn boy who comes out of his shell when he decides to get for Marta, their Ukranian maid, a little shrine for her kitchen such as the one she had had in her European home. Miss Godden's plot is slight: Gregory at first tries to buy a shrine; when that fails, he uses his ingenuity to make one. But as she has shown in her other novels, it is Miss Godden's ability to understand a child's mind and his developing concern for others that makes the book rewarding. Written with the same charm as her earlier books, this is for all fiction and Young Adult collections.

> *Signe L. Steen, in a review of "The Kitchen Madonna," in* Library Journal, *Vol. 92, No. 19, November 1, 1967, p. 4027.*

A flawless book, not about dolls, but about children and making things, love and communication, the nature of homes and humans and much else. . . . Here are wonderful children, wonderful cat, wonderful jewellers, cook, craftsmanship—the lot. . . . A good gift for almost anyone you know. Not a word too many and it would read aloud well if you are able to control your own emotions at the close. (pp. 390-91)

> *A review of "The Kitchen Madonna," in* The Junior Bookshelf, *Vol. 31, No. 6, December, 1967, p. 390-91.*

OPERATION SIPPACIK (1969)

How Rifat's Sippacik, "the sturdiest, prettiest, cleverest donkey in Cyprus" (except when she's a Seytan, a devil) occasions a night exercise by the 27th Battery Royal Artillery, United Nations command, is a story as disparate as it sounds—part child's play, part service record. Even before Grandfather Arif Ali sells Sippacik to the British (as "local transport"), we know as much about each of them as we do about Rifat and his family—actually more: the Turkish Cypriots seem to have fewer idiosyncracies. The longstanding "trouble" between the Turkish and the Greek Cypriots is brewing again, and it may come to a boil if Rifat's patriot-father is intercepted on his way home from Turkish exile. While Rifat is tending Sippacik for the British (he's the only one who can make the donkey go), he finds his father wounded and, trying to get him home, stumbles upon a Greek ambush. That's when the Battery becomes involved: the Captain, to provide cover for Rifat and Sippacik, orders the practice exercise. Not only is Osman Ali rescued but the British, when they pull out, take up a collection to buy Sippacik back for Rifat. Their relationship with Sippacik (strained, after they spoil her) and Rifat's reaction to them ("three helpings of everything except the tea") are vastly amusing and so is the banter among the men. And there's excitement in Rifat's desperate attempt to save his father. But it won't go as the tale of a boy and a donkey. (pp. 440-41)

> *A review of "Operation Sippacik," in* Kirkus Reviews, *Vol. XXXVII, No. 8, April 15, 1969, pp. 440-41.*

Despite such universally appealing ingredients as a boy, an animal, and danger, this short novel, liberally interspersed with Turkish phrases, falls flat. . . . Characterizations are very weak, the setting does not enhance the plot, and Sippacik is just not convincingly lovable.

> *Sandra Meyer, in a review of "Operation Sippacik," in* Library Journal, *Vol. 94, No. 10, May 15, 1969, p. 2100.*

Maintaining strict political neutrality, the author achieves a starker realism than is characteristic of most of her books, without any sacrifice of her customary insight and sympathy. The minutiae of the Cyprian landscape and the contrast between the traditional types of the Turkish family and the humorously differentiated British soldiers create the background for Rifat's love for Sippacik and for Rifat's heroism. (pp. 305-06)

> *Paul Heins, in a review of "Operation Sippacik," in* The Horn Book Magazine, *Vol. XLV, No. 3, June, 1969, pp. 305-06.*

THE OLD WOMAN WHO LIVED IN A VINEGAR BOTTLE (1972)

The Old Woman who Lived in a Vinegar Bottle used to be told every hairwashing night in Rumer Godden's family—it is a version of the greedy fisherman legend, with, in this case, the story ending happily if morally. Miss Godden's effortless, flowing style never slips into banality, remaining firmly rooted in recognizable, everyday life, not in the least fairylike or remote despite its theme.

> *"Old Stories, New Pictures," in* The Times Literary Supplement, *No. 3672, July 14, 1972, p. 808.*

Rumer Godden takes one of the greatest of old folk tales, the one most familiar in its Grimm guise as *The Fisherman and His Wife,* and gives it a homely English setting. The old woman has no husband to bully. Indeed she is no virago, being slowly corrupted by power. Her downfall is caused not by a wish to outdo God; she pushes the fish beyond endurance by asking for a car with a chauffeur and by not saying "please". Finally she apologises to the fish and so ensures a regular hot Sunday dinner for herself and Malt, her cat. The story, you will see, lacks both the fierce vision and the rough poetry of the Grimm version. Instead it is intimate and close to a child's experience. It is written with masterly simplicity and warmth.

> *M. Crouch, in a review of "The Old Woman Who Lived in a Vinegar Bottle," in* The Junior Bookshelf, *Vol. 36, No. 4, August, 1972, p. 220.*

In Rumer Godden's books, small domestic objects always take on immense charm, and in this story any child would respond to her loving recital of change—from rag rug to a carpet scattered with roses, from the small black kettle on the hob and the windfall apples to the new stove and the maid offering a cup of tea. From the cumulative folk-tale Rumer Godden has contrived a tiny domestic novel, with room for quirks of character and lively speech. . . . I would suggest reading this book aloud to a child of five or six to give her a feeling for well-selected, rich prose and many happy touches of character and action; it could also give older children an hour or so of very happy reading and looking. (p. 1985)

> *Margery Fisher, in a review of "The Old Woman Who Lived in a Vinegar Bottle," in* Growing Point, *Vol. 11, No. 3, September, 1972, pp. 1984-85.*

THE DIDDAKOI (1972)

A diddakoi is a derisive name for a child who is part Romany gypsy and part gorgio (non-gypsy). Kizzy Lovell is such a child. After her grandmother's death the authorities plan for Kizzy's future. She is given over to one of the local magistrates, an apparently "liberated" woman. Kizzy is a spitfire, and her attempts at reconciling her two worlds cause her unhappiness and the adults involved a great deal of worry. A series of contrived incidents make the story end "just right", but on the whole it is a cloying, sentimental story that adults will gush over and most children will say "ugh". The book needs more of Kizzy's spirit to make it come alive.

> *A review of "The Diddakoi," in* Children's Book Review Service, *Vol. 1, No. 3, November, 1972, p. 18.*

The Diddakoi, a novel by Rumer Godden, laid in the English countryside of today, is a timeless story of love and the need for companionship, and of the invincibility of the human spirit, as a standoffish and fiercely independent orphaned gypsy girl is befriended by a gruff old admiral and a wise and unusual minister. It is a story of stupidity and ignorance too, as some of the do-good villagers almost wreck the gypsy girl's chance of happiness. As usual this is written with Rumer Godden's special charm and enchantment; the end is perhaps a little neater and more sentimental than in her earlier books but then this is sort of a fairy tale. Anyway it is nice to have an old-fashioned happy ending once in a while.

In the **Diddakoi** as in Jane Gardam's books and in many . . . other novels, the adults as well as the children are important and fully realized. The author is at once a child and at the same time someone outside childhood, looking at it with lucidity and vision. (p. 158)

> *Elizabeth Minot Graves, "Children's Novels: Alive and Well," in* Commonweal, *Vol. XCVII, No. 7, November 17, 1972, pp. 156-58.*

Here again Godden has displayed her unique ability to delve into the thinking and emotions of a sensitive child as Kizzy, under the care of the crusty Admiral and the gentle Miss Brooke, gradually emerges from her shell, while the villagers, on the other hand, come to an appreciation of the Gypsy way of life. Charmingly written and on a level with Godden's other stories of childhood, this novelette should be in all fiction collections. Suitable also for YA and younger children.

> *Signe L. Steen, in a review of "The Diddakoi," in* Library Journal, *Vol. 97, No. 21, December 1, 1972, p. 3930.*

Kizzy's story is told with Rumer Godden's wonted compassion for the misunderstood and with the perceptive knowledge of childhood that is hers. There is warmth and emotion, so often missing in modern children's books, and she is not afraid of romance and a happy ending. Kizzy, a child who does not fit into the conventional pattern, defiant and unhappy and so needing love, is the symbol of many unhappy children.

Needless to say, the book is beautifully written with that unobtrusive craftsmanship which is typical of its author. That a book for children should win one of the three Whitbread Awards for Literature is a welcome indication of the growing status of children's literature. That Rumer Godden, author of so many books loved by children, should have this honour is a fitting recognition of a distinguished writer's contribution to children's books. (pp. 39-40)

> *E. Colwell, in a review of "The Diddakoi," in* The Junior Bookshelf, *Vol. 37, No. 1, February, 1973, pp. 39-40.*

MR. McFADDEN'S HALLOWE'EN (1975)

Rumer Godden is enough of a magician to make our willing suspension of disbelief an easy matter, which is perhaps just as well. Mr McFadden is related to Scrooge and perhaps also to Colin in *The Secret Garden;* he is taught to love and forgive by Tim, the skinny orphan, and Selina, who decides to dress up as a good witch at Hallowe'en. Through her pink magic, which is simply courage and warmth of heart, the old man is saved from death (for he, too, has climbed a wall with disastrous consequences) and brought into a new life. There is another sort of moral in the story, however, though Miss Godden may be unaware of it; terrorism pays. Mr McFadden only gives the village the land for its new park after a vicious campaign against him by the locals in which Tim and Selina are nearly killed. The final joyous opening of the park does not

tally with the nastiness of the community. One feels that the author is too easily satisfied with a pretty surface. Similarly, her vivacious and charming style is in danger of becoming an ornamental habit. She is particularly fond of inserting units of direct speech into sentences in place of clauses, a device refreshing in moderation but tiresome in excess. (pp. 1448-49)

> *Dominic Hibberd, "The Mere Suspension of Disbelief," in* The Times Literary Supplement, *No. 3847, December 5, 1975, pp. 1448-49.*

The dourest recluse in the present-day Scottish village owns but will not sell the only land suitable for the community bowling green and swimming pool, money for which has been left in a bequest to the villagers. From one Halloween to the next, the events that change his life and his mind are enjoyably told in an old-fashioned tale full of zestful characters—human and animal. Principal among these are Tim, a mistreated orphan and a stalwart goblin of a child; Selina, eight, bright, stubborn, and resourceful; her pony, Haggis, of the same age and similar nature; Mr. McFadden, that "thrawn old devil"; and Big Wullie, his fearsome guardian gander. The occasional, usually explained Scots dialect adds color and offers some wonderful epithets: "creeping clype" (tattler); "bossie mooth't (mouthed) bletherer." Streatfield, Spyri, Estes, Burnett, etc. fans—and many adults—will especially enjoy this one.

> *Ruth M. McConnell, in a review of "Mr. McFadden's Hallowe'en," in* School Library Journal, *Vol. 22, No. 5, January, 1976, p. 46.*

Rumer Godden writes like an angel and, unlike Goldsmith, talks like one too. She is that rarity among writers—has there been another since Masefield and Walter de la Mare?—one who is equally at ease with children and adults. She is also rare in that her work flowers in the arid country between the picture book and the full blown novel. Not that she tailors her prose to nine-year-old abilities; she uses all the crafts of a master but disciplines them to the imaginative capacity of the child.

Miss Godden is peculiarly the master, in this half century, of the doll-story, but here she turns to the workaday world of a Scottish Border village and the fortunes and misfortunes of a little girl. . . .

One could go on a long time, listing the manifold excellences of this little book. The 'Lallands' dialect may bother a few young readers, but the sincerity which shines through every page, and the quiet irony which keeps its sweetness clear of sentimentality, are not to be denied. Beautifully written and observed, highly professional in its handling of narrative and dialogue, this is a story to be read wherever little girls love ponies and old men are cussed.

> *M. Crouch, in a review of "Mr. McFadden's Hallowe'en," in* The Junior Bookshelf, *Vol. 40, No. 1, February, 1976, p. 23.*

THE PEACOCK SPRING (1975)

In Miss Godden's contemporary bougainvillaea-scented India, the British and Indian upper castes dreamily enact their passions. Diplomat Sir Edward Gwithiam lives in raj splendor in his post; he's tagged by his fifteen-year-old daughter Una the "God Almighty, God damn blasted Director of United Nations Environment Research for Asia." Una and her sunny twelve-year-old sister Hal (for Halcyon) are tutored by Alix Lamont, a Eurasian, who, it turns out, has little to offer academically. She's Edward's mistress and the girls provide his respectable front. A lonely, frustrated Una—who has pieced together some damning inadequacies in Alix's background and temperament—falls in love with Ravi, a handsome young Indian poet masquerading as second gardener to escape a prison term. Una becomes pregnant and the two young people run away. There's an impending clash of East and West, both in the delicate matter of Una's return and within the girl herself as she attempts to obliterate her English identity behind the docile facade of an Indian bride. Ultimately, she acquires a new respect and understanding of the tension-riddled Alix, now Edward's wife, while he is forced to face the consequences of his own deceptions. Miss Godden's characters, like pond lilies on an elegant surface, suggest deeper currents that are never really touched. Still, this is a pleasurably silky ranee's tale by an accomplished storyteller.

A review of "The Peacock Spring," in Kirkus Reviews, *Vol. XLIV, No. 2, January 15, 1976, p. 89.*

Rumer Godden's **The Peacock Spring** is a fascinating book about a sensitive English girl verging on womanhood, set in beautiful, exotic India. . . . The book portrays India and its characters are from several strata of contemporary Indian society: a prince disposed of his royalty, a Eurasian woman climbing to affluence and acceptance by westerners, a young poet and a young doctor in political trouble with the government. Fifteen-year old Una falls in love with Rani, the handsome poet *cum* gardener. She becomes pregnant by her love. The differences in cultural standards then become very real and shocking to the young people. This may sound sociological but this novel is mainly a moving and romantic story which is well written and should be a joy for many young people to read.

Eileen Noonan and Julienne Monroe, in a review of "The Peacock Spring," in Catholic Library World, *Vol. 48, No. 7, February, 1977, p. 308.*

Quiet fifteen-year-old Una and her younger sister are uprooted from boarding school in England and summoned to India by their diplomat father. Amid the colour and confusion of modern India, Una learns about love, sex, and growing up, with a young Indian gardner, Ravi. Godden deftly handles issues of adolescent sex, abortion, and inter-racial marriage in a clear honest manner, and tells a good tale in addition. Modern India is revealed with sympathy and insight. While containing many elements of the problem novel, it treats them with significance and style.

Robin Bellamy, in a review of "The Peacock Spring," in Emergency Librarian, *Vol. 9, No. 3, January-February, 1982, p. 13.*

THE ROCKING HORSE SECRET (1977)

Rumer Godden could not write a dull story if she tried. She knows about children's deepest wishes: surprises and good food and secrets and friendship and recovered treasures—and she blends these nourishing ingredients in a different delightful way each time.

This little story should please people from the age of eight upwards. It tells about Tibby and her mother who come to look

Godden in her study.

after old Miss Pomeroy and her beautiful dilapidated house. They are helped by Jed whom Miss Pomeroy had saved from Borstal five years before when he had broken in to look at her horses which he loved. Miss Pomeroy remains for a long time a remote, forbidding figure to Tabitha, but at last they meet in understanding and amity in the beautiful abandoned nursery. Miss Pomeroy's dying gift of her rocking horse saves all of them, and Pomeroy Place, from a sad fate, and we leave Miss Pomeroy's nieces forgiven for their thieving behaviour and all the friends just ready to enjoy their great and well-deserved happiness.

Brigid Hardwick, "Magic a-Brewing," in The Times Educational Supplement, *No. 3277, April 21, 1978, p. 21.*

This is a bit like a fairy-story, complete with ugly sisters, a bit like a Victorian moral tale (without the moral), but it could only have been written by Rumer Godden. It has her finger-prints all over it, in the scrupulous honesty and freedom from sentimentality—in a tale crammed full of sentiment, above all in the exquisite writing. (pp. 153-54)

It is always a temptation . . . to tell too much of Miss Godden's tales. Perhaps it does not matter much. Excellent as the story is, the magic lies in the telling, and for this one turns, and turns again and again, to the authentic text, illustrated with fitting simplicity and style by Juliet Stanwell Smith. (p. 154)

M. Crouch, in a review of "The Rocking-Horse Se-cret," in The Junior Bookshelf, *Vol. 42, No. 3, June, 1978, pp. 153-54.*

Godden, a master storyteller, creates a gentle buildup of suspense in this short old-fashioned story with a happy ending. . . . Godden's style is clear and easy; the text has large type and there are many illustrations. This is a light, sweet story that will appeal to youngsters looking for post-primer reading.

Christine McDonnell, in a review of "The Rocking Horse Secret," in School Library Journal, *Vol. 25, No. 1, September, 1978, p. 136.*

A KINDLE OF KITTENS (1978)

Rumer Godden is at her best in the longish short story. The picture book form does not come quite so naturally to her, but it makes maximum demands on what she herself calls 'the discipline' of writing for children. Even so, in *A Kindle of Kittens*—admirable title—she produces rather more text than the picture book purists would care for. Needless to say, the words are supremely well chosen and they would defy any attempt to change or reduce them.

The scene is Miss Godden's own Rye, hardly at all romanticised, and the central character is Cat, later known as She-Cat or even Queen-Cat, a very charming stray tabby who makes her life where she finds it and enjoys good relations with at least part of the human population. After an encounter with He-Cat on the ridgepole of her favourite house, she finds that she has assumed additional responsibilities in the shape of four delightful kittens. After much thought she selects suitable homes for them and employs the most subtle blackmail in getting the owners to adopt her children.

M. Crouch, in a review of "A Kindle of Kittens," in The Junior Bookshelf, *Vol. 43, No. 2, April, 1979, p. 95.*

This is the only "real" story in this group [which includes *All Together Now* by Sue Ellen Bridgers, *Cowardly Clyde* by Bill Peet, and *The Pigs' Wedding* by Helme Heine]—though it still has a dreamy, mythical quality that I think all children's books should have. Still, she-cat is definitely a cat—not a person in fur—and the ending of the story is gently sad.

Ellen Steese, in a review of "A Kindle of Kittens," in The Christian Science Monitor, *May 14, 1979, p. B6.*

THE DRAGON OF OG (1981)

Rumer Godden's retelling of the Scottish folk tale is a stylish and whimsical one, of a shy dragon; the upstart Lord of Tundergarth, Angus Og: and the Laird's lovely young wife, Matilda. When Angus Og comes into his inheritance and takes up residence at Tundergarth, Matilda sets out to civilize the place: "The first thing Lady Matilda did was to clean the inner court in the Castle of its midden—the huge spread of manure the horses and cattle made when they were driven in for shelter from the snow or from wars." Matilda has much to do, but she perseveres in her pursuit of order and beauty

and, one day, walking by the river, she sees the beautiful Dragon of Og. The dragon and Matilda take to one another, and all is well until Angus discovers that the dragon lives by eating his bullocks. He hires Sir Robert Le Douce to kill the dragon and sever its head to keep it from coming back to life. This the knight does, but when Angus declines to pay him, Sir Robert helps the head and the body to rejoin. They do. The tale is good and the style is even better. Godden has a knack for introducing unfamiliar vocabulary and glossing it in the text (as with *midden*) without seeming obvious or pedantic. In addition, her long cumulative sentences roll off the tongue rhythmically and seem perfectly adapted to the folk tale in their evocation of an oral tradition. (pp. 75-6)

Katharyn Crabbe, in a review of "The Dragon of Og," in School Library Journal, *Vol. 28, No. 3, November, 1981, pp. 75-6.*

The Dragon of Og is a product of the writer's move to Scotland. She hints at a folk origin, but the story she tells has gone through a creative process in the writing and it is very much more than a retelling. . . .

This excellent story is told in Miss Godden's immaculate prose. The tone is perhaps a little softened, the brittle elegance of this writer's earlier work turning marginally towards sentimentality, as if for the first time she is tempering her words to a youthful audience. In management of narrative and in development of character, especially Matilda and her lumbering spouse, she is not less than the complete novelist, undisputed master of her craft.

Macmillans show their realisation of the worth of this offering by dressing it splendidly, admirable in typography and paper and with decorations by Pauline Baynes on top of her form—elegant endpapers, a superb title-page and seven richly detailed full-page pictures in colour. A collector's piece this as well as a sure-fire winner with the young. (p. 67)

M. Crouch, in a review of "The Dragon of Og," in The Junior Bookshelf, *Vol. 46, No. 2, April, 1982, pp. 66-7.*

FOUR DOLLS (1983)

Between 1954 and 1960 Rumer Godden published a series of stories with illustrations by Adrienne Adams which were, with the earlier **Dolls' House,** the finest 'doll' stories by a British writer. They were the author's first books for children, although she had occupied an outstanding position among novelists for many years. Now four of those books—**Impunity Jane, The Fairy Doll, The Story of Holly and Ivy** and **Candy Floss** have been brought together, with new illustrations by Pauline Baynes. They make a book of incomparable quality and, by any standards, an unsurpassable bargain. The stories are beautifully crafted, as one would expect from one of the great stylists of our day. They are also tender and funny, tough and moving. My personal favourite, as she has been for nearly thirty years, is Impunity Jane, a little 'pocket doll' who retains her integrity and her perkiness—' "I'm Imp-imp-impunity" '—in the face of all dangers, but each is strongly individual. Discerning small readers will note that Miss Godden never cheats. Her dolls certainly have something magic about them but they live always within the limitations of their doll-nature. In this writing there is an honesty, as well as a self-discipline, which children cannot but recognise and respect, just as they will surely love these very individual dolls who so powerfully influence the lives of the children who pretend to own them. . . . Here is a book to span the generations and to last well into the next century. (pp. 21-2)

> *M. Crouch, in a review of "Four Dolls," in* The Junior Bookshelf, *Vol. 48, No. 1, February, 1984, pp. 21-2.*

THE VALIANT CHATTI-MAKER (1983)

Simpler, more straightforward tellings of the Indian folk tale exist—for example, Christine Price's identically titled book (Warne). But the new fleshed-out version, teeming with life, retains a strong narrative thrust while suggesting India's intriguing multiplicity. Attributed to an ayah, the retelling casts the "chatti-maker's" (potter's) wife in a featured role and takes sly digs at the self-absorbed upper classes—mercenary shopkeepers, proud Rajput warriors, holy Brahmins, and the dallying Raja—who never find the time to deal with a marauding tiger, despite the villagers' desperate appeals. But the poor, humble chatti-maker inadvertently captures the tiger and thereby reaps monetary rewards and the title "Valiant" from the fair-minded Raja. An unlikely and unwilling hero, the potter continues to live simply until—a victim of circumstance—he unwittingly drives off an invading army. Laden with more medals, money, and titles, the man continues to make the pottery that he calls *chattis;* because of his exalted status, other people now call them " 'Treasures of Art.' " A celebration of the common man, the tale—full of wry social commentary—twits rather than scolds. (pp. 67-8)

> *Nancy C. Hammond, in a review of "The Valiant Chatti-Maker," in* The Horn Book Magazine, *Vol. LX, No. 1, February, 1984, pp. 67-8.*

This retelling of an Indian dumb-luck tale gives a vivid picture of the customs, dress and rigid social structure of traditional India. The style and language is farcical yet crisp, but it is a pity that, in a modern retelling, the intelligent and ambitious wife is always referred to as the "Clever Little Wife." The ruse in the latter half of the story is less convincing than the tiger-catching episode, although the tongue-in-cheek humor is very effective. . . . Since the story is readily available elsewhere, there is nothing outstanding about this volume.

> *Annette Curtis Klause, in a review of "The Valiant Chatti-Maker," in* School Library Journal, *Vol. 30, No. 6, February, 1984, p. 70.*

The story, available in other collections and also in such other versions as the Grimms' "The Valiant Tailor," has been expanded by Godden and elaborated. Perhaps the author heard the tale during her childhood in India and is repeating it as she heard it, but such phrases as "Though he was not handsome, having a dark skin . . . " are jarring. Godden's familiarity with Indian customs and language gives the story color and vitality; the writing style is excellent, a deft embroidery of the story of the meek man who, inebriated, behaved so courageously in capturing a tiger that he won wealth and kudos. (pp. 126-27)

> *Zena Sutherland, in a review of "The Valiant Chatti-Maker," in* Bulletin of the Center for Children's Books, *Vol. 37, No. 7, March, 1984, pp. 126-27.*

Pat (Goundry) Hutchins

1942-

English author and illustrator of picture books and author of fiction.

Acknowledged as an original and inventive creator of books for preschoolers and children in the early primary grades, Hutchins has secured a firm reputation as an astute storyteller and a distinctive illustrator. Exceptionally popular among both critics and young children, she is a prolific author whose career is marked by diversity. Hutchins has written and illustrated realistic fiction, animal stories, moral tales, and concept books, and she purposely modifies her style to suit both her subjects and her audience. All of her books are characterized by their innocence, optimism, and simplicity, qualities which have become Hutchins's trademark. As an illustrator, she customarily employs stylized backgrounds, bright colors, black-and-white line drawings, and double-page spreads which are often praised for their design. Hutchins is consistently acclaimed for the impressive integration of text and illustration in her works. Whether she is employing watercolor and ink to create richly patterned pictures resembling folk art, as in her animal stories, or unadorned line drawings of domestic situations, as in her stories of contemporary family life, she develops her plots through her art. Envisioned as analagous to filmstrips, the works are considered nearly flawless in their rhythm and clarity. Hutchins is often lauded for the mastery with which she conceives illustrations replete with messages not found in the text. Her first work, *Rosie's Walk* (1968), is composed of approximately thirty words which constitute one declarative sentence. While the text simply but neatly describes Rosie's stroll through the farmyard, the illustrations show a fox stalking the unsuspecting chicken. As the fox is foiled repeatedly, children are involved in the pleasure of the inside joke while the description of Rosie's ramble "across the yard, around the pond," and the accompanying pictures instruct the reader on the use of prepositions. *Rosie's Walk* is often praised as a classic of the picture book genre as well as a groundbreaking work for the very young. Hutchins has also designed several of her picture books to teach basic math and grammar concepts as well as other lessons. In addition, she is the author of stories for older readers illustrated by her husband, Laurence Hutchins. Most often tales of the adventures of a class of grade school students, these books show Hutchins's humor and confidence in the resourcefulness of children while providing her audience with a sense of the pure entertainment that intrigue and mystery in fiction can offer them. In 1968 *Rosie's Walk* was named a *Boston Globe-Horn Book* honor book. *Titch* was selected for the International Board on Books for Young People (IBBY) honour list in 1974 for its illustrations. In 1974 *The Wind Blew* was awarded the Kate Greenaway Medal, an award for which *One-Eyed Jake* was highly commended in 1979. *The Doorbell Rang* was named a runner-up for the Kurt Maschler Award in 1986.

(See also *Something about the Author,* Vol. 15; *Contemporary Authors New Revision Series,* Vol. 15; and *Contemporary Authors,* Vols. 81-84.)

AUTHOR'S COMMENTARY

[The following excerpt is taken from an interview by Hilary Thompson.]

Since **Rosie's Walk** was published in 1968, Pat Hutchins has written and illustrated over twenty books for children. Her sense of fun is prevalent in all of them, particularly in the award-winning **The Wind Blew . . .** and the popular **Changes, Changes,** in which she conveys the joy and tragedy of domestic life among the building blocks by means of a simple plot structure and small changes in facial expression. In both these stories, Hutchins displays her recurrent interest in simple mathematical concepts: in the former the story literally adds up, as it is an accumulative tale, and in **Changes, Changes** we are concerned with volume: her characters struggle to solve their problems with the materials at hand, namely with building blocks whose number, shape and size never change.

Hutchins' work is surprisingly varied in style. Her stories about contemporary children, like **Titch, Don't Forget the Bacon, Happy Birthday Sam,** and **You'll Soon Grow into Them, Titch,** use simple line drawings which have retained the same use of basic colors throughout the years while becoming more filled with complicated patterns and designs. The plot structure of these stories remains simple and linear.

It is amusing to see that the same flat designs that cover walls and fabric in Hutchins' contemporary stories are also used in her animal stories, but now on feathers, fur, leaves, and other natural phenomena. These are heavily patterned in a stylized technique similar to that of simple woodcuts. Color is always important in a Hutchins' illustration, but in *Rosie's Walk, Goodnight Owl, The Surprise Party* and *The Silver Christmas Tree* color is balanced by a complex use of pattern which, together with the humour of the plot, makes these the most appealing of Hutchins' books.

One other kind of story can be found among Hutchins' works: the moral tale, such as *Tom and Sam, The Tale of Thomas Mead* and *One-Eyed Jake.* The style of illustration for these stories has developed to suit each plot: *Tom and Sam* has the stylized medieval look of a timeless folk-tale world. *The Tale of Thomas Mead* is a present day cartoon-like creation which appeals to children who don't want to read. And *One-Eyed Jake* is an ornately dressed swash-buckling pirate whose acquisitiveness is matched by the detailed drawings of his ship and loot.

Throughout her various plots and styles of illustration, Pat Hutchins reveals her love of the traditional folk-tale: she concentrates on the innocent character who may be undervalued, a third child like Titch, one who is on his or her way to finding good fortune in the world, whether that means literally growing toward autonomy by gaining stature or outwitting crafty pirate captains and foxes. Her predeliction for the traditional devices of anticipation, repetition, and accumulation recur throughout her stories, in both illustration and plot. There is much thoughtful consideration of children and their needs in a Pat Hutchins' story. This becomes clear in the interview which follows.

H.T. You first studied art in Leeds, but can you tell me if you always wanted to be an artist?

P.H. Yes. From the time I was little. (pp. 57-8)

H.T. Did you soon find yourself developing a style?

P.H. Yes, pen and ink, colored ink. Color was always very important to me.

H.T. There must have been the weight of the tradition of previous children's illustrators on you.

P.H. It's a difficult field, but children's books nowadays are better than they were then, don't you think? Then the style was much that of Ardizonne you know.

H.T. Yes.

P.H. You develop your own style, learn all the time. I was tentative about drawing. I still am. I am more interested in color. But I was told in *Rosie's Walk* that I could only use three colors. Under these conditions I had to draw, was forced to, and obviously the shapes give you a stronger line.

H.T. You enjoy patterns of fur and fabric, wings and feathers. I wondered if you were using the effect of woodcuts but in the medium of pen and ink?

P.H. Yes, I enjoy line and woodcuts with simple strong colors. But the illustrating style is always adapted to the story. I use basic simple forms for simple stories. But *One-Eyed*

Jake has a different style. It is more sophisticated, for older children. I am age-conscious. I won't use certain things or words because children wouldn't understand. I write the picture books to be read to the children, so that they can ask about words they do not understand and may then read for themselves. I am conscious of the process because of my own children. They remind you of what is important to a child. (Pat Hutchins' children are now twelve and fifteen.)

H.T. What made you choose to tell a story as well as illustrate it?

P.H. I didn't really expect to be writing books, but then an editor told me I could write. She taught me and encouraged me to write. (p. 58)

H.T. Do you imagine the illustrations as you are writing, or vice versa?

P.H. The process is simultaneous. I like writing stories in traditional forms with a beginning and a satisfying conclusion. The form is circular, all is explained. I like to get the child into the book with continuity, so I see the book like a film strip with no awkward lapses. When he was little my son could not understand changes in size of animals, bears for instance, from one page to another. I try to be consistent, placing the creature on the page in a position where it is logical for it to be.

H.T. Do you think of the interplay of text and illustration?

P.H. Yes, but at a later stage of lay-out.

H.T. Your people are stylized, as in *Tom and Sam,* but in that stylization you create a real place, timeless but particular.

P.H. Yes. I think one finds that place continually when writing.

H.T. Talking of *Tom and Sam,* do you find the simplicity of your stories can sometimes make them 'heavy' and didactic?

P.H. I think the most important thing is to entertain, but I also want to make a point which will make children think.

H.T. Well, often you cause us to think of growth in your stories—physical growth in *Titch* and *Happy Birthday Sam,* accumulation in *The Wind Blew.*

P.H. *The Wind Blew* is my least favourite book. It has a weak story.

H.T. You often write about physical growth, but it also seems that growth operates in other ways in your books. For instance, I would say that there is a lot of mathematics in them.

P.H. Yes. It's interesting that you should say that, because I was surprised that a reviewer of *One-Eyed Jake* said that it was a slim story. The reviewer missed the point altogether. You see one-eyed Jake is a pirate who steals so many things that his ship cannot hold them all. It sinks.

H.T. It's teaching the concept of volume.

P.H. Yes. And then *Clocks and More Clocks* deals with time. One professor uses it in a college to teach child-development. Apparently once a child has realised what the book says about time he or she has passed into another stage of development.

H.T. I wondered if this theme of growth or development could not extend into your attitude to society and the need

From Rosie's Walk, *written and illustrated by Pat Hutchins.*

for co-operation. For instance in *The Best Train Set Ever*. . . .

P.H. That began with a carving set in my husband's family. We would say that he would have the knife, someone else the fork, someone else the sharpener, and that we could only use it if we got together.

H.T. Would you say that incident reflects your moral values?

P.H. Yes, that possessions are only worthwhile if you can share them with people.

H.T. You certainly show compassion and respect for the smaller members of society. And you seem to depict their innocence.

P.H. I try not to be unkind to innocent characters. They are like children, characters like Rosie and Mr. Higgins.

H.T. You don't like tricksters do you?

P.H. No. You hit the nail on the head there. And I can't bear magic, or trickery of any kind.

H.T. Would you say you are a romantic?

P.H. Yes. I like to see good come to the innocent characters.

H.T. Which is your favourite book?

P.H. That's a difficult question. I remember one author answered it by saying that that's like asking who is your favourite child. All are written at different times. *The House That Sailed Away* is my favourite at the moment. ·

H.T. What books do you see yourself working on in the future?

P.H. I would like to do more books for older children. It is easier and more relaxing. Picture books are much more difficult. They require so much simplicity. I hope that I don't run out of ideas for them though, because I want to go on with them too. It's very strange but I have been going through old notebooks recently which were six-seven years old, and in them I read ideas and lines almost word for word for books

I have done and I've forgotten that I had that idea so long ago. *One-Eyed Jake* was different though, it started as a counting book and didn't work. So I tried another way. I have written a counting book, though. You know it is a treat from a publisher to a writer when he/she says "You can have your own counting book." But I found it difficult to do. It is about one hunter who is looking for game and so many giraffes, elephants, etc., are camouflaged on the page. At the end he is chased by them.

H.T. Why was it difficult?

P.H. I had so many ideas of what I wanted to do, but I couldn't do it. One has to compromise pictures somehow . . . no, compromise isn't the right word . . . this is a chance to show off one's art work, but if the art work doesn't quite work when you see it, always keeping the child in mind, then sometimes you have to sacrifice the things you want.

H.T. How would you characterize your style?

P.H. As stylized, but realistic enough to enable the child to recognize the image.

H.T. That recognition is important in stimulating a child to read. Do you enjoy using anticipation, too, to stimulate reading?

P.H. Yes, I like to give them a surprise at the end as a treat! (pp. 58-9)

Pat Hutchins and Hilary Thompson, in an interview in Children's Literature Association Quarterly, *Vol. 10, No. 2, Summer, 1985, pp. 57-9.*

GENERAL COMMENTARY

ELAINE MOSS

"There's a word that describes people like me," said Pat Hutchins, "but I can't for the life of me think what it is." One thing is certain: she rejects, and with justification, the words chosen by a national newspaper feature writer to describe her home, "in bijou Hampstead", and her newest picture book—"a lovely-to-look-at, fun-to-read mini-masterpiece". (p. 32)

Rosie's Walk, her first picture book, is a masterpiece—no "mini-" about it. It looked to me as though it had sprung ready-made from her pen. But I was, apparently, wrong. It now has a text of a mere thirty-two words ("Rosie the hen went for a walk across the yard, around the pond, over the haycock, past the mill, through the fence, under the bee-hives and got back in time for dinner") to accompany a close progression of humorous pictures that is the nearest thing to a film you can imagine. "I wanted a child to be able to see what was happening next, rather than having to take a big leap from one page to the next, which might throw him." *What* the child sees all the time is the one thing of which Rosie the hen, strutting ahead, is utterly oblivious; it is the *fox* (never mentioned in the text, you'll notice) who stalks her and meets with one (opportune-for-Rosie) disaster after the other till he is finally chased away over the hills by a swarm of bees.

Pat Hutchins assures me that this simple, very funny picture book began its life with "a text of enormous length like *War and Peace,* but I looked at it and thought how boring—all those cows, sheep, ducks, and so on—and I cut it down." All this before she made a single illustration—and with the help and encouragement ("She didn't tell me what to do, but kept on and on at me to make it more interesting") of Susan Hirschman of Macmillan, New York. It was she who recognized the real talent she saw in embryo: and sat firmly on the egg till it hatched. (pp. 32-3)

Pat Hutchins does not seem too sure about her favourite among her own picture books. "I'm funny about my books. When I look at them afterwards I don't like them very much." She obviously has a soft spot, though, for ***Changes, Changes,*** which is an ingenious no-text picture book in the course of which two wooden people change their building-block house into a fire-engine (when the house catches fire), their fire-engine into a boat, their boat into a car, their car into a train, and their train into a house again—just as [her son] Morgan might have when playing with a box of bricks on the living-room floor.

But sentimentally, ***Titch*** is her favourite story, though "I hate the pictures," she says. "I don't like drawing children, you see." Suddenly one realizes that the three deliciously individual characters in ***Titch*** are the only children in Pat's entire range of picture books. The other books are full of animals, or of rather stylized adults, like the great big silly grown-up male rivals in ***Tom and Sam*** or the none-too-clever clock collector in ***Clocks and More Clocks.*** (p. 34)

Where does Pat Hutchins find her ideas? "They come at the strangest times and in the oddest places!" A single realization—that a tree is the home of hundreds of birds and insects and animals—can provide material for several picture books: ***Titch*** grew from this, so did ***The Surprise Party,*** in which one animal who is going to give a party whispers his invitation to the next who passes it on—and on, and on—with funny but finally satisfactory results. But the idea has come to full flower in her newest picture book, ***Good-Night, Owl!***

Good-Night, Owl!, in full colour, has enabled her to paint the many different kinds of birds—jays, sparrows, robins, woodpeckers—that live in the same tree as Owl and stop him from getting in a good day's sleep. . . . "Then darkness fell and the moon came up. And there wasn't a sound"—wait for it; turn over the page—until "Owl screeched, screech screech,

and woke everyone up". A Pat Hutchins bedtime story *par excellence:* it will have the kids croo-ing and ark-ing and caw-ing and screech-ing till daybreak! Good-*night,* Owl!

Birds are Pat Hutchins's passion. She loves wild creatures and although Hampstead Heath offers more opportunity than any other part of London for observing wild life, she longs to buy a cottage and land in her native Yorkshire: "At least two acres so that Laurence and Morgan can have their narrow-gauge railway"—and she can then nurse, once again, an injured crow or any other bird or animal that needs her help. (pp. 34-5)

What about Nature books? "I've got hundreds of those," said Pat, "but I only look at the pictures. I don't really *want* to know about all the rest of it. There's a word for people like me—but I can't for the life of me think what it is."

Could it, perhaps, be a "natural"? (p. 36)

> *Elaine Moss, "Pat Hutchins: A Natural," in* Signal, *No. 10, January, 1973, pp. 32-6.*

BARBARA BADER

Pat Hutchins made a grand entrance with ***Rosie's Walk,*** a book of thirty-two pages and thirty-three words—in one sentence. Rosie the hen has only to set out with her beak in the air for us to know what she doesn't, that a fox is stalking her; and for us to see what she never sees either, that disaster awaits him at every other turn of the page. The fox's patterned pelt, the ranked pears on the tree, all the flat stylizations borrowed from peasant art say that this is funny make-believe; and the cheerful conventionalized colors, particularly the absence of blue, suggest that reality will remain at bay. But the text, at alternate openings, supplies rhythm and emphasis to a story that would be comprehensible without words. The text, in fact, makes it a story, for Rosie, on the last page, "got back in time for dinner." To be precise, she "went . . . through the fence/under the beehives/and got back in time for dinner." Through the telling, Rosie's walk becomes more than the titular subject and the downfall of the fox takes second place to her providential return.

Changes, Changes, for its part, is all pantomime, fluid and in flux, and appropriately silent. Given are the wooden couple, their multicolored blocks, and one after another emergency; it's up to the observer to see—and if he wishes, to tell—what the resourceful pair are up to as they transform their burning house into a pumper, the flooded pumper into a ship, the beached ship into a truck, and so on and on. But he'll have to look sharp: would you know on the left-hand page what was coming on the right? ***Changes, Changes*** doesn't just happen, it builds; and on the last page it builds a new house for the couple just like the one that caught fire at the start. Manner, design and format are integral; the book is what block-building is about. And, like *Little Blue and Little Yellow,* its humor is inherent—or, equally, built in.

Who needs words? (p. 542)

> *Barbara Bader, "Away from Words," in her* American Picturebooks from Noah's Ark to the Beast Within, *Macmillan Publishing Co., Inc., 1976, pp. 525-43.*

JEAN RUSSELL

To each of her picture books Pat Hutchins brings a wonderful feeling of spontaneous warmth and gaiety. Who could forget

Rosie, the fat comfortable hen as she stomps her way "across the yard, around the pond, over the haycock, past the mill, through the fence, under the beehives" blissfully unaware of the slinky, sly fox coming to grief behind her. Young children from as young as eighteen months will wriggle with delight and anticipation at the downfall of the fox. . . .

Pat Hutchins uses space and colour to its very best advantage—the dominant orange and yellows in *Rosie's Walk* creating patterns upon the page that balance the bold shapes of the round trees and plants with the squat square farmcarts and beehives.

Her latest book *One Hunter . . .* reflects the same colours and simplicity as Rosie, but instead of the familiar farmyard goat and hen we have the jungle setting. *One Hunter* walks through the jungle, but he doesn't notice the two elephants, three giraffes, or the four ostriches. He stalks on through the trees, looking all around and still fails to see five antelopes, six tigers and seven crocodiles . . . but they all see him. A superb, original counting book with a wealth of detail for looking and finding and talking about.

As a young Mother, Pat Hutchins mirrored the responses of her own twin sons, Sam and Morgan, as they explored the world about them. Only acute observation of the frustration felt by Sam at not yet being tall enough to switch on the light, or reach his clothes in order to dress himself, could have resulted in the sympathetic *Happy Birthday, Sam. . . .Tom and Sam* is dedicated to Pat's artist husband Laurence. Whether their boys are like the heroes of this picture book who are always trying to outdo each other, we shall never know, but in the end Tom and Sam stop thinking about themselves and become friends again. The strong feeling in all these books is that the ideas for them come from actual experiences within the family. (p. 14)

Jean Russell, *"Cover Artist: Pat Hutchins,"* in Books for Your Children, *Vol. 17, No. 1, Spring, 1982, pp. 14-15.*

JON C. STOTT

Discussing her books, Hutchins has stated, "I try to keep my stories logical, even if a story is pure fantasy. . . . I like to build my stories up, so the reader can understand what is happening and, in some cases, anticipate what is likely to happen on the next page." Each story has a steadily progressing narrative which leads to a satisfying conclusion. In *Rosie's Walk,* a chicken takes a stroll, unaware of a fox who several times tries unsuccessfully to pounce on her. In *The Wind Blew,* a cumulative story, an increasing number of people chase after objects the wind has blown from them.

Pat Hutchins' earlier illustrations were somewhat stylized; those for more recent stories are more realistic. However, in all her books, she uses page design to indicate continuity of action from illustration to illustration and thus to create narrative movement. In *Rosie's Walk,* one two-page spread reveals the fox in midair, his eyes intent on the chicken, oblivious to the rake toward which his momentum carries him. The following two-page spread shows him landing and the rake hitting him. Rosie appears on the right-hand edge of each spread, walking toward the scene to be depicted in the following spread, unaware of the peril behind her.

The Wind Blew uses more realistic drawings to tell its simple story. By the end of the book, twelve people, including four children, a bridegroom, a palace guardsman, and a postman,

are chasing objects. The right-hand side of each two-page spread becomes progressively more cluttered as the people follow the wind. Near the edge of the left-hand side of each page is seen the individual who, although he does not yet realize it, is the wind's next victim. The pages contain much humor as the chaos increases. (pp. 147-48)

Jon C. Stott, *"Pat Hutchins,"* in his Children's Literature from A to Z: A Guide for Parents and Teachers, *McGraw-Hill Book Company, 1984, pp. 147-48.*

ROSIE'S WALK (1968)

Rosie's Walk is by a new artist, English but staying temporarily in New York, which may account for an indefinable American quality in her book, especially its colour. Rosie the hen goes for a walk about the farm, tracked at every step by a predatory but consistently unsuccessful fox. One cannot complain here of an overlong text. The tale is told in 32 words, with accompanying pictures which explore the action in exciting and amusing fashion. The drawing is stiff and formal: just a trifle self-conscious in its naivety, as is the very flat colouring. Nevertheless a most interesting new-comer. We look forward eagerly to her next. (pp. 355, 357)

A review of *"Rosie's Walk,"* in The Junior Bookshelf, *Vol. 32, No. 6, December, 1968, pp. 355, 357.*

[Since] the words in picture books are often simple enough to be vague, pictures often have the express purpose of limiting the range of possible meanings. After hearing the story in Sendak's *Where the Wild Things Are* without seeing the pictures, my students say it is too frightening for young children; when they see the pictures, they change their minds. The wild things they imagine on their own are far more frightening than the ones Sendak actually provided. Sendak's comparatively gentle pictures allow his scary words.

Furthermore, my students tell me that Sendak's wild things are more interesting than the ones they imagined themselves. Some people claim that pictures limit imagination. While Sendak's wild things . . . do limit my response to the words, they actually expand the realm of my experience. I could never have imagined Sendak's unusual wild things on my own. . . . If pictures limit our imaginations, then so do words, and the only safe alternative is utterly blank pages. In fact, both words and pictures exercise our imaginations by giving us something definite and new to think about.

Pat Hutchins' *Rosie's Walk* contains only thirty-two simple words: "Rosie the hen went for a walk/across the yard/around the pond/over the haystack/past the mill/through the fence/under the beehives/and got back in time for dinner." This is too vague to be interesting and not much more complex than blank pages; Hutchins' pictures make it a story (and engage our imaginations) by making it more specific. They show us that Rosie is blithely ignorant of the fox who is following her and that every move Rosie takes leads the fox into another slapstick disaster, but they do more than that. . . . [They] change our response to the text. Considered along with the pictures, it is not just an objective description of boring events; the person who speaks these words in this situation is either as blind as Rosie or else deliberately leaves the fox out in order to tease. In either case, the pictures force us to be conscious of the inadequacies of the text and, in fact, to enjoy them; it is the distance between

From Changes, Changes, *written and illustrated by Pat Hutchins.*

the story the words tell and the story the pictures tell that makes the book interesting. (p. 60)

Perry Nodelman, "How Picture Books Work," in Proceedings of the Eighth Annual Conference of the Children's Literature Association, *1981, pp. 57-68.*

There is what has variously been called the deviation of the illustration from the text, or *inspiration* instead of illustration. Both these terms refer to illustrations which are initiated by the textual framework but veer away from it due to the illustrator's own associations and ideas. (p. 16)

[Some] artists, especially writer-illustrators, inventively develop deviation . . . until text and illustration *counterpoint* each other. The text of *Rosie's Walk* by Pat Hutchins portrays Rosie the hen as she innocently walks across the yard and gets back in time for dinner. The illustrations, on the other hand, depict the indefatigable and frustrating efforts of the fox to catch her, until the bees finally drive him off. These are, in fact, two entirely separate stories. One, the verbal text, is peaceful, uneventful, boring. The other one, in pictures, relates the terrible dangers to which Rosie is exposed again and the fox's repeated failures. This is a perfectly understandable wordless story, with some tension and some fun, but of no great interest. However, when the two stories are brought to-

gether, an additional dimension appears: as the illustrations give to Rosie's walk a mood and meaning totally opposite to those found in the text, our fun and satisfaction arise from the fact that *we* know what the poor hen does not, for the pictures let us in on the secret. (pp. 16-17)

Joseph H. Schwarcz, "Relationships between Text and Illustration," in his Ways of the Illustrator: Visual Communication in Children's Literature, *American Library Association, 1982, pp. 9-22.*

In our English-based culture . . . we start at the "front" of the book (some other cultures have their front at what we think of as the back). We "read" from the top of the left-hand page, working in horizontal lines across the page and line by line down the page, then begin again at the top of the right-hand page, and so on, before "turning over" and starting again at the top of the next left-hand page. There is therefore a basic "rule"—our books follow a left to right flow; and when we turn over there is the possibility of surprise. Picture books make use of these elements—and so teach very young children how a book works while entertaining them with pictures.

A book like *Rosie's Walk* by Pat Hutchins not only uses those rules, it breaks one of them in such a way that it adds a new excitement for a young reader who may have just learned how to handle a book. The way the rule is broken works so well because the author-artist has employed a fact of reading that we usually ignore—which is that as we turn over a page the first part of the next two pages we see is not the top left-hand page (where we must begin to read) but the right-hand page. So Hutchins arranges her story-drawings in such a way that as you turn over you first see Rosie, calmly going about her morning's walk apparently safely and happily, and it is only as your eye travels leftwards (the "wrong" way) across the page and into the left-hand page itself that you see the fox who is stalking the hen and trying to catch her. This in turn sends your eye traveling to the right— "reading" the pages—in order that you can confirm to yourself that what you now know to be true is in fact what is happening, and to dwell with ironic amusement on Rosie's apparently ignorant sanguinity. You also very much want to turn over to see what will happen next: Will Rosie be caught? Will Fox miss again? And what this time will be the cause of his slapstick downfall? So *Rosie's Walk* both uses the basic conventions of reading and adds new ones at the same time, melding both into the one story. This is one of the reasons that always makes people think it a "classic" of picture book making. (pp. 178-79)

> *Aidan Chambers, "A Critical Blueprint," in his* Introducing Books to Children, *second edition, The Horn Book, Inc., 1983, pp. 174-93.*

TOM AND SAM (1968)

Neighbors Tom and Sam are friends and equals until Tom digs a lake . . . and Sam builds a tower . . . and Tom plants flowering trees . . . and Sam plants a hedge . . . and where it will all end Levittown only knows until Sam and Tom each steal out one night to steal the other's latest improvement and run right into each other. Tom claims that he is saving Sam's statue from a thief, and Sam claims that he is saving Tom's birdbath, whereupon each promises to make one for the other as a reward, and they become friends and equals again. In dress and stance, Tom and Sam could be Shakespeare's fools and their competition is good-natured buffoonery in pantomime. A sly dig by the author-artist of *Rosie's Walk,* also sparing of words if more intricately drawn. (pp. 1157-58)

> *A review of "Tom and Sam," in* Kirkus Service, *Vol. XXXVI, No. 20, October 15, 1968, pp. 1157-58.*

Another simple, brief cautionary tale: the problem is petty rivalry. Tom and Sam were "the best of friends" until each slyly tried to make his garden more magnificent than the other's. But it's all in jest: With their mincing airs and brilliant pseudo-medieval clothes, the two men cut ridiculous figures and set a mood of good-humored nonsense.

> *Ethel L. Heins, in a review of "Tom and Sam," in* The Horn Book Magazine, *Vol. XLV, No. 2, April, 1969, p. 162.*

There are many qualities in this picture-book which will appeal to the very young reader—the large print, only a few words on each page, and the repetition of many of these words. It is a properly moral story for this age group, in which two neighbours becoming jealous of each other and trying to outdo each other, finally steal from each other. . . . The illustrations are in autumnal browns, mauves, and yellows and greens, Tom is very thin, Sam is very plump, and there is a humorous touch to the whole story.

> *A review of "Tom and Sam," in* The Junior Bookshelf, *Vol. 34, No. 2, April, 1970, p. 81.*

THE SURPRISE PARTY (1969)

In fresh, sunny scenes drawn in green, and colored with yellows and orange, bustling animals (some met earlier in *Rosie's Walk*) pass on a bit of news—the "surprise," that Rabbit is "having a party tomorrow." As in the game of Gossip, each repetition becomes altered in the hearsay. Appropriately for small listeners, the news always begins "Rabbit is . . ." and ends "tomorrow." . . . Although drawn in stylized textural designs, each animal figure has a vivid personality. Gay and original. (pp. 32-3)

> *Virginia Haviland, in a review of "The Surprise Party," in* The Horn Book Magazine, *Vol. XLVI, No. 1, February, 1970, pp. 32-3.*

The rich harvest of picture books already available to babies today creates a special problem for the reviewer: should he examine new books against the best that have gone before, or simply greet each season's arrivals with undimmed enthusiasm? Babies' tastes are not fickle; a constant factor in a changing world, they are happiest with the traditional songs and stories worn into shape by the passing of time.

All the more remarkable to find a new author who can work within these time-honoured patterns and yet produce something truly original. Pat Hutchins's first book, *Rosie's Walk,* was published a couple of years ago; her new book, *The Surprise Party,* confirms its brilliance. Rosie is a fat, most credibly silly hen, pottering round the farm on her daily walk sublimely unaware that crafty Mr. Fox is creeping after her, planning to eat her up. The slapstick pitfalls devised to keep the villain one pounce behind are marvellously funny, and so clearly expressed in firm, bold pictures that any two-year-old can see the joke.

The Surprise Party gives us the fox again, but this time he is out in the fields with rabbit, owl, squirrel, duck, mouse and frog.

> "I'm having a party tomorrow", whispered Rabbit. "It's a surprise". "Rabbit is hoeing the parsley tomorrow", whispered Owl. "It's a surprise". "Rabbit is going to sea tomorrow" whispered Squirrel . . .

and so it goes on, so that when Rabbit tries to collect his friends for the surprise, they all make excuses. Needless to say, all ends well, with a feast set out on a treestump.

Of course, the pictures are the thing—wonderfully bright, clean-looking pictures, drawn with the loving care of a pre-Raphaelite, coloured in bright orange browns and clear yellow greens which never ring false. As for the words, the child will learn them by heart long before he sees the joke, as in the case of an old favourite like *Johnny Crow's Garden;* grownups have the pleasure of seeing the pennies drop at last.

> *"Jokes for Two-Year-Olds," in* The Times Literary Supplement, *No. 3566, July 2, 1970, p. 717.*

This pretty and amusing book would appeal very much to five-to-seven-year-olds. . . . Children delight in playing and making jokes with words so that I suspect this is a book which will be read and read again until it is learnt by heart like a poem. The repeated phrases make it a useful book for a child just beginning to read and recognize words. The decorative drawings of flowers and countryside and of the animals themselves, so serious and so silly, are so detailed that they will be lovingly pored over. This is a charming children's book.

> *Janet Leach, in a review of "The Surprise Party," in* The School Librarian, *Vol. 19, No. 2, June, 1971, p. 183.*

CLOCKS AND MORE CLOCKS   (1970)

As nonsensical and timeless as the Mad Hatter's watch is the author-illustrator's fourth picture book. The story tells of a man whose four clocks apparently refused to synchronize. As fast as he raced from kitchen to hall to bedroom to attic, he always found a discrepancy of a minute or two; and he could not figure out why! Finally he bought " 'a wonderful watch,' " which he solemnly carried with him about the house; and after that all his clocks were correct. A minimum of well-chosen words and bright colored pictures tell the droll tale of a simpleton who was befuddled by time. (pp. 470-71)

> *Ethel L. Heins, in a review of "Clocks and More Clocks," in* The Horn Book Magazine, *Vol. XLVI, No. 5, October, 1970, pp. 470-71.*

An intriguing narrative for children who have learnt to tell the time, but not entirely logical, since a clock *found* in the attic would not be running and set to the correct time! The story is told with great simplicity and economy, and beautifully illustrated in Pat Hutchins's highly individual style; bold forms outlined against the white page, rich detail and texture in careful line, coloured in lucent greens, yellows and browns mainly, all informed by a generous humour and delight in the odd ways of humanity. Not, alas, equal to ***Rosie's walk,*** (will she ever equal that, first, masterpiece?) but a pleasing picture book for children from about six to eight. (p. 15)

> *John A. Cunliffe, in a review of "Clocks and More Clocks," in* Children's Book Review, *Vol. I, No. 1, February, 1971, pp. 14-15.*

Clocks and More Clocks is geared . . . to the child's sense of discovery. The problem of Mr Higgins's clocks, none of which, as he races from one to the other upstairs and downstairs, appears to tell the correct time, provides an elementary lesson in relativity. Predictably, the setting is Victorian (in lime, tangerine and lemon) but there is more good nature than swanky mise-en-scène. And it does set the child thinking: Miss Hutchins has shown again what an inventive writer and illustrator she is. (p. 314)

> *John Fuller, "Images," in* New Statesman, *Vol. 81, No. 2085, March 5, 1971, pp. 314-15.*

CHANGES, CHANGES   (1971)

This is a picture-book without words, but it is certainly not one of those pieces of artistic self-indulgence that some other makers of picture-books seem so bent on producing; it has the simplicity and clarity, the direct appeal to young children, that one expects from Pat Hutchins. She tells an ingenious story, too. We are presented with two wooden figures and a set of coloured bricks, such as many children possess. The figures build a house with the bricks, and stand on it. A series of transformation scenes follows, creating new forms with the

bricks, just as a child's skill and imagination might do. The house is on fire; a few deft changes, and here is a fire-engine to extinguish the flames. The water makes a flood; more changes, and there is a ship to sail away in. And so on, via a lorry and a locomotive, until a house is made again.

The pictures are on a landscape format, in simple paint-box colours, with the bricks and figures outlined against the white page. They have a striking boldness and clarity; neatly disposed on the page, they are refreshingly simple and uncluttered.

The special attraction of this book is that it combines a story and a game; young children will delight in guessing what the next change is to be, and may go on to create their own changes with real bricks and figures, as well as just enjoying the story itself. This book is as good as ***Rosie's Walk,*** which is to say that it is outstanding by any standard, and it is a great pleasure to see Pat Hutchins regaining the high peak of her first book.

> *John A. Cunliffe, in a review of "Changes, Changes," in* Children's Book Review, *Vol. I, No. 2, April, 1971, p. 47.*

No text, but a pattern of illustration easy and exhilarating to follow, devised from a set of building bricks in plain strong colours and two wooden figures, a junior Mr. and Mrs. Noah. By re-arranging the bricks the artist shows us how her characters build a house, how when it catches fire they make a fire engine and put the fire out (a touch of surrealism here), how they construct for themselves a boat, then a lorry, then a train, and finally build an identical house on a new site. The demure joke and the dashing colours make an irresistible book for the very young.

> *Margery Fisher, in a review of "Changes, Changes," in* Growing Point, *Vol. 10, No. 2, July, 1971, p. 1772.*

TITCH   (1971)

With her latest book Pat Hutchins has returned, in part, to the simplicity of her first and most successful picture book—***Rosie's Walk.***

Titch, the youngest of three children, always comes a bad third behind his big brother and sister. The text consists of simple statements each elaborated by an illustration: 'Pete had a big drum. Mary had a trumpet. And Titch had a little wooden whistle.' The repetitive structure should appeal to young children whose enjoyment is often increased by anticipating the predictable.

Graphically ***Titch*** is less original than Pat Hutchins's previous picture books, it takes its visual cue from a transatlantic tradition of figure drawing, relying rather heavily on snub noses, freckles and cute expressions to achieve its effect.

The idea is simple but it calls for the capacity to recognise the emotions of its central character rather than presenting a series of purely external events and this may detract from its appeal to the under fives.

Compared with ***Rosie's Walk, Titch*** is less robust, more self-conscious, its humour is more sophisticated and, unlike ***Rosie,*** its punch line is more likely to appeal to parents than their offspring.

It pulled the new scarves from the twins and tossed them to the other things.

From The Wind Blew, *written and illustrated by Pat Hutchins.*

Eleanor von Schweinitz, in a review of "Titch," in Children's Book Review, *Vol. II, No. 2, April, 1972, p. 37.*

Life for the smallest member of an active family can be a series of frustrations—from bike-riding to kite-flying. But just as the humblest may be exalted, so the youngest can enjoy a moment of triumph—as the perceptive author demonstrates in an understated, childlike picture-story which blends economy of text with bright, uncomplicated illustrations. The amazing growth of Titch's tiny seed, planted as his share of a family project, is a satisfying conclusion to the story as well as a logical symbol of human potentiality for the many small persons who will sympathize with his position and delight in his success. Imaginative realism for pre-schoolers which is reassuring, but never condescending.

Mary M. Burns, in a review of "Titch," in The Horn Book Magazine, *Vol. XLVIII, No. 2, April, 1972, p. 135.*

In my search for books to emphasize the notion that 'readers are people, not books' Pat Hutchins is treasure trove. Her ideas come right from the core of children's puzzling about the world: comparisons of size and worth in **Tom and Sam,** the problem of time-telling in **Clocks and More Clocks,** while **Rosie's Walk** is the pattern of all that young children write of their own adventures. Here now is Titch; he is little and suffers the thirdness of all third children, at the end of the comparison line. Mary and Pete have everything bigger and better. But Titch has a seed, and all small readers are comforted about growing. The text and the drawings match with artistic deliberation. This is what learning to read should be about.

Margaret Meek, in a review of "Titch," in The School Librarian, *Vol. 20, No. 2, June, 1972, p. 190.*

GOOD NIGHT, OWL! (1972)

Pat Hutchins is [a] leading member of the rare breed of illustrators who know how to tell a good story. Her plots are not simply convenient pegs on which to hang a series of pictures, but ingenious constructions which appeal to the sense of the ridiculous in parents and children alike. **Good-night Owl!** is a very simple story written for the youngest reader, but it has plenty of humour and a good final surprise. The illustrations are bright and formal, like embroidered pictures, but so expressive that you can almost hear all the day-time noises made by the other inhabitants of the tree in which poor Owl is trying to take a nap. At the end of the book Owl wins a splendid revenge, one that should amuse the young reader enormously.

"Comedy in Line and Colour," in The Times Literary Supplement, *No. 3719, June 15, 1973, p. 678.*

This is an unexpectedly dull book from a picture book artist who has shown exceptional freshness and invention in many of her earlier publications. (p. 138)

[The] simple theme, involving repetition, animal noises and a funny ending has considerable potential in a picture book for the very young. But the text is pedestrian, lacking an imaginative ear for sounds and rhythms . . .

> The robin peeped,
> pip pip,
> and Owl tried to sleep.
> The sparrow chirped,
> cheep cheep,
> and Owl tried to sleep.

We have heard this sort of thing many times before and Pat Hutchins has nothing new to add.

Nor is the book redeemed by its pictorial qualities and overall design. The details of each illustration match the requirements of the text and have a certain broad humour but are in no way distinguished. Page composition is monotonous and the choice of a rather heavy sans serif type contributes nothing to the balance and unity of each opening.

There is little here to remind one of the liveliness and originality of **Rosie's Walk** or even **Titch.** (pp. 138-39)

Eleanor von Schweinitz, in a review of "Good-Night

Owl," in Children's Book Review, *Vol. III, No. 5, October, 1973, pp. 138-39.*

By making her own text, Pat Hutchins has been able to make words serve her art instead of the other way round—perhaps the ultimate secret of her outstanding achievement in picture-book art. The neat cumulation of protesting neighbours who one by one settle in formal poses on the tree's branches is rendered in the warm yellows she uses so brilliantly, and the compromise between nature and art is both diverting and superbly pictorial. (pp. 2269-70)

> *Margery Fisher, in a review of "Good-night Owl," in* Growing Point, *Vol. 12, No. 5, November, 1973, pp. 2269-70.*

THE WIND BLEW (1974)

Full-color paintings illustrate a rhymed cumulative text depicting the frantic efforts of unwary pedestrians to recover possessions snatched away by a mischievous and unpredictable wind. The airborne impedimenta—including an umbrella, a balloon, a judge's wig, a bridegroom's hat—are crisply detailed, while the slightly caricatured human figures offer an amusing contrast to the illustrator's customary stylized backgrounds. Although the brief text is a pleasant, rhythmic accompaniment to the pictures, the story can be "read" from the doublespread illustrations. A humorous and imaginative treatment of a familiar situation.

> *Mary M. Burns, in a review of "The Wind Blew," in* The Horn Book Magazine, *Vol. L, No. 2, April, 1974, p. 140.*

Although this lacks the originality of **Rosie's walk** and **Goodnight, Owl!,** it will serve as one of those early books requiring short attention span, literal illustration, and simple story line. The verse . . . is saved from banality by a nursery rhyme chant quality. And the odd-looking peoples' caricatured sameness is redeemed by clean lines and graceful settings.

> *A review of "The Wind Blew," in* The Booklist, *Vol. 70, No. 17, May 1, 1974, p. 1003.*

This latest picture book by Pat Hutchins inevitably invites comparison with that classic of the nineteen-forties, *Whoo Whoo the Wind Blew* (alas now out of print)—a book whose rumbustious text by Diana Ross and witty illustrations by Leslie Wood make Pat Hutchins's invention seem a little thin.

The story line is very simple: the wind whisks umbrellas, scarves and wigs into the air, building up a procession of gesticulating owners in its wake.

The text describes each incident in rather flat rhyming couplets but the pictures have a liveliness and humour which carry the reader along; each individual is neatly characterised and the colours are bright and clear.

Although lacking the originality of the best of Pat Hutchins's work, these illustrations display a freshness and variety which was conspicuously absent from her previous picture book, **Goodnight Owl.**

> *Eleanor von Schweinitz, in a review of "The Wind Blew," in* Children's Book Review, *Vol. IV, No. 2, Summer, 1974, p. 55.*

Pat Hutchins is by now an established favourite with young children. She is fond of paradox and is not afraid of presenting her readers with quite complex jokes to unravel. In **The Wind Blew,** however, the narrative is of the simplest, and the jokes are purely visual as the thieving wind arbitrarily redistributes all the articles it has snatched. The story is told in unexceptional verse, but the book's real pleasure lies in the author's lucid, exuberant pictures. . . . (p. 719)

> *"Violence, Anarchy or Just Good Clean Fun," in* The Times Literary Supplement, *No. 3774, July 5, 1974, pp. 718-19.*

Pat Hutchins continues to communicate successfully and also to welcome readers into her exquisite small world. The cumulative story grows beautifully, adding enough on each page to keep the story moving and retain suspense, and the words, as ever, are perfect in their simplicity. If not as funny as some, **The Wind Blew** shows most of this young master's qualities, including the delicate fantasy which is firmly anchored in the real world.

> *M. Crouch, in a review of "The Wind Blew," in* The Junior Bookshelf, *Vol. 38, No. 4, August, 1974, p. 201.*

THE SILVER CHRISTMAS TREE (1974)

Five of the seven animals who appeared in **The Surprise Party** return in a Christmas story for little children. Squirrel, engrossed in decorating a tree as a surprise for his friends, does not notice that night has fallen until the branches are bathed in the silvery light of a great star. But by the next morning the star has disappeared. Vainly Squirrel hopes that one of his friends—Duck, Mouse, Fox, or Rabbit—might have found the star; at last, on Christmas Eve, while "all the animals stared in wonder" the silver star returns—"Bigger, brighter, and more beautiful than ever." A childlike, but somewhat tenuous story, with less substance and impact than one expects from the author-artist.

> *Ethel L. Heins, in a review of "The Silver Christmas Tree," in* The Horn Book Magazine, *Vol. L, No. 6, December, 1974, p. 681.*

The illustrations have clarity and stylised patterning, like the story, forming a well-integrated whole. But, as a story, it has a number of weaknesses. One can possibly accept the star illuminating the tree, as a part of the conventions of Christmas stories; but it is hard to believe that Squirrel would make no effort to win back what he believed to have been stolen from him, or that a fox would be friendly with the animals that he would devour in nature—Duck, Rabbit, and Mouse. This is, after all, the hungry fox of **Rosie's Walk,** or at least he looks like him, and there he was true to his folk-tale character. There is also a visual convention, adopted to show darkness, which may seem very puzzling to young readers. This shows the tree buried in a mound of what looks like dark-blue bubbles, or clouds, whilst the squirrel remains in broad daylight.

Pat Hutchins's art work is as good as ever, though there is little variation in style and colour-range from one book to another; they *almost* begin to look stereotyped. In terms of the story, I find this the most disappointing of all her books.

> *John A. Cunliffe, in a review of "The Silver Christmas Tree," in* Children's Book Review, *Vol. V, No. 1, Spring, 1975, p. 12.*

Pat Hutchins returns to the manner, and to some of the characters, of her *Surprise Party.* The new book is a little less funny but not less charming. . . . No artist today knows better how much to reveal at each opening, and she sustains interest and suspense throughout the book. The text is as always immaculate.

> *M. Crouch, in a review of "The Silver Christmas Tree," in* The Junior Bookshelf, *Vol. 39, No. 2, April, 1975, p. 97.*

THE HOUSE THAT SAILED AWAY (1975)

Their London row house breaks off during a rainstorm, leaving the neighbors without a side wall, and off they go—Father, Mother, Grandmother, Morgan and the baby—to sail the Pacific Ocean and encounter pirates, cannibals, the missing crown jewels, and at last the *Queen E II* whose smitten captain tows them all home and marries Grandmother in the end. While Father and Morgan cope, Grandmother floats through it all on "tonic" wine, rum and champagne, flirting with the cannibal chief and posing in the jewels, and Mother breezes about being forgetful and mildly expressing her pleasure in the novelty of it all. Neither woman has a redeeming feature and no one at all is even a colorful stereotype—which might be one reason why—despite a kidnapping, a desert island reunion and a coconut war (all intended to be delightfully dotty)—*The House That Sailed Away* never takes off.

> *A review of "The House That Sailed Away," in* Kirkus Reviews, *Vol. XLIII, No. 14, July 15, 1975, p. 777.*

In her picture book *Rosie's Walk* Pat Hutchins broke new ground in books for the very young. In *The House That Sailed Away* which she has written and her husband [Laurence Hutchins] illustrated, she has again proved her remarkable originality. It is such a pleasure to find a thoroughly funny read aloud for six to eights and a book that older children will chuckle over on their own; that is if they can resist the temptation of reading out their favourite bits. Very few authors achieve good comic writing for the young without sounding arch. Pat Hutchins' triumph of characterisation in this story is Grandma with her hair in curlers, a tendency to turn to the tonic wine at any opportunity and her sharp tongue, although mother's vagueness and father's hostility to grandma (only just kept under), as well as the baby's singleminded purpose of grabbing the cat by the tail all contribute to the success of the story. Only Morgan, our hero, is without idiosyncracies as the house with all its inhabitants starts to float down Willow Road and out to sea where there are adventures involving hungry cannibals, bloodthirsty pirates and buried treasure with grandma featuring largely in every episode. Tremendous fun for everybody and certainly a story to tempt the most reluctant reader.

> *A review of "The House That Sailed Away," in* Books for Your Children, *Vol. 11, No. 4, Autumn, 1976, p. 5.*

There may be more jokes for the adult reader than for the child in this zany story of a family caught in a house that sails away in a flood and ends up on a treasure island. Grandma drinks and Dad wishes she were elsewhere. The baby and the cat are at loggerheads. The cannibal chief fancies Grandma, but it is the captain of the ship which rescues them who marries her. The book is fun and should read aloud well to infants

and younger juniors. The teacher will enjoy the sly humour but may not be entirely satisfied with the style, which is always gossipy and at times perhaps overdoes it. Can you take, from one page alone 'dreadfully', 'nice' (twice), 'lovely', 'awfully' and 'terribly'?

> *David Churchill, in a review of "The House That Sailed Away," in* The School Librarian, *Vol. 25, No. 1, March, 1977, p. 28.*

DON'T FORGET THE BACON! (1976)

This might not be the most visually striking of Pat Hutchins' highly inventive picture books, but it might well be the most mirth provoking. There's recognition too in the mental mixups of a little boy who is sent out for "six farm eggs, a cake for tea, a pound of pears, and don't forget the bacon"—but who, distracted by the passing scene, gradually turns the first three items into "six fat legs, a cape for me and a flight of stairs," and then to "six clothes pegs, a rake for leaves and a pile of chairs." Returning home with this unlikely market basket he does remember, and substitute, the requested items—except that "I forgot the bacon!" With the bright, mobile pictures providing all the narration needed and the only words the little boy's recitation of the changing shopping list, it's a certain story hour ice-breaker.

> *A review of "Don't Forget the Bacon!" in* Kirkus Reviews, *Vol. XLIV, No. 2, January 15, 1976, p. 68.*

A boy going shopping gets his instructions progressively garbled, his list becoming increasingly bizarre. . . . All this provides many opportunities for humour in words and pictures and also for verbal repetition, which helps the young reader as well as adding to the hilarity of the story. Wit, clarity and conciseness are qualities too well-known in Pat Hutchins's books to need expanding on here. Certainly she has maintained her high standard in this book which is strongly recommended for children from about four upwards.

> *John A. Cunliffe, in a review of "Don't Forget the Bacon!" in* Children's Book Review, *Vol. VI, October, 1976, p. 9.*

FOLLOW THAT BUS! (1977)

Follow That Bus, an adventure tale, is neither slick nor flimsy, and heaven knows it tries, it tries very hard, to be perky, peppy, jaunty, jolly and utterly hilarious about a grade-school outing that turns into cops-and-robbers. Indeed, what I think is wrong with the book is that it tries so hard, its utter absence of free and easy effortlessness and the sense that here is this poor comic plot—with kidnappings, chases, mistaken identities, captures—being dragged and shoved along, creaking and groaning. With action replacing a lot of the words, this might do well as a half-hour television special. But really, does it need to be a book?

> *Judith Viorst, in a review of "Follow That Bus!" in* The New York Times Book Review, *April 17, 1977, p. 51.*

This is any child's fantasy of the most exciting school trip ever, told in a robust style that carries off all improbabilities of plot. The amiable and scatty Miss Beaver (whose lost hold-all is the cause of all that follows) comes across very well, both in the prose and in [Laurence Hutchins's] illustrations;

From 1 Hunter, *written and illustrated by Pat Hutchins.*

while among the children of Class 6 attention-seeking Jessica and pessimistic Avril stand out memorably (I found the three named boys much less distinguishable). (pp. 42, 45)

> *Rodie Sudberry, in a review of "Follow That Bus!" in* The School Librarian, *Vol. 26, No. 1, March, 1978, pp. 42, 45.*

HAPPY BIRTHDAY, SAM   (1978)

Grandfather's birthday gift to Sam is a yellow, cane-seated chair. Standing on it, Sam can reach the knobs and switches which—despite becoming older—were still too high that morning. Equally enabling is this cheerful, gentle book, Pat Hutchins's gift to young children. Its full-toned pictures are rich in detail: pattern on rug, hook in wardrobe, crumpled toothpaste tube. Beginning readers can read to small siblings the logical, low-keyed, and well-paced text which does not mock as it conveys that resourcefulness, not inches, is what does the trick. After a decade of quite the reverse, it is nice to find parents who are shown as being both competent and fond, and a Grandpa who comes to celebrate but does not steal the show.

> *Joan W. Blos, in a review of "Happy Birthday, Sam," in* School Library Journal, *Vol. 25, No. 2, October, 1978, p. 134.*

Growing up has its problems as Sam discovered on his birthday. Despite being a year older he was still too small to reach the light switch or his clothes in the wardrobe. However,

Grandpa's present solved the problem! Once again, Pat Hutchins has shown how well she understands young children, and this book will go straight to the hearts of youngsters as it highlights some of their frustrations and their joy at overcoming them. It is a delightful book. (pp. 17-18)

> *Margaret Walker, in a review of "Happy Birthday, Sam," in* Book Window, *Vol. 6, No. 1, Winter, 1978, pp. 17-18.*

THE BEST TRAIN SET EVER   (1978)

Hutchins' three holiday bundles of family happiness are almost swamped in the general rush of good feeling. On Peter's birthday, though no one in the family can afford the train set he's been dreaming of, his parents secretly spend their $10.00 on the engine ("It would be a start"), brother Tony independently buys the track with his $8.00 savings ("It's a start"), and the three younger ones sneak out separately and return with the coach, caboose, and flat car. Their mutual surprise when the whole train is assembled makes for a happy ending to be sure, but it's obviously been in the works ever since the buying chain was set in motion. The second piece, on Halloween, follows a too-similar line, with each brother and sister giving undecided Maria a leftover piece of his or her costume and Maria finally putting them all together to form a prize-winning ostrich. Then, as if suddenly aware of the drift, Hutchins throws a last-minute curve in the Christmas story, where the whole family comes down with measles just in time to cancel the long-anticipated visit from their out-of-town relatives. There's a moment of gloom—but then, in summer, "they had the best Fourth-of-July Christmas Party ever." The family's very likable but unidealized appearance does make them a lot easier to relate to, and no doubt many will want to identify.

> *A review of "The Best Train Set Ever," in* Kirkus Reviews, *Vol. XLVI, No. 6, March 15, 1978, p. 303.*

A book that should encourage beginner-readers with short bursts of simple prose covering the activities of assorted siblings, each spending according to means on part of a train set which young Peter, due for a birthday, has been longingly watching in the window of a local shop. The repetition of phrases ("not much use on its own but I'll take it . . . it's a start"), of parts (coach, rails, guard's van and so on) and prices (from £1 to £5) should help the reader, while Pat Hutchins's chunky pictures, and her attention to physiognomy and facial expressions, confirm the identity, status and attitudes of each member of the family.

> *Margery Fisher, in a review of "The Best Train Set Ever," in* Growing Point, *Vol. 17, No. 6, March, 1979, p. 3477.*

This talented artist has given us a charming trio of stories which have exceptional quality. The first story is about Peter who badly wants the train set in the local shop. . . . The other stories are centred around a Halloween Party and A Picnic for Christmas, and are equally good—especially for telling to small children, as well as being excellent for reading practice, as the words are repeated again and again.

> *B. Clark, in a review of "The Best Train Set Ever," in* The Junior Bookshelf, *Vol. 43, No. 3, April, 1979, p. 107.*

ONE-EYED JAKE (1979)

It's hard to resist a pirate, and this not-so-swaggering crew of brigands is certainly an eyeful. One-Eyed Jake, the captain, and his ramshackle crew rob everything on the high seas until, one day, the cook, bosun, and cabin boy decide they'd just as soon go straight. Adventure leads to misadventure and, as each of the subordinates contrives to wind up exactly where he wants to be, only believability is forced to walk the plank. Never mind! The final splash, with One-Eyed Jake descending to Davy Jones' Locker, has all the authenticity of a pirate's treasure map—you don't have to believe in it since the fun's in following the arrows to the spot marked X. The text, unfortunately, is awash in empty calorie words, and the absurdities upon which the plot turns require a lighter sense of word play. Still, the intricate detailing of the illustrations makes up for the flattened phrases, and the combination of the subject matter with the simple (to the point of repetitious) text, might just make this buried treasure reluctant beginning readers need.

> *Kristi L. Thomas, in a review of "One-Eyed Jake," in* School Library Journal, *Vol. 26, No. 2, October, 1979, p. 141.*

Children and adults sometimes fall about laughing at the same jokes, but not always; and perhaps comedy for the young is the most difficult of all the genres in which adult proclivities have to be matched with the guessed-at needs and capacities of the young. Among the various types of comic fiction, parody is particularly tricky. Pat Hutchins succeeds

with *One-Eyed Jake* because she is merely extending by comic exaggeration a type which has already been fantasised from reality—the story-book pirate. Jake, who has 'a horrible face, a terrible voice, and an awful temper', should be completely recognisable to children, and his deserved death by drowning, which releases the bosun, cook and ship's cat from a miserable servitude, is described in an extended picturebook in an exuberant style matched with ink and wash pictures whose grotesque figures and forceful colour suit the explicit absurdity of the book.

> *Margery Fisher, in a review of "One-Eyed Jake," in* Growing Point, *Vol. 18, No. 4, November, 1979, p. 3597.*

Almost anyone knowing that pirate stories for young children are difficult to come by would be attracted by the opening panorama showing the embodiment of piratical wickedness against a brilliant, exotic background. . . . The clear, repetitious text should present no problems for early readers, and the double-page spreads done in flamboyant full color are brimming with activity and incidental details. Yet not all of the pages are equally successful; on some of them the intricacy of the drawing combines with the variegation of color to produce pictures that are a bit too elaborate, a bit too fussy, for clarity.

> *Ethel L. Heins, in a review of "One-Eyed Jake," in* The Horn Book Magazine, *Vol. LVI, No. 1, February, 1980, p. 46.*

THE TALE OF THOMAS MEAD (1980)

Exaggeration works well in the comically cautionary *Tale of Thomas Mead* . . .—a boy who refuses to read—and its message is unbeatable. " 'I wish you would!' his teacher sighed. 'Why should I?' Thomas Mead replied." Unable to read "Don't Walk," jaywalking Thomas lands in jail where his cellmates teach him, and Thomas becomes a voracious reader. Pat Hutchins' illustrations show lots of disastrous action. Children will have fun foreseeing the consequences (Thomas heading for the door marked "Ladies") and will take in word repetition painlessly through the conversation balloons which echo lines from the text in every picture.

> *A review of "The Tale of Thomas Mead," in* School Library Journal, *Vol. 27, No. 4, December, 1980, p. 65.*

Hutchins's humorous and colorful drawings add to the fun of a rhyming, mock-didactic text for beginning independent readers. The poetic refrain provides repetition, the vocabulary is simple but not stultified, and the rhyme and scansion are tidy. This is a tallish tale, and a funny one. . . .

> *Zena Sutherland, in a review of "The Tale of Thomas Mead," in* Bulletin of the Center for Children's Books, *Vol. 34, No. 7, March, 1981, p. 135.*

The Tale of Thomas Mead is . . . a book created around a single idea. It is a cautionary verse about a boy who refuses to learn to read. . . . Pat Hutchins's strong, clear and lively illustrations take up the greater part of the space and the couplets of verse, one or two per page, are satisfyingly repetitious (much of the dialogue reappears in balloons in the pictures) and run smoothly. Although some of its American terms may need to be explained, this is a book which will be most enjoyed by those who can read it for themselves.

Lucy Micklethwait, "Transmogrifications," in The Times Literary Supplement, No. 4069, March 27, 1981, p. 342.

THE MONA LISA MYSTERY (1981)

A profusion of humorous illustrations, large print and a simple mystery-puzzle plot make this a good choice for the beginning whodunit fan not ready for a complicated plot and subtle characterization. A busload of third-graders travels to Paris for an outing and becomes caught up in a mystery that involves mistaken identity, art theft and kidnapping. Hutchins is wise to introduce only a half dozen children (out of 20) in the class; more characters to keep track of would be confusing. There are no fine nuances of language here, and there is no more than the most sketchy characterization, but those literary elements seem largely outside of the author's concern. Hutchins has succeeded in writing an entertaining, humorous story; undemanding fare, but having the appearance of a book for older children. In addition, the resourcefulness of the students and the bewilderment of their good-natured teachers will be pleasing to the child reader.

Holly Sanhuber, in a review of "The Mona Lisa Mystery," in School Library Journal, Vol. 27, No. 10, August, 1981, p. 56.

The lively third grade class that had an exciting, if improbable, adventure the year before (in *Follow That Bus!* . . . now takes off by bus and ferry for Paris and another, equally nonsensical swashing and buckling romp. . . . Absolutely nothing is meant to be taken seriously, so that all of the exaggeration, coincidence, contrivance, and stereotyped characterization become part of the fun.

Zena Sutherland, in a review of "The Mona Lisa Mystery," in Bulletin of the Center for Children's Books, Vol. 35, No. 1, September, 1981, p. 11.

"The Mona Lisa Mystery" is a child's dream and possibly a parent's nightmare.

In its charmingly convoluted plot, the third grade of an English elementary school takes a week-long holiday in Paris (imagine supervising such a group and you can see why the book would give teachers shudders, too). Even before the children set foot on French soil, bizarre events begin to occur: they're being shadowed by a series of strangers. It turns out that their substitute teacher—a category of person who must rank next to stepmothers as a most-sinister group—is a thief in league with a forger and an imposter physician in a plot to steal the Mona Lisa.

Before the book's end, the painting is taken, one child is temporarily held hostage, all are made captives in a chateau, and the guiltless instructor who's chaperoning them is arrested by mistake. . . .

If this sounds like superior children's fare, it is—so superior that it may provide some difficulties for its readers. The vocabulary and a few of the descriptions (". . . Jessica, looking like Lady Macbeth in her white nightie . . . ") are probably too sophisticated for a child reading at the level of the book's third-grade protagonists. And although Pat Hutchins has filled the story with enough humorous episodes to make readers of all ages laugh, many of the best jokes will be appreciated more by adults: one student collapsing in horror because she believes that the "poisson" on the French menu means

poison; the manager of the hotel giving his guests the four-star menu of his former place of employ, only to admit, after singing the praises of all the delicacies requested, that the only thing he has to offer is fish and chips.

The solution to this problem may be to pass *The Mona Lisa Mystery* along to slightly older readers, or, better yet, read it out loud and explain the nuances—it's just too good to miss. Even though some parents may blanch at some of the third graders' more grisly imaginings—sharks in the English Channel and blood-stained ghosts at the hotel—children will recognize and enjoy their own speculations. . . . They will be especially pleased to see how many of the young pupils' theories turn out to be true. This is one school field trip that *does* become an adventure—and for what more could a child ask?

Laurel Graeber, "Third-graders Snare Parisian Art Thief," in The Christian Science Monitor, October 14, 1981, p. B9.

---

1 HUNTER (1982)

[*1 Hunter*] follows a Mister Magoo-style gentleman, in pith helmet and baggy shorts, through a jungle where he fails to notice (but readers do) two elephants, three giraffes and so forth. The illustrations strike me as a little stiff and hard-edged. (Our hunter-in-profile never varies from one page to the next, and his jungle is out of Emilio Pucci rather than Henri Rousseau.) But a young child may enjoy discovering that those three branches are really antelope horns, and that the bumpy green stones the hunter treads when fording a swamp are actually crocodiles.

Joyce Maynard, in a review of "1 Hunter," in The New York Times Book Review, April 25, 1982, p. 48.

Many counting books move from one to ten, as this does; some of them recapitulate, as this does. But few of them tell a story that has a gentle message and is amusing, *and* is illustrated with the sort of originality and craftmanship that has won the Kate Greenway Medal for its creator. . . . The visual joke, easy for small children to spot, is that each group of animals is seen twice: first in part (as when the hunter marches between the tall legs of the giraffes or strides across the green stepping stones (crocodiles) of a pond, and second in fully identifiable view after the hunter has passed. As decorative as it is useful.

Zena Sutherland, in a review of "1 Hunter," in Bulletin of the Center for Children's Books, Vol. 35, No, 10, June, 1982, p. 189.

When I first saw this book I so nearly dismissed it, thinking 'Why on earth is Pat Hutchins wasting her talents on a counting book?' But of course I should have known better. In fact, this one has similarities to her classic *Rosie's Walk:* reader and author share a joke, the pictures telling the real story, and a marvellous story it is. . . . On several occasions I have seen young children reduced to helpless laughter over this book, in which there is more to discover and enjoy with each reading.

Jill Bennett, "Picture Books for Learning to Read," in The Signal Review: A Selective Guide to Children's Books, Vol. 1, edited by Nancy Chambers,

From The Doorbell Rang, *written and illustrated by Pat Hutchins.*

The Thimble Press, 1983, pp. 6-12.

YOU'LL SOON GROW INTO THEM, TITCH (1983)

Poor little Titch is the youngest of the family, so he has to have his older brother's and sister's left-off trousers, sweater and socks, and anyway he will soon grow into them. Titch's day was to come: he and Dad went shopping, and bought a brand new sweater, and new trousers, and new socks, so that when Mum came home with a brand new baby brother, Titch could hand over his old clothes for the new baby to grow into. A very slight tale of a very everyday situation, but brought to life as always by Pat Hutchins' illustrations. There is plenty of detail for observant children, as they watch the bird in the window who first appears building her nest, then sitting on it, and then feeding her babies as a background to Mum's arrival home with the latest addition to the family.

> *B. Clark, in a review of "You'll Soon Grow into Them, Titch," in* The Junior Bookshelf, *Vol. 47, No. 4, August, 1983, p. 154.*

Again Pat Hutchins offers beginners the chance to learn one of the untaught reading lessons: the words are not all; what isn't being said can matter a great deal. Children have to be helped to make this discovery, though with a book like this I suspect that some will find it out for themselves. (p. 10)

> *Jill Bennett, "Picture Books 3 to 7: Learning to Read," in* The Signal Review: A Selective Guide to Children's Books, *Vol. 2, edited by Nancy Chambers, The Thimble Press, 1984, pp. 8-11.*

KING HENRY'S PALACE (1983)

Three witty, warming tales of King Henry: a clever old dear and, for youngsters, a brand-new charmer. Because he is "a very nice king," the cook, the gardener, and the servants do their best for him; because he has "such a nice, happy little palace," wicked King Boris ("who lived in a nasty, unhappy palace") covets it; because Henry is clever—and Boris isn't—

King Henry's ten guards (successively hoisting flags, drums, pipes, swords, pistols) pass muster as hundreds . . . and frighten off Boris' horde. Episode II: "It was King Henry's birthday and the cook decided to bake a special cake for him." However, the gardener, the servants, and the soldiers make off first with the cook's cherries ("nice cherries," "very good cherries," "excellent cherries"), and then with his nuts; so King Henry will have pancakes for his birthday—which he shares, of course, with the gardener, the servants, and the soldiers ("Very nice . . . ," "Very good . . . ," "Excellent pancakes"). "'They were,' said the cook, looking at the empty plate." Episode III? **"King Henry's Christmas Present"**—wherein the gardener, the cook, the servants, the guards (doing what *doesn't* come naturally) make King Henry a bench that collapses—which he, with his kindly quick-wittedness, hails as a long-wanted sled. And while the sledding proceeds by turns, the gardener fetches a tree, the servants set the table and decorate the tree . . . until, the feast assembled, "they all went in to eat it." Style, snap, high-seasoned colors, memorable lines, stage-worthy structuring—and a gentlemanly king: a great thing to set by the small thing of Hutchins' memorable debut, **Rosie's Walk.** (pp. J-149-J-150)

> *A review of "King Henry's Palace," in* Kirkus Reviews, *Juvenile Issue, Vol. LI, No. 13-17, September 1, 1983, pp. J-149-50.*

These three vignettes about good King Henry have some mirthful moments. While kids will spot the jokes easily in . . . two chapters, there is a problem in the remaining one, which comes first in the book. The king uses sleight of hand to make his enemies think his army is larger than it actually is. Children may need some help in catching the visual humor that explains just how his majesty pulls off the ruse. The comic, cartoon-style illustrations in Day-Glo-bright colors are used to good effect. Though this is not designated as an easy-to-read, it could work well in that capacity.

> *Ilene Cooper, in a review of "King Henry's Palace," in* Booklist, *Vol. 80, No. 6, November 15, 1983, p. 497.*

Pat Hutchins knows all about the virtue of economy. . . . There are rather more words than usual in her King Henry book, but after all here are in effect three books for the price of one. Each has one nice small joke, put over very effectively with the minimum number of words to accompany the strong simple drawing. King Henry is a 'very nice king' who protects his palace, feeds the community, and shares with them a jolly Christmas, all this with fine design and controlled detail thrown in. I am not sure that we are going to love King Henry as we do some of Miss Hutchins' creations, but we will certainly admire him, and her, for this virtuoso performance.

M. Crouch, in a review of "King Henry's Palace," in The Junior Bookshelf, *Vol. 48, No. 1, February, 1984, p. 12.*

THE CURSE OF THE EGYPTIAN MUMMY (1983)

A camping trip in the country quickly turns sinister for the scouts and leaders of the 15th Hampstead Cub Scouts. When the group makes a rest stop in a village near their campsite, they learn that an unidentified man has been killed by a poisonous snake which is still on the loose. Before boarding the bus one of the scouts finds an Egyptian ibis statue stashed in a trash can and takes it with him. To make matters worse, elderly Miss Hylyard, who allows the scouts to camp on her property, tells them that lack of money will force her to sell her land and house. There will be several more deaths (of the villains), another appearance of the sinister serpent and plenty of high jinks before the scouts unravel *The Curse of the Egyptian Mummy* and save the day for Miss Hylyard. Readers drawn by the intriguing title will not be disappointed by Hutchins' freewheeling story. The solution to the mystery gets a bit thick at the end but this wild and woolly bunch of scouts makes for good times and good reading. (pp. 82-3)

Drew Stevenson, in a review of "The Curse of the Egyptian Mummy," in School Library Journal, *Vol. 30, No. 4, December, 1983, pp. 82-3.*

The 15th Hampshire Cub Scouts are involved in an Agatha Christie type crime adventure bestrewn with clues, false leads and all the mayhem of Egyptian curses, imposters in police uniform and death by a deadly snakebite.

The story gallops through eighteen chapters each with a cliff-hanger ending and the wealth of clues are brought together neatly at the conclusion.

Plenty of action and plenty of fun will be enjoyed by the young reader even if the intricacy of plot eludes them.

D. A. Young, in a review of "The Curse of the Egyptian Mummy," in The Junior Bookshelf, *Vol. 48, No. 1, February, 1984, p. 24.*

THE VERY WORST MONSTER (1985)

Given Hutchins' light touch and humor, the appeal of the subject, and the combining of two sure-fire ideas (sibling dethronement and the worst-is-the-best) this could hardly fail to be amusing and popular. Bright, imaginative pictures, featuring monsters with strong family resemblances illustrate the sprightly text in which Hazel is jealous of a new-born baby brother. Everybody coos at him, gloating over how bad he is, how loudly he growls, how strong his fangs are. Hazel mutters to herself that she's bad, too, and growls even louder.

Alas for her ego, little Billy wins a baby contest title by trying to eat the judge: "Worst Monster Baby in the World." Hazel tries to lose Billy, frighten him, and give him away. Nothing works. Her parents, horrified, say "You gave your own baby brother away! You must be the Worst Monster in the World!" "I told you I was," Hazel points out, and confesses that the family who had taken Billy had given him back. Yeasty fun.

Zena Sutherland, in a review of "The Very Worst Monster," in Bulletin of the Center for Children's Books, *Vol. 38, No. 8, April, 1985, p. 149.*

Finally, there is a book for the child who requests a "scary" book but is too young for one. . . . Echoes of Wells' *Noisy Nora* (Dial, 1973) and a bit of Sendak, but Hutchins is completely original in her treatment. Her watercolor illustrations show a variety of monsters that will delight and pleasantly terrify. Even the youngest children can appreciate these monsters without being frightened. Members of the Monster family, although ugly and green, are both humorous and humanized. A monstrously wonderful addition to any picture book collection.

Nancy Schmidtmann, in a review of "The Very Worst Monster," in School Library Journal, *Vol. 31, No. 9, May, 1985, p. 76.*

Pat Hutchins has never entirely found a style of her own—or perhaps she prefers to experiment from one book to the next. ***The Very Worst Monster*** shows her under the spell of Fungus the Bogeyman, so that for the pleasures of recognition must be substituted the more doubtful rewards of fantasy. Yet despite the ubiquitous pointed ears and long green toenails, this too turns out to be yet another story of sibling rivalry—*My Naughty Little Sister* in bogeyland. Ma and Pa Monster think that the new baby, Billy, is so bad that they enter him for the Worst Monster Baby in the World Competition, but older sister Hazel is determined to prove that she is really the worst, and gives him away—which is, of course, what all older sisters would like to do to their younger siblings. It is reassuring, though also mildly disappointing, to find that the monster world mirrors our own so closely.

Julia Briggs, "Worthy Objects," in The Times Literary Supplement, *No. 4286, May 24, 1985, p. 589.*

THE DOORBELL RANG (1986)

Victoria and Sam are delighted when Ma bakes a tray of a dozen cookies, even though Ma insists that her cookies aren't as good as Grandma's. They count them and find that each can have six. But the doorbell rings, friends arrive and the cookies must be re-divided. This happens again and again, and the number of cookies on each plate decreases as the visitors' pile of gear in the corner of the kitchen grows larger. When each child's share is down to one, and the doorbell rings again, Sam and Victoria are worried—and then elated, when they discover that it's Grandma with a tray of dozens more cookies. Hutchins' illustrations are more than cheerful. Her exuberant colors flow from page edge to page edge with a lavish generosity born out by Grandma's abundant supply of cookies. The double-page spreads are filled with details for children to find, such as the peripatetic cat. Ma's unending battle with the footprints on her clean kitchen floor and the changing facial expressions of the multiracial children. The math concepts shown make this a beautiful choice for curriculum support in the primary grades, and the evident dismay of the children may lead to further discussion in areas other than math. As refreshing, enjoyable and unpredictable as an unexpected visit from a friend.

Ruth Semrau, in a review of "The Doorbell Rang,"
in School Library Journal, *Vol. 32, No. 8, April,*
1986, p. 73.

What child hasn't been introduced to the concept of sharing? On this instantly recognizable notion, Pat Hutchins has constructed a thoroughly satisfying tale for young picture-story audiences, executed with the exuberance which has become her trademark. . . . The brief repetitive text, printed in easy-to-read type with generous leading between the lines, invites participation and encourages independent reading. The illustrations, featuring patterns against patterns—black-and-white checkerboard floor, blue-and-white checked tablecloth, striped or floral clothing—suggest the cheerful crowded coziness of a warm, loving environment. This is not house beautiful, perhaps, but certainly home delightful. Against the busy background, the slightly cartooned characters, including an irrepressible black-and-white cat, emerge as distinct individuals. The double-page spreads allow for a full view of the kitchen—children crowded around the table to the left, while Mother, on the right, wields a squeegee, trying in vain to clean up the rapidly multiplying tracks left by muddy feet. Bright, joyous, dynamic, this wonderfully humorous piece of realism for the young is presented simply but with style and imagination. It should become a staple for story hours.

Mary M. Burns, in a review of "The Doorbell
Rang," in The Horn Book Magazine, *Vol. LXII,*
No. 3, May-June, 1986, p. 318.

WHERE'S THE BABY? (1988)

Hutchins' charming greenish monsters are back, and baby is still living up to the reputation he gained in *The Very Worst Monster*—and he's still receiving raves from his relatives. The clever plot line has Grandma, Ma, and older sister Hazel following the baby, who is blithely traipsing through the house wreaking havoc as he goes, leaving paint footprints on the floor and handprints on the wall, a mess in the kitchen and chaos in the workroom, and more of the same upstairs.

With the discovery of every fresh disaster, this true-to-life grandma praises her grandchild with phrases such as "he's good at painting." Finally, they find baby apparently asleep. But when they tiptoe out of the room, baby reaches for the basket of eggs grandma left behind, and the jacket art shows further developments. While Grandma's comments will particularly appeal to adults, children will be tickled by baby's antics, his path of disaster, the expressions on the monster faces, and the promise of the ending. The text is mostly in rhyming couplets, which flow naturally. Bright watercolor and ink illustrations provide strong support and witty detail, and the well-composed double-page spreads encourage a sense of movement through the house. A satisfying sequel.

Leda Schubert, in a review of "Where's the Baby?"
in School Library Journal, *Vol. 34, No. 7, March,*
1988, p. 167.

The 'baby'—if you can call Billy, the diabolical hero of *The Very Worst Monster* by such an endearing term—has done his worst, but Grandma always finds something nice to say about him. 'He's been cleaning the chimney for you,' she says, 'He's a help!' What will she say when she discovers that he has broken all the eggs in her basket?

Was it necessary to portray quite such ugly creatures as characters? Does this add to the attraction for children? The trend today seems to be to present children with the grotesque in preference to the pleasing.

E. Colwell, in a review of "Where's the Baby?" in
The Junior Bookshelf, *Vol. 52, No. 2, April, 1988,*
p. 84.

Havoc is also the keynote to Pat Hutchins's delightful *Where's the Baby? . . .* Each brightly decked illustration is cluttered with everyday objects for the young reader to identify and the text is a loping doggerel entirely in keeping with the rough-and-ready storyline: "The dress Ma was making was shorter than planned./'He can use scissors,' said Grandma, 'isn't that grand!' "

Jake Hobson, "Monstrously Appealing," in The
Times Literary Supplement, *No. 4435, April 1-7,*
1988, p. 371.

Barbro Lindgren

1937-

Swedish author and illustrator of picture books, fiction, and poetry.

Although Lindgren has written and illustrated several books for readers in the early elementary grades, she is best known in the English-speaking world as the author of two series of exhilarating picture books featuring infant protagonists. The "Wild Baby" books, adapted from the Swedish in America by Jack Prelutsky and in England by Alison Winn, depict an indomitable toddler who, despite his constant mischievousness, enjoys the comforting love of a forgiving mother. His uninhibited disposition and typically imaginative play are portrayed in Lindgren's lighthearted verse and the lively illustrations by Eva Eriksson; as a result, these books have been praised for delighting the youngest reader and listener. In the "Sam" series, which treats the experiences and emotions of a small boy, Lindgren's texts are comprised of short, declarative sentences, but her ability to capture the essence of a toddler's daily diversions remains unaltered. These picture books, characterized by Lindgren's understated approach and her delicate humor, offer preschoolers an enticing introduction to literature. Lindgren has won several international awards including the Astrid Lindgren Prize in 1973 and the Nils Holgersson Plaque in 1977; she was also nominated for the Hans Christian Andersen Award in 1988.

(See also *Something about the Author,* Vol. 46.)

HILDING'S SUMMER (1967)

Hilding's summer is a five-year-old's summer, complete with collections, a trip to the zoo, running away, selling kid sister, burying treasure, finding a baby bird, going on a picnic—a typical batch of warm weather diversions. Hilding has no sense of proportion about money or distance: "You mean it costs money to ride the streetcar?" he demands. After all, a boy of five is very naive; a boy big enough to to read a book this long, however, isn't naive enough to enjoy it. A gently amusing Scandinavian entry which will have trouble finding a suitable audience.

A review of "Hilding's Summer," in Kirkus Service, *Vol. XXXV, No. 6, March 15, 1967, p. 341.*

Hilding and his friends, who seem to be six or seven years old, have daily experiences which reflect life in Sweden. Each chapter is an episode. Third- and fourth-graders can read the book, with its short, simple sentences; younger children would enjoy the story more, however, the choppy style does not lend itself to oral reading.

Eleanor Everett, in a review of "Hilding's Summer," in Library Journal, *Vol. 92, No. 12, June 15, 1967, p. 2451.*

ALBAN (1974)

[*Alban*] conceals a good deal of meat under a deceptively sim-

ple style: a whole life cycle [of a dog] in fact, from Alban's birth (popping in a perfectly matter-of-fact fashion out of his mother's bottom), growing up, having fun, having his own puppies, growing old, dying equally matter-of-factly without any fuss at the end. It may sound a bit sentimental but it isn't. The whole book is rather scrappily laid out but it doesn't matter: the drawings (sharp pen-and-ink animals on fuzzy chalk backgrounds) are expressive enough to survive. (p. 739)

David Gentleman, "Dog Days," in New Statesman, *Vol. 87, No. 2253, May 24, 1974, pp. 739-40.*

I can imagine certain children taking this book to their hearts. It is, in terms of plot at least, a very natural, straightforward chronicle of a dog's life—mating, breeding, growing old, dying—told simply and with songs "by Alban" repeating salient points. It is an odd but attractive mixture of canine behaviour and fancy, illustrated in a naïve style, with chalk effects and with the dogs standing out in outline against a simple background.

Margery Fisher, in a review of "Alban," in Growing Point, *Vol. 13, No. 3, September, 1974, p. 2460.*

The writers who choose animals as their main characters walk a dangerous path. So often they are overcome by feyness, and in their attempts to portray a personality, albeit one clad in fur and walking upon four legs, they are prey to the fatal flaw of coyness. Too often in humanising the animal, they remove its natural dignity, thereby leaving it with no credible identity whatever. It becomes no creature at all, merely rather pathetic like an elephant in a ballet skirt. This Swedish author shows this weakness to be held in common, and not merely a proclivity of our animal-besotted nation. The extreme archness of the text of this story makes it difficult to appreciate as a book to read, but it possesses a certain appeal visually, for its pictures are simple and cheerfully coloured.

> *Gabrielle Maunder, in a review of "Alban," in* The School Librarian, *Vol. 22, No. 3, September, 1974, p. 234.*

THE WILD BABY (1981)

Adapted from Lindgren's Swedish *Mamman och den vilda Bebin,* in Jack Prelutsky's inimitable verse, is the story of baby Ben: always where he shouldn't be, never where he should. He sleeps in the clock and the chandelier, swims in the sink and wanders off at every opportunity. Things tend to get broken around Ben, but Mama loves him dearly. Young readers love him, too. Their response is particularly strong and favorable when he gets stuck in the toilet, cheap shot or not. Ben is fun, and Mama, singlehandedly attempting to keep up with him, is endearing. Reckless, loud and wild fun. (pp. 110-11)

> *Helen Gregory, in a review of "The Wild Baby," in* School Library Journal, *Vol. 28, No. 1, September, 1981, pp. 110-11.*

The Wild Baby concerns a mischievous toddler called Bodger who "Eats toothpaste worms, and snips his hair, / Smashes his toys, torments and teases, / Swinging on pretend trapezes". His mother is permanently on the verge of a nervous breakdown and there is an insensitive scene in which the child is seen falling down the loo ("Help, help, I'm drowning"). The structure is bad and the translation [by Alison Winn] is worse. . . .

> *Lucy Micklethwait, "Second Helpings," in* The Times Literary Supplement, *No. 4094, September 18, 1981, p. 1066.*

Although [Ben's] escapades would intimidate the hardiest of baby-sitters, they will undoubtedly delight preschoolers smugly aware that they no longer succumb to such marvelous temptations. Depicted as a wispy-haired toddler, Ben is a bustling bundle of energy, one of the most deliciously naughty children to appear since Sendak's Pierre. The Swedish text has been adapted into rhythmic rhymed nonsense verse accompanying a series of lightly caricatured watercolor illustrations [by Eva Eriksson] detailed in pen and ink. The effect is broadly humorous to complement the mood of the situations and reflect the nature of the young protagonist, who is totally uninhibited as he follows his adventurous whims. "Reckless, loud and wild," Ben is irresistible.

> *Mary M. Burns, in a review of "The Wild Baby," in* The Horn Book Magazine, *Vol. LVII, No. 6, December, 1981, p. 659.*

SAM'S CAR; SAM'S COOKIE; SAM'S TEDDY BEAR
(1982; British editions as *Sam's Biscuit* and *Sam's Teddy*)

[Three] pert mini-dramas, in mock-primerese, for tiny tots—from which you may wish, however, to select only one or two. **Sam's Cookie** and **Sam's Car** are similar struggles-for-possession. Both begin with scruffy tyke Sam and the object of his attentions: "Sam has a cookie"; "Look, here's Sam's car." Then, after more or less warm-up, "Doggie takes Sam's cookie" and Lisa and Sam fight over Sam's little red car. Each conflict, in its own realistic, funny way, is a stand-off. "Sam is angry. *Dumb doggie.* / Doggie is angry. *Grr.*" Then Doggie chases Sam, Mommy scolds him, Sam gets another cookie, and Doggie (wordlessly) gets a bone. A quietly happy outcome all around As for Sam and Lisa, both in turn "hurt," cry, and—when "Mommy brings another car"—beam. The natty wind-up: "*Toot,* says Lisa's car. *Toot, toot,* says Sam's car." **Sam's Teddy Bear** is slightly more complicated and oblique—and less a story than an incident. But it also has an engaging bit of silent parallelism: while Sam, in bed, kisses, licks, and bites Teddy Bear, Doggie, on the floor alongside, does the same with Sam's slippers. Then, "Sam throws Teddy Bear"—who "falls into the pottie" (presumably empty, though we're not told), from which Doggie extracts him and returns him to a grateful Sam. With every emotion clearly telegraphed (Doggie has, if anything, a larger repertoire of expressions than Sam), these rudimentary tales have considerable story-content.

> *A review of "Sam's Car," "Sam's Cookie," and "Sam's Teddy Bear," in* Kirkus Reviews, *Vol. L, No. 12, June 15, 1982, p. 675.*

The texts here are almost a spoof on the Dick-and-Jane style, with the humor and authenticity of each story making it a captivating reading experience for toddlers. Every episode deals with losing something (a cookie to the dog, a toy car to the little girl next door, and a teddy bear into the potty chair), crying over it, and working things out. This series of emotions is no less relevant for its familiarity. . . . While many early books have to be adapted to suit young concentration spans, Sam's stories can be read straight through—over and over, as demand will warrant. Translated from Swedish, these are imports that pass the child test of universal identification.

> *Betsy Hearne, in a review of "Sam's Car," "Sam's Cookie," and "Sam's Teddy Bear," in* Booklist, *Vol. 79, No. 1, September 1, 1982, p. 46.*

I loved these. There is but one simple sentence per page, and the facing illustrations [by Eva Eriksson] portray precisely what the words convey. The language and situations are totally childlike; the pictures are endearing. These are sure to be welcomed by the youngest listeners.

> *Beverly Woods, in a review of "Sam's Car," "Sam's Cookie," and "Sam's Teddy Bear," in* Children's Book Review Service, *Vol. 11, No. 3, November, 1982, p. 22.*

Three short books about Sam, an endearing wide-eyed waifish-looking toddler, employ simple direct sentences reminiscent of Dick and Jane, but far more engaging and memorable. Lindgren obviously knows what makes little ones tick, and there is no attempt to sentimentalize the innocence of childhood. Done in soft colors with pen outline, each illustration appears on a wordless page facing large type text. Each illustration perfectly amplifies the humor and emotion which is so minimally expressed in the text. These delights can be shared with infants and toddlers, while beginning readers will find simple reading and pleasure in the true-to-life situations. *Sam's Teddy Bear* and *Sam's Cookie* are definite winners, with *Sam's Car* running just behind.

> *Brenda Durrin Maloney, in a review of "Sam's Car," "Sam's Cookie," and "Sam's Teddy Bear," in* School Library Journal, *Vol. 29, No. 10, August, 1983, p. 54.*

WILD BABY GOES TO SEA (1982; British edition as *The Wild Baby's Boat Trip*)

Baby Ben, the impish little hero of *The Wild Baby,* has a single make-believe adventure here, playing sailboat with an old box, two brooms that serve as mast and oar, and Mama's apron for a sail. With his three stuffed animals on board, Ben sails into and out of a whale's "great mouth," on through a wild storm that dumps them all, and into the night where "something gruesome, dark, and weird" beckons them on. But Ben turns down the invitation and steers the ship " . . . back [to] shore, / safe and sound on Mama's floor." As in many fantasies, there's a teasing element—here a rooster Ben hauls on board—that makes the trip back to everyday reality and remains to puzzle Mama. It's a common device and, for that matter, the whole trip follows a familiar picture-book pattern; but readers captivated by the *Wild Baby*'s irrepressible antics won't feel let down by the sequel; with Lindgren, Eriksson, and Prelutsky at the helm, it rolls along with vim and agility.

> *A review of "Wild Baby Goes to Sea," in* Kirkus Reviews, *Vol. LI, No. 7, April 1, 1983, p. 373.*

Lindgren has an excellent sense of what a child's imaginative play is all about. Like Max in *Where the Wild Things Are,* Ben is hero, and triumphs over forces more powerful than himself. He plays at being adult, in control of what happens to him. Yet when things get out of hand, he can call off the voyage, and return to the safety of Mother and a lunch of fried eggs.

> *Alice Digilio, in a review of "Wild Baby Goes to Sea," in* Book World—The Washington Post, *April 10, 1983, p. 10.*

Slightly older than the rollicking *Wild Baby,* this requires nursery-schoolers' understanding the fine distinction between reality and fantasy as baby Ben sets out to sea on his mother's blue rug, which transforms into an ocean as wild as his imagination. He and his crew . . . manage to land safely back on mama's floor by dint of Ben's cavalier management of the gravest dangers. In fact, one of his deeds during the sail is saving a desperate rooster by hauling him aboard the boat (constructed of a box, broom, and apron claimed from mama's housecleaning), and this grateful bird follows him back to the real world, causing mama to wonder "all that day / just how that rooster / came their way!" Prelutsky has adapted the verse in his characteristic comic-narrative rhyme. (pp. 1218, 1220)

> *Betsy Hearne, in a review of "Wild Baby Goes to Sea," in* Booklist, *Vol. 79, No. 18, May 15, 1983, pp. 1218, 1220.*

BAD SAM!; SAM'S BALL; SAM'S BATH; SAM'S LAMP (1983)

A small boy's equally small misdemeanours [in *Sam's Ball* and *Bad Sam!*] described briefly and cogently and illustrated in entertaining caricature in a style that lends personality to the indomitable Sam, reflecting his moods of rage, pain, joy and curiosity with sparkling humour. . . . [Two] irresistible miniatures.

> *Margery Fisher, in a review of "Sam's Ball" and "Bad Sam!" in* Growing Point, *Vol. 22, No. 2, July, 1983, p. 4110.*

Three new picture books starring incorrigible Baby Sam, epitome of perpetual motion, are great news for his many admirers. Lindgren's brief, pungent sentences are easy for the younger set to grasp in *Sam's Lamp*. . . . Sam wants the pretty lamp affixed to the ceiling in his house. Scrambling from a small stool to a chair and then a table, the infant grabs for the lamp but loses his balance and falls on his teddy bear. His screams bring Sam's long-suffering Mommy on the run with kisses and a bandage for both the baby and his wounded bear: "Now Sam is happy." He's happy also in . . . *Sam's Bath,* *très chic* in his rubber cap, splashing in the tub with his puppy and all his toys; again in *Sam's Ball,* playing catch with a kitten.

> *A review of "Sam's Lamp," "Sam's Bath," and "Sam's Ball," in* Publishers Weekly, *Vol. 224, No. 2, July 8, 1983, p. 65.*

Toddler Sam's exploits with ball, lamp and bath are set forth in short, declarative sentences. The terse language and near absence of adjectives and qualifiers make for an offbeat sense of humor. Each book is a tiny vignette of a tiny day. . . . The scenes are free of elaborate trappings of 20th-Century society. The simple, direct stories and [Eva Eriksson's] illustrations should withstand hundreds of repeated readings.

> *Dana Whitney Pinizzotto, in a review of "Sam's Ball," "Sam's Bath," and "Sam's Lamp," in* School Library Journal, *Vol. 30, No. 1, September, 1983, p. 108.*

If anything, this second batch of mini-dramas about scruffy tyke Sam is better than the first—*Sam's Car, Sam's Cookie,* and *Sam's Teddy Bear*—on which the very best of the new trio, *Sam's Bath,* builds. Again Lindgren begins, with primerese grandeur (and humor): "Look, there's Sam. Look, there's Sam's tub." Sam goes happily into the tub; and, in an orgy of possessiveness, Sam's ball, Sam's truck, Sam's teddy bear, and Sam's cookie all go into the tub too. But: "Doggie is scared. Doggie does not like the tub." Though he tries to slink away, Sam won't have it: "Doggie must go into the tub." Then each tumbles in—the last blissful picture is justly captioned, "A bath is fun." *Sam's Ball,* involving a conflict and reconciliation with Kitty, is more along the rumbustious lines of *Sam's Car* and *Sam's Cookie* (with some real violence and sneak-thievery that scrappy toddlers will appreciate). *Sam's Lamp,* in turn, perfectly dramatizes the way small fry personalize and blame objects. Spotting the "pretty" lamp, Sam climbs up "on the stool . . . on the chair . . . on the table" to get a closer look (a wonderful little sequence in itself); but immediately he falls down. "*Bad lamp,* yells Sam." His bleeding knee hurts; he cries; "Mommy puts on a bandage"; and Sam, eyeing his bandaged knee, happily cavorts with teddy bear. Sam is the rare preschool hero, with a range of emotions, *not* set forth in animal guise. These sly, cathartic little tales don't quickly exhaust themselves either.

> *A review of, "Sam's Ball," "Sam's Bath," and "Sam's Lamp," in* Kirkus Reviews, *Juvenile Issue, Vol. LI, No. 13-17, September 1, 1983, p. J-151.*

Sam's Ball, Sam's Bath, and **Sam's Lamp,** three] small books, each a delightful vignette of a young child's behavior, should entertain readers-aloud as well as their audience, and should also serve as good prereading experiences, since the texts have few and simple words, short sentences, repetition that isn't cloying, and humor.

> *Zena Sutherland, in a review of "Sam's Ball," "Sam's Bath," and "Sam's Lamp," in* Bulletin of the Center for Children's Books, *Vol. 37, No. 4, December, 1983, p. 72.*

SAM'S POTTY; SAM'S WAGON (1986)

Sam, the energetic toddler-hero of earlier escapades, stars in two new childlike escapades. In **Sam's Potty** Sam determinedly procrastinates when it comes to using his potty. After eyeing it evilly, he tries to sit his dog on the pot. Having little success with that, he finally sits down himself, with dog in lap. In **Sam's Wagon** the boy takes Doggie and a wagon load of toys for a ride. Things fall out one by one and each time Doggie retrieves them. When the cookie Sam had included tumbles out, Doggie goes to get that too—suddenly there is no more cookie. Sam looks puzzled, but readers will guess where the cookie wound up. The same scruffy line-and-wash drawings [by Eva Eriksson] found in others of the Sam series continue to display the author's knack for speaking directly to a very young audience.

> *Denise M. Wilms, in a review of "Sam's Potty," and "Sam's Wagon," in* Booklist, *Vol. 83, No. 5, November 1, 1986, p. 411.*

These two new books about toddler Sam are as well done, realistic, and as comical as their predecessors. **Sam's Potty** does not have the same instructional intent as does Alona Frankel's *Once Upon a Potty.* Rather, Lindgren tells a delightful anecdote of Sam's frustrating encounter with a potty. . . . The potty is a chamber pot, and this may need explanation for readers familiar only with the conventional toilet. . . . These small and sturdy books are ideal for an audience of one to three year olds. . . . Sam's facial expressions and actions are typical of a toddler. It is good to see this type of picture book, in addition to the board book format, for toddlers.

> *Mary Beth Burgoyne, in a review of "Sam's Potty" and "Sam's Wagon," in* School Library Journal, *Vol. 33, No. 4, December, 1986, p. 91.*

THE WILD BABY'S DOG (1987; U.S. edition as *The Wild Baby Gets a Puppy*)

Rhymed verse in a variety of metres describes how Baby Bodger, furious at being given a home-made toy dog for his birthday instead of the live dog he wanted, has a glorious romp through the galaxies with the despised toy, which reveals an unexpected power over inanimate objects. Mother's comment as she listens to the tale of the adventure ('I wish he wasn't *quite* so wild') anchors the snub-nosed baby and shapeless mongrel to reality and so does the eccentric, viva-cious definition of toys and furniture in a lively piece of fancy. . . .

> *Margery Fisher, in a review of "The Wild Baby's Dog," in* Growing Point, *Vol. 26, No. 1, May, 1987, p. 4807.*

In a turnabout from the usual fantasy excursions, the dog is still very much alive the following morning—to Mother's surprise and to Ben's smug look. Prelutsky's light-hearted translation of Lindgren's Swedish text has a rollicking beat that will capture the attention of little ones. The same is true for the frisky artwork featuring that homely wild baby who can express a variety of emotions with the raising of an eyebrow or the pout of a lip. Executed in subtle watercolors outlined in pen [Eva] Eriksson captures the everyday events and flights of fantasy with panache. A wild and woolly time will be had by all. (pp. 1182-83)

> *Ilene Cooper, in a review of "The Wild Baby Gets a Puppy," in* Booklist, *Vol. 84, No. 13, March 1, 1988, pp. 1182-83.*

The sometimes-forced rhymes require practice to be read smoothly, but they have the same rollicking child-like humor of earlier **Wild Baby** favorites. The facial expressions on these cartoon characters, reminiscent of the Katzenjammer Kids, provide special appeal in these lively and humorous watercolor illustrations. One point that may concern some readers is the haziness of the line between fantasy and reality. The morning after their adventure, the other animals are stuffed toys again, but Baby Ben appears to be somewhat smugly showing his mother that Rags is a real dog on a leash, raising his leg by a tree. (p. 86)

> *Kay E. Vandergrift, in a review of "The Wild Baby Gets a Puppy," in* School Library Journal, *Vol. 35, No. 8, May, 1988, pp. 85-6.*

A WORM'S TALE (1988)

Despite its whimsical premise [and] several funny scenes . . . , this tale of an unlikely friendship—between man and worm—never really takes off. It begins when Arthur, a friendless but likable fellow, literally stumbles across a talking worm in the park. He takes him home, names him Charles and takes him to a tailor to be properly outfitted. Charles proves a double blessing, becoming not just a friend for Arthur but a catalyst for the making of additional friends among children who are captivated by the unusual duo. In a hurried and tacked-on denouement, the friendship (and the worm) are threatened by a bully, whom the children dispatch post-haste—a flat finale to elements that seemed to herald greater hijinks and hilarity.

> *A review of "A Worm's Tale," in* Publishers Weekly, *Vol. 234, No. 18, October 28, 1988, p. 78.*

A kindly story of friendship has two unlikely protagonists, Arthur, a middle-aged gentleman, and Charles, a worm. . . . [The] pleasures of friendship are somehow made clearer by the bizarre juxtaposition of worm and man. (pp. 200-01)

> *Ann A. Flowers, in a review of "A Worm's Tale," in* The Horn Book Magazine, *Vol. LXV, No. 2, March-April, 1989, pp. 200-01.*

Farley (McGill) Mowat

1921-

Canadian author of fiction.

One of Canada's most popular and controversial authors of nonfiction for adults, Mowat is also revered for creating books for children and young adults which reflect his affection and respect for animals, the Canadian wilderness, and his young readers. A well known naturalist whose works are filled with the details of his own experiences, he is regarded as an especially effective storyteller whose seriousness of purpose regarding the relationship of humanity and the environment underscores his exciting adventure stories and humorous autobiographical fiction. Conveying the importance of preserving a connection to and kinship with the land as well as his feeling for the Indians and Inuits who people his books, he presents his audience with such themes as the importance of friendship and of knowing ourselves as well as such attributes as self-reliance, courage, compassion, and justice. He is perhaps best known for his first book *Lost in the Barrens* (1956), the story of a sixteen-year-old Scottish boy and his young Cree friend who are forced to survive a winter alone in northern Manitoba, and for *The Dog Who Wouldn't Be* (1957), a charming tale about Mowat's boyhood and family life which features his unusually talented Prince Albert retriever. Mowat created two sequels to these books, *The Curse of the Viking Grave* (1966), in which Jamie and Awasin go back to the Barrens in search of Viking artifacts, and *Owls in the Family* (1961), an expansion of a chapter in *The Dog Who Wouldn't Be* which describes the amusing adventures of Mowat's anthropomorphic pet owls. He is also the author of *The Black Joke* (1962), a story of whiskey smuggling and piracy which takes place off the coast of Newfoundland during Prohibition. Acclaimed for his knowledge of both human and animal nature as well as for his depictions of Canadian landscape and atmosphere, Mowat has been dubbed the " 'Mr. Canada' of children's literature" by critic Sheila Egoff, a title which few observers would dispute. *Lost in the Barrens* received the Governor-General's Award in 1957 and the Canadian Library Association Book of the Year Medal in 1958 and was named to the Hans Christian Andersen Awards Honours List of outstanding international children's books. In 1970, Mowat received the Vicky Metcalf Award for his contribution to Canadian children's literature.

(See also *Contemporary Literary Criticism,* Vol. 26; *Something about the Author,* Vol. 3; *Contemporary Authors New Revision Series,* Vols. 4, 24; *Contemporary Authors,* Vols. 1-4, rev. ed.; and *Dictionary of Literary Biography,* Vol. 68.)

AUTHOR'S COMMENTARY

The hardest books in the world to write are books for young people. They are also by far the most rewarding. Books written by adults, for adults, rarely have any prolonged effect upon their readers, no matter how good they may be. A good book for youngsters can influence the whole future life of the young reader. This is, of course, almost an axiom. Yet it is all too often ignored by writers in this country, and elsewhere. I happen to believe that it is an absolute duty for good

writers to devote a significant part of their time and talent to writing for young people. It is the hardest kind of work, for it demands qualities of honesty that are not essential in an adult book. But it is of absolutely vital importance if basic changes for the good are ever to be initiated in any human culture. God knows, *our* culture desperately needs changing, for the better.

Of course writing for youngsters is not *all* hard work. In truth it can be, and damned well ought to be, good fun too. There ought to be a large ingredient of fun in everything we do. Alas, it is a quality that seems to be of declining value. For me, the writing of young people's books has been fun—and some of the best and most enduring fun I have ever known. It has also brought me, and I hope, my young readers, the feeling that life is very much worth living.

Farley Mowat, "A Message from the Patron," in Ca-nadian Library Journal, Vol. 30, No. 5, September-October, 1973, p. 391.

GENERAL COMMENTARY

EVA MARTIN

As a creator of fiction for children Farley Mowat is not at his artistic best. The dynamic quality and the humour have become weakened in the effort of conjuring fictional characters and situations. Even *Owls in the Family,* an expansion of a chapter in *The Dog Who Wouldn't Be,* though hilarious, and a memorable story has become weakened in the expanding process.

Lost in the Barrens is an adventure story with a good pace although plot and characters are conventional. What redeems the book as a piece of literature is the delineation of its main character—the North. Although much information is packed into each page for the edification of young readers, the North as an indomitable force comes through strongly perhaps because it has all of Mowat's sympathy and understanding, and as a force of nature it cannot be manoeuvred in the way that human characters can be. As the two boys struggle to survive the winter in the barrenlands they are slowly and almost imperceptibly taught by nature that you can only survive in the North on *its* terms. When man fights back he encounters only disaster. In this book, the conventional picture of the barrenness of the land is vanquished forever, for it is seen to be teeming with a great variety of life. It is the kind of survival story that has great appeal, and could definitely sustain its identity as a Canadian piece of literature when read by children in other countries. The sequel. *The Curse of the Viking Grave,* is a disappointment not only to its readers but to the author himself, for he says in a recent article, "It's a lousy book, a really bad piece of work." At its best it is a flimsy plot held together by ordinary, hackneyed conversation.

The Black Joke has great possibilities as a sea adventure. It has the staple ingredients of smugglers and contraband whiskey, an ill-omened sailing ship, a stubborn sea captain and his two adventure-loving sons, and the sea itself, but the characters are so thoroughly conventional (all white or all black) and so obviously manipulated that many of the ingredients are wasted. The action of the plot is not sustained nearly as successfully as that of *Lost in the Barrens.* Also, the sea, which can be as equally destructive to man as the North, does not emerge with anything like the vitality of the latter. Its presence is not felt consistently throughout the book. Conversation between the villagers of Miquelon and the boys is weakened by a forced French dialect which distracts the reader's attention from the matter under discussion. Whatever the flaws in his creative fiction, Farley Mowat makes an honest attempt to provide Canadians with literature that is distinctive in style and content. (pp. 8-9)

> *Eva Martin, "Farley Mowat—'The Dog Who Wouldn't Be'," in* In Review: Canadian Books for Children, *Vol. 2, No. 2, Spring, 1968, pp. 5-10.*

JOS. E. CARVER

When reading any of Mowat's books one is swept along in the descriptions and events of the tale without too much attention to feasibility. It is only in the cold light of criticism that one is forced to be pro or con and then the criticism is always on the correctness of detail, not on the writer's ability to grasp, hold and guide the reader, and it is here and here only that he should be assessed. Mowat is a story teller. His tales appeal to children and to adults. Some of Mowat's "adult" writings will be adopted by children much the same as Swift's *Gulliver's Travels* or Defoe's *Robinson Crusoe,* and the most likely to be adopted first will be *The People of the Deer, Serpents Coil,* and *The Grey Seas Under.* If these are

read beside *Lost in the Barrens, The Curse of the Viking Grave, The Dog Who Wouldn't Be, Owls in the Family,* and *Never Cry Wolf,* the term adult or children's story is soon lost.

Lost in the Barrens and *The Curse of the Viking Grave* are two books that should be judged as one tale of high adventure in the Canadian north. (p. 11)

Possibly there is one criticism that can be raised about these two books. Mowat, as in *The People of the Deer,* (one is led to believe Peetyuk is part of the Ihalmiut tribe) is still emphasizing Canada's role and responsibility to the Indian and Eskimo. Again, however, the criticism cannot remove the fact that they are good stories, well written and exciting. Mowat in his characterization of the young men has painted three individual personalities that one would immediately recognize if they were to come alive. Young people reading this book surely will not question Jamie's naivety in the Angeline-Zabadee issue. Strange that Mowat did not make Jamie as aware of the facts of life as are Peetyuk and Awasin. (p. 12)

[Mowat] still retains his youthful exuberance, curiosity and inventiveness, delights in exaggeration and slapstick humour, loves tall tales and high adventure and writes his stories in this spirit. Understandably he knows children and what they like and can open doors to adventures both credible and entertaining to his young readers. His stories are credible because Mowat wanted to write them to give permanence to the places, loyalties and experiences of his youth; entertaining because the author enjoys the telling of them.

Two books reveal part of Mowat's childhood, *The Dog Who Wouldn't Be,* and *Owls in the Family.* The two primary influences on Mowat's life were his irascible father and his richly gifted dog. . . .

The elder Mowat is cast in the mould of an eccentric, quick-to-anger, but loveable father, but Mutt is a great original and Mowat describes him with love and respect which never drops to sentimentality.

An expansion of a chapter of *The Dog Who Wouldn't Be* is *Owls in the Family.* These are animal stories with one major ingredient—the verbal wit, situation comedy and simple humour of incongruity that children enjoy.

Young and old alike will find humorous the violent, earthy, farcical adventures of the youthful Mowat and his unusual pets. His stories are crammed with situation comedies, practical jokes and boisterous nonsense. In *Owls in the Family,* the teacher Mr. Miller, safe after his death-defying leap from the tree, concludes that owls can count when the murderous attack by a defiant mother results in the total destruction of his carefully constructed and concealed "blind"; the T. Eaton Co. pet parade erupts into an utter shambles when the judges open the box releasing the Surprise Pet, an ancient but venemous-looking rattlesnake; poor unsuspecting Mutt is stalked by the clever Wol, who delights in seizing the dog's tail in his vice-like talons; and humans and animals alike flee in stomach curdling nausea when the uninvited Wol proudly bears his own lunch to the table in the form of a fragrant still-warm skunk.

These hilarious, outlandish, exaggerated incidents presumably would strain the belief of even a ten-year-old. But they do not. Mowat's stories achieve a remarkable credulity that leave his readers chortling in good humoured affection for the ludicrous-looking Mutt; the handsome, sportive Wol and his perfect foil, the melancholy, pensive, little Weeps.

There is more to Mowat than a love for animals and an understanding of Eskimos. It is his love of the sea and seamen, especially the Newfoundlander. *The Grey Seas Under, The Serpent's Coil* and *The Black Joke* are three sea stories that should delight everyone. *Grey Seas* and *Serpent's Coil* have been classed as adult reading and yet these are the very stories I feel that children will adopt. These two stories have the romance of a sea story but with a difference; the role of the real heroes in the war between man and ocean—the salvage tugboatmen—is revealed. (pp. 12-13)

Mowat writes with sensitivity and simplicity, with the skill to create in a few words the effect he seeks. His perceptive mind and eye and his enthusiastic interest contribute to his skill as a writer. His area is limited because almost all of his writing is autobiographical, but he relives his experiences so vividly and exuberantly that the action rings with an authenticity the reader cannot help but enjoy. . . .

As an author Mowat handles dialogue easily and naturally. The characterization of Wol or Mutt is as unique as Awasin, Peetyuk or Captain Featherstone. Perhaps Mowat is sometimes too exuberant and undisciplined in his writing, but since children themselves indulge in fanciful embroidery of factual incidents, they will not be disturbed by occasional heavy-handed exaggeration and overstretching. Indeed these faults are only minor criticisms of books that children will find credible, educational and exciting. (p. 15)

> Jos. E. Carver, "Farley Mowat: An Author for All Ages," in British Columbia Library Quarterly, Vol. 32, No. 4, April, 1969, pp. 10-16.

PATRICIA MORLEY

I have just read, pondered and inwardly digested all four of Farley Mowat's recently reprinted books for young people: *Lost in the Barrens, Owls in the Family, The Black Joke,* and *The Curse of the Viking Grave.* I encountered the same Mowat who had given me pleasure in adult books such as *A Whale for the Killing* and *Wake of the Great Sealers.* . . . No question about it, the man writes well, for any age. He tells a good story, with verve, humour, and a sharp eye for detail. He also manages to convey a feeling for the texture of the Canadian land and its people. . . .

The Black Joke is a modern adventure story with a feeling for the historic traditions of Newfoundland and the sea. Jonathan Spence is having difficulty surviving the Thirties. The villainous store-keeper of the outport . . . hatches a scheme for getting possession of Jonathan's ship. Jonathan loses "Black Joke" through a legal trick, and is badly hurt while attempting to steal his own ship and escape from the authorities in St. Pierre. Rescue depends upon his teen-aged son Peter and nephew Kye. Jonathan's old friend Pierre finds the marooned boys. Pierre and his fisher-friends on the island of Miquelon plan to hijack "Black Joke" as it is bound for the United States with eight hundred cases of contraband liquor. They will hide the liquor and return it only after Jonathan's fine is paid and the ship legally signed over to him once again. When the expected adult help fails to materialize in time, three boys stowaway on the refitted "Black Joke" in a desperate last-minute venture. They set a flash fire which panics the crew and leaves the boys and Captain Smith to battle the flames alone.

Humorously, the American captain is actually relieved to see Pierre and the Miquelon fishermen: " 'Kidnapper, nothin'!' he replied with feeling. 'It was them *kids* done the nappin'. Drove off my crew, hijacked my boat, and damn near got me burned to a crisp into the bargain! Mister, there ain't nothin' you can do to me that they ain't already thought of!' "

True to the spirit of comedy, the villain is at least partly restored to the good graces of the community. . . . (p. 63)

The fast-paced story has all the classical elements of its type: piracy, rum-running, stowaways, and a brief survival episode à la Robinson Crusoe. . . . (p. 64)

The Black Joke, like Mowat's *Owls in the Family,* is slanted to slightly younger readers than is *The Curse of the Viking Grave.* This adventure for adolescents is a sequel to *Lost in the Barrens,* and it has a more melodramatic plot and a more involved narrative than its predecessor. *Lost in the Barrens* is truly a Canadian Crusoe tale, with the subarctic wilderness of northern Manitoba replacing the desert island as setting-*cum*-challenge. Two boys, one Indian and one white, get separated from the Indian party searching for cariboo to feed their starving band. They are marooned when their canoe is shattered by rapids. They rescue one gun, a little ammunition, and some simple tools. Armed with these, and with their determination to survive, they manage to build a cabin and kill and cache a winter's supply of meat. Much of the interest of the book lies in its How-To aspect, as Mowat describes how Jamie and Awasin make everything from lamps to skin parkas and moccasins.

Its other fascination lies in its loving feeling for the animals and the land, and the sense of man's kinship (that word beloved by Charles G. D. Roberts) with this kingdom. The boys kill only what they need to eat; other killing is murder. Animals help to people the land and reduce loneliness. The description of the cariboo herd, flowing forward as irresistibly as the sea itself, has both power and beauty: the boys feel that they have "looked deeply into one of the great mysteries of the animal world."

The sequel features four young people loose in approximately the same area. Mowat likes to get his adults offstage to leave things up to the teen-aged protagonists. Trapper-teacher Angus McNair becomes sick and is hospitalized. His fifteen-year-old nephew Jamie ignores a letter telling him to report to the Child Welfare authorities in Winnipeg, and heads for the Barrens in search of the Viking relics which he had discovered on the earlier expedition with the Chipeweyan, Awasin. There is a third youth, an Anglo-Eskimo called Peetyuk, and Awasin's sister Angeline—a Canadian mosaic. The romantic attraction between Angeline and Peetyuk (played humorously against Jamie's disgust with girls in general) would appeal to adolescents.

Mowat's depiction of Indian and Eskimo life is both sympathetic and humorous. Indian and Eskimo legends are woven into the main story. As in *The Black Joke,* the youths accomplish fantastic and Homeric feats, including shooting the rapids of a river, which no one has achieved before. Somehow it all seems to be possible, while Mowat has us in his spell. In *Lost in the Barrens,* however, there is an interesting incident where natural conditions almost defeat the two boys, and the Indian cautions: " 'If you fight against the spirits of the north you will always lose. Obey their laws, and they'll look after you.' "

There are fine descriptions of animals and of the northland in *The Curse of the Viking Grave,* as in its predecessor. Mowat's technique ranges between humour and, at times, sublimity. . . . (pp. 64-5)

Patricia Morley, "Verve, Humour, and an Eye for Detail," in Canadian Children's Literature, *No. 1, 1975, pp. 63-5.*

SHEILA EGOFF

No definition quite encompasses or fits animals like Mutt, the Prince Albert (?) retriever, the hero of Farley Mowat's *The Dog Who Wouldn't Be,* written for adults and adopted by children, or Wol and Weeps, the equally surprising owls of Mowat's *Owls in the Family,* written for children and adopted by adults. Both books brought joy and exuberance and a sense of fun and mischief into Canadian children's literature.

Mutt, the dog who wouldn't be, was a dog all right, but he was also sensitive to his appearance and to comments made about him. He early learned to avoid trouble with more combative dogs by balancing on the top of back fences; then he graduated to tree and ladder climbing. He was a traveller, sailing on the Saskatchewan River with Farley's father and on land in the Mowat car, suitably dressed in dark glasses. He became the most noted, but not always the most loved, dog in Saskatoon. . . . Death on a back road in eastern Ontario ends his story—the ending does not come as a surprise: it is inevitable. The fast and furious sense of fun has been gradually disappearing and the reality of the ending casts an aura of credibility, even over the bizarre incidents that have gone before.

All the Mowat animals are presented as eccentric individualists, memorable for their refusal to accept the limitations of an animal's life. The truth or untruth of any particular incident is immaterial; disbelief is suspended and the reader does not doubt either the genuineness or the exaggerations of the Mowat way of life. If animals do take on the characteristics of the family with whom they live, then Mutt is completely credible.

Owls in the Family is an extension of one of the episodes in *The Dog Who Wouldn't Be.* No more readily classifiable than its predecessor, it purports to be a factual account of a family and its peculiar pets. The element of realism does exist—the owls are owls and the boys are boys—and there is a sharp sense of prairie sky and sun and cottonwoods. The details are wholly convincing, from the statement 'You can't walk quietly on the poplar bluff because of all the dead sticks underfoot' to the delineation of the contrasted characters of Wol and Weeps—Wol the extrovert and Weeps the introvert. But it is also a fast-moving adventure story about a search for the baby owls, the boys' animal circus, an encounter with the toughest kids in town. Most of all, it is an autobiography, recalling and conveying with humour, sometimes farcical and sometimes wry, a sympathetic but unsentimental feeling for animals and the values the author holds important: generosity, justice, and compassion. And it always rings true, for the boy who recounts the tale is honest and sensitive, and as colloquial as only a boy can be.

Mowat is a natural writer for children. He writes from his own experience, both childhood and adult. With his direct, simple, and lively style he can reveal aspects of life that are necessary in good children's literature if it is to have any enduring value. Qualities such as cruelty, irony, satire—gentled

of course—give life and depth to children's literature and they are present in all Mowat's animal stories. They are implied in the style and confronted squarely in the realistic details. (pp. 141-43)

Alongside Mowat's highly personal narratives, others seem bland. (p. 143)

[In *Lost in the Barrens,*] Mowat's strength lies in the sense of pace and breathless suspense he gives to his tale. The boys almost reel from crisis to crisis. But Mowat is far too good a writer, and he knows the North too well, to strain credibility in the interest of narrative. Beneath the overlay of adventure there is always the solid substance of the North itself and the kind of character development it imposes on those who live there. Awasin, the son of a Cree chieftain, explains to Jamie, the city boy, that one must conform to the North rather than fight it, and so the interest of the story is fundamentally based on the way that adaptation is made rather than on the events that precipitate it.

Mowat's steady hand on the world of reality can be seen even more clearly in his modern pirate story, *The Black Joke.* Here are the hard economic facts of life in the Newfoundland outports in the 1930s. The power of the traders, the father's need to find a profitable cargo so as to retain his ship, form a springboard for the incidents. *The Black Joke* is also a first-class tale of the sea in the grand, a-little-larger-than-life tradition: seafaring boys navigating in stormy waters, brave seamen and scheming merchants, rum-runners and castaways, a fine schooner shipwrecked and seized but brought home safely to port. Mowat's beautifully outrageous imagination is shown particularly in the gusto with which he delineates character. His villains are properly evil. There is even a touch of grandeur about Captain Smith: 'Back to the ship,' he bellowed, 'or I'll drill the rotten lot of you'—an imprecation in the best tradition of pirates' curses. Yet all this is set against a background of precise detail, whether Mowat is describing a Newfoundland outport or catching a salmon or sailing a ship through the fog. The humour in the story is not particularly subtle, though perhaps it is well calculated for its audience. The two young heroes, Peter and Kye, who are capable of doing a man's job in sailing the *Black Joke,* indulge in pranks dear to their age—squirting bilgewater at the unpleasant trader, Mr Barnes, and frying salt pork when he is seasick. The style, as in *Lost in the Barrens,* is simple, exact, and detailed, in the tradition of the plain English of Defoe and Swift. . . . [The pages in which the boys cause an explosion on the *Black Joke* and rout the villains] are probably the most exciting in Canadian children's literature. *The Black Joke* is a latter-day *Treasure Island,* a story whose gusto and toughness are generally lacking in Canadian books for children.

In such works as *Starbuck Valley Winter* and *The Black Joke,* [Roderick] Haig-Brown and Mowat owe most of their success to their respect for their readers. When that fails, craftsmanship falters, as is evident in Mowat's *The Curse of the Viking Grave,* a sequel to *Lost in the Barrens.* A tedious re-working of material is a fault in many sequels, but here the careless writing, lack of attention to detail, and a dull plot (there is not even a good old-fashioned curse) presumably led Mowat himself to describe it as a 'pot-boiler'. (pp. 157-59)

Sheila Egoff, "The Realistic Animal Story," and "Realistic Fiction," in her The Republic of Childhood: A Critical Guide to Canadian Children's Literature in English, *second edition, Oxford Universi-*

ty Press, Canadian Branch, 1975, pp. 133-52, 153-203.

VALERIE WYATT

Farley Mowat has a remarkably humble view of his place—of man's place in general—in the scheme of things. He believes that man is no more and no less important than any of the other animals that inhabit the planet, and he has lived by this philosophy, elaborating on it in his books.

In books such as *A Whale for the Killing* and *Never Cry Wolf* his commitment to the animal world has surfaced with a passion that cannot be ignored by the reader. He also has an unshakable respect for Canada's Native people, evident in such books as *People of the Deer* and *The Desperate People.*

His children's books are an equally important forum for his ideas. In them he succeeds in communicating his love for the creatures around him. "Most children have a good chance of turning into good adults if we can persuade them that man is not the be-all and end-all," he explains. "Anything you can do to give them a healthier appreciation of the world around them is worthwhile." In Mowat's case, that "healthier appreciation" extends to the Indians and Inuit who also people his books for children.

But while respect for the natural environment and for the animals and people who live in harmony with nature is a central theme in all of his books, there is no "crusading" in his books for children. Instead his ideas are developed through humour, as in *Owls in the Family* and *The Dog Who Wouldn't Be,* or mixed with spine-tingling adventure, as in *Lost in the Barrens* and *The Black Joke.*

Many of the details in Mowat's children's books are drawn directly from his own experience. "When I'm not writing, I'm living life so I'll have something to write about," he says. (pp. 98-9)

At present he is thinking about writing another children's book, his first in ten years. Like *Lost in the Barrens,* it will be a survival story, based on the adventures of a young boy marooned on an island in the Gulf of St. Lawrence in the mid-eighteenth century. And as for all of his other books, the plot for it will emerge as he writes it. "Planning a book would be like writing the obituary before the baby is born," he says, explaining his somewhat unorthodox method.

Farley Mowat admits that he has a special affection for his children's books: "The only ones I re-read are the children's books." He has dedicated them to his sons, Robert Alexander and Peter David, with love. If the 28 foreign-language editions of his children's books are any indication, hundreds of thousands of children around the world also have a special affection for them, and eagerly await his new historical adventure. (p. 101)

> *Valerie Wyatt, "Farley Mowat," in* Profiles, *edited by Irma McDonough, revised edition, Canadian Library Association, 1975, pp. 98-101.*

ALEC LUCAS

With such angry books as *People of the Deer, The Desperate People,* and *A Whale for the Killing* among his works, Farley Mowat is scarcely the kind of author one would normally associate with children's books. Yet, faced perhaps with doubts about effecting any changes in attitudes of society through these very books, he has written several stories for young peo-

ple and has spoken out with his usual forthrightness on the importance of such literature. . . . (p. 40)

From early youth Mowat had been interested in creative writing. At first he had addressed himself to the high ambition of serious poetry. Later he took a course in creative writing at university and early in his career published short stories (to be published soon in revised versions in *The Snow Walker*). Moreover, as the critics of many of his adult books (all non-fiction) delight to proclaim, he liked to stretch the truth in them if he did not actually write fiction. In his children's books, Mowat could, then, indulge his imagination without fear of attack and perhaps also find some fulfillment for his desire to write the fiction that seems to have been his early ambition, but that he never quite realized, either because he found the adult novel as then defined unsuited to his way of conceptualizing or to his social purpose. Beyond these conjectures, however, Mowat's children's books (and all are boy's books) demonstrate his desire, on the one hand, to indoctrinate boys with his social concepts and values and, on the other, to retain the pleasant memories of his childhood.

For the most part Mowat skillfully disguises his didactic intent. He hides it under narrative motifs and themes that have to do with wish-fulfillment, with the search for affection and security, with animals as a way of satisfying a child's wish to love and be loved, and with success achieved through brave and noble deeds or through skill and resourcefulness. These motifs and themes are not only those of much adult fiction, but also (especially those relating to deeds) of much of Mowat's non-fiction, despite what would seem radical differences between his juvenile and his adult books. (pp. 40-1)

Like his motifs and themes, Mowat's subjects are the old time-tested children's story standbys of pets and family life, Eskimos, Indians, and pirates, but in his books they take on new life. Mutt and his "owlish" playmates, Wol and Weeps, defy classification with animals and birds. Mowat's Eskimos may be friendly, but they are far from the fat-cheeked and jolly creatures of the general run of children's books about them, and his Indians live as Indians, not as noble savages, or as blood-thirsty warriors, or as sentimentalized vanishing Americans. Vanishing they may be, but Mowat is indignant rather than sentimental about their plight. Mowat's "pirates" are boys, and their booty, far from the usual, is a treasure-trove of bootleg whiskey!

The settings of Mowat's stories have a freshness about them. His northland is far more realistic than Ballantyne's, E. R. Young's, and Oxley's, and there is also a convincing verisimilitude about the maritime world of *The Black Joke.* As for the animal stories, Mowat relieves his childhood in them and has simply to recreate, not invent, their settings. The fact that Mowat wrote from experience may limit his scope somewhat, but it makes his books more vivid and more interesting. He is no arm-chair naturalist or yacht-club seaman. He lived in the Canadian North and sailed the eastern seaboard and the coasts of Newfoundland, and he succeeds in imparting his knowledge of and feeling for these regions in his stories.

If Mowat is impressive for his handling of his settings, subjects, and themes, he is no less so for his skill as a story-teller and for the liveliness of his humour. He creates suspense by hinting at future events or by withholding information and by dramatizing or describing exciting episodes in which disaster is only a hair's breadth away. As is standard, also, in fiction of event, the characters are types with just enough individuality to set them apart from each other, but not so much as to preclude the reader's identification with them, or to hinder the flow of the narrative. Mowat is little concerned with analyzing personality. His interest centres on the physical world and the life of action. This interest unquestionably attracts young readers, but it also seems to have contributed much to the popularity of his books for adults. (pp. 41-2)

To teach and to delight have long been the aims of literature, but with such early writers of children's books as Traill, Ballantyne, Young, and Saunders, "fun" scarcely ever reached the level of humour, and then only as the cute or farcical. With Mowat "fun," especially in his animal stories, means hijinks, eccentric characters, and a flavouring of satire.

Mowat's first juvenile book, *Lost in the Barrens,* is obviously a by-product of *People of the Deer.* Both are set in the Keewatin District, the barren lands west of Hudson Bay. Both aim not only at creating sympathy for the aborigines of the north, but also at a greater understanding of the north itself and the way of life appropriate to it. It could be argued that *Lost in the Barrens* represents Mowat's response to the failure of officialdom to take prompt and appropriate action following his *exposé* in *People of the Deer* of their inadequacies. An indignant book aimed at immediate remedies, it had received indignant replies in its turn. *Lost in the Barrens,* by the very nature of its genre, is a more moderate book than *People of the Deer,* and though it takes its stand on the same issues, it puts its trust in a future when its young readers, having become adults, will help bring about a changed attitude toward our native peoples. Jamie, a white city boy, and Awasin, a young Indian, survive a winter on the barrens only because the "inventiveness" of the former complements the "experience" of the latter. The combination of the strength of each enables them to cope with injury, illness, storms, and bone-freezing frosts, though they do benefit, too, from the good offices of coincidence or "the spirits of the north," whereby they discover a hidden valley replete with trees and wintering caribou, not to mention the two huskies that seek refuge with them or Peetyuk's igloo that they happen to find just in time to thwart death in a raging blizzard. And, through it all, Jamie learns what Awasin has always known, but what "white men don't as a rule." "If you fight against the spirits of the north you will always lose," Mowat admonishes. "Obey their laws and they'll look after You." Mowat's Indians are not redskin varmints like many in Ballantyne's stories who ungraciously, with white man's firearms, make life difficult for those who bear the white man's burden, nor do they resemble Young's, who are innocents waiting for the word of the Lord. . . . Mowat's Indians in *Lost in the Barrens* are simply human beings with values and customs of their own, living their everyday lives, fishing, hunting, feasting or, when called on, lending a hand to their white friends. (pp. 42-3)

The most distinguished section of the book by far, however, revolves around the boys' lives in Hidden Valley. Mowat, like Defoe, could make the most of a situation in which man and nature meet, not as rivals but as partners. Although storms blow violently in Hidden Valley, it is always cosy in the cabin, thanks to human ingenuity and to nature's bounty in supplying food and fuel and, as evidence of even greater largess, a caribou fawn so that the boys have an opportunity to satisfy their "wish to love and to be loved," the motif of so many pet animal stories. The wolves kill the fawn to Jamie's angry re-

gret, but not to Awasin's, for, as he informs Jamie, "wolves have to eat."

Mowat, again like Defoe, also made the most of a deep psychological realism by describing minutely all the boys' activities in building their wilderness home, getting in their supplies, making their clothes, building their fires, and cooking their meals. Hidden Valley resembles Ballantyne's Silver Lake in *Silver Lake, or Lost in the Snow,* but in Ballantyne's northern Eden the children (a brother and a sister) live almost idyllically, playing house as it were—such was the influence of home, sweet home, in an age of great migration—and enjoy their winter sports of sliding and tobogganing. (They even delight in washing in the clear water of the lake—after they reach it on their snow-shoes in sub-zero weather.) Indeed, they live as happily as the British lads who, in Young's *Winter Adventures of Three Boys in the Great Lone Land,* turn the north into vacationland.

Mowat's boys never live so luxuriously as Ballantyne's and Young's. Their activities resemble the initiation rites of an adolescent Indian as they pass through the hardships of their winter's isolation on the barrens. Ballantyne's and Young's books were addressed to the nineteenth-century British; Mowat's, to the twentieth-century Canadians. On the surface the central theme of the book may appear to be that of survival, but Mowat celebrates no such negative concept, not the merits of mere dogged persistency, for beneath the surface lies evidence that he has dedicated his story to positive values through which one asserts a joy in the vitality of living.

Mowat has unified the different elements in his story with a variation of the epic quest for home as a central motif. Mrs. Traill had introduced this kind of quest into Canadian children's literature with *Canadian Crusoes,* but in her book the children are truly lost—she had drawn on a local and contemporary event—and are only saved through their faith in divine guidance. Ballantyne in *Silver Lake, or Lost in the Snow* follows Mrs. Traill in suggesting that prayer and faith in divine guidance are instrumental in saving the children. Jamie and Awasin in *Lost in the Barrens,* however, triumph largely through faith in themselves and an ability to adjust to their environment—though the supernatural ("the spirits of the north") comes to their aid, not because of the efficacy of prayer, but of common sense. (pp. 43-4)

In *Lost in the Barrens,* breeding does not count, even if race does; the boys succeed largely because of "good sense," "hard work," and self-reliance, as Horatio Alger's boys did in the world of office and factory. Though not interested in the same kind of "success", Mowat's adolescents are cut from the same cloth as Alger's, and their achievement demonstrates two typically North American faiths—that self-reliance counts above all and that luck comes to those who earn it.

Ten years after *Lost in the Barrens,* Mowat turned to the north again in another book for boys, *The Curse of the Viking Grave.* Like the former, it also stems from a preceding adult's book, in this case a history, *Westviking.* *Lost in the Barrens* won a Governor-General's Award among other honours and, according to Egoff, became "one of the few Canadian children's books that have achieved an international reputation." No such acclaim awaited *The Curse of the Viking Grave.* Even Mowat called it "a lousy book, a really bad piece of work," and despite D. H. Lawrence's dictum, "Never trust the author." Mowat can be trusted here.

All the ingredients of *The Curse of The Viking Grave*—

Illustration by Paul Galdone from The Dog Who Wouldn't Be.

sizzling caribou chops over cheery campfires, dangerous rivers, ancient treasures, Indian and Eskimo hunters—ought to have produced another exciting tale. But the book proves the conjurer's old adage, "never twice," for Mowat seems to have lost his magic in it. Perhaps he was exhausted after the big book *Westviking,* or perhaps *Lost in the Barrens* had expended his imaginative capital as regards the north.

The Curse of the Viking Grave again uses quest and chase to create suspense and achieve unity. The heroics of Jamie, Awasin, Peetyuk, and this time Marie, Awasin's sister, derive from a trek to a mysterious viking tomb to secure treasures buried there and at the same time to avoid the RCMP officers who are out to get their man, Jamie—to send him back to school in the south. Not even the RCMP can stir up much excitement, however, for Mowat has too palpable a design upon the reader. Again there is a plea for understanding of the natives who, as the fellowship of the travellers proves, are worthy people by any standard worth holding by white civilization. In this book, however, Mowat has a new cause to take up. He is convinced that the vikings once settled in northern Canada. He accepts the Kensington Stone (and the Beardmore relics) as genuine and as almost certain proof of the viking presence there, as the long recitations of viking legends in the book demonstrate. Even if justified as history, they clog the narrative, for Mowat drags them in as support of a theory and not as part of the plot. The story involving the police trails off completely early in the book, and the story of the treasure hunt loses itself in a thicket of anthropological and geographical details. Furthermore, no account could carry the weight of the description of an almost interminable journey through country that is endlessly the same, particularly since, from the very beginning, the treasure seems hardly worth the trouble, even if it is to be sold to help the native cause, and since the awful curse of the Eskimo medicine man seems little more than a joke to the young people.

Mowat's attempt to write a thriller about the north fails because the story proper is mainly a travelogue and hence lacks any dramatic tension. "Where do the characters go next?" is a bare substitute for "what do they do next?" or "what happens next?" as a narrative device. Moreover the characters do not have the personalities to supply the interest that the plot lacks. They are theme-ridden, Jamie obviously acting as

spokesman for the author when, early in the book, he cries out against white man's indifference and injustice towards the Cree Indians: "Jamie clenched his hands, wadded the letter into a ball and flung it onto the ice. There was bitter defiance in his voice. '*My* people? They aren't mine! They'd let the whole lot of you die without lifting a hand to help. Don't call them *my* people, Alphonse!' " The romance between Peetyuk and Marie is out of place, cute, and heavily propagandistic. Fiction with four protagonists, no villains, and two adolescent lovers sets up obstacles that *The Curse of the Viking Grave* never overcomes.

Mowat's only other adventure story, *The Black Joke,* is a tale of the sea, but, unlike the books set in the north, it centres on the struggles of man with man, not man in nature. If it lacks the psychological insight that the experience of the two boys in their winter camp reveals, it does not have to carry any of the kind of message that *The Curse of the Viking Grave* collapses under. Mowat again makes heroes of the unsophisticated—this time of the Newfoundland fishermen with their skills as seamen and their inherent loyalty and honesty. In *The Black Joke,* however, the qualities he admires are implicit in the story, so that it contains little upstage moralizing.

If the northern books gave the teen-ager a chance to "play" Indian, *The Black Joke,* the story of a boat, lets him identify with three modern boy "pirates" who rescue her from the rum-runners and restore her to her rightful owner, the father of one of these good "pirates." The story focuses on a plot leading to a typical "virtue triumphant" conclusion thanks to the shrewdness and derring-do of the three boys (this time a white, his white-Indian cousin, and a French boy) who prove too much for a whole crew of rum-runners.

The northern books, though stories of event, do not depend on the conflict between hero and villain for their interest. Mowat prefers a positive and general approach to the virtues of the northern people over one in which he would set out the weaknesses of the white man in his treatment of the aborigines by selecting some individual trader or trapper as a villain. Not that the white men were not worthy of the role, but Mowat avoided isolating one for such a part; he feared he would run the risk of defeating his purpose of revealing the general callousness or indifference of the white man outside the world of the natives, if he based his attack on the specific evils of an individual within it. He wishes most of all to disclose the attitudes, customs, and values of a good society, the members of which he thinks have long been treated as inferior citizens. Only once he toys with the idea of a villain—strangely, an Indian—who falls from grace apparently because he made improper proposals to Marie, destined by love (and theme) for Peetyuk, a white-Eskimo.

In *The Black Joke,* white villains take centre stage. Mowat has no need here to concentrate on enlightening the reader about a different way of life in a primitive society. Twice he alludes to the running sore of social injustice by which a government declares as contraband cheap food that could have been a godsend to the impoverished outports of Newfoundland during the Depression era, but otherwise he comes at the problem indirectly by devising a story and by creating characters who in themselves demonstrate the evils of modern materialism—Barnes, a business man (the standard whipping boy for such purposes in fiction), who secretly arranges to seize Jonathan Spence's *Black Joke,* a French judge who puts money above the law and Jonathan's rights, and Smith, a blow-hard American rum-runner, who indirectly controls all three. Mowat squares accounts somewhat with two good Frenchmen (Basques and poor fishermen), but the business man, the lawyers, and the American have no similar counter-balances, although Bill Smith's brave deeds (and his admiration of the three boys for their boldness) "redeem" the American in the end. There are no subtleties here. Mowat makes no attempt to analyze his views; he assumes their validity. The good guys and the bad, all type, static characters like those of most juvenile fiction, are clearly distinguishable, and the issues—unsophisticated integrity and honesty versus sophisticated chicanery and avarice—are no less obvious, despite the fact that the boys set fire to the *Black Joke.* They act for justice, for true law and order and, in doing so, enable the honest poor of Newfoundland to defeat the less morally pure privileged and wealthy who would subjugate them to economic serfdom. Even in his children's books Mowat did not hesitate to deride establishment values.

As Canadian children's books go, *The Black Joke* belongs in the "rough and tough" school. Yet the boys do have a chance to have some fun on the island of Miquelon. They fish and hunt and, moreover, learn that, as Awasin had also admonished, "It is not good to kill more than one needs." In such comments, however, Mowat leaves "need" undefined, perhaps because hunters belong with his red-blooded men of action, or because he still has a yen for hunting himself, associated as it is with his youthful years in Saskatchewan. For all that, his children's books disclose his intense interest in the natural world, not as romantic love of the pretty or as awe of grandeur, but as a sincere appreciation of the whole dynamic process it manifests. In the books about the north he tries to inculcate something of the feeling that vast land with its rivers, lakes, caribou, and Eskimos invoked in him. *The Black Joke* reveals a similar fascination with the sea and the fishermen who meet its challenge knowingly, yet unflinchingly, in their daily lives, and the story ends, after all its turbulence, with a tribute to their world:

> The wind was fresh from the southeast. Under the combined power of her sails and her diesel engine, *Black Joke* was soon logging a full twelve knots. It was still daylight when she began to close with the shores of Newfoundland. The massive sea-cliffs rose up close ahead, and the roar of bursting seas echoed back from the great rocks. Snoring through the water, the black-hulled ship bore down through the shadows of the evening.
>
> *Black Joke* was home at last.

This is the traditionally happy ending of children's stories. Simon Barnes's black joke has failed, turned back on him as it has been by the clever and brave boys. Yet it is more than a formula ending or a variant of the epic conclusion in which the long absent traveller finally returns home. It hints at Mowat's sympathy with the way of life of what he calls the "natural" man—the "simple life" as it is termed in the so-called agrarian myth. If the books about Indians and Eskimos speak for the pleasure of escape into the natural world, *The Black Joke,* the other side of the coin, implies the pleasure of escape from corrupted urban life.

Mowat has written four books about animals. Of these the publisher has classified "For Young Readers" only *Owls in the Family.* Yet since it is a sequel to *The Dog Who Wouldn't Be,* the latter also, as Egoff notes, belongs in the same category. *Never Cry Wolf* and *A Whale for the Killing,* despite being animal stories, however, are books for adult readers, for their subject concerns the adult world and the cause of conservation of natural wildlife.

Within the genre of the animal story, *The Dog Who Wouldn't Be* belongs to the very popular class in which pets are the protagonists. Among the celebrated of the kind is *Beautiful Joe,* Marshall Saunder's earnest and emotional plea for prevention of cruelty to animals, but other books about pets have had their day. Ballantyne's *The Dog Crusoe* is a boy-and-dog story that extols Crusoe largely as a faithful servant. E. R. Young's *Hector, My Dog* is the autobiography of a dog that seems fully converted to the Christian belief. At least, Hector concludes his story with a long rumination about death and his hopes of reaching heaven so that he can continue to love his master. Finally, in Callaghan's *Luke Baldwin's Vow,* Dan, an old dog, is central in a pattern of moral symbols.

Mowat's book stands apart from these and from Roberts's and Seton's stories with their attempts to examine animal psyche and character. It could be argued easily that Mowat satirizes all of these in his book, for it treats light-heartedly and even irreverently everything that they took so seriously, that Mutt, the animal hero or anti-hero (the very name suggests anti-elitism), embodies Mowat's own sense of fun in a world of make-believe, or that Mutt and Wol reflect something of the revolt against the *status quo* of the time as the dogs of the earlier books reflected the attitudes of their day and age.

Whatever the matrix of *The Dog Who Wouldn't Be,* on the surface it is an animal-cum-family children's story that has proved very popular. Although it has won no awards, it has gone through many editions and, like several other of Mowat's books, has become a favourite in Russia. Written in the first person about the author's childhood, it allows both the child and the adult reader to identify with the story teller's "I," as wish-fulfillment for the one in a world of mischievous but affectionate pets, and as a detour into the past for the other, for there is a common denominator in the autobiography of childhood lacking in that of maturity. Actually the book is broken-backed, for the protagonist, Mutt, fades from the middle of the story for some eighty pages. Because the book is episodic and anecdotal, the break does little harm, however, especially since the story never slackens pace from its remarkable *in medias res* beginning, whether Mutt, Father, or the owls are in the spotlight.

Lost in the Barrens, with its crises, issues, and serious purpose had no place for humour, nor had *The Curse of the Viking Grave* or *The Black Joke,* except for a practical joke or two, played against a shy lover in the former and, of course, against the villains in the latter. It is quite otherwise in *The Dog Who Wouldn't Be,* with its alleged recreation of events and people from the writer's happy, boisterous boyhood. Much of the humour is tongue-in-cheek, and, indeed, the whole story is a tall tale, for Mowat describes a dog who uses a diving board to go swimming, who climbs trees, fences, ladders, and mountains, and who challenges the very science of biology with his chattering teeth. This principle of exaggeration leads most frequently to slap-stick scenes, which Mowat occasionally garnishes with fine dialect dialogue, as when Mr. Couzinsky describes his experience with the acrobatic Mutt. "I stand there painted," he explains, "and nowhere looking when it comes up between the legs. Dat dug! Oh my, dat dug! I yomp, what else?"

The verbal, descriptive, and situational humour of *The Dog Who Wouldn't Be* is never subtle. Unfortunately the verbal humour is sometimes forced or obnoxiously prurient, and the descriptive and situational is hackneyed (at least in the tired old "dog and skunk confrontation") or coarse (as when Mutt falls foul of a cormorant in its nest). Humour of character often combines with humour of situation in *The Dog Who Wouldn't Be* in the battle of the sexes (as it does much less successfully in *The Black Joke*) during the mild skirmishes between Father and Mother Mowat, but especially in Father Mowat's misadventures afield and afloat. Although they are not the bland and sentimentalized parents of many children's stories, they are traditional, however, in that their ancestors have had long and distinguished careers in life-with-father comedies—a naive wife (who thinks Mutt chases cows because beef is a "dreadful price"), a blustering husband (who loves boats but moves to the dust-bowl prairies), and a precocious child (who acts as innocent commentator, observer, and prankster). All of these make for the fun Mowat has—hilarious is a favourite work word with the critics—but it is Mutt, not the father in the familiar roles of green-horn nimrod or sailor or foolish eccentric, nor the owls, who gives the story distinction.

For one thing Mutt is no ordinary dog. "His hind legs moved at a slower speed than did his front ones. This was theoretically explicable on the grounds that his hind legs were much longer than his forelegs—but an understanding of this explanation could not dispel the unsettling impression that Mutt's forward section was slowly and relentlessly pulling away from the tardy after-end." For another thing there are Mutt's ingenious methods of dealing with trouble: by lying on his back and waving his legs when he fights, or, like Roberts's Red Fox, by running away along the fence-tops. But most noteworthy are Mutt's achievements (as a Prince Albert retriever) when he frightens the ducks from the blind or herds them ashore for his sportsmen masters in scenes that illustrate Mowat's ability to recreate situations with remarkable vividness.

Essentially, *The Dog Who Wouldn't Be* is a modern beast fable. Although neither typically allegorical nor heavily moralistic, it fits the genre, for it employs an animal to satirize man. Aside from the family comedy, there are inklings of a deeper satiric intent, also, in Mowat's grumbling about Ontario's lack of culture and Paul Sazalski's shrewd business practices: here Mowat, the social critic, surfaces too obviously. But it is Mutt who focuses the irony of the story. If, as Mowat says, Mutt is not human, he has, mingled with the canine, many of the characteristics of the human. Like a small boy he dislikes to wash (and so furtively swallows the soap), eats cherries and spits out their pits (against all rules of etiquette), and chews gum and swallows it (much to Mother's disapproval). As a naive actor he unconsciously makes a mockery of hunting, that holy of holies activity of the outdoors man. He dislikes rising in the cold dawn, he plays a practical joke on the hunters to the benefit of the hunted when he bounces from the duck blind before the firing starts (and it is he who saves the wounded ducks and geese from a slow death), and he even retrieves a mounted grouse from a hardware store, whereby his master saves face in a boastful and silly bet. Finally Mutt enables the son (and the reader) to learn of the father's pretentiousness and false pride and, along with Wol and Weeps, is the vehicle for an irony that pokes good-natured fun at the adult world. Although Mutt's innocence may be Tom Sawyerlike, Mutt does make a case

for astute, individualistic behaviour as against mere eccentricity. For all his extraordinary ways as animal, Mutt makes more sense than the master of the house. Again, when, at the end of the book, a truck kills Mutt, it brings an animal story to a sad conclusion, but it also seems to imply much about this technological age. (pp. 44-9)

Owls in the Family is . . . more than sequel, for not only are the characters identical, but so also are many of the scenes, probably the result of the pleasures of memory rather than a flagging imagination. The owls are good copy, besides, and are never cute and cuddly, and play some very good scenes— Wol contributes a dead skunk to a dinner party, frightens a visiting minister, disrupts a French class, and plays squeeze-tail with poor Mutt. Many of the bizarre events have as common denominator not only the farcical but also the satiric overtones of *The Dog Who Wouldn't Be.* The trick of breaking up the Eaton's parade with a rattlesnake hidden in a box is more than trick. It is a joke played on a tinselly society, for until the box is opened, the "special pet in reserve" wins great praise from a successful business man as "smart merchandising." Actually Mowat speaks out directly once about his conviction that man is an inferior animal, Wol killing only out of need and man out of greed and his aggressiveness, he says, though he must have had war, not hunting, in mind in making the comment. But even iconoclast Mowat has not gone unscathed among modern socio-literary critics. Apparently he has been rocking only one side of the boat with his criticism of middle-class attitudes, for his *Owls in the Family* has recently been singled out for attack for its allegedly stereotyped, bourgeois attitude toward a black boy.

Despite Mutt's highly anthropomorphic traits, Mowat readily secures a willing suspension of disbelief because of the vigour of his narrative and humour, and because the whole story is a wonderful spoof that discloses some inner truths about man and his little ways. *Owls in the Family* maintains the same realistic-fanciful (if not fantastical) perspective, as *The Dog Who Wouldn't Be* but since owls, unlike dogs, are neither familiar pets nor common literary subjects, the remarkable antics and habits of Wol, the brashly confident, and Weeps, the timid (whose role it is to win sympathy for the animal world), add something to the book as realism, but they do not and cannot reveal (few readers having the knowledge needed as a standard of reference) the outlandish imagination that enabled Mowat to make Mutt so attractive and original.

If natural history goes awry in Wol's deliberately calling crows, acting as a mother prairie chicken, or failing to remember "whether he had finished his dinner or not," it certainly does not go astray in the western setting. Here, as in the descriptions of hunting in *The Dog Who Wouldn't Be,* Mowat's feeling for nature comes through clearly. The search for the owl's nest, to give one example, bears witness to the fact.

Some of Mowat's success depends on the choice of suitable themes, but much more depends on his talent in dramatizing them, on his lively descriptions of settings and situations, and on the verve of his narrative and humour. In short, on his prowess as a story teller. Beyond the wit, the farce, and the melodrama, the excitement and the fun, however, Mowat shows a seriousness of purpose: on the one hand he is in sympathy with the down-trodden and abused, and, on the other, he is out of sympathy with white society. Moreover, if his human characters sometimes support stereotyped concepts about certain aspects of human behaviour, his animals never do. They echo the anti-establishment attitude of some of his books for adults. One may disagree with Mowat's views, but it is they that contribute much of the intensity that makes his children's books far superior to the general run in our literature. (pp. 49-50)

Alec Lucas, "Farley Mowat: Writer for Young People," in Canadian Children's Literature, *Nos. 5-6, 1976, pp. 40-51.*

MARGERY FISHER

[*Lost in the Barrens* and *The Curse of the Viking Grave*] have worn well by virtue of a forceful narrative style and a strikingly authentic picture of the Canadian Arctic. Here two boys—orphaned Jamie, whose trapper uncle has trained him well, and his friend Awasin, a Cree Indian with the expertise of his tribe—call on all their courage and skill first to survive an unexpected winter in the wild and then to find again and preserve for posterity, against some opposition, a priceless archaeological treasure. Behind the compulsive detail and strong movement of the book lies a theme, of man's duty to the past, expressed in terms of Indians, Eskimos and white Canadians.

Margery Fisher, in a review of "Lost in the Barrens," and "The Curse of the Viking Grave," in Growing Point, *Vol. 18, No. 2, July, 1979, p. 3560.*

RICHARD ROTERT

Mortal existence remains our enigmatic and most elemental success. It is a spiritual triumph serving as the basis from which all other derive. Once infused with this magical phenomenon, maintaining it becomes the real trick. Still reserved for the fittest, survival has redefined the attributes of its beneficiaries to revere the cognitive as well as physical qualities. The fight to live is won by knowledge as well as knuckles, by brain as well as brawn. Intelligently circumventing a potential disaster occasions elation, self-confidence, and a prolonged life. It is this confidence which animates the accomplished characters in Farley Mowat's books, which are anthologies of survival techniques disguised as wilderness adventure stories.

As author and naturalist, Farley Mowat documents human and phenomenological natures without the perspective altering prejudices of the romantic or the clinician. His observations reveal his boyhood interest in biology and extensive travels in the arctic, two occupations which involved him directly with the environment. Mowat maintains in his twenty-five books that communion with the environment is humanity's primary, if not ultimate, apotheosis. He is skeptical of modern influences, both tangible and theological, neither of which is required for spiritual experience. Actually, they have interposed themselves between man and his previous wilderness experience, thus setting man apart from and at odds with the natural world and, consequently, with his own nature as well. These impositions insidiously have become the terms by which man now defines himself, heedless of prior ties to the natural world which, for Mowat, is man's genuine source of sustenance and inspiration.

When stranded at sea in a raging hurricane or blinded by a whiteout at the top of the world, Mowat's characters rely on knowledge of natural phenomena to secure their survival. Neither heroes nor prophets, they understandably look to the land for solutions to their terrestrial problems rather than ap-

pealing to metaphysical systems. For, in Mowat's understanding, the tundra, prairie, and open sea are more than just backdrops for the visitation of man-made furies that destroy the calm. These wilderness settings also proffer salvation to those would-be victims who, by their resourcefulness, are able to fashion alternatives to catastrophe. They prevail by aligning their native intelligence with the forces at large rather than by physically struggling against them. The resultant complementary relationship reveals the best of both man and his natural environment. . . . Demonstrating a familiarity with nature once common to all mankind, and now represented by his admired Eskimos and Indians, Mowat's survivors seem anachronistic, especially in this era of vanishing human competence in the wild. (pp. 22-3)

Mowat's wilderness characters elude a form of "cultural irreversibility," as described by Robert Ardrey in *The Hunting Hypothesis,* by clearing a man's evolutionary backtrail of cultural obstacles which frustrate inquiry into fundamental principles. Ardrey suggests that dependence upon a cultural adaptation, say the hand-held hatchet, heralds the physical loss of a biological adaptation which provides the same function, in this case the elongated canine tooth once common to humanoids. Once in motion, this process disallows a return to the previous state, thus reinforcing dependence upon the new. On a broader scale, Mowat shows that man has broken from the natural world by creating his own supportive environment and beliefs. These cultural modifications deny man's return to the instinctual realm, and even recognition of that original existence in the wilderness. Consequently a gulf exists between contemporary societies and the knowledge and talents made obsolete by their creation. Farley Mowat spans that cultural Rubicon with his writing, whereby the reader regains some understanding of that primal land, and of those travelers, ourselves, who crossed it, and of our capacity for spiritual triumphs in this existential world. (pp. 25-6)

Richard Rotert, "Farley Mowat in the Wilderness," in Triumphs of the Spirit in Children's Literature, *edited by Francelia Butler and Richard Rotert, Library Professional Publications, 1986, pp. 21-6.*

LOST IN THE BARRENS (1956)

Across northern Canada stretch the Barrens, a region of swamps in summer and windswept, ice-encrusted plains in winter. Into this forbidding country, young Jamie Macnair and his Cree friend Awasin accompany a hunting party of desperate Chipeweyans—the tribe of the Deer Eaters. The boys are separated from the rest of the group, and, with winter coming, are forced to hole up. How they face up to their predicament and learn—the hard way—to go along with nature rather than to fight it is the main theme. Illuminating it are the struggle for life's necessities; encounters with caribou, wolverine, grizzly bear and supposedly hostile Eskimos; and the discovery of Viking cairns.

Survival in the wilds has been a favorite theme since *Robinson Crusoe.* Here Farley Mowat develops it skillfully. . . . [He] seems to know all there is to know about the Barrens—as well as a good deal about human nature under stress. An engrossing, well-constructed tale, sharp with the tang of the north land.

Howard Boston, "Fight for Survival," in The New York Times Book Review, *August 12, 1956, p. 24.*

Few children can resist a good adventure story, and *Lost in the Barrens* is one of the best. Young readers will find themselves living through the struggle for survival which is forced on Jamie and his young Indian friend, Awasin. . . . And, in the process, they will learn more about Indian-white relations and gain a new respect for Canada's North. A popular and exciting book for readers in grades 4 to 6.

> *A review of "Lost in the Barrens," in* Children's Book News, *Toronto, Vol. 2, No. 1, June, 1979, p. 2.*

The sting of danger and the possibility of real emotional change are limited in the average disaster-adventure. This limitation is perhaps more surprising in books where the sensitive areas of personality are still relatively uncomplicated by experience and should therefore be more accessible to the author's scrutiny. Most often a boy or girl will emerge from a period of stress or endurance, whether with cold or heat, flood or fire, very much the same as before, springing back easily like new elastic to a former shape, and a sense of experience, if it is present, is more likely to come from the interaction of personality than from the influence of natural forces in a particular place.

It is rarely that we find a situation like the one described by Farley Mowat in *Lost in the Barrens,* where two boys lost in the Canadian Arctic have to find a way to survive the winter *in relation to* the land itself. Jamie Macnair, at sixteen, has a certain knowledge of the country, for he has already been trapping with his uncle for a year: his friend Awasin, a Cree Indian, has a deeper knowledge with which he can correct the Canadian boy's impetuosity and self-confidence. While they usefully complement each other's skills in camping and hunting, they are not truly equal until Jamie has realised for himself that their attempt at a winter journey was ill-advised. . . . Farley Mowat does not press the point but the book, as an active and exciting adventure, is expanded by the hint that Jamie has had an experience beyond the physical challenge. (pp. 318-19)

> *Margery Fisher, "Techniques of Description," in her* The Bright Face of Danger, *The Horn Book, Inc., 1986, pp. 318-44.*

Lost In The Barrens is an adventure story which rivals *The Boy Scout Handbook* (originally written by another renowned naturalist, Ernest Thompson Seton) in techniques which make life in the wild not only possible, but unexpectedly comfortable. The young orphan Jamie Macnair leaves the metropolis of Toronto for the north Canadian home of his uncle. Embracing the uncustomarily harsh and invigorating lifestyle, Jamie soon gains a companion in Awasin, a young Cree Indian boy who is to be Jamie's tutor to the ways of the wilderness. Braving the subarctic environment and their supposed enemy, the Eskimo, the pair join a starving Chipeweyan hunting party headed for the Barrenlands. A broken promise, an unresisted temptation and a boat-shattering mishap strand the partners in unknown, hostile territory. In the ensuing months of hardship, as Jamie and Awasin overcome each travail and threat to life, Mowat treats the reader to a trove of wilderness lore and logic.

Initially, Jamie is representative of "civilized" men whose primary needs are furnished by society and who, separated from nature, orient themselves by concrete curbs rather than compass points and game trails. He is of the city, that closed system of anthropocentric rationality whose principles are in-

consequential when dealing with the laws of the wilderness. Though a capable individual, Jamie lacks "insight into the course of nature," and ironically would fail for want of the knowledge once common to his ancestors.

When injured and undone by the apparent futility of his predicament, Jamie prematurely resigns himself to destruction. . . . Jamie's fear, the precipitate of his ignorance, is the precondition of his failure.

But these same circumstances warrant a different, more informed conclusion from his talented companion who has retained his ancestral acumen: "As Awasin looked critically over the collection he felt almost confident. There was enough equipment here for any real woodsman to make a living for several weeks at least." It is characteristic of Mowat's works to demonstrate fate as sealed not by external or celestial forces, but rather by one's resourcefulness. Calm decision-making under pressure is allied to personal proficiency, and truly our every outcome lies "not within our stars, but within ourselves."

Because of his familiarity with nature, Awasin repeatedly avoids impending crises. . . . (pp. 23-4)

Misfortunes occur, of course, but the boys prevail and experience euphoric interludes as their confidence increases with their developing talents. And their elation is at a high when they finally encounter the reputedly savage Eskimos who in reality prove hospitable and gracious. From this direct interaction with phenomenological realities, Jamie and Awasin establish self-reliance, a spiritual high, which liberates them from mischievous fate and fallacy, reaffirming man's station as a part of this world, and not apart from it. (p. 24)

> *Richard Rotert, "Farley Mowat in the Wilderness," in* Triumphs of the Spirit in Children's Literature, *edited by Francelia Butler and Richard Rotert, Library Professional Publications, 1986, pp. 21-6.*

Typically (and especially in Canada) [North American] adventure stories link two teenage boys, one white and one native, against the challenge of the frontier. Almost always, the native boy, seen through the white boy's eyes, is romanticized as the teacher of lessons: He is wise in the lore of the wilds, patient, stoic, in tune with nature. The white boy, made vulnerable by the threatening wilderness, learns to be less impulsive or greedy, and to absorb some (but never all) of the native wisdom of the earth.

These stories are eagerly read by youngsters seeking a straight-forward, energetic plot. All, however, are marred by bad or hasty writing, a crude sense of character development, and a flatly exterior view of North American natives.

Farley Mowat's *Lost in the Barrens* avoids condescension but shows signs of hasty writing; some excruciating clichés ("fairly stuttering with excitement") are repeated twice or more, and there are constant jarring lacunae in the time structure of the narrative. Jamie MacNair, seventeen, is eating dinner with his Cree friend Awasin when someone rushes in with the news that a party of Chipewayans has been sighted an hour's distance away. Awasin "bolts his dinner" and runs outside to meet "the Chips," who seem to have miraculously arrived on the instant.

Perhaps adventure stories of this ilk are written at the same furious clip at which they are meant to be devoured ("It took a moment for the idea to register on Jamie's mind, then it registered. A wave of excitement swept over him. Here was the possibility of a real adventure"). Clichés speed the action along with no need for the reader to linger over details or atmosphere. The point, in any case, is not to enter into the characters or their world—the depth isn't there—but to learn something of the survival techniques that keep the boys alive in the harsh landscape of the barrens.

The same lessons are taught in *Frozen Fire* by James Houston. . . . Again, we have the flattering physical description so familiar from adult thrillers and detective novels. . . . (pp. 137-38)

These descriptions are a lazy shorthand: They tell the reader whom to admire, and absolve him from the imaginative work of learning about the hero's character. However, like Mowat, Houston offers a convincing friendship between the two boys, who overcome the cultural gulf that divides them, with the added pleasure of their growing skill and competence as they defy all odds to survive. Compared to the formula pap now being churned out to exploit the young teenage market, these books, despite their literary deficiencies, do express an honest commitment on the part of their authors. (p. 138)

> *Michele Landsberg, "Adventure: The Great Game," in her* Reading for the Love of It: Best Books for Young Readers, *Prentice Hall Press, 1987, pp. 129-56.*

THE DOG WHO WOULDN'T BE (1957)

[Farley Mowat] has written here a book of charm and gayety, the kind that makes family reading aloud one of the happiest of diversions.

Children will delight in the exploits of the animals. Grownups will remember their own boyhood with nostalgia, or with regret that a dog like Mutt, horned owls like Weeps and Wol, and countless, nameless snakes, chipmunks, and other fauna were not part of their own boyhood and that they didn't have a great-uncle Frank to insist that if you couldn't live with wild creatures in their homes, you invited them to live in yours. . . .

The Dog Who Wouldn't Be is a warm, happy, often enchanting book about boyhood, the best antidote imaginable for late-summer or late-life doldrums.

> *Fanny Butcher, "Happy, Nostalgic Tale about Boy and His Dog," in* Chicago Tribune, *part 4, August 18, 1957, p. 2.*

His name was Mutt and Farley Mowat's mother bought him from a peddling boy for four cents. Thus began the saga of the relationship between dog and boy which Mr. Mowat relates in *The Dog Who Wouldn't Be.*

Actually, the title is misleading for Mutt, whom young Farley's father imaginatively christened a Prince Albert Retriever, was very much a dog but in wholly individual fashion. What set him apart from his own four-footed world were several pecularities of temperament and quick-wittedness. He could climb ladders and mountains; he could walk along a fence rail, much to the distress and bewilderment of cats; he liked fruit, especially cherries, and developed a technique of spitting out the pits; he dived for sea fowl; he fished for crawfish; he accepted the companionship of two pet horned owls; he wore goggles when riding in the family car.

To the portrait of Mutt, puppy and dog, Mr. Mowat brings a tender memory, a sharp eye for observation and a gift of expression that holds both poetry and humor. The development of Mutt as a hunting dog, from the day of his first hunt when he frightened the ducks by racing and screaming at them to the high point in his career when, on a bet, he retrieved a stuffed grouse for want of the real thing, is told with a nostalgic warmth rooted in a man's devotion to a beloved childhood friend.

Besides painting the portrait of an unusual dog, Mr. Mowat also paints the portrait of the author as a boy. The same adjective, "unusual," may be applied to him, for his interests and his pursuits were out of the ordinary. Encouraged by teachers and parents, the boy early showed the marks of an ardent naturalist.

Knowledgefully and amusingly, Mr. Mowat writes of his association with snakes, gophers, cormorants, owls and skunks. . . .

This book is one of reminiscence rather than fiction and is the work of an inspired nature writer.

> *Rose Feld, "Yes, Sir, This Dog Could Do Anthing," in* New York Herald Tribune Book Review, *August 18, 1957, p. 8.*

It would be much simpler to describe this book as a dog story, a good tale about an unusual dog, and let it go at that. But Mutt wasn't just a dog—indeed, as Farley Mowat says, Mutt was never content with being just a dog; he always wanted to be something more, and he pretty well succeeded. This is a good deal more than a dog story, for it is the story of a boy and his parents and dozens of neighbors and friends, tame and wild, human and almost-human. And it is a story about Canada, both the high, dry plains and the well watered area.

Mutt was a dog that Farley Mowat's mother bought from a small boy peddling baby ducks. The pup was an afterthought and cost Mrs. Mowat four cents. She bought it because young Farley wanted a dog and because Farley's father wanted to pay some fabulous sum for a hunting dog. Mutt, who came of thoroughly mixed ancestry, took over the household and the hearts of the whole family. He even became a hunting dog, of sorts. This is his story, with the variations noted above; it is, in a sense, also the story of the Mowat family during a number of turbulent, fantastic years. Mutt was naturally in the midst of every predicament, every trial, every triumph. . . .

If this seems to be the usual material of boy-dog tales, set that down to the deadening effect of summarization. Add to it the nature lore . . . and the human anecdote, salt it all with uninhibited humor, and you have a grand tale, one of the best stories of boyhood this reviewer has read in a long time.

> *Hal Borland, "The Story of Mutt," in* The New York Times Book Review, *August 18, 1957, p. 10.*

OWLS IN THE FAMILY (1961)

In his delightful all-ages book, *The Dog Who Wouldn't Be,* Farley Mowat briefly told about the owls, Wol and Weeps. They deserved a book of their own, and here it is—a wonderful tale of boys, owls and warm family life in Saskatoon, Saskatchewan. Mutt, the incredible dog, is here too, but only as a minor character. Wol was rescued as a pathetic owlet from

Illustration by Robert Frankenberg from Owls in the Family.

a storm-wrecked nest. Weeps came out of an old oil barrel in an alley. They grew up together in the Mowat family and, like Mutt, wanted to be people too. Weeps never learned to fly. Wol never learned that people didn't like skunks on the dinner table. Life with them was never tedious.

Mowat's charm and humor make his pictures of boyhood and family life memorable. His story is rich with unobtrusive natural history, and he achieves a rare combination of simplicity, grace and distinction in the writing.

> *Hal Borland, in a review of "Owls in the Family," in* The New York Times Book Review, *March 11, 1962, p. 30.*

An irresistible passion for owl pets is the almost certain result of reading about Mr. Mowat's experiences as a boy in Saskatoon. . . . Wol especially is one of the most endearing and maddening creatures imaginable. Not quite aware that he was an owl (half believing himself to be a boy, preferring walking to flying, cooked food to raw, he could put Mary's little lamb to shame as a loving, persistent and frequently embarrassing companion at school and play. Mr. Mowat's brief book is hilariously funny. It will delight old and young, with anecdotes of Wol and his practical jokes, his feuds with cats, crows and skunks. Whether he was being bathed in tomato juice (to deskunk him), or trying to walk on water and nearly drowning, we came to agree with Mrs. Mowat that "until a woman has tried to bake a cake with two horned owls looking over her shoulder, she hasn't really lived." We managed to avoid getting a lion cub like Elsa, and no otters or seals have joined our family despite *Ring of Bright Water* and *Seal*

Morning. But human nature can stand just so much temptation. Any kindly science teacher who offered to shinny up a tree and secure us a baby horned owl might not be refused.

> *Margaret Sherwood Libby, in a review of "Owls in the Family," in* Books, New York, *April 29, 1962, p. 13.*

[The escapades of the owls] are told with good humour and an accuracy which indicates an affection for the subject. It does not matter that the setting is Saskatchewan; children will respond to the genuine honesty and sensitive manner of the narrative. So rarely are animals allowed to remain their natural selves, that this is not an opportunity to be missed. Though Weeps is quite pathetic in his fondness for Wol, the relationship is never made the subject of slushy sentimentality. . . . Recommended for the ten-to-fourteen age-group, and read aloud to a class it's the kind of book that you could use in many ways.

> *Laurence Adkins, in a review of "Owls in the Family," in* The School Librarian and School Library Review, *Vol. 12, No. 1, March, 1964, p. 99.*

[*Owls in the Family* is a] highly entertaining story. . . . Oral reading of part or all of the story followed by discussion gives children a chance to share their enjoyment and to appreciate what the author is telling them about wild creatures. Emotional response should emerge in the form of laughter at amusing incidents and descriptions and, for some children, in an understanding of Billy's friendship with his owls. Feelings of empathy for one or another of the characters may also be expressed. Through discussion, children may become aware of a literary quality of the story as they see how frequently the author injects humor involving a story character's mishaps. Evaluation can be a part of the response pattern if children are asked how the author has succeeded in giving the owls qualities that are both human and animal-like.

The entire book is suitable for reading aloud and is written with an episodic plot structure so that each chapter stands alone. . . . To set a situation for discussion of the Mowat book, you might want to read the first five chapters aloud, pausing after Chapter 5 to give the children a chance to react. You can begin the discussion by noting parts of the story that brought laughter from the group as you read. Ask why they laughed. What had the author done to create a funny scene? Why did they laugh when Wol falls with a thud as he is learning to fly? Why did they laugh when Weeps refuses to even try to open his wings and falls like a rock instead? Perhaps they will recognize the ridiculousness of each situation and also the fact that we often laugh at another person's misfortune. . . . Why does that make us feel good?

Children may be interested in talking about the relationship Bill has with his owls. Why does he seem to know what they are thinking? Some children may be able to compare their relationships with pets to the example in the story. A natural extension of this questioning tack leads to student evaluation of the way these animals are presented. You can pursue this by asking children in what ways the owls in the story appear human and in what ways they appear like wild animals. If students are able to make these comparisons, you might ask whether they think the author should have included the wild animal episodes (such as the killing of the cat) as well as the accounts of the owls' almost human behavior. What is he telling us? Children who have pets will enjoy writing descriptions of their pets' behavior and appearance. (pp. 605-06)

> *Zena Sutherland and May Hill Arbuthnot, "Introducing Literature to Children," in their* Children and Books, *seventh edition, Scott, Foresman and Company, 1986, pp. 592-662.*

THE BLACK JOKE   (1962)

[Farley Mowat] once again successfully taps the rich vien of a Canadian wilderness—here it is the rockbound coast of Newfoundland during the thirties when "buried treasure" was whiskey, not gold. Jonathan Spence, like his ancestors, made a living by fishing and carrying freight on his schooner, *The Black Joke*. With no cargo to ship, Jonathan accepts business from a man he does not respect. Taking his young sons on as crew, he sets out. Intrigue and trouble dominate the scene even before port is reached, when some rumrunners steal the fast ship. The plot is masterfully controlled; the story sharply etched, and the colorful shore life of Basque fishermen artfully painted by an author who commands the attention of his audience.

> *A review of "The Black Joke," in* Virginia Kirkus' Service, *Vol. XXXI, No. 15, August 1, 1963, p. 721.*

That Farley Mowat knows and loves Newfoundland is half the battle, but not all. If he had matched the excellence of his setting with more convincing invention this would have been a book of real distinction. As it is, *The Black Joke* hardly rises above the level of a good yarn. . . .

The story, largely incredible, is told with some enjoyment, but the best of it is in the sailing and the scrambling among high wave-washed rocks. What a pity these could not have been the basic ingredients.

> *A review of "The Black Joke," in* The Junior Bookshelf, *Vol. 28, No. 2, March, 1964, p. 94.*

For craftsmanship, *The Black Joke* is the best of [the books reviewed]. It is well written, exciting and has a sure and vivid use of setting. . . . This is a splendid yarn, and the descriptions of wind and weather give it a force that really sweeps the reader along.

> *Margery Fisher, in a review of "The Black Joke," in* Growing Point, *Vol. 3, No. 1, May, 1964, pp. 318-19.*

THE CURSE OF THE VIKING GRAVE   (1966)

An unnecessary sequel to *Lost in the Barrens* and an anticlimax compared to that book, *The Black Joke,* and the author's other excellent adventure stories set in the wilderness of northern Canada. In *Barrens,* the Scotch boy Jamie and his Cree Indian friend Awasin had been lost for a winter in the Barrenlands and finally rescued by Peetyuk and his Eskimo tribe. Here, Jamie, Awasin and Peetyuk make plans to go trapping and then in the summer to return to the region to investigate what they believe to be evidence of Vikings. Much of the territory is the same, but this story is padded, not so much with fresh adventure, as with dreary anecdotes and dialogue. Awasin's sister is foisted off on the expedition, and despite the accounts of her athletic prowess as well as physical charm, readers are likely to agree with Jamie that she doesn't belong on this trip. The boys should be approaching the adult years, but sound younger when they talk, particularly when they are around the girl—Jamie is schoolboyishly clumsy and inexperienced about addressing her; Peetyuk, who wants to marry her, carries on an adolescent flirtation while the other two give him a dreary razzing. The mixture of dialects makes the book especially dismal.

> *A review of "The Curse of the Viking Grave," in* Virginia Kirkus' Service, *Vol. XXXIV, No. 13, July 1, 1966, p. 635.*

Sequels are often disappointing and this one lacks the spontaneity, careful planning and craft of *Lost in the Barrens.* Frequently the story seems forced or contrived and the characters suffer too in a plot which to all appearances has been hastily thrown together. This is somewhat compensated for by the author's knowledge of the North and by his concern for the Eskimo.

Not a first rate book but one which will no doubt find temporary quarters in Canadian libraries.

> *Marguerite Bagshaw, in a review of "The Curse of the Viking Grave," in* In Review: Canadian Books for Children, *Vol. 1, No. 1, Winter, 1967, p. 38.*

This sequel to *Lost in the Barrens* is less successful than its predecessor. . . . The author's empathy for the country and the people is again apparent, but the book is padded, the plot somewhat disconnected, and the "curse" exaggerated. Rather startlingly, Jamie who is supposed to be about 17 at the beginning of *Lost in the Barrens* is at the end of this (roughly a year later) "nearly sixteen".

Shirley Ellison, in a review of "The Curse of the Viking Grave," in School Library Journal, *Vol. 13, No. 5, January, 1967, p. 78.*

Jan(ette Louise) Ormerod

1946-

Australian author and illustrator of picture books.

Ormerod's picture books, wordless or with minimal text, offer vivid representations of loving family life to children from infancy to the early elementary grades. Her naturalistic watercolor paintings, full of drama and animated facial expressions, depict the warmth of close relationships between family members while addressing such common frustrations as the battle of wills between parents and toddlers and the rivalry between siblings. In one series of books for preschoolers, Ormerod teaches counting, the use of adjectives, and comparison of actions through her illustration of such phrases as "hair like a hedgehog's" and "jump like a kangaroo"; in her wordless "Baby Book" series, she realistically portrays an infant and parent in comical, tender scenes. Throughout her career, Ormerod has often been praised for creating visually stimulating and amusing books which inspire relaxed, affectionate lap reading. Ormerod won the Australian Picture Book of the Year Award from the Australian Children's Book Council and a Kate Greenaway Award commendation in 1982 for *Sunshine*.

(See also *Something about the Author,* Vol. 44 and *Contemporary Authors,* Vol. 113.)

GENERAL COMMENTARY

MARGARET CARTER

Jan's first book **Sunshine** [is] the pictorial record of a small girl waking up. . . . It was to be followed by **Moonlight**—the winding down of the same little girl's day. The pictures are remarkable for their gentle humorous observation: their appeal is instantly universal. . . .

Be Brave, Billy is a cooperation between herself and her publishers. Once again there is an endearing portrait of a child—this time Billy, who can't be brave about everything. The pictures have the same wry observation that characterised her first two books. Billy is at times diffident, courageous, watchful, tearful—but he's never brash or boastful. If Jan Ormerod were to draw such a child, there would be—underlying the composure—all the uncertainties and small tortures that are masked to all but the most discerning eye.

Painting is both a disguise and a revelation. Jan Ormerod's paintings are gentle, tolerant, tender, observant and shrewd. They say a great deal about their creator.

> Margaret Carter, "Cover Artist—Jan Ormerod," in
> Books for Your Children, *Vol. 18, No. 3, Autumn-Winter, 1983, p. 7.*

SUNSHINE (1981)

Sunshine is an attractive blow-by-blow account without words of a small girl waking early, attempting to amuse herself, going in to wake her father, helping him get breakfast, take it up to a reluctantly surfacing mother then (in a series of 24 small frames) dressing herself inch by inch, till she takes the clock to her parents still in bed, and they rush across the pages in a splendid confusion of undress then, demurely tidy, mother takes Sunshine to school. Beautifully observed, with good strong foreground colours and a mere suggestion of background, and particularly attractive for its patterns of frames, to divide pages and with details spilling out, this is probably as much an adult's book as a child's.

> M. Hobbs, in a review of "Sunshine," in The Junior
> Bookshelf, *Vol. 45, No. 5, October, 1981, p. 187.*

A wordless good-morning book in which a little girl awakens first, rouses her father and then her mother, dresses herself and finally sees to it that her laggard parents—dad's reading the paper in bed, mom's gone back to sleep—also get up and get going. It's a pleasant-enough conceit, clearly spelled out in the pictures; but, as so often happens, nothing is gained by suppressing words altogether except to make a tiny anecdote into a puzzle. A few words would add resonance, would make the figures real people and the happenings a *story;* even the little girl's acquisition of a name would help. A couple of sequences might still have been handled *without* words, because there's an oh-look! element involved: the wide-awake little girl, in full daylight, peering in and seeing her parents still asleep; the toast burning in the kitchen while her father absent-mindedly reads the paper. Otherwise, the wordlessness merely tends to make the whole thing abstract and insubstantial.

A review of "Sunshine," in Kirkus Reviews, *Vol. XLIX, No. 23, December 1, 1981, p. 1463.*

Couldn't be simpler or more clear, the acid test of the wordless book. And the illustrations are simply composed, with large but quiet areas of color and with realistic details; they are distinctive in the use of light and shadow, reminiscent of Brinton Turkle's work in the first pages particularly, as the sunlight creeps across the shadowed bedrooms.

Zena Sutherland, in a review of "Sunshine," in Bulletin of the Center for Children's Books, *Vol. 35, No. 5, January, 1982, p. 92.*

MOONLIGHT (1982)

Domestic truth is achieved by pictures alone in **Moonlight,** and with complete success. Mixing a few full-page pictures with a number of strip sequences, Jan Ormerod sets out her story with total clarity. A small child, having eaten her supper, throws together a couple of boats from skins, shells and toothpicks, sails them untidily in the bath and retires to bed apparently exhausted: night frights, however, require a drink, a cuddle and a story-book before she goes to sleep on the sofa, outstripping her weary parents by a short head. So far so good—an entertaining story, told plainly in relaxed wash and in line. But narrative is only the framework for a statement about family life, about affection and closeness, about co-operation (Father washes up, by the way), about personality, status, domestic habit, about the fun and the chores of being a parent and about the shifting imagination of a child—all in twenty-five pages of quiet, precise, naturalistic, illuminating artwork.

Margery Fisher, in a review of "Moonlight," in Growing Point, *Vol. 21, No. 2, July, 1982, p. 3917.*

This wordless book about bedtime is a companion to the author's **Sunshine.** In a similar format, with lovely, detailed watercolor paintings that are warm and human, Ormerod describes one bedtime in the life of the same family. . . . The book recreates situations familiar to all children and parents and is a welcome addition to the body of books about nighttime rituals. Although the technique of picturing the same

young girl as many as nine times in a sequence on a two-page spread may confuse some young "readers," this book will appeal to young and old and should be most useful in filling requests for a reassuring book about going to bed. (pp. 103-04)

Ellen Fader, in a review of "Moonlight," in School Library Journal, *Vol. 28, No. 10, August, 1982, pp. 103-04.*

Even a wordless book can help the child in the first lessons of reading closely, noticing details, linking them together in sequence and holding them all together in the mind for lightning cross references as the story progresses. *Moonlight . . .* is justly recognized for the charm of its realistic and touching watercolors depicting an evening in the life of a young, modern, middle-class family. The book begins with a family dinner scene that we "read" horizontally from left to right: the mother looking informal and capable with her short-cropped hair and casually crossed legs beneath the table; the four- or five-year-old daughter, relaxed and loved, glancing perkily up at her mother (and she really is a preschooler, as the litter of crumbs and dropped cutlery beneath her chair tells us); then the father, his curly beard and youthful face letting us know that he is gentle and playful.

The great skill of the narrative in **Moonlight** lies in the way the child reader must make the connections, though all the clues to the story are provided in correct sequence. On pages where four or five separate panels tell the story, they lead from left to right with continuing action, and sometimes the little girl even walks from one frame to another, leading the reader's eye visually and the mind temporally. When the child makes two little boats from a melon rind and a triangle of orange peel, we are reminded that the food scraps and other makings (toothpicks, a fallen leaf, red paper napkins) have been in the pictures from the beginning. That's an example of the forward and backward cross referencing I mentioned earlier. Incidentally, the fate of the little boats provides another strand in the continuing story. We see them being sailed in the bath, gradually coming apart, and then being abandoned as the action goes on.

Just as in older fiction, we must read motivation and character from the sequence of events. The father washes the dishes; where is mother? The question is left hanging, like a small subplot in a novel, until it becomes clear, a few pictures later, that she was in the bathroom running the bedtime bath for the little girl. The shower cap and the neatly hung roll of toi-

From Sunshine, *written and illustrated by Jan Ormerod.*

let paper become the tags that carry us to the next picture, where the once-tidy bathroom is strewn with the child's clothes. The toilet paper roll is on the floor (a clue to the unstated intervening action which the reader must infer) and the shower cap, just visible above the rim of the tub, tells us where the little girl is.

Action leads to consequence: Not only is the child's bathtub play deliciously drawn but the reader can anticipate what might come next when the shower cap drifts away, and the girl's hair gets more wet and bedraggled by the minute. When the mother comes back, her hands-on-hip stance clearly spells out her exasperation; the last frame of the bath sequence shows mother (whose face wears a "Well, it's your own fault" expression) combing out the wet tangles, while the child squawks in protest.

The bedtime scene—its rituals, its tenderness, its fears—is just as sensitively narrated. In every frame, the reader is called upon to remember previous details, make connections, deduce causes and consequences, and identify emotionally with the characters. Humor, surprise, comfort, and family love are all there. All count on the reader's active imaginative involvement to make the story live. Without words, the drama of nuance and character are fully present: the father's amused affection, for example, and the mother's more down-to-earth personality, in which the child greatly resembles her. The beauty of **Moonlight** (and its companion volume, **Sunshine**) is that all this is drawn from the reader without any strain. The reader's work is unconscious, just as it is in an engrossing but complex adult work of fiction.

This is the priceless lesson of beginner books: how to read with an awakened imagination. The ABCs of reading, the mechanical mastery, are mere eye exercises compared to this. (pp. 48-9)

> Michele Landsberg, "Books to Encourage the Beginning Reader," in her Reading for the Love of It: Best Books for Young Readers, *Prentice Hall Press, 1987, pp. 35-52.*

RHYMES AROUND THE DAY (1983)

[Rhymes around the Day *is a collection of traditional nursery rhymes selected by Pat Thomson.*]

With illustrations clearly matched to rhymes, we travel through the day with a family—(moustached father and affectionate mother, twin girls of six or so and small brother)—and the stages of the day at school, shopping, meal times, play and bed are represented by suitable nursery rhymes or acting games. The pictures are literal in style; the artist has individualised the members of the family and offers an entertaining and vivacious set of experiences which young children will readily match with their own. (pp. 4142)

> Margery Fisher, in a review of "Rhymes around the Day," in Growing Point, *Vol. 22, No. 3, September, 1983, pp. 4141-42.*

Traditional nursery rhymes—of diverse kinds—with contemporary illustrations in the mode of Ormerod's **Sunshine** and **Moonlight** (about morning and bedtime), but more wishy-washy: faint colorings and outlines, vapid expressions. The real difficulty, though, is in trying to attach rhymes that have no reference to everyday life (like "Humpty-Dumpty"), or to contemporary life ("Dan, Dan, Dirty old Man, / Washed his

face in a frying pan"), to the daily family round. "Humpty Dumpty" becomes what appears to be three runny eggs in three egg cups (more confusingly, one cup rooster-shaped, one chicken-shaped, and one plain); "One, Two, Buckle My Shoe" becomes a sequence in which the twin sisters actually reenact the rhyme ("a big fat hen" also turning up one cue). In other cases, somewhat more imaginatively (and much more sensibly), the rhymes just become part of family play—with Daddy, for instance, bouncing the baby to "Rigadoon, Rigadoon, / Now let him fly." Once, Rojankovsky mixed ordinary kids into a costume Mother Goose, and there have been other truly satisfactory adaptations; this, however, is a strained link-up—where neither the family doings nor the nursery rhymes gain.

> A review of "Rhymes around the Day," in Kirkus Reviews, *Juvenile Issue, Vol. LI, No. 13-17, September 1, 1983, p. J-155.*

Traditional Mother Goose rhymes are given an up-to-date interpretation by the depiction of everyday activities of a contemporary family. . . . Some of the rhymes are familiar . . . ; most, however, are not usually anthologized in small collections. Consequently, the felicitous choice of theme provides the unique opportunity to introduce young children to less frequently quoted verses, such as "One-eyed Jack, the pirate chief, / Was a terrible, fearsome ocean thief" or "1, 2, 3, / I give you a warning, / Do be better children / Before the morning!" The theme is also noteworthy as the inspiration for the fresh, fluid sequence of expressive images executed in soft watercolors against generous expanses of white. Delicate yet never sentimental, they remain true to the spirit of the rhymes while emphasizing their enduring fascination and relevance. Like Rojankovsky's illustrations in The Tall Book of Mother Goose, they humanize rather than idealize—an appropriate technique for capturing the humor and vigor of the subject.

> Mary M. Burns, in a review of "Rhymes Around the Day," in The Horn Book Magazine, *Vol. LIX, No. 6, December, 1983, p. 722.*

BE BRAVE, BILLY (1983)

Coping with fear is one of the earliest problems that beset the growing child. He must learn to distinguish between being brave and being foolhardy: between steering clear of danger and taking the acceptable risk. Well-meaning advice, teasing, bullying and the dare all conspire to confuse the issue. This little book with its reassuring illustrations sets out to help children come to terms with the 101 incidents out of which fear can spring. It stresses that being brave is difficult for everyone some of the time. Grown-ups and older children have to master the things that scare them. We can help each other to overcome our timidities. That is what mothering is all about and here is a book which will prove most helpful.

> D. A. Young, in a review of "Be Brave, Billy," in The Junior Bookshelf, *Vol. 47, No. 5, October, 1983, p. 201.*

In **Be brave, Billy** the feelings and emotions of a brother and sister are explored through a series of questions about everyday activities, the answers to which are in the beautifully observed pictures. What emerges from this sensitive book is that we all, adults and children alike, have our own particular fears and anxieties.

Jill Bennett, in a review of "Be Brave, Billy," in The School Librarian, *Vol. 31, No. 4, December, 1983, p. 341.*

---

101 THINGS TO DO WITH A BABY (1984)

I would have written this review of *101 Things to Do With a Baby* a lot sooner, except for one thing: I could never locate the book. My 5-year-old son kept taking it in order to experiment upon his baby brother. I would find him in the playroom, trying out No. 66 ("touch his nose") or in the living room, testing No. 11 ("spy him in his bouncing chair") or out in the backyard, exploring the possibilities of No. 84 ("let him meet big dogs"), 85 ("babies") or 86 ("snails").

It has always seemed to me that there are two types of children's books—those written for the children who read them and those written for the parents who buy them. *101 Things to Do With a Baby* is a rare and happy blend of both. Around our house, where the baby is now five months old, this tome, both jolly and poignant, is more frequently consulted—and delighted in—than either Dr. Spock or *The Joy of Cooking*.

Jan Ormerod's illustrations are magnificent—evoking both the tenderness and the tumult with which each day in a two-sibling household is filled. They are also painfully realistic. The full page that follows No. 61 ("put him in a crib for a quiet time") shows mother and older daughter enjoying their own special moment together, but surrounded by such debris—the half-eaten apple, half-finished tea, spilled juice, unread magazine, last night's pajamas—as to make any parent who's ever gloried in that 10-minute respite from midday chaos say, "That's *my* house!"

Fathers in particular will appreciate the authenticity of the illustrations accompanying Nos. 15 through 23 ("now do sit ups . . . or stand ups . . . or push ups . . . see how we can stretch . . . twist left . . . twist right . . . and roll over . . . now knees up all together . . . and then relax.") Father, older daughter and baby undertake this series of motions together. While daughter and baby survive it just fine, poor father is grimacing a bit by the push ups, notably red in the face by the stretching, gasping for breath by the knees up and in a state of utter collapse at the end.

If you are yourself, or if you know anyone who is contemplating having a second child, or who is about to, or who has just had one, forget the stretch suits and crib toys: find this book. But be aware of two things. First, you will have a hard time keeping it out of the hands of the older sibling in order to read it as often as you would like to yourself. And second—careful supervision is required for No. 88 ("roll him up in a rug"). With that one, a 5-year old can tend to get carried away.

Joe McGinniss, "How to Survive a Sibling," in The New York Times Book Review, *November 11, 1984, p. 48.*

What to do with a baby may be less of a problem [than the disruption of Katy's life in Annalena McAfee's *The Visitors Who Came to Stay*] but it is quite a time-consuming one. Jan Ormerod's witty book for elder brothers and sisters makes 101 suggestions. . . . The only trouble is that all 101 items can be dispatched (according to my rough calculations) in about 75 minutes flat, which leaves rather a lot of the rest of the day to fill. And in our household the problems only start *after* No 101, 'give him a kiss goodnight.' (p. 28)

William Henry Holmes, "Frog in Paris—Problems at Home," in The Listener, *Vol. 112, No. 2886, November 29, 1984, pp. 27-8.*

This is a tender story of a new sibling as well as a catalog of activities a young girl does with the new baby in her family. . . . Father, Mother and sister are shown caring equally for the baby and performing the multitude of tasks necessary during the day. Ormerod has a good grasp on the many emotions of a six-year-old child who has a new sibling, and the gentle watercolors accurately show ways to play with the baby as well as how the older child feels throughout the day. They clearly capture the nuances of a family with a new baby: a mother's expression while getting her nose tweaked or the minor jealousy of the sibling not carried on dad's shoulders. A pleasant read-aloud book to which young readers will relate.

Blair Christolon, in a review of "101 Things to Do with a Baby," in School Library Journal, *Vol. 31, No. 4, December, 1984, p. 75.*

DAD'S BACK; MESSY BABY; READING; SLEEPING (1985)

In these little books Jan Ormerod has recreated four episodes

From 101 Things to Do with a Baby, *written and illustrated by Jan Ormerod.*

in the lives of a mobile infant and his or her father and done it so fully that we see their loving relationship come to life. She has managed this with a novelist's eye for detail and a painter's grasp of nuance. The result is that rare thing, books that both parent and child can identify with and share.

In *Messy Baby* a dutiful Dad pits himself against a normal baby in the name of cleanliness. He goes through the house picking up and properly instructing her. "Soft toys in the box," he says, putting them there. And, "Clothes in the cupboard," as he neatly folds and lays them on their shelves.

As he completes each chore and turns his back to handle the next, the child and her collaborator, a black-and-white cat (that appears in each book), follow his tracks, undoing every single thing. The soft toys go flying out of the box as Dad is putting books on the shelf; the books are tossed back on the floor as he straightens the clothes.

There is no parent who has not gone through something like this, and looking at the whole charade replayed in Miss Ormerod's marvelous, soft, figurative drawings, you smile with recognition. It is also very funny, as even little children know. Recognition and realistic humor are not all that common in children's books and greatly to be prized.

In *Reading* we see a baby determined to involve herself with Dad, who is deep in his book. She crawls across the room, over, then under and along his leg, and finally to where she can peep over the top of his book.

Her face, till now, tells us she is quite intent on her mission. Dad's face, with a turn of the mouth here, a line on the brow there, devolves from absorbed reader to slightly irritated reader still hanging on to hopes of finishing the book, to a Dad who is absolutely delighted by that pair of eyes now peeping over the top. The two of them then read together, baby cradled on Dad's chest and, of course, wearing his glasses.

Dad's Back reflects the joy that comes from a simple every-day event. There are "jingling keys" to play with, "warm gloves" for her to pull on her feet, and for props, "a cold nose" and "a long, long scarf."

In *Sleeping* baby and cat wake Dad, climbing and bouncing upon him, cuddling, letting him doze off again. Another affectionate ritual you may happily recognize from your own family.

Miss Ormerod is an Australian painter who now lives in England. In her first books, *Sunshine* . . . and *Moonlight,* she spun out the family routines for starting and ending a little girl's day. Without a single written word, her delicate water-colors plunge readers into the middle of a family, letting them feel their love and their lives. . . . These new books celebrate the intimacy of the father and the baby. There is no comment or explanation about where the mother is—you may wonder, but only her artist's report suggests her presence here.

Robert Wool, in a review of "Messy Baby", "Reading," "Dad's Back," and "Sleeping," in The New York Times Book Review, *March 24, 1985, p. 35.*

These four small-format picture books for babies present three pleasant characters encountering mildly pleasurable situations in everyday indoor settings. An even-tempered, slightly mischievous infant of indeterminate age and gender is tended by a consciousness-raised father who tidies, tolerates and generally nurtures his charge. Together they pursue ordinary activities accompanied by an inquisitive but ordinary black-and-white cat.

Jan Ormerod's sensitive illustrations each cover two pages, which allows her to position all objects and protagonists within a long foot-deep slice of space. Her method of organization eliminates foreground and background, a sensible course when dealing with the younger reader. But there is otherwise a steadfast naturalism which seems better suited to the adult than to the child. The charm of a baby's chin in profile or of the backview of a bedraggled baby bouncing on a bed is likely to be lost on those of similar age, who will seek (in vain) for faces with two eyes and won't notice that the baby's socks are falling off in a supposedly comical manner. The cat is not entertaining when sitting still. Nor is the father, who remains prostrate throughout *Sleeping,* despite the amiable torments offered by the baby. In *Reading* too, page after identical page shows the father reading in a semi-reclining pose and even the infant's persistent efforts to distract him are tediously imperceptible. This makes *Reading* both remarkably repetitive in form and oddly anti-book in content.

But *Dad's Back* has more variety of incident, and in *Messy Baby,* Ormerod produces true tension and pathos, as the Messy Baby systematically subverts the father's cleaning routine. If strenuously emphasized by the adult reader, the humour might amuse. Spurred on by only a word or two per page from Ormerod, audience participation is the best way of dealing with her frugal servings of plot and prose. Any tickling in the books could also be reenacted by the reading-partners.

A minor reunion (*Dad's Back*), smiles, a frown, some games (more tickling), a few tender embraces and some attempts to sabotage the wishes of others—the stuff of life no doubt—comprise Ormerod's alternatives to the frights and delights of much children's fiction. Her books seem desirous of serving other social functions rather than preparing children for disasters. Through their good example of quiet play they might well subdue the hyperactive child (Ormerod's characters do not overdose on orange squash). But on the other hand, to stimulate paternal dedication to child care, these books could usefully be dotted around ante-natal clinic waiting-rooms.

Lucy Ellmann, "Tot-Tickling," in The Times Literary Supplement, *No. 4278, March 29, 1985, p. 351.*

Anyone who thinks books are not for babies and that the months between one and two are dull should look at these delectable books and think again. In boldly descriptive wash and pencil pictures we see a father and baby engaged in discovering one another, with occasional assistance from the family cat. There is a wealth of feeling and comment in these expressive pictures, linked by simple statements and showing the enormous appetite for exploration in the very young.

Margery Fisher, in a review of "Reading" and others, in Growing Point, *Vol. 24, No. 1, May, 1985, p. 4442.*

THE STORY OF CHICKEN LICKEN (1986)

[Paul Galdone's *The Elves and the Shoemaker*] is a warm and satisfying presentation of a favourite tale.

I am a little less happy with **Chicken Licken** (a reaction perhaps influenced by my preference for the Joseph Jacobs version of this incomparable tale). The artist's idea is original and excellent. This **Chicken Licken** is a stage production, by masked children to an audience of proud parents. The top-hatted presenter tells the story with a deadpan composure disturbed only when Foxy Woxy lures the animals to his den. Meanwhile, behind the silhouetted audience a secondary drama is enacted as Baby escapes from his carrycot and makes his unsteady way on to the stage to play with the ball which, falling from the sky, had set the play into motion. At the last opening the children, unmasked, take a deserved bow, while one mother looks aghast. The drawing has a calculated crudity which is very effective. This is a book which improves with each re-reading.

> M. Crouch, in a review of "The Story of Chicken Licken," in The Junior Bookshelf, Vol. 50, No. 1, February, 1986, p. 16.

Ormerod's World-Mother-Goose-Theater-treatment of **The Story of Chicken Licken** is a little disappointing. . . . [Her] reporting of this ritual of childhood is the book's most appealing feature. Each double page is designed so that three-fifths of the horizontal spread is on the stage and two-fifths is the audience (with a baby carrier in the foreground). Readers view the book as if watching from the back of the theater (or gym), so they view three arenas in each spread: the baby (who eventually climbs up on the stage) in the foreground, the backs of the audience in silhouette and the action on stage. All three focuses are story lines in themselves—there is just *too much* going on. Having one's eye drawn in so many directions, it is difficult to give any attention to the text, and the story loses any sort of the momentum so necessary in a cumulative tale such as "Chicken Licken." In the end, the telling of the story becomes merely a fragmented *part* of the work. It's not a good version of the story, and it's not good Jan Ormerod, either. There is a neither here nor thereness about the book that makes one wonder just what to do with it.

> Christina Olson, in a review of "The Story of Chicken Licken," in School Library Journal, Vol. 32, No. 10, August, 1986, p. 86.

In a clever, original variation on straightforward storytelling, Jan Ormerod has managed to tell several stories simultaneously. . . . Although the scenery is nil, the players are imaginatively and simply costumed, and the whole affair might be easily copied by youthful theatrical entrepreneurs. The black silhouettes contrast particularly well with the flat, colorful characters on the stage. A charming, cheerful version of an old favorite.

> Ann A. Flowers, in a review of "The Story of Chicken Licken," in The Horn Book Magazine, Vol. LXII, No. 5, September-October, 1986, p. 583.

JUST LIKE ME; OUR OLLIE; SILLY GOOSE; YOUNG JOE (1986)

While each of these toddler books is bright, cleanly designed, and attractive, they are somewhat muddled conceptually. In **Just Like Me,** a little girl wonders why her grandmother says the new baby is just like her, for the baby is bald as an egg, has ears pink as a rabbit—each spread pictures the baby and the simile. But "toothless as a toad"? "And he goes about on all-fours, like a puppy" does not really convey the difference

between crawling and walking. **Silly Goose** is a similar idea; a little girl "swings like a gibbon" and "parades like a peacock." But the difference between "hop like a flea" and "jump like a kangaroo" is not clear. "Paddle like a duck" shows the girl and a duck, each placidly standing, ankle-deep. **Young Joe** is an adequate counting book; Joe counts one fish, two frogs, all the way up to "ten playful piglets" (a glorious picture, this one; the others are overly schematized). *Then* come ten puppies, "and one puppy chooses Joe for its very own." Figure that one out. Concept books for the very young need simplicity, a bold punch that does not allow for fuzziness. For a better example of this, see the author's **Our Ollie**. . . .

[It is simpler] and stronger than the other books in this series. . . . "Our Ollie sleeps like a cat," "yawns like a hippopotamus," "has hair like a hedgehog's," etc. Each spread shows baby Ollie (sleeping, yawning, etc.) opposite the animal (sleeping, yawning, etc.) used in the simile. The paintings of the animals vary in tone and style, but all are clear and attractive, particularly a moody silhouette of a crowing cockerel. While young children may not be familiar with some of the animals' names (hedgehog, cockerel), the similes are always readily apparent. A last picture of all the animals climbing on one another is a real bonus.

> A review of "Just Like Me" and others," in Bulletin of the Center for Children's Books, Vol. 39, No. 9, May, 1986, p. 176.

[These books compare] various animals with small children, teaching counting, adjectives, and comparisons of actions. **Young Joe** is a black child, one is glad to note. In **Just Like Me** the baby and his older sister are blond and in **Silly Goose** and **Our Ollie** they are Ms Ormerod's standard pale-faced black-haired and vaguely oriental child. The drawings and the off-beat composition are beautiful but the progress of thought is at once over-complicated and flat for the age group. Sibling rivalry is still one of Ms Ormerod's main themes.

> Victoria Neumark, in a review of "Just Like Me" and others," in The Times Educational Supplement, No. 3647, May 23, 1986, p. 24.

These four baby books nicely tune into toddlers' sensibilities as they capture familiar nuances of developing personalities and foster a sense of sibling understanding. Animals are the common denominator. . . . Ormerod's lines and washes are controlled and true and leavened by nice touches of humor. Besides capturing toddler experiences, these also will expand object recognition for very young children as they make their acquaintance with the menagerie Ormerod has so deftly incorporated into the presentations.

> Denise M. Wilms, in a review of "Just Like Me" and others," in Booklist, Vol. 82, No. 19, June 1, 1986, p. 1462.

Books for very young children need strong images—of animals, families, toys—to keep a toddler intrigued; but they also need charm, whimsy or beauty of language to keep parents from becoming bored with pages they may have to look at a dozen times a day. This genre's Jane Austen, the ever-fresh Beatrix Potter, could provide not only good stories and winning pictures but also perfect sentences of compactness, simplicity, and power. Recently Jan Ormerod has been establishing herself as a contemporary master of the board book. Her previous series—with titles like **Reading** and **Sleeping**—depicts a father, a little boy, and a cat in various playful

From The Story of Chicken Licken, *written and illustrated by Jan Ormerod.*

moods. This latest quartet extends her range and should be pounced on by parents weary of *Pat the Bunny.*

Our Ollie, for instance, alternates colored drawings of a small boy with his animal counterparts. . . . Toddlers will enjoy the animals, and with some nudging by parents learn to see the parallelism.

Of the other books here, **Young Joe** is a counting primer—from one fish to 10 puppies—with a surprise ending. . . . Try one and you'll want them all.

> *Michael Dirda, "Books for Beach Bag and Knapsack," in* Book World—The Washington Post, *June 8, 1986, p. 10.*

Each book portrays a different age group from infant to approximately four years old. Illustrations are large, colorful, clear, and sure to appeal to young children. The problem lies with the texts, which lack the charm of Ormerod's other books. Except for **Young Joe,** which works well as a simple counting book, the books read like lists of descriptions rather than as unified stories. Other than **Young Joe,** libraries would do well to skip these titles and stay with Ormerod's earlier works, which are more likely to develop a devoted audience.

> *Nancy A. Gifford, in a review of "Just Like Me" and others," in* School Library Journal, *Vol. 33, No. 1, September, 1986, p. 126.*

BEND AND STRETCH; MAKING FRIENDS; MOM'S HOME; THIS LITTLE NOSE (1987)

A pre-toddler and his pregnant mother share activities to-

gether in this series with brief texts composed of what the mother might say.

In **Bend and Stretch,** Mom does exercises while the baby climbs under and over her, warmly welcome at every turn, ending with a playful tickle and mutual relaxation—all shared by a curious black cat. As Baby plays with scraps and spools, Mom constructs a simple rag doll in **Making Friends**—a new friend for Baby to cuddle, but the last picture shows him drowsing in Mom's arms while the cat gets the doll. **Mom's Home** with a basket of shopping for Baby to unpack while Mom, obviously exhausted, relaxes on the floor: tiny clothes for the baby yet to come, cat food, a banana to eat right now. And **This Little Nose** is red and runny, occasion for a growing pile of tissues and playful comparisons with toys and cat.

With deft line, Ormerod places softly rounded figures in beautifully composed arrangements, capturing the joy that a well-loved baby and his inventive, patient, but often weary mother have in time together. With a fine role model for parents and a good variety of clearly depicted objects and activities for the youngest to identify, this should become a staple.

> *A review of "Bend and Stretch" and others," in* Kirkus Reviews, *Vol. LV, No. 15, August 1, 1987, p. 1161.*

Ormerod proves once again that she's well acquainted with babies and parents. These four books, companions to her series featuring Dad and baby spotlight pregnant mother and baby. The simple, minimal text in each book describes the action illustrated, providing just the right narration for sharing with babies and toddlers. . . . A mood of serenity, love, and close companionship pervades this series. Through the choices of soft watercolors and the expressions and gestures of the mother and her child, a gentle, fun-loving mother/child relationship unfolds. Children will love these books, and for all those tired pregnant mothers of infants, Ormerod provides an exemplary role model of patience and humor. First-rate.

> *Jacqueline Elsner, in a review of "Bend and Stretch" and others," in* School Library Journal, *Vol. 34, No. 2, October, 1987, p. 118.*

In Jan Ormerod's hands the most ordinary chunks of everyday life are given vivid shape and substance. Her four most recent books for the youngest picture-book audience provide a delightful, warm glimpse into the world shared by a pregnant mom and her wide-eyed baby. With simple, fresh, colorful illustrations the author-artist portrays the pair creating and playing with a cloth doll, doing floor stretches and exercises, coping with the drips and sniffles of a cold, and investigating the contents of a wicker basket—skillfully managing to communicate the emotions and responses of both adult and baby. A sleek black-and-white cat observes or joins in all the activity as well, providing an additional focus for readers. Similar in format to the author-illustrator's earlier quartet about a dad and a baby, the new books will make an excellent companion set.

> *Karen Jameyson, in a review of "Bend and Stretch" and others," in* The Horn Book Magazine, *Vol. LXIV, No. 2, March-April, 1988, p. 193.*

Meredith Ann Pierce

1958-

American author of fiction and picture books.

Celebrated as one of the most accomplished recent writers of fantasy for children and young adults, Pierce is praised as the creator of imaginative, haunting works which use elements from psychology, history, religion, and folklore to express her distinctive personal vision. Filled with a wide array of fabulous characters and magical beasts, Pierce's books characteristically feature courageous, compassionate heroines whose bravery and love enables them to survive the dangerous quests on which they embark in order to help others. These works, which contain such themes as the power of love and the conflicts in confronting one's destiny, are often acclaimed for their inventiveness and for Pierce's skill as a prose stylist. Her first two books, *The Darkangel* (1982) and *A Gathering of Gargoyles* (1984), are part of a projected trilogy about Aeriel, an orphaned servant girl who releases a handsome vampire from enchantment by a wicked witch, becomes his wife, and seeks to assist her husband and his brothers in defeating the witch's forces. Set on the moon in a far distant time, the novels are often acknowledged for their believability and for Pierce's palpable descriptions of her physical world. Pierce has also created the first volume of another projected trilogy, *Birth of the Firebringer* (1985), in which a rebellious but visionary unicorn comes to realize that he is to lead his exiled people to their ancestral homeland. A similiar theme underscores *The Woman Who Loved Reindeer* (1985), a mystical story loosely based on Lapp culture which describes how a young wisewoman leads her tribal society away from a geothermal cataclysm with the help of the reindeer changeling she loves. Pierce is also the author of *Where the Wild Geese Go* (1988), a picture book about a young girl who gains maturity when she undertakes a magical dreamlike journey to heal her sick grandmother.

(See also *Something about the Author,* Vol. 48; *Contemporary Authors New Revision Series,* Vol. 26; and *Contemporary Authors,* Vol. 108.)

THE DARKANGEL (1982)

"Anyone inheriting the fantastic device of human language can say *the green sun,*" writes Tolkien in an essay on fairy tales, but "to make a Secondary World inside which the green sun will be credible . . . will certainly demand a special skill, a kind of elvish craft." *The Darkangel,* written with plenty of skill and elvish craft, is set on the moon. It is one of the best fantasies I've read in a long time.

This tale, which has the strangeness and authority of a vision, was inspired by a dream recorded in Jung's *Memories, Dreams, Reflections,* and came to the writer "all of a piece" during a long bus ride. It is the story of a servant girl, Aeriel, and her struggle to destroy the handsome vampire who has kidnapped her mistress and to keep his evil power from taking over the world. It is also the story of Aeriel's journey from innocence to experience, involving love's power to heal and evil's terrible attractiveness.

I am haunted by the vampire's 13 wives, reduced to wraiths, robbed of their blood and hearts and of their souls, which he wears in 13 lead vials hanging from his neck. "We are all almost the same," the wraiths tell Aeriel. "Talking to each other is only a little more or less like talking to oneself." For them Aeriel learns to spin and weave and stitch her own feelings into garments, and thereby hangs the tale: "Whereas an ounce of pity had spun only a skein of thread, and loathing even less, a drop of charity made a thread so fine and long that she had not yet reached the end of it."

The book has no illustrations, but never mind. Miss Pierce makes her own word pictures. . . . (pp. 35, 47)

Though I have met many a magical beast, never have I met in any other story the likes of those that live in this one: the water witch's ghostly jackals, the lyon that carries Aeriel over the desert, the starhorse whose death breaks the power of evil. "The fairy tale tells us how to proceed if we want to overcome the power of darkness," says Jung. Like the best fairy tales, *The Darkangel* will last and be loved by readers of all ages. (p. 47)

Nancy Willard, "Vampire on the Moon," in The New York Times Book Review, *April 25, 1982, pp. 35, 47.*

A book I think [Theodore] Sturgeon may have influenced heavily is Meredith Ann Pierce's *The Darkangel*. . . . [It's now out] in mass paperback, and I think it's time you had one.

Aeriel lives on the Moon, whose air is fading. On the heights lives the vampyre, and comes and takes her. Taken, she dwells with him, leaves him, comes back to him. Dark, he is the obverse of light; soaring, he falls, an Icarus of the Sun's pale lover. Bridal in his palace, Aeriel moves through stony collonnades, a figure in an Escher drawing. Outside, in quest of . . . well, what are we all in quest of . . . Pierce suddenly brings her out into a golden, life-repleted universe full of amazing, often charming creatures who aid or attempt to deter her, before she returns to her angel to kill him . . . or not.

But I am in some danger of waxing poetic here; of suggesting that this book is a marvelous tissue of allusions and evocations which cannot be described in terms of plot events and yet are spun from the stuff of the plot events. The thing I worry about, you see, is that with a writer like Sturgeon, or with Pierce if she goes on like this, clever people will tick off all the plot events and produce scores of stories "just like these," and they will be nothing, nothing like.

> *Algis Budrys, in a review of "The Darkangel," in* The Magazine of Fantasy & Science Fiction, *Vol. 67, No. 5, November, 1984, p. 38.*

A potent blend of myth, fantasy, and psychology gives this first novel its haunting quality. . . . *The Darkangel* comes complete with its own mythology and dreamlike population (vampires, witches, lion, unicorn). . . . Aeriel is a brave and resourceful heroine—fascinating because she possesses that fairy-tale compassion for apparently base creatures which enables her to recognize their true nature and, hence, to redeem them. Aeriel also offers an effective picture of an adolescent developing a meaningful adult identity, this growth charted in terms of her relationships with and effect upon others.

Although Aeriel's portrait is finely drawn, *The Darkangel* suffers elsewhere from shallow characterization. As a writer, Pierce as yet lacks discipline. Her prose is, at times, hackneyed and overwritten; her conclusion hurried. Yet this romantic fantasy with its echoes of both traditional and twentieth-century lore (Tolkien and Lewis) maintains a strong hold on the reader—a sure indication of the power of its theme. (pp. 49-50)

> *Elizabeth Hammill, in a review of "The Darkangel," in* The Signal Review: A Selective Guide to Children's Books, *Vol. 2, edited by Nancy Chambers, The Thimble Press, 1984, pp. 49-50.*

A GATHERING OF GARGOYLES (1984)

Those who read with pleasure Meredith Pierce's widely praised fantasy first novel, *The Darkangel,* will recall that the darkangel Irrylath (evil, cold, leaden-hearted, but irresistibly beautiful) was one of seven vampyre brothers under the spell of the White Witch. Irrylath wanted to marry Aeriel because of her strange courage and strength of spirit. Though compelled to love him for some unfathomable reason, Aeriel escapes Irrylath's lunar prison. . . . [She] sets forth, in face of innumerable dangers, to seek the meaning of the riddle-rhyme that is the heart of the story.

A Gathering of Gargoyles is about Aeriel's search for the lost lons of Irrylath, great ugly animals—the "gargoyles" of the book's title—that she had once befriended (as she had befriended his poor brides), fed and set free out of pitying affection for them. They will serve as steeds for Irrylath and his brothers in their battle against the White Witch. Aeriel travels across the vast Sea-of-Dust, discovers the little Dust Shrimp (reminding me of Ged's small pet otak in Ursula K. Le Guin's *A Wizard of Earthsea*), finds a carved staff, out of which a cranelike bird unfolds itself in unexpected crises to aid her, and locates on the far shore the apricocks, the rare fruits that bring the gargoyles to muscled, glossy strength in service of the brothers.

Miss Pierce posits a moon civilization that remains after the Ancient Ones (settlers from Earth, or Oceanus, as the moon people call it) had made a life for themselves under domed temples, netted their atmosphere to the dead surface. They left fruits, vegetables, animals and words that became the moon people's legacy from man. Miss Pierce sustains a tone of beguiling strangeness in her conceits: the Sea-of-Dust with its dust whales and dust shrimps, her double namings—nightfruit, beebirds, lampwings, hungerspice, leatherstalks, firethorn, lightmaidens—and a new instrument, Aeriel's bandolin (banjo-mandolin) and more.

It is no doubt to be expected that within what is new in this fantasy we find echoes of other outstanding fantasies; from Le Guin's Orm Embar and Pendor come Miss Pierce's Orm and Pendar; from the cycles of Susan Cooper and Jane Louise Curry comes the precognitive riddling rhyme that structures Aeriel's searches as she carries out her task. Miss Pierce is intensely visual, even poetic, in her descriptions and imaginative in her surprising plot turns. And she is strong in her overall conception of a courageous, loving girl who is both compassionate and determined despite the coldness of Irrylath, the ugliness of the gargoyles and starved wraiths, the pervading evil of the White Witch.

> *Eleanor Cameron, in a review of "A Gathering of Gargoyles," in* The New York Times Book Review, *December 30, 1984, p. 19.*

The best fantasies for young readers maintain precarious balance between stereotype and archetype, between predictability and the satisfying fulfillment of readers' expectations, between eccentricity and inventiveness. In this sequel to *The Darkangel* Pierce has continued that balance, maybe even improved over her first effort. . . .

The perils, companions, and marvelous creatures [Aeriel] encounters on her journey form the substance of this gripping novel. Aeriel is a brave and sensitive but believable protagonist. This well crafted series will please fantasy aficionados, and for the neophyte, will serve as a pleasant introduction to the genre. (p. 84)

> *Beth Nelms and Ben Nelms, "The Farfaring Imagination: Recent Fantasy and Science Fiction," in* English Journal, *Vol. 74, No. 4, April, 1985, pp. 83-6.*

A Gathering of Gargoyles is, perhaps, an even finer work [than *The Darkangel*] since Pierce seems to have found her own, distinctive voice and to be less indebted to fantasy writers like Tolkien and C. S. Lewis. As in the earlier book, one of her great strengths is her ability to capture the colors and textures of the physical world and the voyage of Aeriel across the perilous Sea-of-Dust is a splendid achievement that confirms Pierce's stylistic growth. Her handling of both the fabulous and human characters is equally secure and the airborne conclusion is exhilarating and moving.

If Pierce does no more than equal her achievement in *A Gathering of Gargoyles* in the third volume, the three novels will surely be ranked with the small number of enduring fantasy classics.

> *Walter Albert, "One of a Small Number of Fantasy Classics," in* Fantasy Review, *Vol. 8, No. 5, May, 1985, p. 20.*

BIRTH OF THE FIREBRINGER (1985)

A hotheaded young unicorn discovers that he is the legendary Firebringer, destined to restore his tribe to their homeland.

Jan's recklessness and disobedience have prevented him from being allowed to join the Ring of Warriors. Ashamed of his impetuousness, Jan desperately wants to prove himself to his father, Prince of the Unicorns. At last Jan redeems himself, and is allowed to join the band of initiates making the dangerous pilgrimage to their ancient homeland, now inhabited by evil wyverns. When the initiates are to see a vision of their destiny reflected in a sacred well, Jan sees water. Aghast, he runs away, ready to give up the struggle to follow his tribe's ways. A powerful wyvern tries to seduce him into betraying his people, but Jan resists and kills her. He is sent magnificent visions and comes to understand his own contradictory nature and his destiny as Firebringer.

The language here is as elegant as the unicorn people it chronicles. Unicorn rituals and mythology are woven skillfully into the story, strengthening characterization and making the fantasy believable. The book is complex in theme and in structure; consequently the plot is sometimes hard to follow, and descriptions of Jan's visions may be heavy going. But readers capable of handling its demands will be well rewarded.

> *A review of "Birth of the Firebringer," in* Kirkus Reviews, *Vol. LIII, No. 19, October 1, 1985, p. 1090.*

The untangling of the satisfying plot and Pierce's ability to foster belief in her unicorns, consistently describing the action as these horse-like animals feel and sense it, are enhanced by her stately use of language and the sense of their history and culture which she creates and sustains. The tale of a heritage realized and a prophecy fulfilled is not new, but the vital characters and the unique device of a narrator whose identity remains hidden until story's end give it a fresh appeal.

> *Holly Sanhuber, in a review of "Birth of the Firebringer," in* School Library Journal, *Vol. 32, No. 5, January, 1986, p. 70.*

This lacks the concentration of Pierce's *Darkangel.* The language is poetic, with wonderful rhythm and sweeping images of sky and plain, but it is sometimes overheightened and awkwardly archaic. Perhaps because it is the first in a projected trilogy, there is much explanation and discussion about the fantasy world, its history and structure. But the world is a compelling one, and Jan is a dramatic hero. His coming-of-age from uncertain child to a leader who has grown beyond his father will have strong appeal for many young people.

> *Hazel Rochman, in a review of "Birth of the Firebringer," in* Booklist, *Vol. 82, No. 12, February 15, 1986, p. 870.*

THE WOMAN WHO LOVED REINDEER (1985)

Meredith Ann Pierce, like Nancy Willard and Robin McKinley, is one of the foremost young authors of fantasy today. Her work combines a mythic inventiveness with such elemental themes as love, conflict and quest.

The Woman Who Loved Reindeer presents the reader with a forceful yet feminine heroine. . . . The setting is a Tribal society living on the tundra north of a Pole on a two-mooned land. The novel suggests both the primeval transhumance way of the Lapps and the religious closeness to earth and animal of the Native Americans. Pierce's style, dramatic and descriptive, is poetic. . . .

Mature readers will find this a tale of courage and caring in the face of change, as appropriate to our age as to that of the protagonist wisewoman *i'dris,* Caribou, and her gold-eyed lover-guide, Reindeer.

> *Joan Nist, in a review of "The Woman Who Loved Reindeer," in* The ALAN Review, *Vol. 13, No. 2, Winter, 1985, p. 31.*

A novel based on the husk-myth of an animal that can cast its skin to take human form traces the fate of a reindeer changeling, or *trangl,* brought as a baby to the lonely young woman Caribou. Caribou raises the child but cannot bind him when he becomes a man, nor keep his golden stag self from running with the wild deer in spring and fall. Still, the power of her love draws him back, and because of his travels he is able to show her how to lead her people away from a devastating series of earthquakes into a new land. The love story is convincing, the dangers of the long trek suspenseful, but the style is overdramatic, with much blanching, trembling, and throat-closing in addition to unnecessary exposition, like "None of this could be happening." Still, readers of the author's *Darkangel* will revel in her flair for odd romance and the sometimes striking descriptions of a barren northland.

> *A review of "The Woman Who Loved Reindeer," in* Bulletin of the Center for Children's Books, *Vol. 39, No. 4, December, 1985, p. 75.*

Caribou's consuming passion for the enigmatic Reindeer and his gradual assumption of human emotions is believable and satisfying. The author's imaginary world is an intriguing combination of realistic, folkloric, and fantastic elements; her style is smooth, clear, and elegant, with never a word in the wrong place. A remarkably fine fantasy by an emerging master of the genre. (p. 209)

> *Ann A. Flowers, in a review of "The Woman Who Loved Reindeer," in* The Horn Book Magazine, *Vol. LXII, No. 2, March-April, 1986, pp. 208-09.*

WHERE THE WILD GEESE GO (1988)

A stag's-horn comb, scattered geese feathers and a crystal globe are all that is left of a magical trip undertaken by a young girl named Truzjka, who wakes to find herself safely home in bed after a dreamlike journey. Truzjka's undertaking had been to find the land where the wild geese go, a task that would heal her sick grandmother. Pierce's narrative weaves an enchanting aura, full of descriptive imagery and mysterious allusions, all of which fit together into a cohesive whole. Perceptive readers will find much to digest as Truzjka journeys into a frozen tundra, aided by talismans given her by a stranger, and encounters innumerable obstacles in her quest. The theme of the snow geese recurs throughout the finely detailed illustrations [by Jamichael Henterley], which perfectly mirror the haunting tale.

> *A review of "Where the Wild Geese Go," in* Publishers Weekly, *Vol. 233, No. 6, February 12, 1988, p. 82.*

[Truzjka] is a heedless child, dreamy and careless, the despair of her grandmother. One morning she awakens to find her grandmother ill because she wishes to find out where the wild geese go. Truzjka runs away to find the wild geese to cure her grandmother. . . . [Truzjka's] magical adventures gradually transform her into a responsible child, and the girl returns home, only to find she has been ill and that the journey was perhaps a dream. Most of the motifs introduced in the first few pages of the book cleverly recur in the course of Truzjka's adventures, but some are difficult to understand. . . . Although the symbolic theme is a bit unclear, the book will be enjoyed for the sympathetic heroine and the beautiful illustrations.

> *Ann A. Flowers, in a review of "Where the Wild Geese Go," in* The Horn Book Magazine, *Vol. LXIV, No. 3, May-June, 1988, p. 349.*

[***Where the Wild Geese Go***] combines elements of mystical fantasy and moral tale. Truzjka is helped on her way by assorted magical creatures, but the dangers she encounters are all related to her own shortcomings—faults she abandons on the journey. The full-page illustrations match the romanticism of the tale. . . . While the storytelling lacks the structure and richness of works by George MacDonald and Andersen, it shares their timeless and mystical qualities and will appeal to somewhat younger readers of fantasy.

> *Eleanor K. MacDonald, in a review of "Where the Wild Geese Go," in* School Library Journal, *Vol. 35, No. 9, June-July, 1988, p. 94.*

Philip Pullman

1946-

English author of fiction and nonfiction.

Pullman is best known as the writer of exciting, detailed historical novels for young adults which are set in nineteenth-century London and feature the independent, resourceful Sally Lockhart as their heroine. His first two works in a projected trilogy, *The Ruby in the Smoke* (1986) and *The Shadow in the Plate* (1986; U. S. edition as *The Shadow in the North*), are often considered fascinating contributions to the genre of historical fiction which reflect Pullman's talents as a storyteller and a creator of atmosphere and larger-than-life characters. In *The Ruby in the Smoke,* Sally, a sixteen-year-old orphan, pursues the mystery of her father's death and tries to recover a legendary gem that is rightfully hers with the help of Frederick, a young photographer, and his actress sister Rosa. The protagonists become involved in a series of rousing adventures which take them through the London underworld, where they encounter opium dens, Chinese pirates, and murder. Like its predecessor, *The Shadow in the Plate* is a dramatic, intricately structured thriller; in this novel, Sally Lockhart is now a twenty-two year old financial consultant. Attempting to recover money lost by one of her clients, she and Frederick become embroiled in such issues as blackmail and industrial fraud and are forced to confront the evil, wealthy industrialist Axel Bellman, who is producing a steam-powered gun capable of incredible destruction. Behind Pullman's suspenseful plots, which he often laces with humor, are such themes as Sally's feminism versus the conventions of the time, England's involvement with the opium trade, and the Victorian fascination with spiritualism, elements credited with providing young readers with a strong sense of period. In addition to his books about Sally Lockhart, Pullman has written an informational book about the ancient cultures of several Mediterranean, Eastern, Middle Eastern, and South American countries; a mock horror story for young adults set in nineteenth-century Switzerland; and an adult novel.

The Junior Bookshelf, *Vol. 46, No. 2, April, 1982, p. 75.*

ANCIENT CIVILIZATIONS (1982)

The manner in which affairs were conducted in ancient Greece and Rome still influences our life today. In this handsome, well produced book Philip Pullman describes these civilizations and six others: those of Mesopotamia, Egypt and Crete, Mexico, Peru and China.

The book contains a substantial text, and many illustrations [by G. Long] which show artefacts produced by ancient peoples and imaginative reconstructions of their appearance and surroundings. . . . [This is] a lively and informative work. It is enriched by intriguing details like the meaning of the word civilization, a description of the predestined Inca life pattern, and an account of the existence led by fearless Spartan aristocrats, so bleak and unpleasant that their willingness to leave this world during battle is perhaps understandable.

R. Baines, in a review of "Ancient Civilizations," in

One reason for the continued interest in ancient civilizations must be the great variety of possible approaches to them, emphasized, of course, in small books, where selection is inevitable. . . .

To justify the cost of hard covers, a larger book needs to offer either a picture of cultural development or a chance to compare self-contained civilizations. The aim of **Ancient Civilizations** seems to have been the latter, to judge not only from its scope, as it includes America and China as well as the more familiar Middle Eastern and Mediterranean cultures, but also from its difficult introductory essay on concepts of civilization. In fact, though, this demanding approach is not maintained, and all that most readers will acquire is a sense of the variety of societies described as civilized. Successive chapters offer potted histories and descriptions of cultural achievements, but the compression is not really satisfactory. . . . The verdict must be that this book fails to meet any existing need or to persuade us that it has identified a new one.

Ian Pratt, "Ancient World Tour," in The Times Educational Supplement, *No. 3431, April 2, 1982, p. 26.*

Civilization, [**Ancient Civilizations**] reminds us, is 'the art of living in cities'. In necessarily brief chapters it describes and contrasts the ways in which this art developed in Mesopotamia and Egypt, Crete, Greece and Rome, Mexico, Peru and China. It would be churlish to complain that space has not been lopped off for the inclusion of Indian and other ancient cultures. Enough has been said to whet the young reader's appetite and for fuller information he can turn to other books, like Hugh Bodey's *Roman People,* which treat a single civilization.

> *Geoffrey Trease, in a review of "Ancient Civilizations," in British Book News, Spring, 1982, p. 18.*

COUNT KARLSTEIN   (1982)

Classy writers of course, make the most unlikely events seem feasible. For instance, Philip Pullman's **Count Karlstein** is, on the face of it, an account of how two girls avoid ending up as a late-night snack for Zamiel, Prince of the Mountains and Demon Huntsman. The place is Switzerland, the year 1816, and the point is not so much the plot as how the narrative unfolds. It is supplied by a number of hands, including a comic policeman and a ladylike governess. . . . And at least one of the heroines stays cool, even after discovering that the key to her cell is concealed in a bowl of soup. . . . To compare this book with T. H. White's *Mistress Masham's Repose* is to risk hyperbole, yet it shares a similar concern with making the improbable seem remarkably precise. Which may not be such a bad way of shaping up to the world ahead. (pp. 21-2)

> *Charles Fox, "Once and Future Image," in New Statesman, Vol. 104, No. 2698, December 3, 1982, pp. 21-2.*

Verging only occasionally on parody, this novel is written in a quaint, fulsome style that will delight readers with a taste for the unconventional. . . . Proliferating subplots, changing chroniclers, and a cast of characters that includes a bumbling police sergeant, a strong-minded English governess, a cosmopolitan con man, and a missing heir make up a deliciously complex yarn saturated with adventure and suspense. Never mind that most readers will guess the happy ending well in advance; in this skillful mock-gothic romp, the pleasure is all in the telling. (pp. 815-16)

> *Karen Stang Haley, in a review of "Count Karlstein," in Booklist, Vol. 80, No. 11, February 1, 1984, pp. 815-16.*

Lucy and Charlotte, young orphans, have been sent to live with their uncle, Count Karlstein, a dark and evil man. He had made a bargain with Zamiel, the Demon Huntsman, ten years earlier, that in return for a great estate, an honorable name and wealth, he would provide Zamiel with a human soul on All Souls' Eve. Hildi, a young servant at Castle Karlstein, discovers that Karlstein intends to sacrifice his nieces and sets about to rescue them from this horrible fate. This spellbinding tale takes place in Switzerland in the early 19th Century and is told by Hildi in Part One. Part Two, "Narratives by Various Hands," provides some interesting, often humorous, viewpoints from other characters; Hildi resumes the narration in Part Three. In the end, Hildi witnesses the terri-

fying scene in which the Prince of Darkness arrives on a huge horse amidst baying hounds and the ominous sound of his hunting horn. After a horrifying death scene, everything comes together for a satisfactory conclusion. Pullman's combination of suspense and humor work well, making this a good addition to horror story collections.

> *Phyllis K. Kennemer, in a review of "Count Karlstein," in School Library Journal, Vol. 30, No. 7, March, 1984, p. 174.*

THE RUBY IN THE SMOKE   (1986)

Set in nineteenth-century London, this atmospheric and exciting thriller weaves together two dark intrigues, one concerning the whereabouts of a priceless ruby that mysteriously disappeared in the Indian Mutiny, and the other the sinking of the schooner *Lavinia* in Far Eastern waters. Two things link these mysteries: the deadly opium trade, and sixteen-year-old Sally Lockhart. Sally, the victim of a sinister family history, finds her life at risk from two sets of mortal enemies. Fortunately she has had an unconventional childhood, which has taught her little about music or sewing, but a great deal about business management and guns. Both these accomplishments prove handy in her brave and resourceful struggle against terrible odds. This is a splendid book, full of memorable characters, furious action and heroic deeds in murky London settings. It is a first-rate adventure story, and will appeal to boys and girls across a wide age-range from ten upwards. (pp. 33-4)

> *Peter Hollindale, in a review of "The Ruby in the Smoke," in British Book News Children's Books, March, 1986, pp. 33-4.*

It would not be difficult to make fun of Mr. Pullman's tale, and for the first third of this book I was unwilling to take it seriously. But his young heroine has an appeal that grows on the reader and before the end I was as much her devoted slave as are the young men in the story. For the rest, I just couldn't take Mrs. Holland, whether as leader of the underworld or as misused beauty of the regiment, and the London scenes, opium den and all, were more comic than enthralling. But whether you find the story absurd or convincing you will surely not want to resist its thrills. Mr. Pullman tells a great tale. (p. 81)

> *Marcus Crouch, in a review of "The Ruby in the Smoke," in The Junior Bookshelf, Vol. 50, No. 2, April, 1986, pp. 80-1.*

I found this book fascinating and thoroughly entertaining in every way. The atmosphere and background, although richly detailed and authentic in feel, are never laboured because they are so varied. The characters are delightful and the whole style and approach are brimming with intelligence and vitality. There are not many books that offer such promise of satisfaction to so many children, of both sexes, of secondary age. It is absorbing, admirably written and excellently produced.

> *David Churchill, in a review of "The Ruby in the Smoke," in The School Librarian, Vol. 34, No. 2, June, 1986, p. 174.*

The Ruby in the Smoke is one of those all-too-few British novels which should appeal just as greatly to American teens as it does to British teens. Pullman uses a cliff-hanger at the end of each chapter to keep readers enthralled in this fast-paced, intricate, and suspenseful novel. Sally's complex characterization as a resourceful, yet occasionally unsure, young woman, makes her both likable and memorable. The incident with the opium smoking is acceptable within the context of the novel, and the discussion of the British government's opium trade makes the novel appropriate as Social Studies supplemental reading. The beautifully crafted writing and the fact that Pullman respects his teenaged audience enough to treat them to a complex, interwoven plot will certainly make readers anxious for the upcoming sequel, **The Shadow on the Plate,** and the third novel of the trilogy, currently underway.

> *Brooke L. Dillon, in a review of "The Ruby in the Smoke," in* Voice of Youth Advocates, *Vol. 10, No. 4, October, 1987, p. 206.*

THE SHADOW IN THE PLATE (1986; U. S. edition as *Shadow in the North)*

Like its predecessor, . . . [**The Shadow in the Plate**] is a melodrama, its lurid and often violent action taking place in a seedy underworld of fraud, crime and squalor. Its extravagant and complicated plot centres on a clever and brutal arms manufacturer. Ranged against this formidable villain are two people we first met and grew to like in the earlier book: Sally Lockhart, a girl of eccentric education and independent spirit who has now set up as a financial consultant, and Frederick Garland, young photographer turned detective.

The convention of melodrama tolerates grotesque violence and inhumanity, provided that their deformities are clear and they do not kill genuine bravery and goodness. In the first book the convention was meticulously observed. This time it is strained throughout, and finally broken by an event of unexpected and appalling dreadfulness. This is a compelling and in some ways excellent book, but could mystify and distress young children who may have liked the earlier one. Older and tougher readers will relish it; but the effect is disturbing. This, after all, is part of a children's trilogy, not *Bleak House.* (pp. 30-1)

> *Peter Hollindale, in a reveiw of "The Shadow in the Plate," in* British Book News Children's Books, *December, 1986, pp. 30-1.*

According to tradition reviewers divide books into two categories: those you can't put down, and those you can't pick up. Philip Pullman's new instalment of his Victorian trilogy is a splendid example of the former. . . . (p. 229)

Well researched, told with gusto, and with a string of colourful, larger-than-life characters. More like Wilkie Collins than Dickens, and with an unexpected sting in the tail. Wonderfully readable, almost totally believable, it is the kind of tale in which the reader willingly suspends critical judgement in favour of a wholehearted good 'read'. (p. 230)

> *M. Crouch, in a review of "The Shadow in the Plate," in* The Junior Bookshelf, *Vol. 50, No. 6, December, 1986, pp. 229-30.*

We are in the London of Conan Doyle and George Gissing. Sally Lockhart, Frederick Garland and friends (Sally a financial consultant and Frederick a photographer-detective) piece together a mystery which leads to revelations involving the aristocracy, the turf, spiritualism, the music hall, high finance and a conspiracy leading to the production of a Victorian 'ultimate weapon'. The atmosphere tingles with authenticity; the story has a pace and a slickness of plot (sometimes too slick?) which are very impressive. There are feelings and developing relationships and, from the main protagonists, a modern view of society which shows what 'Victorian values' really were in that vigorous, competitive and ultimately heartless period. A super read and a story to mull over afterwards for a significance which belies its outward form. This is the second in a trilogy. I shall read the first and look forward eagerly to the third.

> *Dennis Hamley, in a review of "The Shadow in the Plate," in* The School Librarian, *Vol. 33, No. 4, December, 1986, p. 368.*

As he did in **The Ruby in the Smoke,** Pullman once again demonstrates his mastery of atmosphere and style. Readers of that first book may be put off, however, by the more somber tone and the thematic and symbolic weight of the second, which demand special maturity and sophistication of its readers not only to grapple intellectually with such issues as the moral implications of the Industrial Revolution and the dehumanization of man by machine but also to deal with both the sexual expression of Sally's growing love for Frederick and the violent deaths of leading characters. Too many of the characters seem to be manipulated for thematic ends, and one wonders if the conventions of the mystery/adventure genre are not too fragile to bear the weight of Pullman's thematic ambition. Such issues are sure to inspire spirited discussion, the resolution of which may have to await the final volume in the trilogy.

> *Michael Cart, in a review of "Shadow in the North," in* School Library Journal, *Vol. 35, No. 8, May, 1988, p. 112.*

Mary Rodgers

1931-

American author of fiction and screenwriter.

The creator of humorous fiction for grade school and middle grade readers, Rodgers is recognized for providing her audience with works which present insights on the relationship between parents and children in a witty and original manner. In most of her stories, fantastical events suddenly emerge from chic upper-middle class New York settings and propel Rodgers's protagonists into a series of complicated dilemmas. Her second book, *Freaky Friday* (1972), became the prototype for her later works; in this popular story, thirteen-year-old Annabel Andrews discovers one morning that she has, inexplicably and without forewarning, turned into her mother. As Rodgers follows Annabel through ludicrous predicaments such as a parent-teacher conference in which Annabel finds herself trying to explain her own misbehavior in school, readers are concurrently entertained and instructed on the value of traditional morals; at the same time, Rodgers voices her approval of the unconventional behavior and attitudes of young people in both *Freaky Friday* and her subsequent works about the Andrews family and their friends. In *A Billion for Boris* (1974), Annabel's upstairs boyfriend acquires a television set that broadcasts tomorrow's programs and uses it to win money for his mother, while in *Summer Switch* (1982), Annabel's twelve-year-old brother Ben, whom she has dubbed Ape Face, switches roles with his father. Confronted with the persistent conflicts of the generation gap, Rodgers's characters awaken to such common realizations associated with maturation as the existence of paternal love and the merit of loyal friendships. In addition to her fiction, Rodgers wrote the screenplay for the film of *Freaky Friday* and is well known as a composer and lyricist for both children and adults. She received the Christopher Award in 1973 for *Freaky Friday* and in 1975 for *A Billion for Boris*.

(See also *Contemporary Literary Criticism,* Vol. 12; *Something about the Author,* Vol. 8; *Contemporary Authors New Revision Series,* Vol. 8; and *Contemporary Authors,* Vols. 49-52.)

AUTHOR'S COMMENTARY

[*The following excerpt is from an interview by Lee Bennett Hopkins.*]

Mary Rodgers was born in New York City into a theatrical world. Her father, Richard Rodgers, together with Oscar Hammerstein, created such Broadway smashes as *South Pacific, Oklahoma, The King and I* and *The Sound of Music.* Her mother, Dorothy, is a professional writer and an interior decorator. But Rodgers says she and her sister did not feel a part of her parents' exciting world.

> I had a rather boring childhood. I had a regimented life, raised in a regimented house. The only way I could escape the regimentation was to read and read and read. And I did! I was always, I suppose, the family rebel, and like Annabel, I yearned to live

not worrying about what to wear, not caring how my room looked, just being what *I* wanted to be.

> Although children certainly aren't a minority, they are unrecognized. There's always someone around to tell them what and what not to do. I'm an advocate of hostility and anger in children. Emotions like those are healthy means of communication, and they should be fostered.

This philosophy is reflected in Rodgers's first book for children, **The Rotten Book.** Published in 1969 with pictures by Steven Kellogg, the story relates the deliciously rotten dreams of rebellious young Simon—destroying his room, putting Silly Putty in his sister's hair and cutting it all off and locking her in the closet.

Following **The Rotten Book** was *Freaky Friday,* in 1972, to which the classmates of one of Rodgers's children responded, "Your mother wrote that book!?" Its hilarious sequel is *A Billion for Boris,* a fantasy adventure involving Annabel, her friends and a TV that foretells the future.

> My books are based on the "what if" principle. "What if you became invisible?" or "What if you did change into your mother for one day?"

> I then take it from there. Each book takes several

months in the long process of writing, rewriting, writing, rewriting, and each has its own set of problems.

The one thing I dislike about the process is the sometimes loneliness of it all. Readers only get to see the glamour part of a bound book, not some of the agonizing moments one has while constructing it.

(pp. 81-2)

Lee Bennett Hopkins, "'Freaky Friday' from Book to Film," in Teacher, *Vol. 95, No. 2, October, 1977, pp. 80-2.*

THE ROTTEN BOOK (1969)

The Rotten Book is really two books, a worldly satire and a simple, rather old-fashioned cautionary tale. The trouble starts—for Simon and the reader—at the breakfast table where Simon is dawdling with his egg and his father is holding forth on a "rotten" little boy who's ungrateful for what he has (which matches what Simon has) and who's "going to land up in jail one of these days." Whereupon Simon, wondering what the boy did, goes through a day of being absolutely rotten to everyone and everything. When he's put Silly Putty in his sister's hair, cut it all off, locked her in a closet, and turned on the hi-fi and TV and FM so that no one can hear her, he gets his come-uppance; policemen and firemen are called to find her and when they do, Simon is taken away handcuffed while his family cheers. "He'd probably spend the rest of his life in jail (and) never even get an egg for breakfast." Cut to the breakfast table where Simon praises the egg and proceeds to behave like a model boy. The father's self-righteous condemnation of a *little* boy is odd to start with, and if he and Simon's mother are going through this elaborate charade on behalf of an egg, it's ludicrous. Either way, father's letter-perfect pompous and in today's context (and today's plots), the child is supposed to rebel, not capitulate. If he were to rebel, jail's not the timeliest deterrent; if it's meant simply as a warning, there are others more suitable. And suppose he didn't eat the **** egg—would he have to feel rotten?

A review of "The Rotten Book," in Kirkus Reviews, *Vol. XXXVII, No. 17, September 1, 1969, p. 926.*

How rotten can one small boy be? Very . . . very. Particularly when his rottenness is all in his mind! . . . Simon is believable, and the story is funny, as it builds rotten adventure on top of rotten adventure to a logical conclusion. (It's true that young listeners may be introduced to tantalizingly rotten schemes they might not have otherwise dreamed of!)

Marjorie Lewis, in a review of "The Rotten Book," in School Library Journal, *Vol. 16, No. 3, November, 1969, p. 112.*

This is the first children's book by Mary Rodgers, who wrote the score for **"Once Upon a Mattress."** She appears to have a sharp ear for the peculiar tone adults use on children—"Children, children we don't grab," says the teacher, "we take turns." The book is fresh and fun. . . . (p. 54)

Betsy Wade, in a review of "The Rotten Book," in The New York Times Book Review, *November 16, 1969, pp. 54, 56.*

FREAKY FRIDAY (1972)

Set in Manhattan, this contemporary fantasy features 13-year-old Annabel Andrews who wakes up as her 35-year-old mother after an argument about the relative responsibilities of children and adults. Beginning with her delighted anticipation of absolute freedom, Annabel's day predictably turns into one disaster after another—from the washing machine's breakdown, through an interview with officials at Annabel's private school, to the disappearance of her six-year-old brother. Through Mommy's intervention at the crucial moment, however, all ends well, and Annabel winds up finding a bit of romance with the boy upstairs, admitting affection for her brother, and gaining a better understanding of herself and her parents and teachers. Although the magic is never satisfactorily explained and Annabel's problems are rather simplistically removed with her braces, the first-person narrative keeps plot and characters moving with humor and believability for a fast-paced, enjoyable read that should be popular with middle-graders.

Margaret A. Dorsey, in a review of "Freaky Friday," in School Library Journal, *Vol. 18, No. 8, April, 1972, p. 138.*

Mary Rodgers has the knack of catching the sound of a real child talking. When Annabel says, "Oh, wow," it is because writer, character, page of print, and reader have all been catapulted into an Oh, wow mood. Plenty of other writers try to hit young readers with "now" ideas and phrases—make love, not war; I mean; you know; Fascist pig. You wish they hadn't. Why didn't they try to be, like, universal and timeless? But in this book the pages rush by, right now in 1972, and it might all be happening in the apartment next door. *Freaky Friday* is unputdownable. It is a gem.

Jane Langton, "Grand Girls All," in Book World—Chicago Tribune, *May 7, 1972, p. 5.*

As bright and breezy as the title, a truly funny story about a girl who awakens one morning in her mother's body, and who—during an incredible day of revelation and opportunity—sees herself as others see her and faces her mixed-up adolescent problems squarely. . . . There is wisdom as well as humor in this fresh, original story, and the impact, despite the story's fantastic basis, is successful and convincing.

Beryl Robinson, in a review of "Freaky Friday," in The Horn Book Magazine, *Vol. XLVIII, No. 4, August, 1972, p. 378.*

There's nothing didactic here; the story bubbles along in fine style as Annabel sees herself as others see her (a more complimentary set of attitudes than she might have anticipated) and adjusts to the rigors of her mother's problems and the inevitable complications of changed roles. A fresh, imaginative, and entertaining story.

Zena Sutherland, in a review of "Freaky Friday," in Bulletin of the Center for Children's Books, *Vol. 26, No. 1, September, 1972, p. 15.*

How many young people read *Vice Versa* these days? Not many I imagine. This is a modern trendy version of the theme set in New York. . . . Annabel sees herself as others see her and is forced to face her adolescent problems squarely. The dialogue is excellent; Mary Rodgers is able to get on the wavelength of a thirteen-year-old without appearing at all pretentious, but into this fresh, original and very funny story she also manages to slip quite a lot of wisdom. Girls of 12 to

15 with a sense of humour and a taste for the fantastic should really enjoy this. (pp. 119-20)

> *J. M., in a review of "Freaky Friday," in* The Junior Bookshelf, *Vol. 38, No. 2, April, 1974, pp. 119-20.*

A BILLION FOR BORIS (1974)

When Boris, Annabel's upstairs boyfriend in *Freaky Friday*, acquires a TV set that broadcasts tomorrow's programs, Annabel wants to use their foreknowledge for good deeds like helping the police entertain a lost child or providing a *Daily News* journalist with scoops, but Boris has bigger plans. It seems that Sascha, his mother (he was allergic to her in the last book), is not after all evil but just a flighty writer, and the only way he sees to straighten her out and make his own life bearable is to win $12,000 on the races at OTB—and spend it all on redecorating and furnishing their apartment, buying Sascha a new wardrobe (including mink jacket) at Lord & Taylor, and providing her with a good shrink, a new accountant, a decent housekeeper and a secretary. "It sounds like a lot" but never mind; when he loses his sudden wealth in the end on a disqualified front runner, Sascha (who really prefers her old junk) comes up not only with a $50,000 check from Hollywood to pay the bills but also with the apparent revelation that she loves him. This leaves Boris, who has essentially learned his lesson without suffering for his mistakes, blubbering with joy—but it's poor reward for readers who have taken in all the cheap crises and social insensitivity of *Freaky Friday* without any of the compensating laughs.

> *A review of "A Billion for Boris," in* Kirkus Reviews, *Vol. XLII, No. 20, October 15, 1974, p. 1104.*

It's too bad we don't reserve a special set of adjectives for books that really *are* commendable—witty, original, entertaining, well-plotted and well-wrought; as it is, copywriters (and I freely admit my own transgressions in that profession) have so diluted those terms that when the genuine article comes along it's like crying wolf. Wolf!

While I'm not saying this is *Eloise* of the seventies, *A Billion for Boris* does assume an urban and sophisticated frame of reference on the part of the reader, and it evokes so much New York City local color (from the Village to 125th Street by way of Central Park West, Lord & Taylor and a walk-up on west 53rd) that it really is the perfect New York City book.

Ah, but its smart high-school repartee is so snappy (and so true!) it ought to delight the cognoscenti and their eccentric, rotten-housekeeper mothers from coast to coast.

> *Alix Nelson, in a review of "A Billion for Boris," in* The New York Times Book Review, *November 24, 1974, p. 8.*

The sprightly and articulate heroine of *Freaky Friday* reports another fantastic adventure that seems completely believable; Mary Rodgers has to a remarkable degree the ability to blend fantasy and realism. Spiced with humor, sophisticated dialogue, and an unusual mother-son relationship, the story is, in the British sense, a "good read." (p. 136)

> *Zena Sutherland, in a review of "A Billion for Boris," in* Bulletin of the Center for Children's Books, *Vol. 28, No. 8, April, 1975, pp. 136-37.*

A Billion for Boris . . . [has a] bizarre plot which is based

on several important points—prominent among them the idea that if parents don't understand their children, neither do children understand their parents. . . . All the characters in this crazily logical drama end up a little wiser than before, while the reader, beguiled by the sparkling American dialogue and the proliferation of astonishing scenes, should be well content to absorb the lesson along with the fun, since fantasy has so skilfully embellished both. (p. 2690)

> *Margery Fisher, in a review of "A Billion for Boris," in* Growing Point, *Vol. 14, No. 3, September, 1975, pp. 2689-90.*

American children are apt to move through their fictional lives with great gusto, much wise-cracking and a columnist's wit. . . . As in all the best folk tales the possession of wishes that come true or powers of foretelling the future never seem to work out. There is a lot of hilarious backchat and exchanges of verbal fireworks between children and parents. Why is that, to all American fictional children, adults are slightly soft in the head? As devoid of real emotion as a P.G. Wodehouse anti-hero, these superficial fun-loving urban descendants of Huck Finn will provide an amusing read for a wet English Sunday.

> *D. A. Young, in a review of "A Billion for Boris," in* The Junior Bookshelf, *Vol. 39, No. 5, October, 1975, p. 336.*

SUMMER SWITCH (1982)

And now, ten years later, a companion volume to *Freaky Friday*. . . . Here the younger child, Ben, also known as "Ape Face," turns into his father and vice versa. This happens just as Ben is going off to camp and his father is going off to the West Coast to negotiate for a big part in the shakeup of the film company he represents in New York. The chapters are told alternately by Ben and his father, with contrasting type-faces used to help the reader distinguish between the two. It *does* get confusing, as each struggles to maintain his changed image; Ben is thunderstruck, for example, when the doorman at his Beverly Hills hotel gives him the keys to a car, since he's only twelve, and his father is equally frustrated when he has to make a telephone call to Ben and call him "Daddy" to give him advice on business matters while the camp director listens. Ben finds it hard to get used to having body hair and a deep voice; Daddy finds it hard to cope with a bully in his cabin. This is just as funny as *Freaky Friday*, it's told in a yeasty style, it takes some enjoyably acid pokes at the wonderful world of Hollywood, and it shows—in a light way that is not didactic—how much insight can be gained into personal relationships if one can really step into someone else's shoes.

> *Zena Sutherland, in a review of "Summer Switch," in* Bulletin of the Center for Children's Books, *Vol. 36, No. 1, September, 1982, p. 19.*

In evoking the reactions of father and son to their predicaments Miss Rodgers demonstrates psychological shrewdness, and she injects a message: sensitive, vulnerable is best. There is an impeccable feminist subtext that wives should not be expected to give up their own jobs and be dragged up the corporate ladder with their spouses. Also, successful women executives, she hints, can be as nice as, well, your second-grade teacher.

Often, however, the author's human insights tend to get lost in an overly glib style that conceals rather than reveals the truths implied in the situations flowing from the initial premise. And the first-person narration, alternating between the father's and the son's points of view, isn't always in character. For example, on the plane Ape Face explains, "I verbatimed what Dad had said about the devastatingly attractive shark in sheep's clothing, pussycat on the surface, coldest fish in filmdom, et cetera, et cetera, blah-blah-blah"—a verbatim I doubt that a 12-year-old-kid would ever verbatim, even in his father's skin. What Mary Rodgers needs is more strength of characterization.

> *Richard Lingeman, "Growing Up and Down," in* The New York Times Book Review, *November 14, 1982, p. 60.*

Who am I? The voices of fiction are never more varied in tone than when they are answering this perennial question. [Here it is] the voice of comedy—teasing, light-hearted but with a serious note to be heard by the discerning. **Summer Switch** is a companion piece to Mary Rodgers' earlier **Freaky Friday,** once more scrutinising through the medium of a bizarre change the distances and difficulties in communication between children and their elders. . . . Many readers will think of the worst moments of Anstey's *Vice Versa* as they watch the efforts of a grown man in a boy's body shaping up to strenuous athletic tests and the rather more insouciant attempts of the schoolboy to understand high finance and office protocol. The American way of life is neatly packaged and examined with cool satirical acumen in scene after inventive scene and the intricacies of the plot are controlled by a formal arrangement by which father and son alternately describe their ordeal, in alternate type-faces. This sharp comedy is crafted with a sure hand and should be enjoyed as an unusual way of mapping that mysterious geographical feature, the generation-gap. (pp. 4067-68)

> *Margery Fisher, in a review of "Summer Switch," in* Growing Point, *Vol. 22, No. 1, May, 1983, pp. 4067-68.*

Jack Denton Scott

1915-

American author of nonfiction.

Well known for creating instructional nature books for middle grade and high school readers, Scott expresses his respect for animals and concern for endangered species in works applauded for their depth and lucidity. Frequently concentrating on a certain species of mammal, bird, or reptile, he writes straightforward descriptions of the evolutionary history, physical characteristics, habitat, diet, mating, and reproduction of his subjects, which include such animals as the cormorant, the horse, the pig, the seal, the swan, the buffalo, the turtle, and the egret. Scott, who is also renowned as a naturalist, an author of adult nonfiction, and a columnist on outdoor life and wildlife, has collaborated most often with photographer Ozzie Sweet; the blending of Scott's texts with Sweet's black-and-white pictures is intended by the collaborators to provide an almost cinematic experience for the reader. Scott's books are considered paens to the natural world which offer young people detailed and unusual views of both domestic and wild animals.

(See also *Something about the Author,* Vol. 31 and *Contemporary Authors,* Vol. 108.)

AUTHOR'S COMMENTARY

Demands [of writing nonfiction for children] are precise: Be accurate. Be relaxed; write fluently; never write down to your readers; never try to write up either. Know your audience; also know your subject; but even if you do know it, research it so that you will know perhaps more than you or anyone else will want to know. Put these all together and they may be an axiom for writing nonfiction for your readers.

But there is more: There can be no cloudy language; writing must be simple, crisp, clear. This, in fact, should be a primer for all writing. Children demand the best from a writer. If young readers become bored, confused, puzzled by style, or showered with a writer's self-important, complicated words you've lost readers. Young readers instinctively shy away from the pretentious and the phony.

In the dozen photo-essays that photographer Ozzie Sweet and I have produced . . ., we have worked with one object in mind: Entertain and inform. We believe that children want to learn; and everyone knows that they want to be entertained. We have tried to do this with clarity in words and with dramatic but thoughtfully conceived photographs by perhaps the most talented man with the camera in the U.S.

We have also introduced our series of books to children with a new technique. Action, constant movement, words flowing into photographs, photographs flowing into words, no labored captions, no slowing of pace. Almost a cinematic technique. This is difficult, demanding that photographer and writer work closely together.

I, personally, also have the belief that too much weird way-out fiction is pushed at children. (I have nothing against fiction; in fact I also write adult fiction.) But children have their own vivid and creative imaginations that they bring to their reading. One 10-year-old boy wrote me that while he was reading our book, **Canada Geese,** he actually flew south with the geese. I bet he did. I *hope* he did.

Ozzie Sweet and I also object to violence in children's literature; it's boring, it's burdensome, and it's unwanted by children. I write of the free, wild creatures and try to give children straight information that will interest them and educate them, staying away from cuteness or giving animals or birds human traits which, of course, they don't have. There is an entire essay on our shrinking world and what wildlife means to children, wildlife that may not even be around when our readers become adults.

Finally, we believe that children who are forming habits and outlooks that will serve them forever are more important than adult readers and we feel fortunate that we have the opportunity to give them worthwhile subjects to think about. Thus we choose those subjects carefully for our intelligent and demanding audience. (pp. 590-91)

Jack Denton Scott, "Through the Eyes of an Author: Writing Natural History for Young Readers," in Through the Eyes of a Child: An Introduction to

Children's Literature, *by Donna E. Norton, second edition, Merrill Publishing Company, 1987, pp. 590-91.*

LOGGERHEAD TURTLE: SURVIVOR FROM THE SEA (1974)

It's a rare achievement to write so extensive and informative a book as this without forfeiting color and lyricism. Scott's visual account of the loggerhead's fight for survival sparkles with wit and admiration for a creature which has remained unaffected by evolution. And [Ozzie] Sweet's photos make the most of the text, especially in pictures of the "Turtle Boys," a group of young conservationists who guard the nests and hatchlings on Jupiter Island, off Florida. The boys watch over the infants and protect them from predators—seabirds, crabs and man. Once the young loggerheads reach the sea, they are on the intricate, perilous path to adulthood. This saga of their life cycle is truly for people of all ages, of all levels of zoological knowledge.

> *A review of "Loggerhead Turtle: Survivor from the Sea," in* Publishers Weekly, *Vol. 205, No. 7, February 18, 1974, p. 74.*

Like Victor Scheffer's *Little Calf,* this is both a poetic essay and an impressively informative book about a marine creature. The photographs are excellent and are nicely integrated with the text. Scott describes in vivid prose the lumbering, ferocious looking loggerhead turtle on land, laboriously scraping a nest and laying her eggs—and waddling back to the sea to move with grace and power in her watery element. As background for his description of the habits and habitat of the loggerhead, he discusses the endurance of a creature that has survived almost unchanged for 150 million years, the dangers it faces today, and the conservation work that is being done to protect it. A fine book.

> *Zena Sutherland, in a review of "Loggerhead Turtle: Survivor from the Sea," in* Bulletin of the Center for Children's Books, *Vol. 27, No. 11, July-August, 1974, p. 185.*

The text contains much accurate information; the author knows his subject. Generally, the book is interesting to read, although the somewhat anthropomorphic style might deter some readers. It is, however, a good concise account of the life and times of the loggerhead turtle, and as such, it can be recommended as useful general reading.

> *D. L. Pawson, in a review of "Loggerhead Turtle: Survivor from the Sea," in* Science Books & Films, *Vol. XI, No. 2, September, 1975, p. 78.*

THAT WONDERFUL PELICAN (1975)

We've already learned the story of the brown pelican's fight against extinction from Robert McClung's *Scoop* (1972), but this is a truly unique view of the bird at home in his nesting ground on Pelican Island, Florida. Scott tells us just how this remarkable fisherman dives for his food from a height of up to 60 feet (inflatable air sacs cushion his impact with the water), how the young, looking like "little antediluvian horrors" are hatched and, pathetically, how the more aggressive hatchling will appropriate all the food, reducing his nestmate to an emaciated shadow. Scott's passion for specifics is only part of his love for these "ancient and lyrical" animals

whom he respects as grand survivors from prehistoric times as well as dockside clowns. Ozzie Sweet's photos capture the pelican in all these aspects, and include a poignant record of the struggle for survival between two nestlings. This is a match for the same team's *Loggerhead Turtle,* and in some ways superior since the pelican's habitat makes him so much more accessible.

> *A review of "That Wonderful Pelican," in* Kirkus Reviews, *Vol. XLIII, No. 6, March 15, 1975, p. 315.*

The author-photographer team that produced last year's outstanding *Loggerhead Turtle: Survivor from the Sea* has provided an equally beautiful and eloquent book on the endangered pelican. Its comic ugliness on land and its magnificence in flight are captured in startlingly sharp black-and-white photographs on every page. The accompanying text describes the pelican life cycle and the efforts necessary to save the world's largest web-footed bird from extinction. It's first-rate writing with the information visualized through superb photography.

> *Lillian N. Gerhardt, in a review of "That Wonderful Pelican," in* School Library Journal, *Vol. 21, No. 9, May, 1975, p. 58.*

Although the title might imply broader coverage, this book deals essentially with only the brown pelican on the coast of Florida. An outstanding feature is the exceptionally sharp black-and-white photography that illustrates the book. The text, written to accompany the photographs, is an independent narrative rather than a series of extended captions. There are a few errors of fact (e.g., birds did not make their "first historic leap into the air" in the Paleocene), but these really do not detract from the story the author has to tell about the life history, behavior, conservation and esthetic appeal of the pelicans. This book would be useful as a reference for junior high school students and as collateral reading at the high school level. To the adult reader, it is a brief, delightful impression of the pelican and the world in which it lives.

> *John L. Zimmerman, in a review of "That Wonderful Pelican," in* Science Books & Films, *Vol. XII, No. 1, May, 1976, p. 26.*

THE SURVIVORS: ENDURING ANIMALS OF NORTH AMERICA (1975)

Crows and gulls, shrews and porcupines are among the 12 familiar North American animals discussed in this readable survey. A miscellany of information about the physical characteristics and behavior of each family is given with an emphasis on the traits which enable these animals to survive and flourish under circumstances which have brought about the near extinction of other species. Scott combines anecdotal material and personal observations into an integrated text which succeeds exceptionally well at conveying interest in and sympathy for the subjects.

> *Margaret Bush, in a review of "The Survivors: Enduring Animals of North America," in* School Library Journal, *Vol. 22, No. 2, October, 1975, p. 101.*

As is evident from his earlier books, *Loggerhead Turtle* and *That Wonderful Pelican,* Scott has both a profound knowledge of the animal world and a writing style that is both spontaneous and fluent. The admiration he feels for wild creatures is never excessive; his views on conservation or respect for animals never become didactic. Here he examines, in separate chapters, some of the creatures that have flourished in a time when so many species have become endangered or extinct: in the descriptions of the twelve survivors (chipmunk, cottontail, coyote, crow, white-tailed deer, gull, opossum, porcupine, raccoon, short-tailed shrew, skunk, and woodchuck) the reasons that they have been successful emerge.

> *Zena Sutherland, in a review of "The Survivors: Enduring Animals of North America," in* Bulletin of the Center for Children's Books, *Vol. 29, No. 8, April, 1976, p. 133.*

With all the furor over our endangered wildlife, this book comes as a refreshing change. The author discusses those wild animals whose populations have been maintained at a high level, despite occasional attempts at extermination. Scott discusses the ecology and behavior of 12 species, emphasizing the economic benefits we accrue from each. Sometimes his advocacy of an animal obscures his good judgment, as in the case of that scourge of farmers, the woodchuck. In other cases, the account is apparently based on limited information, although there has been much work done on these animals. (The feeding habits of the short-tailed shrew provide a case in point.) More fundamentally, Scott sometimes fails to point out which characteristics of the species he discusses have contributed most to the animal's extraordinary abilities to survive in an ecological system distorted by human interference. The wolf, which preys mainly upon large animals, is declining in numbers, while its cousin, the coyote, which feeds primarily on small animals, is burgeoning. The author fails to correlate the differences in food habits with the differences in numbers. Similarly, while mentioning that deer browse on twigs, Scott does not describe the secondary succession that followed the cutting of the climax forest and the enormous increase in available twigs in low, secondary growth. Because of these defects and other annoyances, such as the author's occasional anthropomorphisms and generally teleological arguments, the book cannot be recommended. It's a pity, because there is much good, sound information in this book. . . . (pp. 87-8)

> *D. Covalt-Dunning, in a review of "The Survivors: Enduring Animals of North America," in* Science Books & Films, *Vol. XII, No. 2, September, 1976, pp. 87-8.*

DISCOVERING THE AMERICAN STORK (1976)

The same species appreciation that marked *Loggerhead Turtle; Survivor from the Sea* and *That Wonderful Pelican* is apparent here. The American wood stork has survived, Scott tells us, largely because it has not attracted the undue attention of man: its plumage is not sought after, its feeding habits do not place it in competition with fishermen, and its flesh is unpalatable. And though developers threaten its breeding areas in the Florida cyprus swamps, conservationists have been successful in establishing a sanctuary to preserve the birds' endangered habitat. The personable documentary goes on to describe the mating and nesting habits of the stork, the care of its young, and its special skills as a flier and fisherman. Occasional awkward phrasing and loosely organized information show a need for more careful editing, but the author's involvement with his subject and Sweet's arresting photographs have their effect.

> *Denise M. Wilms, in a review of "Discovering the*

American Stork," in The Booklist, *Vol. 72, No. 14, March 15, 1976, p. 1050.*

Since this team's investigation of *The Loggerhead Turtle* Scott seems to have lost interest in keeping his vocabulary to a level easily manageable by grade school students. Still, his up-to-date report on the stork's prospects and digest of Kahl's research on their habits is valuable, and the intimacy of fine documentary photographs should hold readers through the text's difficult spots. In all, a worthy if less graceful companion to *That Wonderful Pelican.*

> *A review of "Discovering the American Stork," in* Kirkus Reviews, *Vol. XLIV, No. 8, April 15, 1976, p. 487.*

As is true of other books by Scott, this is profusely illustrated with handsome photographs, and the fluent, deceptively casual text is authoritative, lucid, and up to date. . . . Scott describes nesting, courtship, and mating procedures (the male chooses a nest site, the female then woos him), and the care and feeding of the young when they hatch. Also discussed are flight patterns and feeding habits. Fascinating.

> *Zena Sutherland, in a review of "Discovering the American Stork," in* Bulletin of the Center for Children's Books, *Vol. 30, No. 2, October, 1976, p. 31.*

CANADA GEESE (1976)

This beautiful, informative volume by the nature-loving team of [Scott and photographer Ozzie Sweet] equals in excellence their books on the loggerhead, the pelican, the American stork and others. Now they zero in on the Canadian goose, a species which no one with an ounce of romance has ever been able to resist. Pictures and text are devoted to the geese's precision flights, the instinct which urges them to flee south before the first killing frosts, the way they choose leaders for their exhausting V-formation flight (which sometimes takes them as high as 9000 feet) and other facts about the superb navigators. This is a book which adults, as well as younger readers, should find irresistible.

> *A review of "Canada Geese," in* Publishers Weekly, *Vol. 209, No. 19, May 10, 1976, p. 84.*

In an elegant contrast to [Thomas D. Fegely's *The Wonders of Geese and Swans*], Scott stays close to one flock of (Todd's) Canada geese and uses intimate glimpses of their lives as a take-off point for more expansive questions—among them, how migratory birds find their way (part of the answer, uncovered by watching birds inside a planetarium, seems to be a genetic "star map"). We also find out how scientists have categorized the different goose cries; see the step-by-step progress of a mating ritual (though not mating itself); and learn how geese defend their nest (Audubon nearly had his arm broken by an angry nester) and present themselves to their goslings for imprinting. All this occurs in a poetic setting—there are shots of geese circling at sunset, and references to the "piercing and mournful" calls of a gander who has lost his mate to hunters (though, of course, "no one can tell what that . . . goose feels or if he has the capacity for sorrow"); and the beauty is never a distraction or a substitute for accuracy, but a canvas on which the facts and emotional response meld.

> *A review of "Canada Geese," in* Kirkus Reviews, *Vol. XLIV, No. 11, June 1, 1976, p. 639.*

The numerous photographs are perhaps the best part of this latest collaboration between the author and photographer who gave us **Discovering the American Stork** and **That Wonderful Pelican.** In contrast to Fegely's *The Wonders of Geese and Swans,* the author follows one flock of Todd's Canada Geese, and discusses, in considerably more detail than Fegely, certain aspects of anatomy, the process of imprinting, and current theories on how migrating flocks find their way. Unfortunately what is intended to be a poetic photo essay is marred by emotionalism in the discussion of hunting, by considerable anthropomorphism, and even some sexism. The goose is "demure" and "snuggles up" to the gander. . . . While the work contains much useful information, this is a mood piece rather than a reference book.

> *Rea Alkema, in a review of "Canada Geese," in* Appraisal: Children's Science Books, *Vol. 10, No. 2, Spring, 1977, p. 47.*

RETURN OF THE BUFFALO (1976)

Scott and Sweet follow the format of their successful photo-essays . . . in this account of the revival of the once nearly extinct bison commonly known as the American buffalo. History and information on physiology and behavior are presented in a text which tends to wax a bit over-eloquent at times. . . . Scott lays bare the wastefulness of the white man's mass slaughter of the thriving buffalo population and praises those instrumental in protecting and nourishing the few remaining animals, but he goes too far in leaving readers with the sense that buffaloes are safe from exploitation (e.g., nowhere does he mention that buffalo meat is now being featured in supermarkets). Still, no other title at present is devoted to the animal, and the book is, undeniably, handsome.

> *Margaret Bush, in a review of "Return of the Buffalo," in* School Library Journal, *Vol. 23, No. 4, December, 1976, p. 56.*

This is a rather undistinguished book with an undistinguished cover and undistinguished illustrations. The text contains a fair bit of information on the life and times of our native cow, but it is marred by questionable comments and generalizations. The illustrations (one per page) are uncaptioned but generally relate to the adjacent text. . . . This is not a book I would give a child as a gift, nor would I expect a child to deliberately choose it in the library. On the other hand, it is inexpensive and contains subject matter that kids enjoy. It might be called a serendipity book—the kind you find in a library tucked next to the book you were really looking for. So I suspect that a fair number of junior readers will stumble on this book, take it home, and know more about buffalo than they otherwise would.

> *John D. Buffington, in a review of "Return of the Buffalo," in* Science Books & Films, *Vol. XIII, No. 2, September, 1977, p. 99.*

LITTLE DOGS OF THE PRAIRIE (1977)

As they have for the American Stork, Canada Geese, and other creatures of the wild, Scott and Sweet team up here with superior photos and a brief but informative text for an appreciative introduction to the prairie dog. Though Scott's prose is occasionally awkward, he does clarify some minor issues that are more carelessly handled elsewhere: where Eber-

le (*Prairie Dogs in Prairie Dog Town,* 1974) shows her semi-fictionalized subjects trapping and burying a rattlesnake, Scott goes into the conflicting reports on how they actually do react to rattlers; he also points out that there are more than the two subspecies reported in Chace's *Wonders of Prairie Dogs* (1976), which is closest to this in level and coverage but far less attractive. In addition to the seven subclasses of prairie dogs, Scott reports eight separate barks (each with a different meaning) and at least four ways in which their digging benefits the soil; his description of the animal's feeding habits includes also the non-nutritional function of grass-eating and aspects of its unique digestive system. With Sweet's intimate, appealing photos, this comes closest yet to the treatment that these clannish, industrious, and most engaging creatures seem to call for.

> *A review of "Little Dogs of the Prairie," in* Kirkus Reviews, *Vol XLV, No. 9, May 1, 1977, p. 491.*

For older readers and with more extensive treatment than the books about prairie dogs by Eberle and by Chace, this is written in a graceful style, gives accurate information, and is illustrated with photographs of good quality. As he has in earlier books, Scott not only describes the habits and habitat of his subjects but also places them in their ecological environment and discusses them in relation to conservation of species.

> *Zena Sutherland, in a review of "Little Dogs of the Prairie," in* Bulletin of the Center for Children's Books, *Vol. 31, No. 3, November, 1977, p. 53.*

Excellent photographs and clear, readable text complement each other in this introduction to the prairie dog. . . . The author alerts the reader to the current ecological plight of this amusing animal; poisoning of prairie dogs, a practice originating in the 1880s, is still popular with ranchers and farmers who incorrectly blame this animal for depleted grazing lands. The book's use with younger children may be supplemented by Alston's *Come Visit a Prairie-Dog Town* (Harcourt, 1976), a pleasant, informative and easy book illustrated with line drawings. There is no index or table of contents but the text is brief enough that browsing gives adequate access to specific details. Highly recommended for both school and public libraries. (pp. 43-4)

> *Christine McDonnell, in a review of "Little Dogs of the Prairie," in* Appraisal: Children's Science Books, *Vol. 11, No. 1, Winter, 1978, pp. 43-4.*

THE GULLS OF SMUTTYNOSE ISLAND (1977)

Sweet's photographs are beautiful, varied, clear, and informative; Scott's writing is lucid, authoritative, skillfully organized and often poetic in its phrasing and vision. In his description of the herring gulls and black-backed gulls that take over an Atlantic island rookery each summer, Scott includes every aspect of the gulls' lives: mating and breeding patterns, group behavior, territorial prerogatives, flight, feeding and nesting. . . . It's a superb book.

> *Zena Sutherland, in a review of "The Gulls of Smuttynose Island," in* Bulletin of the Center for Children's Books, *Vol. 31, No. 6, February, 1978, p. 101.*

The Gulls of Smuttynose Island belongs in every bird lover's library! The poetic text by Jack Denton Scott and the beautiful black and white photographs by Ozzie Sweet capture the magic of the rocky islands off the New England coast where thousands of gulls take up residence. . . . Although the book has a certain poetic beauty, it also provides a wealth of scientific information. Mr. Scott quotes Niko Tinbergen, the world-renowned expert on gull behavior. Only a few small mistakes mar the book. On page eleven, Scott explains how the laughing gulls steal food from pelicans. This is true—in the southern part of the gull's range, but there are no pelicans near Smuttynose Island. Also on page twenty, *Charadriifommmes* is called a "species" when it is actually an Order. Due to the very sophisticated vocabulary, the book would present problems even for older children. Teachers and parents could help alleviate these problems; the pictures could be "read" by younger students. Overall, **The Gulls of Smuttynose Island** will be sure to excite young "birders." (pp. 34-5)

> *Martha T. Kane, in a review of "The Gulls of Smuttynose Island," in* Appraisal: Children's Science Books, *Vol. 12, No. 1, Winter, 1979, pp. 34-5.*

Scott and Sweet detail the lives of herring gulls and great black-backed gulls on the rookery on Smuttynose Island, off the New England Coast. Beginning with the springtime arrival of the gulls at the rookery, they describe the major inter- and intraspecific behaviors and physiological phenomena that occur during the gulls' summer occupancy of the island. The treatment of both the behavior and the physiology is appropriately substantial for the intended audience and nicely documented by citations from biological research. Perhaps the most outstanding and useful feature of this large-format book is the close linkage between the text and the fine black-and-white photographs. Even in the more dense sections of the text (of which there are very few), the placement and choice of photographs reduce confusion and make interest and understanding more likely. The one discrepant feature in this otherwise fine book is the disparity between the physical features of the book, which are made to appeal to a juvenile audience, and the level of text presentation, which seems at times more appropriate for an older audience.

> *Fred Rasmussen, in a review of "The Gulls of Smuttynose Island," in* Science Books & Films, *Vol. XIV, No. 4, March, 1979, p. 232.*

CITY OF BIRDS AND BEASTS: BEHIND THE SCENES AT THE BRONX ZOO   (1978)

Until now, naturalist Scott and photographer Sweet have been famous for their documentaries on wild creatures. Now they take readers behind the scenes at the Bronx Zoo, the 252-acre preserve in New York. In vivid photos and a skillful text, the team describes, almost moment by moment, the incredible events during one day at the great park. At dawn, the staff is alerted by screams from the rheas (ostrichlike birds) and arrest a man who is caught pulling out the creatures' tail feathers. At 6:20 A.M., the curator of reptiles solves the mystery of 30 timber rattlers found in a shopping center. From sunup to sundown, incidents infuriating, amusing, worrying, and sometimes tragic keep the people on the alert. Readers of all ages will be fascinated by this book, a work that should increase our awareness of and respect for animals and their protectors.

> *A review of "City of Birds and Beasts," in* Publishers Weekly, *Vol. 215, No. 8, February 20, 1978, p. 127.*

This presumably composite day-in-the-life exposé of zoo inner workings makes easy, interesting reading; it proceeds

like a log book, beginning with the 4:50 predawn setting in which Animal Commissary head George Fielding begins food preparation for the inhabitants' morning meals. Continuing entries introduce the keepers, curators, and other personnel who handle everyday routines, problems, or emergencies. . . . Scott obviously likes what he found inside the zoo, and his vignettes consistently highlight a dedicated staff and management; add to this humane aura smooth writing and Sweet's clean black-and-white photographs. The introduction is most pleasing.

> *Denise M. Wilms, in a review of "City of Birds and Beasts: Behind the Scenes at the Bronx Zoo," in* Booklist, *Vol. 74, No. 18, May 15, 1978, p. 1497.*

Scott's attempt to depict what happens during a day at the Bronx Zoo actually shows an inflated, unrealistic and particularly awful day for the zoo staff. The zoo director or curator who has to cope with five or six escapes, two major deaths (a gorilla and an elephant), six animal injuries, a snake bite and two employee hospitalizations in a "typical day" would be driven completely insane in a week. Most zoos are far more efficiently and professionally run to ever experience most of these activities in any week, month or year. The author is trying to make his story exciting, and his prose often calls for excesses that are simply not there. Employees are described in glowing, superhuman terms: One is "widely respected," another "expert" and a "quick thinker": others "strive constantly, missing no detail." The attempt to show behind-the-scene activities ranges from a ludicrous discussion between the assistant curator of education and the director of the zoo to the slightly more believable interchanges between curators and keepers. The relatively few errors are mostly misspellings and wishful half-truths. The author uses the word "animal" interchangeably with "mammal," "vertebrate" and "organism." . . . The book does hint at the complexity of operations in any large zoo, but does not do justice to the complexity of the Bronx Zoo. The writing, when it is not idolizing or exaggerating, is clear and occasionally manages to evoke some of the many sides of zoo life. In summary, the book has little to recommend it as a realistic picture of operation of the Bronx Zoo. There are better general zoo books, and an Annual Report of the New York Zoological Society will probably be more informative about the Bronx Zoo's real work.

> *James W. Waddick, in a review of "City of Birds and Beasts: Behind the Scenes at the Bronx Zoo," in* Science Books & Films, *Vol. XV, No. 1, May, 1979, p. 42.*

DISCOVERING THE MYSTERIOUS EGRET   (1978)

Cattle egrets, at the heart of this latest Scott-Sweet photoessay, confound scientists with their precedent-breaking behavior. The birds, native to Africa, turned up in British Guiana in 1930; in 20 years they had spread through Surinam, Venezuela, and Colombia, and in 1950 Sudbury Valley, Massachusetts, bird-watchers took astonished note of them there. Their continued success has been due in part to the surprising fact that they've settled into an unoccupied biological niche: their feeding routine—sticking close to grazing herds who stir up insects—does not infringe on food supplies of indigenous species; moreover, their breeding and young-raising patterns work to foster survival. Scott explains it all in simple, often lyrical prose, and by the end he's once more sparked a sense of wonder at nature's machinations.

> *Denise M. Wilms, in a review of "Discovering the Mysterious Egret," in* Booklist, *Vol. 74, No. 17, May 1, 1978, p. 1438.*

A native of East Africa, the cattle egret, weighing approximately four pounds, lives amongst herds of grazing Masai cattle, hippopotamus and rhinoceros. Scott and Sweet have chosen this slender white bird as the subject of their latest collaboration, a marvelous photo-essay on one of nature's most beautiful creatures. The text is lengthy and very inclusive, covering the egret from birth to maturity to death. The photographs both complement and expand the factual information. An excellent resource for both African and ornithological information.

> *Amy Scholar, in a review of "Discovering the Mysterious Egret," in* School Library Journal, *Vol. 25, No. 2, October, 1978, p. 150.*

ISLAND OF WILD HORSES (1978)

"What manner of horse can survive on an island for as long as 300 years, living on thin grass, marsh plants, and leaves?" Darwin was as stumped by the success of the Chincoteague equine breed as naturalists are today. Beginning with theories and local legends of how the small stallion-ruled bands first landed in their unlikely Virginia location, Scott and Sweet go on to describe the habitat in detail, from grazing grounds of soggy marshes to groves of loblolly pines that shelter the animals from storms. Even more fascinating than the ecology of this species' survival is the politics involved in their conservation. The town fire department has an admirably non-violent approach to population control—an annual round-up and auction; and, if winters are severe, the brigade chops holes in frozen ponds and drops care packages of hay to the herds. . . . This is a fine, handsomely illustrated and well-designed factual essay on a lively subject bound to be appealing to a wide audience including those with fond memories of Marguerite Henry's Misty.

> *Laura Geringer, in a review of "Island of Wild Horses," in* School Library Journal, *Vol. 25, No. 3, November, 1978, p. 68.*

A staunch conservationist, Scott discusses, as he has in earlier books, both the environmental adaption of the animals he is writing about and the protective legislation that enables them to continue to have their freedom and comparative safety. The writing style is straightforward, the information accurate, the tone sympathetic but not saccharine.

> *Zena Sutherland, in a review of "Island of Wild Horses," in* Bulletin of the Center for Children's Books, *Vol. 32, No. 7, March, 1979, p. 126.*

Once again this author/photographer team has created another stirring wildlife book, this time about the wild horses which live on the Island of Assateague off the coast of Virginia. Various theories on how the horses got to the Island are discussed. The photo-essay describes their life on the Island. Especially interesting is the struggle the horses face with the harsh Atlantic winter weather. The well-written smoothly flowing prose is scientifically accurate. The superb black and white photographs are both interpretive and informative. In-

dividuals of all ages will want to read this attractive book. (p. 53)

> *Herbert J. Stolz, in a review of "Island of Wild Horses," in* Appraisal: Children's Science Books, *Vol. 12, No. 3, Fall, 1979, pp. 52-3.*

THE BOOK OF THE GOAT (1979)

A very attractive, rather erudite book that is definitely pro goat. The author first tries to undo some negative stereotypes about goats and challenges the dog's position as human's best and oldest friend. He does this by tracing the goat through history where it obviously held a very popular place, even achieving divinity among the Egyptians, Greeks, and Romans. The six most common breeds are then presented—Saanen, Nubian, Alpine, La Mancha, Toggenburg and Angora—with all their specifications. The rest of the book is devoted to praising goat intelligence, cleanliness, personality and character, milk and fleece, breeding and kidding, feeding habits and herd behavior. The photographs are excellent and add greatly to the book's appeal; there is an especially fine series showing the birth of a pair of kids. The pictures should spur less accomplished readers on to tackle the text which, though generally interesting, is difficult and sometimes reads like an obstacle course, particularly in the history section, e.g., "Archaeologists do, however, make the flat statement that based on evidence gathered it is obvious that the goat was definitely the first ruminant to be domesticated" (both "archaeologists" and "ruminant" have been previously defined). Nonetheless, this is a high quality book, and the only one available specifically on goats, except for the more limited *Dairy Goats* by Gregory (Arco, 1976).

> *Marilyn R. Singer, in a review of "The Book of the Goat," in* School Library Journal, *Vol. 26, No. 2, October, 1979, p. 162.*

The excellent photos make this a very appealing book, and the text, though it contains some difficult vocabulary, is interesting and informative. This is a good book to combat misinformation about goats. The author and photographer present an image of an intelligent, clean, affectionate and photogenic animal. (pp. 733-34)

> *A review of "The Book of the Goat," in* The Reading Teacher, *Vol. 33, No. 6, March, 1980, pp. 733-34.*

THE SUBMARINE BIRD (1979)

The author and photographer who have been honored for their photo essays on wildlife present an outstanding book on the astonishing cormorant. Scott's polished text is particularly interesting where it describes features of the bird that substantiate the theory of avian evolution from reptiles. The book contains information on the cormorant's mating, nesting habits, care of the fledglings, etc. The many engrossing facts about the "submarine bird" are illustrated by Sweet's remarkable photos taken at rookeries where thousands of birds are massed and in various parts of the world.

> *A review of "The Submarine Bird," in* Publishers Weekly, *Vol. 216, No. 23, December 3, 1979, p. 52.*

Clear, action-filled black-and-white photographs aid the text in describing the cormorants' courtship and breeding rituals, the raising of young, their diving ability and feeding habits, and other interesting bits of information about their history and their ecological niche (they do not, contrary to popular belief, rob fishermen of valuable food fish, their diet consisting of mostly "trash" fish). Two minor flaws: in some places, the writing is not as smooth as it could be, with a few awkward sentences and unclear pronoun references; and one photograph of an anhinga (which very closely resembles a cormorant), included for the purpose of comparison, is not clearly identified.

Karen Ritter, in a review of "The Submarine Bird," in School Library Journal, *Vol. 26, No. 5, January, 1980, p. 75.*

With an abundance of illustrations, Scott presents the natural history of cormorants, including their use by fishermen in the Orient. The author concentrates on one species—the double-crested cormorant. . . . Unfortunately, the text includes questionable statements about evolutionary history and errors of spelling and grammar. I find it difficult to believe that cormorants can look like vultures, diamondback rattlers, *Archaeopteryx* and vampires. This book is acceptable primarily because of the excellent photographs.

Dennis Sustare, in a review of "The Submarine Bird," in Science Books & Films, *Vol. 16, No. 1, September-October, 1980, p. 34.*

WINDOW ON THE WILD (1980)

"I hope that the reader will also be patient with my frequent intrusions into the pages that follow." Indeed the author does intrude into these essays on 11 animals (earthworm, monarch butterfly, beaver, badger, red fox, gray squirrel, weasel, ruffed grouse, bald eagle, loon and great horned owl). He is admittedly sentimental and extols the marvels of nature in lush terms ("the feather-brush football of the field mouse"; "that bit of ebony-and-gold gossamer"). He reminisces and cites the experiences and conversations of friends and other naturalists. His purpose is to teach better habits of observation, and he repeatedly exhorts readers to this effect. Some genuinely interesting observations and bits of information on animal behavior are also to be found. Scott's intent is laudable and his respect for the animals genuine; but his book will appeal most to certain adults who think that paeans to nature are nice for children.

Margaret Bush, in a review of "Window on the Wild," in School Library Journal, *Vol. 27, No. 4, December, 1980, p. 64.*

Scott calls this a lesson in "seeing"—his term for observing nature—and he begins each of these eleven animal sketches with a first-person account of some encounter of his own. But the discussions of different animals don't focus on those features that might be observed by an amateur in the wild; nor do they include any tips on finding the creatures or any hints as to how they are to be observed. Instead, they mix anecdotes of past observations with reports on life cycles or special features, and with much appreciative exclamation—on the worm's contribution to the soil, the monarch butterfly's migration feat, the badger's strength and skill, the fox's cunning, the loon's affecting cry, and so on. It's all pleasantly readable in a chatty, personal way, which might give it some appeal for the casual naturalist who has not read the more informative juveniles on these animals. Serious readers might wish for more sense of direction.

A review of "Window on the Wild," in Kirkus Reviews, *Vol. XLIX, No. 3, February 1, 1981, p. 146.*

Writing as a naturalist rather than a biologist, Scott presents descriptions of 11 different animals, ranging in complexity from the earthworm and butterfly to the great horned owl and the bald eagle. His facile style provides very interesting and easy reading, and his language portrays that beauty and peace found in nature. Scientific terminology never becomes burdensome for, if he uses a new or unusual term, Scott defines it as he progresses. A unique feature of his book is the constant stress on the importance of observation and proof that so much is missed by the unobservant. A minor shortcoming of this book is the illustrations [by Geri Greinke]: more linocuts would have increased the appeal of the book, and photographs certainly would have added to the attractiveness of the text and would have enhanced the book particularly for younger readers. All in all, however, the author is to be complimented for a book that is a delight to any lover of nature.

Sr. Laura Herold, in a review of "Window on the Wild," in Science Books & Films, *Vol. 16, No. 5, May-June, 1981, p. 264.*

THE BOOK OF THE PIG (1981)

Naturalists Scott and Sweet add to their acclaimed essays on animals with their outstanding text and photos on the maligned pig. The clear, information-packed text and fine photos in black-and-white should alter ideas of pigs as greedy, dirty, stupid and so on. Actually, they are highly intelligent, affectionate and predisposed to domestication. Pigs' feeding habits are fastidious; they wallow, but in clean mud (except in desperation when they roll in anything soothingly wet), to survive the heat because they are unable to sweat. Examples of the pig's importance to humans, historical facts and anecdotes document Scott's report. And two unforgettable photos illustrate an affable, independent, 1000-lb. sow who trots around her New England village, calling on residents and asking for handouts.

A review of "The Book of the Pig," in Publishers Weekly, *Vol. 219, No. 16, April 17, 1981, p. 63.*

Scott and Sweet employ their familiar photo-essay format to pay tribute to the temperament, intelligence and usefulness of the domestic pig. The photographs—exceptionally pleasing in quality and content—convey the distinctive character of many breeds and individuals, the winsome nature of the young and the impressive girth of the adult animal. The text is difficult in syntax and vocabulary but clear and smoothly developed. History, behavior, breeding and raising of the young are covered as well as the animal's usefulness to man for food, medical products and psychological and biological research. The jolting connection between these appealing animals and bacon and ham is avoided—commercial practices and uses are downplayed with no mention at all of slaughtering procedures. The portion of the text describing characteristics of particular breeds does not generally coordinate with the relevant photographs, making this information less clear than it might be. On the whole, the often maligned pig is well served by this attractive appreciative introduction.

Margaret Bush, in a review of "The Book of the Pig," in School Library Journal, *Vol. 27, No. 9, May, 1981, p. 69.*

With frequent kudos from uninformed pig-lovers as well as from more scientific observers who attest to the intelligence, amicability, and natural (if belied) cleanliness of the pig, this informative text just—but just—avoids being fulsome. It avoids the pitfall by providing facts in a straightforward style, giving details about popular breeds, behavior patterns, mating, care of young, and temperament. The text is continuous, the print large, the illustrations of good quality, well-placed but not captioned.

> *Zena Sutherland, in a review of "The Book of the Pig," in* Bulletin of the Center for Children's Books, *Vol. 35, No. 1, September, 1981, p. 16.*

MOOSE (1981)

This seasoned team of nature reporters presents yet another species profile. Sweet's photographs offer a number of engaging as well as reverential poses of this animal that "seems to be made up of the spare parts of other animals." The text has a personable force that will attract readers; unfortunately, sloppy editing has resulted in a number of awkward sentences and outright grammatical errors. Also, biological terminology sometimes goes undefined. Attractive looking and informative despite the above-mentioned problems, this will fill the bill as introductory fare.

> *Denise M. Wilms, in a review of "Moose," in* Booklist, *Vol. 78, No. 10, January 15, 1982, p. 655.*

The author and photographer pool their dependable skills to produce another good book in their series of photo-essays on animals. Here the majestic scenery of the far north adds to the beauty of the photographs; the text is Scott's usual amalgam of carefully detailed facts about habits, habitat, mating and reproductive patterns, appearance, eating habits, et cetera. The writing is serious but not dry, dignified but not formal, and imbued with naturalist Scott's own enthusiastic interest in the subject.

> *Zena Sutherland, in a review of "Moose," in* Bulletin of the Center for Children's Books, *Vol. 35, No. 6, February, 1982, p. 116.*

In prose, photographs and picture-book format, just about all you want to know about moose. And you can enjoyably "read" *Moose* simply by looking at the illustrations. However, the adult-level vocabulary and text of long and rambling sentences could deter some young readers. A more detailed and objective book than Irmengarde Eberle's *Moose Live Here* (Doubleday, 1971), *Moose* is overall of the same caliber as Scott and Sweet's fine *Little Dogs of the Prairie.* The popularity of this topic with hunters and others is attested by numerous articles in such publications as *Field and Stream, Outdoor Life* and *National Wildlife; Moose* could be useful to flesh out such articles.

> *George Gleason, in a review of "Moose," in* School Library Journal, *Vol. 28, No. 8, April, 1982, p. 85.*

ORPHANS FROM THE SEA (1982)

It all began in 1971 when 25-year-old Ralph Heath found a crippled cormorant on a Florida beach and took it home to his parents' rec room. Others heard about his project and sent more birds, and soon the Suncoast Seabird Sanctuary was in full swing. Scott describes the sanctuary's fourfold pro-

gram—Rescue (now expanded to search and rescue), Repair, Recuperation, and Release (over 10,000 birds have been returned to the wild so far, though many disabled ones must be kept on for life)—and Sweet contributes his crisp pictures of the birds and of the staff at work. Most of the sanctuary's patients are Brown Pelicans, a once-populous species hard hit by pesticides and PCB's; 85 percent of their injuries are from fish hooks or monofilament fishing line. Funded entirely by donations, the center also feeds wild birds and breeds disabled ones whose healthy chicks are eventually released. Among animal rescue documentaries, this is tight, unsentimental, and visually attractive.

> *A review of "Orphans from the Sea," in* Kirkus Reviews, *Vol. L, No. 17, September 1, 1982, p. 999.*

Profusely illustrated by photographs of excellent quality, this description of a wildlife haven, the Suncoast Seabird Sanctuary, is divided into sections that correspond to the organization's four purposes: rescue, repair, recuperation, and release. Some of the many varieties of birds (and an occasional snake or turtle) have been hurt by natural causes, some (often unintentionally) by people. The sanctuary's dedicated staff and successful program are described in a text that is lively, sympathetic, and informative, its message loud and clear.

> *Zena Sutherland, in a review of "Orphans from the Sea," in* Bulletin of the Center for Children's Books, *Vol. 36, No. 6, February, 1983, p. 117.*

THE FUR SEALS OF PRIBILOF (1983)

The slaughtering of baby seals for the fur industry is a perennial banner for animals rights supported by many proactive organizations. Thus, ***The Fur Seals of Pribilof*** is relevant and can be useful for helping young readers become more effective adult decision makers. This is neither an advocate's nor an adversary's book for animal rights activists. It is an informational source, and a fair and good one. Many black and white photographs [by Ozzie Sweet] are used, although most are enriching rather than correlated with the text. Topics include harvesting history, life cycle, survival, herding, territorialism, and daily behavior. The format and type-size are suited for younger readers; however, the sentence structure and vocabulary will challenge ages 12-15.

> *John R. Pancella, in a review of "The Fur Seals of Pribilof," in* Appraisal: Science Books for Young People, *Vol. 17, No. 2, Spring-Summer, 1984, p. 41.*

Millions of northern fur seals were indiscriminately slaughtered for their thick, lustrous fur before 1911, then the seal-hunting nations signed an international agreement to regulate the hunt and to protect breeding females. Of the four now protected populations of *Callorhinus ursinus,* Scott focuses on the largest, the seals of the Pribilof Islands off Alaska. The many visually excellent (although not well reproduced) black-and-white photographs, along with the vivid text, portray details of courtship and the lives of the baby seals; the chaos of bulls establishing their breeding territories and sequestering their females; the details of ears, fur, and flippers; adaptations for surviving Arctic temperatures; and the seals' ability to dive for fish down to 600 feet. Unfortunately, the section that describes the seals' evolution is marred by a number of confusing phrases, including this vast oversimplification: "the seals that still crawl . . . are thought to have evolved from otters, while those that move on all four flippers . . . are thought to have evolved from bears." Some of the confusion of this section appears to be the result of the author's trying to simplify a passage from Victor Scheffer's *The Year of the Seal.* Despite several unclear passages and the lack of index or maps, Scott has produced an interesting, live- ly book on this remarkable species.

> *Aryln M. Christopherson, in a review of "The Fur Seals of Pribilof," in* Science Books & Films, *Vol. 20, No. 1, September-October, 1984, p. 22.*

ALLIGATOR (1984)

Complete with sharp black-and-white photographs [by Ozzie Sweet], this slim volume chronicles the alligator's time on Earth from the Mesozoic era to its present resurgence be- cause of the protection of the Endangered Species Act. All facets of alligator life are covered: physical appearance, habi- tat, breeding and reproduction. Discussion includes how they were first pursued for their valuable hides and are now being pursued for alligator meat, a recent food fad. The problems of "nuisance" alligators and misconceptions are also dealt with, along with the development of alligator farms. There are a few problems with this book. It does not have a table of contents, and the index is inadequate. Some of the photo- graphs need clarification or captions. Sentence structure and vocabulary are more suitable for adults. There is no list of sources. However, the concise treatment of this remarkable animal makes the book a good addition to reptile collections for older children.

> *Olive Hull, in a review of "Alligator," in* School Li- brary Journal, *Vol. 31, No. 6, February, 1985, p. 86.*

In *Alligator,* Scott presents a sympathetic, fairly comprehen- sive exposition of the problems that are associated with more than 100 years of the harvesting and poaching of alligators and traces the development and the effects of recent conserva- tion laws designed to protect them. Woven into the narrative, which presents the life history and habits of alligators in an interesting manner, are discussions of some prevalent mis- conceptions. Photographer Sweet creates an excellent pictor- al study in black and white of these surviving prehistoric "liz- ards." However, there is a limit to the information that can be conveyed without color or by not including underwater photographs. The vocabulary and sentence length make the book difficult for young readers. Nevertheless, the author's easy, flowing style and the interesting subject matter make this a good supplementary book.

> *Charlotte M. Boener, in a review of "Alligator," in* Science Books & Films, *Vol. 20, No. 5, May-June, 1985, p. 310.*

SWANS (1988)

Swans, a favorite subject of Michelangelo and da Vinci, are perceived as a symbol of serene beauty. Depicted as the em- bodiment of grace in paintings, poetry, music, and dance, swans are also powerfully accomplished fliers. Scott notes

that ornithologists consider their speed and altitude the "most astonishing flight of all birds"—a whistling swan was struck by an airplane at 30,000 feet. An impressive wingspan and a complicated collection of more than 25,000 feathers contribute to the swans' miracle of flight. Accomplished wildlife photographer Sweet's dramatic black-and-white shots augment the text's enlightening description of physical characteristics and behavior. Constantly vigilant and aggres- sive, swans are strongly motivated by territorial imperatives and a zealous protective instinct for their fuzzy, vulnerable young. The life-style of the swans and cygnets is seen in an abundance of striking close-ups. The author terms swans as "birds of character," and he and Sweet succeed in portraying them as such; straightforward for reports, engrossing for browsing.

> *Philis Wilson, in a review of "Swans," in* Booklist, *Vol. 84, No. 18, May 15, 1988, p. 1612.*

As usual, Scott and Sweet have produced a book in which the text and photographs have equal strength, even to the unusu- al care with which the pictures are placed to make captions unnecessary in almost every instance. The subject lends itself to action pictures of grace and beauty, and to still shots, also beautiful, that extend the text. The continuous text is smooth, seldom formal, never cute or repetitive. Scott gives facts about anatomical structure and flight, about characteristics of species, about habitats and migrations, and about all the patterns of courting, mating, nesting, and rearing cygnets in a book that is pleasant to read and dependably accurate in the information it provides.

> *Zena Sutherland, in a review of "Swans," in* Bulle- tin of the Center for Children's Books, *Vol. 41, No. 10, June, 1988, p. 216.*

Naturalist Scott and photographer Sweet explain the charac- teristics and life cycle of the seven species of swans found worldwide. Utilizing their now familiar combination of lucid, accurate text and sometimes startling close-up black-and- white photographs, the duo creates a readable and intriguing portrait of these majestic birds. Interestingly, more than half of this exploration is spent detailing the habits of the mute swan, the species most commonly seen in this country but which is not native to the United States. Some previous knowledge about birds will be helpful for readers, since terms such as *slipstream, primary feathers,* and *preening* are not de- fined, and the majority of photographs are not labeled. Inter- esting digressions include a discussion of the expression "swan song" and the history of the mute swan as a Royal Bird in Britain. Report writers will find what they need here and will be additionally rewarded with a respectful and up-to- date look at these stately birds. The integrity of this presenta- tion surpasses Coldrey's *World of Swans* and *Swan on the Lake* (both Gareth Stevens, 1986), and is for an older audi- ence than either. (pp. 194-95)

> *Ellen Fader, in a review of "Swans," in* School Li- brary Journal, *Vol. 35, No. 1, September, 1988, pp. 194-95.*

Tejima

1931-

(Also writes as Keizaburo Tejima) Japanese author and illustrator of picture books.

One of the most acclaimed international creators of picture books to have emerged in recent years, Tejima is applauded for works which use colorful woodcuts, distinctive page design, and simple yet poetic texts to express the beauty of nature and its cycles for children in preschool through the early grades. Considered an artist of exceptional virtuosity, he is recognized for expanding the possibilities of the woodcut technique with his commanding illustrations. Tejima spins delicate tales which have as their protagonists animals from and around his birthplace of Hokkaido in Japan. His earliest books, *The Bears' Autumn* (1986) and *Owl Lake* (1987), provide quiet observations about a bear cub and his mother and a night in the life of an owl family. However, he underscores his later books *Fox's Dream* (1987) and *Swan Sky* (1988) with deeper themes of renewal: *Fox's Dream* (1987) describes how a lonely fox, hunting a snow hare in a mountain forest, meets a vixen after having a vision, while *Swan Sky* (1988) outlines how a family of swans waits for one that is sick, flies away, and then returns to stay with her until she dies; after her death, they continue on their journey. Celebrations of life and death, Tejima's works are characteristically illustrated with double-page spreads which contain a dramatic use of color contrast, shifts in perspective, and bold line art.

THE BEARS' AUTUMN (1986)

This simple tale about a bear cub's first salmon-fishing expedition is greatly enhanced by beautifully executed woodcuts. It is fall in the northern forests of Japan, and a mother and her baby cub are finding food to sustain themselves during their winter hibernation. From a high tree, Baby Bear spies a river, and that evening the two venture down to the water's edge. After several false attempts, Baby Bear finally catches his first salmon and enjoys the results. The contrasts of color that Tejima achieves in his woodcuts are exemplary and heighten the story's drama as do the sure, bold lines that effectively form the figures and emphasize the action. This book offers sharing possibilities with children on several levels: as an example of outstanding woodcuts, as an offering from another country, and as a nature story. Its conclusion, when the baby bear mistakes a shaft of moonlight for a fish and then dreams of the "big fish that got away," adds a bit of fantasy that is also evocatively displayed in the graphics.

Barbara Elleman, in a review of "The Bears' Autumn," in Booklist, *Vol. 83, No. 13, March 1, 1987, p. 1057.*

[*The Bears' Autumn* is a] simple, pared-down, original story, and the text, which is stilted, does not rise above average. But oh, the woodcuts! There are 19 of them, all double-page spreads. The large size of the page and the lack of margins add to the drama inherent in Tejima's strong, heavy lines and superb designs. In the strange, underwater world of the river, the green bodies of the fish curve like the lines of white foam;

Baby Bear's astonished eyes, round and white, echo the shape of the white bubbles of his breath. The colors used throughout suggest both the season and the setting: the dark reddish-orange, purple, brown, and gold of the autumn forest, the green and blue of the water. The lavender and white endpapers with a mountain scene predicting the coming winter contribute another special note to an already beautiful book. Haunting, mysterious, powerful.

Ellen D. Warwick, in a review of "The Bears' Autumn," in School Library Journal, *Vol. 33, No. 11, August, 1987, p. 75.*

OWL LAKE (1987)

Proving that simplicity can be stunning, Tejima gives us this beautiful story of an owl family through one night. The sun sets, and Father Owl succeeds in catching a fish for his family. The night goes on; the sun rises. With astounding control and virtuosity, Tejima makes this scant tale live in his woodcuts, so that the overwhelming blackness of the night is alive and glittering with the myriad feathers of the owls, the shading of bark on trees, the soft wooded hills beyond, all tinted in cream, gold and, underwater, an aqueous blue. The authority of Father Owl resonates from his fierce eyes, his gripping talons and his swooping, beautifully detailed wings.

As the stars fade, the mood changes completely. The lake and sky are transposed to a lovely blue, in a strikingly symmetrical pattern. The exceptional art work in this book brings drama to the simple story and should excite any child.

A review of "Owl Lake," in Kirkus Reviews, *Vol. LV, No. 8, April 15, 1987, p. 645.*

Dramatic woodcuts illustrate this simple story. . . . The subtle colors of sky and lake that change from sunset to night and from moonlight to dawn are an effective contrast to the black woodcuts of the owls, lake, and shore. The owl is magnificent in flight, his wingspread breaking through the borders. The center spread, showing the owl catching the fish, is made even more spectacular by the use of triangular, stark white borders that focus all attention on the catch; you can practically hear the water splash. The text is somewhat uneven; ranging from poetic to static, it lacks the strength of the illustrations.

Elizabeth S. Watson, in a review of "Owl Lake," in The Horn Book Magazine, *Vol. LXIII, No. 4, July-August, 1987, p. 457.*

A simple yet poetic story line chronicles one night in the life of a Blakiston's fish owl. . . . But the text is just the *basso continuo* for this book's delightful series of woodcuts, which portray the moods and textures of the environment in which this owl lives and hunts food for his family. The sequence of three figures against the nightfall are particularly effective. My only regret is what I suspect is an error in translation from the Japanese, where the father owl is said to swoop down to rest upon "a drifting log," when the log pictured is

From Owl Lake, *written and illustrated by Tejima.*

actually firmly beached on the shore. North American readers should be made aware that this peculiar fish-eating owl is unknown in the Western Hemisphere; it is found only on the artist's home island of Hokkaido and adjacent areas of the Asian mainland. . . . [This] book will be enjoyed by readers of all ages.

John L. Zimmerman, in a review of "Owl Lake," in Science Books & Films, *Vol. 23, No. 2, November-December, 1987, p. 109.*

FOX'S DREAM (1987)

[*Fox's Dream*] reminds us of the vital, expressive possibilities of the woodblock print. From the blue-gray endpapers that capture the tranquillity of a forest snowfall and set the book's reflective mood, to the swirling tendrils of ice that he carves into the branches of other trees, on almost every page of *Fox's Dream* Tejima creates striking, often dazzling effects.

The simple story provides a vehicle for artistic virtuosity. On a cold winter night, a lonely fox hunts the mountain forest of what may be Hokkaido, the most northern of Japanese islands and Tejima's birthplace. After a series of frozen moments, in which we watch the fox wander through the woods, he finally happens on the trail of a snow hare. Tejima sudden-

ly sends the fox sailing from the trees into a clearing of luminous blue snow. The shadow beneath his feet tells us that the artist has caught him in midair, before the driving energy of the chase propels him off the page in pursuit of the rabbit. One wants to turn the page, quickly, for Tejima has led the reader's eye, with the rabbit's prints in the snow, to a vanishing point, where the snow, the black sky and the right margin of the page come together.

And yet one hesitates and looks again. Tejima turns this into a transfixing moment, its tension captured in the very grain of the wood that he must cut to make this picture. Perhaps no other kind of illustration is quite as static as the woodcut; the thickness and roughness of its lines, the weight of its monochromatic masses tend to hold it to the page. And yet Tejima and his fox have made it move.

Quickly, we turn the page, and there is the hare, huge and in flight across the vast, black space of the next double-page picture. The ghostly whiteness of the creature gives it an unearthly quality. Though real, it is also magical and could quite reasonably vanish into the distant mountains, as Tejima has it do. But before it disappears, the rabbit leads the reader to the center of the book and the fox to the unfamiliar place where he discovers his dream, etched into the vast frozen branches of "a forest of ice."

The fox's dream—or, perhaps, one should call it his vision—is about what he does not have: a family, and all the comfort, warmth and security that implies. As he stares into the swirling tendrils of the icy trees, he sees a mother fox and her cubs, an image that reminds him of his own youth. The ice melts into a glowing orange meadow of memory, where he leaps in a joyful dance with his brother and sister. Within a few pages after his return from his dream, and just over the next hill, the fox meets a vixen as a violet dawn arrives and the two of them "nuzzle in the sunshine."

The contrived happy ending of **Fox's Dream** is less convincing than the open-ended, more naturalistic conceptions of Tejima's two earlier books, **Owl Lake** and **The Bears' Autumn,** both of which are available in this country. But Tejima's exceptional talents and his deep feeling for the dynamics of the picture book transcend this reservation. **Fox's Dream** is an astonishing work, a near-perfect picture book. Like the fox's run through the snow, like the air in those frosty mountain valleys, it will take your breath away.

> *John Cech, "Frozen Moments in a Forest of Ice," in* The New York Times Book Review, *November 8, 1987, p. 49.*

A bold, yet gentle, book. . . . It is the compelling power of the colored woodcuts that will attract readers to this book; but on more careful consideration, readers will find that the text conveys the quiet sensitivity of haiku poetry which perfectly matches the Japanese woodcuts. The cold lavender and blue backgrounds and the stretch of shadows on the frozen snow add to the stillness of the place and the loneliness of the fox. The only other living creature seen in the forest is a snow hare who seems almost to bound from the page as the fox chases him, leaving the fox alone once more in a strange place. Looking at the frozen trees, he imagines ice animals in the branches. With the coming of morning, however, comes the promise of another springtime and a mate. Thus, the cyclical nature of the text leaves readers with both a sense of satisfaction and with the anticipation of promises yet to be fulfilled. This is a perfect read-aloud for the quiet contemplation of nature for, like all poetry, these words need to be heard as well as seen; and the illustrations are even more startling and powerful from across the room than they are close-up.

> *Kay E. Vandergrift, in a review of "Fox's Dream," in* School Library Journal, *Vol. 34, No. 4, December, 1987, p. 78.*

The simple story of life's seasons is told in a spare text against a striking backdrop of bold woodcuts. Winter shades of white, black, golden brown, and blue predominate, with the blue blending to gray or purple in some scenes; orange and yellow denote the summer days the fox remembers. The strong design of the pages is compelling and evocative. The

From Fox's Dream, *written and illustrated by Tejima.*

frontal view of the fox against the night, the hare leaping into space, the ice animals in the trees, the mother fox suckling her young in a field of flowers, and the young foxes leaping against the sun in an orange sky are in fine counterpoint to the lonely scenes of the fox wandering among the imposing trees. The story anthropomorphizes the fox just a bit and borders on the banal with a tidy ending. . . . Yet there are the eternal verities of loneliness and dreams and the life cycle, all rendered with clarity and fine artistry.

> *Margaret A. Bush, in a review of "Fox's Dream," in* The Horn Book Magazine, *Vol. LXIV, No. 1, January-February, 1988, p. 58.*

SWAN SKY (1988)

As much a story about nature's way of accepting death as about the behavioral characteristics of swans, this is a stunning picture book with strong elements of linear design. The text is a simple one: a family of swans waits for one that is sick, flies away, and then recircles back to stay with her till she dies. As he did in *Fox's Dream,* Tejima comes dangerously close to anthropomorphism here; the family is "saddened" but later in the "the morning light . . . thinks of the little swan." Of course, this will only deepen children's empathy with a situation already dramatized by vivid graphics. The play of turquoise, blue, and black with sudden spurts of orange is arresting. So are the shapes, patterned for contrast and repetition, tension and resolution, across the double spreads. The rhythmic cycle of life and death is clearly projected for young listeners to think or talk about.

> *Betsy Hearne, in a review of "Swan Sky," in* Bulletin of the Center for Children's Books, *Vol. 42, No. 2, October, 1988, p. 55.*

Tejima's previous books, *Owl Lake* and *Fox's Dream* established his place as a gifted artist and storyteller. This book, too, is an artistic achievement. The black intensity of the woodcuts is tempered by muted golds, grayed blues, and smoky oranges; each illustration is memorable and haunting. The story is one of death and acceptance. A band of swans winter on a distant lake. When it is time for them to go north to their summer home, one young swan is ill and unable to leave. Her family, after delaying their departure, sadly flies off; but soon returns to stay with her as she dies. . . . The final scene agains shows the swan family gazing above at a cloud formation with a swan-like appearance. Whether swans would stay with a dying family member is of no consequence to the point which Tejima is trying to make. But the final illustrations are a disappointment, for they leave nothing to readers' imagination and in contrast to the earlier powerful images seem disturbingly sentimental. This is a handsome book, but its impact is diminished by its obvious symbolism.

> *Phyllis G. Sidorsky, in a review of "Swan Sky," in* School Library Journal, *Vol. 35, No. 3, November, 1988, p. 96.*

The Japanese artist Keizaburo Tejima is fast becoming one of the world's pre-eminent contemporary picture book designers. With each succeeding title, from *The Bears' Autumn* to *Owl Lake* to *Fox's Dream* to the latest, *Swan Sky,* he has adroitly tested the rigorousness of the woodcut technique in his cool, crisp, clean studies of nature.

His rendering of landscape will never be confused with Hokusai's. Tejima works within a fully contemporary sensibility. His forms may be conventional and his no-nonsense line lacks the virtuosity of, say, Barry Moser's in his *Alice in Wonderland,* but Tejima wisely tempers the inherent severity of his contrasting blacks and whites with flat fields of bright harmonious colors, as here in *Swan Sky,* where he uses primarily ice-blue and pumpkin. Some cheating is apparent, unfortunately, where the artist relies on the brush rather than the block to apply touches of secondary color.

Still, whatever the immediate and modest disappointments in style and technical risk, Tejima's efforts remain superb examples of the art of the picture book. He knows how to pace his pictures, interplaying scale and perspective from spread to spread, and he often boldly offers double-page panoramas free of any text. . . .

Swan Sky is arguably Tejima's best book to date. [It is a] fitting companion to the much-honored *Fox's Dream,* a simple but moving tale about the renewal of the family. . . .

[What] at first appears to be a picture book exploring the agony of abandonment quickly develops another, deeper theme. Just as *Fox's Dream* celebrates birth, *Swan Sky* acknowledges death. . . .

Tejima's language is so quiet, his pictures so unassuming that the reassuring conclusion comes as an epiphany. Taking so simple an incident from natural history, Tejima's touching narrative unfolds in illustrations as lulling as his storytelling. The only jarring detail in this otherwise straightforward observation of nature is the description of the swans as "saddened" by the loss of their sister. Birds do not mourn. Grief is a human emotion. What *Fox's Dream* and finally *Swan Sky* prove is that in nature there is only renewal.

> *Michael Patrick Hearn, "After Many a Winter. . . ." in* The New York Times Book Review, *November 13, 1988, p. 58.*

Brenda Wilkinson

1946-

Black American author of fiction.

Wilkinson is best known as the creator of the *Ludell* trilogy, young adult novels about Ludell Wilson, an illegitimate young black woman from rural Georgia who faces changes in lifestyle and attitudes in the mid-fifties to early sixties. In these works—*Ludell* (1975), *Ludell and Willie* (1976), and *Ludell's New York Time* (1980)—Wilkinson describes how Ludell discovers her ability as a writer while living with her grandmother in Waycross, Georgia, falls in love with her next-door neighbor, Willie, and moves to Harlem to live with her mother after her grandmother dies. Written in dialogue that reflects the language pattern of southern blacks, the novels address such themes as the importance of loving and of being loved, the clash of urban and rural cultures, the facing of racial tension, the evolvement of black identity, and the supportiveness of the black community. Wilkinson is praised both for her success with dialogue and for her spirited portrayal of Ludell, whose strength, sensitivity, honesty, and confidence help her to face transition without the loss of her self-esteem. Wilkinson is also the author of *Not Separate, Not Equal* (1987), a novel about the abduction of six black teenagers who integrated a Georgia high school during the civil rights struggle of the 1960s.

(See also *Something about the Author,* Vol. 14; *Contemporary Authors New Revision Series,* Vol. 26; *Contemporary Authors,* Vols. 69-72; and *Black Writers.*)

AUTHOR'S COMMENTARY

Like my protagonist Ludell, I am a product of the last of the segregated school system in the South. What I've attempted in the trilogy I've written is to give a "factional" account of this period. I think my work will ultimately stand as a kind of continuation of the works that Wright, Killens, and other Southern black writers began. While they captured the 1930s and 40s, I have picked up at the 50s/60s. I felt it especially important that this period be recorded as it was the end of an era (segregation).

Presently I'm working on a novel of the "new South" drawn from the experiences of my younger sisters and brothers, who, unlike most of my generation and those before, view the north as "no promised land." The changes that have resulted from integration, both positive and negative, make for an interesting and important story.

While I don't want my work to become too political, preachy, or instructional—my overall objective in writing is to give young people a sense of where we've been in this country, and why. In giving them this history, I attempt to help them see that their experiences, fears, desires, and frustrations aren't that unique. Hopefully the writing will continue to come out in an entertaining and interesting manner, so that indeed my work will be a source of some direction in what I'm convinced is a difficult time to be young. (pp. 443-44)

Brenda Wilkinson, in an excerpt in Literature for

Today's Young Adults, *by Kenneth L. Donelson and Alleen Pace Nilsen, Scott, Foresman and Company, 1980, pp. 443-44.*

GENERAL COMMENTARY

RONI NATOV

Ludell's strength in Brenda Wilkinson's recent trilogy, *Ludell, Ludell and Willie,* and *Ludell's New York Time,* seems to come from her ability to express freely the full range of her emotions. In a fit of pleasure at the way she looks in her new clothes, for example, Ludell enjoys what might seem sinfully vain to her traditional religious grandmother who raises her and to her rural southern black neighbors. She struts around in her pink dress, pink socks, and pink hairbow, noting, in her plucky voice:

> "Ye-eah, I look nice if I hafta say so myself. . . .
> And I don't have to say so myself," she thought,
> "cause enough people done said it for me!"

Equally unacceptable to those around her are her feelings about her mother, which she freely expresses to her boyfriend, Willie:

"I'on hate her—don't love her, don't nothing her,"
Ludell said.

"Now that don't make no sense to me," he said.

"I guess it don't," she replied. "But that's the way
I feel about her. Plain empty."

Whatever Ludell sees and feels, she acknowledges it all. And
because she does not block or flatten out reality, her perceptions are rich and interesting. She notices the pretensions, aspirations, and the desperation of those around her: the extreme poverty and humiliation of her closest friends, the racial discrimination in her hometown, the scapegoating by
children of other children, and the beatings and betrayals of
adults. At times, indeed, she shivers from the cruelty she sees
around her.

In many ways, Ludell is powerless to change the destructive
conditions of her life. As a child she has been pushed and
pulled between her traditional Southern grandmother and
her flashy mother who fled to New York to escape the small
town ways of Waycross, Georgia. As an adolescent, she is
faced with the senility of her grandmother, who, in her para-
noia, allows Ludell almost no privacy. Ludell alone is saddled
with the adult responsibility of caring for her, though she is,
in turn, watched over like a child. In fact, the adult world
seems oppressive and hostile, particularly to the most nurturing aspect of Ludell's life, her relationship with Willie. Ludell
learns to assert herself the best way she can—by remaining
honest with herself and by lying to the adults. In addition,
the threat of poverty forces her into working for white
women who embody the racist attitudes of southern whites
of the 1950s. But in the face of all this, Ludell's high spirits
persist. Unlike the other black women who survive the degra-
dation of working for their oppressors by transforming them,
in their anecdotal bragging, into appreciative and gracious
benefactors, Ludell remains true to her perceptions. . . .
(pp. 119-20)

After her grandmother's death, Ludell is forced to go to New
York with her mother and to leave behind Willie and her life
in Waycross. Though she is powerless to inspire in her mother respect for her relationship with Willie, Ludell asserts her
need to be with him. *Ludell's New York Time* is almost entirely about how Ludell remains faithful to her own sense of
self in the face of strong pressures from her mother and her
peers to fit into the social life in New York. At the end of the
book when her mother insists that she should lay some "sensible" foundation for her life, Ludell concludes: " 'Concrete
/ plan / foundation, her sharp words bounced on my ears,
while my heart dictated love / faith / determination. . . .' "
Whether Ludell is wise or foolish to follow her own leanings,
at least she knows her own mind and acknowledges her own
feelings. And it has been this kind of self-assertion that has
kept her from despairing and has allowed her to take pleasure
in what she has been able to retrieve from the restricted and
limited conditions of her life. (p. 120)

> *Roni Natov, "The Truth of Ordinary Lives: Autobio-*
> *graphical Fiction for Children," in* Children's litera-
> ture in education, *Vol. 17, No. 2, Summer, 1986, pp.*
> *112-25.*

LUDELL (1975)

Ludell, which seems autobiographical is a beautiful little

novel about a sensitive young girl whose individuality and talent blossom in spite of the abyssmal circumstances under
which she has to live and go to school.

It will inform young readers in other sections of the world
and, in other circumstances about life that is raw in many
ways—an environment where children become adults much
sooner than they would like.

Some of Ludell's schoolmates can do no more than just get
by from day to day. Some are crushed by disadvantages, but
others—especially Ludell—find worth and joy despite their
drab prospects.

Young readers may find the dialect difficult to read at first,
but one soon gets used to it. That dialect—and the circumstances portrayed in *Ludell* are completely genuine.

> *Leon W. Lindsay, "Growing Up and Going to*
> *School in the South," in* The Christian Science
> Monitor, *November 5, 1975, p. B10.*

Here is a rough-cut first novel about children of the South
that, despite its flaws, reflects life. The illegitimate daughter
of a teen-ager who went North, Ludell was left to be raised
by her grandmother, whom she calls "mama." By the time
she is in the fifth grade, she can not remember her mother's
face. (p. 16)

Unlike many novels of the South, *Ludell* is not a tragedy in
any sense, not an angry book, nor is it soft-centered. An episodic, dialect-ridden account of three years—mostly two winters and a cotton-picking summer—in the life of a left-behind
child in a left-behind pocket of the United States in 1955.
Even the characters' names seem left behind—Ludell (her
mother hated that "country name"), Monkey Juice, Hawk,
Buddie Boy, Mis Lizzie. These are blacks who did not protest
with violence and anger, families whose husbands have died
or deserted, who are not upwardly mobile.

There are children like these all over the South, many who
have not emerged whole from their lives as Ludell promises
to do at the end of the book when her seventh grade teacher
says, "It's your own lil red wagon. You can roll it, pull it, or
drag it. You can even stand still—not move it a'tall and go
no place at all!"

The stage is small: Ludell's house, strictly run by "mama"
whose "old-timey ways" keep Ludell working hard, and God
and grandmother fearing; across the yard to the Johnsons'
loosely run house where Ludell's best friend, Ruthie Mae,
lives; the streets and backyards of Waycross, Georgia; "Mis
Kelly's grocery store" where anyone can "credit"; school,
where the biggest challenge is what you can afford to buy for
lunch.

The place is Georgia, and Georgia is its sound, sometimes so
thick I had to reread passages to be sure of the meaning.
There are overheard conversations that stretch credibility,
spelling conflicts within the same line of dialogue.

I wished for an intensity of emotion that I never felt, but by
the end of the book I liked Ludell. I was glad to have known
her and her friends. . . . (pp. 16, 18)

> *Cynthia King, in a review of "Ludell," in* The New
> York Times Book Review, *February 22, 1976, pp.*
> *16, 18.*

Brenda Wilkinson's novel is a remarkable accomplishment

and bears comparison with an earlier novel—it too a remarkable accomplishment—*Native Son.* I make the comparison despite the fact that Richard Wright, the author of *Native Son,* is a literary legend, a writer tested in three genres, whose reputation was forged in the political, social and literary hell of America during the 1930s, 1940s and 1950s, while Ms. Wilkinson, on the other hand is not yet into her 30s, has written only a few poems, one short story, and now her first novel.

Still, there are comparisons to be drawn between the older and the younger writer, and the age difference between them may account for the fact that **Ludell** seems an extension of *Native Son* rather than an antithesis of it. Both writers were transplanted Southerners—Wright from Mississippi, Wilkinson from Georgia. Both write in the naturalistic idiom, though Wilkinson has the better eye for detail and is more proficient in handling dialogue. In their first fictional offerings, both writers demonstrated awareness of the varied tensions prevalent in the black community, and both sought to explicate the lives of those who lived there, with equal candor and sincerity. More important, both writers arrived on the literary scene at a time when the black novel seemed to have lost its moorings, when competing philosophies regarding its function had led to the kind of internecine warfare among black novelists and critics that marred the achievements of the writers of the Harlem Renaissance.

During the Harlem Renaissance, the period of black creativity between 1922—the publication of Claude McKay's *Harlem Shadows* and 1940, the publication date of *Native Son*—the black novel reached maturity in terms of structure, form and acceptance on the part of readers. Not surprisingly, therefore, the serious critical debate concerning the nature and function of black literature in general, began in earnest.

The novel, as viewed by the old guard (James Weldon Johnson, W. E. B. Du Bois, Jesse Fauset and Alaine Locke) functioned primarily as the uplift vehicle of the black middle class; in portraying artificial, near-white characters who possessed the mannerisms, language and status of the men and women of the novels of Jane Austen, Anthony Trollope and Henry James, the old guard sought to inform white America that assimilationism had worked for some, though not all, blacks. "The party line" was pronounced in Ms. Fauset's introduction to her novel, *The Chinaberry Tree:* "But of course there are breathing spells, in between spaces where colored men and women work and love and go their ways with no thought of the [race] problem. . . . What are they like then? So few of the other Americans know. . . ." The question, "What are they like then?" leads to a description of characters now legion in the lexicon of the black middle class: the professional man, the upward-bound striver, the socialite and the patriot, differing in no major essentials from other Americans, for they are simply "dark American[s] who wear [their] joy and rue very much as does the white American . . . it is the same joy and rue."

Such assimilationist pronouncements came under attack from the younger members of the Harlem Renaissance (Rudolph Fisher, Claude McKay and Langston Hughes). . . . (p. 469)

By 1940, the views of the younger writers were ascendant, the novel had begun explication of the lives of those whom Hughes labeled, "the low-down folk." In this accomplishment, however, the younger writers midwifed a litter of new stereotypes: the romanticized pimp, the forlorn prostitute, the ostentatious "sweetman" and the social parasite. Whether such characters were an improvement over those offered in the literature of the old guard is open to conjecture; spurred on, however, by such novels as *Nigger Heaven, Not Without Laughter, The Walls Of Jericho* and *Home to Harlem,* those who would have the black novel function as an instrument for entertainment, escapism and naive romanticism succeeded very well.

But neither school realistically confronted the black community. The old guard only succeeded in perpetuating the ideal of assimilationism, deeming human worth measurable solely according to criteria established by white Americans. The younger writers were only successful in giving visibility to and romanticizing the least desirable elements in the black community; without intending to do so they suggested that hustling, parasitism and exoticism were major characteristics of a black way of life. For older and younger writer alike, the hulking, demonic figure of Bigger Thomas, the black Frankenstein monster, was buried deep in the literary subconscious, relegated to eternal darkness and invisibility.

The publication of *Native Son* ended the debate among the Harlem Renaissance writers by redefining the function and nature of the black novel. The entrance of Bigger Thomas onto the literary stage demolished the stereotypes of both schools, though those offered in the writings of the younger members, with seemingly indestructible resilience, would reappear in the 1950s in such books as *Manchild in the Promised Land* and *Another Country,* and would stake out new territory in black movies and television shows. Devoted more to the realities of black life than its predecessors, *Native Son* depicted men and women trapped in the hell of racism and deprivation; it portrayed a sensitive young man, neither exotic nor parasitic, who craved not the supposed joy of jazz or Harlem night spots, but the opportunity to move freely in a world which appeared to him as one long elevator shaft—the place, where, ironically enough, he throws the dead body of his second victim, the black Bessie Mears.

That *Native Son* marked a significant break with the traditional form and theme of the black novel is evidenced by the caliber of the men and women who began to model their own fiction after Wright's accomplishment. The old guard of the Harlem Renaissance had found their paradigms in the works of Carl Van Vechten, Gertrude Stein and Jean Toomer. William Attaway, Ann Petry, Chester Himes and William Gardner Smith, who comprised the Richard Wright school of writers, followed their leader into paths charted by Theodore Dreiser, Hart Crane and Feodor Dostoevsky. In their novels, the Dostoevskian man came to represent an important dimension of black life. Their canvases were painted in dark gray colors, and upon their landscapes men walked in hatred and rage, immobilized by an inability to stamp their humanity upon a racist society. (pp. 469-70)

The members of the Wright school . . . were moral warriors who believed that the novel should function as an instrument for improving the human condition. Ralph Ellison's statement concerning his own novel, " . . . If a moral or perception is needed, let them [the readers] supply their own. For me, of course, the narrative is the meaning," was met with derision, probably by Wright and, as we know from *Amistad I,* by Chester Himes. For here, and more explicitly in his other critical works, Ellison makes concessions to the academic proponents of an "art for art's sake" theology, notwithstanding the fact that nothing in the lives of black people suggests that their writers should dedicate themselves to such specious theories. Such a dedication would mean that the black writer had leaped outside the history of the society in which he lives.

Invisible Man, therefore, fails to become the model for the post-Wright generation of black writers, for such novelists as John A. Williams, John Killens and Louise Merriwether. For it depicts the black man alone, a character more Kafkaesque than Dostoevskian, existing in a world exemplified more by the paintings of Jackson Pollock than by the writings of Theodore Dreiser. In such a universe the terror of modern man becomes "universal," not specific, and the lives of black people are threatened by demons more omnipresent than those of American racism.

The truth of the matter, however, is not that racism has become less threatening, but that black people, like the post-Wright school of black writers, have come to accept it as one of the eternal givens of American society. Such acceptance mandated that the black writer redirect the search for identity away from the computerized mechanistic culture of the West and toward the culture peopled by those whom Frantz Fanon labeled "the wretched of the earth." After the abortive push for equal rights in the 1960s, the return of white liberals to support of the *status quo,* the acceptance of the Nixon-Agnew formula for re-establishing the past pattern of black-white relationships, it was clear to the younger writers of sensibility that the black novel could achieve universality only by depicting the style of life, the heroism and the courage of those who remained outside the American nightmare and were able, therefore, to offer 200 years of fateful encounters within the Diaspora as models for that three-quarters of the world that is neither white nor Western.

But the failure of the civil rights struggle in the 1960s left a legacy of despair, now being articulated by some of the most promising black novelists. Unable to surrender the quixotic dream of an egalitarian America, and more apt to blame the failures of the 1960s upon black people themselves rather than upon the white majority, they have produced works which re-create the stereotypes of old and depict a universe in which the major antagonists are black men and black women. These novels, *Sula, The Last Days of Louisiana Red* and *Corregidora* are, basically, unhealthy works, suggesting the inability of the authors to accept their own identity and their own humanity.

The attempt to establish a new tradition in black fiction based upon such narcissistic offerings, therefore, makes Brenda Wilkinson's novel, *Ludell,* of immediate importance. The novel negates the mythology accepted by the writers of the Harlem Renaissance that black life is artificial or sterile, sensationalistic or atavistic. It argues fervently against the assimilationist contentions of the post-Wright school, that blacks have imbibed the worst characteristics of that West in which they have dwelled for so long.

Like Wright's short story, "Big Boy Leaves Home," *Ludell* is primarily a novel about children. These young innocents, existing in the South, the first African-American home away from home, are such because they have not yet become inoculated with the values of the West. Theirs is an innocence much like that whispered in the poetry of Claude McKay and Mrs. Paul Laurence Dunbar, unsullied by too close association with the white world outside. But, too, the universe of this novel is alive with innocence, which emanates from the

community even in the persons of the stern schoolmistresses, and it is highlighted by the love and care that each black person exhibits toward the other—characteristics of black life from the days of slavery until the present time.

Here, as John Killens, Louise Merriwether and George Caine realized, is the *sine qua non* of the black tradition, the determining mark of black heroes and heroines from Frederick Douglass and Harriet Tubman to Fannie Lou Hamer and Martin Luther King, and it is such characteristics, love and caring, that form the organizing principle of *Ludell.* As is traditional in the black community, the grandmother in this novel steps in to care for the young child, when the child's mother joins the migration heading north. Here, in this Southern land of so much pain and misery, containing a heritage for black people of so much brutality, black families love and care for one another, support one another, encourage one another, give sustenance one to another. In the person of Mis Hattie, tough field boss of an itinerant cotton crew, love and caring is elevated to an all-encompassing metaphor. When Ludell, a member of the work crew, becomes ill and is unable to pick her day's quota of cotton, Mis Hattie " . . . suggested that everybody give her some cotton, since she'd taken sick—and they all had, but no one was supposed to mention it."

Such incidents, as Wilkinson knows, are neither rare nor confined only to the South. They are daily occurrences among black people and comprise those many unsung episodes which render facile and self-serving the works of those who would use the black novel as a vehicle for resolving their personal conflicts and who seek to paint the black world in the time-sanctioned stereotypes of hatred, unmitigated rage and brutality. Such novels have received a hearing in the past few years only because they appeal to the sensibility of white liberals and the black middle class, groups who are largely incapable of fathoming the depths of the currents running strong and swift within the black community. *Ludell,* a novel of substance, suggests that their short-lived vogue, among black people, is ended, and that the black novel will return to an explication of the ethics and values which have assured black survival in this society.

The black writer, Richard Wright wrote more than thirty years ago, must create "those values by which his people are to live and die." The word, "create" obscures this important definition of the function of black literature. Far more to the point, the job of the black writer is to articulate those values, germane to the success of a people in forestalling the final *Götterdämmerung,* and among them has been a communal love and caring unsurpassed and unparalleled by other racial groups in American society. The function of the novel, then, is to return to the values of racial compassion and concern as defined in the fiction of the pre-Harlem Renaissance writers, in the works of Martin Delaney and Sutton Griggs, and in this respect *Ludell* is an important contribution. For this novel reminds those in the black community—who need reminding—that the Sulas and Corregidoras, the Superflys and the Melindas, are images of men and women who live in large measure, not in the black community but in the fitful, fanciful imaginations of those who after so many years regard themselves, still, as the bastard children of the West. (pp. 470-71)

Addison Gayle, " 'Ludell': Beyond 'Native Son'," in The Nation, *New York, Vol. 222, No. 15, April 17, 1976, pp. 469-71.*

Dialogue that is rhythmical and euphonious with black dialect carries the burden of Ludell's highly detailed story. Though slow starting and lacking in climax, the story gives a clear sense of some of the problems, joys, and hopes of a black community and blacks individually without being preachy, simplistic, or sensational. Ludell's sudden talent for writing strains credulity, but she is a round, dynamic, likeable character who grows up believably. Some characters are purely types, but Mama and Mis Johnson are particularly sympathetic, strongly delineated figures who command respect for their earnest attempts to achieve decent lives for their families. (p. 390)

> *Alethea K. Helbig and Agnes Regan Perkins, in a review of "Ludell," in their* Dictionary of American Children's Fiction, 1960-1984: Recent Books of Recognized Merit, *Greenwood Press, 1986, pp. 389-90.*

LUDELL AND WILLIE (1976)

The only complaint one can file against Wilkinson's brilliant novel is that it ends. Readers who loved her first story, **Ludell,** meet the young black heroine again in the sequel, set during the 1950s in a small town in the deep South. Ludell, now a teenager, is in love with Willie but the sweetness of their romance is shadowed by racial tensions and by the pious fanaticism of Ludell's grandmother, her guardian. Willie is devoted to Ludell but she fears she will lose him to other girls who are free to enjoy the social life forbidden her. She also has to cope with the urgings of her mother who's living a "glamorous" life up north and wants Ludell to join her and to forget Willie and their plans to marry. Through the twists of an artfully constructed plot, Ludell does end up in New York but the love between her and Willie remains constant. A moving and convincing story, this will leave readers impatient for the next installment.

> *A review of "Ludell and Willie," in* Publishers Weekly, *Vol. 211, No. 6, February 7, 1977, p. 95.*

The style of the telling might even be too simple if it were not couched in an idiom both rich and strange to the non-black (or is it merely the non-Southern?) ear. As it is, we should be grateful to Ludell and Willie, their families and friends, for living and talking like themselves, thus transcending weighty generalizations about black teen-agers, Southern mores or social justice. I'm looking forward to the next book about Ludell, even though I'm not a sociologist.

> *Georgess McHargue, in a review of "Ludell and Willie," in* The New York Times Book Review, *May 22, 1977, p. 29.*

Although the story line is more substantial than that of the earlier book, this is primarily a facet of the black experience, for Ludell works for a white family and resents the way she is treated, sympathizes with Willie in his worrying about his future, and participates in the mutually supportive life of the black community in her town. While the use of phonetically spelled dialect is more controlled in this second novel, there are still some instances of this ("Everybody dark who be with Lilly nem do,") or of colloquialism in exposition ("He kissed her like he longed to.") . . . While this is a story about a black adolescent, it is a story about problems all teenagers share: loving and being loved, moving toward independence, being concerned about the pattern of adult life that suddenly seems so close.

> *Zena Sutherland, in a review of "Ludell and Willie," in* Bulletin of the Center for Children's Books, *Vol. 30, No. 11, July-August, 1977, p. 184.*

LUDELL'S NEW YORK TIME (1980)

Wilkinson picks up roughly where she left off in **Ludell and Willie** with Ludell's arrival in New York City in the early 1960s. Upset about her separation from Willie and unhappy about leaving Waycross, Ludell has a difficult time adjusting to "citified" attitudes that she encounters living in Harlem, at work, and in social settings. While her attempts to cope are not very imaginative (her decision to return home to marry Willie comes as no surprise) and Ludell is never particularly likable (she's as selfish and opinionated as those around her), she radiates strength and purpose that set her sharply apart. Wilkinson has tempered the dialect used in previous books without damaging the flavor of this latest one, and readers of the earlier novels will feel fully comfortable with the by now familiar, forthright Ludell.

> *A review of "Ludell's New York Time," in* Booklist, *Vol. 76, No. 14, March 15, 1980, p. 1045.*

Just six weeks before high school graduation and their anticipated marriage, Ludell and Willie find themselves separated. The death of Ludell's grandmother, "Mama," has necessitated Ludell's leaving Willie and her hometown, Waycross, Ga., to live with her long-absent mother, Dessa, in Harlem. She has every expectation that Willie will come North shortly after graduation and they will be married.

This dream helps her cope with being away from Willie, with her rather tenuous relationship with her mother, and with the totally different way of life in Harlem. . . .

Willie's arrival is delayed again and again. When the worst happens—Willie is drafted—Ludell once again must face change and uncertainty.

Wilkinson has crafted a special kind of love story with wide-ranging appeal. The clash of Ludell's Waycross background with the Harlem of the '60s reveals the social fabric of both places, as Ludell shares her experiences with her friends, writes to Willie, and questions the manners and morals of New York life.

A number of people and events change Ludell: her attempts to understand and be understood by Harlem teen-agers; her experiences with racism in the New York job market; and her friendship with Carolyn, a young woman from a similar rural South background, whose concern for social change and evolving black identity are new to Ludell.

Though it is truly Ludell's story, Wilkinson has created a memorable group of supporting characters. Their speech, lifestyles, and aspirations are true to their varied backgrounds and circumstances. Dialogue is Wilkinson's forte, and she uses it with consummate skill. It is natural and convincing, an expression of her strongly defined sense of each of her characters. She combines this with a keen eye for detail and a carefully paced presentation of events to totally involve us with Ludell and her life.

Ludell Wilson is a warm, disarmingly straightforward, determined young woman who is deeply in love, and we are convinced that she is capable of meeting whatever challenges await her. Today's young readers will find her story a welcome addition to their reading lists.

Jerrie Norris, "Love Story Set in Harlem," in The Christian Science Monitor, *April 14, 1980, p. B7.*

When I was a teenager, it would have been nice—real nice—to have had an author like Brenda Wilkinson shining her spicy, authentic dialogue from the pages of the books I read. We needed some books where solid characters struggled to solve the same problems that other teenagers had *and* those problems specific to Black teenagers—solid characters in books written from an African American perspective. Whew! It would have been nice.

The characters in **Ludell's New York Time** become known through their words. The dialogue is full of the rhythm, form, idioms, proverbs and syntax of Ebonics (meaning Black sounds and referring to the varied language forms spoken by people of African descent). The writing of Ebonics is handled well and therefore, "reads" the way many of us speak. The text, in most instances, is free of the quotation marks and apostrophes that some publishers use to emphasize the so-called dialect.

The book even conveys many of the tonal inflections that we African Americans have retained. " 'Pul-eze take off those funeral shoes, chile,' she moaned" is really different from " 'Please take off those funeral shoes, child,' she said." It truly is! It means, Ain nobody died, so put those shoes away til you need 'em, and put on a pair that look like you been in New York long enough to know how to really dress! Wilkinson handles the African-based English spoken by her characters with finesse and *always* with the dignity and respect it deserves. In so doing, she provides accurate and much needed positive linguistic feedback for Black teenagers.

In this, the third novel about Ludell, the major character continues to grow. She strides into young womanhood with great resilience. In her journey North after the death of her grandmother who reared her, Ludell learns to manage loss, grief, homesickness, her mother's style of childrearing, missing her boyfriend Willie and the mechanics of surviving in New York—Harlem, New York. We need more books that describe—from the perspective of teenagers—how those transitions can be managed.

Ludell symbolizes all the Black folks who have left the South, migrating North and West. The author describes the paternal, often brutal, process by which rural and small town people are put down as they learn city ways. Wilkinson does a good job of illustrating that kind of urban arrogance, and she skillfully reveals the institutional support of that arrogance. (p. 18)

Ludell is a great example of the time-honored Black practice of passive resistance. She is drawn as a person with moral fiber and toughness. Some of the temptations with which she is confronted just don't "make sense" to her. Oh, she understands them, but Ludell's been taught not to diminish herself by doing destructive things just because "everybody else" does them. Another aspect of Black life illuminated in this book is the way, very often, in Black families, that significant family members who've "passed on" are kept alive through invocation (Mama said) and the use of childrearing proverbs. Ludell's grandmother and her standards are a living presence in the book and continue as a force in Ludell's life. Her childrearing principles are put to the test, through Ludell's resis-

tance, in the contemporary and real situations created by the author.

In most situations in the book, Ludell stands out sharply—sometimes almost too sharply—as the SURVIVOR. She has good sense, and in most instances she has good judgment. Wilkinson draws the classic picture of the evil, sinful big city, and she depicts the city as an appropriator and diluter of rural and African American values.

Many people think books for young people should not be "didactic" or convey explicit "moral" messages. That might be OK if there weren't lots of teenage alcoholics (Black, white, Latino, rich, middle-income and poor). That might be fine if there weren't irresponsible, exploitative adults involved in selling drugs and making prostitutes of teenage boys and girls. But Brenda Wilkinson is a responsible writer who knows the African American story-telling tradition, and she writes well within that tradition, part of which has a direct teaching function. The lesson she wants to teach, the messages she wants teenagers to think about are conveyed without boring the reader and that is a strength of the book.

It would have strengthened the book had there been some positive response from Ludell about the various cultural groups that are so vibrantly visible in New York. The rather strict and sometimes negative portrayal of a few of the Black characters seems appropriate to the style of the moral tale, but the technique presents a problem when extended to the two Jewish and the one Puerto Rican characters. Writers for children must continue to work to create multi-dimensional characters, particularly those whose cultural/racial identity differ from the author's. The Jewish and Puerto Rican characters in this book, unfortunately, do not depart much from traditional negative stereotypes.

The story is thoughtfully constructed, moving and moves well. By the end of the story you worry a little about Ludell's aloneness. You wish she'd go see her friend Shirley more often. You wish that Willie . . . well, read it, keeping in mind that Ludell's decision to marry Willie does not exclude the probability of work and school for her, as is traditional to women in the African American community. Let's look forward to another installment in the life of Ludell. (pp. 18-19)

Geraldine L. Wilson, in a review of "Ludell's New York Time," in Interracial Books for Children Bulletin, *Vol. 12, No. 2, 1981, pp. 18-19.*

NOT SEPARATE, NOT EQUAL (1987)

As one of six black teenagers chosen to integrate Georgia's Pineridge High, Malene Freeman encounters both subtle and overt harassment. And harassment escalates to violence when a crazy white man abducts the six teens on their way home from school, prompting local blacks, outside civil-rights activists and the Klan-infested police force to take up the search. Wilkinson paints an honest, unvarnished picture of the obstacles and hatred with which the struggle for civil rights was met in the '60s. Rather than reducing the issue to a simplistic battle between good and evil, she suggests the complexities that attend it, and portrays the confusion and inner turmoil of even the well-intentioned. . . . A provocative and sobering story, but one that holds the promise of hope.

A review of "Not Separate, Not Equal," in Publishers Weekly, *Vol. 232, No. 22, November 27, 1987, p. 83.*

When the black children talk among themselves, telling of what is going on in their lives, this story blossoms. But the plot fizzles after the children are rescued—they disperse to college and other futures, and integration goes on. The author's **Ludell** books were more vivid and believable, yet Malene's story is nonetheless one that young people today should hear.

A review of "Not Separate, Not Equal," in Kirkus Reviews, *Vol. LV, No. 23, December 1, 1987, p. 1680.*

Wilkinson imbues Malene with the same appealing candor and fortitude found in her other popular heroine, Ludell. However, the emphasis of this latest novel is plot, not character. Dogs attack Malene, bomb threats disrupt the school, the black students are kidnapped, and the tense search involves the irate black community and a flustered white law enforcement officer. Stereotypes abound in this chronicle of a southern town awaking to the equal importance of all its citizens. Malene's sensitive and intelligent perspective on the rights of all and the motivations of many personalize this explosive period in civil rights history. Readers will find this novel an action-packed account and a palatable history lesson.

Gerry Larson, in a review of "Not Separate, Not Equal," in School Library Journal, *Vol. 34, No. 8, April, 1988, p. 115.*

Arthur Yorinks

1953-

(Also writes as Alan Yaffe) American author of picture books and screenwriter.

Yorinks is recognized as a writer of surrealistic, wryly humorous modern fables which mesh fantasy and reality as they characteristically describe adult characters in the midst of discovering their true identities. Presenting young readers with such themes as being satisfied with ourselves and the importance of tolerance, the stories, which are praised for their distinctiveness, warmth, and wit, are usually illustrated by Richard Egielski. Yorinks and Egielski, whose colorful pictures are often applauded for blending perfectly with Yorinks's texts, work together to challenge their audience with fantastic premises which are often considered bizarre but hilarious examples of irony and black humor. In *Louis the Fish* (1980), for example, a story inspired by Kafka's *The Metamorphosis,* an unhappy butcher who hates meat is transformed into a fish—an animal with which he is fascinated—after being forced to take over his family's butcher shop. Transformation is also at the heart of *Hey, Al* (1986), a book for which Egielski was awarded the Caldecott Medal in 1987. In this story, Al, a New York City janitor, and his dog Eddie are dissatisfied with their small, cluttered apartment and accept an offer from a giant colored bird to go with him to a paradise in the sky. When they realize that they are beginning to become birds themselves, they escape and go back home, happy to be who they are. Yorinks has also worked with illustrator David Small on *Company's Coming* (1988), a gentle yet pointed satire about how a middle-aged housewife graciously welcomes a pair of bug-like aliens into her home and is treated by them in kind. Also a playwright for adults, Yorinks invests his works with droll, understated texts and deadpan dialogue while underscoring them with what observers often consider a personal and idiosyncratic world view. *It Happened in Pinsk* received a plaque from the Biennale of Illustrations Bratislava (BIB) in 1985.

(See also *Something about the Author,* Vols. 33, 49 and *Contemporary Authors,* Vol. 106.)

GENERAL COMMENTARY

SELMA G. LANES

Some years ago, a teenager named Arthur Yorinks rang [Maurice] Sendak's bell on West Ninth Street—where the artist had, for a long period, rented two floors of a brownstone—and left several manuscripts with him. Sendak was struck by Yorinks's originality and gift for fantasy and helped bring his later efforts to the attention of several children's book editors. Curiously, Yorinks's first picture-book text, published several years after Sendak met him, was illustrated by one of the artist's Parsons pupils, Richard Egielski. The partnership proved to be a happy one. . . . (p. 258)

> Selma G. Lanes, *"Portrait of the Artist as a Private Person," in her* The Art of Maurice Sendak, *edited by Robert Morton, Harry N. Abrams, Inc., 1980, pp. 251-70.*

BILL OTT

Determining the difference between a children's book and a book for adults is often tricky business. After all, many people once considered *Huckleberry Finn*—that bible of individualism, perhaps the most delightfully subversive, anti-authoritarian work in American literature—to be a charming children's story. Later generations may be just as surprised to discover that we once classified the mature work of Arthur Yorinks and Richard Egielski as picture books—"read-alouds" for young children.

Not that children won't enjoy such works as **Hey, Al** and the even better **It Happened in Pinsk,** but under their children's-book veneer lurks some of the best black humor to appear since Woody Allen was writing "casuals" for The New Yorker. It's difficult to say whether Mr. Yorinks (the writer) and Mr. Egielski (the artist) . . . intend to write straightforward children's books but are powerless to keep their dark sides from usurping control—sort of like the way Milton's Satan "steals" "Paradise Lost" from Adam and Eve—or whether they are camouflaging their decidedly pessimistic world view by cloaking it in the simplistic moral terms that so often are the stuff of picture books. Either way, the rare pleasure of finding a perverse subtext trapped in the straitjacket of "positive moral values" is a distinctly adult experience.

To prepare for that experience, it is necessary to remember the wise admonition of D. H. Lawrence: trust the tale, not the teller. As one reads the words and views the pictures that make up their four books, it is imperative to look beyond whatever conclusions the tellers draw for us and determine whether the tales bear them out. Usually we will find the opposite: while the author and the artist are busy constructing tidy morals, if we listen carefully we can hear the books' main characters screaming, "No! That's not what I think at all!"

There's no such screaming in either of their first two books, *Sid & Sol* and *Louis the Fish.* The former is an eminently forgettable tale of a meek little man (Sid) who saves the world from an ill-tempered giant (Sol). There is nothing in the text to suggest the ambiguity and irony that are at the heart of the later books; only in some of Mr. Egielski's drawings, in which a devilish smirk seems to be trying to form at the corners of Sid's mouth, can one find even a vague foreshadowing of what is to come.

Louis the Fish on the other hand, clearly stems from the same subversive imagination that produced *Pinsk* and *Hey, Al.* The story, of course, is simple. Louis is the son of a butcher and becomes a butcher himself: "Small shop on Flatbush. Steady customers. Good meat." Unfortunately, "Louis was not a happy man. He hated meat." Here is the fundamental human situation, as Mr. Yorinks and Mr. Egielski see it: "Surrounded by steaks, all Louis thought about was fish." No matter what we have, it's not what we want—irony in its purest form. Soon enough, however, that ironic view has been replaced by the world according to Walt Disney: Louis becomes a salmon and lives happily ever after.

It's a different story for Irv Irving, a shoe salesman from Pinsk, in the next book, *It Happened in Pinsk.* Like Louis, Irv and wife Irma seem well situated: "Nice clothes. Good food. A telephone. They had everything. Did Irv care? No." As he looks from his apartment balcony to the street below, Irv sees only people he would rather be, things he would rather do: Kaminski the wrestler ("such muscles"); Belchek ("all that money, those cars, those suits"); and even the widow Veskey ("She has to have a mansion and I don't? Unfair!").

It gets worse. Instead of waking up with muscles, Irv wakes up without a head. After Irma obligingly makes him a new one from pillowcases, Irv has a chance to fulfill his dream, to be someone else. In scenes that drip with bitter but hilarious irony, that is exactly what happens. People mistake Irv for a criminal, a long-lost uncle and, worst of all, Leo Totski, a "low-life" who owes Seymour the barber for five shaves.

We are now set up for the Walt Disney ending. It comes but with a difference. Irv finds his head, proudly declares, *"I'm Irv Irving,"* and, according to Mr. Yorinks, hardly ever complains again. Sure—and if you buy that, try turning into a salmon. It's easy enough to see *It Happened in Pinsk* as a parable about coming to terms with one's identity, but it doesn't quite work. The characterization of Irv as the perennially dissatisfied modern man—a grouser of the magnitude of Saul Bellow's Herzog or Ignatius J. Reilly in John Kennedy Toole's *Confederacy of Dunces*—is too strong to be undercut by a little authorial interference. Mr. Yorinks can say what he wants. Give Irv Irving a week or two, and he'll find plenty to complain about. Life is one long complaint—that's what this tale tells us.

Hey, Al tells us the same thing, but again we have to be on the lookout for the author's tendency to deal happy endings

from the bottom of the deck. Al is a janitor, living on the West Side with his loyal dog, Eddie: "They ate together. They worked together. They watched TV together. What could be bad? Plenty." No surprise there. Eddie wants a house, a little yard, anything beyond what they have: "Pigeons live better than us!"

Help is on the way in the form of a large, brightly colored bird bearing an invitation to visit paradise: "Al, Al, *Al!* You need a change." Al is cautious, but Eddie needs no convincing; soon the bird has transplanted them to paradise in the sky, where they bask in the sun, nibble fruit, frolic with the birds. Things have changed since *Louis the Fish,* however; there is no happily-ever-aftering here. "But ripe fruit soon spoils," we are reminded, and before you know it Al and Eddie are turning into birds. They quickly retreat to the safety of the West Side, where their feathers fall off and they decide to paint their room bright yellow.

But wait. Mr. Yorinks and Mr. Egielski have their thumbs on the moral scales again. They ask us to believe that Al and Eddie are now happy with what they once scorned. The last sentence of the book declaims piously: "Paradise lost is sometimes Heaven found." A new coat of paint is nice, but can it really be expected to take the place of tropical drinks served by a waterfall? Syrupy morals may be just the ticket to win Caldecott medals (as *Hey, Al* did last year), but don't expect us to buy that a smart mutt like Eddie is going to be satisfied counting blessings (meager ones, at that) for the rest of his life.

By ignoring the tellers in these tales, we allow their fictional world to emerge in all its depth, richness and complexity. There is a tremendous vitality to Irv and Al in the illustrations as well as in the texts that can only be felt if we acknowledge the inherently ironic nature of their lives. It may be true that we never get what we want when we want it, or that when we do it's not what we wanted after all, but there's lots of good fun to be had grousing about it. What would Woody Allen do for jokes if he didn't have to worry about dying? Even when we're at our most contented, our ears are listening for the words, "Al, Al, *Al!* You need a change."

Bill Ott, "A Convention of Grousers," in The New York Times Book Review, *January 10, 1988, p. 37.*

SID AND SOL (1977)

Take a giant terrorizing today's world, a "short guy" who (from a small plane) taunts him into building a precarious tower—and you have, with a mighty crash, one dead giant and one Grand Canyon. Also, of course, hero Sid set up for life with his reward. Newcomers Yorinks and Egielski are onto a satirical something in the Ungerer vein (see the city streets in smithereens, the world's leaders at a loss) and the switches in scale, the shifts in format are visually exciting— but the book has wit without humor, a somberness that extends from the sharply defined, gray-toned pictures to the world-view projected. No love, no warmth, no reason to save this ugly world at all.

A review of "Sid and Sol," in Kirkus Reviews, *Vol. XLV, No. 23, December 1, 1977, p. 1265.*

Mr. Yorinks's narrative is pure Mel Brooks; Mr. Egielski's cartoonish illustrations a mixture of Disney, Mad Comics and R. Crumb; but the combination of the two is original and irresistible.

Christopher Lehmann-Haupt, in a review of "Sid & Sol," in The New York Times, *December 8, 1977, p. C21.*

Sid and Sol is a wonder—a picture book that heralds a hopeful, healthy flicker of life in what is becoming a creatively exhausted genre. The magic rests in the seamless bond of Arthur Yorinks's and Richard Egielski's deft and exciting collaboration.

Sol is a giant. "Tremendous. He was bigger than a thousand midgets on each other's shoulders. He was bigger than the tallest building. He was BIG." (These short, spikey opening sentences delight me. They have, to my ear, the sharp staccato sound of movie language, as though the book were being introduced by no less a star than James Cagney.) Sol delights in his size and strength. "He likes to tremble the world." And the world, desperate, advertises for a giant-killer. After a long wait, Sid comes along. (Sid *is* James Cagney—see him softshoe his way in and out of the world leaders' office.) "Sid, the whole world wishes you good luck," the moguls tell him, but Mr. Yorinks, never the false optimist, wryly adds, "The world thought the worst."

That very day, however, Sol gets his comeuppance in a sly,

original fashion—which I won't spoil for the reader. Enough to say that the results are bizarre and immensely funny. Like the hectic hodgepodge mountain Sol wildly piles up—composed, shockingly, of some of the world's most ponderously pious totems (Mount Rushmore and the Sphinx, to name just two)—the book, too, is a hodgepodge of variations on the runt/giant theme; not just David and Goliath, but Jack the Giant Killer and even King Kong. It is all seen through the nostalgic glow of a 1940's movie.

Curiously, the book reminds me of old, good things. But the childhood feelings it evokes, and the nostalgia for a past time and place, can have nothing to do with the two young artists who created this superb book; they are of another generation.

The surprise in ***Sid and Sol*** is that both Arthur Yorinks's daring text and Richard Egielski's innovative pictures convey the very essence of another time in American books and film. It is not the heavy-handed, commercial, star-struck nostalgia for the 1930's and 40's that currently threatens to inundate us, but rather the clear-eyed, unsentimental and perhaps somewhat astonished view of another, younger generation.

Mr. Yorinks has the cool audacity to mix purest nonsense with cockeyed fact. Almost as an aside, the book offers an upside-down National Geographic explanation of the creation of the Grand Canyon. It is perfect stand-up comic stuff and gorgeous writing. Mr. Yorinks is refreshingly free with both

Yorinks with illustrator Richard Egielski.

sentence structure and language—i.e. "with a shivery timber"—but there is no random conceit at work here. The deceptive dryness and droll, terse emphasis in the writing are cleverly calculated. And the pictures do the fleshing out—that's what picture books are all about. . . .

Page by page, the illustrator matches the daring of the writer. . . .

The story ends happily, sort of. But the true miracle is how, together, these two artists tell their tale without ever telegraphing ahead what's about to happen—or, for that matter, even trying to convince us of that traditional, tacked-on happy ending. Despite the words about Sid's good fortune and the picture of him, cocktail in hand, on his Taj Mahalian estate, our hero seems definitely lonely and disenchanted with the world he has conquered.

The picture book, as I can attest, is a fiendishly difficult form. There is no margin for error; one small slip and the work collapses. The dearth of successful picture books these days is sad proof of just how perilous the esthetic problems are. *Sid and Sol* is a brand new venture for both its young artists, and it works. Welcome Mr. Yorinks and Mr. Egielski!

> *Maurice Sendak, "The Giant and the Runt," in* The New York Times Book Review, *December 10, 1978, p. 72.*

LOUIS THE FISH (1980)

Louis comes from a family of butchers, but he hates meat. He loved his job cleaning fish tanks, though. When his parents die suddenly, he is forced to take over the butcher shop. He carries on his fascination with fish to the point of hallucination and, finally, transformation: Louis becomes a fish, and a most happy one at that. While the plot appears slender, *Louis the Fish* is a rich blending of text and pictures and an exciting tale. No words are wasted in Yorinks' crisp, clear writing: "One day last spring, Louis, a butcher, turned into a fish. Silvery scales. Big lips. A tail. A salmon." This astounding and seductive introduction is followed by proof—Egielski's double-spread illustration of a giant fish asleep in pajamas. The book then flashes back to establish Louis' previous human life, and the humor of his predicament is developed. He was forever getting gifts of meat. The reporting style of the prose is matched by an expose-style illustration showing the unfortunate boy holding a gift-wrapped salami near a chalkboard that states the vital information: "Louis. 7 years old!" . . . Yorinks and Egielski work together as if they were one. Their joint pacing and a variety of verbal and visual viewpoints makes *Louis the Fish* an outstanding and refreshingly unusual picture book.

> *George Shannon, in a review of "Louis the Fish," in* School Library Journal, *Vol. 27, No. 3, November, 1980, p. 68.*

The stream of children's literature is well-stocked with fish stories but never has there been a yarn remotely resembling this one.

A second collaboration between Mr. Yorinks and Mr. Egielski . . . , the present work is in full color and more pointed and original than their maiden effort. . . .

Despite a bizarre premise, the story works beautifully. A total

commitment by both author and artist to Louis and his developing mania is the key to the book's near mesmerizing power.

> *Selma G. Lanes, in a review of "Louis the Fish," in* The New York Times Book Review, *November 23, 1980, p. 36.*

Whether or not children grasp the bizarre quality of this picture-book story of an unhappy man-turned-fish, there is a compelling aspect to the book. Transformation of the kind that Louis experiences may even prove fascinating to some young children. . . . Louis' unhappiness is understandable in spite of the fact that his problem is exclusively adult. This is not a comfortable or comforting story, though it has humorous aspects; one wonders whether fishdom is all that permanent a "good life." But fewer children than adults are likely to project beyond the story's resolution.

> *Judith Goldberger, in a review of "Louis the Fish," in* Booklist, *Vol. 77, No. 7, December 1, 1980, p. 519.*

IT HAPPENED IN PINSK (1983)

"Ah, Pinsk. Could there be a lovelier city? No." A Russian shoe salesman, Irv Irving, and his wife lead a peaceful life there. "Nice clothes. Good food. A telephone. They had everything. Did Irv care? No."

No, as Arthur Yorinks and Richard Egielski portray him in *It Happened in Pinsk,* he'd rather be a wrestler, a tycoon, even a mansion-dwelling widow. As if discontent were not enough, one morning, just as he's about to eat a roll, Irv realizes his head is missing. Lucky for him his wife is so resourceful. With socks and a pillowcase, she makes him a head and sends him to work.

But does Irv go to work? He does not. Wandering around trying to find his head, he is taken for a criminal, for the skinflint Leo Totski, then for the long-lost uncle of an overly solicitous . . . country clan. All of Irv's escapes are narrow, and when he finally finds his head, he hangs onto it as others might their hats in a piercing Russian wind. And Irv, after this, is (at least a little) less of a kvetch.

This is the third bit of picture-book magic by Mr. Yorinks and Mr. Egielski. . . . Mr. Egielski's pictures are active, richly colored and detailed. . . . The book's imagery and its idiom (a bit of Russian Jewish) are perfectly wedded to each other as well as to the setting. Mr. Yorinks's and Mr. Egielski's is a most remarkable collaboration. Their work is unusual, vivacious, hilarious and touching.

> *Marguerite Feitlowitz, in a review of "It Happened in Pinsk," in* The New York Times Book Review, *December 18, 1983, p. 20.*

The sole complaint one could lay against Yorinks and Egielski is that time is too long between their bracing, mad collaborations. The author and illustrator are not alone in implying the precept "Be yourself" in their books but they do that like nobody else. . . . Readers are bound to roar with laughter at the predicaments Irv faces, and at the surprising road that leads him to his own head at last, but they'll also discover something to think about in this grand successor to *Sid and Sol* and *Louis the Fish.*

> *A review of "It Happened in Pinsk," in* Publishers Weekly, *Vol. 224, No. 26, December 23, 1983, p. 58.*

While individual episodes are humorous, the text and illustrations as a whole lack rationale and purpose; virtually no reason is given for any of Irv's unlikely experiences. . . . The illustrations, many of which depict genuinely funny incidents, evoke a feeling of an earlier Russia, capturing the sense of its architecture and people. This story will probably be lost on children, though, as it is rooted in a mid-life identity crisis.(pp. 64-5)

> *Maria Salvadore, in a review of "It Happened in Pinsk," in* School Library Journal, *Vol. 30, No. 6, February, 1984, pp. 64-5.*

HEY, AL (1986)

A New York City janitor and his dog, Eddie, make a temporary escape to a fantastic land of birds, but discover that the price is too high.

Al is content, but Eddie wants more space than their one messy room; so when a giddily colored bird offers the two a worry-free alternative, they accept. He transports them to a paradise of sorts: lush vegetation, a marvelous array of gaudy, surreal birds to respond to their every whim. "But ripe fruit soon spoils." Noticing that they are being transformed into birds, Eddie and Al make a quick escape to their dingy home. "Paradise lost is sometimes Heaven found," and Al is last seen patching and painting.

This fable is related with sly wit made more pungent by its brevity. . . . Both verbally and pictorially, the relationship between the friends is funny and touching. A clever idea well realized by an inspired pair in their fourth collaboration. Kids will chuckle over this one.

> *A review of "Hey, Al," in* Kirkus Reviews, *Vol. LIV, No. 22, November 15, 1986, p. 1726.*

Two top picture-book collaborators team up in another irresistible entry. . . . Egielski's watercolors are humorous, marvelously detailed and a perfect foil for Yorinks's art. . . . Like **Louis the Fish, Hey, Al** is sure to please both parents and kids with its wry wit. (pp. 52-3)

> *A review of "Hey, Al," in* Publishers Weekly, *Vol. 230, No. 24, December 12, 1986, pp. 52-3.*

[This is a] rather odd but touching tale of a deeply devoted couple, an airborne Circe and a perfect (or is it?) island in the sky. Like Maurice Sendak's *Where the Wild Things Are*, this picture book explores the pleasures and the costs of leaving home.

The team of Richard Egielski and Arthur Yorinks . . . have worked their magic again. Playfully written in the sharpie cadences of New-York-City-ese, and illustrated with rich and loving attention to every detail, **Hey, Al** is a perfect melding of words and pictures, fantasy and reality, tenderness and humor. There's a heavy-hitting moral here—about the charms of even the humblest home. But the message is benevolent, delivered with warmth and wit and imagination. And so, as the author would put it, "What could be bad?"

> *Judith Viorst, in a review of "Hey, Al," in* The New York Times Book Review, *January 11, 1987, p. 38.*

The theme here is, "be happy with who you are," or maybe, "there's no free lunch." . . . Egielski's solid naturalism provides just the visual foil needed to establish the surreal char-acter of this fantasy. . . . Text and pictures work together to challenge readers' concept of reality, with touches such as the stacks of delivered newspapers outside Al's door when he returns from—his "dream"? (pp. 152-53)

> *Kenneth Marantz, in a review of "Hey, Al," in* School Library Journal, *Vol. 33, No. 7, March, 1987, pp. 151-52.*

COMPANY'S COMING (1988)

In the most deliciously funny picture-book about extraterrestrials since the Marshalls' *Space Case,* a pair of friendly, foot-high, insectlike creatures arrive in a bright red flying saucer (at first mistaken for an outsized barbecue) and are invited by a nice middle-aged lady to join a family party. Her husband, more apprehensive, notifies the FBI, so that by the time the creatures report for the appointed meal a mighty arsenal awaits them. Still, when the gift they bring proves to be not a bomb but just a blender ("We weren't sure if you had one of these . . . it was on sale!"), everyone from cousins to marines settles down together for a friendly spaghetti dinner. . . . A pointed story with its point well made.

> *A review of "Company's Coming," in* Kirkus Reviews, *Vol. LVI, No. 2, January 15, 1988, p. 130.*

Yorinks displays his talent for droll, surprising humor in this off-beat tale about trust and hospitality. Through deliberate exaggeration and absurdity, he pokes fun at paranoid and militaristic responses to perceived threats from those different from ourselves—a timely message indeed.

> *A review of "Company's Coming," in* Publishers Weekly, *Vol. 233, No. 4, January 29, 1988, p. 429.*

I have always admired people who, in the face of uninvited guests, are cool and calm. I'm one who flies into a tizzy at the mere thought of a dinner party. Last-minute drop-ins never bothered my mother, because my father was in the restaurant business and could bring home extras of whatever they were serving.

But I'm not sure my mother could ever have been as cool and unruffled as Shirley, the heroine of Arthur Yorinks's new story, **Company's Coming**. . . .

I admire Shirley. "Moe, you had to buy *that* barbecue?" she chides [her husband] when she sees the flying saucer sitting next to the toolshed. "It's too big." Moe replies, "Shirl, it's not a barbecue." (The deadpan dialogue is irresistible, and at this point, readers and listeners tend to crack up.) Then two creatures from outer space, looking suspiciously like cockroaches wearing helmets, emerge from the oversized barbecue. " 'Greetings,' they spoke in English. 'We come in peace. Do you have a bathroom?' "

Now, if you think about that request, it doesn't make any sense—clearly these creatures have been traveling for years on their way to another galaxy. What have they been doing all that time? Doesn't their spaceship have a bathroom? Yet it's absolutely logical. The first thing most children ask for whether they've been traveling for 10 minutes or 10 years is a bathroom. The genius of Arthur Yorinks's understated texts . . . is that he knows what's truly important to youngsters.

The second thing children want is food, and that's just what

Shirley, the consummate hostess, offers the travelers. "How about a sandwich, you must be hungry. . . . Would you like to stay for dinner?" The invitation is graciously accepted and the spacemen take off until 6 P.M., while Shirley and Moe rush inside to deal with this turn of events: Shirley goes straight to the kitchen, Moe rushes straight to the bedroom to phone the F.B.I., which in turn calls the Pentagon, which calls out the Army, the Air Force and the Marines. Moe is convinced that the creatures will vaporize not only their town, Bellmore, but the whole earth. The Pentagon seems worried as well. Not Shirley. Company's coming, and she has lots of work to do! . . .

The spacemen are very polite; they've even brought a hostess gift. Shirley is equally gracious, while Moe tries to rush them on their way and "Cousin Sheldon the loudmouth" tries to make conversation by asking about their trip.

"Well, we're on our way to check out a new planet," they say. "Our population has grown so quickly that we must branch out and find new places to live." This response only convinces me that the spacemen are cockroaches. Moe takes it much more seriously. "An invasion—we're doomed," he informs

Cousin Harriet, while Shirley announces dinner. The visitors want her to open their gift first. "It'll knock you out," they tell her, and at that very moment, the soldiers and tanks armed with ballistic missiles invade. Amid the chaos, Shirley discovers that the gift is a blender. "And we don't even have one," she exclaims. "It was on sale!" the spacemen beam, and they all sit down to eat spaghetti and meatballs. Shirley has made extra!

This picture book is as satisfying as Shirley's meal. Arthur Yorinks's dialogue is as well timed as the best comedy act, and David Small has used pen and ink to outline his pale watercolors to capture the rhythm of the humor in, for example, the shrug of Shirley's shoulder, the twist of Moe's moustache or the way his hand fits in his pocket. You know these people. You've been to their house for dinner. So, if a spaceship could land in their backyard, what could happen at your house?

Alice Miller Bregman, "Dinner Guests from Outer Space," in The New York Times Book Review, *May 8, 1988, p. 38.*

CUMULATIVE INDEX TO AUTHORS

This index lists all author entries in *Children's Literature Review* and includes cross-references to them in other Gale sources. References in the index are identified as follows:

CA: *Contemporary Authors* (original series), Volumes 1-127
CANR: *Contemporary Authors New Revision Series,* Volumes 1-28
CAP: *Contemporary Authors Permanent Series,* Volumes 1-2
CA-R: *Contemporary Authors* (revised editions), Volumes 1-44
CDALB: *Concise Dictionary of American Literary Biography,* Volumes 1-4
CLC: *Contemporary Literary Criticism,* Volumes 1-57
CLR: *Children's Literature Review,* Volumes 1-20
DLB: *Dictionary of Literary Biography,* Volumes 1-84
DLB-DS: *Dictionary of Literary Biography Documentary Series,* Volumes 1-6
DLB-Y: *Dictionary of Literary Biography Yearbook,* Volumes 1980-1987
LC: *Literature Criticism from 1400 to 1800,* Volumes 1-11
NCLC: *Nineteenth-Century Literature Criticism,* Volumes 1-25
SAAS: *Somthing About the Author Autobiography Series,* Volumes 1-8
SATA: *Something about the Author,* Volumes 1-56
TCLC: *Twentieth-Century Literary Criticism,* Volumes 1-35
YABC: *Yesterday's Authors of Books for Children,* Volumes 1-2

CUMULATIVE INDEX TO NATIONALITIES

Lofting, Hugh **19**
Macaulay, David **3, 14**
Mark, Jan **11**
Milne, A. A. **1**
Nesbit, E. **3**
Norton, Mary **6**
Oakley, Graham **7**
Ottley, Reginald **16**
Pearce, Philippa **9**
Peyton, K. M. **3**
Pienkowski, Jan **6**
Potter, Beatrix **1, 19**
Pullman, Philip **20**
Ransome, Arthur **8**
Serraillier, Ian **2**
Sewell, Anna **17**
Streatfeild, Noel **17**
Sutcliff, Rosemary **1**
Tenniel, Sir John **18**
Townsend, John Rowe **2**
Travers, P. L. **2**
Treece, Henry **2**
Walsh, Jill Paton **2**
Westall, Robert **13**
Wildsmith, Brian **2**
Willard, Barbara **2**
Williams, Kit **4**

FILIPINO
Aruego, Jose **5**

FINNISH
Jansson, Tove **2**

FRENCH
Berna, Paul **19**
Brunhoff, Jean de **4**
Brunhoff, Laurent de **4**
Saint-Exupery, Antoine de **10**
Ungerer, Tomi **3**

GERMAN
Benary-Isbert, Margot **12**
Ende, Michael **14**
Heine, Helme **18**
Kastner, Erich **4**
Kruss, James **9**
Rey, H. A. **5**
Rey, Margret **5**
Zimnik, Reiner **3**

GREEK
Aesop **14**
Zei, Alki **6**

HUNGARIAN
Galdone, Paul **16**
Seredy, Kate **10**

INDIAN
Mukerji, Dhan Gopal **10**

IRISH
O'Shea, Pat **18**

ISRAELI
Shulevitz, Uri **5**

ITALIAN
Collodi, Carlo **5**
Munari, Bruno **9**
Ventura, Piero **16**

JAPANESE
Anno, Mitsumasa **2, 14**
Iwasaki, Chihiro **18**
Maruki, Toshi **19**
Tejima **20**
Watanabe, Shigeo **8**
Yashima, Taro **4**

NEW ZEALAND
Mahy, Margaret **7**

NIGERIAN
Achebe, Chinua **20**

POLISH
Pienkowski, Jan **6**
Shulevitz, Uri **5**
Singer, Isaac Bashevis **1**
Suhl, Yuri **2**
Wojciechowska, Maia **1**

RUSSIAN
Korinetz, Yuri **4**

SCOTTISH
Barrie, J. M. **16**
Burnford, Sheila **2**
Stevenson, Robert Louis **10, 11**

SOUTH AFRICAN
Lewin, Hugh **9**

SPANISH
Sanchez-Silva, Jose Maria **12**

SWEDISH
Beskow, Elsa **17**
Gripe, Maria **5**
Lagerlof, Selma **7**
Lindgren, Astrid **1**
Lindgren, Barbro **20**

SWISS
Spyri, Johanna **13**

WELSH
Dahl, Roald **1, 7**

WEST INDIAN
Guy, Rosa **13**

Nationality Index

CUMULATIVE INDEX TO TITLES

Title Index

Title Index

Title Index